Management Strategies for Libraries

A Basic Reader

Edited by
Beverly P. Lynch

Neal-Schuman Publishers, Inc.
New York London

Published by Neal-Schuman Publishers, Inc.
23 Cornelia Street
New York, NY 10014

Printed and bound in the United States of America.

Library of Congress Cataloging in Publication Data
Main entry under title:

Management strategies for libraries.

    Includes index.
    1. Library administration—Addresses, essays, lectures. I. Lynch, Beverly P.
Z678.M278 1985   025.1   85-5668
ISBN 0-918212-86-3

Contents

Preface

M*ANAGEMENT Strategies for Libraries* is designed for students, teachers, and practitioners of library and information science who seek to know the literature of library management. Since much of our knowledge about library management has been derived from the theory and research of other fields, the readings in this book are taken from the literature of sociology, psychology, political science, and public administration, as well as from the literature of librarianship. Thirty-eight articles have been brought together here so that the classics on the theory of organizations and the functions and processes of management are available in one volume. The intent is to place side-by-side the management classics and the prominent writings in the library field that are based in these classics.

The decisions to include or exclude articles were very difficult to make. I have used almost every selection at one time or another in my own work. Many are those articles frequently cited in textbooks in library management or in studies of libraries. Those which are included reflect, for the most part, my theoretical and research interests which are centered in the study of the sociology of complex organizations.

The book is organized in three parts. Part One, Theoretical Perspectives, includes fifteen articles; nine of these are theoretical perspectives that form the foundations for library organization and management, six are from the library literature that reflects the theory. Part Two, The Management Process, presents seven articles on the management process in general and five articles applying that process in the library context. Part Three, The Work of Management, contains articles on specific management functions. Included in this section also are articles on job design and job satisfaction. Seven of the eleven papers are from the library literature. The influences of the earlier theoretical perspectives, particularly the human relations approach, are apparent here.

I wish to thank those authors and publishers who granted permission to use these articles. This book could not have been completed without their generosity.

—Beverly P. Lynch

Introduction

Beverly P. Lynch

LIBRARIANS do not agree on what constitutes the best approach to the study of library management. There is agreement though, that libraries are modern, complex organizations. Libraries have organizational structures and processes such as technology, decision making, and communications. Libraries have environments and clientele. They are staffed by highly skilled professionals, technical assistants, and clerical personnel and maintain tables of organization that seek to describe staff relationships. Libraries change, sometimes rapidly, sometimes not rapidly enough. They grow or shrink. They have too many or not enough rules. Libraries, often in direct competition with other organizations for scarce resources, have budgets and spend them easily. Large portions of these budgets go to employees for salaries, benefits, and such perquisites as travel and educational programs. Yet, not all employees are satisfied, and may be more discontented and apathetic than contented and committed.

Depending on our experience and what we observe, all of us have "studied" organizations and believe we know organizations. Each of us believes we could improve the performance of the library, for we have observed what is right about it and what isn't. Each person coming in contact with a library already has some very definite ideas about hiring interviews, performance appraisals, bureaucratic "red-tape," bosses, conflict between department head and staff member, administrator and professional.

Modern libraries, however, are complicated; to know about them systematically requires study and investigation. The difficulties of managing these complex organizations have been studied and written about by managers, educators, and librarians. To a certain extent, librarians have been more interested in management topics than in issues relating to professional competencies, for we recognize that librarianship is practiced in organizational settings of great variety and complexity. When problems of library management are dealt with well, the work of the library is enhanced. When dealt with badly, the work of the library and the library itself may suffer.

Solving the organizational and managerial problems of libraries, while of interest to many, is the primary responsibility of library managers. It is the managers who must observe and understand the different viewpoints, the paradoxes, and influences on the libraries and translate and communicate all of this to others, for the managers are responsible for the successful performance of the libraries in which they work.

Library managers tend to see their most pressing problem as getting the work done as efficiently as possible. They have looked to the management of industrial organizations in the for-profit sector for help in creating greater efficiencies in their own library operations. The techniques, policies, and managerial practices of large-scale industrial organizations have influenced in major ways the management of libraries, for it is in large industrial organizations that efficiencies and effectiveness are paramount.

THE BASIC THEORIES

Two major viewpoints have dominated the study of the organization of large industrial organizations and hence the study of libraries as organizations. One emphasizes the importance of organizational structure and considers methods of coordination and control in goal attainment. This approach has its base in the work of the theorists of classical management, such as Frederick Taylor, and of bureaucracies, such as Max Weber, both represented in this book. The approach takes a reasoned and rational approach to the study of organizations. Its theorists study and design organizations as rational systems.

The second viewpoint, the human relations approach, begins with the people who work in organizations. These theorists are anxious to identify the human needs of the employee and to tailor the work to fit those needs. The human relations theorists, while believing to a certain extent that organizations are rational, emphasize the need to reduce organizational malfunctions which may occur when the individual and the organization display different needs.

There is another theoretical perspective in the study of organizations that is important to our understanding of libraries: the political perspective. It has its base in the study of governmental agencies and other organizations in the not-for-profit sector. Predominantly a perspective found in the literature of public administration and political science, this theoretical approach considers organizational conflict and the use of power and influence in the allocation of scarce resources. The political school emphasizes the decisions made in organizations that affect the allocation of resources. It recognizes that individuals in organizations may differ in their values and orientation but will come together in coalitions when decisions are required. Depending upon the decision, coalitions will shift, break apart, and combine in different ways. Some coalitions will remain stable over time; others will not. Power and conflict are critical variables in the political approach to the study of complex organizations.

The political approach has been less influential in the study of libraries as organizations than it should be. To understand the management of libraries, we must add to the analysis of the library's organizational structure, and the role of the individual in the library, the study of organizational politics and the analysis of power, coalitions, and bargaining. Issues such as the political and institutional forces in the environment and the absence of economic markets for the library's output loom large. The literature of public administration, together with the literature of classical management and human relations, offer important insights and theoretical perspectives for library managers. Several papers in this book emphasize the concept of power, including Jeffrey Raffel's political analysis of the library. Most of the papers, however, emphasize the structural and human relations perspective—for these still are the dominant theories upon which we base our understanding of library management.

The Structural Approach

The structural approach to the study of libraries and other organizations is based upon several central themes or propositions:

- Organizations, including libraries, are created and exist to achieve certain goals.
- The structure of the organization and the processes in it of planning, communicating, deciding, coordinating, and controlling are influenced or determined by the organization's goals, as well as by its size, technology, and environment.
- The behavior of the organization is essentially rational; it is determined more by the organization's goals, size, technology, environment, and structure than by the needs of the individuals in the organization.

This tradition is followed in the work of Woodward,[1] Perrow,[2] Lawrence and Lorsch,[3] Blau and Schoenherr,[4] Burns and Stalker,[5] Thompson,[6] March and Simon,[7] Pugh, Hickson, and Hinings,[8] and Hage and Aiken.[9] The studies of libraries by Lynch[10] and Sloan[11] carry the structural perspective into libraries.

The Human Relations Approach

The human relations approach to the study of libraries and other organizations has its base in these themes or propositions:

- The organization exists basically to serve the needs of the people working in it.
- Individuals in the organization can influence in major ways the organization's goals and objectives and processes.
- Individuals are dependent on the organization for their personal satisfactions and for meaning in their lives.
- If individual needs are matched with organizational needs, the individual will be satisfied and the organization's goals will be achieved.

The work of McGregor,[12] Argyris,[13] Herzberg,[14] and Likert[15] follow the human relations tradition. The studies of Marchant[16] on the participation of librarians in decision making and Martell[17] on job design in libraries carry the human relations perspective into the study of libraries.

The structural perspective has taught us a great deal about organizations and has extended our knowledge of the relationships between organizational goals, technologies, and structures. Structural theorists, however, for the most part ignore the matter of people in organizations and pay little attention to the issues of power and conflict in organizations. The human relations perspective, by looking at organizational issues from the viewpoint of the individual in the organization, considers the relationships between organizational problems and human relations remedies. But human relations theorists tend to dismiss structural constraints and ignore problems of authority. Like the structuralists, the human relations school pays little attention to the issues of the allocation of scarce resources, power, or conflict.

Large-scale comparative investigations of organizations have been undertaken based on the theories of the structuralists. Organizations have been compared on many variables using large samples, but many of the investigators have encountered difficult methodological problems. Their measures generally have been based on survey data or secondary analyses of organizational data. Few of the measures have been used in more than one study and few of the studies have been replicated. In fact, most attempts at replication have not been successful. Child[18] found as many differences as similarities in his replication of Pugh, Hickson, and Hinings. Beyer and Trice,[19] in their attempt to replicate Blau and Schoenherr, also found more differences than similarities. Overton, Schneck, and Hazlett[20] could not replicate Lynch's measures.

Empirical support also is lacking for the human relations theories and many of the propositions lack conceptual clarity. The review of Marchant's work by Lynch[21] and Marchant's comment on the review[22] illustrate some of the methodological problems encountered in organizational studies based in libraries which stem from a single theoretical perspective. Perrow sums up the viewpoint: "One cannot explain organizations by explaining the attitudes and behavior of individuals or even small groups within them. We learn a great deal about psychology and social psychology but little about organizations per se in this fashion."[23]

The Political Approach

The structuralists and the human relations theorists, when considering organizational conflict, tend to see the conflict as something wrong, as an indicator of a problem to be solved. Conflict to the classical management theorist is a failure in planning and control. To the human relations theorist, it is a lack of participation in decision making or a failure in leadership. The political theorist, on the other hand, takes the view that conflict is central to the organization and that bargaining, negotiating, and the formation of coalitions are essential to organizational decision making.

The central theories or propositions shaping the political approach to the study of organizations are:

- The allocation of scarce resources is the most critical decision made in the organization.
- Decisions are made through the formation of various organizational coalitions.
- Within the organization, individuals and groups differ on values, beliefs, and perceptions of reality.
- Organizational goals are multiple and conflicting. Decisions about them emerge from the on-going process of bargaining and negotiating.

The work of Baldridge,[24] Meyer,[25] Kaufman,[26] and Pfeffer and Salancik[27] reflect this approach.

The political perspective is gaining importance in the study of organizations, having emerged out of the general dissatisfaction with the explanations offered by the structural and human relations approaches. As theorists turn their attention to interrelationships and other issues external to organizations, and as they compare public agencies with for-profit businesses, the importance of political perspectives becomes more apparent.

Library managers already have begun to recognize the inevitability of politics in complex organizations. Libraries, with the notable exceptions of those serving the for-profit sector and private educational institutions, are public agencies. Taking account of political influences, they must compete with other governmental groups for their resources, but without the objective measures of success available for enterprises with an economic market for their products and services. The literature of public administration is rich in the description of the influence of nonmarket and political factors on public agencies. This literature is only beginning to influence our current understanding of libraries as organizations. Library managers find they are helped by knowledge of some of the fundamental issues detailed by the theorists of public administration, such as the absence of market-based performance measures, patronage and corruption in government, the tendency toward inefficiency, lack of innovation, and unresponsiveness to public wants caused by narrow political self-interest.[28]

APPLYING THEORY TO PRACTICE

According to the studies of Stewart,[29] Kotter,[30] and Mintzberg,[31] managers make too little use of broad insights offered by the various theorists. Managers tend to be superficial in their actions—they seek interruptions, respond quickly, deal only with the tangible, and avoid the abstract. Studies of managerial work suggest that managers rarely make grand, bold decisions; instead, they decide in small increments. Contrary to popular belief, managers do not work in a leisurely fashion, designing rational plans and organizing, coordinating, and controlling the work of subordinates. Instead they have busy, fragmented days with little time to contemplate or reflect.

Managers can be helped in their work, though, through an

understanding of theoretical perspectives they bring to a managerial problem and by trying to see the problem from *more than one* theoretical perspective. A theoretical understanding of complex organizations can help the manager know and understand his or her own response to a managerial problem. As Mintzberg observes, "The manager's effectiveness is significantly influenced by his insight into his own work."

For example, depending upon which theoretical perspective is dominating the manager's thought, the manager may view the process of performance appraisal as the basis for the distribution of rewards or as a basis for punishment to control behavior (structural perspective), as a means for helping the individual grow and develop (the human relations perspective), or as an opportunity to exert power (the political perspective). The manager might use meetings to make decisions or to inform others about decisions already made (structural), to share information informally so as to involve all participants (human relations), or as a competition (political). From the structural view, decision making is a rational process to produce the right decision; the human relations perspective sees it as a process to produce commitment from individuals in the organization; the political perspective sees organizational decision making as an opportunity to gain or to exercise power.[32] It may be that for a given situation, any one of the perspectives will be useful. In practice, what a successful manager does is apply what he or she believes to be the appropriate strategy.

Library managers working from a human relations perspective can be frustrated in their efforts to redesign jobs, enrich jobs, or restructure units in a library which is governed by civil service regulations or agreements. The systems of rules imposed upon the manager have their basis in rationality. These systems were anticipated by Max Weber (see his article "Characteristics of Bureaucracies"), yet they do not fit the manager's view of successful performance. Many libraries emphasize rules and regulations, a division of labor based on specialized training and expertise, on carefully recognized systems of authority. These emphases are based in the structural perspective. A manager who does not agree with the perspective may seek either to circumvent the system—possibly a counterproductive move or a conflict-laden one—or the manager will seek to understand the basis of the system and strive to shape the system to serve the library's objectives.

The popular book by Peters and Waterman, *In Search of Excel-*

lence,[33] has become essential reading for many managers and is an adopted text in some management courses, for it offers inspiration to managers who seek to improve the performance of their organizations. Library managers, too, will find provocative Peters and Waterman's insights on the importance to successful companies of a value system that is nurtured and enhanced, the importance of the details of execution, ensuring that the routine aspects of the work are done well. In successful companies there is a belief in the importance of people as individuals, of superior quality and service. Excellent companies believe that most members of the organization should be innovative. Thus the best-run organizations display a willingness to support failure. Library managers should review whether such beliefs are important or are applicable to their libraries.

As Van de Ven[34] points out in his review reprinted in this book, Peters and Waterman offer a fine opportunity for the development of a synthesis of theoretical pespectives. They provoke the theorist, the researcher, and the manager. No one theoretical perspective explains the performance of a successful company. The contradictions and paradoxes are obvious, yet the managers interviewed by Peters and Waterman had learned to manage within them.

Based on what is emerging from various studies in the public administrative field, political strategies may be even more useful in many library situations. The study of governmental agencies generally is based in case studies, rich in anecdotal evidence, leaner in rigorous methodology and conceptual definition. The reports of this research, considered along with other studies, promises an integration of theoretical views which has been lacking in most library literature.

Several points emerge from the study of the classics of the management literature. There is no established theory or prescription for the one best way to run an organization. Management is an applied field, drawing its theory and research from sociology, psychology, political science, economics. To be successful, the manager must know and understand the organization in which he or she works and seek to understand it within its environment and within the set of organizations in which it operates. Interorganizational interactions are as important as the interpersonal ones are. To perform successfully as a manager, the manager must link together the various and diverse disciplines, must understand the theoretical perspectives he or she brings to each issue, and must develop an ability to bring about a synthesis of perspectives. *Management Strategies for Libraries* should help the manager achieve success in these efforts.

References

1. Woodward, Joan, ed. *Industrial Organization: Behavior and Control.* London: Oxford University Press, 1970.
2. Perrow, Charles. *Complex Organizations; a Critical Essay.* 2d. ed. Glenview, Il., Scott, Foresman, 1979.
3. Lawrence, Paul R. and Jay W. Lorsch. *Organization and Environment.* Boston: Harvard Business School, Division of Research, 1967.
4. Blau, Peter M. and Richard A. Schoenherr. *The Structure of Organizations.* New York: Basic Books, 1971.
5. Burns, Tom and G. M. Stalker. *The Management of Innovation.* London: Tavistock Publications, 1961.
6. Thompson, James D. *Organizations in Action.* New York: McGraw-Hill, 1967.
7. March, James G. and Herbert A. Simon. *Organizations.* New York: Wiley, 1958.
8. Pugh, D.S., D. J. Hickson, and C. R. Hinings. "An Empirical Taxonomy of the Structure of Work Organizations," *Administrative Science Quarterly,* 14 (1969): 115-25.
9. Hage, Jerald and Michael Aiken. "Routine Technology, Social Structure, and Organizational Goals," *Administrative Science Quarterly* 14 (1969): 366-76.
10. Lynch, Beverly P. "An Empirical Assessment of Perrow's Technology Construct," *Administrative Science Quarterly* 19 (1974): 338-56.
11. Sloan, Elaine A. "The Organization of Collection Development in Large University Libraries," Ph.D. Dissertation (University of Maryland 1973.
12. McGregor, Douglas. *The Human Side of Enterprise.* New York: McGraw-Hill, 1960.
13. Argyris, Chris. *Integrating the Individual and the Organization.* New York: Wiley, 1964.
14. Herzberg, Frederick. *Work and the Nature of Man.* New York: T. Crowell Co., 1966.
15. Likert, Rensis. *The Human Organization.* New York: McGraw-Hill, 1967.
16. Marchant, Maurice P. *Participative Management in Academic Libraries.* Westport, Conn.: Greenwood Press, 1976.
17. Martell, Charles. *The Client-Centered Academic Library.* Westport, Conn.: Greenwood Press, 1983.
18. Child, John. "Organization Structure and Strategies of Control: A Replication of the Aston Study," *Administrative Science Quarterly* 17 (1972): 163-77.
19. Beyer, Janice M. and Harrison M. Trice. "A Re-examination of the Relations Between Size and Various Components of Organizational Complexity," *Administrative Science Quarterly* 24 (1979): 48-64.

20. Overton, Peggy, Rodney Scheneck, and C. B. Hazlett. "An Empirical Study of the Technology of Nursing Subunits," *Administrative Science Quarterly* 22 (1977): 203-19.
21. Lynch, Beverly. "Participative Management in Relation to Library Effectiveness," *College & Research Libraries* 33 (1972): 382-90.
22. Marchant, Maurice P. "And a Response," *College & Research Libraries* 33 (1972): 391-97.
23. Perrow, op. cit. p. 133.
24. Baldridge, J. Victor. *Power and Conflict in the University.* New York: Wiley, 1971.
25. Meyer, Marshall W. *Change in Public Bureaucracies.* Cambridge: Cambridge University Press, 1979.
26. Kaufman, Herbert. *The Forest Ranger; a study in Administrative Behavior.* Baltimore: Published for Resources for the Future by John Hopkins University Press, 1960.
27. Pfeffer, Jeffrey and Gerald Salancik. *The External Control of Organizations: A Resource Dependence Perspective.* New York: Harper & Row, 1978.
28. Rainey, Hal G. "Public Organization Theory: The Rising Challenge," *Public Administrative Review* 43 (March/April 1983): 176-82.
29. Stewart, Rosemary, *Managers and Their Jobs.* London: Macmillan, 1967.
30. Kotter, John P. *The General Managers.* New York: Free Press, 1982.
31. Mintzberg, Henry. *The Nature of Managerial Work.* New York: Harper & Row, 1973.
32. Bolman, Lee G. and Terrence E. Deal. *Modern Approaches to Understanding and Managing Organizations.* San Francisco: Jossey-Bass, 1984.
33. Peters, Thomas J. and Robert H. Waterman, Jr. *In Search of Excellence: Lessons From America's Best Run Companies.* New York: Harper and Row, 1982.
34. Van de Van, Andrew H. *(Review of) In Search of Excellence: Lessons from America's Best-Run Companies,* by Thomas J. Peters and Robert H. Waterman, Jr. in *Administrative Science Quarterly* 28 (December 1983): 621-24.

PART I   THEORETICAL PERSPECTIVES

In this section, the classics of organizational literature and writings on the emerging theoretical perspectives in the study of organizations are presented. Within that context I also have included writings from the library literature to illustrate the influence other theories have had on the thought of librarianship.

Organizational theory is changing and expanding rapidly; widely diverse perspectives are available. The emerging theories, however, continue to be guided by the work of Frederick Taylor, Max Weber, Peter Blau, and others. Taylor's approach to the work of the organization emphasizes breaking down complex tasks into simpler ones. He expects that careful definition of each job and the tasks associated with that job will produce greater efficiency and effectiveness. Donald Coney's paper, "Management in College and University Libraries," reflects the early adoption by libraries of the perspectives of scientific management. Similarly, Richard Dougherty and Fred Heinritz apply Taylor's theoretical perspectives to the work of libraries. Having observed that many library processes are mechanical and repetitive, they propose that applying scientific management to these tasks will result in improved efficiency in the library.

Weber's theory of bureaucracy dominates the study of complex organizations. The selection presented here describes and analyzes the characteristics of a bureaucracy. My article "Libraries as Bureaucracies," shows the general influence Weber's work has had on librarianship: his description of the characteristics of bureaucracy seem to many librarians to reflect the nature of organizations in which they work. His analysis of authority can illuminate the recent interest in participative management and the role of power in organizations.

Blau's paper on the hierarchy of authority expands upon Weber's work. Its insights into the conditions that lead to certain configurations of authority in organizations and to variations in organizational structure are important to the understanding of libraries and other organizations. Rose B. Phelps' analysis of the organizational structure of libraries anticipated many recent theoretical and empirical investigations.

This section includes several readings on the interrelationships of the organization and the individual working in it. The human relations approach, in contrast to scientific management, suggests that nonfinancial, social rewards also can motivate workers to do good work. Fritz J. Rothlisberger and William J. Dickson, in their article "Human Relations," concentrate on the informal organization, particularly on the behavior of groups. The influence of the human relations theorists on the approach to the management of libraries is apparent in Part 3 of this book, which includes papers on job design and job satisfaction.

Fremont E. Kast and James E. Rosenzweig consider general systems theory. The theory has been influential in the investigation of the organization of libraries. It forms the base for Maurice P. Marchant's study of academic libraries, "The Library as Open System."

R.M. Cyert and James B. March emphasize decision theory and its influence on complex organizations. Their work on the relationships of human problem-solving and rational choice continues to be important. A second selection by March, from a 1980 lecture, called "Organizations and Change," offers a viewpoint on the inevitability of change. Six perspectives are presented on how the organization responds routinely to its environment. March suggests that an organization's success may depend on just how well it accomplishes "the trivia of day-to-day relationships with clients and day-to-day problems in maintaining and operating its technology." His observations suggest that the library cannot ignore its core activity—the point implicit in the work of Dougherty and Heinritz. While change has dominated much of the thinking and writing of library managers, as reflected in the work of Arthur M. McAnally and Robert B. Downs in Part 2, there has been little systematic investigation of libraries along the lines March proposes.

It was inevitable that theorists would seek to understand more fully the interactions of an organization with its environment. The environmental perspective developed out of the general systems model and the inconclusive results of many studies which assumed the organization to be a closed system. These investigations simply could not explain much of the phenomenon being studied. Howard E. Aldrich and Jeffrey Pfeffer summarize these environmental perspectives in "Environments and Organizations"; in "the Academic Library and Its Environment," I place these perspectives in the context of the library.

Charles Perrow's provocative article "The Short and Glorious History of Organizational Theory," summarizes much of the literature on complex organizations. He says to management: 1. much of the organization's behavior depends on its environment; 2. the organization's technology can predict variation in and between organizations; 3. change generally will be ineffective if induced by job enrichment or interpersonal relations; 4. leadership still is an illusive, albeit crucial, concept; and 5. critical variables related to organizational change are likely to be authority, degrees of specialization, rules and regulations, reward structures, and conflict.

Scientific Management

Frederick W. Taylor

THE writer has found that there are three questions uppermost in the minds of men when they become interested in scientific management.

First. Wherein do the principles of scientific management differ essentially from those of ordinary management?

Second. Why are better results attained under scientific management than under the other types?

Third. Is not the most important problem that of getting the right man at the head of the company? And if you have the right man cannot the choice of the type of management be safely left to him?

One of the principal objects of the following pages will be to give a satisfactory answer to these questions . . . .

Before starting to illustrate the principles of scientific management, or "task management" as it is briefly called, it seems desirable to outline what the writer believes will be recognized as the best type of management which is in common use. This is done so that the great difference between the best of the ordinary management and scientific management may be fully appreciated.

In an industrial establishment which employs say from 500 to 1000 workmen, there will be found in many cases at least twenty to thirty different trades. The workmen in each of these trades have had their knowledge handed down to them by word of mouth, through the many years in which their trade has been developed from the primitive condition, in which our far-distant ancestors each one practised the rudiments of many different trades, to the present state of great and growing subdivision of labor, in which each man specializes upon some comparatively small class of work.

The ingenuity of each generation has developed quicker and better methods for doing every element of the work in every trade. Thus the methods which are now in use may in a broad sense be said to be an evolution representing the survival of the fittest and best of the ideas

Pages 30–48 and 57–60 from THE PRINCIPLES OF SCIENTIFIC MANAGEMENT, by Frederick Winslow Taylor. Copyright © 1911, by Frederick W. Taylor. Renewed, 1939, by Louise M. S. Taylor. Copyright © 1947, by Harper & Row, Publishers. Inc. Reprinted by permission of Harper & Row, Publishers, Inc.

which have been developed since the starting of each trade. However, while this is true in a broad sense, only those who are intimately acquainted with each of these trades are fully aware of the fact that in hardly any element of any trade is there uniformity in the methods which are used. Instead of having only one way which is generally accepted as a standard, there are in daily use, say, fifty or a hundred different ways of doing each element of the work. And a little thought will make it clear that this must inevitably be the case, since our methods have been handed down from man to man by word of mouth, or have, in most cases, been almost unconsciously learned through personal observation. Practically in no instances have they been codified or systematically analyzed or described. The ingenuity and experience of each generation—of each decade, even, have without doubt handed over better methods to the next.This mass of rule-of-thumb or traditional knowledge may be said to be the principal asset or possession of everyday tradesman. Now, in the best of the ordinary types of management, the managers recognize frankly the fact that the 500 or 1000 workmen, included in the twenty to thirty trades, who are under them, possess this mass of traditional knowledge, a large part of which is not in the possession of the management. The management, of course, includes foremen and superintendents, who themselves have been in most cases first-class workers at their trades. And yet those foremen and superintendents know, better than any one else, that their own knowledge and personal skill falls far short of the combined knowledge and dexterity of all the workmen under them. The most experienced managers therefore frankly place before their workmen the problem of doing the work in the best and most economical way. They recognize the task before them as that of inducing each workman to use his best endeavors, his hardest work, all his traditional knowledge, his skill, his ingenuity, and his goodwill—in a word, his "initiative," so as to yield the largest possible return to his employer. The problem before the management then, may be briefly said to be that of obtaining the best *initiative* of every workman. And the writer uses the word "initiative" in its broadest sense to cover all of the good qualities sought for from the men.

On the other hand, no intelligent manager would hope to obtain in any full measure the initiative of his workmen unless he felt that he was giving them something more than they usually receive from their employers. Only those among the readers of this paper who have been managers or who have worked themselves at a trade realize how far the average workman falls short of giving his employer his full initiative. It is well within the mark to state that in nineteen out of twenty industrial establishments the workmen believe it to be directly against their interests to give their employers their best initiative, and that instead of working hard to do the largest possible amount of work and the best quality of work for their employers, they deliberately work as slowly as they dare while they at the same time try to make those over them believe that they are working fast.[1]

The writer repeats, therefore, that in order to have any hope of obtaining the initiative of his workmen the manager must give some *special incentive* to his men beyond that which is given to the average of the trade. This incentive can be given in several different ways, as, for example, the hope of rapid promotion or advancement; higher wages, either in the form of generous piecework prices or of a premium or bonus of some kind for good and rapid work; shorter hours of labor; better surroundings and working conditions than are ordinarily given, etc., and, above all, this special incentive should be accompanied by that personal consideration for, and friendly contact with, his workmen which comes only from a genuine and kindly interest in the welfare of those under him. It is only by giving a special inducement or "incentive" of this kind that the employer can hope even approximately to get the "initiative" of this workman. Under the ordinary type of management the necessity for offering the workman a special inducement has come to be so generally recognized that a large proportion of those most interested in the subject look upon the adoption of some one of the modern schemes for paying men (such as piece work, the premium plan, or the bonus plan, for instance) as practically the whole system of management. Under scientific management, however, the particular pay system which is adopted is merely one of the subordinate elements.

Broadly speaking, then, the best type of management in ordinary use may be defined as management in which the workmen give their best *initiative* and in return receive some *special incentive* from their employers. This type of management will be referred to as the management of *"initiative and incentive"* in contradistinction to scientific management, or task management, with which it is to be compared.

The writer hopes that the management of "initiative and incentive" will be recognized as representing the best type in ordinary use, and in fact he believes that it will be hard to persuade the average manager that anything better exists in the whole field than this type. The task which the writer has before him, then, is the difficult one of trying to prove in a thoroughly convincing way that there is another type of management which is not only better but overwhelmingly better than the management of "initiative and incentive."

The universal prejudice in favor of the management of "initiative and incentive" is so strong that no mere theoretical advantages which can be pointed out will be likely to convince the average manager that any other system is better. It will be upon a series of practical illustrations of the actual working of the two systems that the writer will depend in his efforts to prove that scientific management is so greatly superior to other types. Certain elementary principles, a certain philosophy, will however be recognized as the essence of that which is being illustrated in all of the practical examples which will be given. And the broad principles in which the scientific system differs from the ordinary or "rule-of-thumb" system are so simple in their nature that it seems desirable to describe them before starting with the illustrations.

Under the old type of management success depends almost entirely upon getting the "initiative" of the workmen, and it is indeed a rare case in which this initiative is really attained. Under scientific management the "initiative" of the workmen (that is, their hard work, their good-will, and their ingenuity) is obtained with absolute uniformity and to a greater extent than is possible under the old system; and in addition to this improvement on the part of the men, the managers assume new burdens, new duties, and responsibilities never dreamed of in the past. The managers assume, for instance, the burden of gathering together all of the traditional knowledge which in the past has been possessed by the workmen and then of classifying, tabulating, and reducing this knowledge to rules, laws, and formulæ which are immensely helpful to the workmen in doing their daily work. In addition to developing a *science* in this way, the management take on three other types of duties which involve new and heavy burdens for themselves.

These new duties are grouped under four heads:

First. They develop a science for each element of a man's work, which replaces the old rule-of-thumb method.

Second. They scientifically select and then train, teach, and develop the workman, whereas in the past he chose his own work and trained himself as best he could.

Third. They heartily cooperate with the men so as to insure all of the work being done in accordance with the principles of the science which has been developed.

Fourth. There is an almost equal division of the work and the responsibility between the management and the workmen. The management take over all work for which they are better fitted than the workmen, while in the past almost all of the work and the greater part of the responsibility were thrown upon the men.

It is this combination of the initiative of the workmen, coupled with the new types of work done by the management, that makes scientific management so much more efficient than the old plan.

Three of these elements exist in many cases, under the management of "initiative and incentive," in a small and rudimentary way, but they are, under this management, of minor importance, whereas under scientific management they form the very essence of the whole system.

The fourth of these elements, "an almost equal division of the responsibility between the management and the workmen," requires further explanation. The philosophy of the management of "initiative and incentive" makes it necessary for each workman to bear almost the entire responsibility for the general plan as well as for each detail of his work, and in many cases for his implements as well. In addition to this he must do all of the actual physical labor. The development of a science, on the other hand, involves the establishment of many rules, laws, and formulæ which replace the judgment of the individual workmen and which can be effectively used only after having been systematically recorded, indexed, etc. The practical use of scientific data also calls for a room in which to keep the books, records,[2] etc., and a desk for the planner to work at. Thus all of the planning which under the old system was done by the workman, as a result of his personal experience, must of necessity under the new system be done by the management in accordance with the laws of the science; because even if the workman was well suited to the development and use of scientific data, it would be physically impossible for him to work at his machine and at a desk at the same time. It is also clear that in most cases one type of man is needed to plan ahead and an entirely different type to execute the work.

The man in the planning room, whose specialty under scientific management is planning ahead, invariably finds that the work can be done better and more economically by a subdivision of the labor; each act of each mechanic, for example, should be preceded by various preparatory acts done by other men. And all of this involves, as we have said, "an almost equal division of the responsibility and the work between the management and the workman."

To summarize: Under the management of "initiative and incentive" practically the whole problem is "up to the workman," while under scientific management fully one-half of the problem is "up to the management."

Perhaps the most prominent single element in modern scientific management is the task idea. The work of every workman is fully planned out by the management at least one day in advance, and each man receives in most cases complete written instructions, describing in detail the task which he is to accomplish, as well as the means to be used in doing the work. And the work planned in advance in this way constitutes a task which is to be solved, as explained above, not by the workman alone, but in almost all cases by the joint effort of the workman and the management. This task specifies not only what is to be done but how it is to be done and the exact time allowed for doing it. And whenever the workman succeeds in doing his task right, and within the time limit specified, he receives an addition of from 30 percent to 100 percent to his ordinary wages. These tasks are carefully planned, so that both good and careful work are called for in their performance, but it should be distinctly understood that in no case is the workman called upon to work at a pace which would be injurious to his health. The task is always so regulated that the man who is well suited to his job will thrive while working at this rate during a long term of years and grow happier and more prosperous, instead of being overworked. Scientific management consists very largely in preparing for and carrying out these tasks.

The writer is fully aware that to perhaps most of the readers of this paper the four elements which differentiate the new management from the old will at first appear to be merely high-sounding phrases; and he would again repeat that he has no idea of convincing the reader of their value merely through announcing their existence. His hope of carrying conviction rests upon demonstrating the tremendous force and effect of these four elements through a series of practical illustrations. It will be shown, first, that they can be applied absolutely to all classes of work, from the most elementary to the most intricate; and second, that when they are applied, the results must of necessity be overwhelmingly greater than those which it is possible to attain under the management of initiative and incentive.

The first illustration is that of handling pig iron, and this work is chosen because it is typical of perhaps the crudest and most elementary form of labor which is performed by man. This work is done by men with no other implements than their hands. The pig-iron handler stoops down, picks up a pig weighing about 92 pounds, walks for a few feet or yards and then drops it on the ground or upon a pile. This work is so crude and elementary in its nature that the writer firmly believes that it would be possible to train an intelligent gorilla so as to become a more efficient pig-iron handler than any man can be. Yet it will be shown that the science of handling pig iron is so great and amounts to so much that it is impossible for the man who is best suited to this type of work to understand the principles of this science, or even to work in accordance with these principles without the aid of a man better educated than he is. And the further illustrations to be given will make it clear that in almost all of the mechanic arts the science which underlies each workman's act is so great and amounts to so much that the workman who is best suited actually to do the work is incapable (either through lack of education or through insufficient mental capacity) of understanding this science. This is announced as a general principle, the truth of which will become apparent as one illustration after another is given. After showing these four elements in the handling of pig iron, several illustrations will be given of their application to different kinds of work in the field of the mechanic arts, at intervals in a rising scale, beginning with the simplest and ending with the more intricate forms of labor.

One of the first pieces of work undertaken by us, when the writer started to introduce scientific management into the Bethlehem Steel Company, was to handle pig iron on task work. The opening of the Spanish War found some 80,000 tons of pig iron placed in small piles in an open field adjoining the works. Prices for pig iron had been so low that it could not be sold at a profit, and it therefore had been stored. With the opening of the Spanish War the price of pig iron rose, and this large accumulation of iron was sold. This gave us a good opportunity to show the workmen, as well as the owners and managers of the works, on a fairly large scale the advantages of task work over the old-fashioned day work and piece work, in doing a very elementary class of work.

The Bethlehem Steel Company had five blast furnaces, the product of which had been handled by a pig-iron gang for many years. This gang, at this time, consisted of about seventy-five men. They were good, average pig-iron handlers, were under an excellent foreman who himself had been a pig-iron handler, and the work was done, on the whole, about as fast and as cheaply as it was anywhere else at that time.

A railroad switch was run out into the field, right along the edge of the piles of pig iron. An inclined plank was placed against the side of a car, and each man picked up from his pile a pig of iron weighing about 92 pounds, walked up the inclined plank and dropped it on the end of the car.

We found that this gang were loading on the average about 12½ long tons per man per day. We were surprised to find, after studying the matter, that a first-class pig-iron handler ought to handle between 47 and 48 long tons per day, instead of 12½ tons. This task seemed to us so very large that we were obliged to go over our work several times before we were absolutely sure that we were right. Once we were sure, however, that 47 tons was a proper day's work for a first-class pig-iron handler, the task which faced us as managers under the modern scientific plan was clearly before us. It was our duty to see that 80,000 tons of pig iron was loaded on to the cars at the rate of 47 tons per man per day, in place of 12½ tons, at which rate the work was then being done. And it was further our duty to see that this work was done without bringing on a strike among the men, without any quarrel with the men, and to see that the men were happier and better contented when loading at the new rate of 47 tons than they were when loading at the old rate of 12½ tons.

Our first step was the scientific selection of the workman. In dealing with workmen under this type of management, it is an inflexible rule to talk to and deal with only one man at a time, since each workman has his own special abilities and limitations, and since we are not dealing with men in masses, but are trying to develop each individual man to his highest state of efficiency and prosperity. Our first step was to find the proper workman to begin with. We therefore carefully watched and studied these seventy-five men for three or four days, at the end of which time we had picked out four men who appeared to be physically able to handle pig iron at the rate of 47 tons per day. A careful study was then made of each of these men. We looked up their history as far back as practicable and thorough inquiries were made as to the character, habits, and the ambition of each of them. Finally we selected one from among the four as the most likely man to start with. He was a little Pennsylvania Dutchman who had been observed to trot back home for a mile or so after his work in the evening about as fresh as he was when he came trotting down to work in the morning. We found that upon wages of $1.15 a day he had succeeded in buying a small plot of ground, and that he was engaged in putting up the walls of a little house for himself in the morning before starting to work and at night after leaving. He also had the reputation of being exceedingly "close," that is, of placing a very high value on a dollar. As one man whom we talked to about him said, "A penny looks about the size of a cart-wheel to him." This man we will call Schmidt.

The task before us, then, narrowed itself down to getting Schmidt to handle 47 tons of pig iron per day and making him glad to do it. This was done as follows. Schmidt was called out from among the gang of pig-iron handlers and talked to somewhat in this way:

"Schmidt, are you a high-priced man?"

"Vell, I don't know vat you mean."

"Oh yes, you do. What I want to know is whether you are a high-priced man or not."

"Vell, I don't know vat you mean."

"Oh, come now, you answer my questions. What I want to find out is whether you are a high-priced man or one of these cheap fellows here. What I want to find out is whether you want to earn $1.85 a day or whether you are satisfied with $1.15, just the same as all those cheap fellows are getting."

"Did I vant $1.85 a day? Vas dot a high-priced man? Vell, yes, I vas a high-priced man."

"Oh, you're aggravating me. Of course you want $1.85 a day—everyone wants it! You know perfectly well that has very little to do with your being a high-priced man. For goodness' sake answer my questions, and don't waste any more of my time. Now come over here. You see that pig iron?"

"Yes."

"You see that car?"

"Yes."

"Well, if you are a high-priced man, you will load that pig iron on that car tomorrow for $1.85. Now do wake up and answer my question. Tell me whether you are a high-priced man or not."

"Vell—did I got $1.85 for loading dot pig iron on dot car tomorrow?"

"Yes, of course you do, and you get $1.85 for loading a pile like that every day right through the year. That is what a high-priced man does, and you know it just as well as I do."

"Vell, dot's all right. I could load dot pig iron on the car tomorrow for $1.85, and I get it every day, don't I?"

"Certainly you do—certainly you do."

"Vell, den, I vas a high-priced man."

"Now, hold on, hold on. You know just as well as I do that a high-priced man has to exactly as he's told from morning till night. You have seen this man here before, haven't you?"

"No, I never saw him."

"Well, if you are a high-priced man, you will do exactly as this man tells you tomorrow, from morning till night. When he tells you to pick up a pig and walk, you pick it up and you walk, and when he tells you to sit down and rest, you sit down. You do that straight through the day. And what's more, no back talk. Now a high-priced man does just what he's told to do, and no back talk. Do you understand that? When this man tells you to walk, you walk; when he tells you to sit down, you sit down, and you don't talk back at him. Now you come on to work here tomorrow morning and I'll know before night whether you are really a high-priced man or not."

This seems to be rather rough talk. And indeed it would be if applied to an educated mechanic, or even an intelligent laborer. With a man of the mentally sluggish type of Schmidt it is appropriate and not unkind, since it is effective in fixing his attention on the high wages which he wants and away from what, if it were called to his attention, he probably would consider impossibly hard work.

What would Schmidt's answer be if he were talked to in a manner which is usual under the management of "initiative and incentive"? say, as follows:

"Now, Schmidt, you are a first-class pig-iron handler and know your business well. You have been handling at the rate of 12½ tons per day. I have given considerable study to handling pig iron, and feel sure that you could do a much larger day's work than you have been doing. Now don't you think that if you really tried you could handle 47 tons of pig iron per day, instead of 12½ tons?"

What do you think Schmidt's answer would be to this?

Schmidt started to work, and all day long, and at regular intervals, was told by the man who stood over him with a watch, "Now pick up a pig and walk. Now sit down and rest. Now walk—now rest," etc. He worked when he was told to work, and rested when he was told to rest, and at half-past five in the afternoon had his 47½ tons loaded on the car. And he practically never failed to work at this pace and do the task that was set him during the three years that the writer was at Bethlehem. And throughout this time he averaged a little more than $1.85 a day, whereas before he had never received over $1.15 per day, which was the ruling rate of wages at that time in Bethlehem. That is, he received 60 percent higher wages than were paid to other men who were not working on task work. One man after another was picked out and trained to handle pig iron at the rate of 47½ tons per day until all of the pig iron was handled at this rate, and the men were receiving 60 percent more wages than other workmen around them.

The writer has given above a brief description of three of the four elements which constitute the essence of scientific management: first, the careful selection of the workman, and, second and third, the method of first inducing and then training and helping the workman to work according to the scientific method. Nothing has as yet been said about the science of handling pig iron. The writer trusts, however, that before leaving this illustration the reader will be thoroughly convinced that there is a science of handling pig iron, and further that this science amounts to so much that the man who is suited to handle pig iron cannot possibly understand it, nor even work in accordance with the laws of this science, without the help of those who are over him.

• • •

The law is confined to that class of work in which the limit of a man's capacity is reached because he is tired out. It is the law of heavy laboring, corresponding to the work of the cart horse, rather than that of the trotter. Practically all such work consists of a heavy pull or a push on the man's arms, that is, the man's strength is exerted by either lifting or pushing something which he grasps in his hands. And the law is that for each given pull or push on the man's arms it is possible for the workman to to be under load for only a definite percentage of the day. For example, when a pig iron is being handled (each pig weighing 92 pounds), a first-class workman can only be under load 43 percent of the day. He must be entirely free from load during 57 percent of the day. And as the load becomes lighter, the percentage of the day under which the man can remain under load increases. So that, if the workman is handling a half pig weighing 46 pounds, he can then be under load 58 percent of the day and only has to rest during 42 percent. As the weight grows lighter the man can remain under load during a larger and larger percentage of the day, until finally a load is reached which he can carry in his hands all day long without being tired out. When that point has been arrived at this law ceases to be useful as a guide to a laborer's endurance, and some other law must be found which indicates the man's capacity for work.

When a laborer is carrying a piece of pig iron weighing 92 pounds in his hands, it tires him about as much to stand still under the load as it does to walk with it, since his arm muscles are under the same severe tension whether he is moving or not. A man, however, who stands still under a load is exerting no horse-power whatever, and this accounts for the fact that no constant relation could be traced in various kinds of heavy laboring work between the foot-pounds of energy exerted and the tiring effect of the work on the man. It will be clear that in all work of this kind it is necessary for the arms of the workman to be completely free from load (that is, for the workman to rest) at frequent intervals. Throughout the time that the man is under a heavy load the tissues of his arm muscles are in process of degeneration, and frequent periods of rest are required in order that the blood may have a chance to restore these tissues to their normal condition.

To return now to our pig-iron handlers at the Bethlehem Steel Company. If Schmidt had been allowed to attack the pile of 47 tons of pig iron without the guidance or direction of a man who understood the art, or science, of handling pig iron, in his desire to earn his high wages he would probably have tired himself out by eleven or twelve o'clock in the day. He would have kept so steadily at work that his muscles would not have had the proper periods of rest absolutely needed for recuperation, and he would have been completely exhausted early in the day. By having a man, however, who understood this law, stand over him and direct his work, day after day, until he acquired the habit of resting at proper intervals, he was able to work at an even gait all day long without unduly tiring himself.

Now one of the very first requirements for a man who is fit to handle pig iron as a regular occupation is that he shall be so stupid and so phlegmatic that he more nearly resembles in his mental make-up the ox than any other type. The man who is mentally alert and intelligent is for this very reason entirely unsuited to what would, for him, be the grinding monotony of work of this character. Therefore the workman who is best suited to handling pig iron is unable to understand the real science of doing this class of work. He is so stupid that the word "percentage" has no meaning to him, and he must consequently be trained by a man more intelligent than himself into the habit of working in accordance with the laws of this science before he can be successful.

The writer trusts that it is now clear that even in the case of the most elementary form of labor that is known, there is a science, and that when the man best suited to this class of work has been carefully selected, when the science of doing the work has been developed, and when the carefully selected man has been trained to work in accordance with this science, the results obtained must of necessity be overwhelmingly greater than those which are possible under the plan of "initiative and incentive."

References

1. The writer has tried to make the reason for this unfortunate state of things clear in a paper entitled "Shop Management," read before the American Society of Mechanical Engineers.
2. For example, the records containing the data used under scientific management in an ordinary machine-shop fill thousands of pages.

Scientific Management of Library Operations

Richard M. Dougherty and Fred J. Heinritz

T HE high-sounding term Scientific Management should not be allowed to mislead anybody. It is not something that can be bought wholesale and utilized retail, but simply means: study your problem according to scientific methods, eliminating guess, setting each man a proper task, and allowing suitable awards for the accomplishment of these tasks. This done, increased efficiency is bound to follow.—Henry L. Gantt

SCIENTIFIC MANAGEMENT:
A HISTORICAL PERSPECTIVE

The scientific manager applies the principle of science to problems of administration. Most of us are aware of these principles, even if we cannot recite them. The scientific method is little more than the use of common sense and strategy to solve problems: one formulates a hypothesis, gathers data, evaluates the data, implements a solution, and evaluates the solution.

Before a problem can be solved there must first be a decision maker who is dissatisfied and desires some change. The decision maker must crystallize the change in the form of objectives and develop a strategy to solve the problem. The tools of scientific management are designed to facilitate this process. A problem cannot exist unless the decision maker has a choice between at least two courses of action: dissatisfaction with an existing situation may be present, but it is a *problem* only when alternatives are possible. The need to cope with finite resources by choosing among courses of action is a part of growing up in the latter half of twentieth-century America.

The roots of management science reach back to the late nineteenth century. Frederick Taylor (1856–1915), an engineer, is often referred to as the Father of Scientific Management. Most pioneers in the field began by studying the physical rather than the psychological aspects of work, although they soon recognized that this emphasis was misplaced and spoke out against such a narrow approach. The immediate tangible gains achieved by applying scientific-management principles created a misleading image in the eyes of the public, which often thought of them as a mechanistic approach to solving work-related problems. It was not until the labor movement became a formidable bargaining force and until research and experience increased our physical, psychological, and sociological sophistication that the human side of management gradually assumed greater importance.

Experiments conducted at the Hawthorne plant of the Western Electric Company between 1927 and 1932 helped explode the myth that the worker was concerned only with the size of the paycheck (F. J. Roethlisberger and W. J. Dickson, *Management and the Worker* [Cambridge: Harvard University Press, 1939]). The Hawthorne experiment revealed that the motivations of an individual or a group are complex and that there are many factors—physical, psychological, and, social—that influence productivity. Today's scientific manager is concerned with all of these factors and strives to satisfy the objectives of an organization without ignoring the aspirations of its workers.

In recent years some management scientists have criticized the work of Taylor and his colleagues. These critics have influenced some managers to dismiss the principles that the early researchers espoused and also to ignore the entire field of human engineering. Consequently it is important for the librarian new to the profession, as well as the experienced practitioner who may not be familiar with the principles of scientific management, to learn more about the work of these pioneers so that their contributions can be placed in a better perspective. Otherwise there might be a temptation to avoid or even reject a powerful set of principles and tools that is available to today's library manager.

In the introduction to *The Principles of Scientific Management* Taylor quoted Theodore Roosevelt, in an address to a group of governors at the White House:

> The conservation of our national resources is only preliminary to the larger question of national efficiency.
>   The whole country at once recognized the importance of conserving our material resources and a large movement has been started which will be effective in accomplishing this object. As yet, however, we have but vaguely

appreciated the importance of "the larger question of increasing our national efficiency."

We can see our forests vanishing, our water-power going to waste, our soil being carried by floods to the sea; and the end of our coal and our iron is in sight. But our larger wastes of human effort, which goes on every day through such acts as are [sic] blundering, ill-directed or inefficient are less visible, less tangible, and are but vaguely appreciated.

We can see and feel the waste of material things. Awkward, inefficient, or ill-directed movements of men, however, leave nothing visible or tangible behind them [F. W. Taylor, *The Principles of Scientific Management* (New York: Norton, 1967), p. 5].

Although these words were uttered over seventy years ago, they are equally applicable to present-day society. The recent decline in worker productivity has given even greater urgency to the search for better ways of doing work than was the case in Taylor's time.

Taylor offered four objectives to guide managers in their quest to improve productivity: 1) the development of management as a science; 2) the scientific selection of workers; 3) scientific education and development of workers; and 4) intimate friendly cooperation between management and workers (Taylor, *Principles*, p. 130).

One of today's foremost management experts, Peter Drucker, has postulated what he believes to be the framework in which work can be made more productive:

First, it requires analysis. We have to know the specific operations needed for work, their sequence, and their requirement.

Second, we also need synthesis. The individual operations have to be brought together into a process of production.

Third, we need to build into the process the control of direction, of quality and quantity, of standards, and of exceptions.

Fourth, the appropriate tools have to be provided [P. F. Drucker, *Management: Tasks, Responsibilities, Practices* (New York: Harper and Row, 1974), p. 199].

The parallels between the principles set forth by Taylor in 1911 and by Peter Drucker in 1974 are inescapable. Students of scientific management should strive to gain a clear understanding of how these principles can be applied toward improving library operations. In order to accomplish this objective one must first recognize that scientific management is more than a mechanistic set of tools—it is a philosophy, an approach to problem solving generating a special attitude toward work by workers and managers. Managers in all types of organizations have applied many of the tools successfully. It was in large part their misapplication by some administrators that led to the criticisms against the scientific-management movement. Drucker touched on this point when he noted: "It is fashionable today to look down on Taylor and to decry his outmoded psychology, but Taylor was the first man in known history of mankind who did not take work for granted, but looked at it and studied it" (*Management*, p. 24).

Taylor believed that the casual rule-of-thumb approach to management that was so prevalent in the late nineteenth century should be replaced by scientific analysis. Among his many contributions were the development of time study and the application of work standards. He tried to determine what constituted a fair day's work based not upon a supervisor's best estimate but on empirical studies of the work actually performed.

Many of Taylor's closest associates made noteworthy contributions to the movement. Among these were Carl Barth, Horace Hathaway, Morris Cooke, and Henry Gantt. Gantt is best known for the development of techniques for planning and scheduling work; organizational planners still use the Gantt chart. Gantt was also one of the earliest management scientists to focus his attention on the concerns of the worker.

Frank (1868–1924) and Lillian Gilbreth (1878–1972), who achieved a sort of accidental immortality via the best-selling book *Cheaper by the Dozen*, rank with Taylor as contributors to the development of scientific-management philosophy and techniques. Early in their careers the Gilbreths became interested in the elimination of nonproductive motions. In order to perform their studies they devised and perfected the flow process chart. Frank Gilbreth always tried to achieve what he termed the "one best method of doing a job." The Gilbreths' contributions resulted in improvements in many industries and led to the development and refinement of such techniques as micromotion and the use of motion pictures in the study of work.

The discipline of scientific management had its origin in industrial settings. Only later were its principles applied to social agencies. We do not know when libraries first entered the movement. It is known, however, that librarians in the late nineteenth and early twentieth centuries were concerned with the cost of operations. It is reasonable to assume that there were attempts to analyze and simplify work in order to achieve economies. The literature since World War II reflects a much greater interest by librarians in applying scientific-management principles in a library environment.

A detailed history of scientific management is beyond the scope of this text. Readers interested in gaining a historical overview of the field will find several comprehensive works listed in the bibliography at the end of this chapter.

SCIENTIFIC MANAGEMENT
IN LIBRARIES

Most readers will have little difficulty in understanding why the tools of scientific management have played such an important role in the industrial world. When correctly applied, they improved productivity, speeded distribution, and reduced costs, allowing industrial firms to market their products at lower unit prices. This in turn stimulated product demand—and profits. Increased profits made possible the payment of larger dividends and larger salaries. On the other hand, libraries, as well as other social agencies, are not operated for the purpose of producing a favorable balance sheet. This important distinction has led some to argue, speciously, that the principles of scientific management do not apply to nonprofit organizations.

The employees of social organizations should make every effort to guarantee fellow taxpayers a maximum return on their tax dollars. This responsibility is now termed accountability. As tax rates have continued to spiral upward, the public clamor for greater accountability has intensified. The tax squeeze has already taken its toll in some communities: budget cuts, staff layoffs, cutbacks in library services, have become all too common. Library and school bond issues are often defeated at the polls, and operating budgets have come under close citizen scrutiny. No, American taxpayers will not subscribe to the notion that scientific management applies only to profit-making firms!

Some librarians are reluctant to use scientific-management tools because they do not believe that library work lends itself to systematic analysis, citing book selection and reference services as types of work that cannot be adequately quantified. They overlook, however, the high percentage of library tasks that consist of repetitive, mechanical routines that do lend themselves to such analysis—for example, searching, ordering, cataloging, filing, binding, circulation, and shelving. Others ask how to measure the benefits of library service derived by a community or by an individual library user. Some library activities are and will continue to be hard to measure, but these limitations should not dissuade analysts. The same difficulties are associated with most educational processes, yet intensive efforts to document the cost and social benefits of education continue in spite of measurement problems. The tools of analysis are becoming every more sophisticated. The computer, for example, has made it possible to analyze activities that could not be measured a few short years ago.

The data collected through scientific management will help a library administrator in many ways: to modify procedures so as to improve efficiency, to work up accurate job descriptions so as to better match employees with tasks, to train new workers, and to develop and update procedure manuals. At budget time these data can be used to justify the continuation of funding at an existing level or the need for additional funds. State legislatures and city councils are usually more impressed by budget requests accompanied by supporting quantitative data than they are by panegyrics on librarianship.

On an individual level library professionals will also find that scientific management can improve their own productivity. There is personal satisfaction in doing one's job well. Better performance can also lead to more rapid promotion. And, when promoted, the librarian who has practiced increasing his or her own productivity will make a better manager.

WHEN SHOULD A LIBRARY AUTOMATE?

Although this text emphasizes improvements of manual library procedures, the authors recognize the importance that many librarians attach to automation. Unfortunately, some librarians in their haste to automate have ignored the importance of first analyzing carefully their manual operations. The analytical tools presented in this text are germane to both manual and automated procedures: one must be able to document and fully understand the former before beginning to design the latter. The specifications of an improved system may or may not be dependent on the application of computer technology. Even with an automated system, current documentation is very desirable.

One should neither jump on the automation bandwagon nor ignore the power of computer technology. Many failures reported in the literature since the mid-1960s illustrate the pitfalls of automating library operations. On the other hand, some polemical essays have overstated the negative aspects of automation. Since the cost of library personnel is increasing more rapidly than the cost of computer technology, it is inevitable that more libraries will be able to automate selected operations.

The prudent library manager should compare carefully the economic and service potential of automated systems with the library's current procedures. The potential of some computer systems is enormous. Many successful applications can be cited; some were developed locally, others developed and marketed by commercial vendors, and still others developed to serve large numbers of libraries organized into networks—OCLC and the Research Library Group (RLG), for example.

Because the purchasing power of library budgets in recent years has been significantly eroded by inflation, and because library operations are so labor intensive, there is a special incentive to adopt techniques that will reduce, or at least lower, the rate of increase in labor costs. It is also true that many library procedures lend themselves to computerization: they tend to be repetitious, be frequently performed, and make multiple use of the same data elements—author, title, imprint, and so on.

Nevertheless, a library manager must weigh a number of factors before making a long-range commitment to automation:

1. There should be access to the necessary analysis, programming, and computer expertise needed to reach the desired goal.
2. There should be adequate and stable computer power for a period of at least five years. Many library automation projects have floundered or failed because access to a computer facility could not be maintained.
3. Careful planning and the preparation of specifications should precede the selection of a machine system. The computer hardware and supporting software package must be capable of handling all the required workload.
4. The computer hardware configuration should be expandable.
5. The computer system should deliver information in a time-frame acceptable to users and at a cost libraries are willing and able to pay.

Computer technology is changing so rapidly that today's state of the art may be tomorrow's Model A. Minicomputers have replaced large central processors for some library applications, and microcomputers are already beginning to replace minis as the equipment of choice. More library operations will certainly be computerized in this decade. It is therefore prudent for managers to familiarize themselves with developments in this field and stay abreast of changes.

We urge those who are interested to examine the literature of library automation and computer science.

Management in College and University Libraries

Donald Coney

MANAGEMENT, as a field in itself, is generally identified with the last four decades, beginning with F. W. Taylor and time-and-motion study and ending—for the moment—with "operations research."[1,2] Management is a broad area with a vague configuration; no attempt is made in this paper to define it with any precision. Information at hand shows that management in college and university libraries gathers around the focuses of personnel, work measurement, costs, machines, and plant. "Organization," often considered a part of management, and a popular subject in libary administration, is the topic of another article in this journal. For the most part, the evidence of interest in management areas is drawn from articles in the library press and a few books, and is limited to the period following World War II.

The management of libraries has never benefited from the wealth of attention devoted to such areas of librarianship as the development of book collections, classification, cataloging, bibliography, and the like. For a long time this inattention was not important; the small size of collections, staff, buildings, and clienteles made for simplicity of operation and demanded no very sophisticated approach to the ways of doing things. Librarians were directed to new methods of management as early as 1911 by the then Librarian of Cornell.[3] The Williamson report,[4] in 1923, spelled out the advantages of training in the techniques of management. In one of the most recent treatments of library management, Leigh sets the stage again for the need of management—though he speaks of public libraries, his views are as true for those of learned institutions:

> Like other institutions—especially those not under the constant spur of profit seeking—we might expect public library operations to be compounded of clear-cut, rational, economical processes and traditional, rule-

Reprinted with permission from *Library Trends*, vol. 1, no. 1, July 1952, pp. 83–94.
© 1952 The Board of Trustees of The University of Illinois.

of-thumb, wasteful practices never subjected to rigid analysis. This is the more likely because of the historical evolution of the public library. Its early leadership had a major background of interest and training in literary, cultural fields rather than in science, technology, and administration. The same tendency survives in the most of the present library personnel.[5–]

Leigh develops the argument for management education as follows:

The introduction of these expert techniques of management presents subtle problems of adaptation. It is one of the assumptions of the Inquiry that librarians, like other professional groups, are sensitive with regard to the values of their traditional ways and will be slow to accept changes in accustomed practices recommended by outside specialists. It is also assumed that some changes would be desirable. It is, therefore, of great importance that the skills of management analysis and scientific personnel administration be assimilated within the general administration of libraries and professional training of librarians rather than occasionally presented as an intrusion of outsiders to measure work, to analyze and classify positions, or to establish salary grades.[6]

He is able to report that "In some of the newer programs an attempt has been made to draw into one general course in library administration the essential material formerly in several elective courses dealing with the organization and the operating problems of the several types of libraries."[7] This is hopeful because such a concentration is likely to result in some specialization of instruction and to lead the instructor into familiarity with the literature of professional management. Columbia University School of Library Service offered, in the summer of 1951, a workshop in policy-making, operations analysis, and work simplification directed by R. R. Shaw, Librarian of the U.S. Department of Agriculture, who had recently offered a course in work measurement and standards of performance in the Department of Agriculture's Graduate School. His article, "Scientific Management in the Library,"[8] discusses management concepts for analyzing activity to determine a fair day's work and the "best method"—the classic objectives of early management. Columbia has projected, but has not yet financed, a cooperative management research center.

It will be interesting to see if one of Leigh's management recommendations is accepted by the profession. "The Inquiry studies indicated," he says, "that the greatest possibilities for improvement in the years ahead depend not so much upon analysis of internal formal structure as of flow of work, definition of duties, disposition of personnel and simplification of processes."[9] Traditionally, the organization structure has been the area of greatest management concern in libraries, if the evidence of the literature is to be trusted. It would appear, however, from the writing reported below, that personnel administration already is well entrenched in administrators' minds as an important management technique, and that the work flow and process study are gaining attention. The process chart was the subject of a Chicago master's thesis;[10] and a master's paper was written on the process and personnel of the University of Illinois Library's Purchase Division.[11]

Little attention, apparently, was paid directly to standards, though Clapp[12] reported briefly on the reactivation of the American Standards Association's Committee Z39 with a wide representation of library organizations and enlarged terms of reference. It will be recalled that this committee's one completed piece of work—before the war forced its suspension—was the standard on reference data and arrangement of periodicals. The revived committee has commenced study of standardizing of periodical title abbreviations, of transliterating Cyrillic characters, of bibliographical presentation in serials, and of library statistics.

In his iconoclastic study of organization theory[13] Simon offers what might serve as a text for all discussions of personnel: "In the study of organization, the operative employee must be at the focus of attention, for the success of the structure will be judged by his performance within it." It is a matter of concern, then, that Wilson and Tauber[14] (whose book reflects professional writing to 1944) concluded that librarians had paid little attention to many important personnel matters. Leigh, more recently, reports that "it seemed evident that public libraries have not yet developed fully the agencies or the patterns for the execution of modern personnel policy."[15] In 1944 Trent had to report, after a survey of sixteen university libraries, that librarians tend to believe "that the library staff, because of its training, interests, and general cultural background, does not need any kind of personnel system,"[16] despite the fact that library staffs are subject to the kind of human frailties that affect the employees of industry. Yet librarians have been concerned about training and the direction of staffs for years. The American Library Association has formalized the personnel interests of the profession for a long time in a committee or board. In 1927 the earliest job classification and compensation plan for libraries was published under the auspices of the Committee on Classification of Library Personnel by the Bureau of Public Personnel Administration—the so-called "Telford report."[17] There is discernible a reflection of good personnel practice in libraries, even though at times or in certain areas the reflection is faint or cloudy.

A broad view of personnel administration in libraries was taken by the tenth Institute of the Graduate Library School at Chicago at the beginning of what was then considered a post-war period. The papers of the institute[18] bring together a group of professional personnel people, who present standard material on the leading concepts of personnel management (career service, selection, job classification, morale) and some librarians of more than usual information and interest in the personnel field. Despite a good deal of "warming-over" the result furnishes librarians with a useful introduction. It should be noted that the volume contains the most suggestive treatment of unions and related library employee groups in O. W. Phelps' article on organization of employees.

The American Library Association's Board on Personnel Administration has been active in providing librarians with materials on job classification and pay plans.[19] Its most recent publication in the field[20] is reported to have "come out of an expressed need for such a tool"—a not surprising situation in view of the post-war problems of living costs, expansion of library services, and labor shortages. One application of job classification and pay plan technique is reported in detail for the University of California by Bryant and Kaiser.[21]

Concern for competence in supervision is reflected by Stanford,[22] speaking for the Board on Personnel Administration. He describes the duties and traits of the supervisor, and, noting the failure to treat of this subject in library school programs, argues that the principles and techniques can be taught. Osteen,[23] after a comparison of the executive in-service training practices of large public libraries with those of business agencies, concludes that librarianship could profit by adopting certain techniques in this field. Hirsch[24] reported, in somewhat tentative language, on the successful conclusion of the first year of a limited in-service program at the University of Pennsylvania. However, Wight[25] questions the need for a systematic program of in-service training for professional librarians, given adequate education, pay, intellectual stimulation, and good morale conditions. The wartime "training within industry" technique is related to library needs for skilled supervision by Heintz.[26]

As might be expected, the largest library expresses most extensively in its administration the concepts and devices of personnel administration. In 1940 the Library of Congress transferred personnel work from the Chief Clerk's Office to a new Personnel Office with a broadly defined program.[27] The activities of this office afford an example of accepted personnel practice translated into library terms. Even a library of modest size can profit from study of Library of Congress personnel work as recounted in the annual reports of the Librarian, especially those of 1947–48 and 1949–50.[28]

Employee attitude questionnaires to determine staff views of work conditions and administration do not appear to be much used in libraries. One example is found in the "What Do You Think?" questionnaire designed and administered by the Staff Association of the University of California Library at Berkeley in 1949. Interpretations of the results were reported to the staff; were related to the building program of the library, and to the Bureau of Labor Statistics' survey of library salaries and working conditions; and were used by department heads for the improvement of administration.[29]

There is a notable absence of emphasis on incentive devices, perhaps because the most common one, incentive payment, is usually impossible under governmental policy which controls most libraries.

Time-and-motion study, job analysis, process analysis, etc. are terms in management literature which cluster around the focus of work measurement—the analysis of work into elements, either large or small, for study and measurement in time or money. This notion was F. W. Taylor's great contribution to management, and the foundation of the scientific management movement. The minute analysis of work actions as developed by Frank Gilbreth is more generally applicable to the innumerable repetitive motions of industry than to a great deal of library work, especially that work ideally identified with professional activity. Nevertheless, the manual part of work done in libraries is susceptible to microanalysis, while all activities can be measured in large units of work. A report of what is believed to be the first time-and-motion study of a library process using formal techniques by Battles, Davis, and Harms,[30] which appeared in 1943, analyzes the loan routine at Bradley University Library. Price[31] reports a later study of periodical routing at the Beltsville Branch of the U.S. Department of Agriculture Library using a simpler and grosser technique. In recent years library schools, influenced by a growing employment of the attitudes and methods of science, have applied work measurement methods to library situations. Hardkopf[32] studied the application of motion techniques to the preparation processes at the New York Public Library, and Frantz[33] made a motion study of acquisition work at the University of Illinois. Two reports on a time study of the Urbana Free Library came from the University of Illinois Library School.[34,35] Time-and-motion study methods were employed at the U.S. Department of Agriculture Library in 1944 to speed up the photographic processes.[36] A work simplification clinic, sponsored in 1951 by the University of California School of Librarianship and its alumni association, centered on the flow chart as an analytical tool for examining a process.[37]

University libraries lack a comprehensive, comparative cost study of their operations in any way comparable to the one by Baldwin and Marcus for public libraries.[38] Nevertheless, university libraries have pioneered in exploiting work measurement and unit cost methods, chiefly in the matter of cataloging costs. In 1949 a group of Association of Research Libraries members privately exchanged cataloging cost data developed on the gross unit cost basis used in connection with the catalog inquiry at the University of California at Berkeley.[39] Knapp reported the results of a cost study of the preparation department of a small college library in 1943.[40]

The 1947 report of the U.S. Department of Agriculture Library[41] carries a table showing a decline in the unit cost of circulation and reference combined from 1941 ($1.42) to 1947 ($0.31), an improvement in efficiency attributed to the "continued application of scientific management." The gross cost method, by which all library expenditures are distributed over the number of loans made and reference questions answered, is used. This relates cataloging, binding, supervision, etc., as well as the work of loan and reference assistants, to the end-product of the library: loans and answers to inquiries.

The advantage of machines is that they perform repetitive operations more rapidly and accurately than humans do. Their drawbacks are their high initial cost, the need to supply them with a large volume of their particular kind of work if their operating cost is to be kept down, and their limited use. While library work is replete with drudgery, much of it is of a kind which springs from manifestations of the human mind—books, questions—and it is not repetitive in ways acceptable to the machine. Except in the largest libraries there is not enough money to pay the purchase price of many machines, nor enough work of their kind to justify them. This, at any rate, appears to be the situation. But whether it is cheaper to buy hours of labor or machines, whether the volume of repetitive work has reached the point of machine justification, are often matters requiring job analysis and cost studies; that is, more arduous observation and calculation than librarians are prepared to make.

In this connection it is interesting to know that certain European experts who examined documentation techniques here in 1950 reported that "it was emphasized that in the United States labor is more expensive than machines and materials, and that efforts are therefore constantly made to mechanize operations as far as possible," and that "the main reason for using automatic machines is to economize manpower. In Europe the costs of equipment are comparatively more important than the costs of labor."[42]

There is still a good deal of journal literature on the commoner sorts of office machinery. The American Library Association and some state library assocations maintain committees on apparatus useful to libraries. This must mean that the use of machinery is percolating down into the smaller organizations.

The machines which have exercised the greatest fascination over librarians in the past fifteen years are punched card equipment. Actuated by holes punched in cards, these machines identify, sort, and correlate whatever data is represented by the combinations of holes on the cards. These machines exist at present in two types widely separate in complexity. The edge-punched card is characteristic of the simplest form; the apparatus required is little more than a tray for cards and a skewer for sorting them. There is no middle ground between this simple device and the electronic complexities of the machinery required to handle field-punched cards, of which International Business Machines provide the best-known example.

Perry, Ferris, and Stanford furnish a handy summary of punched card use in American libraries.[43] The section on applications to administration reveals that, as in the use of cost studies, university and scholarly libraries are the most active in exploiting these machines. The Perry bibliography is extended in Casey and Perry, *Punched Cards*;[44] and Klausner's article[45] in the same work reviews IBM applications to charging files.

An early application of IBM was to accounting in library order departments, at Boston Public Library, the Universities of Georgia and, most recently, California (Berkeley) where a multiple-copy card is used.[46] Illinois has made use of the simpler edge-punched system.[47] There are two theses on punched cards.[48,49] The greatest current interest in this machinery is in its development for the location and correlation of information, a subject outside the scope of this article.

Eleven libraries are collaborating in a two-year experiment with an office-appliance type of camera called the "Photoclerk," developed by R. R. Shaw, and intended to offer a cheap substitute, in the form of photographic copies on paper, for other ways of duplicating small-size records. It is expected that improvements of processes will result from the use of this machine and from the accompanying analysis of processes.

Attention to building was inevitable after the war, after a long freeze of materials and labor. The post-war period was, until the metal shortages brought about by the Korean War, characterized by great activity in planning new structures and alterations to old. Some librarians, suddenly required to consider plant more than academically, found themselves confronted by questions of fundamental library policy as to collections and service. Many planners felt genuinely handicapped by the absence of tested facts about the habits, behavior, and needs of the users of the library materials. It was apparent, however, as descriptions of the new buildings unfolded in library and architectural press, that the old standard for the large university library building—the California prototype, reflected at Harvard, Michigan, Minnesota, and elsewhere—had been pretty much abandoned in favor of a fluid plan of more intimate character. The Doe library building at Berkeley (1911) reflected a concept of library service based on the forms of material (books, periodicals, etc.) and kinds of library activity (loan, reference, etc.). The University of Colorado building (1940) symbolizes a subject or "divisional" concept of service in which all kinds of materials and service activities bearing on an area of knowledge are grouped together in one place. This concept has had, and is having, a powerful influence on library management.

Two landmarks appeared in this period. In 1944 the Cooperative Committee on Library Building Plans came into existence at the suggestion of Princeton's President Dodds. Around a core of chief librarians representing fifteen universities with new library buildings in progress flowed architects, engineers, illumination men, and other experts in a series of discussions synthesized in what will for many years stand as the best book on the subject.[50]

The other landmark is the 1946 Library Institute at the University of Chicago whose subject was library building.[51] Some of the speakers and many of the ideas advanced were the same as those of the Cooperative Committee. Taken together, these two books sum up the extent to which thinking about library buildings has gone. In a very real way these books state the philosophy of university library service as it exists today.

No account of trends in physical working conditions should omit reference to the program of improving work environment at the Library of Congress reported in its *Information Bulletin*, and the series of lectures in the relationship between environment and production given in 1950 at the Library of Congress.[52-54] Summaries of these lectures on noise, color, air conditioning, and accident prevention were released in the form of news stories at the time. Nor should the Librarian of Congress' daring but vain attempt to introduce industrial music into the Card Division be ignored.[55]

Conclusion. There is good reason to believe, from the evidence of the literature cited and in news from the field, that librarians are not unaware of the nature of management, its devices and techniques. It is very probable that, if a sufficiently detailed description of management were constructed and advertised to university libraries, much additional evidence of management activity could be discovered. For example, Yale University Library expects to add a management specialist to its staff in the near future; New York Public Library has carried on management studies since 1946 in the areas of administration, consolidation of operations, technical procedures, and staff organization, sometimes employing professional management specialists for the purpose.

There is a regrettable lack of first-hand acquaintance with management literature, and of orientation in the management field, on the part of library administrators and those who write on library management. Much of librarians' writing on this subject is more descriptive than analytical and, often, more naïve than sophisticated. There is a real lack of "bridging" literature; that is, articles that relate the concepts and practices of "professional" management literature to library situations. There is probably a need for some means of directing librarians to those parts of management writing that have application to library work. It hardly seems necessary to add that management is only one of the aspects of librarianship, and that "library work" and an appreciation of the uses of books are of even greater importance.

References

1. Morse, P. M., and Kimball, G. E.: *Methods of Operations Research.* New York, John Wiley and Sons, 1951, Chapter I.
2. Ridenour, L. N., *et al.: Bibliography in an Age of Science.* Urbana, University of Illinois Press, 1951, p. 20.
3. Austen, W.: Efficiency in College and University Library Work. *Library Journal,* 36:566-569, Nov. 1911.
4. Williamson, C. C.: *Training for Library Service;* A Report Prepared for the Carnegie Corporation of New York. New York [Boston, D. B. Updike, The Merrymount Press], 1923, p. 96.
5. Leigh, R. D.: *Public Library in the United States;* General Report of the

Public Library Inquiry. New York, Columbia University Press, 1950, p. 172.

6. *Ibid.*, p. 238.

7. *Ibid.*, p. 215.

8. Shaw, R. R.: Scientific Management in the Library. *Wilson Library Bulletin,* 21:349-352+, Jan. 1947.

9. Leigh, *op. cit.*, p.237

10. Oboler, E.: *Process Chart as Management Device for College and University Libraries; with Special Reference to Circulation Routines.* Unpublished M.S. Thesis, University of Chicago Graduate Library School, 1949.

11. Burg, K. O.: *Processing of a Book Through the Acquistions Department of the University of Illinois Library; Examination of the Processes and Personnel of the Purchase Division.* Unpublished M.S. paper, University of Illinois Library School, 1949.

12. Clapp, V. W.: Standardization in Library Work and Documentation-Reactivation of ASA Committee Z39. *Library of Congress Information Bulletin,* 10:6-7, April 9, 1951.

13. Simon, H. A.: *Administrative Behavior.* New York, Macmillan, 1947, p. 3.

14. Wilson, L. R., and Tauber, M. F.: *The University Library.* Chicago, University of Chicago Press, 1945, p. 543 ff.

15. Leigh, *op. cit.*, p. 203.

16. Trent, R. M.: Personnel Administrator in University Libraries and in Business. *College and Research Libraries,* 5:322-326, Sept. 1944.

17. Bureau of Public Personnel Administration: Proposed Classification and Compensation Plans for Library Positions. Washington, D.C., The Bureau, 1927.

18. Martin, L., ed.: *Personnel Administration in Libraries.* Chicago, University of Chicago Press, 1946.

19. American Library Association. Board on Personnel Administration: *Classification and Pay Plans for Libraries in Institutions of Higher Education.* 3 Vols. Ed. 2. Chicago, American Library Association, 1947.

20. American Library Association. Board on Personnel Administration: *Position Classification and Salary Administration in Libraries.* Chicago, American Library Association, 1951.

21. Bryant, D. W., and Kaiser, B. S.: University Library Position Classification and Compensation Plan. *Library Quarterly,* 17:1-17, Jan. 1947.

22. Stanford, E. B.: Supervision in Libraries: What It Is—and What It Takes! *A.L.A. Bulletin,* 44:119-121, April 1950.

23. Osteen, Phyllis L.: *In-Service Training of Executives.* Unpublished M.S. Thesis, Columbia University School of Library Service, 1947.

24. Hirsch, R.: In-Service Training Program of the University of Pennsylvania Library. *College and Research Libraries,* 10:103-107, April 1949.

25. Wight, E. A.: In-Service Training of Professional Librarians in College and University Libraries. *College and Research Libraries*, 10:103-107, April 1949.
26. Heintz, E. C.: Industrial Training Applied to Libraries. *Wilson Library Bulletin*, 21:353-357, Jan. 1947.
27. U.S. Library of Congress. *Annual Report of the Librarian of Congress, 1940-41*. Washington, Government Printing Office, 1942, pp. 330-335.
28. U.S. Library of Congress: *op. cit.*, 1947-48, pp. 30-33; 1949-50, pp. 155-160.
29. California. University. General Library. *CU News*, Vol. 4, May 17; Oct. 5; and Oct. 25, 1949.
30. Battles, D. D., *et al.*: Motion and Time Study of a Library Routine. *Library Quarterly*, 13:241-244, July 1943.
31. Price, R. F.: Man-Hour Analysis of Periodical Circulation. *Library Quarterly*, 16:239-244, July 1946.
32. Hardkopf, Jewel C.: *Application of Methods and Motion Techniques in Preparing Books in the New York Public Library*. Unpublished M.S. Thesis, Columbia University School of Library Service, 1949.
33. Frantz, R. W.: *Motion Study of the Acquisition Department Related to Physical Structure of the Rooms Concerned*. Unpublished M.S. paper, University of Illinois Library School, 1949.
34. Oller, Kathryn: *Time Study of the Urbana (Illinois) Free Library*. University of Illinois Library School *Occasional Papers* No. 16, Nov. 1950.
35. Cleveland, T. S.: *Time Study of the Urbana Free Library*. Unpublished M.S. paper, University of Illinois Library School, 1950.
36. Shaw, R. R.: Continuous Fotoprinting at the U.S.D.A. Library. *Library Journal*, 70:738-741, Sept. 1, 1945.
37. Hale, Carolyn L.: Motion Study Inspires Library Workshop. *Library Journal*, 76:1302-1303, Sept. 1, 1951.
38. Baldwin, E. V., and Marcus, W. E.: *Library Costs and Budgets; a Study of Cost Accounting in Public Libraries*. New York, R. R. Bowker, 1941.
39. California. University. General Library. Catalog Inquiry Memo. No. 5, March 28, 1949.
40. Knapp, Patricia B.: Cost Study in Preparations Department of Small College Library. *Library Quarterly*, 13:335-337, Oct. 1943.
41. U.S. Department of Agriculture Library. *Report of the Librarian, 1947*. Washington, Government Printing Office, 1947, p. 2.
42. *Documentation Techniques in the USA*. Organization for European Economic Cooperation. Paris, 1951.
43. Perry, J. W., *et al.*: Use of Punched Cards in American Libraries. *Association of Special Libraries and Information Bureaux Report of Proceedings of the Twenty-Second Conference, 1947*. London, The Association, 1947, pp. 40-50.

44. Ferris, L. A., *et al.*: Bibliography on Uses of Punched Cards, *in* Casey, R. S., and Perry, J. W., eds., *Punched Cards, Their Application to Science and Industry.* New York, Reinhold Publishing Corporation, 1951.
45. Klausner, Margaret: Routine Library Operations: Application of Machine-sorted Cards, *in* Casey and Perry, *op.cit.,* ref. 44, pp. 221-229.
46. Keller, Dorothy B.: IBM Order Forms and the Microphotostat. Transcription of speech at American Library Association Heads of Acquisition Departments of Research Libraries Round Table, Jan. 30, 1951.
47. Brown, G. B.: Use of Punched Cards in Acquisition Work: Experience at Illinois. *College and Research Libraries,* 10:219-220+, July 1949, part I.
48. Blasingame, R. U., Jr.: *Application of IBM's in Libraries.* Unpublished M.S. Thesis, Columbia University School of Library Service, 1950.
49. Stokkeland, Margaret C.: *Use of Punched Cards for Recording Informatio* Unpublished M.S. Thesis, Carnegie Institute of Technology, 1950.
50. Burchard, J. E., *et al.: Planning the University Library Building.* Princeton, N.J., Princeton University Press, 1949.
51. Fussler, H. H., ed.: *Library Buildings for Library Service.* Chicago, American Library Association, 1947.
52. Andreassen, J. C. L.: Program on Work Environment. *Library of Congress Information Bulletin,* 9:8-10, Nov. 20, 1950.
53. Andreassen, J. C. L.: The Library's Management Improvement Program (Part I). *Library of Congress Information Bulletin,* 9:21-24, May 15, 1950.
54. Andreassen, J. C. L.:Management Notes (Part II). *Library of Congress Information Bulletin,* 9:I. Appendix, May 29, 1950.
55. U.S. Congress. House. *Hearings Before the Subcommittee of the Committee on Appropriations . . . on the Legislative Branch Appropriation Bill for 1950.* 81st Cong., 1st sess. Washington, U.S. Government Printing Office, 1949, pp. 213-215.

Characteristics of Bureaucracy

Max Weber

MODERN officialdom functions in the following specific manner:

I. There is the principle of fixed and official jurisdictional areas, which are generally ordered by rules, that is, by laws or administrative regulations.

1. The regular activities required for the purposes of the bureaucratically governed structure are distributed in a fixed way as official duties.

2. The authority to give commands required for the discharge of these duties is distributed in a stable way and is strictly delimited by rules concerning the coercive means, physical, sacerdotal, or otherwise, which may be placed at the disposal of officials.

3. Methodical provision is made for the regular and continuous fulfilment of these duties and for the execution of the corresponding rights; only persons who have the generally regulated qualifications to serve are employed.

In public and lawful government these three elements constitute "bureaucratic authority." In private economic domination, they constitute bureaucratic "management." Bureaucracy, thus understood, is fully developed in political and ecclesiastical communities only in the modern state, and, in the private economy, only in the most advanced institutions of capitalism. Permanent and public office authority, with fixed jurisdiction, is not the historical rule but rather the exception. This is so even in large political structures such as those of the ancient Orient, the Germanic and Mongolian empires of

Excerpted from *From Max Weber: Essays in Sociology*, edited and translated by H.H. Gerth and C. Wright Mills. Copyright © 1946 by Oxford University Press, Inc.; renewed 1973 by Hans H. Gerth. Reprinted by permission of the publisher.

conquest, or of many feudal structures of state. In all these cases, the ruler executes the most important measures through personal trustees, table-companions, or court-servants. Their commissions and authority are not precisely delimited and are temporarily called into being for each case.

II. The principles of office hierarchy and of levels of graded authority mean a firmly ordered system of super- and subordination in which there is a supervision of the lower offices by the higher ones. Such system offers the governed the possibility of appealing the decision of a lower office to its higher authority, in a definitely regulated manner. With the full development of the bureaucratic type, the office hierarchy is monocratically organized. The principle of hierarchical office authority is found in all bureaucratic structures: in state and ecclesiastical structures as well as in large party organizations and private enterprises. It does not matter for the character of bureaucracy whether its authority is called "private" or "public."

When the principle of jurisdictional "competency" is fully carried through, hierarchical subordination—at least in public office—does not mean that the "higher" authority is simply authorized to take over the business of the "lower." Indeed, the opposite is the rule. Once established and having fulfilled its task, an office tends to continue in existence and be held by another incumbent.

III. The management of the modern office is based upon written documents ("the files"), which are preserved in their original or draught form. There is, therefore, a staff of subaltern officials and scribes of all sorts. The body of officials actively engaged in a "public" office, along with the respective apparatus of material implements and the files, make up a "bureau." In private enterprise, "the bureau" is often called "the office."

In principle, the modern organization of the civil service separates the bureau from the private domicile of the official, and, in general, bureaucracy segregates official activity as something distinct from the sphere of private life. Public monies and equipment are divorced from the private property of the official. This condition is everywhere the product of a long development. Nowadays, it is found in public as well as in private enterprises; in the latter, the principle extends even to the leading entrepreneur. In principle, the executive office is separated from the household, business from private correspondence, and business assets from private fortunes. The more consistently the modern type of business management has been carried through the more are these separations the case. The beginnings of this process are to be found as early as the Middle Ages.

It is the peculiarity of the modern entrepreneur that he conducts himself as the "first official" of his enterprise, in the very same way in which the ruler of a specifically modern bureaucratic state spoke of himself as "the first servant" of the state. The idea that the bureau activities of the state are intrinsically different in character from the management of private economic offices is a continental European notion and, by way of contrast, is totally foreign to the American way.

IV. Office management, at least all specialized office management—and such management is distinctly modern—usually presupposes thorough and expert training. This increasingly holds for the modern executive and employee of private enterprises, in the same manner as it holds for the state official.

V. When the office is fully developed, official activity demands the full working capacity of the official, irrespective of the fact that his obligatory time in the bureau may be firmly delimited. In the normal case, this is only the product of a long development, in the public as well as in the private office. Formerly, in all cases, the normal state of affairs was reversed: official business was discharged as a secondary activity.

VI. The management of the office follows general rules, which are more or less stable, more or less exhaustive, and which can be learned. Knowledge of these rules represents a special technical learning which the officials possess. In involves jurisprudence, or administrative or business management.

The reduction of modern office management to rules is deeply embedded in its very nature. The theory of modern public administration, for instance, assumes that the authority to order certain matters by decree—which has been legally granted to public authorities—does not entitle the bureau to regulate the matter by commands given for each case, but only to regulate the matter abstractly. This stands in extreme contrast to the regulation of all relationships through individual privileges and bestowals of favor, which is absolutely dominant in patrimonialism, at least in so far as such relationships are not fixed by sacred tradition.

THE POSITION OF THE OFFICIAL

All this results in the following for the internal and external position of the official:

I. Office holding is a "vocation." This is shown, first, in the requirement of a firmly prescribed course of training, which demands the entire capacity for work for a long period of time, and in the generally prescribed and special examinations which are prerequisites of employment. Furthermore, the position of the official is in the nature of a duty. This determines the internal structure of his relations, in the following manner: Legally and actually, office holding is not considered a source to be exploited for rents or emoluments, as was normally the case during the Middle Ages and frequently up to the threshold of recent times. Nor is office holding considered a usual exchange of services for equivalents, as is the case with free labor contracts. Entrance into an office, including one in the private economy, is considered an acceptance of a specific obligation of faithful management in return for a secure existence. It is decisive for the specific nature of modern loyalty to an office that, in the pure type, it does not establish a relationship to a *person*, like the vassal's or disciple's faith in feudal or in patrimonial relations of authority. Modern loyalty is devoted to impersonal and functional purposes. Behind the functional purposes, of course, "ideas of culture-values" usually stand. These are *ersatz* for the earthly or supramundane personal master: ideas such as "state," "church," "community," "party," or "enterprise" and thought of as being realized in a community; they provide an ideological halo for the master.

The political official—at least in the fully developed modern state—is not considered the personal servant of a ruler. Today, the bishop, the priest, and the preacher are in fact no longer, as in early Christian times, holders of purely personal charisma. The supramundane and sacred values which they offer are given to everybody who seems to be worthy of them and who asks for them. In former times, such leaders acted upon the personal command of their master; in principle, they were responsible only to him. Nowadays, in spite of the partial survival of the old theory, such religious leaders are officials in the service of a functional purpose, which in the present-day "church" has become routinized and, in turn, ideologically hallowed.

II. The personal position of the official is patterned in the following way:

1. Whether he is in a private office or a public bureau, the modern official always strives and usually enjoys a distinct *social esteem* as compared with the governed. His social position is guaranteed by the prescriptive rules of rank order and, for the political official, by special definitions of the criminal code against "insults of officials" and "contempt" of state and church authorities.

The actual social position of the official is normally highest where, as in old civilized countries, the following conditions prevail: a strong demand for administration by trained experts; a strong and stable social differentiation, where the official predominantly derives from socially and economically privileged strata because of the social distribution of power; or where the costliness of the required training and status conventions are binding upon him. The possession of educational certificates—to be discussed elsewhere—are usually linked with qualification for office. Naturally, such certificates or patents enhance the "status element" in the social position of the official. For the rest this status factor in individual cases is explicitly and impassively acknowledged; for example, in the prescription that the acceptance or rejection of an aspirant to an official career depends upon the consent ("election") of the members of the official body. This is the case in the German army with the official corps. Similar phenomena, which promote this guildlike closure of officialdom, are typically found in patrimonial and, particularly, in prebendal officialdoms of the past. The desire to resurrect such phenomena in changed forms is by no means infrequent among modern bureaucrats. For instance, they have played a role among the demands of the quite proletarian and expert officials (the *tretyi* element) during the Russian revolution.

Usually the social esteem of the officials as such is especially low where the demand for expert administration and the dominance of status conventions are weak. This is especially the case in the United States; it is often the case in new settlements by virtue of their wide fields for profit-making and the great instability of their social stratification.

2. The pure type of bureaucratic official is *appointed* by a superior authority. An official elected by the governed is not a purely bureaucratic figure. Of course, the formal existence of an election does not by itself mean that no appointment hides behind the election—in the state, especially, appointment by party chiefs. Whether or not this is the case does not depend upon legal statutes but upon the way in which the party mechanism functions. Once firmly organized, the parties can turn a formally free election into the mere acclamation of a

candidate designated by the party chief. As a rule, however, a formally free election is turned into a fight, conducted according to definite rules, for votes in favor of one or two designated candidates.

In all circumstances, the designation of officials by means of an election among the governed modifies the strictness of hierarchial subordination. In principle, an official who is so elected has an autonomous position opposite the superordinate official. The elected official does not derive his position "from above" but "from below," or at least not from a superior authority of the official hierarchy but from powerful party men ("bosses"), who also determine his further career. The career of the elected official is not, or at least not primarily, dependent upon his chief in the administration. The official who is not elected but appointed by a chief normally functions more exactly, from a technical point of view, because, all other circumstances being equal, it is more likely that purely functional points of consideration and qualities will determine his selection and career. As laymen, the governed can become acquainted with the extent to which a candidate is expertly qualified for office only in terms of experience, and hence only after his service. Moreover, in every sort of selection of officials by election, parties quite naturally give decisive weight not to expert considerations but to the services a follower renders to the party boss. This holds for all kinds of procurement for officials by elections, for the designation of formally free, elected officials by party bosses when they determine the slate of candidates, or the free appointment by a chief who has himself been elected. The contrast, however, is relative: substantially similar conditions hold where legitimate monarchs and their subordinates appoint officials, except that the influence of the followings are then less controllable.

Where the demand for administration by trained experts is considerable, and the party followings have to recognize an intellectually developed, educated, and freely moving "public opinion," the use of unqualified officials falls back upon the party in power at the next election. Naturally, this is more likely to happen when the officials are appointed by the chief. The demand for a trained administration now exists in the United States, but in the large cities, where immigrant votes are "corralled," there is, of course, no educated public opinion. Therefore, popular elections of the administrative chief and also of his subordinate officials usually endanger the expert qualification of the official as well as the precise functioning of the bureaucratic mechanism. It also weakens the dependence of the officials upon the hierarchy. This holds at least for the large administrative bodies that are difficult to supervise. The superior qualification and integrity of federal judges, appointed by the President, as over against elected judges in the United States is well known, although both types of officials have been selected primarily in terms of party considerations. The great changes in American metropolitan administrations demanded by reformers have proceeded essentially from elected mayors working with an apparatus of officials who were appointed by them. These reforms have thus come about in a "Caesarist" fashion. Viewed technically, as an organized form of authority, the efficiency of "Caesarism," which often grows out of democracy, rests in general upon the position of the "Caesar" as a free trustee of the masses (of the army or of the citizenry), who is unfettered by tradition. The "Caesar" is thus the unrestrained master of a body of highly qualified military officers and officials whom he selects freely and personally without regard to tradition or to any other considerations. This "rule of the personal genius," however, stands in contradiction to the formally "democratic" principle of a universally elected officialdom.

3. Normally, the position of the official is held for life, at least in public bureaucracies; and this is increasingly the case for all similar structures. As a factual rule, *tenure for life* is presupposed, even where the giving of notice or periodic reappointment occurs. In contrast to the worker in a private enterprise, the official normally holds tenure. Legal or actual life-tenure, however, is not recognized as the official's right to the possession of office, as was the case with many structures of authority in the past. Where legal guarantees against arbitrary dismissal or transfer are developed, they merely serve to guarantee a strictly objective discharge of specific office duties free from all personal considerations. In Germany, this is the case for all juridical and, increasingly for all administrative officials.

Within the bureaucracy, therefore, the measure of "independence," legally guaranteed by tenure, is not always a source of increased status for the official whose position is thus secured. Indeed, often the reverse holds, especially in old cultures and communities that are highly differentiated. In such communities, the stricter the subordination under the arbitrary rule of the master, the more it guarantees the maintenance of the conventional seigneurial style of living for the official. Because of the very absence of these legal guarantees of tenure, the conventional esteem for the official may rise in the same way as, during the Middle Ages, the esteem of the nobility of office rose at the expense of esteem for the freemen, and as the king's judge surpassed that of the people's judge. In Germany, the military officer or the administrative official can be removed from office at any time, or at least far more readily than the "independent judge," who never pays with loss of his office for even the grossest offense against the "code of honor" or against social conventions of the salon. For this very reason, if other things are equal, in the eyes of the master stratum the judge is considered less qualified for social intercourse than are officers and administrative officials, whose greater dependence on the master is a greater guarantee of their conformity with status conventions. Of course, the average official strives for a civil-service law, which would materially secure his old age and provide increased guarantees against his arbitrary removal from office. This striving, however, has its limits. A very strong development of the "right to the office" naturally makes it more difficult to staff them with regard to technical efficiency, for such a development decreases the career opportunities of ambitious candidates for office. This makes for the fact that officials, on the whole, do not feel their dependency upon those at the top. This lack of a feeling of dependency, however, rests primarily upon the inclination to depend upon one's equals rather than upon the socially inferior and governed strata. The present conservative movement among the Badenia clergy, occasioned by the anxiety of a presumably threatening separation of church and state, has been expressly determined by the desire not to be turned "from a master into a servant of the parish."

4. The official receives the regular *pecuniary* compensation of a normally fixed *salary* and the old age security provided by a pension. The salary is not measured like a wage in terms of work done, but according to "status," that is, according to the kind of function (the "rank") and, in addition, possibly, according to the length of service. The relatively great security of the official's income, as well as the rewards of social esteem, make the office a sought-after position, especially in countries which no longer provide opportunities for colonial profits. In such countries, this situation permits relatively low salaries for officials.

5. The official is set for a *"career"* within the hierarchical order of the public service. He moves from the lower, less important, and lower paid to the higher positions. The average official naturally desires a mechanical fixing of conditions of promotion: if not of the offices, at least of the salary levels. He wants these conditions fixed in terms of "seniority," or possibly according to grades achieved in a developed system of expert examinations. Here and there, such examinations actually form a character *indelibilis* of the official and have lifelong effects on his career. To this is joined the desire to qualify the right to office and the increasing tendency toward status group closure and

economic security. All of this makes for a tendency to consider the offices as "prebends" of those who are qualified by educational certificates. The necessity of taking general personal and intellectual qualifications into consideration, irrespective of the often subaltern character of the educational certificate, has led to a condition in which the highest political offices, especially the positions of "ministers," are principally filled without reference to such certificates. (pp. 196-204)

•   •   •

THE QUANTITATIVE DEVELOPMENT OF ADMINISTRATIVE TASKS

The proper soil for the bureaucratization of an administration has always been the specific developments of administrative tasks. We shall first discuss the quantitative extension of such tasks. In the field of politics, the great state and the mass party are the classic soil for bureaucratization.

This does not mean that every historically known and genuine formation of great states has brought about a bureaucratic administration. The permanence of a once-existing great state, or the homogeneity of a culture borne by such a state, has not always been attached to a bureaucratic structure of state. However, both of these features have held to a great extent, for instance, in the Chinese empire. The numerous great Negro empires, and similar formations, have had only an ephemeral existence primarily because they have lacked an apparatus of officials. And the unity of the Carolingian empire disintegrated when its organization of officials disintegrated. This organization, however, was predominantly patrimonial rather than bureaucratic in nature. From a purely temporal view, however, the empire of the Caliphs and its predecessors on Asiatic soil have lasted for considerable periods of time, and their organization of office was essentially patrimonial and prebendal. Also, the Holy Roman Empire lasted for a long time in spite of the almost complete absence of bureaucracy. All these realms have represented a cultural unity of at least approximately the same strength as is usually created by bureaucratic polities.

The ancient Roman Empire disintegrated internally in spite of increasing bureaucratization and even during its very execution. This was because of the way the tax burdens were distributed by the bureaucratic state, which favored the subsistence economy. Viewed with regard to the intensity of their purely *political* unities, the temporal existences of the empires of the Caliphs, Carolingian and other medieval emperors were essentially unstable, nominal, and cohesive conglomerates. On the whole, the capacity for political action steadily diminished, and the relatively great unity of *culture* flowed from ecclesiastic structures that were in part strictly unified and, in the Occidental Middle Ages, increasingly bureaucratic in character. The unity of their cultures resulted partly from the far-going homogeneity of their social structures, which in turn was the aftermath and transformation of their former political unity. Both are phenomena of the traditional stereotyping of culture, which favors an unstable equilibrium. Both of these factors proved so strong a foundation that even grandiose attempts at expansion, such as the Crusades, could be undertaken in spite of the lack of intensive political unity; they were, one might say, performed as "private undertakings." The failure of the Crusades and their often irrational political course, however, is associated with the absence of a unified and intensive state power to back them up. And there is no doubt that the nuclei of intensive "modern" states in the Middle Ages developed concomitantly with bureaucratic structures. Furthermore, in the end these quite bureaucratic political structures undoubtedly shattered the social conglomerates, which rested essentially upon unstable equilibriums.

The disintegration of the Roman Empire was partly conditioned by the very bureaucratization of its army and official apparatus. This bureaucratization could only be realized by carrying through at the same time a method of taxation which by its distribution of burdens was bound to lead to relative increase in the importance of a subsistence economy. Individual factors of this sort always enter the picture. Also the "intensity" of the external and the internal state activities play their part. Quite apart from the relation between the state influence upon culture and the degree of bureaucratization, it may be said that "normally"—though not without exception—the vigor to expand is directly related to the degree of bureaucratization. For two of the most expansive polities, the Roman Empire and the British world empire, during their most expansive periods, rested upon bureaucratic foundations only to a small extent. The Norman state in England carried through a strict organization on the basis of a feudal hierarchy. To a large extent, it received its unity and its push through the bureaucratization of the royal exchequer, which, in comparison to other political structures of the feudal period, was extremely strict. Later on, the English state did not share in the continental development towards bureaucratization, but remained an administration of notables. Just as in the republican administration of Rome, this English rule by notables was a result of the relative absence of a continental character, as well as of absolutely unique pre-conditions, which at the present time are disappearing. The dispens-ability of the large standing armies, which a continental state with equally expansive tendencies requires for its land frontiers, is among these special preconditions. In Rome, bureaucratization advanced with the transition from a coastal to a continental ring of frontiers. For the rest, in the domination structure of Rome, the strictly military character of the magistrate authorities—in the Roman manner unknown to any other people—made up for the lack of a bureaucratic apparatus with its technical efficiency, its precision and unity of administrative functions, especially outside the city limits. The continuity of administration was safeguarded by the unique position of the Senate. In Rome, as in England, one presupposition for this dispensability of bureaucracy which should not be forgotten was that the state authorities increasingly "minimized" the scope of their functions at home. They restricted their functions to what was absolutely demanded for direct "reasons of state."

At the beginning of the modern period, all the prerogatives of the continental states accumulated in the hands of those princes who most relentlessly took the course of administrative bureaucratization. It is obvious that technically the great modern state is absolutely depen-dent upon a bureaucratic basis. The larger the state, and the more it is or the more it becomes a greater power state, the more unconditionally is this the case.

The United States still bears the character of a polity which, at least in the technical sense, is not fully bureaucratized. But the greater the zones of friction with the outside and the more urgent the needs for administrative unity at home become, the more this character is inevitably and gradually giving way formally to the bureaucratic structure. Moreover, the partly unbureaucratic form of the state structure of the United States is materially balanced by the more strictly bureaucratic structures of those formations which, in truth, dominate politically, namely, the parties under the leadership of professionals or experts in organization and election tactics. The increasingly bureaucratic organization of all genuine mass parties offers the most striking example of the role of sheer quantity as a leverage for the bureaucratization of a social structure. In Germany, above all, the Social Democratic party, and abroad both of the "historical" American parties are bureaucratic in the greatest possible degree.

QUALITATIVE CHANGES OF
ADMINISTRATIVE TASKS

Bureaucratization is occasioned more by intensive and qualitative enlargement and internal deployment of the scope of administrative tasks than by their extensive and quantitative increase. But the direction bureaucratization takes and the reasons that occasion it vary widely.

In Egypt, the oldest country of bureaucratic state administration, the public and collective regulation of waterways for the whole country and from the top could not be avoided because of technical economic factors. This regulation created the mechanisms of scribes and officals. Once established, this mechanism, even in early times, found its second realm of business in the extraordinary construction activities which were organized militarily. As mentioned before, the bureaucratic tendency has chiefly been influenced by needs arising from the creation of standing armies as determined by power politics and by the development of public finance connected with the military establishment. In the modern state, the increasing demands for administration rest on the increasing complexity of civilization and push towards bureaucratization.

Very considerable expansions, especially overseas, have, of course, been managed by states ruled by notables (Rome, England, Venice), as will become evident in the appropriate context. Yet the "intensity" of the administration, that is, the transfer of as many tasks as possible to the organization of the state proper for continuous management and discharge, has been only slightly developed among the great states ruled by notables, especially Rome and England, if we compare them with bureaucratic polities.

Both in notable and bureaucratic administrations the *structure* of state power has influenced culture very strongly. But it has done so relatively slightly in the form of management and control by the state. This holds from justice down to education. The growing demands on culture, in turn, are determined, though to a varying extent, by the growing wealth of the most influential strata in the state. To this extent increasing bureaucratization is a function of the increasing possession of goods used for consumption, and of an increasingly sophisticated technique of fashioning external life—a technique which corresponds to the opportunities provided by such wealth. This reacts upon the standard of living and makes for an increasing subjective indispensability of organized, collective, interlocal, and thus bureaucratic, provision for the varied wants, which previously were either unknown, or were satisfied locally or by a private economy.

Among purely political factors, the increasing demand of a society, accustomed to absolute pacification, for order and protection ("police") in all fields exerts an especially persevering influence in the direction of bureaucratization. A steady road leads from modifications of the blood feud, sacerdotally, or by means of arbitration, to the present position of the policeman as the "representative of God on earth." The former means placed the guarantees for the individual's rights and security squarely upon members of his sib, who are obligated to assist him with oath and vengeance. Among other factors, primarily the manifold tasks of the so-called "policy of social welfare" operate in the direction of bureaucratization, for these tasks are, in part, saddled upon the state by interest groups and, in part, the state usurps them, either for reasons of power policy or for ideological motives. Of course, these tasks are to a large extent economically determined.

Among essentially technical factors, the specifically modern means of communication enter the picture as pacemakers of bureaucratization. Public land and water-ways, railroads, the telegraph, et cetera—they must, in part, neccessarily be administered in a public and collective way; in part, such administration is technically expedient. In this respect, the contemporary means of communication frequently play a role similar to that of the canals of Mesopotamia and the regulation of the Nile in the ancient Orient. The degree to which the means of communication have been developed is a condition of decisive importance for the possibility of bureaucratic administration, although it is not the only decisive condition. Certainly in Egypt, bureaucratic centralization, on the basis of an almost pure subsistence economy, could never have reached the actual degree which it did without the natural trade route of the Nile. In order to promote bureaucratic centralization in modern Persia, the telegraph officials were officially commissioned with reporting all occurrences in the provinces to the Shah, over the heads of the local authorities. In addition, everyone received the right to remonstrate directly by telegraph. The modern Occidental state can be administered the way it actually is only because the state controls the telegraph network and has the mails and railroads at its disposal.

Railroads, in turn, are intimately connected with the development of an interlocal traffic of mass goods. This traffic is among the causal factors in the formation of the modern state. As we have already seen, this does not hold unconditionally for the past.

TECHNICAL ADVANTAGES OF
BUREAUCRATIC ORGANIZATION

The decisive reason for the advance of bureaucratic organization has always been its purely technical superiority over any other form of organization. The fully developed bureaucratic mechanism compares with other organizations exactly as does the machine with the non-mechanical modes of production.

Precision, speed, unambiguity, knowledge of the files, continuity, discretion, unity, strict subordination, reduction of friction and of material and personal costs—these are raised to the optimum point in the strictly bureaucratic administration, and especially in its monocratic form. As compared with all collegiate, honorific, and avocational forms of administration, trained bureaucracy is superior on all these points. And as far as complicated tasks are concerned, paid bureaucratic work is not only more precise but, in the last analysis, it is ofter cheaper than even formally unremunerated honorific service.

Honorific arrangements make administrative work an avocation and for this reason alone, honorific service normally functions more slowly; being less bound to schemata and being more formless. Hence it is less precise and less unified than bureaucratic work because it is less dependent upon superiors and because the establishment and exploitation of the apparatus of subordinate officials and filing services are almost unavoidably less economical. Honorific service is less continuous than bureaucratic and frequently quite expensive. This is especially the case if one thinks not only of the money costs to the public treasure—costs which bureaucratic administration, in comparison with administration by notables, usually substantially increases—but also of the frequent economic losses of the governed caused by delays and lack of precision. The possibility of administration by notables normally and permanently exists only where official management can be satisfactorily discharged as an avocation. With the qualitative increase of tasks the administration has to face, administration by notables reaches its limit—today, even in England. Work organized by collegiate bodies causes friction and delay and requires compromises between colliding interests and views. The administration, therefore, runs less precisely and is more independent of superiors; hence, it is less unified and slower. All advances of the Prussian administrative organization have been and will in the future be advances of the bureaucratic, and especially of the monocratic, principle.

Today, it is primarily the capitalist market economy which demands that the official business of the administration be discharged precisely, unambiguously, continuously, and with as much speed as possible. Normally, the very large, modern capitalist enterprises are themselves unequalled models of strict bureaucratic organization. Business management throughout rests on increasing precision, steadiness, and, above all, the speed of operations. This, in turn, is determined by the peculiar nature of the modern means of communication, including, among other things, the news service of the press. The extraordinary increase in the speed by which public announcements, as well as economic and political facts, are transmitted exerts a steady and sharp pressure in the direction of speeding up the tempo of administrative reaction towards various situations. The optimum of such reaction time is normally attained only by a strictly bureaucratic organization.*

Bureaucratization offers above all the optimum possibility for carrying through the principle of specializing administrative functions according to purely objective considerations. Individual performances are allocated to functionaries who have specialized training and who by constant practice learn more and more. The "objective" discharge of business primarily means a discharge of business according to *calculable rules* and "without regard for persons."

"Without regard for persons" is also the watchword of the "market" and, in general, of all pursuits of naked economic interests. A consistent execution of bureaucratic domination means the leveling of status "honor." Hence, if the principle of the free-market is not at the same time restricted, it means the universal domination of the "class situation." That this consequence of bureaucratic domination has not set in everywhere, parallel to the extent of bureaucratization, is due to the differences among possible principles by which polities may meet their demands.

The second element mentioned, "calculable rules," also is of paramount importance for modern bureaucracy. The peculiarity of modern culture, and specifically of its technical and economic basis, demands this very "calculability" of results. When fully developed, bureaucracy also stands, in a specific sense, under the principle of *sine ira ac studio*. Its specific nature, which is welcomed by capitalism, develops the more perfectly the more the bureaucracy is "dehuman-

---

*Here we cannot discuss in detail how the bureaucratic apparatus may, and actually does, produce definite obstacles to the discharge of business in a manner suitable for the single case.

ized," the more completely it succeeds in eliminating from official business love, hatred, and all purely personal, irrational, and emotional elements which escape calculation. This is the specific nature of bureaucracy and it is appraised as its special virtue.

The more complicated and specialized modern culture becomes, the more its external supporting apparatus demands the personally detached and strictly "objective" *expert,* in lieu of the master of older social structures, who was moved by personal sympathy and favor, by grace and gratitude. Bureaucracy offers the attitudes demanded by the external apparatus of modern culture in the most favorable combination. As a rule, only bureaucracy has established the foundation for the administration of a rational law conceptually systematized on the basis of such enactments as the latter Roman imperial period first created with a high degree of technical perfection. During the Middle Ages, this law was received along with the bureaucratization of legal administration, that is to say, with the displacement of the old trial procedure which was bound to tradition or to irrational presuppositions, by the rationally trained and specialized expert. (pp. 209-216)

• • •

THE CONCENTRATION OF THE MEANS OF ADMINISTRATION

The bureaucratic structure goes hand in hand with the concentration of the material means of management in the hands of the master. This concentration occurs, for instance, in a well-known and typical fashion, in the development of big capitalist enterprises, which find their essential characteristics in this process. A corresponding process occurs in public organizations.

The bureaucratically led army of the Pharaohs, the army during the later period of the Roman republic and the principate, and, above all, the army of the modern military state are characterized by the fact that their equipment and provisions are supplied from the magazines of the war lord. This is in contrast to the folk armies of agricultural tribes, the armed citizenry of ancient cities, the militias of early medieval cities, and all feudal armies; for these, the self-equipment and the self-provisioning of those obliged to fight was normal.

War in our time is a war of machines. And this makes magazines technically necessary, just as the dominance of the machine in industry promotes the concentration of the means of production and management. In the main, however, the bureaucratic armies of the past, equipped and provisioned by the lord, have risen when social and economic development has absolutely or relatively diminished the stratum of citizens who were economically able to equip themselves, so that their number was no longer sufficient for putting the required armies in the field. They were reduced at least relatively, that is, in relation to the range of power claimed for the polity. Only the bureaucratic army structure allowed for the development of the professional standing armies which are necessary for the constant pacification of large states of the plains, as well as for warfare against far-distant enemies, especially enemies overseas. Specifically, military discipline and technical training can be normally and fully developed, at least to its modern high level, only in the bureaucratic army.

Historically, the bureaucratization of the army has everywhere been realized along with the transfer of army service from the propertied to the propertyless. Until this transfer occurs, military service is an honorific privilege of propertied men. Such a transfer was made to the native-born unpropertied, for instance, in the armies of the generals of the late Roman republic and the empire, as well as in modern armies up to the nineteenth century. The burden of service has also been transferred to strangers, as in the mercenary armies of all ages. This process typically goes hand in hand with the general increase in material and intellectual culture. The following reason has also played its part everywhere: the increasing density of population, and therewith the intensity and strain of economic work, makes for an increasing "indispensability" of the acquisitive strata for purposes of war. Leaving aside periods of strong ideological fervor, the propertied strata of sophisticated and especially of urban culture as a rule are little fitted and also little inclined to do the coarse war work of the common soldier. Other circumstances being equal, the propertied strata of the open country are at least usually better qualified and more strongly inclined to become professional officers. This difference between the urban and the rural propertied is balanced only where the increasing possibility of mechanized warfare requires the leaders to qualify as "technicians."

The bureaucratization of organized warfare may be carried through in the form of private capitalist enterprise, just like any other business. Indeed, the procurement of armies and their administration by private capitalists has been the rule in mercenary armies, especially those of the Occident up to the turn of the eighteenth century. During the Thirty Years' War, in Brandenburg the soldier was still the predominant owner of the material implements of his business. He owned his weapons, horses, and dress, although the state, in the role, as it were, of the merchant of the "putting-out system," did supply him to some extent. Later on, in the standing army of Prussia, the chief of the company owned the material means of warfare, and only since the peace of Tilsit has the concentration of the means of warfare in the hands of the state definitely come about. Only with this concentration was the introduction of uniforms generally carried through. Before then, the introduction of uniforms had been left to a great extent to the arbitrary discretion of the regimental officer, with the exception of individual categories of troops to whom the king had "bestowed" certain uniforms, first, in 1620, to the royal bodyguard, then, under Frederick II, repeatedly.

Such terms as "regiment" and "battalion" usually had quite different meanings in the eighteenth century from the meanings they have today. Only the battalion was a tactical unit (today both are); the "regiment" was then a managerial unit of an economic organization established by the colonel's position as an "entrepreneur." "Official" maritime ventures (like the Genoese maonae) and army procurement belong to private capitalism's first giant enterprises of far-going bureaucratic character. In this respect, the "nationalization" of these enterprises by the state has its modern parallel in the nationalization of the railroads, which have been controlled by the state from their beginnings.

In the same way as with army organizations, the bureaucratization of administration goes hand in hand with the concentration of the means of organization in other spheres. The old administration by satraps and regents, as well as administration by farmers of office, purchasers of office, and, most of all, administration by feudal vassals, decentralize the material means of administration. The local demand of the province and the cost of the army and of subaltern officials are regularly paid for in advance from local income, and only the surplus reaches the central treasure. The enfeoffed official administers entirely by payment out of his own pocket. The bureaucratic state, however, puts its whole administrative expense on the budget and equips the lower authorities with the current means of expenditure, the use of which the state regulates and controls. This has the same meaning for the "economics" of the administration as for the large centralized capitalist enterprise.

In the field of scientific research and instruction, the bureaucratization of the always existing research institutes of the universities is a function of the increasing demand for material means of management. Liebig's laboratory at Giessen University was the first example of big enterprise in this field. Through the concentration of such means in the hands of the privileged head of the institute, the mass of researchers and docents are separated from their "means of production," in the same way as capitalist enterprise has separated the workers from theirs.

In spite of its indubitable technical superiority, bureaucracy has everywhere been a relatively late development. A number of obstacles have contributed to this, and only under certain social and political conditions have they definitely receded into the background.

THE LEVELING OF
SOCIAL DIFFERENCES

Bureaucratic organization has usually come into power on the basis of a leveling of economic and social differences. This leveling has been at least relative, and has concerned the significance of social and economic differences for the assumption of administrative functions.

Bureaucracy inevitably accompanies modern *mass democracy* in contrast to the democratic self-government of small homogeneous units. This results from the characteristic principle of bureaucracy: the abstract regularity of the execution of authority, which is a result of the demand for "equality before the law" in the personal and functional sense—hence, of the horror of "privilege," and the principled rejection of doing business "from case to case." Such regularity also follows from the social preconditions of the origins of bureaucracies. The nonbureaucratic administration of any large social structure rests in some way upon the fact that existing social, material, or honorific perferences and ranks are connected with administrative functions and duties. This usually means that a direct or indirect economic exploitation or a "social" exploitation of position, which every sort of administrative activity gives to its bearers, is equivalent to the assumption of administrative functions.

Bureaucratization and democratization within the administration of the state signify and increase the cash expenditures of the public treasury. And this is the case in spite of the fact that bureaucratic administration is usually more "economical" in character than other forms of administration. Until recent times—at least from the point of view of the treasury—the cheapest way of satisfying the need for administration was to leave almost the entire local administration and lower judicature to the landlords of Eastern Prussia. The same fact applies to the administration of sheriffs in England. Mass democracy makes a clean sweep of the feudal, patrimonial, and—at least in intent—the plutocratic privileges in administration. Unavoidably it puts paid professional labor in place of the historically inherited avocational administration by notables.

This not only applies to structures of the state. For it is no accident that their own organizations, the democratic mass parties have completely broken with traditional notable rule based upon personal relationships and personal esteem. Yet such personal structures frequently continue among the old conservative as well as the old liberal parties. Democratic mass parties are bureaucratically organized under the leadership of party officials, professional party and trade union secretaries, et cetera. In Germany, for instance, this has happened in the Social Democratic party and in the agrarian mass movement; and in England, for the first time, in the caucus democracy of Gladstone-Chamberlain, which was originally organized in Birmingham and since the 1870's has spread. In the United States, both parties since Jackson's administration have developed bureaucratically. In France, however, attempts to organize disciplined political parties on the basis of an election system that would compel bureaucratic organization have repeatedly failed. The resistance of local circles of notables against the ultimately unavoidable bureaucratization of the parties, which would encompass the entire country and break their influence, could not be overcome. Every advance of the simple election techniques, for instance the system of proportional elections, which calculates with figures, means a strict and interlocal bureaucratic organization of the parties and therewith an increasing domination of party bureaucracy and discipline, as well as the elimination of the local circles of notables—at least this holds for great states.

The progress of bureaucratization in the state administration itself is a parallel phenomenon of democracy, as is quite obvious in France, North America, and now in England. Of course one must always remember that the term "democratization" can be misleading. The demos itself, in the sense of an inarticulate mass, never "governs" larger associations; rather, it is governed, and its existence only changes the way in which the executive leaders are selected and the measure of influence which the demos, or better, which social circles from its midst are able to exert upon the content and the direction of administrative activities by supplementing what is called "public opinion." "Democratization," in the sense here intended, does not necessarily mean an increasingly active share of the governed in the authority of the social structure. This may be a result of democratization, but it is not necessarily the case.

We must expressly recall at this point that the political concept of democracy deduced from the "equal rights" of the governed, includes these postulates: (1) prevention of the development of a closed status group of officials in the interest of a universal accessibility of office, and (2) minimization of the authority of officialdom in the interest of expanding the sphere of influence of "public opinion" as far as practicable. Hence, whenever possible, political democracy strives to shorten the term of office by election and recall and by not binding the candidates to a special expertness. Thereby democracy inevitably comes into conflict with the bureaucratic tendencies which, by its fight against notable rule, democracy has produced. The generally loose term "democratization" cannot be used here, in so far as it is understood to mean the minimization of the civil servants' ruling power in favor of the greatest possible "direct" rule of the *demos*, which in practice means the respective party leaders of the *demos*. The most decisive thing here—indeed it is rather exclusively so—is the *leveling of the governed* in opposition to the ruling and bureaucratically articulated group, which in its turn may occupy a quite autocratic position, both in fact in and in form. (pp. 221-226).

•   •   •

THE PERMANENT CHARACTER OF THE BUREAUCRATIC MACHINE

Once it is fully established, bureaucracy is among those social structures which are the hardest to destroy. Bureaucracy is *the* means of carrying "community action" over into rationally ordered "societal action." Therefore, as an instrument for "societalizing" relations of power, bureaucracy has been and is a power instrument of the first order—for the one who controls the bureaucratic apparatus.

Under otherwise equal conditions, a "societal action," which is methodically ordered and led, is superior to every resistance of "mass" or even of "communal action." And where the bureaucratization of administration has been completely carried through, a form of power relation is established that is practically unshatterable.

The individual bureaucrat cannot squirm out of the apparatus in which he is harnessed. In contrast to the honorific or avocational "notable," the professional bureaucrat is chained to his activity by his entire material and ideal existence. In the great majority of cases, he is only a single cog in an ever-moving mechanism which prescribes to him an essentially fixed route of march. The official is entrusted with specialized tasks and normally the mechanism cannot be put into motion or arrested by him, but only from the very top. The individual bureaucrat is thus forged to the community of all the functionaries who are integrated into the mechanism. They have a common interest in seeing that the mechanism continues its functions and that the societally exercised authority carries on.

The ruled, for their part, cannot dispense with or replace the bureaucratic apparatus of authority once it exists. For this bureaucracy rests upon expert training, a functional specialization of work, and an attitude set for habitual and virtuoso-like mastery of single yet methodically integrated functions. If the official stops working, or if his work is forcefully interrupted, chaos results, and it is difficult to improvise replacements from among the governed who are fit to master such chaos. This holds for public administration as well as for private economic management. More and more the material fate of the masses depends upon the steady and correct functioning of the increasingly bureaucratic organizations of private capitalism. The idea of eliminating these organizations becomes more and more utopian.

The discipline of officialdom refers to the attitude-set of the official for precise obedience within his *habitual* activity, in public as well as in private organizations. This discipline increasingly becomes the basis of all order, however great the practical importance of administration on the basis of the filed documents may be. The naïve idea of Bakuninism of destroying the basis of "acquired rights" and "domination" by destroying public documents overlooks the settled orientation of *man* for keeping to the habitual rules and regulations that continue to exist independently of the documents. Every reorganization of beaten or dissolved troops, as well as the restoration of administrative orders destroyed by revolt, panic, or other catastrophes, is realized by appealing to the trained orientation of obedient compliance to such orders. Such compliance has been conditioned into the officials, on the one hand, and, on the other hand, into the governed. If such an appeal is successful it brings, as it were, the disturbed mechanism into gear again.

The objective indispensability of the once-existing apparatus, with its peculiar, "impersonal" character, means that the mechanism—in contrast to feudal orders based upon personal piety—is easily made to work for anybody who knows how to gain control over it. A rationally ordered system of officials continues to function smoothly after the enemy has occupied the area; he merely needs to change the top officials. This body of officials continues to operate because it is to the vital interest of everyone concerned, including above all the enemy.

During the course of his long years in power, Bismarck brought his ministerial colleagues into unconditioned bureaucratic dependence by eliminating all independent statesmen. Upon his retirement, he saw to his surprise that they continued to manage their offices unconcerned and undismayed, as if he had not been the master mind and creator of these creatures, but rather as if some single figure has been exchanged for some other figure in the bureaucratic machine. With all the changes of masters in France since the time of the First Empire, the power machine has remained essentially the same. Such a machine makes "revolution," in the sense of the forceful creation of entirely new formations of authority, technically more and more impossible, especially when the apparatus controls the modern means of communication (telegraph, et cetera) and also by virtue of its internal rationalized structure. In classic fashion, France has demonstrated how this process has substituted *coups d'état* for "revolutions"; all successful transformations in France have amounted to *coups d'état*. (pp. 228–230)

Libraries as Bureaucracies

Beverly P. Lynch

Two major themes can be discerned in much of the literature on the organization and management of libraries. The first considers libraries in terms of their formal characteristics, emphasizing the relationships of hierarchy and authority, size, rules and the division of labor. The objective of the study of the formal structure of libraries is to find ways to organize the library in order to achieve maximum administrative efficiency. The study of the formal structure is guided by the concept of achieving specific objectives at minimum cost.

The second theme considers the informal processes in the library. This approach seeks to describe the experiences, attitudes and behavior of individual staff members as they participate in a complex organization. The objective of the study of informal processes and unofficial practices is to find those organizational characteristics or elements which inhibit the achievement of the library's goals of service.

Each of these approaches to the study of libraries as complex organizations complements the other. Each tells much about the organization and management of libraries. Rarely are studies of formal structure and of informal process carried out simultaneously, however, for the approaches are derived from different theoretical frameworks and require different methods of research. The management literature has sought to synthesize the two theoretical perspectives since each contributes to the understanding of organizational behavior. The literature of librarianship, for the most part, has reflected one or the other theme with little synthesis of perspectives into a single framework.

Bureaucracy as a colloquial expression means inefficiency and red tape; it is used most often in a pejorative sense. The sociological meaning of the term refers to the administrative aspects of an

Reprinted with permission from *Library Trends*, Vol. 27, no. 4, Winter 1979. © 1979 The Board of Trustees of the University of Illinois.

organization; it emphasizes those tasks that maintain the organization and coordinate the activities of its members. The tasks of maintaining the library are considered to be separate and distinct from those which relate directly to the achievement of the library's overall goals.

Max Weber's ideal type of organization is a bureaucracy characterized by a hierarchy of office, careful specification of office functions, recruitment on the basis of merit, promotion according to merit and performance, and a coherent system of discipline and control.[1] Weber is not the only theorist who finds the study of bureaucracies of interest, but it is his work on bureaucracy as an ideal type which has served as a basis for important segments of administrative theory and as a theoretical source for the study of the formal structure of organizations. Weber and others, including the leaders of the scientific management school, identify size as a fundamental characteristic of bureaucracies. Weber suggests that large size leads to greater organizational complexity, more specialization, training and professionalization of staff, an increase in rules and regulations, and an expansion of administrative staff and apparatus.

Weber's theory of increase of size as a determinant of increased bureaucracy guided Paul Spence's systematic study of libraries as bureaucracies.[2] Although there are flaws in his research design and method (for example, the independent variable, size, was controlled by selecting as libraries for study sixty-two members of the Association of Research Libraries, by definition the largest academic libraries in the United States), several conclusions drawn by Spence are similar to those reported by Peter Blau in his studies of governmental finance departments and personnel agencies.[3] Both Blau and Spence find high correlations between the professionalization of staff and the size of the organization's administrative component. It is this similarity of results which makes Spence's study of libraries as bureaucracies so interesting. Librarians often assume that the hiring of experts (defined as professionally trained librarians) should reduce the administrative component necessary to run the library. The professional's authority, stemming from his or her certification as an expert, is expected to prompt others to follow voluntarily the professional's directive, thus eliminating the need for an organizational hierarchy, authority, or specific rules and regulations. Yet Blau and Spence find that organizations which hire experts remain organized in a hierarchical fashion. The administrative components of these organizations are not reduced. These findings are of great theoretical interest and can help in the understanding of libraries as bureaucracies.

The work of Weber has greatly influenced the study of the formal structures of organizations. Influential too are the writings of Frederick Taylor, Luther Gulick, Lyndall Urwick, and James D. Mooney, which form the basis of scientific management—an important influence in the management of libraries. Most of these writers were managers who took time to record what they did and then organized their observations into sets of principles. The major thrust of scientific management rests in the attempt to establish normal times for various production tasks through the use of job analysis and time and motion studies. Scientific management became popular in the 1930s and 1940s when large governmental and industrial organizations emerged. Plants or divisions had to be coordinated from the top. New specialists, sales executives, engineers and scientists were added to organizations. The proponents of scientific management, seeking ways to enhance the efficiency of management practices, made the first contributions to the analysis of management in these new and large organizations. Libraries also were growing during this time, and library administrators sought techniques used elsewhere which might help them to administer libraries which were becoming increasingly complex.

In an early review of scientific management in research libraries,[4] several elements are identified which characterize the application of scientific management to libraries. The first is the determination of standards of performance for specific library operations. Such standards, established by the library's administration either through time and motion studies or through less formal means, identify average levels of performance for specific library operations. Another characteristic of the use of scientific management in libraries is the careful definition and assignment of work in each department. Work definition is expected to facilitate the measurement of performance. It fixes responsibility of performance and influences the hiring and assignment of personnel. The efforts to identify and to differentiate the work of the professional from that of the clerical employee reflects this characteristic and leads to a centralization of personnel functions and a codification of personnel policies, both elements of the classical theory of bureaucracy. Work definition and organizational design require careful planning, and the separation of the planning function from the operational function is another characteristic of scientific planning and management.

Library managers seeking useful management techniques to apply in their own libraries recognize intuitively the influence of the size factor on the formal structure of libraries. In the 1950s those libraries with collections over 200,000 volumes were identified as being large enough to apply the concepts of scientific management.[5] Librarians in these libraries were interested in achieving maximum efficiency at minimum cost. They accumulated data on unit costs, particularly costs associated with the cataloging and processing of materials (which amounts to a large part of the library's budget), in order to identify ways which would reduce these costs. Time and motion studies were carried out in many libraries, textbooks were written for library managers,[6] and studies were undertaken regularly to create efficiencies in library operations through time reductions.

The work of Mayo, Barnard and others followed that of the scientific managers and brought to industry (and later, to libraries) the human relations theories, as well as the inevitable attack on the principles of scientific management and on the elements of bureaucracy, such as hierarchy of authority and formal rules and regulations. The influence of the human relations approach in the study of informal processes in organizations has been felt widely in libraries. Professionals tend to chafe under perceived bureaucratic constraints and strive for greater participation in library affairs so as to eliminate some of the constraints. The quest for efficiency and improved performance pervades the organization and does influence the work on participation in libraries. Therefore, many of the demands for greater participation are justified by the argument that the library's overall performance will improve, because greater participation by library staff members in the overall decision-making of the library will lead to greater job satisfaction and better performance.

Library managers seeking organizational efficiency and librarians seeking the best in service programs may disagree on solutions to particular library problems. Although the decisions in many academic libraries to change from old classification systems to the Library of Congress system were for the most part noncontroversial, the decision to switch to the Library of Congress system offers good examples of both the managerial approach to decision-making with a base in efficiency, and a professional expert approach with a base in a service idea. In many libraries the decision to change classification schemes was made on the grounds of greater efficiency, as managers sought ways to reduce the costs in technical services operations. The decision to change sometimes reflected the need for updating the classification schedules for scientific materials. Rarely was the decision based on an extensive analysis of classification schemes or on an assessment of how the particular library's clientele used the old scheme to find needed materials and information. The decision was made primarily on the basis of operational costs. Whether the change in classification scheme is an inhibition of any consequence to the library user is a professional concern, but not one which appears to be of any major interest. The administrator strives to achieve maximum efficiency at minimum cost. Whenever the cost of attaining a particular objective rises in terms of time, effort or money, the administrator seeks less to attain that objective.

There has been surprisingly little discussion on the impact of classification schemes. It may be that all librarians, managers or not, are in general agreement that lower technical services costs are of paramount importance and should take precedence in any decision involving cataloging and classification; or, the profession may not understand clearly enough the strengths and weaknesses of particular classification systems; or, the classification scheme may have become only a shelving device, having lost the ability to help users find a variety of materials on a particular subject. In any case, the reasons for the decision on classification schemes are of little importance to the present discussion. The example only illustrates a potential conflict which has its base in a decision influenced by managerial efficiencies instead of organizational goals. Had the decision been more controversial, the conflicts may have been more readily observed.

Bureaucracy and professionalism have several elements in common. Each requires impersonal detachment and specialized technical competence. Each bases its decision-making in a rational application of standards. There are also differences, however. Bureaucratic authority rests not so much on technical skills or competencies as on the official position. Bureaucratic authority requires subordinates to comply with directives under threat of some sanction. Professional authority rests upon possession of expertise. It requires an abstract body of knowledge to support the technical skills. Professional authority is self-governing through an association of peers, professional standards of practice and ethical conduct. Professionalism has a service orientation.[7]

The service orientation of the professional can lead to an opposite approach to work from that based in strict compliance with work procedures, a bureaucratic characteristic, and conflict can occur when these approaches are joined. Conflict can occur when decisions are made on the basis of purely professional standards, ignoring the administrative requirements of the organization. Yet large libraries, like all organizations of a certain size, are bureaucratic to some degree, even though they are staffed with professionals. There is someone at the top who decides what the library program will be and who assigns jobs. Specializations in tasks are determined and jobs are designed within the library to carry out these tasks. Rules and regulations are introduced and are useful in dealing with organizational issues such as staff turnover, consistency in performance and output. Among organizations the degree of bureaucratization does vary, and interesting questions center on why variations occur. For example, what conditions shape the organizational hierarchy? Does the work influence the division of labor or the nature of rules? How might the qualifications of the library's staff influence the structure of authority in it? Within large libraries are often found reference departments in which a high percentage of staff are professionals with expert training and experience. The catalog department, by contrast, although staffed with some professional people, generally has a higher percentage of clerical staff. These units should be expected to differ in terms of their bureaucratic characteristics, i.e., authority structures. Reference departments should exhibit a greater degree of participation in decision-making than catalog departments.

The relationship between the professional skills and competencies of the librarian and the bureaucratic authority vested in the hierarchy of office in the library occupies considerable attention and is a useful theoretical issue in the study of libraries as bureaucracies. The organization model which influences the library literature is the model of the autonomous professional. The work of the librarian is most often described in terms of a librarian/client relationship, a one-to-one relationship. Yet much of the work performed in libraries is divided into specialized tasks and is conducted outside the framework of the client relationship. Rarely does a librarian participate in all the tasks required in the selection of materials, in their cataloging and classification, or even in the answering of a reference question. The library profession itself seeks ways to divide the work into those tasks which are professional and those which are clerical in order to reduce costs, achieve greater efficiency, and utilize to the greatest extent possible the knowledge of the professional. Much effort is given to separating the routine tasks from the less routine, and then to designing jobs according to the nature of the tasks. The amount of job specialization will vary in libraries and it is to be expected that the specialization of tasks or the division of labor would be greater in large libraries than in small ones—consistent with Weber's theory that the larger the size of the organization the greater the specialization. Spence, in his library study on bureaucratic characteristics, found no support for Weber's theory of bureaucracy regarding size and specialization, but methodological problems in Spence's study make his results suspect.

Although Weber implies that professional authority, with its basis in technical competence, and bureaucratic authority, with its basis in a positional hierarchy, would exist concurrently in organizations, the prevailing attitude among librarians is that the professional's work suffers from the constraints of bureaucratic conditions. Yet much of the work in libraries is governed by written rules and regulations. The rules are more or less stable, more or less exhaustive, and can be learned. Knowledge of the rules and regulations forms the technical skills identified by Weber as a bureaucratic characteristic. Within libraries, technical knowledge and professional knowledge exist concurrently, although variation in degree will exist.

Some of the support in libraries for the human relations approach and the study of informal processes has its basis in the inherent difference of opinion between library managers and staff members over the type of organizational structure needed to achieve organizational goals.[8] Given the different theoretical perspectives governing the knowledge available about library organization and behavior, such conflict is predictable. The library is an organization in which tasks are arranged in a rational way and one in which a marshalling of scarce resources is the responsibility of management. The literature of librarianship reflects the effort expended by librarians to find and report more efficient ways of getting work done. The library is also an organization in which professional experts seek to provide the best service possible, sometimes with little regard to cost. The recent library literature emphasizes the conditions which affect the attitudes and initiative of librarians and derides some of the bureaucratic conditions which exist in libraries. Nevertheless, every library exhibits the characteristics of a bureaucracy to a certain degree; each has a certain pattern of behavior based on specialized tasks and role design. Libraries are expected to vary in the degree to which they are bureaucratized, i.e., in stuctural characteristics. Some libraries will have a greater degree of job specialization than others. Some will restrict the discretion of staff members more than others in terms of required adherence to rules and regulations. Some will centralize authority in a small cadre of administrators, while others will delegate authority to the lower levels.

The research conducted so far which attempts to compare libraries or their structural characteristics is inconclusive, though tantalizing. Research which compares organizational structure by type of library will be even more interesting. In the absence of specific research on libraries as bureaucracies, the studies of other types of organizations must be examined for insights and theories to guide one's understanding.

Although many professionally trained librarians seek work environments which are flexible, democratic and completely participatory, it is rare for libraries to be structured in this way. Such work environments are generally inefficient, and libraries are designed to be as efficient as possible. Efficiency demands a stable and constant environment. The library is heavily influenced by its environment and much of the library manager's time is spent trying to reduce these environmental influences. Library managers commonly use both staff specialists and rules and regulations to cope with environmental problems. Some rules and regulations, of course, are designed to assist the librarians in carrying out their work. Cataloging rules and the like are examples of library rules which are related to the work of the library. Other rules are those which do not contribute to the library's goals and objectives, but are designed to maintain the library itself. Particularly important are rules and regulations related to the hiring of staff. In a completely democratic organization each individual staff member is in the best position to determine the knowledge, skills and abilities needed to do the job. The hiring process, being affected by such outside factors as ability to judge potential successors, union contracts, civil service requirements, affirmative action procedures, availability of a pool of qualified candidates from which to hire, is aided by organizational rules regarding appointments and by staff specialists who are responsible for determining minimum qualifications for various positions and for finding suitable candidates for the position. Libraries often reflect homogeneity in terms of personnel, partly because of geographic reasons and the self-selection on the part of applicants, and partly because of the personnel specialists' determination to hire people with similar backgrounds and characteristics in order to increase predictability, i.e., to limit the uncertainty which a variety of backgrounds inevitably brings to an organization.

Turnover in staff entails other rules and regulations. The efficient organization will codify the way a particular person does a job and make that way the "right way." The codification is designed to minimize the differences in job performance a new person will bring to a position and to reduce the uncertainty and adjustment problems the new person might have. An organization designs many rules and regulations in order to exert control over the external influences upon organizational behavior. Such rules and regulations often are described as bureaucratic red tape since they appear to be unrelated to the actual work of the organization. Nonetheless, these rules serve to control and to stabilize environmental influences, enabling the organization to deal with the environment in a more predictable and routine fashion.

The emphasis in most organizations, including libraries, is to make tasks routine, reduce uncertainty, increase predictability, and centralize authority. There is an inevitable tendency toward internal efficiency. The question of efficiency depends on a stable environment.

Libraries are bureaucracies. The bureaucratic elements which critics identify have their sources, not in the red tape or pettiness of officials, but in the attempt of the library to control its environment. The elements of bureaucracy emerge from the library's attempt to ensure its efficiency and its competency and from its attempt to minimize the impact of outside influences. Although variations will exist in the bureaucratic conditions, libraries will remain bureaucratic in form.

References

1. Weber, Max. "Bureaucracy." In *From Max Weber: Essays in Sociology.* H. H. Gerth and C. Wright Mills, trans. New York, Oxford University Press, 1962, pp. 196–244.
2. Spence, Paul H. "A Comparative Study of University Library Organizational Structure." Ph.D. diss., University of Illinois, 1969.
3. Blau, Peter M. "The Hierarchy of Authority in Organizations," *The American Journal of Sociology* 73:453–67, Jan. 1968.
4. Kipp, Laurence J. "Scientific Management in Research Libraries," *Library Trends* 2:390–400, Jan. 1954.
5. McAnally, Arthur M. "Organization of College and University Libraries," *Library Trends* 1:21–36, July 1952.
6. Dougherty, Richard M., and Heinritz, Fred J. *Scientific Management of Library Operations.* New York, Scarecrow Press, 1966.
7. Blau, op. cit.
8. Webster, Duane et al. "Effecting Change in the Management of Libraries: The Management Review and Analysis Program." In "Coping with Change: The Challenge for Research Libraries," *Minutes of the Eighty-Second Meeting, Association of Research Libraries*, May 11–12, 1973, pp. 41–80.

The Hierarchy of Authority in Organizations

Peter M. Blau

Aᴅᴠᴀɴᴄᴇѕ in the social sciences do not occur in straight lines of uniform progress, as the recurrent rediscoveries of half-forgotten classics indicate, be it Simmel's analysis of conflict or Durkheim's of the division of labor, the insights of Karl Marx, Adam Smith, or even Plato. But neither does the development of sociology move in circles or simply fluctuate between alternative theoretical approaches. There is some continuity, and there is some progress. The analysis of pattern variables by Parsons and Shils surely is a refinement of Toennies's concepts of *Gemeinschaft* and *Gesellschaft*, for example, and the research of Lipset, Trow, and Coleman clearly advances our knowledge of union democracy far beyond Michels's theory of oligarchy which inspired it. The pattern of scientific development may be described as dialectical. Mounting criticisms of one approach lead to concentration on another designed to overcome the first's shortcomings; yet the second approach is likely, in due time, to reveal limitations of its own that encourage still other lines of scientific attack. But slowly some progress is made.

The study of formal organizations is a case in point. Weber's theoretical analysis, which has long dominated the field, was increasingly criticized for presenting an idealized conception of bureaucracy and for examining only its formal characteristics and ignoring the informal modifications that occur in actual practice. In response to this criticism, research on organizations concentrated on informal relations and unofficial practices, the attitudes of individual members and their observable behavior. The resulting studies of the informal organization of work groups and the actual performance of duties in bureaucracies have undoubtedly contributed much to our under-

Reprinted with permission from the *American Journal of Sociology*, V. 73, (Jan. 1968), pp. 453–467. © 1968 by The University of Chicago.

standing of these complex structures. While complementing Weber's approach, however, the new focus neglected the basic theoretical problem to which he addressed himself. One question a student of organizations may ask is how the existing conditions in a bureaucracy affect attitudes and conduct, for instance, why bureaucratic conditions stifle initiative and what the processes involved are.[1] But there is another question that can be asked, namely, why certain conditions emerge in organizations in the first place, for example, what determines the development and the characteristics of the authority structure. Weber was concerned with the second problem—explaining the configurations of bureaucratic conditions—whereas recent research focused on the first—investigating their consequences for individuals and groups—to the virtual exclusion of the second, in part because the case study method usually employed is not suitable for answering the second question.

A theory of formal organization, as distinguished from a theory of group life in a bureaucratic context, seeks to explain why organizations develop various characteristics, such as a multilevel hierarchy or decentralized authority. To furnish these explanations requires that the characteristics of organizations are not taken as given but the conditions that produce them are the very object of the inquiry. Thus one may ask how the qualifications of an organization's staff influence the structure of authority in it, or generally what conditions affect the shape of the hierarchy, which are the two problems posed in this paper. In order to answer this kind of question, it is necessary to compare different organizations and not merely to study the influence exerted on behavior by the conditions found in a single case. The method of comparison might involve analyzing bureaucracies in different historical periods, which was Weber's approach; or intensive examination of two contrasting forms of organization, as in Stinchcombe's study cited below; or quantitative comparisons of many organizations and multivariate analysis of their characteristics. The last procedure is adopted here.

The assumption made in choosing this procedure is that the analysis of the interdependence between organizational attributes based on systematic comparisons of large numbers of organizations promises to contribute most to organizational theory. If the ultimate aim of this theory is to derive general principles that explain the emergence of structures with various characteristics, the first step must be to advance more limited generalizations that specify the conditions that affect the development of different characteristics. Quantitative comparisons permit such specification. The analysis of the authority structure to be presented is based on data collected from several hundred government agencies. Only agencies of a specific type are directly compared, to eliminate the disturbing influence of differences between types; but the results of one such study are confronted with those of another, to discern whether conclusions are confined to a single type. The inquiry is restricted to the formal attributes of organizations, since it was not possible to collect data on informal patterns and individual attitudes in hundreds of government agencies. This limitation of the approach to organizational research here adopted may well give rise in the future to different approaches not similarly limited to easily accessible data. But the prospect of a possible countertrend in the future should not deter us now from exploiting the scientific contribution that systematic comparisons of even relatively simple organizational traits can make at the present stage of knowledge.

The exposition is deliberately designed to call attention to continuities in bureaucratic theory and research, and the paper also seeks to reveal the role that theoretical speculations which go beyond the empirical evidence play in establishing continuities between different investigations. The research reported is conceived within the framework of Weber's theoretical tradition; it follows his approach of studying the interrelations between formal conditions in bureaucratic structures, rather than the individuals and human relations within them, and it deals with two substantive issues his theory poses—the relationship between expertness and authority, and the significance of the formal hierarchy of offices. Moreover, the continuities from one empirical investigation to another are indicated as the tentative interpretations of earlier findings are tested and refined in a subsequent study. I shall try to illustrate that advancing highly speculative generalizations in interpreting empirical findings serves important scientific functions, for such inferential conjectures are the basis for the cumulation of scientific knowledge, provided that they are followed up by further research. The only connection between different empirical investigations, and hence the only source of cumulation, is the generalizations derived from each that go beyond its limited evidence.

PROFESSIONAL AND BUREAUCRATIC AUTHORITY

The relationship between the expert qualifications of a professional staff and the bureaucratic authority vested in a hierarchy of offices poses an interesting theoretical issue. Professionalism and bureaucracy have much in common, such as impersonal detachment, specialized technical expertness, and rational decision-making based on universalistic standards. There are also divergent elements, however, and professional principles often come into conflict with the requirements of bureaucratic authority. Weber implied that the professional authority rooted in expert technical knowledge and the bureaucratic authority rooted in a hierarchy of offices with legitimate claims to disciplined compliance tend to occur together, both being distinctive characteristics of complex rational organizations. "The role of technical qualifications in bureaucratic organizations is continually increasing."[2] But, in addition, "each lower office is under the control and supervision of a higher one."[3] The assumption that professional expertness and bureaucratic discipline are simply two aspects of the rational organization of large-scale tasks not only conflicts with the prevailing impression that professional work suffers if subjected to bureaucratic discipline, but it also has been questioned on both systematic theoretical and empirical grounds.

In a well-known footnote, Parsons criticizes Weber for confounding two analytically distinct types of authority.[4] Professional authority rests on the certified superior competence of the expert, which prompts others voluntarily to follow his directives because they consider doing so to be in their own interest. Bureaucratic authority, in contrast, rests on the legitimate power of command vested in an official position, which obligates subordinates to follow directives under the threat of sanctions. Superior knowledge is not required for bureaucratic authority (expert knowledge is not what authorizes the policeman to direct traffic, for example, or what induces us to obey his signals), whereas it is essential for professional control, and mandatory compliance is enforced by coercive sanctions in the bureaucratic but not in the professional case. Gouldner similarly stresses the difference between the influence exerted on the basis of technical competence and the compelling authority in a bureaucratic hierarchy, and he derives from this distinction two contrasting forms of bureaucracy—"representative" and "punishment-centered."[5]

Research results also challenge Weber's assumption that technical expertness and hierarchically enforced discipline typically occur together. Stinchcombe's comparison of two industries suggests, for example, that the technical skills of construction workers, which contrast with the low level of skill in mass production, promote rational performance and therefore serve as a substitute for the bureaucratic hierarchy through which the work in mass production is rationally organized.[6] Thus technical expertness and hierarchical authority seem to be alternative, not complementary, principles of organization. Udy's research on the organization of production in 150 nonindustrial societies arrives at parallel results.[7] He finds that several bureaucratic characteristics, including a hierarchical authority structure, are directly correlated with one another but not, or even inversely, with several rational characteristics, including specialization, which may be considered a primitive forerunner of technical expertness, and so may rational work procedures in general. Udy concludes: "Bureaucracy and rationality tend to be mutually inconsistent in the same formal organization."[8] It is noteworthy that both of these studies do not deal with advanced levels of professionalization but with rather rudimentary forms of expert qualifications.

The various components of professionalism must be distinguished in analyzing its implications for heirarchical authority in organizations. Full-fledged professionalization entails not only expert skills but also a body of abstract knowledge underlying them, a self-governing association of professional peers, professional standards of workmanship and ethical conduct, and an orientation toward service. Some of these factors may easily come into conflict with the discipline required by bureaucratic authority. Research indicates that a professional orientation toward service and a bureaucratic orientation toward disciplined compliance with procedures are opposite approaches toward work and often create conflict in organizations.[9] Besides, the identification of professionals with an external reference group may well lessen their loyalty to the organization.[10] It is also reasonable to expect that conflicts arise as decisions made strictly on the basis of professional standards are recurrently set aside for the sake of administrative considerations by bureaucratic authorities. All these conflicts refer to fairly advanced aspects of professionalization. But Weber's concern was not so much with these components of professionalism as with technical expertness, which he held to be an integral part of hierarchically organized bureaucracies. The findings of Stinchcombe and Udy imply, however, that even a moderate degree of technical expertness conflicts with bureaucratic authority.

Yet there can be no question that hierarchically organized bureaucracies do employ personnel with expert training and qualifications. As a matter of fact, formal organizations typically *require* their staff to meet certain educational or technical qualifications, and these requirements indicate that a minimum of expertness is indeed an integral part of the bureaucratic structure. If expertness itself is, nevertheless, incompatible with some elements of strict bureaucratic authority, as the findings cited suggest, the question is how it modifies the structure of authority in organizations. The present paper addresses itself first to this problem of how variations in the qualifications of the personnel affect the authority structure in formal organizations, and it then turns to the question of how other conditions affect the hierarchy of authority.

A simple working hypothesis for investigating the first problem can be derived from a few plausible considerations. Entrance requirements that assure that the agency staff (meaning all personnel, in line as well as "staff" positions) has relatively high minimum qualifications might be expected to lessen the need for guidance and close supervision. The implication is that such expert requirements widen the span of control of managers, increasing the number of subordinates under each,[11] and therefore reduce the proportion of managerial personnel in the organization, because each superior can supervise more subordinates if they are experts than if their lower skills necessitate much guidance and checking. These inferences, which appear straightforward and perhaps even self-evident, suggest as an initial hypothesis that expert requirements decrease the ratio of managerial to nonsupervisory personnel in organizations, which widens the average span of control.

STUDY OF PUBLIC
PERSONNEL AGENCIES

This hypothesis was tested as part of a previously published study of 156 public personnel agencies,[12] and a brief summary of the pertinent results suffices to introduce the problem investigated in subsequent research. The data were collected by the Public Personnel Association through questionnaires to its members. They pertain to the executive agencies of the civil service commissions of most state and major local American governments, with the bias of selection favoring larger agencies and those identified with merit principles. These agencies are small bureaucracies, with a median staff of not quite seventeen (even after the ninety-six with a staff of less than five were eliminated from the analysis). The measure of expertness is whether the operating staff, excluding both managerial and clerical personnel, is required to have a college degree with a specified job-related major.[13] The only available information on the hierarchy of authority is the ratio of managers to nonsupervisory officials.[14]

The employment of experts with stipulated educational qualifications does not reduce the proportionate size of the managerial staff in public personnel agencies. On the contrary, under most conditions, though not under all, agencies that require their employees to meet relatively high qualifications are more likely than others to have a high ratio of managers. Expertness, moreover, seems to prevent other conditions from reducing the proportion of managers. An increase in the division of labor tends to decrease the managerial ratio in the absence of expert requirements but increase it in their presence. The hypothesis that the expertness of the operating staff widens the span of supervisory control and consequently is reflected in a low ratio of managers is clearly negated by these results.

In the light of these negative findings we reconceptualized the meaning attributed to the managerial ratio. Since it does not appear reasonable that better-trained personnel officers are more closely supervised than those lacking similar qualifications, the initial assumption that a higher ratio of managers is indicative of closer supervision must be questioned. An alternative interpretation of the significance of this measure, which is compatible with the findings, is that a low ratio of managers implies a centralized authority structure, with managerial authority concentrated in the hands of comparatively few officials. When administrative authority is centralized in few positions, management presumably is carried out largely by a central headquarters that issues directives to the operating staff, whereas management in a structure with a large proportion of authority positions probably entails more reciprocal adjustments as the result of the greater opportunities for communication between managerial and operating personnel.

The difference in assumptions between the original and the revised interpretations of the managerial ratio should be made explicit. The initial formulation assumed that few managers with a wide span of control imply less close supervision, which permits subordinates to exercise more autonomy in their work. The reconceptualization assumes that few managers imply a centralized authority structure, which encourages management through one-sided directives with little feedback from operating levels, thus reducing the autonomy of subordinates. The empirical data, though they were the basis for the revision, are not adequate to validate either set of assumptions. However, the reconceptualization permits some suggestive conjectures.

Appointing employees with expert qualifications and instituting a centralized authority structure appear to be alternative modes of organization, which are somewhat incompatible. This conclusion is in broad agreement with the one reached by both Stinchcombe and Udy in their empirical studies, as well as with the theoretical distinction Parsons makes between professional and bureaucratic authority. But our research specifies the source of the incompatibility. What is inappropriate for an organization staffed by experts is a hierarchy in which official authority is centralized in the hands of few managers. It seems paradoxical that more managers are required to direct employees with superior qualifications than those less well trained. The explanation lies in the implications of a low ratio of managers already adumbrated and in the implications of expert qualifications.

Expert training may be expected to make a man not only more independent in the performance of his duties but also more aware of the broader implications of his work and more capable of detecting operating problems and finding solutions for them than is an untrained person. Experts are more likely to resent having their discretion limited by managerial directives than are employees whose lesser skills make some guidance welcome. In addition, experts can make greater contributions to the improvement of operation procedures than men without specialized training. Hence, feedback communication from the operating staff is especially valuable for management if this staff consists of experts. To take full advantage of the contribution experts can make to operations, management must facilitate the flow of upward communication. A low ratio of managers tends to discourage upward communication, however, inasmuch as a small contingent of managers can most easily direct operations by issuing orders from a central headquarters to the staff. A high ratio of managers increases opportunities for communication between officials responsible for administrative and those responsible for operating decisions. Such extensive two-way communication is of special importance if the personnel has expert qualifications, not alone because experts tend to be more alienated by one-sided directives but particularly because they make greater contributions through feedback than persons with poorer qualifications.

In short, the interpretation suggested is that the added significance the expertness of the staff lends to the free flow of upward communication in organizations accounts for the association between expert requirements and a high ratio of managers. We were able to muster a bit of indirect evidence in support of this interpretation in the study of public personnel agencies. An expert staff improves operating economy in very small agencies, with a personnel of less than twenty, but it impedes economy in larger agencies unless the clerical staff is relatively large. In agencies of sufficient size to make communication a serious problem, the absence of an adequate clerical apparatus to maintain channels of communication has an adverse effect on operating economy if and only if the staff consists of experts.[15] This finding implies that expert qualifications of operating officials enhance the importance of communication, indirectly supporting our interpretation.

Nevertheless, the generalizations we advanced rest on shaky grounds. They are based on data from only one kind of organization, a specific type of government agency. Besides, public personnel agencies are very small, while bureaucratic theory presumably deals with large organizations. (It should be noted, however, that the stereotype of the huge government bureaucracy with a staff of thousand is misleading as far as particular agencies of state and local governments are concerned, most of which probably have less than one hundred employees.) Moreover, the only measure of the hierarchy of authority available, the proportion of managers, is clearly insufficient to analyze this complex institution. Finally, the inference that expertness promotes a decentralized authority structure is highly speculative, since the implication is that decision making is decentralized, but a large proportion of managers is not necessarily indicative of decentralization of *decisionmaking*. One might even argue that, on the contrary, the *smaller* the proportion of managers, the more likely will they be to delegate responsibilities to subordinates in order to lighten the burden of their duties.

STUDY OF GOVERNMENT
FINANCE DEPARTMENTS

A study of 254 finance departments of state and local governments made it possible to test the hypothesis that staff expertness leads to decentralization of responsibilities, and further to explore the conditions that influence the structure of authority in organizations. Original data were collected for the purpose of this study by National Opinion Research Center interviewers from informants (senior managers) in the major finance department of each government. The universe consists of the departments in all states, all counties with a population of more than 100,000 and all cities with a population of more than 50,000, in the United States, except those with a staff of fewer than twenty or with no subdivision of responsibilities into two or more units.[16] The sample comprises the entire universe, and information was obtained from 96.6 percent of these organizations. Although responsibilities vary, nearly all departments maintain financial records and preaudit disbursements, and the majority are also responsible for postauditing other departments, investment management, and fixed-asset accounting. The median department has a staff of sixty, six major subdivisions, and four hierarchical levels.

A number of the questions raised by the conclusions of the earlier study can be answered by this research. Another type of government agency has now been investigated, making it possible to check whether the previous findings merely reflect some special conditions in personnel work. The organizations under examination are larger, with a minimum size of twenty instead of five and a median of sixty instead of seventeen, and a larger number of cases is available for analysis, increasing the reliability of findings. Of greatest importance is the fact that a variety of measures of the structure of authority were deliberately designed to permit refinement of the earlier inferences. Information was obtained on the proportion of managerial personnel, specifically defined as all officials with supervisory duties; the number of levels in the hierarchy (the mean for the various divisions); the average span of control—number of subordinates—of first-line supervisors and that of middle managers; the proportion of their time managers spend on supervision; and the hierarchical level on which various specified decisions are made, furnishing direct indications of delegation of responsibilities and decentralization of authority. The index of expert requirements is the proportion of the staff expected to have a college degree, roughly parallel to the index used in the other study,[17] and departments are dichotomized on the basis of whether at least one-fifth of the total personnel (which is about two-fifths of the nonclerical personnel) is expected to meet the requirement of college graduation.

The basic finding reported from the study of public personnel agencies is confirmed by this research on another type of government agency; a high ratio of managerial personnel is more often found in finance departments with a large proportion of college-trained experts than in those with comparatively few employees so qualified (Table 1, row 1).[18] The more extensive data of the second study make it possible to stipulate the structural implications of the higher ratio of managers in organizations with many experts. The employment of an expert staff seems to give rise to vertical differentiation, increasing the number of managerial levels in the organization. The number of hierarchical levels tends to be larger in departments requiring of its personnel relatively high educational qualifications than in those with lower requirements (row 2). The span of control of first-line super-

TABLE 1   Training Requirements and Authority Structure

PERCENTAGE OF FINANCE DEPARTMENTS (IN COLS. [1] AND [2]) IN WHICH:	PROPORTION OF STAFF REQUIRED TO HAVE B.A.*		YULE'S Q (GAMMA)
	Low (1)	High (2)	(3)
1. The proportion of managers exceeds one-quarter of the total personnel.................	35 (147)	48 (106)	.27
2. The number of levels is four or more	36 (148)	51 (106)	.29
3. The mean span of control of first-line supervisors is six or more.....................	56 (147)	44 (106)	−.23†
4. The mean span of control of middle managers is 1.6 or more...........................	38 (135)	54 (100)	.32
5. The average manager spends more than two-fifths of his time supervising...............	52 (145)	38 (106)	−.29
6. Division heads make budgeting or accounting decisions.............................	40 (122)	54 (86)	.26†
7. An official below the director recommends promotions and dismissals................	30 (147)	45 (104)	.32

* Since this variable is not associated with size, it is not necessary to control size.

† All relationships are significant below the .05 level except these two, which are significant on the .08 and .06 levels, respectively.

visors is, on the average, somewhat narrower if the staff has superior qualifications than if it does not (row 3).[19] The span of control of middle managers (those between the top executive and first-line supervisors) is, by contrast, wider in agencies with well-trained personnel than in others (row 4). But these middle managers have many fewer subordinates in any case, averaging less than two, than first-line supervisors, whose median is six subordinates. Supervisors have typically broader responsibilities than operating officials, and very few of them report to the same superior; expert qualifications presumably broaden the responsibilities of operating employees, which is reflected in a parallel reduction in the number reporting to the same supervisor. This consistent inverse association between scope of responsibilities and width of span of control clearly indicates that a narrow span of control must not be assumed to be indicative of closeness of supervision.[20]

The employment of personnel with superior qualifications raises the proportion of managers in an organization apparently because it tends to increase the number of managerial levels and decrease the span of control of first-line supervisors. The question arises how the extra managerial manpower is utilized in departments with a highly qualified staff. The time estimates of informants permit tentative answers to this question. If much of the staff is college trained, managers are less likely to spend most of their time in actual supervision than if it is not (Table 1, row 5, based on the mean for all managers), and this is the case for first-line supervisors as well as higher managers. The finding that superiors of experts devote comparatively little time to actually supervising them helps to explain why their narrow span of control does not imply close supervision. Managers in departments with highly qualified personnel seem to spend more time than other managers on professional work of their own which keeps them in touch with the problems encountered by the operating level.[21] Such greater involvement in actual operations on the the part of managers of an expert staff, compared to other managers, may well improve their qualifications to discuss technical problems of the work with their subordinates and thus to take full advantage of the greater opportunities for communication that the smaller numbers of subordinates per superior create.

The question of prime interest is whether the hypothesis that expertness promotes decentralization, which rested merely on inferential conjecture, is confirmed by the directly pertinent data from finance departments. This is in fact the case. Responsibilities of various kinds tend to be delegated by management to lower levels in agencies where the staff has relatively high qualifications. Thus budgeting and accounting decisions are more likely to be made by division heads rather than the department director himself if the staff includes many college-trained men than if it includes few (Table 1, row 6). The likelihood that an official below the top executive recommends promotions and dismissals is also greater in agencies with many experts than in others (row 7). Parallel relationships with expertness, though they are somewhat less pronounced, are revealed by other indications of decentralization of responsibilities, such as the top executive's policy to let his division heads make most decisions, and the fact that first-line supervisors, not higher officials, formally evaluate the performance of nonsupervisory employees. In sum, managerial authority over decision-making appears indeed to be more decentralized in organizations with large proportions of trained experts than in others.

MULTILEVEL HIERARCHIES

The finding that superior qualifications of the personnel in government agencies encourage delegation of responsibilities is not surprising. But what is unexpected is that such superior qualifications are also associated with vertical differentiation into multilevel hierarchies. It is generally assumed that the proliferation of hierarchical levels in organizations is a sign of over-bureaucratization that is incompatible with the rational work of trained experts, and the results of Udy's study of primitive production organizations point to this conclusion.[22] However, the finding here implies the opposite, namely, that multilevel hierarchies in organizations occur together with superior training which contributes to rational operations. This raises the question of what conditions in contemporary American agencies promote hierarchical differentiation.

A multilevel hierarchy is associated with eight basic characteristics of finance departments: (1) The number of levels increases with increasing size, that is, the number of employees (Pearsonian zero-order correlation, .51).[23] (2) Although the zero-order correlation between number of levels and number of major subdivisions[24] is virtually nil (−.05), there is an inverse association between the two when size is controlled (−.34). (3) The wider the average span of control of middle managers, the larger is the number of levels in the hierarchy (.27). (4) Automation in the form of computers is associated with multiple levels (.34). (5) Explicit written promotion regulations

TABLE 2   Correlations with Number of Levels in the Hierarchy

Independent Variable	Zero-Order Correlation	Partial Correlation	Standardized B^*	Regression Error	DATA ON EMPLOYMENT AGENCIES: Zero-Order Correlation
Number of employees	.51	.50	.53	.06	.60
Number of major divisions	−.05	−.32	−.30	.06	.19
Span of control of middle managers	.27	.11	.09	.05	.31
Automation (computers)[a]	.34	.23	.19	.05	.53
Explicit promotion regulations[a]	.22	.04	−.03	.06	.33
Weight of examinations in promotions	.24	.13	.12	.06	[b]
Decentralization of promotion decisions[a]	.18	.12	.09	.05	.19
Proportion of staff required to have B.A.	.16	.03	.02	.05	−.00

[a] These three factors are dichotomous and were used as dummy variables in the regression analysis. All others are continuous variables except weight of examinations, which was coded in four categories.
[b] No corresponding variable is available for the employment security study.

encourage hierarchical differentiation (.22). (6) The number of levels increases the more weight written examinations have for promotions (.24), and it decreases the more weight seniority (−.22) and supervisory evaluations (−.16) have for promotions.[25] (7) Decentralization of responsibility for promotions and dismissals is correlated with multiple levels (.18). (8) The larger the proportion of employees required to have college degrees, finally, the larger the number of levels. (.16).

Since so many factors are associated with hierarchical levels, partial correlations were computed between each of the eight and number of levels holding constant the other seven. The results of this regression analysis, which provide the basis for the further discussion, are presented in Table 2. The multiple correlation between all eight factors and levels is .65. These characteristics of finance departments explain 43 percent of the variance in hierarchical levels, with most of the difference being due to three factors—size, divisions, and automation.

Some reflections on the considerations that probably influence the decision to add new levels in the hierarchy can serve as a starting point for interpreting these associations. As an organization expands in size and complexity, it is likely that additional major divisions are established, which increases the number of officials directly responsible to the department director and overburdens him with supervisory responsibilities. To lighten this administrative load of the top executive and free him to devote more time to his primary executive functions, a few assistant directors may be installed on a new level to whom the division directors report and who in turn report to the director, just as the creation of the U.S Secretary of Health, Education, and Welfare constituted an intermediate level between the President and officials who formerly reported directly to him. The introduction of such a new level of assistant directors would account for the inverse association observed between levels and major subdivisions because the few "superdivisions" headed by the assistant directors, not the former divisions, would now be defined as the "major subdivisions" by the criterion used. This change would also help to explain why number of levels and span of control of middle managers, which includes assistant directors, are correlated without controls (.27) but are no longer significantly related once size, subdivisions, and other conditions are controlled (.11). The assumptions here are that the assistant directors, whose establishment increases levels, have a particularly wide span of control—hence the zero-order correlation—but that the introduction of this new level occurs usually in large agencies and reduces the number of major subdivisions—hence the considerably lower correlation under these controls.

Differentiation into a multilevel hierarchy has evident advantages for expanding organizations, according to these conjectures. In fact the number of levels in finance departments increases with increasing size, as previously noted; so does the number of major subdivisions, however (the zero-order correlation between size and subdivisions being .43, nearly as large as that between size and levels, .51). Not all large agencies have many levels and few major divisions. The inverse association between levels and subdivisions when size is controlled implies the existence of two contrasting departmental structures, one that is primarily differentiated horizontally into many major divisions and one that is primarily differentiated vertically into many levels. The question is what conditions discourage horizontal differentiation—which places an excessive administrative burden on top management—and encourage vertical differentiation instead.

The clue for answering this question is provided by the other major correlate of number of levels, namely, automation, which reveals a substantial association with it (.34) that persists when other conditions are controlled (.23). Although extending the hierarchy has administrative advantages for the top executive of a large organization, it also removes him increasingly from the operating level and makes it difficult for him directly to control operations and keep tight reins on them. This loss of close contact with the operating level is a serious disadvantage for a director who relies largely on direct supervision for control, but it is not such a disadvantage if top management has instituted indirect mechanisms of control and can exercise with their aid sufficient influence on operations by setting policies and formulating programs. The automation of accounting procedures through computers is just such an impersonal mechanism of control in finance departments. It places much controlling influence over operations into the hands of the top executives whose decisions determine the overall setup of the automated facilities and the nature of the computer programs, thereby obviating the need for much direct supervision. The assembly line serves similar functions in factories.[26] Since automation serves as a control mechanism that greatly reduces the main disadvantage of multilevel hierarchies, it furthers their development.[27]

The general principle suggested is that conditions in organizations that make the reliable performance of duties relatively independent of direct intervention by top management further the development of multilevel hierarchies. Advanced technological equipment, inasmuch as it mechanizes operations and makes them to some degree self-regulating, often serves this function. The mechanization of facilities is not the only condition that affects the reliability of performance, however. Regardless of how automated operations are, top management must rely on its managerial staff to implement its objectives and administer its policies. Herein lies the significance of promotion procedures for the hierarchy. Explicit promotion regulations furnish uniform standards that all higher officials must have met. But these standards assure top management that higher officials will have adequate qualifications for their responsibilities only if they stipulate that promotions be based primarily on examinations designed to test these qualifications rather than on seniority or the possibly idiosyncratic evaluations of supervisors. A significant correlation between the weight of written examinations in promotions and number of levels remains when other conditions are controlled (.13), but the correlation between the existence of promotion regulations and levels disappears when the weight of examinations and other conditions are controlled (.04). The reason probably is that only promotion regulations that give merit examinations such weight guarantee that all managerial officials have certain minimum qualifications and thus reduce top management's reluctance to lose direct contact with the operating level by establishing intervening layers in the hierarchy.

The more top management trusts the middle managers who constitute its administrative arm to discharge their responsibilities in accordance with its guidelines and directives, the more inclined it will be in all likelihood to delegate responsibilities to them. The implication is that the degree of confidence top executives place in their managerial assistance will promote decentralization of authority as well as multilevel hierarchies. If this surmise is correct, it could explain why the zero-order correlation between number of levels and decentralization (.18) is reduced to a point that falls just short of significance at .05 when other conditions that affect management's trust are controlled (.12).

Entrance requirements that demand comparatively high qualification of employees undoubtedly improve their abilities to perform their duties without close supervision. The interpretation advanced implies, therefore, that the proportion of the agency personnel expected to have college degrees and the number of levels in the hierarchy are positively related. As a matter of fact, such a positive zero-order correlation has been observed (.16), but controlling other conditions reduces this correlation to the vanishing point (.03). The proportion of employees with college training is not strongly associated with any of the other control variables under consideration, but it is somewhat correlated with four of them (between .12 and .14), its most pronounced zero-order correlation being that with decentralization (.14). A plausible explanation of this pattern of findings can be derived if expert qualifications are viewed as simply one element in a configuration of conditions indicative of operations that are relatively self-regulating and independent of direct intervention by management. As part of this configuration, the qualifications of employees are associated with the development of multilevel hierarchies. But once the other factors that manifest independence of managerial intervention are controlled, including those to which expert qualifications directly contribute, such as decentralization, the entire significance of qualifications for the hierarchy has been taken into account, and they are no longer associated with the number of levels.

TWO CONTRASTING TYPES

In conclusion, some inferences about two contrasting types of formal organization will be drawn from the associations with multilevel hierarchy observed. One of these types may be considered the modern organization governed by universalistic standards; the other represents the old-fashioned bureaucracy.

A fundamental issue confronting the executives of organizations is whether to manage primarily by means of direct or indirect controls. Management through direct controls entails keeping in close touch with operations and issuing corrective orders whenever necessary. Management through indirect controls involves devising impersonal control mechanisms that constrain operations to follow automatically the policies and programs specified by top executives. The substitution of indirect mechanisms of control for direct control requires that an orientation to abstract universalistic standards replace reliance on personal judgments. The development of these impersonal control mechanisms is most likely if technical considerations and effective performance are supreme values, whereas ideological commitments and particularistic solidarities have little significance.[28]

Today the prototype of an impersonal control mechanism is the computer, which dramatically illustrates how technological facilities automate operations and simultaneously give top management—whose decisions govern the basic computer setup—much control over them without requiring frequent direct intervention. Not only the operations themselves but also the recruitment of employees and that of the managerial staff tend to become standardized in the modern organization in terms of universalistic principles of effective performance. Explicit personnel regulations stipulate merit criteria for employment and for advancement to managerial positions, relieving top management of administrative tasks, lessening the influence of personal bias and variations in judgment over personnel decisions, and assuring minimum qualifications. Both the automation of the work process and the merit standards that the managerial and operating staff must meet contribute to the reliable performance of duties and help to make operations comparatively self-regulating within the framework of the organization's objectives and management's policies. These conditions reduce management's need to keep close direct control over operations and, consequently, often give rise to major changes in the hierarchy. To wit, vertical differentiation creates a multilevel hierarchy, which usually decreases the number of major divisions whose heads report to the agency director and increases the span of control of these division heads, and responsibilities become decentralized. The strongest pressure to institute impersonal mechanisms of control, and thus the conditions that facilitate these structural changes, comes from the expanding size of organizations.

In short, the modern organization is characterized by a tall, slim hierarchy with decentralized authority. The opposite type, which may be called an old-fashioned bureaucracy, has a squat hierarchy with authority centralized at the top. In this case, which is most prevalent in smaller organizations, the top executive maintains tight control over operations by directly supervising many division heads, assigning each of them only few subordinates, refraining from introducing intermediate levels that would increase his distance from the operating personnel, and delegating few responsibilities. The lesser interest in impersonal mechanisms of control under these circumstances is reflected in the rare instances of automation and in the nature of the personnel policies. Explicit regulations that specify personnel qualifications are infrequent; promotions are largely left under the discretion of management; and insofar as promotion standards do exist, they tend to give weight to seniority and personal judgments of superiors rather than objective merit criteria, thus implicitly enhancing the importance of loyalty at the expense of that of technical competence.

A final question to be raised is whether these conclusions concerning two contrasting types of formal structure apply to all work organizations (those employing people to perform tasks), or only to government agencies, or perhaps only to government finance departments. The methodological point made in the introduction bears repeating in this connection: generalizing beyond the data is necessary for scientific cumulation because such generalizing supplies the sole connection between different empirical studies. The finding that multilevel finance departments in the United States have fewer major divisions than others of the same size, for example, can neither be negated nor confirmed by research on other organizations, for the association between levels and divisions in another type of agency simply has no direct bearing on it. Only if the investigator is willing to advance generalizations that refer to broader concepts than his empirical data—all work organizations or vertical differentiation of any kind—is it possible to replicate or refute conclusions and ultimately to develop a scientific theory.

Hence the empirical findings from the study of finance departments are deliberately used to suggest tentative principles about work organizations in general, to be tested and appropriately modified in future research, just as the inferences drawn in our earlier study were tested and refined this one. Some indication that the conclusions about hierarchical structure are at least not restricted to finance departments is provided by a preliminary analysis of data on quite another type of government agency. The state employment security agencies in this country are large roof organizations, each consisting of a state headquarters and an average of forty local offices dispersed throughout the state, and their median size is more than ten times that of finance departments. Despite these differences, most of the factors associated with multiple levels in finance departments reveal similar zero-order correlations in state employment agencies, even though several of the measures are far from identical (compare the last with the first column in Table 2). Controlling size tends to increase the similarity; for instance, number of divisions and number of levels are inversely correlated when size (after logarithmic transformation) is controlled in employment security agencies ($-.37$), as they are in finance departments ($-.34$).

These parallels lend some credibility to the claim that the propositions about hierarchical differentiation suggested in this paper are fairly general principles about work organizations, or in any case about the government agencies among them, though further research will undoubtedly call for revisions and refinements. The tentative conclusion is that impersonal mechanisms of control, such as automation and merit personnel standards, help transform flat structures in which the chief executive exercises much personal control into multilevel hierarchies with decentralized authority.

References

1. See Robert K. Merton, *Social Theory and Social Structure,* 3d ed. (New York: Free Press, 1957), pp. 195, 249–260.
2. Max Weber, *The Theory of Social and Economic Organization* (New York: Oxford University Press, 1947), p. 335.
3. *Ibid.,* p. 331.
4. Talcott Parsons, "Introduction," *ibid.,* pp. 58–60.
5. Alvin W. Gouldner, *Patterns of Industrial Bureaucracy* (Glencoe: Free Press, 1954), esp. pp. 21–24.
6. Arthur L. Stinchcombe, "Bureaucratic and Craft Administration of Production," *Administrative Science Quarterly* 4 (1959), 168–187.
7. Stanley H. Udy, Jr., "'Bureaucracy' and 'Rationality' in Weber's Organization Theory," *American Sociology Review* 24 (1959), 791–795.
8. *Ibid.,* p. 794.
9. See e.g., Roy G. Francies and Robert C. Stone, *Service and Procedure in Bureaucracy* (Minneapolis: University of Minnesota Press, 1956).
10. See Alvin W. Gouldner, "Cosmopolitans and Locals," *Administrative Science Quarterly* 2 (1957-58), 281–306, 444–480; Theodore Caplow and Reece J. McGee, *The Academic Marketplace* (New York: Basic Books, 1958), esp. p. 85; Everett C. Hughes, *Men and Their Work* (Glencoe: Free Press, 1958), esp. p. 137; and Peter M. Blau and W. Richard Scott, *Formal Organizations* (San Francisco: Chandler, 1962), pp. 64–74.
11. The assumption that less close supervision widens the span of control is made explicit by A. Janger, among others. "If the manager practices close supervision, . . . then he is decreasing the number of people he can supervise. He broadens his span by granting them more authority" ["Analyzing the Span of Control," *Management Record* 22 (July-August, 1960), 9].
12. Peter M. Blau, Wolf V. Heydebrand, and Robert E. Stauffer, "The Structure of Small Bureaucracies," *American Sociological Review* 31 (1966), 179–191 (see Chapter 13).
13. The measure was dichotomized in contingencies tables on the basis of whether at least half of the operating staff has to meet this requirement,

but the actual distribution is bimodal, and in most organizations either all of the staff or none of it has to meet his educational requirement.

14. The criterion of manager was being head of a division rather than a journeyman or apprentice, which probably includes most supervisory personnel in these small agencies, though some chiefs of small sections may have been excluded, particularly in the few large agencies (only seventeen have a staff of more than one hundred).

15. Blau *et al., op. cit.,* p. 189, Table 8 (see Table 13.8 above). Among larger agencies *with* an expert staff, 60 percent of those with a low but only 23 percent of those with a high clerical ratio operate at high cost; whereas in larger agencies *without* an expert staff, high cost is as unlikely with a low (24 percent) as with a high clerical ratio (33 percent).

16. Data on these smaller departments were also obtained, in this case by mail questionnaire, but they are not included in the present analysis.

17. Although the number required to have a college degree in accounting was ascertained as well, which would furnish an index exactly parallel to that used in the previous study, this number was so low (an average of one-tenth of the staff) that the less stringent requirement—college degree whatever the major—is considered to be the preferable index of staff expertness.

18. The implicit assumption that proportion of managers is inversely associated with span of control over the operating level is strongly supported by the data. The proportion of departments in which first-line supervisors average six or more subordinates is 72 percent in the 151 with a managerial ratio of less than one-quarter and 20 percent in the 102 with a higher managerial ratio.

19. A parallel result, showing complexity of task to be inversely related to width of span of control, is presented in Gerald D. Bell, "Determinants of Span Control," *American Journal of Sociology* 73 (1967), 100–109.

20. Bell has some direct evidence on closeness of supervision, which shows it to be unrelated to span of control (*ibid.,* p. 106).

21. One might think that the finding could also be interpreted to show that departments with many experts have more complex responsibilities and their managers devote more time to planning and administration, but the instructions were that such activities be included under supervision, and virtually the only activity excluded, except for top executives, would be work of one's own.

22. Udy, *loc. cit.*

23. Regression analysis is used here, partly because the number of levels is a genuine continuous variable and so are most independent variables, and particularly because this procedure makes it possible to examine partial associations while holding all seven other correlates constant.

24. The criterion of "major subdivision" is a division whose head reports directly to the department director (or his deputy, if he has a single deputy).

25. Only the weight of written promotion examinations is considered in the subsequent analysis, since the two other factors are complementary to it.
26. Blau and Scott, *op. cit.*, pp. 176–178.
27. It is also possible that the causal direction is the opposite from that assumed above, which would mean that agencies with multiple levels are more likely than others to introduce automation, quite possibly because they benefit particularly from its function as a control mechanism.
28. It is evident that this orientation is inappropriate for certain kinds of organizations, such as religious congregations or ideological political parties.

The Effect of Organizational Patterns on the Adequacy and Efficiency of Reference Service in the Large American Public Library[1]

Rose B. Phelps

DURING the war years American public libraries have found it difficult enough to carry on their work with depleted staffs, without trying to expand their services. But during this period many have been planning a reorganization and modernization which they may soon be able to execute, and it is known that some public libraries are considering complete subject departmentation. In view of this fact, the present may be an opportune time to present the results of a study of the effects of central library organization on reference service which was completed in 1943, although the materials on which conclusions are based were largely collected in 1939 and 1940. Generally speaking, the decennial year 1940 may therefore be considered the date of this investigation.

"Subject departmentation" is a term generally used to describe a form of central library organization in which reference and circulation functions are united in each of several subject departments operating on the same organizational level. Each such department has its chief and a staff of professional and clerical assistants. The chiefs of these departments may be directly responsible to the director of the library, or they may be supervised by a subordinate administrator who reports

Reprinted with permission from *The Library Quarterly*, V. 17 (Oct. 1947), pp. 281–295. © by The University of Chicago.

to the director. Most libraries of this type still maintain a general reference department for ready-reference and information service, although the bulk of their reference work is performed in the special subject departments. The clerical routine of charging and discharging books may be conducted either in a central lobby surrounded by the subject departments or by clerical assistants in the departments themselves.

The utility of this type of central library organization was first demonstrated by William Howard Brett in Cleveland during the period from 1913 to 1918.[2] In 1913, when the Cleveland Public Library moved into rented quarters in the Kinney and Levan building on Euclid Avenue, Mr. Brett divided his book stock into subject units which combined circulation and reference materials and thus established specialized reference divisions, all of which are functioning today.[3] The only additions to their number have been the John G. White Library of Folklore and Orientalia and a Business Bureau. The development of subject departmentation in Los Angeles resembles that in Cleveland, but its evolution has been more gradual and much less definite and purposeful. However, it is the Los Angeles Public Library which has been adopted as the best example of this form of organization, partly because it is the only completely subject-departmentalized library in the United States, having abolished its general reference department in 1927.

The original study on which this paper is based may be described as a comparative case-study of three libraries, each representing one of the major types of public library organization found in the larger American cities. Its purpose was to discover which type of organization provides the most adequate and efficient reference service for the large American public library. To represent the functional type of organization, the St. Louis Public Library was selected; Los Angeles Public Library is the example of the subject-departmental type; a third type, referred to as the mixed type, which is particularly common in the eastern United States, is exemplified by the Boston Public Library.

Though this study deals largely with forms of internal organization of central libraries and with their capacity to produce an adequate reference service, it should not be assumed that the sociological differences in metropolitan communities which affect the use of library facilities have been totally ignored. The racial composition, educational achievement, and occupational interests of the population of a city undoubtedly influence its reading. Likewise, the city's standing as a financial, commercial, industrial, religious, and educational center may vitally affect its use of reference facilities. A brief survey of these sociological factors in each of the three cities shows that they differ in many respects, and that, on the whole, Boston and Los Angeles probably furnish a somewhat better field for the development of library service than does St. Louis. However, an assumption with which this study was begun, that no public library, however successful, has as yet developed its reference service to the point where the potential demands of the public are fully supplied, still appears to be justified, and internal improvements in organization and better public relations may therefore be expected to produce increased use.

In order to simplify the presentation of this subject for the benefit of public library administrators and students of library administration, and to condense the contents of the study sufficiently for periodical publication, this report will begin with a brief description of the organization of each of the three central libraries; it will then proceed immediately to present the chief findings which deal with the use of reference facilities and the relative costs of service in each library. The more important conclusions of earlier chapters which investigated the effect of organization on the administration of central library service, on circulation and reference personnel, and on book collections are briefly summarized in a final section which seeks to explain the possible reasons for the greater adequacy and efficiency of the subject-departmentalized library.

ORGANIZATION

Los Angeles.—In 1940 the Adult Education Department of the Los Angeles Public Library (see Fig. 1) was the only wholly functional department exclusively concerned with central library service to adults. In the case of the Fiction and Periodicals and Newspaper departments, departmentation was based on the type of materials serviced. The subject departments were Art and Music, Foreign (largely foreign literature), History, Literature and Philology, Philosophy and Religion, Science and Industry, Sociology, and the Teachers' section of the Teachers' and Children's Department. General reference books such as general encyclopedias, dictionaries, and bibliographies were kept in the Literature and Philology Department.

The Los Angeles Public Library had no supervisory officer charged with the co-ordination of the work of these central library depart-

Figure 1 Organization of the Los Angeles Public Library, 1940

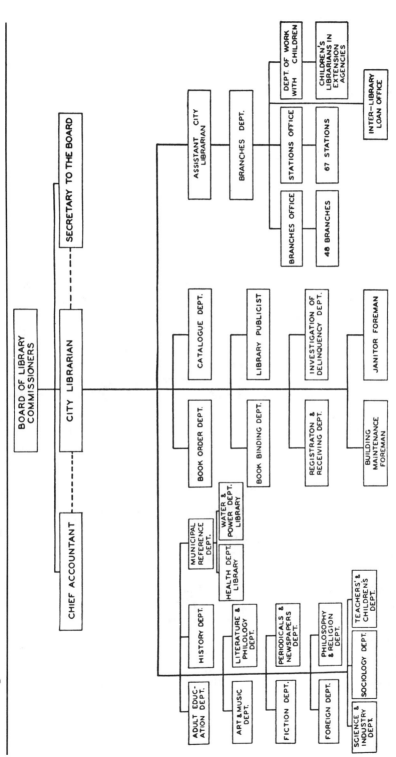

ments, although an assistant librarian in charge of extension was appointed in 1940 to supervise the work of the branches. The imposing and beautiful Los Angeles building was planned for subject specialization but is not as well adapted to the requirements of this type of organization as the "open-plan" building of the Enoch Pratt Free Library at Baltimore, completed in 1932.

Boston.—The organization of the Reference Division of the Boston Public Library may be studied in Figure 2. In 1940 this division had two departments of a functional character, an "issue" and a general reference department called the Main Reading Room, which took the place of the former Bates Hall Reference Department and Bates Hall Center Desk. It likewise maintained two departments based on the type of material serviced, a Rare Book Department and a Periodical and Newspaper Department. Special subject departments were as follows: Fine Arts, History, Music, Statistical, Science and Technology, and Teachers'. The Statistical Department was chiefly concerned with economic and government publications. The special collections of the Rare Book Department were highly useful in the library's reference work, being especially rich in the fields of early American, English, and European literature and in early American history. The well-stocked Business Branch occupies the Kirstein Memorial Building in the center of Boston's commercial and financial district.

In comparison with like units in the true subject-departmental library, the scope of these Boston departments is generally narrower and their work is more largely of a reference nature. It should also be noted that some of them owe their foundation either to the gift of special collections or to the bequest of special book funds rather than to any deliberate plan of specialization to meet the needs of the community. In 1940 the main building of the Boston Public Library had been in use for almost fifty years and tended to perpetuate the rather conservative type of organization for which it had been planned.

Essentially, the Boston Public Library in 1940 consisted of two almost completely separate operating libraries—a Reference Division and a Circulating Division—served by a common Division of Business Operations. Each of the first two divisions had a chief librarian, and the last was administered by the comptroller. The Reference Division also had a supervisor responsible to the chief librarian. The director's narrow span of control is an excellent feature of the Boston plan: only

FIGURE 2 Organization of the Boston Public Library, 1940

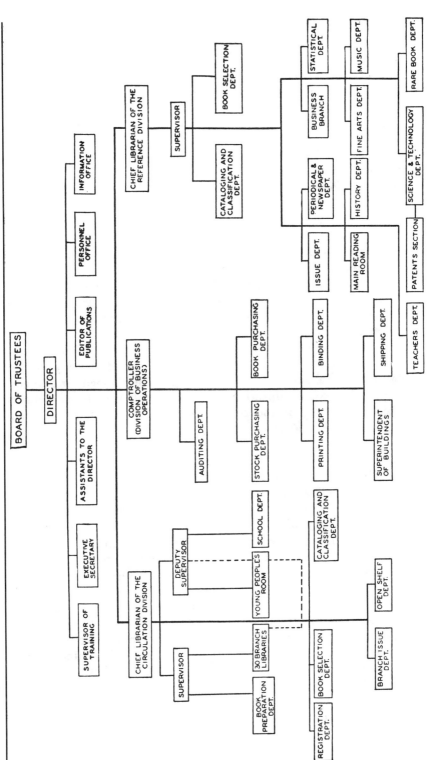

the chiefs of the three main divisions and a few staff officers report to him directly. In 1940 the Boston Public Library was the only one of the three studied which adequately co-ordinated the work of public departments in the central library.

St. Louis.—Figure 3 shows that in 1940 the adult public service departments of the St. Louis central library were the following: Circulation and Reference departments, functional in their character; Periodical, Newspaper, and Open-Shelf departments in which departmentation was based on the type of material made available, and three subject departments, Applied Science, Art, and a Teachers' department, in addition to a Municipal Reference Library. Of these the Art Department most closely resembled the true subject department as developed in Cleveland and Los Angeles, inasmuch as its circulation policy was fairly liberal. The Teachers' Room, established by the Stations and Traveling Library Department in the central library, was intended as a circulation agency, but such a unit inevitably develops some reference and advisory functions. In 1940 the St. Louis Public Library had neither a supervisor of branches nor one of central library departments. Some fifteen branches and an equal number of central library departments reported directly to the librarian. The central library building, though planned for a largely functional type of organization, is fairly adaptable and could probably be converted to suit the requirements of another type of organization.

USE OF REFERENCE MATERIALS IN THE THREE CENTRAL LIBRARIES

The difficulty of evaluating reference service has been much discussed in library literature[4] and is frankly recognized. Since some measurements of the quantity of reference service were necessary in order to test the hypothesis that the volume of service varies directly with the degree of subject specialization, three measures of use were selected for the purposes of this study. The first was the number of reference questions asked in the central library building in a week which library authorities considered typical. Since every reference librarian knows that patrons differ widely in their inclination and ability to answer their own questions and likewise that the degree of availability of reference materials is a factor influencing the reader's independence in the use of books, two other measures—the attendance in reading rooms and the number of books used in reading rooms but

FIGURE 3 Organization of the St. Louis Public Library, 1940

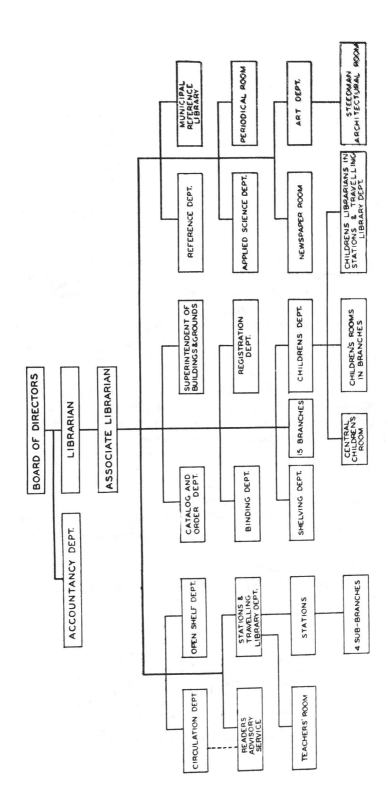

not circulated—have all been employed. Table I compares the three libraries with regard to these three measures of volume.

Though it is evident that the completely subject-departmentalized Los Angeles Public Library surpasses both the functionally organized St. Louis Public Library and the Boston Public Library in the volume of its central library reference work, this comparison may be considered unfair because Los Angeles is a much larger city than either St. Louis or Boston.[5] To make a just comparison, annual per capita estimates of use based on figures presented in Table I have been made for each of the three measures used. These are presented in Table 2. These figures show not only that the subject-departmentalized Los Angeles Public library leads the group in the volume of its central library service but that the three libraries rank in the order of the degree of subject specialization which they have achieved.

Another measure often employed in studies of this type is the proportion of the number of reference questions to the number of books circulated during a given period. Table 3 presents data on this point. Though the subject-departmentalized Los Angeles central library has attained a relatively large circulation as contrasted with that of St. Louis, its reference service has grown even more rapidly. The highest proportion is shown by the Boston Reference Division, but this appears to be due to the highly conservative attitude and practice of this division with regard to the circulation of its books.

Table 4 serves to sharpen the contrast between the subject-departmentalized and functional type of organization by omitting the library representing the mixed type; it likewise summarizes the findings of this section of the report.

While this study does not afford conclusive evidence on the relative quality of reference service in the three representative libraries, some

TABLE 1   Reference Use of the Three Central Libraries During a Typical Week

Measures	Los Angeles	Boston	St. Louis
Reading-room attendance	41,982	17,951	5,748
Books used in reading rooms...............	37,743	13,350	11,253
Reference questions*....	11,225	3,699	2,169

* Figures do not include questions asked by telephone.

TABLE 2   Estimated Annual Per Capita Use of Reference Facilities in Three Central Libraries

Measures	Los Angeles	Boston	St. Louis
Reading-room attendance	1.75	1.54	0.45
Books used in reading rooms...............	1.57	1.145	0.886
Reference questions.....	0.467	0.317	0.171

information on the character of service was obtained. The large amount of special indexing done by clerical assistants in the Los Angeles departments appears to have secured for it the quickest service of the three. Statistics compiled from 1,048[6] question blanks, covering the more important and difficult reference questions asked in each library during a typical week, suggest that it is probably true that the subject department uses more highly specialized reference tools than does the general reference department. Subject departments in all three libraries also made greater use of research and statistical materials than the St. Louis Reference Department, a fact which suggests that the subject-departmental library may be a better instrument for the dissemination of knowledge than the functionally organized library. Of the three libraries studied, the Boston Public Library was the largest user of scholarly printed bibliographies, while the Los Angeles Public Library made the greatest use of indexes and bibliographies created in the library itself. A comparison of inter-library loan statistics showed that the Boston Public Library is by far

TABLE 3   Relation of the Number of Reference Questions Asked to the Number of Books Circulated During a Typical Week in the Three Central Libraries

LOS ANGELES			BOSTON			ST. LOUIS		
Number of Reference Questions	Circulation	Per Cent	Number of Reference Questions	Circulation	Per Cent	Number of Reference Questions	Circulation	Per Cent
11,225	27,672	40.6	3,699	7,013	52.1	2,169	6,659	33.0

TABLE 4   Per Capita Measurements of Service
in the Los Angeles and St. Louis Central Libraries, 1940–41

Measurement	St. Louis	Los Angeles	Approximate Ratio St. Louis to Los Angeles
Attendance..........	0.45	1.75	1:4
Books used in reading rooms............	.886	0.57	1:2
Circulation..........	.506	1.423	1:3
Reference questions..	0.171	0.467	1:3

the greatest lender of the three, possibly because its rich special collections have been so fully described in printed catalogs.

Summary.—The preceding figures comparing the use made of the various forms of central reference service appear to justify the hypothesis that the subject-departmental type of organization provides the most adequate service. It has been shown that the use of the reference service in the three libraries generally corresponds to the degree of their specialization, the Boston Reference Division, with its numerous subject departments usually standing much closer to the completely subject-departmentalized Los Angeles central library than to the functionally organized St. Louis central library. Although the evidence on the quality of reference service in the three libraries is by no means conclusive, its general trend is to favor the libraries of the subject-departmental and mixed types. As has been previously stated, other factors, such as the quality of library staffs, the educational level of the city's population, and the financial support the library receives contribute to the greater reference use in Los Angeles. But when all these factors are considered, it is still impossible to imagine that so great a volume of service could result from a simple functional organization.

COSTS

Judged by the criterion of public use, the foregoing section has shown that the subject-departmental type of organization provides better reference service than the functional and mixed types. The present section seeks to determine whether subject departmentation is more expensive than the other types and, in particular, whether it is more efficient, in the sense of producing a greater volume of service for a given expenditure. It should be noted that the findings of this study cannot be considered wholly conclusive because only the two major costs—personnel and printed materials—have been investigated. The relative costs of processing materials[7] and of housing central library departments in the three representative libraries have not been investigated.

It is also essential to point out that all costs of central library personnel include both circulation and reference service. Since circulation and reference functions were inextricably combined in the majority of public departments of both the Boston and Los Angeles libraries and in several of those in St. Louis library, it was found impossible to separate the costs of these two types of service. Likewise, only departments which serve adults have been considered in this study; the cost of central library service to children is not included in any of the figures except those which deal with total library expenditures.

ABSOLUTE AND PROPORTIONAL COSTS

Total operating costs.—During the thirteen-year period from 1927 through 1939 the average annual expenditure of the three libraries was as follows: Los Angeles: $1,145,251; Boston: $1,262,708; and St. Louis: $528,258.

The cities of Boston and St. Louis, which are of comparable size, differed markedly in the amount expended on their public libraries, the amount spent in Boston being nearly two and one-half times as great as that in St. Louis. The average expenditure on the Boston Public Library even exceeded that of Los Angeles, a city approximately twice its size.

Total cost of salaries and books in circulation and reference departments.—Table 5 presents statistics secured from the accounting departments of the three libraries which show the cost of salaries and of books, periodicals, and binding for public departments of each of the three central libraries during the five years previous to 1940. For purposes of comparison the total operating expenditures are also included in the table. This table shows that on central library costs the three libraries rank in the same order as on total expenditures, Boston being first, Los Angeles second, and St. Louis third.

Proportional expenditures for central library circulation and reference departments.—It is often charged that the subject-departmental type of organization is unduly expensive,[8] and there are several different methods of approaching the investigation of this question. One of these is to inquire what proportion of each library's salary-and-wage fund and what proportion of its general fund for books, periodicals, and binding is expended for these adult circulation and reference departments in the central library. By using the data contained in Table 5 and additional figures showing the total amounts expended for each purpose in each library system during the years 1935-39, the results presented in Table 6 have been obtained. It will be noted that while the St. Louis Public Library devotes about one-fifth of its salary-and-wage fund to the service of these central library departments, the Boston and Los Angeles libraries both spend about a fourth of their personnel money on them. This difference is considerable, but, as has already been shown, both of the last-mentioned libraries do a much larger volume of work in proportion to the size of the city served than does the St. Louis Public Library. Moreover, it can hardly be contended that a quarter of the library's personnel fund is too much to devote to salaries for the staff of the central library which performs such important circulation, reference, and research functions.

Table 6 also shows that the proportion of the book fund used for printed materials for the central library is quite similar in St. Louis

TABLE 5   Total Cost of Salaries and Books for Circulation and Reference Departments of the Three Central Libraries, 1935-39*

YEAR	LOS ANGELES			BOSTON			ST. LOUIS		
	Salaries	Books, Periodicals, and Binding	Total Operating Expenses (System)	Salaries	Books, Periodicals, and Binding	Total Operating Expenses (System)	Salaries	Books, Periodicals, and Binding	Total Operating Expenses (System)
1934-35†.....	$193,430	$48,303	$ 926,406	$195,000	$ 82,272	$1,194,202	$63,571	$30,914	$465,785
1935-36......	196,230	75,755	1,006,144	205,053	92,423	1,248,328	65,272	33,570	472,333
1936-37......	184,330	70,227	1,036,217	216,888	100,531	1,329,567	66,373	34,591	474,355
1937-38......	187,660	66,862	1,068,173	241,077	130,849	1,383,861	67,581	37,296	489,183
1938-39......	193,400	68,102	1,077,032	248,936	161,563	1,391,169	67,316	30,203	505,556
Average..	$191,010	$65,850	$1,022,794	$221,391	$113,528	$1,309,425	$66,023	$33,315	$481,442

* Source: For statistics of total operating expenses, annual reports of the three libraries; for departmental expenses, statistics furnished by accounting or order departments of each library.
† In the Los Angeles Public Library the fiscal year is from July 1 to June 30; in St. Louis it begins on April 1, but figures for Boston are for the calendar years from 1935 through 1939.

TABLE 6   Percentage of Expenditures for Salaries
and Books Allocated to Central Circulation
and Reference Departments (averages: 1935–39)

PURPOSE	LOS ANGELES	BOSTON	ST. LOUIS
	Percent-age	Percent-age	Percent-age
Salaries and wages. . .	25.0	24.1	19.4
Books, periodicals, and binding.	38.9	54.5	36.3

and Los Angeles, but much higher in Boston. In neither St. Louis nor Los Angeles could the money available for books, periodicals, and binding be considered adequate to the library's needs; only in Boston was the central library book fund ample for the purpose. Probably the reason why the ratio of the central library fund to the total book fund is so high in Boston is that, while gift and endowment funds provide a sufficient income for book-buying for the Reference Division, branches are almost wholly dependent on city appropriations, and in recent years comparatively small amounts have been spent on books for the branches.[9]

The conclusion reached in regard to proportional costs is that, though the subject-departmental library probably requires a larger share of the library's total salary-and-wage fund, it may not require a much greater share of the book fund, and that the larger proportion of total library expenditure which it consumes may possibly be justified by the greater amount of service which it is capable of supplying to the public. Further evidence on this point will be presented hereafter.

DIFFERENCES IN OPERATING COSTS IN
TERMS OF SERVICE RENDERED

Thus far absolute and proportional costs of central library service have been discussed, but no measurement of costs in terms of service demanded and performed has been undertaken. Since it is possible that a large volume of service will have the effect of decreasing unit costs of operation, it is important to devise some such measures. The two measures proposed, the per capita cost of central library service and the cost per unit of service, are indeed somewhat arbitrary and provide only a rough approximation of relative costs. Taken in conjunction with each other, however, they furnish some basis for judgment as to the comparative efficiency of the three types of organization.

Cost per capita of central library service.—Table 7, based on figures already presented in Table 5, gives per capita cost of central library service, including salaries, books, periodicals, and binding in the year 1939. It shows that the per capita cost of salaries for the circulation and reference departments of the central library is a little less than half again as great in Los Angeles as in St. Louis. In both of these libraries the per capita cost of books, periodicals, and binding is very small, and the difference in cost is relatively slight. Compared with all costs in Boston—that of salaries, of books, periodicals, and binding, and of these combined—the costs in Los Angeles and St. Louis are so moderate that the difference between the two seems of little importance and hardly worth emphasizing. Judged by per capita as well as by absolute costs, it appears that the library of the mixed type which supports both strong functional departments and numerous subject departments is the most expensive to operate. The per capita cost of the subject-departmental type of organization, though somewhat greater than that of the functional type, is by comparison very moderate.

Cost of unit of service rendered.—Costs of central library personnel for public departments, as given in Table 5, embrace both the

TABLE 7 Per Capita Costs of Central Library Service in the Three Libraries, 1939

Cost or Percentage of Cost	Los Angeles	Boston	St. Louis
Total per capita cost of library service.	$ 0.717	$ 1.80	$ 0.62
Per capita cost of central library service (salaries, books, periodicals, and binding).	.174	0.532	.12
Per capita cost of salaries, central library circulation and reference departments.	.129	0.324	.083
Per capita cost of books, periodicals, and binding in central library.	0.045	0.208	0.037
Percentage which per capita cost of central library service forms of total per capita costs of library service.	24.3	29.6	19.4

cost of circulation and reference service because, in a study of libraries so differently organized, it was found impossible to separate the costs of types of service which are at many points so closely associated with each other. If a unit cost of service is to be used, it must therefore be one which can be used to measure both circulation and reference work.

A recent study of costs in thirty-seven American public libraries[10] shows the average cost in time spent on a reference question to be four times the average cost in time taken for the circulation of a book. If this proportion of four to one be taken as a standard, the number of reference questions asked during a given period should be multiplied by four and added to the circulation for the period, and the cost of personnel for circulation and reference purposes should then be divided by this weighted measure of service. The period used in this calculation was the year 1939, and the estimate of the number of reference questions for the year was based on the proportion of reference questions to circulation in a typical week of that year. When this calculation is employed in the three libraries the resulting approximate cost of a unit of service in each is as follows: Los Angeles: $0.042; Boston: $0.154; and St. Louis: $0.093.

The unit cost of service is again the highest in Boston, but it is over twice as high in St. Louis as in Los Angeles. This estimate taken together with figures on per capita costs shows that with the great expansion of both circulation and reference service which accompanies subject departmentation, the per capita cost of central library personnel naturally increases, but the unit cost of service may be greatly decreased.

SUMMARY

Assuming that the three libraries selected for study are fair representatives of their types of organization, one may justly conclude that, of the three, the subject-departmental type is the one best adapted to securing adequate and efficient reference service for the large public library. The functional type of organization, examined in the St. Louis central library, appears to be inadequate to supply the needs of so large a city, while the mixed type of organization exemplified by the Boston Reference Division, though more nearly adequate to its task, is very expensive. Of the three, only the subject-departmental form of organization, exemplified by the Los Angeles central library, proved to be capable of providing for a large expansion of reference service at a low unit cost.

WHY SUBJECT DEPARTMENTATION PRODUCES A MORE ADEQUATE AND EFFICIENT SERVICE

Though it is perhaps impossible to give any simple explanation of the greater potentiality of the subject-departmentalized central library for securing a satisfactory reference service, experience and observation tend to suggest that certain of its features and characteristics are well adapted to producing a service which is at once efficient and adequate. Many of the following statements, particularly those concerned with personnel and book collections, could be supported with statistical data, but for the sake of brevity the evidence is omitted. Those characteristics of subject departmentation which are thought to have increased the volume of reference service are ranged under the heading, "Adequacy"; those which it is judged have contributed to economy will be found under "Efficiency."

Adequacy

1. The subject-departmental type of organization furnishes an ample framework within which reference service adequate to the needs of the population of a large city may evolve.
2. The subject-departmentalized library arranges for the display of a large proportion of the library's live, valuable, and interesting books on open shelves in departmental reading rooms, and thereby stimulates both home circulation and self-service in reference work.
3. In the functionally organized library the reference department favors a conservative circulation policy in the interest of its own service; in the subject-departmentalized library, where reference and circulation functions are united in each department, both types of service develop harmoniously without crippling each other.
4. To a certain degree specialization by subject divides the library's clientele into manageable segments, with like interests and preferences, and enables the library to reach the individual through service to the groups and associations which fall within the scope of each of the subject departments. Such an organization also promotes well-directed and effective publicity in specialized subject media.

5. The subject-departmental library develops a strong group of subordinate executives, interested in public service and capable of valuable assistance in library planning. This group also constitutes an able book-selection council, since the chief of each subject department possesses an intimate knowledge of the reading habits and requirements of patrons in his subject field.

6. Whatever the basic form of the library's organization, the creation of a subject department improves the library's holdings of printed materials in the subject field. In the fuctionally organized library this tendency of the isolated subject department to strengthen its collection slightly disturbs the balance of the collection as a whole. In the completely subject-departmentalized library the same tendency at work in every department produces a general improvement in the quality of the library's holdings and secures a proper balance in the representation of various subjects.

7. Both observation of library collections and service and the checking of book lists in the three libraries would suggest that book selection in the subject-departmental library is probably more practical and utilitarian in its character than in libraries of either of the other types.

Efficiency

1. Subject departmentation divides the universal field of the general reference department into fairly homogeneous sections and thus encourages the professional staff of each department to master the bibliography and literature of its subject field. The result is increased intelligence, skill, and speed in dealing with reference questions, and a consequent decreased cost per unit of service.

2. The subject-departmental public library has shown a disposition to economize by making a proper distinction between professional and clerical duties. It has set up appropriate standards and qualifications for both professional and clerical positions, and thus secured personnel with suitable education and training for both types of positions.

3. Since specialized reference service interests a larger proportion of a city's population than does the service of the functional reference department, it provides for a more continuous and therefore a more economical use of the valuable time of librarians who man the reference desks.

4. In subject departments clerical assistants, under the supervision of professional librarians, have achieved a thorough organization of knowledge through the creation of countless special indexes, bibliographies, and files of ephemeral materials. The greater speed and efficiency of subject-departmental service stems in part from this thorough organization of information and from the employment of other labor-saving methods and devices.

5. The subject-departmental library, with its many like units on the same organization level, produces a friendly rivalry between departments which results in unusual staff interest in the continuous and accurate evaluation of the library's public service.

6. The subject-departmentalized public library with its more ample provision for clerical service, its wider sharing of authority and responsibility, and its more vital public contacts appears to be capable of developing a more active and dynamic professional staff than either of the other types of organization studied.

References

1. A summary of a dissertation submitted to the Graduate Library School of the University of Chicago in December, 1943, in partial fulfilment of the requirements for the degree of Doctor of Philosophy.
2. This experiment was not without its forerunners. In the plan which William Frederick Poole proposed for the Newberry Library in 1881 (*The Construction of Library Buildings* [U.S. Bureau of Education, "Circulars of Information," No. 1.]) it was suggested that the book collection be housed in several separate subject rooms, but, since this was to be strictly a reference library, no combination of circulation and reference functions was involved. In the Providence Public Library, completed in 1900, three departments situated on the third floor, the Art, Music, and Industry departments, combined circulation and reference materials and service and were all originally supervised by a custodian of special libraries (Providence Public Library, *Twenty-third Annual Report, Dec. 31,1900*, p. 6).
3. Most of the information concerning the organization and service of the libraries considered in this paper has been taken from their annual reports.
4. See for instance: Edith Guerrier, "The Measurement of Reference Service," *Library Journal*, LXI (July, 1936), 531; E. A. Henry, "Judging Reference Service," *Library Journal*, LXIV (May, 1939), 358; Enoch Pratt Free Library, *The Reorganization of a Large Public Library: Ten Year Report of the Enoch Pratt Free Library, 1926-1935* (Baltimore: Enoch Pratt Free Library, 1937), pp. 43, 45; Fremont Rider, "Library Cost Accounting," *Library Quarterly*, VI (October, 1936), 379.

5. In 1940 the population of the three cities was as follows: Los Angeles, 1,504,277; Boston, 770,816; St. Louis, 816,048. But since this investigation deals exclusively with adult service, the population over 15 years of age in 1940 has been used in these estimates. For Los Angeles this figure is 1,250,054; for Boston, 606,040; for St. Louis, 660,372. See U.S. Bureau of the Census, *Sixteenth Census of the United States: 1940. Population,* Vol. II, *Characteristics of the Population,* Part I, *United States Summary* (Washington: Government Printing Office, 1943), pp. 121, 132-33, 143.
6. Of these, 482 were from the Los Angeles central library, 290 from the Boston Reference Division, and 276 from the St. Louis central library.
7. In the newer "open-plan" building designed for the subject-departmental type of library, separate subject-department catalogs are not considered absolutely necessary for public service.
8. See Althea Warren, "Departmental Organization of a Library by Subject," in *Current Issues in Library Administration,* ed. by C. B. Joeckel (Chicago: University of Chicago Press, 1939), pp. 122, 124.
9. Serious concern over the inadequate book funds provided for branch libraries was expressed by the Examining Committee (an advisory citizens' group) to the Board of Trustees in 1939. See Boston Public Library, *Annual Report, 1939,* pp. 22-26, 30-31.
10. Emma V. Baldwin and William E. Marcus, *Library Costs and Budgets: A Study of Cost Accounting in Public Libraries* (New York: R.R. Bowker Co., 1941), p. 175, Table IV.

Human Relations

Fritz J. Roethlisberger and William J. Dickson

AN INDUSTRIAL ORGANIZATION AS A
SOCIAL SYSTEM

We shall now attempt to state more systematically than was
possible in a chronological account the results of the research and
some of their implications for practice. Each stage of the research
contributed to the development of a point of view in terms of which the
data could be more usefully assessed. In presenting the studies, this
aspect of the research program was given primary emphasis and an
effort was made to show how each successive step in the research
resulted in the discovery of new facts which in turn brought forth new
questions and new hypotheses and assisted in the development of
more adequate methods and a more adequate conceptual scheme. The
point of view which gradually emerged from these studies is one from
which an industrial organization is regarded as a social system. In this
chapter a statement of this point of view will be made. . . . Various
management problems which have been discussed in connection with
the various research studies will be restated in terms of this new point
of view . . . .The application of the concept of an industrial concern as
a social system to problems of personnel practice will be considered.

The study of the bank wiremen showed that their behavior at work
could not be understood without considering the informal organization
of the group and the relation of this informal organization to the total
social organization of the company. The work activities of this group,
together with their satisfactions and dissatisfactions, had to be viewed
as manifestations of a complex pattern of interrelations. In short, the
work situation of the bank wiring group had to be treated as a social
system; moreover, the industrial organization of which this group was
a part also had to be treated as a social system.

By "system" is meant something which must be considered as a
whole because each part bears a relation of interdependence to every

Reprinted by permission of the publishers from MANAGEMENT AND THE WORKER,
by Fritz J. Roethlisberger and William J. Dickson, Cambridge, Mass.: Harvard
University Press, Copyright © 1939, 1967 by the President and Fellows of Harvard
College.

other part.[1] It will be the purpose of this chapter to state this conception of a social system, to specify more clearly the parts of the social system of which account has to be taken in an industrial organization, and to consider the state of equilibrium which obtains among the parts.

The Two Major Functions of an Industrial Organization

An industrial organization may be regarded as performing two major functions, that of producing a product and that of creating and distributing satisfactions among the individual members of the organization. The first function is ordinarily called economic. From this point of view the functioning of the concern is assessed in such terms as cost, profit, and technical efficiency. The second function, while it is readily understood, is not ordinarily designated by any generally accepted word. It is variously described as maintaining employee relations, employee good will, cooperation, etc. From this standpoint the functioning of the concern is frequently assessed in such terms as labor turnover, tenure of employment, sickness and accident rate, wages, employee attitudes, etc. The industrial concern is continually confronted, therefore, with two sets of major problems: (1) problems of external balance, and (2) problems of internal equilibrium. The problems of external balance are generally assumed to be economic, that is, problems of competition, adjusting the organization to meet changing price levels, etc. The problems of internal equilibrium are chiefly concerned with the maintenance of a kind of social organization in which individuals and groups through working together can satisfy their own desires.

Ordinarily an industrial concern is thought of primarily in terms of its success in meeting problems of external balance, or if the problems of internal equilibrium are explicitly recognized they are frequently assumed to be separate from and unrelated to the economic purpose of the enterprise. Producing an article at a profit and maintaining good employee relations are frequently regarded as antithetical propositions. The results of the studies which have been reported indicated, however, that these two sets of problems are interrelated and interdependent. The kind of social organization which obtains within a concern is intimately related to the effectiveness of the total organization. Likewise, the success with which the concern maintains external balance is directly related to its internal organization.

A great deal of attention has been given to the economic function of industrial organization. Scientific controls have been introduced to further the economic purposes of the concern and of the individuals within it. Much of this advance has gone on in the name of efficiency or rationalization. Nothing comparable to this advance has gone on in the development of skills and techniques for securing cooperation, that is, for getting individuals and groups of individuals working together effectively and with satisfaction to themselves. The slight advances which have been made in this area have been overshadowed by the new and powerful technological developments of modern industry.

The Technical Organization of the Plant

In looking at an industrial organization as a social system it will first be necessary to examine the physical environment, for this is an inseparable part of any organization. The physical environment includes not only climate and weather, but also that part of the environment which is owned and used by the organization itself, namely, the physical plant, tools, machines, raw products, and so on. This latter part of the factory's physical environment is ordered and organized in a certain specified way to accomplish the task of technical production. For our purposes, therefore, it will be convenient to distinguish from the human organization this aspect of the physical environment of an industrial plant and to label it the "technical organization of the plant." This term will refer only to the logical and technical organization of material, tools, machines, and finished product, including all those physical items related to the task of technical production.

The two aspects into which an industrial plant can be roughly divided—the technical organization and the human organization—are interrelated and interdependent. The human organization is constantly molding and re-creating the technical organization either to achieve more effectively the common economic purpose or to secure more satisfaction for its members. Likewise, changes in the technical organization require an adaptation on the part of the human organization.

The Human Organization of the Plant

In the human organization we find a number of individuals working together toward a common end: the collective purpose of the total organization. Each of these individuals, however, is bringing to the work situation a different background of personal and social experiences. No two individuals are making exactly the same demands of their jobs. The demands a particular employee makes depend not only upon his physical needs but upon his social needs as well. These social needs and the sentiments associated with them vary with his early personal history and social conditioning as well as with the needs and sentiments of people closely associated with him both inside and outside of work.

The Individual

It may be well to look more closely at the sentiments the individual is bringing to his work situation. Starting with a certain native organic endowment the child is precipitated into group life by the act of birth. The group into which the child is born is not the group in general. The child is born into a specific family. Moreover, this specific family is not a family in isolation. It is related in certain ways to other families in the community. It has a certain cultural background—a way of life, codes and routines of behavior, associated with certain beliefs and expectations. In the beginning the child brings only his organic needs to this social milieu into which he is born. Very rapidly he begins to accumulate experience. The process of accumulating experience is the process of assigning meanings to the socio-reality about him; it is the process of becoming socialized. Much of the early learning period is devoted to preparing the child to become capable of social life in its particular group. In preparing the child for social participation the immediate family group plays an important role. By the particular type of family into which the child is born he is "conditioned" to certain routines of behavior and ways of living. The early meanings he assigns to his experience are largely in terms of these codes of behavior and associated beliefs. As the child grows up and participates in groups other than the immediate family his meanings lose although never quite entirely, their specific family form. This process of social interaction and social conditioning is never-ending and continues from birth to death. The adult's evaluation of his surroundings is determined in a good part by the system of human interrelations in which he has participated.

The Social Organization of the Plant

However, the human organization of an industrial plant is more than a plurality of individuals, each motivated by sentiments arising from his own personal and private history and background. It is also a social organization, for the members of an industrial plant—executives, technical specialists, supervisors, factory workers, and office workers—are interacting daily with one another and from their associations certain patterns of relations are formed among them. These patterns of relations, together with the objects which symbolize them, constitute the social organization of the industrial enterprise. Most of the individuals who live among these patterns come to accept them as obvious and necessary truths and to react as they dictate. Both the kind of behavior that is expected of a person and the kind of behavior he can expect from others are prescribed by these patterns.

If one looks at a factory situation for example, one finds individuals and groups of individuals who are associated at work acting in certain accepted and prescribed ways toward one another. There is not complete homogeneity of behavior between individuals or between one group of individuals and another, but rather there are differences of behavior expressing differences in social relationship. Some relationships fall into routine patterns, such as the relationship between superior and subordinate or between office worker and shop worker. Individuals conscious of their membership in certain groups are reacting in certain accepted ways to other individuals representing other groups. Behavior varies according to the stereotyped conceptions of relationship. The worker, for example, behaves toward his foreman in one way, toward his first-line supervisor in another way, and toward his fellow worker in still another. People holding the rank of inspector expect a certain kind of behavior from the operators—the operators from the inspectors. Now these relationships, as is well known from everyday experiences, are finely shaded and sometimes become complicated. When a person is in the presence of his supervisor alone he usually acts differently from the way he acts when his supervisor's supervisor is also present. Likewise, his supervisor acts toward him alone quite differently from the way he behaves when his own supervisor is also there. These subtle nuances of relationship are so much a part of everyday life that they are commonplace. They are taken for granted. The vast amount of social conditioning that has taken place by means of which a person maneuvers himself gracefully through the intricacies of these finely shaded social distinctions is seldom explicitly realized. Attention is paid only when a new social situation arises where the past social training of the person prevents him from making the necessary delicate interpretations of a given social signal and hence brings forth the "socially wrong" response.

In the factory, as in any social milieu, a process of social evaluation is constantly at work. From this process distinctions of "good" and "bad," "inferior" and "superior," arise. This process of evaluation is carried on with simple and ready generalizations by means of which values become attached to individuals and to groups performing certain tasks and operations. It assigns to a group of individuals performing such and such a task a particular rank in the established prestige scale. Each work group becomes a carrier of social values. In industry with its extreme diversity of occupations there are a number of such groupings. Any noticeable similarity or difference, not only in occupation but also in age, sex, and nationality, can serve as a basis of social classification, as, for example, "married women," the "old-timer," the "white-collared" or clerical worker, the "foreign element." Each of these groups, too, has its own value system.

All the patterns of interaction that arise between individuals or between different groups can be graded according to the degree of intimacy involved in the relationship. Grades of intimacy or under-standing can be arranged on a scale and expressed in terms of "social distance." Social distance measures differences of sentiment and interest which separate individuals or groups from one another. Between the president of a company and the elevator operator there is considerable social distance, more for example than between the foreman and the benchworker. Social distance is to social organization what physical distance is to physical space. However, physical and social distance do not necessarily coincide. Two people may be physically near but socially distant.

Just as each employee has a particular physical location, so he has a particular social place in the total social organization. But this place is not so rigidly fixed as in a caste system. In any factory there is considerable mobility or movement. Movement can occur in two ways: the individual may pass from one occupation to another occupation higher up in the prestige scale; or the prestige scale itself may change.

It is obvious that these scales of value are never completely accepted by all the groups in the social environment. The shop worker does not quite see why the office worker, for example, should have shorter hours of work than he has. Or the newcomer, whose efficiency on a particular job is about the same, but whose hourly rate is less than that of some oldtimer, wonders why service should count so much. The management group, in turn, from the security of its social elevation, does not often understand what "all the fuss is about."

As was indicated by many of the studies, any person who has achieved a certain rank in the prestige scale regards anything real or imaginary which tends to alter his status adversely as something unfair or unjust. It is apparent that any move on the part of the management may alter the existing social equilibrium to which the employee has grown accustomed and by means of which his status is defined. Immediately this disruption will be expressed in sentiments of resistance to the real or imagined alterations in the social equilibrium.

From this point of view it can be seen how every item and event in the industrial environment becomes an object of a system of senti- ments. According to this way of looking at things, material goods, physical events, wages, hours of work, etc., cannot be treated as things in themselves. Instead they have to be interpreted as carriers of social value. The meanings which any person in an industrial organization assigns to the events and objects in his environment are often determined by the social situation in which the events and objects occur. The signifiance to an employee of a double-pedestal desk, of a particular kind of pencil, or of a handset telephone is determined by the social setting in which these objects appear. If people with double- pedestal desks supervise people with single-pedestal desks, then double-pedestal desks become symbols of status or prestige in the organization. As patterns of behavior become crystallized, every object in the environment tends to take on a particular social significance. It becomes easy to tell a person's social place in the organization by the objects which he wears and carries and which surround him. In these terms it can be seen how the introduction of a technical change may also involve for an individual or a group of individuals the loss of certain prestige symbols and, as a result, have a demoralizing effect.

From this point of view the behavior of no one person in an industrial organization, from the very top to the very bottom, can be regarded as motivated by strictly economic or logical considerations. Routine patterns of interaction involve strong sentiments. Each group in the organization manifests its own powerful sentiments. It is likely that sometimes the behavior of many staff specialists which goes under the name of "efficiency" is as much a manifestation of a very strong sentiment—the sentiment or desire to originate new combina- tions—as it is of anything strictly logical.

This point of view is far from the one which is frequently expressed, namely, that man is essentially an economic being carrying around with him a few noneconomic appendages. Rather, the point of view which has been expressed here is that noneconomic motives, interests, and processes, as well as economic, are fundamental in behavior in business, from the board of directors to the very last man in the organization. Man is not merely—in fact is very seldom—motivated by factors pertaining strictly to facts or logic. Sentiments are not merely things which man carries around with him as appendages. He cannot cast them off like a suit of clothes. He carries them with him wherever he goes. In business or elsewhere, he can hardly behave without expressing them. Moreover, sentiments do not exist in a social vacuum. They are the product of social behavior, of social interaction, of the fact that man lives his life as a member of different groups. Not only does man bring sentiments to the business situation because of his past experiences and conditioning outside of business, but also as a member of a specific local business organization with a particular social place in it he has certain sentiments expressing his particular relations to it.

According to this point of view, every social act in adulthood is an integrated response to both inner and outer stimuli. To each new concrete situation the adult brings his past "social conditioning." To the extent that this past social conditioning has prepared him to assimilate the new experience in the culturally accepted manner, he is said to be "adjusted." To the extent that his private or personal view of the situation is at variance with the cultural situation, the person is called "maladjusted."

The Formal Organization of the Plant

The social organization of the industrial plant is in part formally organized. It is composed of a number of strata or levels which differentiate the benchworker from the skilled mechanic, the group chief from the department chief, and so on. These levels are well defined and all the formal orders, instructions, and compensations are addressed to them. All such factors taken together make up the formal organization of the plant. It includes the systems, policies, rules, and regulations of the plant which express what the relations of one person to another are supposed to be in order to achieve effectively the task of technical production. It prescribes the relations that are supposed to obtain within the human organization and between the human organization and the technical organization. In short, the patterns of human interrelations, as defined by the systems, rules, policies, and regulations of the company, constitute the formal organization.

The formal organization of an industrial plant has two purposes: it addresses itself to the economic purposes of the total enterprise; it concerns itself also with the securing of co-operative effort. The formal organization includes all the explicitly stated systems of control introduced by the company in order to achieve the economic purposes of the total enterprise and the effective contribution of the members of the organization to those economic ends.

The Informal Organization of the Plant

All the experimental studies pointed to the fact that there is something more to the social organization than what has been formally recognized. Many of the actually existing patterns of human interaction have no representation in the formal organization at all, and others are inadequately represented by the formal organization. This fact is frequently forgotten when talking or thinking about industrial situations in general. Too often it is assumed that the organization of a company corresponds to a blueprint plan or organization chart. Actually, it never does. In the formal organization of most companies little explicit recognition is given to many social distinctions residing in the social organization. The blueprint plans of a company show the functional relations between working units, but they do not express the distinctions of social distance, movement, or equilibrium previously described. The hierarchy of prestige values which tends to make the work of men more important than the work of women, the work of clerks more important that the work at the bench, has little representation in the formal organization; nor does a blueprint plan ordinarily show the primary groups, that is, those groups enjoying daily face-to-face relations. Logical lines of horizontal and vertical coordination of functions replace the actually existing patterns of interaction between people in different social places. The formal organization cannot take account of the sentiments and values residing in the social organization by means of which individuals or groups of individuals are informally differentiated, ordered, and integrated. Individuals in their associations with one another in a factory build up personal relationships. They form into informal groups, in terms of which each person achieves a certain position or status. The nature of these informal groups is very important, as has been shown in the Relay Assembly Test Room and in the Bank Wiring Observation Room.

It is well to recognize that informal organizations are not "bad," as they are sometimes assumed to be. Informal social organization exists in every plant, and can be said to be a necessary prerequisite for effective collaboration. Much collaboration exists at an informal level, and it sometimes facilitates the functioning of the formal organization. On the other hand, sometimes the informal organization develops in opposition to the formal organization. The important consideration is, therefore, the relation that exists between formal and informal organizations.

To illustrate, let us consider the Relay Assembly Test Room and the Bank Wiring Observation Room. These two studies offered an interesting contrast between two informal working groups; one situation could be characterized in almost completely opposite terms from the other. In the Relay Assembly Test Room, on the one hand, the five operators changed continuously in their rate of output up and down over the duration of the test, and yet in a curious fashion their variations in output were insensitive to many significant changes introduced during the experiment. On the other hand, in the Bank Wiring Observation Room output was being held relatively constant and there existed a hypersensitivity to change on the part of the worker—in fact, what could almost be described as an organized opposition to it.

It is interesting to note that management could draw from these studies two opposite conclusions. From the Relay Assembly Test Room experiment they could argue that the company can do almost anything it wants in the nature of technical changes without any perceptible effect on the output of the workers. From the Bank Wiring Observation Room they could argue equally convincingly that the company can introduce hardly any changes without meeting a pronounced opposition to them from the workers. To make this dilemma even more striking, it is only necessary to recall that the sensitivity to change in the one case occurred in the room where no experimental changes had been introduced whereas the insensitivity to change in the other case occurred in the room where the operators had been submitted to considerable experimentation. To settle this question by saying that in one case the situation was typical and in the other case atypical of ordinary shop conditions would be to beg the question, for the essential difference between the two situations would again be missed. It would ignore the social setting in which the changes occurred and the meaning which the workers themselves assigned to the changes.

Although in both cases there were certain informal arrangements not identical with the formal setup, the informal organization in one room was quite different from that in the other room, especially in its relation to the formal organization. In the case of the Relay Assembly Test Room there was a group, or informal organization, which could be characterized as a network of personal relations which had been developed in and through a particular way of working together; it was an organization which not only satisfied the wishes of its members but also worked in harmony with the aims of management. In the case of the Bank Wiring Observation Room there was an informal organization which could be characterized better as a set of practices and beliefs which its members had in common—practices and beliefs which at many points worked against the economic purposes of the company. In one case the relation between the formal and informal organization was one of compatibility; in the other case it was one of opposition. Or to put it in another way, collaboration in the Relay Assembly Test Room was at a much higher level than in the Bank Wiring Observation Room.

The difference between these two groups can be understood only by comparing the functions which their informal organizations performed for their members. The chief function of the informal group in the Bank Wiring Observation Room was to resist changes in their established routines of work or personal interrelations. This resistance to change, however, was not the chief function of the informal group in the Relay Assembly Test Room. It is true that at first the introduction of the planned changes in the test room, whether or not these changes were logically in the direction of improvement, was met with apprehension and feelings of uneasiness on the part of the operators. The girls in the beginning were never quite sure that they might not be victims of the changes.

In setting up the Relay Assembly Test Room with the object of studying the factors determining the efficiency of the worker, many of the methods and rules by means of which management tends to promote and maintain efficiency—the "bogey," not talking too much at work, etc.—were, in effect, abrogated. With the removal of this source of constraint and in a setting of heightened social significance (because many of the changes had differentiated the test room girls from the regular department and as a result had elevated the social status within the plant of each of the five girls) a new type of spontaneous social organization developed. Social conditions had been established which allowed the operators to develop their own values and objectives. The experimental conditions allowed the operators to develop openly social codes at work and these codes, unhampered by interference, gave a sustained meaning to their work. It was as if the experimenters had acted as a buffer for the operators and held their work situation steady while they developed a new type of social organization. With this change in the type of social organization there also developed a new attitude toward changes in their working environment. Toward many changes which constitute an unspecified threat in the regular work situation the operators became immune. What the Relay Assembly Test Room experiment showed was that when innovations are introduced carefully and with regard to the actual sentiments of the workers, the workers are likely to develop a spontaneous type of informal organization which will not only express more adequately their own values and significances but also is more likely to be in harmony with the aims of management.

Although all the studies of informal organization at the Hawthorne Plant were made at the employee level, it would be incorrect to assume that this phenomenon occurs only at that level. Informal organization appears at all levels, from the bottom to the very top of the organization.[2] Informal organization at the executive level, just as at the work level, may either facilitate or impede purposive cooperation and communication. In either case, at all levels of the organization informal organizations exist as a necessary condition for collaboration. Without them formal organization could not survive for long. Formal and informal organizations are interdependent aspects of social interaction.

The Ideological Organization of the Plant

There is one aspect of social organization in an industrial plant which cuts across both the formal and informal organizations: the systems of ideas and beliefs by means of which the values residing in the total organization are expressed and the symbols around which these values are organized. Both the formal and informal organizations of a plant have systems of ideas and beliefs. Some are more capable of logical and systematic expression than others. Those of the formal organization in general are more logically explicit and articulate than those of the informal organization, but they are not for that reason more powerful in their effects than those of the informal organization. The sentiments underlying the beliefs and ideas of informal organizations are often very powerful determinants of overt behavior.

Some of these systems of ideas and beliefs represent what the organization should be; that is, what the relations of people to one another should be or how people should behave. Some express the values of one part of the total organization, for each specialist tends to see the total organization from the point of view of the logic of his own specialty. Still others express the values residing in the interhuman relations of the different social groups involved.

Some of these ideas and beliefs represent more closely the actual situation than others. In all cases, however, they are abstractions from the concrete situation. In this respect they are to the concrete situation as maps are to the territories they represent.[3] And like maps these abstractions may be either misleading or useful. They may be misleading because sometimes the person using them fails to realize they are representing only one part of the total organization. Sometimes in the minds of certain individuals these abstractions tend to become divorced from the social reality and, in effect, lead an independent existence.

In their studies the investigators frequently ran into these different systems of ideas and beliefs. Although they were never made the object of systematic study, three general systems which seemed to cling together could be discerned.

The logic of cost. In the industrial plant there is a certain set of ideas and beliefs by means of which the common economic purposes of the total organization are evaluated. This we shall call the "logic of cost." Although the logic of cost is applied mostly to the technical organization, it is also sometimes applied to the human organization. When applied to the human organization it is frequently done under the label of "efficiency."

The word "efficiency" is used in at least five different ways, two of which are rather vague and not clearly differentiated: (*a*) sometimes when talking about a machine it is used in a technical sense, as the relation between output and input; (*b*) sometimes when talking about a manufacturing process or operation it is used to refer to relative unit cost; (*c*) sometimes when referring to a worker it is used to indicate a worker's production or output in relation to a certain standard of performance; (*d*) sometimes its reference becomes more vague and it is used as practically synonymous with "logical coordination of function"; (*e*) sometimes it is used in the sense of "morale" or "social integration."

We shall use the term "logic of cost" to refer only to the system of ideas and beliefs which are explicitly organized around the symbol of "cost" and are applied to the human organization from this point of view.[4] This logic represents one of the values of the formal organization: the system of ideas and beliefs which relates the human organization to the task of technical production.

The logic of efficiency. Closely associated with the logic of cost is another system of ideas and beliefs by means of which the collaborative efforts of the members of an organization are evaluated. This we shall call the "logic of efficiency."[5] This system of ideas and beliefs, which is organized around the symbol of "cooperation," represents another value of the formal organization. It is addressed primarily to the problem of how cooperation between individuals and groups of individuals can be effectively secured and is manifested in plans, such as wage payment plans, designed to promote collaboration among individuals.

A system of beliefs and ideas such as this is usually based upon certain assumptions about employee behavior. In the case of the wage payment plan in the Bank Wiring Observation Room, for example, it was assumed that the employee was a logical being and therefore could see the system, as its creators saw it, as a logical, coherent scheme which he could use to his economic advantage. It was assumed that, given the opportunity, the employee would act in such a way as to obtain the maximum of earnings consistent with his physical capacity. Carrying this basic assumption still further, it followed that the slower workers, who would interfere with the logical functioning of that system, would be disciplined by the faster workers and that daywork claims would be kept at a minimum. It was assumed that the division of labor would permit the employees to increase production through specialization. The possibility that division of labor might result in social stratification, which in turn might generate nonlogical forces that would interfere with the logical functioning of that system, was unforeseen. Practically every aspect of the wage plan followed from the basic assumption that nothing would interfere with the economic motives. It is such assumptions as these that go to make up the "logic of efficiency."

The logic of sentiments. There is another system of ideas and beliefs which we shall give the label "the logic of sentiments." It represents the values residing in the interhuman relations of the different groups within the organization. Examples of what is meant here are the arguments employees give which center around the "right to work," "seniority," "fairness," "the living wage." This logic, as its name implies, is deeply rooted in sentiment and feeling.

Management and employee logics. At first glance it might seem that the logics of cost and efficiency are the logics of management groups, whereas the logic of sentiments is the logic of employee groups. Although in one sense this may be accurate, in another sense it is an oversimplification. All groups within the industry participate in these different logics, although some participate to a greater or less extent than others. One has only to interview a supervisor or executive to see that he has a logic of sentiments which is expressing the values residing in his personal interrelations with other supervisors or executives. Employee groups, moreover, are not unknown to apply the logic of cost.

However, it is incorrect to assume that these different logics have the same significance to different groups in an industrial plant. The logics of cost and efficiency express the values of the formal organization; the logic of sentiments expresses the values of the informal organization. To management groups and technical specialists the logics of cost and efficiency are likely to be more important than they are to employee groups. In form the logic of sentiments expressed by an executive is indistinguishable from that expressed by a worker, but in content it is quite different. As anyone knows who has had industrial experience, much time is spent in industry in debating the relative weights attaching to the logics of cost, efficiency, and sentiments when they are applied to a particular concrete situation.

Definition of Terms

For convenience, it may be well to summarize the different parts into which the industrial plant as a social system can be divided and the way in which the labels attaching to them will be used . . . .The following outline will help the reader to see the levels of abstraction of the different parts of the system:

1. Technical Organization
2. Human Organization
   2.1. Individual
   2.2. Social Organization
      2.21. Formal Organization
         2.211. Patterns of Interaction
         2.212. Systems of Ideas and Beliefs
         (Ideological Organization)
         2.2121. Logic of Cost
         2.2122. Logic of Efficiency
      2.22. Informal Organization
         2.221. Patterns of Interaction
         2.222. Systems of Ideas and Beliefs
         (Ideological Organization-
         2.2221. Logic of Sentiments

1. The term "technical organization" will refer to the logical and technical organization of materials, tools, machines, and finished products including all those physical items related to the task of technical production.

2. The term "human organization" will refer, on the one hand, to the concrete individual with his rich personal and social background and, on the other hand, to the intricate pattern of social relations existing among the various individuals and groups within the plant.

2.1. The term "individual" will refer to the sentiments and values which the person is bringing to the work situation because of his past social conditioning and present social situation outside of the plant; i.e., the past and present patterns of interaction in which he has participated or is participating outside of work.

2.2. The term "social organization" will refer to the actual patterns of interaction existing within and between employee groups, supervisory groups, and management groups in a plant here and now. It will include those relations that remain at a common human level (friendships, antagonisms, etc.), those that have been built up into larger social configurations (social codes, customs, traditions, routines, and associated ideas and beliefs), as well as those patterns of relations formally prescribed by the rules, regulations, practices, and policies of the company.

2.21. The term "formal organization" will refer to those patterns of interaction prescribed by the rules and regulations of the company as well as to the policies which prescribe the relations that obtain, or are supposed to obtain, within the human organization and between the human organization and the technical organization.

2.22 The term "informal organization" will refer to the actual personal interrelations existing among the members of the organization which are not represented by, or are inadequately represented by, the formal organization.

2.212 and 2.222. The term "ideological organization" will refer to the systems of ideas and beliefs by means of which the values of both the formal and informal aspects of the social organization are expressed and the symbols around which these values are organized.

2.2121. The term "logic of cost" will refer to that system of ideas and beliefs by means of which the common economic purposes of the total organization are evaluated.

2.2122. The term "logic efficiency" will refer to that system of ideas and beliefs by means of which the collaborative efforts of the members of the organization are evaluated.

2.2221. The term "logic of sentiments" will refer to that system of ideas and beliefs which expresses the values residing in the interhuman relations of the different groups within the plant.

A Condition of Equilibrium

The parts of the industrial plant as a social system are interrelated and interdependent. Any changes in one part of the social system are accompanied by changes in other parts of the system. The parts of the system can be conceived of as being in a state of equilibrium, such that "if a small (not too great) modification different from that which will otherwise occur is impressed on the system, a reaction will at once appear tending toward the conditions that would have existed if the modification had not been impressed.[6]

Some parts of the system can change more rapidly than others. The technical organization can change more rapidly than the social organization; the formal organization can change more rapidly than the informal; the systems of beliefs and ideas can change more rapidly than the patterns of interaction and associated sentiments, of which these beliefs and ideas are an expression. In the disparity in the rates of change possible there exists a precondition for unbalance which may manifest itself in many forms.

In their studies the investigators identified two such possibilities of unbalance. One was the disparity in the rates of change possible in the technical organization, on the one hand, and the social organization, on the other. This condition was manifested in the workers' behavior by distrust and resistance to change. This resistance was expressed whenever changes were introduced too rapidly or without sufficient considerations of their social implications; in other words, whenever the workers were being asked to adjust themselves to new methods or systems which seemed to them to deprive their work of its customary social significance. In such situations it was evident that the social codes, customs, and routines of the worker could not be accommodated to the technical innovations introduced as quickly as the innovations themselves, in the form of new machines and processes, could be made. The codes, customs, and traditions of the worker are not the product of logic but are based on deeply rooted sentiments. Not only is any alteration of the existing social organization to which the worker has grown accustomed likely to produce sentiments of resistance to the change, but too rapid interference is likely to lead to feelings of frustration and an irrational exasperation with technical change in any form.

Another possibility of unbalance lies in the relation of the ideological organization to the actual work situation. The logics of the ideological organization express only some of the values of the social organization. They frequently fail to take into account not only the feelings and sentiments of people within the plant but also the spontaneous informal social groups which form at all levels of the organization. Thus they tend to become divorced from the concrete situation and to lead an independent existence. As a result of failing to distinguish the human situation as it is from the way it is formally and logically represented to be, many human problems are stated either in terms of the perversities of human nature or in terms of logical defects in the formal organization. The facts of social organization are ignored, and consequently the result in terms of diagnosis or remedy is bound to be inadequate.

It became clear to the investigators that the limits of human collaboration are determined far more by the informal than by the formal organization of the plant. Collaboration is not wholly a matter of logical organization. It presupposes social codes, conventions, traditions, and routine or customary ways of responding to situations. Without such basic codes or conventions, effective work relations are not possible.

References

1. "The interdependence of the variables in a system is one of the widest inductions from experience that we possess; or we may alternatively regard it as the definition of a system." Henderson, L. J., *Pareto's General Sociology,* Harvard University Press, 1935, p. 86.
2. Barnard, C. I., *The Functions of the Executive,* Harvard University Press, 1938, pp. 223–24.
3. This distinction has been borrowed from Korzybski, A., *Science and Sanity,* The Science Press Printing Co., New York, 1933.
4. According to this definition, "logic of cost" does not conform to any single one of the above uses of the word "efficiency" but conforms most closely to a combination of (b) and (c).
5. The "logic of efficiency" conforms most closely to a combination of uses (c), (d), and (e) of the word "efficiency" as given in the previous section.
6. For a discussion of equilibrium, see Pareto, V., *The Mind and Society,* Harcourt, Brace & Co., New York, 1935, pp. 1435–42. The quotation used above is Dr. L. J. Henderson's adaptation of Pareto's definition of equilibrium.

General Systems Theory: Applications for Organizations and Management

Fremont E. Kast and James E. Rosenzweig

BIOLOGICAL and social scientists generally have embraced systems concepts. Many organization and management theorists seem anxious to identify with this movement and to contribute to the development of an approach which purports to offer the ultimate—the unification of all science into one grand conceptual model. Who possibly could resist? General systems theory seems to provide a relief from the limitations of more mechanistic approaches and a rationale for rejecting "principles" based on relatively "closed-system" thinking. This theory provides the paradigm for organization and management theorists to "crank into their systems model" all of the diverse knowledge from relevant underlying disciplines. It has become almost mandatory to have the word "system" in the title of recent articles and books (many of us have compromised and placed it only in the subtitle).[1]

But where did it all start? This question takes us back into history and brings to mind the long-standing philosophical arguments between mechanistic and organismic models of the nineteenth and early twentieth centuries. As Deutsch says:

> Both mechanistic and organismic models were based substantially on experiences and operations known before 1850. Since then, the experience of almost a century of scientific and technological progress has so far not been

Reprinted with permission from the *Academy of Management Journal*, V. 15 (Dec. 1972), pp. 447–465. © 1972 by the Academy of Management.

utilized for any significant new model for the study of organization and in particular of human thought (12, p. 389).

General systems theory even revives the specter of the "vitalists" and their views on "life force" and most certainly brings forth renewed questions of teleological or purposeful behavior of both living and nonliving systems. Phillips and others have suggested that the philosophical roots of general systems theory go back even further, at least to the German philosopher Hegel (1770-1831) (29, p. 56). Thus, we should recognize that in the adoption of the systems approach for the study of organizations we are not dealing with newly discovered ideas—they have rich genealogy.

Even in the field of organization and management theory, systems views are not new. Chester Barnard used a basic systems framework.

A cooperative system is a complex of physical, biological, personal, and social components which are in a specific systematic relationship by reason of the cooperation of two or more persons for at least one definite end. Such a system is evidently a subordinate unit of larger systems from one point of view; and itself embraces subsidiary systems—physical, biological, etc.— from another point of view. One of the systems comprised within a cooperative system, the one which is implicit in the phrase "cooperation of two or more persons," is called an "organization" (3, p. 65).

And Barnard was influenced by the "systems views" of Vilfredo Pareto and Talcott Parsons. Certainly this quote (dressed up a bit to give the term "system" more emphasis) could be the introduction to a 1972 book on organizations.

Miller points out that Alexander Bogdanov, the Russian philosopher, developed a theory of tektology or universal organization science in 1912 which foreshadowed general systems theory and used many of the same concepts as modern systems theorists (26, p. 249–250).

However, in spite of a long history of organismic and holistic thinking, the utilization of the systems approach did not become the accepted model for organization and management writers until relatively recently. It is difficult to specify the turning point exactly. The momentum of systems thinking was identified by Scott in 1961 when he described the relationship between general systems theory and organization theory.

> The distinctive qualities of modern organization theory are its conceptual-analytical base, its reliance on empirical research data, and above all, its integrating nature. These qualities are framed in a philosophy which accepts the premise that the only meaningful way to study organization is to study it as a system . . . Modern organization theory and general system theory are similar in that they look at organization as an integrated whole (33, p. 15–21).

Scott said explicitly what many in our field had been thinking and/or implying—he helped us put into perspective the important writings of Herbert Simon, James March, Talcott Parsons, George Homans, E. Wight Bakke, Kenneth Boulding, and many others.

But how far have we really advanced over the past decade in applying general systems theory to organizations and their management? Is it still a "skeleton," or have we been able to "put some meat on the bones"? The systems approach has been touted because of its potential usefulness in understanding the complexities of "live" organizations. Has this approach really helped us in this endeavor or has it compounded confusion with chaos? Herbert Simon describes the challenge for the systems approach:

> In both science and engineering, the study of "systems" is an increasingly popular activity. Its popularity is more response to a pressing need for synthesizing and analyzing complexity than it is to any large development of a body of knowledge and technique for dealing with complexity. If this popularity is to be more than a fad, necessity will have to mother invention and provide substance to go with the name (35, p. 114).

In this article we will explore the issue of whether we are providing substance for the term *systems approach* as it relates to the study of organizations and their management. There are many interesting historical philosophical questions concerning the relationship between the mechanistic and organistic approaches and their applicability to the various fields of science, as well as other interesting digressions into the evolution of systems approaches. However, we will resist those temptations and plunge directly into a discussion of the key concepts of general systems theory, the way in which these ideas have been used by organization theorists, the limitations in their application, and some suggestions for the future.

KEY CONCEPTS OF GENERAL SYSTEMS THEORY

The key concepts of general systems theory have been set forth by many writers (6, 7, 13, 17, 25, 28, 39) and have been used by many

organization and management theorists (10, 14, 18, 19, 22, 23, 24, 32).
It is not our purpose here to elaborate on them in great detail because
we anticipate that most readers will have been exposed to them in
some depth. Figure 1 provides a very brief review of those characteristics of systems which seem to have wide acceptance. The review is
far from complete. It is difficult to identify a "complete" list of
characteristics derived from general systems theory; moreover, it is
merely a first-order classification. There are many derived second- and
third-order characteristics which could be considered. For example,
James G. Miller sets forth *165* hypotheses, stemming from open
systems theory, which might be applicable to two or more levels of
systems (25). He suggests that they are *general* systems theoretical
hypotheses and qualifies them by suggesting that they are propositions applicable to general systems *behavior* theory and would thus
exclude nonliving systems. He does not limit these propositions to
individual organisms, but considers them appropriate for social
systems as well. His hypotheses are related to such issues as structure,
process, subsystems, information, growth, and integration. It is
obviously impossible to discuss all of these hypotheses; we want only
to indicate the extent to which many interesting propositions are being
posed which might have relevance to many different types of systems.
It will be a very long time (if ever) before most of these hypotheses are
validated; however, we are surprised at how many of them can be
agreed with intuitively, and we can see their possible verification in
studies of social organizations.

We turn now to a closer look at how successful or unsuccessful we
have been in utilizing these concepts in the development of "modern
organization theory."

A BEGINNING:
ENTHUSIASTIC BUT INCOMPLETE

We have embraced general systems theory but, really, how completely? We could review a vast literature in modern organization
theory which has explicitly or implicitly adopted systems theory as a
frame of reference, and we have investigated in detail a few representative examples of the literature in assessing the "state of the art" [18,
19, 22, 23, 31, 38]. It was found that most of these books professed to
utilize general systems theory. Indeed, in the first few chapters, many
of them did an excellent job of presenting basic systems concepts and
showing their relationship to organizations; however, when they
moved further into the discussion of more specific subject matter, they

FIGURE 1   Key Concepts of General Systems Theory

Subsystems or Components: A system by definition is composed of interrelated parts or elements. This is true for all systems—mechanical, biological, and social. Every system has at least two elements, and these elements are interconnected.

Holism, Synergism, Organicism, and Gestalt: The whole is not just the sum of the parts; the system itself can be explained only as a totality. Holism is the opposite of elementarism, which views the total as the sum of its individual parts.

Open Systems View: Systems can be considered in two ways: (1) closed or (2) open. Open systems exchange information, energy, or material with their environments. Biological and social systems are inherently open systems; mechanical systems may be open or closed. The concepts of open and closed systems are difficult to defend in the absolute. We prefer to think of open-closed as a dimension; that is, systems are relatively open or relatively closed.

Input-Transformation-Output Model: The open system can be viewed as a transformation model. In a dynamic relationship with its environment, it receives various inputs, transforms these inputs in some way, exports outputs.

System Boundaries: It follows that systems have boundaries which separate them from their environments. The concept of boundaries helps us understand the distinction between open and closed systems. The relatively closed system has rigid, impenetrable boundaries; whereas the open system has permeable boundaries between itself and a broader suprasystem. Boundaries are relatively easily defined in physical and biological systems, but are very difficult to delineate in social systems, such as organizations.

Negative Entropy: Closed, physical systems are subject to the force of entropy which increases until eventually the entire system fails. The tendency toward maximum entropy is a movement to disorder, complete lack of resource transformation, and death. In a closed system, the change in entropy must always be positive; however, in open biological or social systems, entropy can be arrested and may even be transformed into negative entropy—a process of more complete organization and ability to transform resources—because the system imports resources from its environment.

Steady State, Dynamic Equilibrium, and Homeostasis: The concept of steady state is closely related to that of negative entropy. A closed system eventually must attain an equilibrium state with maximum entropy—death or disorganization. However, an open system may attain a state where the system remains in dynamic equilibrium through the continuous inflow of materials, energy, and information.

Feedback: The concept of feedback is important in understanding how a system maintains a steady state. Information concerning the outputs or the process of the system is fed back as an input into the system, perhaps leading to changes in the transformation process and/or future outputs. Feedback can be both positive and negative, although the field of cybernetics is based on negative feedback. Negative feedback is informational input which indicates that the system is deviating from a prescribed course and should readjust to a new steady state.

Hierarchy: A basic concept in systems thinking is that of hierarchical relationships between systems. A system is composed of subsystems of a lower order and is also part of suprasystem. Thus, there is a hierarchy of the components of the system.

Internal Elaboration: Closed systems move toward entropy and disorganization. In contrast, open systems appear to move in the direction of greater differentiation, elaboration, and a higher level of organization.

Multiple Goal-Seeking: Biological and social systems appear to have multiple goals or purposes. Social organizations seek multiple goals, if for no other reason than that they are composed of individuals and subunits with different values and objectives.

Equifinality of Open Systems: In mechanistic systems there is a direct cause and effect relationship between the initial conditions and the final state. Biological and social systems operate differently. Equifinality suggests that certain results may be achieved with different initial conditions and in different ways. This view suggests that social organizations can accomplish their objectives with diverse inputs and with varying internal activities (conversion processes).

---

departed substantially from systems theory. The studies appear to use a "partial systems approach" and leave for the reader the problem of integrating the various ideas into a systemic whole. It also appears that many of the authors are unable, because of limitations of knowledge about subsystem relationships, to carry out the task of using general systems theory as a conceptual basis for organization theory.

Furthermore, it is evident that each author had many "good ideas" stemming from the existing body of knowledge or current research on organizations which did not fit neatly into a "systems model." For example, they might discuss leadership from a relatively closed-system point of view and not consider it in relation to organizational technology, structure, or other variables. Our review of the literature suggests that much remains to be done in applying general systems theory to organization theory and management practice.

SOME DILEMMAS IN APPLYING GST TO ORGANIZATIONS

Why have writers embracing general systems theory as a basis for studying organizations had so much difficulty in following through? Part of this difficulty may stem from the newness of the paradigm and our inability to operationalize "all we think we know" about this approach. Or it may be because we know too little about the systems under investigation. Both of these possibilities will be covered later, but first we need to look at some of the more specific conceptual problems.

Organizations as Organisms

One of the basic contributions of general systems theory was the rejection of the traditional closed-system or mechanistic view of social organization. But, did general systems theory free us from this constraint only to impose another, less obvious one? General systems theory grew out of the organismic views of von Bertalanffy and other biologists; thus, many of the characteristics are relevant to the living organism. It is conceptually easy to draw the analogy between living organisms and social organizations. "There is, after all, an intuitive similarity between the organization of the human body and the kinds of organizations men create. And so, undaunted by the failures of the human-social analogy through time, new theorists try afresh in each epoch" [2, p. 660]. General systems theory would have us accept this analogy between organism and social organization. Yet, we have a hard time swallowing it whole. Katz and Kahn warn us of the danger:

> There has been no more pervasive, persistent, and futile fallacy handi-capping the social sciences than the use of the physical model for the understanding of social structures. The biological metaphor, with its crude

comparisons of the physical parts of the body to the parts of the social system, has been replaced by more subtle but equally misleading analogies between biological and social functioning. This figurative type of thinking ignores the essential difference between the socially contrived nature of social systems and the physical structure of the machine or the human organism. So long as writers are committed to a theoretical framework based upon the physical model, they will miss the essential social-psychological facts of the highly variable, loosely articulated character of social systems (19, p.31).

In spite of this warning, Katz and Kahn do embrace much of the general systems theory concepts which are based on the biological metaphor. We must be very cautious about trying to make this analogy too literal. We agree with Silverman who says, "It may, therefore, be necessary to drop the analogy between an organization and an organism: organizations may be systems but not necessarily *natural* systems" (34, p. 31).

Distinction between Organization and an Organization

General systems theory emphasizes that systems are organized—they are composed of interdependent components in some relationship. The social organization would then follow logically as just another system. But, we are perhaps being caught in circular thinking. It is true that all systems (physical, biological, and social) are by definition organized, but are all systems organizations? Rapoport and Horvath distinguish "organization theory" and "the theory of organizations" as follows:

We see organization theory as dealing with general and abstract organizational principles; it applies to any system exhibiting organized complexity. As such, organization theory is seen as an extension of mathematical physics or, even more generally, of mathematics designed to deal with organized systems. The theory of organizations, on the other hand, purports to be a social science. It puts real human organizations at the center of interest. It may study the social structure of organizations and so can be viewed as a branch of sociology; it can study the behavior of individuals or groups as members of organizations and can be viewed as a part of social psychology; it can study power relations and principles of control in organizations and so fits into political science (30, pp. 74-75).

Why make an issue of this distinction? It seems to us that there is a vital matter involved. All systems may be considered to be organized, and more advanced systems may display differentiation in the activities of component parts—such as the specialization of human organs. However, all systems *do not* have purposeful entities. Can the heart or lungs be considered as purposeful entities in themselves or are they only components of the larger purposeful system, the human body? By contrast, the social organization is composed of two or more purposeful elements. "An organization consists of elements that have and can exercise their own wills" (1, p. 669). Organisms, the foundation stone of general systems theory, do not contain purposeful elements which exercise their own will. This distinction between the organism and the social organization is of importance. In much of general systems theory, the concern is primarily with the way in which the *organism* responds to environmentally generated inputs. Feedback concepts and the maintenance of a steady state are based on internal adaptations to environmental forces. (This is particularly true of cybernetic models.) But, what about those changes and adaptations which occur from *within* social organizations? Purposeful elements within the social organization may initiate activities and adaptations which are difficult to subsume under feedback and steady state concepts.

Opened and Closed Systems

Another dilemma stemming from general systems theory is the tendency to dichotomize all systems as opened or closed. We have been led to think of physical systems as closed, subject to the laws of entropy, and to think of biological systems as open to their environment and, possibly, becoming negentropic. But applying this strict polarization to social organizations creates many difficulties. In fact, most social organizations and their subsystems are "partially open" and "partially closed." Open and closed are a matter of degree. Unfortunately, there seems to be a widely held view (often more implicit than explicit) that *open-system thinking is good and closed-system thinking is bad.* We have not become sufficiently sophisticated to recognize that both are appropriate under certain conditions. For example, one of the most useful conceptualizations set forth by Thompson is that the social organization *must seek* to use closed-system concepts (particularly at the technical core) to reduce uncertainty and to create more effective performance at this level.

Still Subsystems Thinking

Even though we preach a general systems approach, we often practice subsystems thinking. Each of the academic disciplines and each of us personally have limited perspective of the system we are studying. While proclaiming a broad systems viewpoint, we often dismiss variables outside our interest or competence as being irrelevant, and we only open our system to those inputs which we can handle with our disciplinary bag of tools. We are hampered because each of the academic disciplines has taken a narrow "partial systems view" and find comfort in the relative certainty which this creates. Of course, this is not a problem unique to modern organization theory. Under the more traditional process approach to the study of management, we were able to do an admirable job of delineating and discussing planning, organizing, and controlling as separate activities. We were much less successful in discussing them as intergrated and inter-related activities.

How Does Our Knowledge Fit?

One of the major problems in utilizing general systems theory is that we know (or think we know) more about certain relationships than we can fit into a general systems model. For example, we are beginning to understand the two-variable relationship between technology and structure. But, when we introduce another variable, say psychosocial relationships, our models become too complex. Consequently, in order to discuss all the things we know about organizations, we depart from a systems approach. Perhaps it is because we know a great deal more about the elements or subsystems of an organization than we do about the interrelationships and interactions between these subsystems. And, general systems theory forces us to consider those relationships about which we know the least—a true dilemma. So we continue to elaborate on those aspects of the organization which we know best—a partial systems view.

Failure to Delineate a Specific System

When the social sciences embraced general systems theory, the total system became the focus of attention and terminology tended toward vagueness. In the utilization of systems theory, we should be more precise in delineating the specific system under consideration. Failure to do this leads to much confusion. As Murray suggests:

> I am wary of the word "system" because social scientists use it very frequently without specifying which of several possible different denotations they have in mind; but more particularly because, today, "system" is a highly cathected term, loaded with prestige; hence, we are all strongly tempted to employ it even when we have nothing definite in mind and its only service is to indicate that we subscribe to the general premise respecting the interdependence of things—basic to organismic theory, holism, field theory, interactionism, transactionism, etc . . . .When definitions of the units of a system are lacking, the term stands for no more than an article of faith, and is misleading to boot, insofar as it suggests a condition of affairs that may not actually exist (27, pp. 50-51).

We need to be much more precise in delineating both the boundaries of the system under consideration and the level of our analysis. There is a tendency for current writers in organization theory to accept general systems theory and then to move indiscriminately across systems boundaries and between levels of systems without being very precise (and letting their readers in on what is occurring). James Miller suggests the need for clear delineation of levels in applying systems theory. "It is important to follow one procedural rule in systems theory in order to avoid confusion. Every discussion should begin with an identification of the level of reference, and the discourse should not change to another level without a specific statement that this is occurring" (25, p. 216). Our field is replete with these confusions about systems levels. For example, when we use the term "organizational behavior" are we talking about the way the organization behaves as a system or are we talking about the behavior of the individual participants? By goals, do we mean the goals of the organization or the goals of the individuals within the organization? In using systems theory we must become more precise in our delineation of systems boundaries and systems levels if we are to prevent confusing conceptual ambiguity.

Recognition That Organizations Are "Contrived Systems"

We have a vague uneasiness that general systems theory truly does not recognize the "contrived" nature of social organizations. With its predominate emphasis on natural organisms, it may understate some characteristics which are vital for the social organization. Social organizations do not occur naturally in nature; they are contrived by man. They have structure; but it is the structure of events rather than of physical components, and it cannot be separated from the processes of the system. The fact that social organizations are contrived by human beings suggests that they can be established for an infinite variety of purposes and do not follow the same life-cycle patterns of birth, growth, maturity, and death as biological systems. As Katz and Kahn say:

> Social structures are essentially contrived systems. They are made of men and are imperfect systems. They can come apart at the seams overnight, but they can also outlast by centuries the biological organisms which originally created them. The cement which holds them together is essentially psychological rather than biological. Social systems are anchored in the attitudes, perceptions, beliefs, motivations, habits, and expectations of human beings (19, p. 33).

Recognizing that the social organization is contrived again cautions us against making an exact analogy between it and physical or biological systems.

Questions of Systems Effectiveness

General systems theory with its biological orientation would appear to have an evolutionary view of system effectiveness. That living system which best adapts to its environment prospers and survives. The primary measure of effectiveness is perpetuatuion of the organism's species. Teleological behavior is therefore directed toward survival. But, is survival the only criterion of effectiveness of the social system? It is probably an essential but not all-inclusive measure of effectiveness.

General systems theory emphasizes the organism's survival goal and does not fully relate to the question of the effectiveness of the system in its suprasystem—the environment. Parsonian functional-structural views provide a contrast. "The *raison d'etre* of complex organizations, according to this analysis, is mainly to benefit the society in which they belong, and that society is, therefore, the appropriate frame of reference for the evaluation of organizational effectiveness" (41, p. 896).

But, this view seems to go to the opposite extreme from the survival view of general systems theory—the organization exists to serve the society. It seems to us that the truth lies somewhere between these two viewpoints. And it is likely that a systems viewpoint (modified from the species survival view of general systems theory) will be most appropriate. Yuchtman and Seashore suggest:

> The organization's success over a period of time in this competition for resources—i.e., its bargaining position in a given environment—is regarded as an expression of its overall effectiveness. Since the resources are of various kinds, and the competitive relationships are multiple, and since there is interchangeability among classes of resources, the assessment of organizational effectiveness must be in terms not of any single criterion but of an open-ended multidimensional set of criteria (41, p. 891).

This viewpoint suggests that questions of organizational effectiveness must be concerned with at least three levels of analysis. The level of the environment, the level of the social organization as a system, and the level of the subsystems (human participants) within the organization. Perhaps much of our confusion and ambiguity concerning organizational effectiveness stems from our failure to clearly delineate the level of our analysis and, even more important, our failure really to understand the relationships among these levels.

Our discussion of some of the problems associated with the application of general systems theory to the study of social organizations might suggest that we completely reject the appropriateness of this model. On the contrary, we see the systems approach as the new paradigm for the study of organizations; but, like all new concepts in the sciences, one which has to be applied, modified, and elaborated to make it as useful as possible.

SYSTEMS THEORY PROVIDES THE NEW PARADIGM

We hope the discussion of GST and organizations provides a realistic appraisal. We do not want to promote the value of the systems approach as a matter of faith; however, we do see systems theory as vital to the study of social organizations and as providing the major new paradigm for our field of study.

Thomas Kuhn provides an interesting interpretation of the nature of scientific revolution (20). He suggests that major changes in all fields of science occur with the development of new conceptual schemes or "paradigms." These new paradigms do not just represent a step-by-step advancement in "normal" science (the science generally accepted and practiced) but, rather, a revolutionary change in the way the scientific field is perceived by the practitioners. Kuhn says:

The historian of science may be tempted to exclaim that when paradigms change, the world itself changes with them. Led by a new paradigm, scientists adopt new instruments and look in new places. Even more important, during revolutions scientists see new and different things when looking with familiar instruments in places they have looked before. It is rather as if the professional community has been suddenly transported to another planet where familiar objects are seen in a different light and are joined by unfamiliar ones as well . . . . Paradigm changes do cause scientists to see the world of their research-engagement differently. Insofar as their only recourse to that world is through what they see and do, we may want to say that after a revolution scientists are responding to a different world (20, p.110).

New paradigms frequently are rejected by the scientific community. (At first they may seem crude and limited—offering very little more than older paradigms.) They frequently lack the apparent sophistication of the older paradigms which they ultimately replace. They do not display the clarity and certainty of older paradigms which have been refined through years of research and writing. But, a new paradigm does provide for a "new start" and opens up new directions which were not possible under the old. "We must recognize how very limited in both scope and precision a paradigm can be at the time of its first appearance. Paradigms gain their status because they are more successful than their competitors in solving a few problems that the group of practitioners has come to recognize as acute. To be more successful is not, however, to be either completely successful with a single problem or notably successful with any large number" (20, p. 23).

Systems theory does provide a new paradigm for the study of social organizations and their management. At this stage it is obviously crude and lacking in precision. In some ways it may not be much better than older paradigms which have been accepted and used for a long time (such as the management process approach). As in other fields of scientific endeavor, the new paradigm must be applied, clarified, elaborated, and made more precise. But, it does provide a fundamentally different view of the reality of social organizations and can serve as the basis for major advancements in our field.

We see many exciting examples of the utilization of the new systems paradigm in the field of organization and management. Several of these have been referred to earlier (7, 13, 19, 22, 23, 24, 31, 38), and there have been many others. Burns and Stalker made substantial use of systems views in setting forth their concepts of mechanistic and organic managerial systems (8). Their studies of the characteristics of these two organization types lack precise definition of the variables and relationships, but their colleagues have used the systems approach to look at the relationship of organizations to their environment and also among the technical, structural, and behavioral characteristics within the organization (24). Chamberlain used a system view in studying enterprises and their environment, which is substantially different from traditional microeconomics (9). The emerging field of "environmental sciences" and "environmental administration" has found the systems paradigm vital.

Thus, the systems theory paradigm is being used extensively in the investigation of relationships between subsystems within organizations and in studying the environmental interfaces. But, it still has not advanced sufficiently to meet the needs. One of the major problems is that the practical need to deal with comprehensive systems of relationships is overrunning our ability to fully understand and predict these relationships. *We vitally need the systems paradigm but we are not sufficiently sophisticated to use it appropriately.* This is the dilemma. Do our current failures to fully utilize the systems paradigm suggest that we reject it and return to the older, more traditional, and time-tested paradigms? Or do we work with systems theory to make it more precise, to understand the relationships among subsystems, and to gather the informational inputs which are necessary to make the systems approach really work? We think the latter course offers the best opportunity.

Thus, we prefer to accept current limitations of systems theory, while working to reduce them and to develop more complete and sophisticated approaches for its application. We agree with Rapoport who says:

> The system approach to the study of man can be appreciated as an effort to restore meaning (in terms of intuitively grasped understanding of wholes) while adhering to the principles of *disciplined* generalizations and rigorous deduction. It is, in short, an attempt to make the study of man both scientific and meaningful (7, p. xxii).

We are sympathetic with the second part of Rapoport's comment, the need to apply the systems approach but to make disciplined generalizations and rigorous deductions. This is a vital necessity and yet a major current limitation. We do have some indication that progress (although very slow) is being made.

WHAT DO WE NEED NOW?

Everything is related to everything else—but how? General systems theory provides us with the macro paradigm for the study of social organizations. As Scott and others have pointed out, most sciences go through a macro-micro-macro cycle or sequence of emphasis (33). Traditional bureaucratic theory provided the first major macro view of organizations. Administrative management theorists concentrated on the development of macro "principles of management" which were applicable to all organizations. When these macro views seemed incomplete (unable to explain important phenomena), attention turned to the micro level—more detailed analysis of components or parts of the organization, thus the interest in human relations, technology, or structural dimensions.

The systems approach returns us to the macro level with a new paradigm. General systems theory emphasizes a very high level of abstraction. Phillips classifies it as a third-order study (29) that attempts to develop macro concepts appropriate for all types of biological, physical, and social systems.

In our view, we are now ready to move down a level of abstraction to consider second-order systems studies or midrange concepts. These will be based on general systems theory but will be more concrete and will emphasize more specific characteristics and relationships in social organizations. They will operate within the broad paradigm of systems theory but at a less abstract level.

What should we call this new midrange level of analysis? Various authors have referred to it as a "contingency view," a study of "patterns of relationships," or a search for "configurations among subsystems." Lorsch and Lawrence reflect this view:

> During the past few years there has been evident a new trend in the study of organizational phenomena. Underlying this new approach is the idea that the internal functioning of organizations must be consistent with the demands of the organization task, technology, or external environment, and the needs of its members if the organization is to be effective. Rather than searching for the panacea of the one best way to organize under all conditions, investigators have more and more tended to examine the functioning of organizations in relation to the needs of their particular members and the external pressures facing them. Basically, this approach seems to be leading to the development of a "contingency" theory of organization with the appropriate internal states and processes of the

organization contingent upon external requirements and member needs (21, p. 1).

Numerous others have stressed a similar viewpoint. Thompson suggests that the essence of administration lies in understanding basic configurations which exist between the various subsystems and with the environment. "The basic function of administration appears to be co-alignment, not merely of people (in coalitions) but of institutionalized action—of technology and task environment into a viable domain, and of organizational design and structure appropriate to it (38, p. 157).

Bringing these ideas together we can provide a more precise definition of the contingency view:

> The contingency view of organizations and their management suggests that an organization is a system composed of subsystems and delineated by identifiable boundaries from its environmental suprasystem. The contingency view seeks to understand the interrelationships within and among subsystems as well as between the organization and its environment and to define patterns of relationships or configurations of variables. It emphasizes the multivariate nature of organizations and attempts to understand how organizations operate under varying conditions and in specific circumstances. Contingency views are ultimately directed toward suggesting organizational designs and managerial systems most appropriate for specific situations.

But, it is not enough to suggest that a "contingency view" based on systems concepts of organizations and their management is more appropriate than the simplistic "principles approach." If organization theory is to advance and make contributions to managerial practice, it must define more explicitly certain patterns of relationships between organizational variables. This is the major challenge facing our field.

Just how do we go about using systems theory to develop these midrange or contingency views? We see no alternative but to engage in intensive comparative investigation of many organizations following the advice of Blau:

> A theory of organization, whatever its specific nature, and regardless of how subtle the organizational processes it takes into account, has as its central aim to establish the constellations of characteristics that develop in organizations of various kinds. Comparative studies of many organizations are necessary, not alone to test the hypotheses implied by such a theory, but also to provide a basis for initial exploration and refinement of the theory by indicating the conditions on which relationships, orginially assumed to hold

universally are contingent . . . . Systematic research on many organizations
that provides the data needed to determine the interrelationships between
several organizational features is, however, extremely rare (5, p. 332).

Various conceptual designs for the comparative study of organizations and their subsystems are emerging to help in the development
of a contingency view. We do not want to impose our model as to what
should be considered in looking for these patterns of relationships.
However, the tentative matrix shown in Figure 2 suggests this
approach. We have used as a starting point the two polar organization

FIGURE 2   Matrix of Patterns of Relationships between Organization
Types and Systems Variables

Organizational Supra- and Subsystems	Continuum of Organization Types	
	Closed/Stable/ Mechanistic	Open/Adaptive/ Organic
Environmental relationships		
General nature	Placid	Turbulent
Predictability	Certain, determinate	Uncertain, indeterminate
Boundary relationships	Relatively closed; limited to few par- ticipants (sales, pur- chasing, etc.); fixed and well-defined	Relatively open; many participants have ex- ternal relationships; varied and not clearly defined
Goals and values		
Organizational goals in general	Efficient performance, stability, maintenance	Effective problem- solving, innovation, growth
Goal set	Sincle, clear-cut	Multiple, determined by necessity to satisfy a set of constraints
Stability	Stable	Unstable
Technical		
Structural		
Psychosocial		
Managerial		

types which have been emphasized in the literature—closed/stable/ mechanistic and open/adaptive/organic.

We will consider the environment suprasystem and organizational subsystems (goals and values, technical, structural, psychosocial, and managerial) plus various dimensions or characteristics of each of these systems. By way of illustration we have indicated several specific subcategories under the Environmental Suprasystem as well as the Goals and Values subsystem. This process would have to be completed and extended to all of the subsystems. The next step would be the development of appropriate descriptive language (based on research and conceptualization) for each relevant characteristic across the continuum of organization types. For example, on the "stability" dimension for Goals and Values we would have High, Medium, and Low at appropriate places on the continuum. If the entire matrix were filled in, it is likely that we would begin to see discernible patterns of relationships among subsystems.

We do not expect this matrix to provide *the* midrange model for everyone. It is highly doubtful that we will be able to follow through with the field work investigations necessary to fill in all the squares. Nevertheless, it does illustrate a possible approach for the translation of more abstract general systems theory into an appropriate midrange model which is relevant for organization theory and management practice. Frankly, we see this as a major long-term effort on the part of many researchers, investigating a wide variety of organizations. In spite of the difficulties involved in such research, the endeavor has practical significance. Sophistication in the study of organizations will come when we have a more complete understanding of organizations as total systems (configurations of subsystems) so that we can prescribe more appropriate organizational designs and managerial systems. Ultimately, organization theory should serve as the foundation for more effective management practice.

APPLICATION OF SYSTEMS CONCEPTS TO MANAGEMENT PRACTICE

The study of organizations is an applied science because the resulting knowledge is relevant to problem-solving in on-going institutions. Contributions to organization theory come from many sources. Deductive and inductive research in a variety of disciplines provide a theoretical base of propositions which are useful for understanding organizations and for managing them. Experience gained in management practice is also an important input to organization theory. In short, management is based on the body of knowledge generated by practical experience *and* eclectic scientific research concerning organizations. The body of knowledge developed through theory and research should be translatable into more effective organizational design and managerial practices.

Do systems concepts and contingency views provide a panacea for solving problems in organizations? The answer is an emphatic *no*; this approach does not provide "ten easy steps" to success in management. Such cookbook approaches, while seemingly applicable and easy to grasp, are usually shortsighted, narrow in perspective, and superficial—in short, unrealistic. Fundamental ideas, such as systems concepts and contingency views, are more difficult to comprehend. However, they facilitate more thorough understanding of complex situations and increase the likelihood of appropriate action.

It is important to recognize that many managers have used and will continue to use a systems approach and contingency views intuitively and implicitly. Without much knowledge of the underlying body of organization theory, they have an intuitive "sense of the situation," are flexible diagnosticians, and adjust their actions and decisions accordingly. Thus, systems concepts and contingency views are not new. However, if this approach to organization theory and management practice can be made more explicit, we can facilitate better management and more effective organizations.

Practicing managers in business firms, hospitals, and government agencies continue to function on a day-to-day basis. Therefore, they must use whatever theory is available, they cannot wait for the *ultimate* body of knowledge (there is none!). Practitioners should be included in the search for new knowledge because they control access to an essential ingredient—organizational data—and they are the ones who ultimately put the theory to the test. Mutual understanding among managers, teachers, and researchers will facilitate the development of a relevant body of knowledge.

Simultaneously with the refinement of the body of knowledge, a concerted effort should be directed toward applying what we do know. We need ways of making systems and contingency views more usable. Without oversimplification, we need some relevant guidelines for practicing managers.

The general tenor of the contingency view is somewhere between simplistic, specific principles and complex, vague notions. It is a midrange concept which recognizes the complexity involved in managing modern organizations but uses patterns of relationships and/or configurations of subsystems in order to facilitate improved practice. The art of management depends on a reasonable success rate for actions in a probabilistic environment. Our hope is that systems concepts and contingency views, while continually being refined by scientists/researchers/theorists, will also be made more applicable.

Notes

1. An entire article could be devoted to a discussion of ingenious ways in which the term "systems approach" has been used in the literature pertinent to organization theory and management practice.

References

1. Ackoff, Russell L., "Towards a System of Systems Concepts," *Management Science (July 1971)*.
2. Back, Kurt W., "Biological Models of Social Change," *American Sociological Review* (August 1971).
3. Barnard, Chester I., *The Functions of the Executive* (Cambridge, Mass.: Harvard University Press, 1938).
4. Berrien, F. Kenneth, *General and Social Systems* (New Brunswick, N.J.: Rutgers University Press, 1968).
5. Blau, Peter M., "The Comparative Study of Organizations," *Industrial and Labor Relations Review* (April 1965).
6. Boulding, Kenneth E., "General Systems Theory: The Skeleton of Science," *Management Science* (April 1956).
7. Buckley, Walter, ed., *Modern Systems Research for the Behavioral Scientist* (Chicago: Aldine Publishing Company, 1968).
8. Burns, Tom and G. M. Stalker,*The Management of Innovation* (London: Tavistock Publications, 1961).
9. Chamberlain, Neil W., *Enterprise and Environment: The Firm in Time and Place* (New York: McGraw-Hill Book Company, 1968).
10. Churchman, C. West, *The Systems Approach* (New York: Dell Publishing Company, Inc., 1968).
11. DeGreene, Kenyon, ed., *Systems Psychology* (New York: McGraw-Hill Book Company, 1970).
12. Deutsch, Karl W., "Toward a Cybernetic Model of Man and Society," in Walter Buckley, ed., *Modern Systems Research for the Behavioral Scientist* (Chicago: Aldine Publishing Company, 1968).
13. Easton, David, *A Systems Analysis of Political Life* (New York: John Wiley & Sons, Inc., 1965).
14. Emery, F. E. and E. L. Trist, "Socio-technical Systems," in C. West Churchman and Michele Verhulst, eds., *Management Sciences: Models and Techniques* (New York: Pergamon Press, 1960).
15. Emshoff, James R., *Analysis of Behavioral Systems* (New York: The Macmillan Company, 1971).

16. Gross, Bertram M., "The Coming General Systems Models of Social Systems," *Human Relations* (November 1967).
17. Hall, A. D. and R. E. Eagen, "Definition of System," *General Systems, Yearbook for the Society for the Advancement of General Systems Theory*, Vol 1 (1956).
18. Kast, Fremont E. and James E. Rosenzweig, *Organization and Management Theory: A Systems Approach* (New York: McGraw-Hill Book Company, 1970).
19. Katz, Daniel and Robert L. Kahn, *The Social Psychology of Organizations* (New York: John Wiley & Sons, Inc., 1966).
20. Kuhn Thomas S., *The Structure of Scientific Revolutions* (Chicago: University of Chicago Press, 1962).
21. Lorsch, Jay W. and Paul R. Lawrence, *Studies in Organizational Design* (Homewood, Illinois: Irwin-Dorsey, 1970).
22. Litterer, Joseph A., *Organizaions: Structure and Behavior,* Vol 1 (New York: John Wiley & Sons, Inc., 1969).
23. _____, *Organizations: Systems, Control and Adaptation,* Vol 2 (New York: John Wiley & Sons, Inc., 1969).
24. Miller, E. J. and A. K. Rice, *Systems of Organizations* (London: Tavistock Publications, 1967).
25. Miller, James G., "Living Systems: Basic Concepts," *Behavioral Science* (July 1965).
26. Miller, Robert F., "The New Science of Administration in the USSR," *Administrative Science Quarterly* (September 1971).
27. Murray, Henry A., "Preparation for the Scaffold of a Comprehensive System," in Sigmund Koch, ed., *Psychology: A Study of a Science,* Vol 3 (New York: McGraw-Hill Book Company, 1959).
28. Parsons, Talcott, *The Social System* (New York: The Free Press of Glencoe, 1951).
29. Phillips, D. C., "Systems Theory—A Discredited Philosophy," in Peter P. Schoderbek, *Management Systems* (New York: John Wiley & Sons, Inc., 1971).
30. Rapoport, Anatol and William J. Horvath, "Thoughts on Organization Theory," in Walter Buckley, ed., *Modern Systems Research for the Behavioral Scientist* (Chicago: Aldine Publishing Company, 1968).
31. Rice, A. K., *The Modern University* (London: Tavistock Publications, 1970).
32. Schein, Edgar, *Organizational Psychology,* rev. ed. (Englewood Cliffs, New Jersey: Prentice-Hall, Inc., 1970).
33. Scott, William G., "Organization Theory: An Overview and an Appraisal," *Academy of Management Journal* (April 1961).
34. Silverman, David, *The Theory of Organizations* (New York: Basic Books, Inc., 1971).
35. Simon, Herbert A., "The Architecture of Complexity," in Joseph A. Literer, *Organizations: Systems, Control and Adaptation,* Vol 2 (New York: John Wiley & Sons, Inc., 1969).

36. Springer, Michael, "Social Indicators, Reports, and Accounts: Toward the Management of Society," *The Annals of the American Academy of Political and Social Science (March 1970)*.
37. Terreberry, Shirley, "The Evolution of Organizational Environments," *Administrative Science Quarterly* (March 1968).
38. Thompson, James D., *Organizations in Action* (New York: McGraw-Hill Book Company, 1967).
39. von Bertalanffy, Ludwig, *General System Theory* (New York: George Braziller, 1968).
40. _____, "The Theory of Open Systems in Physics and Biology," *Science* (January 13, 1950).
41. Yuchtman, Ephraim and Stanley E. Seashore, "A System Resource Approach to Organizational Effectiveness," *American Sociological Review* (December 1967).

The Library As an Open System

Maurice P. Marchant

THE THEORY

Systems theory is implicit in both scientific management and participative management. Both recognize the concept of organization as the interlinking of a series of causal relationships, and both are concerned with analyzing and simplifying them so as to optimize organizational efficiency and effectiveness.

The open system of organizations goes somewhat further, however, than scientific management. Generalized from the Likert theory of participative management, it itemizes several subsystems with varying characteristics, including the production, supportive, maintenance, adaptive, and managerial subsystems.[1] The open system recognizes a cyclical character in organizational behavior. Within its construct, continuing cycles of production occur which are related to the broader environment. A major relationship is the processing of production and informational inputs into some product (or service) which can be utilized by the environment and whose acceptance triggers the infusion of new inputs.

Specialized structures such as maintenance and adaptive subsystems are developed to give support to the organization's well-being. Maintenance activities are directed not at the end product but at the equipment for getting the work done. Usually, this equipment consists of patterned human behavior, and the effectiveness of maintenance activities can be measured in terms of the extent to which personnel are tied into the system as functioning parts. Adaptive subsystems are concerned with sensing relevant changes in the environment, translating the meaning of those changes for the organization, and

Maurice P. Marchant, "The Library as an Open System," in *Participative Management in Academic Libraries* (Greenwood Press, Westport, CT, 1976), pp. 13–28. Reprinted by permission of the publisher.

designing new patterns of behavior. While neither of these subsystems is part of the production subsystem, their effectiveness can be expected to affect end-product performance measurements.

Two concepts require special emphasis. The first is that the value of a product is established in the environment and manifested in terms of the input for which it is traded. Internal efficiency is all well and good, but its usefulness really depends on its effect on the value the environment places on the product exported. The second concept is that organizational viability depends upon the ratio of input to output. If the product has less value than the cost expended on its production, the organization is running down. Another way to perceive this concept is in terms of the ratio between the values of the input acquired in exchange for a product and the input required in producing the product. In an open system, the relationship between the organization and its environment is extremely important.

All organizations that require input from outside themselves are open. However, the extent of that openness varies and, to some degree, can be manipulated by the organization. A library can open or close boundaries, for example, depending on the limits they place as regards the clientele they are willing to serve or the sources of service or materials with which they deal. However, the extent to which boundaries, can be controlled by the organization varies. A university library may have considerably more control over its choice of book jobbers than over it relations with the university administration. Some parts of an organization may be more open than others. Public service areas of the library are at the boundary with its clients and acquisitions interact with jobbers and other suppliers, but cataloging is rather well insulated.

One failing of past theories on organizational administration has been to underemphasize or ignore the importance of environmental factors and to treat the organization as a closed system. In such cases, the organization concentrates on internal functions as if they were independent of environmental changes. Goal displacement tends to occur by which means to the end are treated as ends in themselves. Thus, emphasis on collection development rests with the efficiency of the acquisitions and cataloging processes without consideration of its effect on user satisfaction. This narrow emphasis on subprocesses, known as reductivism, can result in inattention to the more important matter of the library's primary objectives. It may even produce behavioral patterns that inhibit the library's service goals. In addition, it may lead to the failure to recognize that more than one way is open to a given outcome. These failings are likely to result in a decline in input from a dissatisfied environment.

Another failing caused by viewing an organization as a closed system is the assumption that irregularities in organizational functions resulting from environmental influences are error variances. The open system theory maintains that environmental influences are not sources of error variance. Rather, adaptation to a changing environment is understood to be an integral part of organizational control. One cannot understand a system without recognizing its place within its environment, and this recognition requires systematic acquistion and analysis of appropriate feedback information for the purposes of readjustment and successful planning.

THE MODERN LIBRARY AS AN OPEN SYSTEM

It would be presumptuous to suggest that this chapter does more than describe in a cursory and tentative way the nature of the academic library as an open system. Research toward that end is only fragmentary and in its beginning stages. Part of the purpose for discussing the matter here is to provide a point of departure for future research. An equally important purpose is to attempt to change the librarians' perspectives regarding the organizational behavior of their libraries, so that they will place a greater emphasis on external relationships, and to provide a theoretical model for future control of administrative behavior.

Librarians have historically paid inadequate attention to environmental factors, though there has been some improvement during the past two decades. Library directors reflect this historical weakness when they deny that political and community contacts are part of their professional roles. The librarians' recent performance is better regarding the study of community library and information needs and interests, even searching for ways of reaching nonuser groups. Even so, program planning in libraries especially long-range planning, has much room for improvement. Recognition of the library as an open system, of the extent and character of its openness, and of the interrelationships between the library and relevant aspects of its environment provides libraries and librarians with greater control over their own future. Lack of such appropriate insight weakens the library as a community force and places it at the mercy of forces over which it has little influence.

The open system theory, as described by Katz and Kahn, recognizes a cyclical character in organizational behavior. Within its construct, continuing cycles of production occur which are related to the broader environment. The openness to a system varies, depending on the extent of that relationship.[2] A major relationship is the processing of production inputs, which results in some outcome that can be utilized by the environment and whose use triggers acquisition of new inputs. The library acquires books, processes them, and makes them available for use by its patrons. In response, the environment provides more books, staff, and other needs.

The stability or recurrence of activities is measurable in terms of energy[3] flow. The open system theory indentifies social systems and determines their functions and objectives by tracing the pattern of energy exchange or activity of people as it results in some output (or product) and by ascertaining how the output is translated into energy which reactivates the pattern. This cyclical effect provides the insight by which a social structure can be defined as a series of interrelated events rather than the static structure characterized by an organization chart.

The open system approach first identifies and maps the energy cycle of input-throughput-output and renewed input that characterizes the organizational pattern. In addition, open systems are characterized by the following elements: negative entropy, feedback, a steady state, differentiation, and equifinality.

Production Cycle

The input-throughput-output cycle is the basic production cycle. Energy is injected into a system as personnel, raw materials, and information; it is then transformed into a product and exported into the environment. In response to the output, elements within the environment reenergize the system to begin a new cycle.

Inputs

In an academic library, the major inputs are the staff, collection, quarters, furniture, equipment, and supplies. Input is usually determined primarily by the institution's administration and board of control through their approval of the library budget. Less apparent as input but of considerable importance are the limits placed on the delegation of authority and responsibility for planning and operating the library.

The flexibility delegated to the library staff in trading the budget for inputs varies widely. Generally, the library recruits its own staff within a salary schedule and general staff and budgetary limitations imposed by the institutional administration. It shares with the faculty, to varying degrees, the task of developing the collection. Major library construction and renovation projects are nearly always budgeted separately and are not directly competitive with the library's operational budget, although an expansion can be expected generally to lead to an increase in operational inputs. Moreover, the nature of a facility is likely to impose conditions that dictate how the library's funding must be allocated. If the library is physically decentralized so that it has many small branch libraries scattered around the campus, there will be higher personnel costs and a greater duplication of books than will be the case in a highly centralized system.

Information concerning many different matters comes into the library from a variety of sources. Data on quality of service are fed in by students, faculty, the library advisory committee, and, occasionally, university administration. The data are submitted largely to public service librarians but also directly to top management. Collection development data are provided by the publishing industry, review media, the library world, faculty, student, and others. Administrative coordination data from the university administration comes largely to top management.

Throughputs

Throughput involves the transformation of energy and information received as input into an exportable product. Activities in a library are divided broadly into three areas: technical processes, public services, and administration.

The major elements of technical processing are acquisitions, cataloging and classification, and collection maintenance. Its most visible elements are the catalog and the collection. Its activities are generally somewhat isolated from the system's boundaries and are therefore not easily observed. The most important boundaries are with book dealers, jobbers, subscription agencies, other material suppliers, and centralized cataloging sources.

Public services include circulation routines, reference services, reader's advisory services, and direct aid in using the library. They are characterized by direct interaction between staff members and users.

Administration is involved in planning, organizing, motivating, and controlling activities. Boundaries with this group are often more filtered and formalized than with technical processes and public services. While provision for access may be possible for users, adminstrative relations are more frequent and meaningful with university administrators, committees, and faculty assigned to represent departments of instruction. Public relations and fund-raising activities are also centered largely at this level, and the extent of involvement varies widely among libraries.

The relationship of the patron to technical processes and public services, respectively, is quite different. The patron only infrequently comes in contact with technical processing personnel, who work primarily behind the scenes. But the patron reacts to the activities of technical processing whenever he uses the catalog or the collection, since technical processing is responsible for acquiring materials, giving order to the collection, and developing information retrieval mechanisms. In large measure, technical processing gives the library its characteristics of self-service. On the other hand, public services are provided to enrich the self-service aspects with individualized service. The very nature of the public services-patron interaction brings a new set of factors to bear, namely, the librarian's personality. Whereas technical processing services are evaluated according to the end result of their activities, public services are also evaluated according to the on-going procedures. The work of public services with users consists of two facets: question-negotiation for the purpose of discovering the nature of the user's informational need and structuring of a search strategy to satisfy the need.[4] Beyond competence in the use of reference materials, psychological factors such as are injected by a pleasant smile and a desire to serve have values independent of the library's success in satisfying the patron's initial need. As a result, public services offer librarians greater opportunity to affect public attitudes toward librarians as individuals and librarianship as a profession than do technical processing activities, which are more readily evaluated as the impersonal character of the library.

Outputs

From the patron's point of view library services consist of circulation for home use, use of materials within the library, instruction and help in the use of the library, answers to reference questions, and literature research services. Another conceptual framework might consider the change the patron undergoes as a result of his use of the library. The more pronounced effects of reading have been itemized as (1) the instrumental effect (e.g., fuller knowledge of a practical problem and greater competence to deal with it), (2) the prestige effect (e.g., relief of inferiority feelings by reading what increases self-approval), (3) the reinforcement effect (e.g., reinforcement of an attitude or conversion to another attitude toward controversial issues), (4) the aesthetic effect (e.g., obtaining aesthetic experience from specimens of literary art), and (5) the respite effect (e.g., finding relief from tensions by reading whatever offers pleasant distraction).[5] These effects are also valid for the other media that libraries provide, such as recordings, pictures, and films.

In the final analysis, perhaps the best measures of library output are in terms of the satisfaction and dissatisfaction generated in library use. Included are frustration and anger resulting from interactions with library personnel and processes and from difficulties in locating needed materials and information. Satisfaction and dissatisfaction are not simply complementary, however. The professor who never uses the library likely has little feeling toward it one way or the other. The patron who uses it extensively and has a high need for its services can be expected to experience both feelings. Adequate appraisal of these matters requires more than the subjective evaluation of informally stated comments. As in other service organizations, good service is assumed; and a breakdown in service is more likely to elicit patron reaction than is continuing high quality service.[6]

Organizations attempt to develop outputs for the purpose of fulfilling objectives, be they formally approved or simply insinuated. Libraries seldom have formally established objectives. Those which exist are often too general for the development of behavior criteria. Moreover, outputs are sometimes unplanned by-products. Outputs must be determined by an appraisal of interactions at the boundaries.

Systems As Cycles of Events

The open system model offers an approach to evaluation of output by relating it to input. In this concept, an output's value is measured according to its ability to reenergize the system.

In a profit-making organization, this cycle is direct and immediate. A toy manufacturer, for example, sells his product and uses the funds to buy raw materials, pay his workers, and keep his equipment in good condition. The relationship between income and cost becomes his evaluative criterion. If the cost of a given toy is greater than the income it produces, the manufacturer must either correct the ratio, cover the loss by surpluses from other operations, or cease production of that toy. If he continues production despite continued losses, he does so because of intrinsic values not accepted by the environment or out of ignorance. Were a general imbalance throughout the company to persist, the company would go broke or, in the language of the open system, would "run down."

Input is improved in two ways. One is to change the internal processes so as to improve the output such that it has greater exchange value in the environment. The other is to change the environment's evaluation of the current product so as to enhance its value.

The first type might involve changes in input as well as the processes. For example, an academic library may decide that its input might be increased by improving reader's advisory service to faculty. The library staff may have observed that some of the faculty are having considerable difficulty locating research materials because they lack skill in using specialized indexing services or are unaware of their existence. As a result, the library may institute a program of direct service to faculty to help them map out search strategies and to help them with the search. The library might expect that the faculty would sufficiently value such a service to support its request for increased input from the administration. If the increase in resultant support is as great as the cost of supplying it, the change is effective. But placing the service in operation might require changes in resource commitment. If the current staff is not adequate to provide the new service, the new emphasis may require a reallocation of energy involving a retrenchment in other activities. For example, book purchases might be reduced or cataloging might be simplified, and these changes might be expected to affect output.

Change in the output calls for manipulation of the organization. Change in the environment's perception of a product's value requires manipulation of the environment, essentially through public relations. A library changes the acceptance of its service in a variety of ways. One is by making displays. A more important and more direct method is through reports directed at the university administration. An example might be the presentation of a planning paper recommending an enriched program of direct service to faculty, describing its operation, estimating the cost, and requesting additional funding to set it in motion. This approach emphasizes satisfaction with antic-ipated services.

Increased input cannot be expected unless a change can be made in the perceived value of some output. Such a change might occur without planning for it, but unplanned improvement is hardly reliable.

Academic libraries, as open systems, follow these same patterns, but the relationships are not readily determined, and little has been done to map the energy exchange. Moreover, the exchange is sometimes indirect and difficult to anticipate and sometimes involves a long time lag. Most library funding is approved annually by the university administration and board of trustees, a group that probably makes little direct use of the library. Yet, the open system affirms that the library's budget is acquired in exchange for the library's products. To the extent that librarians understand the exchange rates of the library's products, the exchange patterns, and the cost of production, they should be able to make decisions on which outputs to emphasize and which to cancel.

The difficulty in ability to anticipate these processes in libraries has resulted in an emphasis on internal operational efficiency, based on the assumption that input is fixed and only mildly affected by performance, and on evaluations which are more related to inputs than to outputs.

Perhaps the easiest way to study the energy trail is to go backward. The library is given a budget, approved by the institution's administration and governing board, which the library may exchange for inputs of staff, collection, equipment, materials, and so forth. The freedom available to the library in making this transfer is controlled by a variety of factors. The budget may be approved by category (line item), such that transfers from one category to another are not allowed or may be allowed only if approved at a level higher than the library administration. Such categories might be very specific or fairly broad. For example, a line item might cover one specific professional position or it might cover all salaried personnel. It might cover expenditures for all books or only books on philosophy. These restrictions also constitute input and reflect the level of trust in which the library's personnel are held. Funds from gifts and endowments often must be used for specific purposes because of a sense of distrust. The receipt of the gift may simultaneously reflect the donor's sense of satisfaction and dissatisfaction with the library.

Most library operating funds come from institutional general funds. Assuming that the governing board approves its administrative staff's recommendations for budget allocations, the adminstration must be acknowledged as the decision-makers. But the president and his top advisors are not free agents. It would be unusual to discover a president who determines the library budget on the basis of his personal observations of library services and needs. His decision is affected by a variety of pressures.

Two influences on the president's decision are the library budget request and annual report received from the library director. These documents should tell the administration what the past level and cost of service has been, and they should provide projected service levels and costs. The quality of planning evidenced in these reports may have substantial effect on the final budget allocation.

Accreditation reports and standards also affect institutional adminstrative decisions on the library. Library directors often find them convenient supporting documents for budget increase requests because accreditation teams seek out inadequacies, many of which can be attributed to inadequate funds.

The director and his staff, as they meet in committee or faculty meetings and at informal gatherings, seek other means to influence the university administration. These possibilities are too numerous to discuss in detail. A particularly important possibility which must be mentioned here is the indirect influence of the staff on the administration by way of the faculty. The effect on the administration of good library staff-faculty relations has not been studied systematically but is probably an important factor in determining library input. One rationale often used to justify faculty status for librarians is that it would improve communications with faculty, thereby resulting in more favorable faculty attitudes and behavior toward the library as an instrument of education. The institution might be more inclined to give librarians faculty status if it resulted in better education and research or, at a more immediate level, in better library service.

Most academic library directors report to the vice-president for academic affairs or a comparable officer rather than directly to the president. This same officer receives budget requests from the instructional departments, schools, and colleges and must make his recommendations on the basis of relative need. The president, in setting the library budget, must rely heavily on his evaluation. This officer is even more likely than the president to have a faculty background and faculty orientation. He hears about the library through academic deans, department heads, friends among the faculty, and possibly an occasional student. They may advise him that the collection is deficient in their areas of interest, that the building is uncomfortable, crowded, remote from their offices and laboratories, or not open long enough in the evenings. They may even have occasional words of praise, but largely their feedback will be complaint-oriented.

An additional influence on the officer will be his own limited experience in interacting with the library. Most of this experience will be retrospective, in the form of memories of libraries he knew as a professor and student, since as an administrator he is not likely to find much time or incentive to use the library. The attitudes he developed toward the library in earlier times may affect his response to the library's present requests.

Competitive factors are also important. Total institutional requests can always be expected to outrun available funds. Faculty salaries need to be improved; course offerings need to be expanded; maintenance of buildings and grounds are less than desirable; and the library is too small to seat the expanded student body. The administration must finally balance its allocation of available funds as best it can in response to the overall objectives of the institution and the relevant information received. In making the final decision, the president and his advisors will act to minimize the stress placed upon them.[7]

It would be wrong to suggest that library inputs are provided as payments for past services rendered. At least, this situation does not occur on a conscious level. Library funding is provided in anticipation of future services. In this respect, libraries and some other nonprofit organizations are different from profit-making organizations. An important influence in determining library inputs is the magnitude of need for services which the institution expects the library to satisfy. Another is inertia. An increase in library funding is not likely to occur without some measure of dissatisfaction with past performance. The increase will also require some measure of assurance that improvement will result. The use of performance budgeting has grown partially out of the feeling that it helps satisfy the need for this assurance.

Negative Entropy

All forms of organization tend to resist the movement toward disorganization and death. One procedure of resistance is to store a surplus that may be called upon during a lean period. In a library, the surplus is seen mainly as buildings, equipment, the collection, and endowment. An academic library is not likely to be allowed to run down as long as the institution survives, at least at present. Its inputs may drop to low levels, however, so that its service is of low quality. In addition, dissatisfaction with activities may result in changes in personnel or in forced reorganization.

During periods of recession, most libraries cut back on their collection development and attempt to get along on whatever is already available. While this expediency might work temporarily, it is a short-range one. The dynamic force in the collection is information, and information in most disciplines appears to have a half-life. Therefore, the collection as a whole loses value fairly rapidly unless it is energized continuously by new inputs. Moreover, besides the relatively greater value of newly packaged information, it appears to be a prime motivator in encouraging users to come to the library where, once there, they find use for the older materials as well as the new.

Information Input, Negative Feedback, and the
Coding Process

Some inputs are informative and signal the structure regarding the environment and its own functioning in relation to the environment. Negative feedback refers to information on the efficiency and effectiveness of organizational behavior, and its purpose is to identify those areas that need readjustment to get it back on course. It occurs when the librarian discovers that a patron cannot find the book he requires, and its appropriate use in this case is to change library behavior in such a way as to expedite patron retrieval of the needed book. The lack of corrective devices eventually leads to termination of the system. However, since a university library is part of a larger organization, the lack of correction is more likely to lead to a change in personnel, which is a corrective device of the university. Some libraries that adapt poorly to their environments appear to exist in a semistate of suspended animation wherein few patrons frequent them, funding is poor, and cost in terms of service rendered is high. Disfunction can occur despite adequate information. The selective mechanism by which a system accepts or rejects feedback information and translates it is known as coding.

The development of an information system for collecting and analyzing pertinent data is related to the quality of planning and varies widely between libraries. Formal library planning is in need of improvement, and one of its weaknesses is inadequate provision for feedback on which to base readjustment. A more prevalent weakness is the reliance on informal planning and *ad hoc* decision-making.[8]

The upward communication of information, especially from public services personnel at the library's boundaries, to top management is particularly important in making wise adjustments and good plans. However, the quality of upward communications is strongly affected by the magnitude of threat resulting from the library's managerial style.

The Steady State and Dynamic Homeostasis

Importation of sufficient energy to arrest entropy produces a steady state. The continual flow of energy through the system, into the environment, and back to the system differentiates this from a true equilibrium, which is static. The steady state is characterized by the ratio of the energy exchange, the relation of the parts, and the character of the system. Thus, a library in a steady state retains the same services at the same level operating in the same way. The basic principle is to preserve the character of the system rather than the outward behavioral manifestations. Toward this end, the library will attempt to import more energy than is required for export and will store the surplus against future lean times or heavier than normal demands. Libraries will expand acquisitions, enrich present services, initiate services of secondary importance, extend service hours, acquire equipment and furniture the purchase of which could be put off, and initiate supportive activities. Thus, the steady state becomes a matter of preserving the character of the system through growth and expansion.

Many libraries have large backlogs of uncataloged books as a result of an imbalance between book and personnel funds. Most librarians are aware of the harm occurring from long waits between publication date and availability of books to patrons and would like to erase their backlogs. Were they able to do so, they would probably create another imbalance for themselves, as a result of an uneven acquistions rate throughout the year. High priority on speed of processing is likely to result in a lowering of efficiency because of overstaffing to take care of peak periods. The library therefore tends to retain a measure of backlog to provide for a steady flow of work to the catalog department.

A measure of instability occurs as a result of changes in patron use of the library. Term paper assignments cause heavy demand for service toward the end of the terms. While variation in demand during the day can be satisfied by staffing to meet that changing condition, the library finds itself hard pressed to add personnel to public services at peak periods during the term or year. Consequently, the quality of service tends to vary with pressure for service. Unfortunately, those patrons who need custom service most are likely to show up when demand for service is highest and service is being rationed.

A fluctuating book budget causes a particularly great hardship on academic libraries that have high serials acquisitions rates and are heavily involved in standing order or gathering plans. Libraries feel breaks in serial runs particularly severely and are likely to expend time and money later trying to fill them in when funds are more plentiful. Acquiring the materials as they are published is more efficient and more sure. Therefore, a cut in book funds usually has a greater effect on the purchase of monographs than serials. Besides, once an order for a serial has been placed, it normally comes automatically until the process has been adjusted. To keep a monograph from coming requires only that it not be ordered, unless it is part of a standing order or gathering plan. The materials hardest hit by a decline in the book budget are generally those which faculty and librarians consciously and specifically choose as appropriate to institutional needs.

It is apparent that instability is particularly hard on libraries, and its effect is out of proportion to the total library budget.

Differentiation

Open systems also tend to differentiate and elaborate, replacing general patterns by more specialized functions. Thus, libraries separate out technical processing and establish divisional or departmental collections. As the total workload grows, individual librarians are assigned increasingly narrow areas of responsibility and are chosen because of training, education, or experience in that special area.

The supportive subsystems acquire specialized staffs. The head librarian's involvement at the circulation and reference desks gives way to managerial duties. A personnel office is established to support the maintenance functions. And, as has occurred more recently, systems analysts and planning budget officers are added to aid the administration in planning, which is an adaptive function.

Equifinality

A system can reach the same final state from differing initial conditions and by a variety of paths. Similarly functioning research libraries of today have originated in support of institutions as diverse as theological seminaries, land grant colleges, private liberal arts colleges, state universities, and teachers' colleges.

SUMMARY

The open system approach to the study of libraries, in common with the general systems approach, emphasizes the dynamic nature of interrelationships and organizational behavior. It goes beyond the causal paths that occur internally within the library and studies the relationship of the library to its environment. That environment for academic libraries is largely the college or university of which it is a part, but is also includes forces such as the library world, the publishing industry, the federal government, and learned and professional societies. Emphasis on the cycles of input, transformation, output, and repeated input highlights the library's dependency on its environment and suggests that the proper orientation from which to evaluate library functions is their effect on the environment and the environment's effect on them. The past tendency has been to overconcentrate on efficiency of internal functions and to fail to develop adequate feedback processes by which libraries can adjust appropriately to changing environmental conditions.

References

1. Daniel Katz and Robert L. Kahn, *The Social Psychology of Organizations* (New York: Wiley, 1966). This section relies especially on Chapter 2, pp. 14-29.
2. Ibid.
3. The term *energy* as used here and following in discussing the nature of the open system does not have the same precision as it does in physics and chemistry. It was chosen because it carries a sense of dynamism and is more general than other terms that might have been used. It includes the concept of activity, but it also is concerned with potential activities and activities that previously resulted in a current state. Energy comes in multiple forms, including people and materials, as well as such standard forms as electricity and heat.
4. Robert S. Taylor, "Question-Negotiation and Information Seeking in Libraries," *College & Research Libraries* 29 (May 1968): 178-194.
5. Douglas Waples, et al., *What Reading Does to People* (Chicago: University of Chicage Press, 1940), p. 13.
6. J. Douglas Brown, *The Liberal University; an Institutional Analysis* (New York: McGraw-Hill, 1969), p. 65.
7. Robert L. Kahn, et al., *Organizational Stress: Studies in Role Conflict and Ambiguity* (New York: Wiley, 1964).

8. Robert E. Kemper, "Strategic Planning for Library Systems" (DBA dissertation, University of Washington, Seattle, 1967.) See also Booz, Allen & Hamilton Inc., *Problems in University Library Management* (Washington, D.C.: Association of Research Libraries, 1970).

A Behavioral Theory of Organizational Objectives

R. M. Cyert and James G. March

O RGANIZATIONS make decisions. They make decisions in the same sense in which individuals make decisions: The organization as a whole behaves as though there existed a central coordination and control system capable of directing the behavior of the members of the organization sufficiently to allow the meaningful imputation of purpose to the total system. Because the central nervous system of most organizations appears to be somewhat different from that of the individual system, we are understandably cautious about viewing organization decision making in quite the same terms as those applied to individual choice. Nevertheless, organizational choice is a legitimate and important focus of research attention.

As in theories of individual choice, theories of organizational decision making fall into two broad classes. Normative theorists—particularly economic theorists of the firm—have been dedicated to the improvement of the rationality of organizational choice. Recent developments in the application of mathematics to the solution of economic decision-problems are fully and effectively in such a tradition (Cooper, Hitch, Baumol, Shubik, Schelling, Valavanis, and Ellsberg, 1958). The empirical theory of organizational decision making has a much more checkered tradition and is considerably less well-developed (March and Simon, 1958).

The present efforts to develop a behavioral theory of organizational decision making represent attempts to overcome the disparity between the importance of decision making in organizations and our understanding of how, in fact, such decisions are made. The research as a whole, as well as that part of it discussed below, is based on three initial commitments. The first of these is to develop an explicitly

Cyert, R.M. and James G. March, "A Behavioral Theory of Organizational Objectives," in *Modern Organizational Theory*, edited by Mason Haire, pp. 79-90 by John Wiley and Sons, Inc., publishers. Reprinted by permission of John Wiley and Sons, Inc.

empirical theory rather than a normative one. Our interest is in understanding how complex organizations make decisions, not how they ought to do so. Without denying the importance of normative theory, we are convinced that the major current needs are for empirical knowledge.

The second commitment is to focus on the classic problems long explored in economic theory—pricing, resource allocation, and capital investment. This commitment is intended to overcome some difficulties with existing organization theory. By introducing organizational propositions into models of rather complex systems, we are driven to increase the precision of the propositions considerably. At present, anyone taking existing organization theory as a base for predicting behavior within organizations finds that he can make a number of rather important predictions of the general form: If x varies, y will vary. Only rarely will he find either the parameters of the functions or more elaborate predictions for situations in which the *ceteris paribus* assumptions are not met.

The third commitment is to approximate in the theory the process by which decisions are made by organizations. This commitment to a process-oriented theory is not new. It has typified many organization theorists in the past (Marshall, 1919; Weber, 1947). The sentiment that one should substitute observation for assumption whenever possible seems, a priori, reasonable. Traditionally, the major dilemma in organization theory has been between putting into the theory all the features of organizations we think are relevant and thereby making the theory unmanageable, or pruning the model down to a simple system, thereby making it unrealistic. So long as we to deal primarily with classical mathematics, there was, in fact, little we could do. With the advent of the computer and the use of simulation, we have a methodology that will permit us to expand considerably the emphasis on actual process without losing the predictive precision essential to testing (Cyert and March, 1959).

In models currently being developed there are four major subsystems. Since they operate more or less independently, it is possible to conceive them as the four basic subtheories required for a behavioral theory of organizational decision making: first, the theory of organizational objectives; second, the theory of organizational expectations; third, the theory of organizational choice; fourth, the theory of organizational implementation. In this paper we discuss the first of these only, the theory of organizational objectives.

THE ORGANIZATION AS A COALITION

Let us conceive the organization as a coalition. It is a coalition of individuals, some of them organized into subcoalitions. In the business organization, one immediately thinks of such coalition members as managers, workers, stockholders, suppliers, customers, lawyers, tax collectors, etc. In the governmental organization, one thinks of such members as administrators, workers, appointive officials, elective officials, legislators, judges, clientele, etc. In the voluntary charitable organization, one thinks of paid functionaries, volunteers, donors, donees, etc.

This view of an organization as a coalition suggests, of course, several different recent treatments of organization theory in which a similar basic position is adopted: in particular, inducements-contributions theory (Barnard, 1938; Simon, 1947), theory of games (von Neumann and Morgenstern, 1947), and theory of teams (Marschak, 1959). Each of these theories is substantially equivalent on this score. Each specifies:

1. That organizations include individual participants with (at least potentially) widely varying preference orderings.
2. That through bargaining and side payments the participants in the organization enter into a coalition agreement for purposes of the game. This agreement specifies a joint preference ordering (or organizational objective) for the coalition.
3. That thereafter the coalition can be treated as a single strategist, entrepreneur, or what have you.

Such a formulation permits us to move immediately to modern decision theory, which has been an important part of recent developments in normative organization theory. In our view, however, a joint preference ordering is not a particularly good description of actual organization goals. Studies of organizational objectives suggest that to the extent to which there is agreement on objectives, it is agreement on highly ambiguous goals (Truman, 1951; Kaplan, Dirlam, and Lanzillotti, 1958). Such agreement is undoubtedly important to choice within the organization, but it is a far cry from a clear preference ordering. The studies suggest further that behind this agreement on rather vague objectives there is considerable disagreement and uncertainty about subgoals; that organizations appear to be pursuing one goal at one time and another (partially inconsistent) goal at another; and that different parts of the organization appear to be pursuing different goals at the same time (Kaplan, Dirlam, and Lanzillotti, 1958; Selznick, 1949). Finally, the studies suggest that most organization objectives take the form of an aspiration level rather than an imperative to "maximize" or minimize," and that the aspiration level changes in response to experience. (Blau, 1955; Alt, 1949).

In the theory to be outlined here, we consider three major ways in which the objectives of a coalition are determined. The first of these is the bargaining process by which the composition and general terms of the coalition are fixed. The second is the internal organizational process of control by which objectives are stabilized and elaborated. The third is the process of adjustment to experience, by which coalition agreements are altered in response to environmental changes. Each of these processes is considered, in turn, in the next three sections of the paper.

FORMATION OF COALITION OBJECTIVES
THROUGH BARGAINING

A basic problem in developing a theory of coalition formation is the problem of handling side payments. No matter how we try, we simply cannot imagine that the side payments by which organizational coalitions are formed even remotely satisfy the requirements of unrestricted transferability of utility. Side payments are made in many forms: money, personal treatment, authority, organization policy, etc. A winning coalition does not have a fixed booty which it then divides among its members. Quite to the contrary, the total value of side payments available for division among coalition members is a function of the composition of the coalition; and the total utility of the actual side payments depends on the distribution made within the coalition. There is no conservation of utility.

For example, if we can imagine a situation in which any dyad is a viable coalition (e.g., a partnership to exploit the proposition that two can live more cheaply in coalition than separately), we would predict a greater total utility for those dyads in which needs were complementary than for those in which they were competitive. Generally speaking, therefore, the partitioning of the adult population into male-female dyads is probably more efficient from the point of view of total utility accruing to the coalition than is a partition into sexually homogeneous pairs.

Such a situation makes game theory as it currently exists virtually irrelevant for a treatment of organizational side payments (Luce and Raiffa, 1957). But the problem is in part even deeper than that. The second requirement of such theories as game theory, theory of teams, and inducements-contributions theory, is that after the side payments are made, a joint preference ordering is defined. All conflict is settled by the side payment bargaining. The employment-contract form of these theories, for example, assumes that the entrepreneur has an objective. He then purchases whatever sevices he needs to achieve the objective. In return for such payments, employees contract to perform whatever is required of them—at least within the range of permissible requirements. For a price, the employee adopts the "organization" goal.

One strange feature of such a conception is that it describes a coalition asymmetrically. To what extent is it arbitrary that we call wage payments "costs" and dividend payments "profits"—rather than the other way around? Why is it that in our quasi-genetic moments we are inclined to say that in the beginning there was a manager and he recruited workers and capital? For the development of our own theory we make two major arguments. First, the emphasis on the asymmetry has seriously confused our understanding of organizational goals. The confusion arises because ultimately it makes only slightly more sense to say that the goal of a business organization is to maximize profit than it does to say that its goal is to maximize the salary of Sam Smith, Assistant to the Janitor.

Second, despite this there are important reasons for viewing some coalition members as quite different from others. For example, it is clear that employees and management make somewhat different demands on the organization. In their bargaining, side payments appear traditionally to have performed the classical function of specifying a joint preference ordering. In addition, some coalition members (e.g., many stockholders) devote substantially less time to the particular coalition under consideration than do others. It is this characteristic that has usually been used to draw organizational boundaries between "external" and "internal" members of the coalition. Thus, there are important classes of coalition members who are passive most of the time. A condition of such passivity must be that the payment demands they make are of such a character that most of the time they can be met rather easily.

Although we thereby reduce substantially the size and complexity of the coalition relevant for most goal setting, we are still left with something more complicated than an individual entrepreneur. It is primarily through bargaining within this active group that what we call organizational objectives arise. Side payments, far from being incidental distribution of a fixed, transferable booty, represent the central process of goal specification. That is, a significant number of these payments are in the form of policy commitments.

The distinction between demands for monetary side payments and demands for policy commitments seems to underlie management-oriented treatments of organizations. It is clear that in many organizations this distinction has important ideological and therefore affective connotations. Indeed, the breakdown of the distinction in our generation has been quite consistently violent. Political party-machines in this country have changed drastically the ratio of direct monetary side payments (e.g., patronage, charity) to policy commitments (e.g., economic legislation). Labor unions are conspicuously entering into what has been viewed traditionally as the management prerogatives of policy-making, and demanding payments in that area. Military forces have long since given up the substance—if not entirely the pretense—of being simply hired agents of the regime. The phenomenon is especially obvious in public (Dahl and Lindblom, 1953; Simon, Smithburg, and Thompson, 1950) and voluntary (Sills, 1957; Messinger, 1955) organizations; but all organizations use policy side payments. The marginal cost to other coalition members is typically quite small.

This trend toward policy side payments is particularly observable in contemporary organizations, but the important point is that we have never come close to maintenance of a sharp distinction in the kinds of payments made and demanded. Policy commitments have (one is tempted to say always) been an important part of the method by which coalitions are formed. In fact, an organization that does not use such devices can exist in only a rather special environment.

To illustrate coalition formation under conditions where the problem is not scarce resources for such payments, but varying complementarities of policy demands, imagine a nine-man committee appointed to commission a painting for the village hall. The nine members make individually the following demands:

Committeeman A: The painting must be an abstract monotone.
Committeeman B: The painting must be an impressionistic oil.
Committeeman C: The painting must be small and oval in shape.
Committeeman D: The painting must be small and in oil.
Committeeman E: The painting must be square in shape and multicolored.
Committeeman F: The painting must be an impressionistic square.

Committeeman G: The painting must be a monotone and in oil.
Committeeman H: The painting must be multicolored and impressionistic.
Committeeman I: The painting must be small and oval.

In this case, each potential coalition member makes two simple demands. Assuming that five members are all that are required to make the decision, there are three feasible coalitions. A, C, D, G, and I can form a coalition and commission a small, oval, monotone, oil abstract. B, C, D, H, and I can form a coalition and commission a small, oval, multicolored, impressionistic oil. B, D, E, F, and H can form a coalition and commission a small, square, multicolored, impressionistic oil.

Committeeman D, it wil be noted, is in the admirable position of being included in every possible coalition. The reason is clear; his demands are completely consistent with the demands of everyone else.

Obviously at some level of generality the distinction between money and policy payments disappears because any side payment can be viewed as a policy constraint. When we agree to pay someone $35,000 a year, we are constrained to that set of policy decisions that will allow such a payment. Any allocation of scarce resources (such as money) limits the alternatives for the organization. But the scarcity of resources is not the only kind of problem. Some policy demands are strictly inconsistent with other demands. Others are completely complementary. If I demand of the organization that John Jones be shot and you demand that he be sainted, it will be difficult for us both to stay in the organization. This is not because either bullets or haloes are in short supply or because we don't have enough money for both.

To be sure, the problems of policy consistency are *in principle* amenable to explicit optimizing behavior. But they add to the computational difficulties facing the coalition members and make it even more obvious why the bargaining leading to side payment and policy agreements is only slightly related to the bargaining anticipated in a theory of omniscient rationality. The tests of short-run feasibility that they represent lead to the familiar complications of conflict, disagreement, and rebargaining.

In the process of bargaining over side payments many of the organizational objectives are defined. Because of the form the bargaining takes, the objectives tend to have several important attributes. First, they are imperfectly rationalized. Depending on the skill of the leaders involved, the sequence of demands leading to the new bargaining, the aggressiveness of various parts of the organization, and the scarcity of resources, the new demands will be tested for consistency with existing policy. But this testing is normally far from complete. Second, some objectives are stated in the form of aspiration-level constraints. Objectives arise in this form when demands which are consistent with the coalition are stated in this form. For example, the demand, "We must allocate ten percent of our total budget to research." Third, some objectives are stated in a nonoperational form. In our formulation such objectives arise when potential coalition members have demands which are nonoperational or demands which can be made nonoperational. The prevalence of objectives in this form can be explained by the fact that nonoperational objectives are consistent with virtually any set of objectives.

STABILIZATION AND ELABORATION OF OBJECTIVES

The bargaining process goes on more or less continuously, turning out a long series of commitments. But a description of goal formation simply in such terms is not adequate. Organizational objectives are, first of all, much more stable than would be suggested by such a model, and secondly, such a model does not handle very well the elaboration and clarification of goals through day-to-day bargaining.

Central to an understanding of these phenomena is again an appreciation for the limitations of human capacities and time to devote to any particular aspect of the organizational system. Let us return to our conception of a coalition having monetary and policy side payments. These side payment agreements are incomplete. They do not anticipate effectively all possible future situations, and they do not identify all considerations that might be viewed as important by the coalition members at some future time. Nevertheless, the coalition members are motivated to operate under the agreements and to develop some mutual control systems for enforcing them.

One such mutual control system in many organizations is the budget. A budget is a highly explicit elaboration of previous commitments. Although it is usually viewed as an asymmetric control device (i.e., a means for superiors to control subordinates), it is clear that it represents a form of mutual control. Just as there are usually severe costs to the department in exceeding the budget, so also are there severe costs to other members of the coalition if the budget is not paid in full. As a result, budgets in every organization tend to be self-confirming.

A second major, mutual control system is allocation of functions. Division of labor and specialization are commonly treated in management textbooks simply as techniques of rational organization. If, however, we consider the allocation of functions in much the way we would normally view the allocation of resources during budgeting, a somewhat different picture emerges. When we define the limits of discretion, we constrain the individual or subgroup from acting outside those limits. But at the same time, we constrain any other members of the coalition from prohibiting action within those limits. Like the allocation of resources in a budget, the allocation of discretion in an organization chart is largely self-confirming.

The secondary bargaining involved in such mutual control systems serves to elaborate and revise the coalition agreements made on entry (Thompson and McEwen, 1958). In the early life of an organization, or after some exceptionally drastic organizational upheaval, this elaboration occurs in a context where very little is taken as given. Relatively deliberate action must be taken on everything from pricing policy to paper clip policy. Reports from individuals who have lived through such early stages emphasize the lack of structure that typifies settings for day-to-day decisions (Simon, 1953).

In most organizations most of the time, however, the elaboration of objectives occurs within much tighter constraints. Much of the situation is taken as given. This is true primarily because organizations have memories in the form of precedents, and individuals in the coalition are strongly motivated to accept the precedents as binding. Whether precedents are formalized in the shape of an official standard operating procedure or are less formally stored, they remove from conscious consideration many agreements, decisions, and commitments that might well be subject to renegotiation in an organization without a memory (Cyert and March, 1960). Past bargains become precedents for present situations. A budget becomes a precedent for future budgets. An allocation of functions becomes a precedent for future allocation. Through all the well-known mechanisms, the coalition agreements of today are institutionalized into semipermanent arrangements. A number of administrative aphorisms come to mind: an unfilled position disappears; see an empty office and fill it up; there is nothing temporary under the sun. As a result of organizational precedents, objectives exhibit much greater stability than would typify a pure bargaining situation. The "accidents" of organizational genealogy tend to be perpetuated.

CHANGES IN OBJECTIVES
THROUGH EXPERIENCE

Although considerably stabilized by memory and institutionalization phenomena, the demands made on the coalition by individual members do change with experience. Both the nature of the demands and their quantitative level vary over time.

Since many of the requirements specified by individual participants are in the form of attainable goals rather than general maximizing constraints, objectives are subject to the usual phenomena associated with aspiration levels. As an approximation to the aspiration-level model, we can take the following set of propositions:

1. In the steady state, aspiration level exceeds achievement by a small amount.
2. Where achievement increases at an increasing rate, aspiration level will exhibit short-run lags behind achievement.
3. Where achievement decreases, aspiration level will be substantially above achievement.

These propositions derive from simpler assumptions requiring that current aspiration be an optimistic extrapolation of past achievement and past aspiration. Although such assumptions are sometimes inappropriate, the model seems to be consistent with a wide range of human goal setting behavior (Lewin, Dembo, Festinger, and Sears, 1944). Two kinds of achievement are of course, important. The first is the achievement of the participant himself. The second is the achievement of others in his reference group (Festinger, 1954).

Because of these phenomena, our theory of organizational objectives must allow for drift in the demands of members of the organization. No one doubts that aspirations with respect to monetary compensation vary substantially as a function of payments received. So also do aspirations regarding advertising budget, quality of product, volume of sales, product of mix, and capital investment. Obviously, until we know a great deal more than we do about the parameters of the relation between achievement and aspiration we can make only relatively weak predictions. But some of these predictions are quite useful, particularly in conjunction with search theory (Cyert, Dill, and March, 1958).

For example, two situations are particularly intriguing. What happens when the rate of improvement in the environment is great enough so that it outruns the upward adjustment of aspiration? Second, what happens when the environment becomes less favorable? The general answer to both of these questions involves the concept of organizational slack (Cyert and March, 1956). When the environment outruns aspiration-level adjustment, the organization secures, or at least has the potentiality of securing, resources in excess of its demands. Some of these resources are simply not obtained—although they are available. Others are used to meet the revised demands of those members of the coalition whose demands adjust most rapidly— usually those most deeply involved in the organization. The excess resources would not be subject to very general bargaining because they do not involve allocation in the face of scarcity. Coincidentally perhaps, the absorption of excess resources also serves to delay aspiration-level adjustment by passive members of the coalition.

When the environment becomes less favorable, organizational slack represents a cushion. Resource scarcity brings on renewed bargaining and tends to cut heavily into the excess payments introduced during plusher times. It does not necessarily mean that precisely those demands that grew abnormally during better days are pruned abnormally during poorer ones; but in general we would expect this to be approximately the case.

Some attempts have been made to use these very simple propositions to generate some meaningful empirical predictions. Thus, we predict that, discounting for the economies of scale, relatively successful firms will have higher unit costs than relatively unsuccessful ones. We predict that advertising expenditures will be a function of sales in the previous time period at least as much as the reverse will be true.

The nature of the demands also changes with experience in another way. We do not conceive that individual members of the coalition will have simple listing of demands, with only the quantitative values changing over time. Instead we imagine each member as having a rather disorganized file case full of demands. At any point in time, the member attends to only a rather small subset of his demands, the number and variety depending again on the extent of his involvement in the organization and on the demands of his other commitments on his attention.

Since not all demands are attended to at the same time, one important part of the theory of organizational objectives is to predict when particular units in the organization will attend to particular goals. Consider the safety goal in a large corporation. For the safety engineers, this is a very important goal most of the time. Other parts of the organization rarely even consider it. If, however, the organization has some drastic experience (e.g., a multiple fatality), attention to a safety goal is much more widespread and safety action quite probable.

Whatever the experience, it shifts the attention focus. In some (as in the safety example), adverse experience suggests a problem area to be attacked. In others, solutions to problems stimulate attention to a particular goal. An organization with an active personnel research department will devote substantial attention to personnel goals not because it is necessarily a particularly pressing problem but because the subunit keeps generating solutions that remind other members of the organization of a particular set of objectives they profess.

The notion of attention focus suggests one reason why organizations are successful in surviving with a large set of unrationalized goals. They rarely see the conflicting objectives simultaneously. For example, let us reconsider the case of the pair of demands that John Jones be either (*a*) shot or (*b*) sainted. Quite naturally, these were described as inconsistent demands. Jones cannot be simultaneously shot and sainted. But the emphasis should be on *simultaneously*. It is quite feasible for him to be first shot and then sainted, or vice versa. It is logically feasible because a halo can be attached as firmly to a dead man a to a live one and a saint is as susceptible to bullets as a sinner. It is organizationally feasible because the probability is low that both of these demands will be attended to simultaneously.

The sequential attention to goals is a simple mechanism. A consequence of the mechanism is that organizations ignore many conditions that outside observers see as direct contradictions. They are contradictions only if we imagine a well-established, joint preference ordering or omniscient bargaining. Neither condition exists in an organization. If we assume that attention to goals is limited, we can explain the absence of any strong pressure to resolve apparent internal inconsistencies. This is not to argue that all conflicts involving objectives can be resolved in this way, but it is one important mechanism that deserves much more intensive study.

CONSTRUCTING A PREDICTIVE THEORY

Before the general considerations outlined above can be transformed into a useful predictive theory, a considerable amount of precision must be added. The introduction of precision depends, in turn, on the future success of research into the process of coalition formation. Nevertheless, some steps can be taken now to develop the theory. In particular, we can specify a general framework for a theory and indicate its needs for further development.

We assume a set of coalition members, actual or potential. Whether these members are individuals or groups of individuals is unimportant. Some of the possible subsets drawn from this set are viable coalitions. That is, we will identify a class of combinations of members such that any of these combinations meet the minimal standards imposed by the external environment on the organization. Patently, therefore, the composition of the viable set of coalitions will depend on environmental conditions.

For each of the potential coalition members we require a set of demands. Each such individual set is partitioned into an active part currently attended to and an inactive part currently ignored. Each demand can be characterized by two factors: first, its marginal resource requirements, given the demands of all possible other combinations of demands from potential coalition members; second, its marginal consistency with all possible combinations of demands from potential coalition members.

For each potential coalition member we also require a set of problems, partitioned similarly into an active and an inactive part.

This provides us with the framework of the theory. In addition, we need five basic mechanisms. First, we need a mechanism that changes the quantitative value of the demands over time. In our formulation, this becomes a version of the basic aspiration-level and mutual control theory outlined earlier.

Second, we need an attention focus mechanism that transfers demands among the three possible states: active set, inactive set, not-considered set. We have said that some organizational participants will attend to more demands than other participants and that for all participants some demands will be considered at one time and others at other times. But we know rather little about the actual mechanisms that control this attention factor.

Third, we need a similar attention focus mechanism for problems. As we have noted, there is a major interaction between what problems are attended to and what demands are attended to, but research is also badly needed in this area.

Fourth, we need a demand-evaluation procedure that is consistent with the limited capacities of human beings. Such a procedure must specify how demands are checked for consistency and for their resource demands. Presumably, such a mechanism will depend heavily on a rule that much of the problem is taken as given and only incremental changes are considered.

Fifth, we need a mechanism for choosing among the potentially viable coalitions. In our judgment, this mechanism will probably look much like the recent suggestions of game theorists that only small changes are evaluated at a time (Luce and Raiffa, 1957).

Given these five mechanisms and some way of expressing environmental resources, we can describe a process for the determination of objectives in an organization that will exhibit the important attributes of organizational goal determination. At the moment, we can approximate some of the required functions. For example, it has been possible to introduce into a complete model a substantial part of the first mechanism, and some elements of the second, third, and fourth (Cyert, Feigenbaum, and March, 1959). Before the theory can develop further, however, and particularly before it can focus intensively on the formation of objectives through bargaining and coalition formation (rather than on the revision of such objectives and the selective attention to them), we require greater empirical clarification of the phenomena involved.

References

1. Alt, R. M., "The Internal Organization of the Firm and Price Formation: An Illustrative Case," *Quarterly Journal of Economics,* 63 (1949), pp. 92–110.
2. Barnard, C. I., *The Functions of the Executive* (Cambridge: Harvard University Press, 1938).
3. Blau, P. M., *The Dynamics of Bureaucracy* (Chicago: University of Chicago Press, 1955).
4. Cooper, W. W., C. Hitch, W. J. Baumol, M. Shubik, T. C. Schelling, S. Valavanis, and D. Ellsberg, "Economics and Operations Research: A Symposium," *The Review of Economics and Statistics,* 40 (1958), pp. 195–229.
5. Cyert, R. M., and J. G. March, "Organizational Factors in the Theory of Oligopoly," *Quarterly Journal of Economics, 70 (1956), pp. 44–64.*
6. Cyert, R. M., W. R. Dill, and J. G. March, "The Role of Expectations in Business Decision Making," *Administration Science Quarterly,* 3 (1958), pp. 307–340.
7. Cyert, R. M., and J. G. March, "Research on a Behavioral Theory of the Firm," *Management Review* (1959).
8. Cyert, R. M., E. A. Feigenbaum, and J. G. March, "Models in a Behavioral Theory of the Firm," *Behavioral Science,* 4 (1959), pp. 81–95.
9. Cyert, R. M., and J. G. March, "Business Operating Procedures," *Industrial Psychology,* ed. B. von H. Gilmer (New York: McGraw-Hill, 1960).
10. Dahl, R. A., and C. E. Lindblom, *Politics, Economics, and Welfare* (New York: Harper, 1953).
11. Festinger, L., "A Theory of Social Comparison Processes," *Human Relations,* 7 (1954), pp. 117–140.

12. Kaplan, A. D. H., J. B. Dirlam, and R. F. Lanzillotti, *Pricing in Big Business* (Washington: Brookings Institution, 1958).
13. Lewin, L., T. Dembo, L. Festinger, and P. Sears, "Level of Aspiration," *Personality and the Behavior Disorders,* ed. J. M. Hunt (New York: Ronald, 1944), Vol. 1.
14. Luce, R. D., and H. Raiffa, *Games and Decisions* (New York: Wiley, 1957), Ch. 7 and 10.
15. March, J. G., and H. A. Simon, *Organizations* (New York: Wiley, 1958).
16. Marschak, J., "Efficient and Viable Organization Forms," *Modern Organization Theory,* ed. Mason Haire (New York: Wiley, 1959).
17. Marshall, A., *Industry and Trade* (London: Macmillan, 1919).
18. Messinger, S. L., "Organizational Transformation: A Case Study of a Declining Social Movement," *American Sociology Review, 20 (1955), pp. 3–10.*
19. Selznick, P., *TVA and the Grass Roots* (Berkeley: University of California Press, 1949).
20. Sills, D. L., *The Volunteers* (Glencoe, Ill.: Free Press, 1957).
21. Simon, H. A., *Administrative Behavior* (New York: Macmillan, 1947).
22. Simon, H. A., D. W. Smithburg, and V. A. Thompson, *Public Administration* (New York: Knopf, 1950), Ch. 18 and 19.
23. Simon, H. A., "Birth of an Organization: The Economic Cooperation Administration," *Public Administration Review,* 13 (1953), pp. 227–236.
24. Thompson, J. D., and W. J. McEwen, "Organizational Goals and Environment: Goal Setting as an Interaction Process," *American Sociology Review,* 23 (1958), pp. 23–31.
25. Truman, D. B., *The Governmental Process* (New York: Knopf, 1951), pp. 282–287.
26. Von Neumann, J., and O. Morgenstern, *Theory of Games and Economic Behavior,* 2nd ed. (Princeton: Princeton University Press, 1947).
27. Weber, M., *The Theory of Social and Economic Organization,* trans. A. M. Henderson and T. Parsons (New York: Oxford University Press, 1947).

Organizations and Change

James G. March

Recent literature on organizations often details the ways that hopes for change are frustrated by organizational behavior. The contrariness of organizations in confronting sensible efforts to change them fills our stories and our research. What most of those experiences tell us, however, is not that organizations are rigid and inflexible. Rather, they picture organizations as impressively imaginative. Organizations change in response to their environments, including their managements; but they rarely change in a way that fulfills the intentional plan of a single group of actors. Sometimes organizations ignore clear policies; sometimes they pursue them more forcefully than was intended. Sometimes they protect policymakers from the follies of foolish policies; sometimes they do not. Sometimes they stand still when we want them to move. Sometimes they move when we want them to stand still.

Organizational tendencies to frustrate arbitrary administrative intention, however, should not be confused with rigidity. Organizations change frequently. They adopt new products, new procedures, new objectives, new postures, new styles, new personnel, new beliefs. Even in a short perspective, the changes are often large. Some of them are sensible; some are not. Bureaucratic organizations are not always efficient. They can be exceptionally obtuse. Change is ubiquitous in organizations; and most change is the result neither of extraordinary organizational process of forces, nor of uncommon imagination, persistence, or skill. It is a result of relatively stable processes that relate organizations to their environment. If economic, political, or social contexts change rapidly, organizations will change rapidly and routinely.

In such a spirit, recent efforts to understand organizations as

---

Reprinted by permission of the author from James G. March, "How We Talk and How We Act: Administrative Theory and Administrative Life." 7th David D. Henry Lecture, Urbana, IL., University of Illinois at Urbana-Champaign, 1980, pp. 14–17.

routine adaptive systems emphasize six basic perspectives for interpreting organizational action:

1. Action can be seen as the application of standard operating procedures or
   other rules to appropriate situations. The terms of reference are duties,
   obligations, and roles. The model is a model of evolutionary selection.
2. Action can be seen as problem solving. The terms of reference are
   alternatives, consequences, and preferences. The model is one of intended
   rational choice.
3. Action can be seen as stemming from past learning. The terms of reference
   are actions and experiences. The model is one of trial and error learning.
4. Action can be seen as resulting from conflict among individuals or groups.
   The terms of reference are interests, activation, and resources. The model
   is one of politics—bargaining and power.
5. Action can be seen as spreading from one organization to another. The
   terms of reference are exposure and susceptibility. The model is one of
   diffusion.
6. Action can be seen as stemming from the mix of intentions and competencies found in organizational actors. The terms of reference are
   attitudes, abilities, and turnover. The model is one of regeneration.

These standard processes of organizational action are understandable and mostly reliable. Much of the time they are adaptive. They
facilitate organizational survival. Sometimes the changes that are
produced seem little connected either to the intentions of organizational actors or to the manifest problems facing an organization. A
propensity to change does not assure survival, and the processes of
change are complicated by a variety of confusions and surprises.
Solutions sometimes discover problems rather than the other way
around. Organizations imitate each other, but innovations and
organizations change in the process. Environments are responded to,
but they are also affected. The efforts of organizations to adapt are
entangled with the simultaneous efforts of individuals and larger
systems of organizations. In these ways, the same processes that
sustain the dull day-to-day activities of an organization produce
unusual events.

These six perspectives portray an organization as coping with the
environment routinely, actively adapting to it, avoiding it, seeking to
change it, comprehend it, and contain it. An organization is neither
unconditionally rigid nor unconditionally malleable; it is a relatively
complicated collection of interests and beliefs acting in response to
conflicting and ambiguous signals received from the environment and
from the organization, acting in a manner that often makes sense and

usually is intelligent. Organizations evolve, solve problems, learn, bargain, imitate, and regenerate. Under a variety of circumstances, the processes are conservative. That is, they tend to maintain stable relations, sustain existing rules, and reduce differences among similar organizations. But the fundamental logic is not one of stability in behavior; it is one of adaptation. The processes are stable; the resulting actions are not.

Organizations change routinely and continually; and the effectiveness of an organization in responding to its environment, as well as much of the effectiveness of management, is linked to the effectiveness of routine processes. As a result, much of the job of an administrator involves the mundane work of making a bureaucracy work. It is filled with activities quite distant from those implied in a conception of administration as heroic leadership. It profits from ordinary competence and a recognition of the ways in which organizations change by modest modifications of routines rather than by massive mucking around. Studies of managerial time and behavior consistently show an implicit managerial recognition of the importance of these activities. The daily activities of a manager are rather distant from grand conceptions of organizational leadership. Administrators spend time talking to people about minor things, making trivial decisions, holding meetings with unimportant agendas, and responding to the little irritants of organizational life. Memoirs of administrators confirm the picture of a rewarding life made busy by large numbers of inconsequential things.

These observations describe administrative life as uncomfortably distant from the precepts of administrative theory and from hopes for personal significance. They have led to efforts to change the ways managers behave. Numerous training programs attempt to teach managers to bring their personal time allocation closer to the ideal. They provide procedures designed to increase the time for decision making, planning, thinking, and the other things that appear more characteristic of theories of administration than of administrative jobs. These efforts may be mistakes. Making bureaucracy work involves effectiveness in executing a large number of little things. Making bureaucracies change involves attention to the minor routines by which things happen. Rules need to be understood in order to be interpreted or broken; simple breakdowns in the flow of supplies need to be minimized; telephones and letters need to be answered; accounts and records need to be maintained.

The importance of simple competence in the routines of organizational life is often overlooked when we sing the grand arias of management, but effective bureaucracies are rarely dramatic. They are administrative organizations that require elementary efficiency as a necessary condition for quality. Efficiency as a concept subject to considerable sensible criticism on the grounds that it is either meaningless or misleading if we treat it independently of the objectives being pursued. The point is well taken as a critique of the "cult of efficiency," but it is much too simple if we take it as an assertion that all, or even most, efforts in an administrative organization need a clear specification of global goals to be done well. An administrative organization combines large numbers of tasks into some kinds of meaningful combinations, but much of the effectiveness of the combination depends on the relatively automatic, local correction of local inefficiencies without continuous attention to the "big picture."

Much of what distinguishes a good bureaucracy from a bad one is how well it accomplishes the trivia of day-to-day relations with clients and day-to-day problems in maintaining and operating its technology. Accomplishing these trivia may involve considerable planning, complex coordination, and central direction, but it is more commonly linked to the effectiveness of large numbers of people doing minor things competently. As a result, it is probably true that the conspicuous differences around the world in the quality of bureaucratic performance are due primarily to variance in the competence of the ordinary clerk, bureaucrat, and lower manager, and to the effectiveness of routine procedures for dealing with problems at a local level. This appears to be true of armies, factories, postal services, hotels, and universities.

Environments of Organizations

Howard E. Aldrich and Jeffrey Pfeffer

INTRODUCTION

The relationship between organizations and environments has drawn increasing attention in the recent literature of the sociology of organizations. We consider the subject of interorganizational relations to be a special case of the more general study of organizations and their environments. Dimensions of interorganizational relations have been listed (Marrett 1971), and partially developed paradigms for analyzing organization-environment relations have been proposed. The natural selection model, developing the strongest argument for an environmental perspective, posits that environmental factors select those organizational characteristics that best fit the environment. (Hannan & Freeman 1974, Aldrich 1971b). A complementary model, variously called a political economy model (Benson 1975, Wamsley & Zald 1973), a dependence exchange approach (Jacobs 1974, Hasenfeld 1972), and a resource dependence model (Pfeffer 1972b), argues for greater attention to internal organizational political decision-making processes and also for the perspective that organizations seek to manage or strategically adapt to their environments.

The two models agree on the importance of organizational environments for understanding organizational decisions and structure, but differ in their evaluation of the importance of the role of environmental selection. Current literature has elements of both incompletely developed perspectives and the shape of organizational sociology will be determined by the implicit debate taking place. As it is impossible to ascertain the ultimate resolution of this argument, we have chosen to examine both perspectives in this chapter, and to include literature from industrial organization, and administrative

Reproduced, with permission, from the ANNUAL REVIEW OF SOCIOLOGY, Vol. 2 © 1976 by Annual Reviews, Inc.

science and organizational behavior, as well as from organizational sociology.

Historical Precedents

The emphasis on organizational environments is not a recent development, since Weber's (1968) historical and comparative studies examined the effect of social structure on bureaucracy. Selznick's studies of the TVA (1949) and the Communist Party (1960) explicitly included the environment as an important external constraint, and the work of Bendix (1956) on the relationship between entrepreneurial and managerial ideologies and social structure is also in this tradition. The theory of the firm in economics treats the relationship of a single organization to its environment and posits that organizational decisions concerning price and output are the outcome of market forces (e.g., Stigler 1966). Industrial organization economists have been concerned with the ability of organizations to acquire market power and modify their environments (Phillips 1960, Scherer 1970). Anthropologists brought the environment into their theories with the concept of societal evolution (White 1949, Sahlins & Service 1960), and a similar interest in societal evolution occurred in the 1960s in sociology (Parsons 1966).

One could pose several questions about the extent to which this work has been cumulative, beginning with the intriguing question of why there has been little cross-fertilization between the fields of industrial organization in economics and organizational sociology. It is also interesting to consider why research on the effects of environments on social structure waxes and wanes, with attention sometimes focused on external effects, and at other times on internal processes. These questions are best left for sociologists of science to answer (cf Hirsch 1975a). There is currently great interest in environmental effects and the journals are filled with papers containing the words *environment* or *interorganizational* in their titles.

THE NATURAL SELECTION MODEL

Two possible approaches to the study of organizational change are the natural selection model of evolutionary theory and the decision-making perspective on organizations that subsumes the resource dependence model. The natural selection model will be presented first and serve as point of contrast for other perspectives. While Campbell (1969) has applied the term *evolution* to the process of natural selection operating on social structures, we will use either the terminology *natural selection* or *ecological* to refer to this process. Evolution contains some connotation of a progression; for example, in biology, from less to more complex forms. Evolution also carries some connotation of progress, as each succeeding generation is presumably more advanced in the evolutionary process. By using the term natural selection or ecological, we emphasize that the process of organizational change, while controlled by the environment, does not necessarily involve progress to more complex or higher forms of social organizations or to better organizations. The process of natural selection means the social organizations are moving toward a better fit with the environment, but nothing more.

The natural selection model in its original form applies at the population level of organizations rather than at the level of single units. Environments differentially select organizations for survival on the basis of the fit between organization structure (and activities) and environmental characteristics (Hannan & Freeman 1974, Buckley 1967). Those organizations that have the appropriate social structure, for whatever reason, are selected over those that do not.

As developed by Campbell (1969), the natural selection model has three stages. The model is not intended to account for short-run changes, which are temporary responses to local conditions, but rather for long-run transformations in the form of the elements being examined. In biology the forms that are changing are typical species genotypes, whereas in social science we are interested in changes in the form of social organization. In organizational sociology, forms are currently identified through various typologies, such as mechanistic-organic or bureaucratic-professional, or through an empirically developed typology (cf Hall 1972, chap. 2). Such typologies are often not complex or developed sufficiently to permit a very comprehensive ecological analysis.

The first stage in the natural selection process is the occurrence of variations for whatever reason, planned or unplanned. In organic evolution, variations occur through the genetic mutation process, while in the learning process variation occurs in the exploratory responses made to stimuli. Variations are the raw material from which the selection process culls those structures or behaviors that are most suitable.

The second stage is the operation of consistent selection criteria that differentially select some variations over others or selectively eliminate certain variations. In organic evolution the differential survival of certain mutant forms that are better able to exploit the food supply in their environment reflects the operation of a resource-based selection criterion. Differential reinforcement of particular exploratory responses by animals, in a consistent manner, is the selection stage in the learning process.

The third stage in the ecological process involves the operation of a retention mechanism for the selective retention of the positively selected variations. Retention occurs when certain variations are preserved, duplicated, or reproduced. In organic evolution the retention mechanism is the chromosome-gene system. Positively selected variations survive and reproduce similar others. For the learning process the memory system is the means whereby positively selected responses can be recalled for future use.

The process as described is perfectly general and can be applied to any situation where the three stages are present. The three-stage model completely describes the evolutionary process. As Campbell (1969:73) noted, "Given these three conditions, an evolution in the direction of better fit to the selective system becomes inevitable."

Before considering some of the theoretical problems of the ecological model, we should note three problems that have limited the application of this model in organizational sociology. First, it is most appropriately applied at the field or population level, as it is not the fitness of any single organization, but rather the distribution of fitness across a population of organizations that is of interest. This requires the study of relatively heterogeneous populations of organizations over a fairly long time span, something few investigators have the funding or the time to do, although Stinchcombe (1965) attempted a partial version of such an analysis in his paper on social structure and organizations. There are few longitudinal studies of organizations beyond isolated case studies, although recently interest has been growing in such work (Aldrich & Reiss 1976, Meyer 1972, Warren, Rose & Bergunder 1974). It might be noted that the availability of archival data, particularly on economic organizations, potentially reduces the cost of such research.

Second, the natural selection model focuses on outcomes involving the selective propagation of changes, however generated, in the structure of a large number of organizations, rather than on the route taken by any single organization in adapting. Indeed, the focus on survival, in contrast to adaptation, as the mechanism of change is one of the unique contributions of this perspective. However, investigators run the risk of merely compiling a chronicle of changes whose causes cannot be ascertained. We would suggest that without a complementary theory of managerial behavior, such an outcome is highly probable.

Third, a proper application of the natural selection model requires a system of classification and categorization of organizational forms analogous to species in biology. In studies of biological evolution, when one particular type of organism disappears and another rises into prominence in the same niche, the system of categorization is able to assess, to some extent, whether the new organism is really a different species, a mutation directly related to the old species, or a temporary phenotypic adaptation. No such system of classification exists in the study of organizations. The difference between structural modifications and the emergence of fundamentally new organizations is frequently unclear. Another way to think of this problem is to note that we do not know the length of an organizational "generation," if such a thing exists.

Summary

As a model of organizational change, the natural selection perspective is indifferent regarding the source of variation or change in the first place. Selection of social structures is accomplished by differential survival of structural forms, rather than by the adaptation of a single organizational unit. While in this model selection is determined by fitness to the environment, no further specification is provided as to the selection criteria. Retention, the opposite of variation (Weick 1969), is accomplished through organizational stability, manifested in the use of unchanging standard operating procedures or formal rules.

Since selection is made by the environment according to some dimension of fitness, a theorist using this model could, in explaining only long-run changes, safely neglect intraorganizational managerial processes. In the long run only those organizations that fit the environment will survive and, consequently, one need not be as concerned with the processes by which such an organization-environment match is achieved. Stated in this form, the ecological perspective can be seen to be virtually isomorphic with the economic theory of perfect competition (Winter 1971) and similar to elements of what has been called structural contingency theory (Pennings 1975). Microeconomic theory, or the theory of the firm, also neglects internal decision-making realities. Friedman (1953) argued that since firms are forced to behave as if they are maximizing profit because of competition, the assumptions of profit maximization will lead to correct predictions in equilibrium, regardless of the process by which such equilibrium states are reached. In both natural selection theory and microeconomics, the environment selects the most fit, or optimal organizations, and both implicitly assume that the individual social unit is itself powerless to affect the selection process. Both models focus strongly on the process of selection, concerning themselves less with variation. Indeed, one might characterize the theory of the firm as a theory of the selection criteria that are inevitable given certain assumptions about decision making and the competitive nature of the environment. Both structural contingency theory and ecological models posit an optimal fit between the organization and its environment and structural contingency theory differs chiefly in its emphasis on managerial adaptation to find the fit, rather than on change being accomplished through differential survival.

THE RESOURCE DEPENDENCE MODEL

The natural selection model leaves out questions about how decisions are made in organizations. If all decisions are confined to some limited set of solutions (in the case of microeconomic theory, a single optimal solution), then it would be proper to treat them as irrelevant, if one assumes further that equilibrium is achieved relatively rapidly and the process of adjustment is not interesting in its own right. However, there are few industries in the United States that fit the model of perfect competition (Galbraith 1967), and furthermore, public and social service organizations face situations of little or no competition. In the absence of environmental demands that must inevitably be heeded if the organization is to survive, how and why decisions are made in organizations becomes a more important focus of research attention.

The resource dependence model proceeds from the indisputable proposition that organizations are not able to internally generate either all the resources or functions required to maintain themselves, and therefore organizations must enter into transactions and relations with elements in the environment that can supply the required resources and services. Since organizations are constructed or enacted systems that must satisfy the demands of members, owners, or constituents (White 1974) and are subject to evaluation (Thompson 1967), administrators face the task of ensuring a continued supply of resources and performances and ensuring the satisfaction of powerful groups in their environment. The resource dependence perspective argues that in addition to the interdependencies among organizations that are based on differentiation and the interorganizational division of labor, some interdependencies are sought or avoided by administrators because of the power and control possibilities inherent in the situation of dependence (Blau 1964). Administrative strategies range from vertical integration to deny the competitor the use of raw materials to horizontal mergers undertaken to restrict competition.

The resource dependence model portrays the organization as active, and capable of changing, as well as responding to, the environment. Administrators manage their environments as well as their organizations, and the former activity may be as important, or even more important, than the latter (Pfeffer 1976). The presumed end result of such strategies is the acquisition of resources and the survival of the organization, as well as the stabilization of relationships with environmental elements.

Since the environment, according to the resource dependence perspective, does not impose as strict requirements for survival, many possible actions and structures are consistent with the survival of the organization. Therefore, the criteria by which decisions are made and structures determined become important and problematic. Internal power differences become important, because there is no longer a single optimal structure or set of actions that will fit the organization with its environment. There is a range of choices or strategies available (Child 1972, Chandler 1962), and the influence of internal subunits may come to determine, in interaction with the demands of various external groups, the outcome (cf. Jacobs 1974, Pfeffer & Salancik 1974). The resource dependence model calls attention to the importance of environmental contingencies and constraints, at the same time leaving room for the operation of strategic choice on the part of organizational members as they maneuver through known contexts.

If the ecological model is analogous to the microeconomic theory of the firm, then the resource dependence model is analogous to theories of oligopoly and the behavioral theory of the firm (Cyert & March 1963). The resource dependence model posits, therefore, that while environmental influences are important, environmental constraints do not reduce the feasible set of social structures to a set consisting of only one form. The possibility that there are a variety of internal structures and actions consistent with the survival of the organization means that while the organization may have the goal of survival, survival does not imply only a single or very limited set of social structural forms. Not all internal decisions are relevant to survival, and thus not all are affected by the environment.

The goal of survival and the corollary idea of environmental constraint provide a calculus for understanding organizational structures over the long run. In the absence of such strict restraint, another way of understanding internal organizational structures and actions is required. The political economy model (Zald 1970), which emphasizes the acquisition and use of power in understanding organizational processes, provides such an alternative perspective. The relationship between the political economy model and the resource dependence model should be clear. Only if one assumes that the environment is not completely binding does the operation of internal organizational political processes become interesting. If the environment inevitably constrains social structures to a unique configuration, then internal political processes relevant to organizational decision making become uninteresting, as they must all lead to the same end result or the organization will fail.

The resource dependence model also posits an active role of the organization affecting its environment, as well as arguing that environmental constraints leave a range of possible social structures consistent with survival. In contrast to the ecological perspective, the resource dependence model posits an active, managerial process of selection, as opposed to a process of natural selection controlled by the environment. While it is of course possible to argue that political and decision-making structures are themselves the outcome of a process of natural selection, such an attempt to subsume the resource dependence approach under the natural selection model would only tend to hide the fundamental difference between them. We might note that this difference between emphasizing personal action versus environmental effects is found throughout the social sciences—in history, in the contrast between the great man approach versus the approach that stresses the effect of context, and in psychology, in the difference between operant conditioning, stressing the control of behavior by the environment, and theories of personality and cognitive choice that emphasize more the effect of intended, conscious action.

In the following sections we review recent research on organizations in terms of its relationship to the three stages of the natural selection process, variation, selection, and retention, noting disagreements among the perspectives. The greatest amount of theoretical divergence is with respect to the selection stage, with the resource dependence model assigning more importance to managerial and organizational decision making than the ecological perspective.

VARIATION

The natural selection model is indifferent to the source of variation, as both random and planned variation serve equally well in providing the raw material from which selection is made. The general principle is that the greater the heterogeneity and number of variations, the richer the opportunities for a close fit to the environmental selection criteria.

Following suggestions made by Buckley (1967) and Hannan & Freeman (1974), we believe that the natural section model can be applied not just to the survival or failure of entire organizations but also to the partial modification of structure and activities that falls short of elimination of the total organization. This modification of the biological model takes into account the capacity of social organizations to alter structure, a process that is qualitatively different from homeostatic changes made by biological organisms in response to environmental change. Whereas organic evolution proceeds by a process of differential survival of the entire unit, the changing of social organizations can also occur through adaptations of structure or conduct in one part of the organization while the rest of the structure remains unchanged.

Modifying the natural selection model in this fashion complicates an ecological analysis, since the criterion for successful adaptation to the environment is changed from the easier-to-observe survival or failure to the more problematic criterion of structural change or stability. Rather than being able to observe a population of organizations adapting by the selective elimination of the less fit, we may find that almost all survive, but that each has undergone significant internal transformations of structure. Nevertheless, modifying the ecological model is a necessary step toward recognizing the difference between organic and social evolution (Zachariah 1971) and toward making natural selection theory useful for organizational analysis.

Ecological change may arise from variation both between and within organizations. There are likely to be significant variations within a differentiated organization in individual abilities to fill particular roles, just as there will be variations over time in carrying out important activities (Campbell 1969). Hirschman's (1970) assertion that all organizations drift into deterioration through random errors in the performance of everday duties is consistent with the ecological approach.

While the natural selection model does not specify the source of variation, economists, management scientists, and many sociologists have argued for the importance of variation as a planned response to environmental contingencies. Penrose (1952:819), for instance, wrote, "Our knowledge of why men do what they do is very imperfect, but there is considerable evidence that consciously formulated human values do affect men's actions, that many decisions are reached after a conscious consideration of alternatives, and that men have a wide range of genuine choices." Similarly, sociological theories of organization treat leadership and organizational design as rational, conscious, planned actions (Gouldner 1954, Selznick 1957).

Variation between organizations is inherent in the interorganizational division of labor across industries and since the distribution of organizations by industry changes over time, we might infer that selection at this level is occurring. There are also variations within industries or generic types, e.g., within the manufacturing sector and within firms manufacturing particular products. Emery & Trist's (1965) example of the firm manufacturing canned foods and the firms manufacturing frozen foods is a case of such within-industry variation.

Innovating organizations may introduce variation into a population by deliberately varying from customary modes of behavior. Innovation, however, need not be a conscious strategy and may be a result of imperfect attempts to imitate other organizations perceived to be successful as pointed out by Alchian (1950:218-19): "While there certainly are those who consciously innovate, there are those who, in their imperfect attempts to imitate others, unconsciously innovate by unwittingly acquiring some unexpected or unsought unique attributes which under the prevailing circumstances prove partly responsible for the success." A continuing cycle of imitation-innovation may occur if other organizations, in turn, attempt to imitate the unwitting innovator.

Variations may be introduced into the organizational population through the creation of new organizations. Economic organizations are presumably created by entrepreneurs seeking profit and confronted with the risks of undertaking a new venture. Theories of the formation of new economic organizations have been presented by Schumpeter (1934) and Knight (1921), while Stinchcombe (1965) has treated the problem of organizational formation more generally. Given the risks and uncertainties involved, the rate of creation of new organizations is surprisingly high. While there are no systematic data on the formation of nonbusiness organizations, in the period between 1944 and 1954 over 5.4 million new small firms were established in the United States and another 4.5 million were transferred to a new owner (Aldrich 1971b). The larger number of voluntary associations (Hausknecht 1962) and social movements that come and go quite regularly (Zald & Ash 1966,

Zurcher & Curtis 1973) provide further evidence that a great deal of variation in the form of new organizations is introduced into the organizational population over time.

The resource dependence model posits that organizations attempt to manage their environments and that variations are conscious, planned responses to environmental contingencies. Organizations attempt to absorb interdependence and uncertainty, either completely, as through merger (Pfeffer 1972b), or partially, as through cooptation (Pfeffer 1972a, Allen 1974) or the movement of personnel among organizations (Pfeffer & Leblebici 1973b). Attempts are made to stabilize relations with other organizations, using tactics ranging from tacit collusion (Scherer 1970:157) to legal contracts (Macaulay 1963). Research on strategies has been designed to test the hypothesis that observed variations are planned responses to environmental conditions or at least that organizations behave as if they were guided by norms of rationality. Pfeffer (1972a) found that regulated firms were more likely to include representatives of outside groups on their boards than nonregulated firms and that the pattern of merger activity followed the pattern of resource transactions (Pfeffer 1972b). Alexander (1971) noted that after traditional forms of mergers were challenged by the antitrust authorities, firms switched to the rarely challenged conglomerate merger.

Since the ecological model is indifferent to the source of variations, studies showing that specific variations appear to be responses to environmental conditions are not inconsistent with the model. More troublesome is the fact that no attempt has been made to test the alternative hypothesis, namely that random or unplanned variations play an important part in organizational change. A well-known study in economics is the attempt by Mansfield (1962) and others to test Gibrat's Law, which states that given equal starting points, the size distribution of a population of firms can be fairly well approximated by allowing growth over time to be determined by a random sampling from a distribution of growth rates. In reviewing some experiments, Scherer (1970:126) noted that "contrary to what untutored intuition might advise, the firms do not long remain equal in size and market share, even though their growth prospects are identical *ex ante*. Patterns resembling the concentrated structures of much American manufacturing industry emerge within a few (experimental) decades." However, Scherer concludes by calling for caution in the use of Gibrat's Law, as it patently excludes many variables of interest to economists.

SELECTION

A critical distinction between the resource dependence and natural selection models of organizational change is the relative importance of environmental selection as opposed to strategic decision making by organizational members. For systematic environmental selection criteria to have an effect, two conditions must be present (Campbell 1969): (a) there must be numerous instances involved, i.e., a high rate of variation, and (b) there must be a fairly high mortality rate for the organizations or structures involved. Without variation, there is no raw material for the selection process, and without a high mortality rate environmental selection criteria would be irrelevant.

The purest form of environmental selection is the selective survival or elimination of complete organizations, depending on their fit with the environment. For instance, if the selection criteria were based on administrative rationality, nonbureaucratic organizations might fail to survive, leaving only bureaucracies. This type of selection process is limited in its applicability to organizational populations of industrial societies because (a) the population of business organizations is bifurcated into a segment of very large organizations with a very low mortality rate and another segment of small organizations with high variation and turnover; and (b) as the size of the public sector of the societies grows, more and more organizations are protected from the possibility of failure since they rely on public funding.

As an example of our first point, in 1964 there were about 1.5 million incorporated businesses in the United States. Of these, the largest 325 nonfinancial corporations controlled 42 percent of the assets of all U.S. nonfinancial corporations (Scherer 1970:39). There were another 10 million or so proprietorships and partnerships, most with less than four employees. Large businesses rarely disappear, and when they do it is generally because of mergers or acquisitions. Collins & Preston (1961) compiled lists of the 100 largest manufacturing, mining, and distribution firms for six fairly evenly spaced periods from 1909 through 1958. An average of 2.5 firms per year disappeared from the list and the rate of turnover declined over time. Mergers and acquisitions account for most of the disappearances. At the other end of the size distribution the rate of turnover among small businesses is extremely high. It is estimated that as many as half of all new small business fail within two years of their creation (Mayer & Goldstein 1961).

Our second limitation of the applicability of the natural selection model is related to the expanding role of government in all industrialized nations. Governmental bureaucracies rarely go out of existence. Organizations that come under the protection of various federal, state, or local governments, e.g., public hospitals, social service agencies, schools, or manpower programs, can also be expected to have very low failure rates. National governments have come to the aid of private enterprise as well, particularly large firms, further reducing the mortality rate in that sector.

Environmental selection of entire organizations exists mainly for small businesses, organizations not linked to or subsidized by governmental units, and voluntary associations. Less complete forms of selection, however, exist for all organizations, as particular structures or behaviors may be eliminated, added, or modified under the impact of environmental forces (Burns & Stalker 1961, Pfeffer & Leblebici 1973a). As is the case in organic evolution, selection among organizations is on the basis of relative, rather than absolute, advantage, except in the case of completely nonviable forms.

Selection Processes

The work of Hickson et al (1971) and others who have noted the importance of choice and power in organizations (e.g. Child 1972) provides an important theoretical link between the organization-environment literature and theories of organizational behavior. In Hickson's strategic contingencies theory, power within the organization comes from a subunit's capability for coping with critical organizational uncertainties, as well as from the importance of the uncertainty and the extent to which other subunits can substitute. Power within the organization, in other words, is related to the uncertainties and contingencies the organization faces (Crozier 1964, Thompson 1967). Power within the organization, in turn, affects the choices made within organizations about structures (Child 1972) and about resource allocations (Pfeffer & Salancik 1974). Thus, the process by which environment comes to affect social structure may be the following:

1. The environment provides many of the constraints, uncertainties, and contingencies because of the necessity for transacting with the environment.
2. These contingencies affect the distribution of power and influence within organizations, providing some subunits with more power and others with less.

3. Power is used in determining organizational social structures, particularly to the extent that there is uncertainty and the decisions concern critical issues.

Therefore, by affecting the distribution of influence within organizations, organizational environments come to affect structure and decisions.

Organizations may actively monitor the environment and borrow successful innovations in structure or conduct from other organizations (Aldrich & Reiss 1971). Alternatively, we need only posit that organizations that adopt the innovations of relatively successful organizations will have at least a short-run advantage over others. If information flows relatively freely throughout the population, we would expect selective diffusion of innovations among organizations to be an important selection mechanism for changes that do not involve the elimination of entire organizations. As Mueller (1972: 200) noted, the initial advantage of an organization, derived from an innovation, is eventually lost when information about the innovation is diffused. Selective diffusion and borrowing will occur most readily when organizations are relatively similar and when communications are inexpensive, permitting the flow of information (Stinchcombe 1965).

Within the organization the process of selection may occur through the selective promotion to leadership roles of persons whose past behavior has been most adaptive and successful in a given environment (Campbell 1969). Similarly, variations in task performance that prove more successful will be selected if they occur frequently enough and there exists a mechanism for retaining the processes of the successful new activities or structures. Variations in the environment must be matched by parallel variations in organizational structure or activity if adaptive selection is to occur (Buckley 1967).

One of the major problems of using the ecological model's conception of selection processes is the difficulty of avoiding circularity or tautological arguments (Campbell 1969). Since organizations or partial structures that are not suited to the environment presumably fail, the surviving organizations or structures are, almost by definition, suited. It is easy to retrospectively construct rationales for the characteristics that caused organizations to fail or survive. Since evolutionary theory focuses on differential survival rates which can only be known retrospectively, the temptation to construct tautological explanations for survival and death is great. We may find ourselves saying that bureaucratic organizations were produced by selective criteria favoring bureaucratic organizations. At that point the concepts of environmental fitness, survival, and selection criteria become conceptually indistinguishable (Alland & McCay 1973).

For evolutionary theory to be successfully applied, it appears that it is necessary that variables be identified that are generalizable across contexts and that permit the formulating of a priori as well as ex post hypotheses. Since organizations typically require resources in order to survive, a linkage between evolutionary theory and the various models of resource dependence can be made. It is possible that the critical variable affecting survival probability is the relative resource abundance or scarcity for the particular organization in the environment. In order to develop this idea, it will be necessary to derive measures of resource scarcity or munificence that are generalizable across contexts and types of organizations (Staw & Szwajkowski 1975), and then to examine the extent to which these resource measures account for survival or organizational death.

Strategic Choice

Selection in the ecological model is a matter of certain organizational variations being either positively or negatively selected, depending on their match with environmental conditions. The model is indifferent as to how the variations arose in the first place and the emphasis in selection is on the role of the environment. We have already noted that in the case of large or public organizations the notion of selection being accomplished through differential survival is probably incorrect. Further criticisms of the basic concepts of the selection process as developed in evolutionary models are implicit in the work of theorists writing in the strategic choice (Child 1972) or political economy (Zald 1970) traditions.

Child (1972) raised three arguments to counter the claim that environmental influence is an overwhelming constraint on organizations. First, he noted that organizational decision makers have more autonomy than might be inferred from the perspective of environmental determinism. Decision makers can both select from a range of viable alternatives compatible with the niche they currently occupy and choose the type of environment in which the organization is to operate. Businessmen, for example, may choose to enter or leave markets. Further, Cyert & March (1963), Williamson (1964), and Hirschman (1970) have proposed that there is typically slack in organizational operations and that few, if any, organizations operate at the limits of efficiency. While contingency theorists have argued that there is no universal, best way to organize, they have searched for the best structure for a given environment (Lawrence & Lorsch 1967). The point made here is that there may be a variety of structures that are viable in a given environment. The inconsistent support for theories of structural contingency (Mohr 1971, Pennings 1975), and the literature which indicates that there are a variety of structural mechanisms that may accomplish an organizational purpose, such as control (e.g. Meyer 1972, Child 1973) are both consistent with this first challenge to evolutionary theory.

Strategies such as product differentiation and market segmentation can be viewed as attempts by business firms to achieve a wider range of discretion. The traditional marketing strategy was to convince consumers that a product served their needs better than products of competing firms. Market segmentation involves an attempt to meet the perceived specialized requirements of consumers in a disaggregated market. Market segmentation was the strategy used by adult education programs in California (Clark 1956), in which programs meeting the needs of different groups were offered. Voluntary associations must often choose between these two strategies. If the association stresses the general needs of all, it may lose potential members with specialized requirements. If special programs are established to meet the needs of subgroups, the overall objectives of the association may be diluted (Aldrich 1971a, Demerath & Thiessen 1966).

The second point is that organizations are not always passive recipients of environmental influence but also have power to reshape the environment (Hirsch 1975b). Perrow (1970) has made the same point, while Galbraith (1967) has argued that large business corporations are able to create demand for their products and control their competitive environments. Theories of oligopoly were developed by economists precisely to examine the conditions under which groups of firms can acquire the power to alter market parameters (Phillips 1960).

If the number of firms in a particular market is small, competition can be regulated through informal interfirm arrangements (Phillips 1960). Such informal arrangements tend to be more effective when the organizations have similar objectives and similar operating characteristics. Semiformal interfirm linkages, such as joint ventures (Pfeffer & Nowak 1967) and the movement of executive personnel (Pfeffer & Leblebici 1973b) can be used when there are more, but still relatively few, organizations to be coordinated. The problem of managing the environment under the uncertain conditions produced by a large and heterogeneous population of firms has been solved in many instances by turning to government regulation or other political interventions in the marketplace. Regulation has frequently operated to restrict entry and to stabilize market prices and product characteristics (cf Pfeffer 1974).

Slightly more subtle is the role played by the Commodity Standards Division of the U.S. Department of Commerce in reducing the number of different products manufactured for a given market and in standardizing their characteristics. These standards remove a major obstacle to interfirm collusion by ensuring that there are standard products, hence easing the task of monitoring market sharing agreements, and also tending to stabilize production characteristics across organizations. Public organizations and private nonprofit organizations may form clearinghouse associations, review committees, and other centralized structures to reduce the uncertainty that might otherwise exist in a multi-organizational field (Warren 1967). Also, both private and public organizations seek assistance of various kinds from the government, ranging from direct financial assistance as in the case of cities and universities to the protection of markets from foreign competition using tariffs and quotas.

Child's (1972) third argument against environmental determinism is that the theories stressing the importance of environment have frequently blurred the distinction between characteristics of the environment and the perception and evaluation of these characterisitcs by persons within the organization. This distinction would not be crucial if people always accurately perceived environmental dimensions. Such is not likely to be the case, however, and Pennings (1973) has indicated that there are minimal correlations between objective and subjective measures even of dimensions of organizational structure. One interesting but thus far unexplored research question is the causes and consequences of the extent to which organizational members accurately perceive the environment.

Conceptions of the Environment

Following up Child's insight, Aldrich & Mindlin (1976) identified two different conceptions of the environment in the organizational literature. One approach, exemplified by Dill (1958), Weick (1969), and Duncan (1972), treats an organization's environment as the flow of information perceived by members at the organization's boundaries. The other approach, exemplified by Pfeffer (1972a, b) and Aiken & Hage (1968), treats an organization's environment as the resources available, more or less ignoring the process by which information about the environment is apprehended by decision makers. Analysts from both approaches tend to stress the active role played by an organization is selecting structure, rather than the role of the environment in selecting appropriate organizations and organizational responses.

When the environment is considered as a stock of resources, the basic concept used by investigators is dependence, defined in terms of the bargaining position of the focal organization with respect to interacting organizations (Mindlin & Aldrich 1975, Jacobs 1974). Although the term dependence has not always been used, references are made to resource exchange (Levine & White 1961), power and control over sources of support (Selznick 1949, Evan 1972), and importance of input and output transactions for determining organizational structure (Katz & Kahn 1966). Dependence on external agents for resources is hypothesized to lead to such interorganizational actions as mergers, joint ventures, and cooptation.

When the environment is considered as a source of information, the basic concept used by investigators has been uncertainty. Theorists have generally assumed that complexity and instability of the environment generates uncertainty (Duncan 1972), though it might be argued that uncertainty is caused by the organization's search and analysis methods. Uncertainty has been hypothesized to lead to less formalized and less centralized structures (Burns & Stalker 1961), though it might be argued that complex and contingent structures simply perceive more of the uncertainty in the environment.

Both Weick (1969) and Child have argued that environments are enacted or created through a process of attention. It does seem reasonable to argue that organizational actions will be determined by perceived reality, which may or may not be the same environment that the researcher perceives. It is also reasonable to argue that in different organizations with different structures and information systems, decision makers will perceive the environment differently. Organizational monitoring and scanning systems are highlighted by the concept of environmental enactment and deserve further exploration. Of course, if the organization is severely constrained by the environment, as in a very competitive market, then perception is not important. The personnel in the organization will operate and perceive effectively or else it will soon go out of existence. Perception becomes important to the extent that the organization is insulated from or immune to environmental effects. To the extent that the organization is not tightly constrained, variations in perceptions of organizational reality have more importance in understanding organizational structures and processes.

Limits to Strategic Choice

While the arguments raised against the general applicability of the evolutionary model to the study of social organization are persuasive, these alternative points of view also have their limitations. While environments are selected by organizational decision makers, there are constraints on the operation of this selection process. Potential environments may be excluded by law because of funding restrictions or legal barriers to entry. For business organizations, economists have identified a number of barriers that prevent potential entrants from gaining a position in a market already served by existing organizations. Caves (1972) discusses three such barriers.

Economy-of-scale barriers exist when an organization's unit production costs remain higher than those of competitors until the organization accounts for a substantial share of the market. Until its costs are competitive, the firm must absorb higher costs and hope that a larger share of the market is obtained before it exhausts its capital. Alternatively, a firm could build a large plant of efficient size at the outset and hope to achieve enough market share to dispose of its output. For example, an entrepreneur wishing to enter the cigarette market must build a plant that produces about 15 to 20 percent of the cigarettes sold in the national market if economies of scale are to be realized. While scale economies are present in many industries (Caves 1972), two points should be noted. First, scale economies apply primarily to plant size rather than firm size. Second, Bain (1956) found that the factor of economies of scale could not account for the large size of many major industrial corporations. Scale economies are typically not great and are achieved at a scale of operations far smaller than that which prevails in many industries.

While introduced in economic analysis to explain entry into markets by profit-seeking firms, the concept of economies of scale applies to other organizational forms as well. State and federal legislation may only grant a place on the ballot or campaign subsidies to political parties that achieve a given level of self-financing or votes, and this effectively limits the growth of new political parties. The United Fund requires new applicants for funds to demonstrate the existence of a sufficiently large market for their services, while universities only subsidize those student associations that are able to demonstrate sufficient student interest.

Absolute cost barriers to entry exist when a new firm's costs are higher than those of existing firms, regardless of the firm's output, or when the cost of entry to achieve economies of scale or to achieve market acceptance is so great as to exclude most entrants. Existing firms may possess knowledge not available to new entrants, perhaps because of patents or the prohibitive expense involved in doing the research or building a plant big enough to compete. A classic example is the Coca Cola Bottling Company with a formula for the product that is known only to a few persons in the organization. Existing firms may have acquired control over the supply of an important resource, thus denying its use to a new firm. Until the end of the second World War the Aluminum Company of America maintained its position as the single supplier of aluminum through its monopolization of the bauxite supply. The amount of capital required to start a new firm may be so enormous as to be prohibitive. For example, in 1954 it was estimated that the capital required to build an efficient automobile plant was $250-500 million. Thus it is not surprising that there has been limited entry into the automobile market.

Product differentiation barriers to entry exist when established firms have achieved high visibility and their brands have gained wide recognition. For a new firm to enter the market, regardless of the production economics involved, the firm must spend an enormous amount on advertising to develop brand recognition and market acceptance. The existing competitor need spend only enough to maintain an image that has been developed over a long period of time. This added expenditure required for overcoming advertising economies of scale provides the new entrant with cost disadvantages that must be absorbed or reflected in higher selling prices. Voluntary associations face similar problems, as particular objectives or causes come to be identified with particular associations (Aldrich 1971a). Consider, for example, the problem a new group working in the ecology area would have winning members away from the Sierra Club. Many public sector organizations further raise the barriers to entry by being recognized legally or socially as monopolies for the service or product they offer.

The existence of barriers to entry makes clear the limits to organizational choice of environment. Further, barriers to entry provide a partial explanation for why rates of change in some populations are much slower than in others. Barriers to entry limit the range of variation in a population and are a negative selective force operating against new organizations. The higher the barriers to entry, the lower the pressure for change in the structure or activities of existing organizations.

The idea of choice of an environment may be an overstatement of the actual degree of planning and rationality exercised by organizations in moving into new niches (Starbuck 1975). Behavioral theories of the firm typically assume that organizations examine their environments only when they are under some pressure (Cyert & March 1963) or that search for new opportunities occurs only when the organization faces problems with its current activities. Studies of organizational managers find that the managers often operate on the basis of folk theories or conventional wisdom (Mintzberg 1973), taking their environment as given and working within the constraints. Organizations occasionally move into a new environmental niche on the basis of misperceptions of their fitness for the niche, such as RCA's entry into the computer business.

The second criticism of environmental determinism, that organizations have the power to modify their environments, is true chiefly for the largest organizations or those that are politically well connected. However, only slightly more than 3 percent of all business enterprises, as enumerated by the U.S. Social Security Administration, have over 50 employees. It is unlikely that firms of under this size have much power to affect their environments, although this varies by local circumstances. At the same time, we should recognize that there is some evidence that concentration of resources in fewer large organizations is increasing, and that clearly these larger organizations and comparable organizations in the public sector dominate many aspects of current life.

While it is true that actions are based on managerial perceptions of reality, and that Child (1972) is correct in stressing the role of perceptions, it is also the case that such perceptions are not likely to be completely idiosyncratic to a particular organization. A variety of social processes combine to induce a common perception of the environment within a subpopulation of organizations. Organizations tend to hire management personnel from within the same industry (Pfeffer & Leblebici 1973b) or subpopulation (Baty, Evan & Rothermel 1971). Imitation and borrowing are important sources of new ideas and business, trade, and professional publications promote the development of a common frame of reference. Managers and staff are sent to the same institutes and training institutions, and various types of coalitions depend on shared perceptions for the coordination of interorganizational behavior.

The effect of these processes is to homogenize perceptions across organizations and to make each organization less sensitive to the unique characteristics of its local environment (Starbuck 1975). If a local environment is benign and has a wide tolerance for deviations from the ideal structure or performance, then socially induced mis-perceptions are not fatal. When perceptions are universally shared, no single organization is at a relative disadvantage in the competition for resources. When an environment is changing rapidly or is less munificent, deviant organizations that do not share the common misperceptions may be positively selected and take over the niche.

Our review of the selection stage of the natural selection process has disclosed three major issues that confront research on organizational change. First, environmental selection is not only between organizations as wholes but also between particular structures or behaviors within organizations. While selection may occur through the failure of an entire organization, the more typical case is for the organization to adapt by means of structural or behavioral modifications. Organizational change, therefore, must be examined at both levels: selection at the population level between competing firms and selection at organizational level between the variations internal to the organization.

Second, the organizational population is structured in such a way as to make selection much more probable in one subpopulation than in the other. One subpopulation, consisting of very large organizations, associations, and public agencies, contains organizations that are relatively unlikely to fail, and, moreover, frequently have the power to alter their environments to fit their own dimensions and capabilities. The other subpopulation consists of smaller organizations that have a significant probability of failure and a high rate of turnover. The latter group is much larger in number than the former, though the former is of greater total societal significance. While large firms and public agencies may not fail, this does not mean these organizations are immune to environmental effects on structure or activity. As we have indicated, autonomous strategic choice is problematic even for very large organizations.

Third, Child's point about the importance of perceptions is probably true, in general. As Starbuck (1975) has noted, however, the critical questions concern the extent to which organizational perceptions vary from objective indicators of environment and the factors that cause variations in perceptions and in divergence from other indicators. Unless such differences are critical, the point is not likely to affect analyses of organizational change.

RETENTION

The retention stage of the natural selection process can be thought of as stability in the structure or decision rules of an individual organization, as the preservation of organizational forms over time, or as stability in the pattern of interdependencies between organizations in an environment. Retention in social evolution is at this time more difficult to conceptualize than in organic evolution and we do not want to force the issue by searching for the organizational analogues to chromosomes and genes. Instead, we consider some general character-istics of retention mechanisms in social systems, identify possible social retention mechanisms, and then consider anew the data on the retention of organizational characteristics presented by Stinchcombe (1965).

Retention of successful adaptations in social systems depends upon the retention and transmission of knowledge from one generation to the next (Campbell 1969). Calling this knowledge *culture* and the retention process *institutionalization* links evolutionary theory to traditional sociological concepts but does not constitute an explan-ation (Parsons 1966). In preliterate societies with few written records, knowledge is passed through the generations via an oral tradition and there are strong sanctions against innovation or variation in the information passed along (Campbell 1969). The evolutionary model explains sanctions against varying successful traditional practices in terms of the extreme vulnerability of societies with few surplus resources to short-run misfortune. A series of unsuccessful variations may mean not the selective elimination of particular practices but the failure of the entire society. Negative sanctions need not have been consciously designed with this objective in mind, as the evolutionary model predicts simply that societies without such sanctions will not survive. As surplus resources accumulate, variation and innovation are less threatening and innovators may find a niche in the societal division of labor (Lenski 1966).

Campbell (1969) argues that as societal forms have matured, there has probably been a trend toward the externalization and rationali-zation of culture. Material culture rather than the oral tradition now carries societal traditions and history, and there is less danger of adaptations being lost because of random variations. Written records, machinery, the physical and material components of cities, and what one might call the capital improvements in a society represent the externalization of past successful adaptations to the environment. This process is similar to that described by Berger & Luckmann (1967) for the social construction of knowledge.

The continuing existence of certain forms does not mean that the form has retained the original function for which it was selected. Forms can and do change functions as evolution takes place and as the environment and other forms change. For example, some theorists

(Bellah 1970) have argued that in the past century traditional religious organizations have been displaced in their function of providing meaning and value by secular institutions; their chief function is now social welfare services. Such transformations of function mean we must guard against assuming continuity in the development and meaning of previously successful adaptations.

Perhaps the most important point made by Campbell (1969) with regard to the retention of forms is that complex structures are only maintained by consistent environmental pressure. Without consistent pressure, two factors combine to disrupt the complexity of a structure. First, the continuous occurrence of random variation, if unchecked by selective elimination, gradually takes a system to a simpler and less organized state. Second, internal selection pressures are biased toward simplicity in the interests of stabilizing intraorganizational conduct. Deviance is rooted out and there are strong pressures toward a uniformity of outlook among all members. These pressures, if not countered by strong environmental pressure rewarding complexity, will eventually remove a structure's complexity. For example, complex oligopolistic arrangements are highly vulnerable to short-term deviations from policy by individual members, and pressures toward a common product development policy may leave the oligopolists at the mercy of a new entrant with a technologically superior product. In general, if we observe a complex and long-lived structure, we should look to the environment for the source of pressures that have maintained it.

Mechanisms of Social Retention

Internal and external retention mechanisms in organizations can be identified, although the structures and behaviors we describe here have not usually been considered in an evolutionary framework. Most of the characteristics of bureaucracy described by Weber (1947) can be thought of as contributing to the retention of a specific organizational form. Documents and files are the archetypal characteristic of bureaucracy and as the material embodiment of past practices, they serve as ready references for the appropriate procedure to be followed for normal contingencies. Specialization and standardization of the duties of each role limit the discretion of officeholders and thus protect the organization against random variations from policy. Given that top managers have a clear image of their organization's character (Selznick 1957), centralization of authority allows them to preserve it. Making membership in the bureaucracy a career and basing mobility through the ranks on universalistic performance criteria rewards persons for conforming to the specialized and standardized duties they are assigned. We are not arguing that these characteristics are optimal for all organizations; rather, we are emphasizing the way in which bureaucratic structures help to preserve a given form.

The informal organization and informal culture also help to preserve stability in behavior on the part of organizational members. Just prior to and immediately upon entering an organizational position, a person goes through a process of acquiring an organizational role (Thornton & Nardi 1975). As part of this process, expectations concerning actions and attitudes appropriate to that position are communicated. Persons entering an organization are socialized (Dornbusch 1955), and as an outcome of this socialization process the culture of the organization is transmitted to new members.

Continuity in an organization's leadership may be another retention mechanism that preserves patterns of behavior and structure. Similarity in leadership is enhanced by a stable selection promotion system that rewards and filters people according to their similarity in outlook and background. Because the filtering is typically done by those already in leadership positions and because people are attracted to others who are similar to themselves, the likelihood of perpetuating current patterns of leadership are great. Furthermore, since the promotion of leaders is based on their experience and expertise in dealing with critical organizational contingencies, to the extent that the definition of organizational uncertainties remains the same, similarity in leadership characteristics is further assured. Organizations that are marketing-oriented, such as consumer goods companies, may tend to promote people with sales or marketing experience who, because of similar backgrounds and socialization, will have fairly similar ideas about organizational policy. Grocery store chains are run by persons with experience in store management rather than those who were promoted from staff positions. In many organizations there are clearly defined paths to the top positions, which ensure some similarity in background and information on the part of those who achieve those positions.

External pressures for retaining a given structure include all the environmental demands that originally selected (or were compatible with) that structure or behavior. Competitive pressures on business firms, member pressures on voluntary associations, and political pressures on public agencies may help to explain the rentention of past structures by these organizations. Indeed, it is possible for the organization to seek to generate external pressures intentionally as a way of helping it to maintain present form.

As implied in our discussion of social forces that induce common perceptions among persons in an industry or subpopulation, information processing and transmitting organizations may assist in the retention of a limited range of forms. Business schools, training and educational institutes, consulting firms, and trade or professional associations promote specific procedures and organizational forms that become part of the culture of an organizational population. Some of these procedures catch the popular fancy and spread to most organizations, where they become entrenched and encrusted with organizational mythology, e.g., divisional as opposed to functional forms of departmentalization. Others, e.g., business schools, are popularized in one subpopulation, but do not achieve a long-lasting place in the larger population, e.g., the Planning, Programming, Budgeting Systems movement of the 1960s.

Folk wisdom and industry rules of thumb (Scherer 1970) are also part of organizational culture, perpetuated by all the forces discussed in the section on selective perception. They play a role in the retention of specific forms because they become part of the habitual behavior of members of organizations and are resistant to change. Since selective elimination or retention depends on variation in the forms of a population, a widespread habit can effectively insulate a population against a changing environment, if no competing forms arise in other industries or subpopulations and new entrants adopt the traditional behavior or structure.

Examination of Stinchcombe's Analysis

In considering why different organizational forms appear in different periods in history, Stinchcombe (1965:160) concluded that "certain kinds of organizations . . . could not be invented before the social structure was appropriate to them." From the perspective of the evolutionary model, one would argue that the environment must have changed to give a selective advantage to particular forms at a given time. The specific characteristics of the form depended upon the nature and distribution of resources available in the environment, technological development, wealth and power, and the structure of labor markets (Stinchcombe 1965:160-64). Stinchcombe also considered why certain forms, once created, persist over time, i.e. have the same structural characteristics as when they were founded. We shall use the ideas of the evolutionary model to reexamine this analysis, as there is compatibility between Stinchcombe's position and the concepts of evolutionary theory.

As evidence for the stability of organizational forms over time, Stinchcombe presents U.S. Census data on the work force characteristics of four groups of industries: pre-factory, early nineteenth century, railroad age, and modern. Some general differences are apparent between these groups. Pre-factory industries, such as agriculture and retail trade, still use more unpaid family labor than industries founded later. Early nineteenth century industries, such as woodworking and apparel, are still family firms, but differ from earlier forms in that they are bureaucratized below the top management level. Railroad age industries, such as railroads and coal mining, have career officials rather than family members at the very top, but their staff departments are not as professionalized as modern industries. Modern industries, such as motor vehicles and air transport, are extensively bureaucratized, with a high proportion of clerical and professional workers at the top and with almost no family labor or management.

Stinchcombe derived an ad hoc set of three hypotheses to explain why these historical differences have persisted. First, the original form may still be the most efficient, given the competition it has had to face. Second, institutionalization may have preserved the form, whether through traditionalizing forces, vested interests, or a strongly legitimated ideological position. Third, the original form may have had no competitors because it is a natural monopoly or is assured of a stable funding source. While these explanations are not tested empirically, they appear to be plausible and are similar to explanations that would be deduced from consideration of the natural selection model of organizational change.

Before looking at these explanations from an ecological perspective, we should note the presence of a problem previously mentioned— the arbitrary nature of the definitions of organizational forms. Stinchcombe used the definitions of industries as adopted by the Bureau of the Census, and therefore classified railroads and air transport as different industries. A different outcome might emerge if organizations were classified by their functional niche in the interorganizational division of labor. At the very least, one could argue that innovative organizations and new forms have appeared in niches adjacent to existing niches, perhaps making use of different resources at the outset, but eventually expanding to take over the adjacent niches. For example, the trucking industry has made inroads into the functions once performed by the railroad industry. If we call these new forms new industries, then Stinchcombe's analysis remains unchanged. However, one could argue for the functional continuity of certain industries that Stinchcombe separated. Thus, water, rail, and air transport might be considered evolving forms of transportation and printing and publishing might be considered the forerunner of telecommunications. Similarly, coal mining, crude petroleum, and natural gas might be considered alternatives within the energy industry.

If such a reclassification is made, different inferences emerge from Stinchcombe's data. Now there is evidence of forms evolving toward more bureaucratic structures. This argument might be examined by considering rates of growth in each of the component industries within the larger functional classifications. If the argument is correct, then newer forms should be gradually displacing older forms and achieving a larger share of the market. At some point, in fact, the new form might completely eliminate the older form. The stability of forms uncovered by Stinchcombe may not be an accurate portrayal of the evolutionary process that is actually occurring. An investigator might still choose to focus on the reasons for the stability of the declining forms, but the implications of such an analysis would be quite different.

If we focus on the explanation of stability, the question can be recast to consider the selective retention of organizational forms. We could first examine the possible sources of variation within an industry. Environmental selection has maximum effect where the rate of variation is high and the life span of any one unit is relatively short. (If we were examining change in a single organization, our premise would be that only an organization with a short memory can move in concert with environmental changes impinging on it.) An industry may be stable because the length of a generation is relatively long or there are few failures and few new starts. This may be due to barriers to entry, slow rate of technological change, or a high proportion of owner-controlled firms. An organization that is controlled by its owner is relatively well protected from takeover by external organizations through tender offers or by management coups within the organization. There is some evidence that owner-controlled business firms can survive for a long time in spite of relatively poor economic performance (Hindley 1970). Another example of a factor suppressing variation is the passing of the business between successive generations of the family, as when a son takes over the father's firm, a practice especially noticeable in agriculture.

Forms may also change slowly because there is little variation across organizations within the industry or subpopulation. This result might occur because the environment at one point had a powerful effect in selecting a homogeneous population of organizations and the environment is now stable, or some factor insulates the organizations from environmental change, for instance the provision of government subsidies.

Variation may be relatively infrequent because there are few entrepreneurs willing to undertake the risk of starting a new organization. Without variation, which is most likely to occur in new organizations, environmental selection criteria are irrelevant in affecting the direction of change in a subpopulation.

Stinchcombe's explanations for stability in forms can thus be reduced to the following cases: (a) conditions where environmental selection operates freely and the original form continues to be chosen because environmental parameters have not changed or new entrants have not developed a more advantageous form; and (b) conditions where environmental selection is severely restricted either because there are barriers to entry or because organizations are insulated from environmental effects. Stability of organizational forms can be explained by the natural selection model, though care must be taken in classifying organizations because of the arbitrary definitions of organizational forms. Whether forms are treated as stable or evolving depends partly on how widely an environmental niche is defined. It is possible that some of Stinchcombe's stable forms are actually declining, if we use a functional classification of industries.

In using the ecological model care must be exercised not to automatically equate stability of form with stability of other features of the organization. For instance, agriculture, a pre-factory industry, has exhibited the highest rate of productivity improvement of virtually any industry in the United States. Thus, the form or structure of an organization may at times remain unchanged, while improvements in the functioning of the form continue.

Forms may be retained because the range of variation had been restricted, environmental selection criteria cannot operate, or the form is still the most fit. Propositions from a resource dependence perspective may be developed about the types of strategies organizations will pursue to ensure their retention in the population. One strategy may be to carefully monitor the environment and change the activities and structure to fit environmental demands. This strategy may be the only feasible action for smaller organizations in competitive settings. Creating barriers to entry, either through interfirm arrangements or through the use of governmental power is probably the most common strategy and we have previously considered the different forms of barriers to entry. Following the ecological perspective, one might argue that these forms of entry barriers, as well as other strategies, themselves evolve over time as environmental conditions change.

CONCLUSIONS

The environment of organizations is important because of its effects on organizational structures and decisions. Progress in the study of organizations derives from focusing on substantive problems rather than from the elaboration of conceptual schemes. Models of environmental selection are useful only as they enrich our understanding of stability and change in organizational forms, or, as Hannan & Freeman (1974:10) ask, "Why are there so many kinds of organizations?" The natural selection model answers this question by examining the nature and distribution of resources in the environment, while the resource dependence model focuses on the decisions and power and influence relationships that affect organizational actions and strategies that seek to manage the environment.

The stages of variation, selection, and retention constitute a general model not entirely incompatible with the resource dependence approach. A review of the differences between the two perspectives indicated that an explanation of organizational change must address issues of the level of analysis, sources of variation, selection criteria and mechanisms, and the time frame for analysis that is used.

The natural selection model has usually been applied at the population level of analysis, as in biological research on the evolution of species. Since forms of social organization undergo major change in other ways besides the elimination of entire units, the model must be modified to treat social evolution as also occurring through morphogenesis (Buckley 1967), or major transformations of the structure and behaviors of existing organizations. Most investigators of organizational change have examined change at the level of individual organizations. This level of analysis is encouraged by the attention investigators have paid to leadership, decision making, and case studies of successful organizations. As research expands to encompass samples of diverse organizations, investigators are more likely to confront issues raised by the ecological model.

The resource dependence model stresses variations that arise through active alternative generation and search procedures. These types of variation could be subsumed under the more general approach to variation of the evolutionary model, in which both planned and random variations are considered. Some theorists would argue that planning for an unexpected future is largely an illusion and that planning occurs only retrospectively (Weick 1969). However, since people do have the capacity to maintain consistency in behavior, evolutionary studies of organizations might incorporate the idea of planned variations.

Selection according to the ecological model occurs as a consequence of the environment. If the organization fits environment requirements, it is selected. The basis of structure selection, experienced as success from the viewpoint of a single organization, may be imperfectly understood by organizational members. Without knowledge of alternative forms that were not positively selected, it is difficult for a single organization's members to accurately attribute the source of their success. The resource dependence model also argues for the necessity of a fit between organization and environment. The principle difference is that the resource dependence model argues that organizations can shape their environments to fit their capabilities, and that environmental constraints leave the possibility of a variety of activities and structures consistent with environmental requirements.

The time frame of most research on organizations, given its emphasis on leadership and decision making, is fairly short. Before natural selection processes can be examined, enough time must pass so that variation, selection, and retention can occur. The requirement for this longer perspective suggests that the use of archival data, as well as the development of research projects that are longitudinal, will be useful.

The ecological model, like models of operant conditioning in learning theory, emphasizes the external control of organizations. The environment selects those forms and activities that fit best. The role of decision making and choice is downplayed and the possibility that people shape, as well as are shaped by, their environments is ignored. Regardless of the empirical validity of the natural selection or resource dependence perspectives, it is likely that the active, planning orientation of the resource dependence approach will make it more palatable to most organizational managers as well as to many social scientists; however, the empirical validity of both approaches must be examined in order to understand organizational change.

Acknowledgement
The authors appreciate the helpful comments of John Freeman, John Child, and Les Metcalfe. The support of the International Institute of Management, Berlin, and the Centre for Environmental Studies, London, is gratefully acknowledged.

References

Aiken, M., Hage, J. 1968. Organizational interdependence and intraorganizational structure. *Am. Sociol. Rev.* 33:912-30

Alchian, A. 1950. Uncertainty, evolution, and economic theory. *J. Polit. Econ.* 58:211-21

Aldrich, H. E. 1971a. The sociable organization: a case study of MENSA and some propositions. *Sociol. Soc. Res.* 55:429-41

Aldrich, H. E. 1971b. Organizational boundaries and interorganizational conflict. *Hum. Relat.* 24:279-87

Aldrich, H. E., Mindlin, S. 1976. Uncertainty and dependence: two conceptions of the environment. In *Organization and Environment,* ed. L. Karpik, New York: Russell Sage Found.

Aldrich, H. E. Reiss, A. J. Jr. 1971. Police officers as boundary personnel. In *The Police in Urban Society,* ed. H. Hahn, pp. 193-208. Beverly Hills, Calif: Sage

Aldrich, H. E., Reiss, A. J. Jr. 1976. Continuities in the study of ecological succession: changes in the race composition of neighborhoods and their businesses. *Am. J. Sociol.* 81:846-66

Alexander, K. 1971. Conglomerate mergers and collective bargaining. *Ind. Lab. Rel. Rev.* 24:354-74

Alland, A. Jr., McCay, B. 1973. The concept of adaptation in biological and cultural evolution. In *Handbook of Social and Cultural Anthropology,* ed. J. Honigmann, pp. 143-78. Chicago: Rand McNally

Allen, M. P. 1974. The structure of interorganizational elite cooptation: interlocking corporate directorates. *Am. Sociol. Rev.* 39:393-406

Bain, J. S. 1956. *Barriers to New Competition.* Cambridge: Harvard Univ. Press

Baty, G., Evan, W. M., Rothermel, T. 1971. Personnel flows as interorganizational relations. *Admin. Sci. Q.* 16:430-43

Bellah, R. N. 1970. *Beyond Belief: Essays on Religion in a Post-Traditional World.* New York: Harper & Row

Bendix, R. 1956. *Work and Authority in Industry.* New York: Wiley

Benson, J. K. 1975. The interorganizational network as a political economy. *Admin. Sci. Q.* 20:229-49

Berger, P. L., Luckmann, T. 1967. *The Social Construction of Reality.* London: Penguin

Blau, P. M. 1964. *Exchange and Power in Social Life.* New York: Wiley

Buckley, W. 1967. *Sociology and Modern Systems Theory.* Englewood Cliffs, NJ: Prentice-Hall

Burns, T., Stalker, G. M. 1961. *The Management of Innovation.* London: Tavistock

Campbell, D. 1969. Variation and selective retention in socio-cultural evolution. *Gen. Sys.* 16:69-85

Caves, R. 1972. *American Industry: Structure, Conduct, and Performance.* Englewood Cliffs, NJ: Prentice-Hall

Chandler, A. 1962. *Strategy and Structure.* Cambridge: MIT Press

Child, J. 1972. Organization structure, environment, and performance—the role of strategic choice. *Sociology* 6:1-22

Child, J. 1973. Strategies of control and organizational behavior. *Admin. Sci. Q.* 18:1-17

Clark, B. 1956. Organizational adaptation and precarious values. *Am. Sociol. Rev.* 21:327-36

Collins, N. R., Preston, L. E. 1961. The size structure of the largest industrial firms, 1909-1958. *Am. Econ. Rev.* 51:986-1011

Crozier, M. 1964. *The Bureaucratic Phenomenon.* Chicago: Univ. Chicago Press

Cyert, R. M., March, J. G. 1963. *A Behavioral Theory of the Firm.* Englewood Cliffs, NJ: Prentice-Hall

Demerath, N. J., Thiessen, V. 1966. On spitting against the wind: organizational precariousness and American irreligion *Am. J. Sociol.* 71:674-87

Dill, W. R. 1958. Environment as an influence on managerial autonomy. *Admin. Sci. Q.* 2:409-43

Dornbusch, S. 1955. The military academy as an assimilating institution. *Soc. Forces* 33:316-21

Duncan, R. 1972. Characteristics of organizational environments and perceived environmental uncertainty. *Admin. Sci. Q. 17:313-27*

Emery, F. E., Trist, E. L. 1965. The casual texture of organizational environments. *Hum. Relat.* 18:21-32

Evan, W. 1972. An organization-set model of interorganizational relations. In *Interorganizational Decision Making,* ed. M. Tuite, R. Chisholm, M. Radnor, pp. 181-200. Chicago: Aldine

Friedman, M. 1953. *Essays in Positive Economics.* Chicago: Univ. Chicago Press

Galbraith, J. K. 1967. *The New Industrial State.* Boston: Houghton Mifflin

Gouldner, A. W. 1954. *Patterns of Industrial Bureaucracy.* Glencoe, Ill: Free Press

Hall, R. 1972. *Organizations: Structure and Process.* Englewood Cliffs, NJ: Prentice-Hall

Hannan, M. T., Freeman, J. H. 1974. Environment and the structure of organizations: a population ecology perspective. Presented at Ann. Meet. Am. Sociol. Assoc., Montreal, Canada, Aug.

Hasenfeld, Y. 1972. People processing organizations. *Am. Sociol. Rev.* 37:256-63

Hausknecht, M. 1962. *The Joiners.* New York: Bedminster

Hickson, D. J., Hinings, C. R., Lee, C. A., Schneck, R. E., Pennings, J. M. 1971. A strategic contingencies theory of intraorganizational power. *Admin. Sci. Q.* 16:216-29

Hindley, B. 1970. Separation of ownership and control in the modern corporation. *J. Law Econ.* 13:185-222

Hirsch, P. M. 1975a. Organizational analysis and industrial sociology: an instance of cultural lag. *Am. Sociol.* 10:3-12

Hirsch, P. M. 1975b. Organizational effectiveness and the institutional environment. *Admin. Sci. Q.* 20:327-44

Hirschman, A. O. 1970. *Exit, Voice, and Loyalty.* Cambridge: Harvard Univ. Press

Jacobs, D. 1974. Dependency and vulnerability: and exchange approach to the control of organizations. *Admin. Sci. Q.* 19:45-59

Katz, D., Kahn, R. L. 1966. *The Social Psychology of Organizations.* New York: Wiley

Knight, F. H. 1921. *Risk, Uncertainty, and Profit,* Boston: Houghton Mifflin

Lawrence, P. R., Lorsch, J. W. 1967. *Organization and Environment.* Boston: Harvard Univ. Press

Lenski, G. E. 1966. *Power and Privilege: A Theory of Social Stratification.* New York: McGraw-Hill

Levine, S., White, P. E. 1961. Exchange as a conceptual framework for the study of interorganizational relationships. *Admin. Sci. Q.* 5:583-610

Macaulay, S. 1963. Non-contractual relations in business: a preliminary study. *Am. Sociol. Rev.* 28:55-67

Mansfield, E. 1962. Entry, Gibrat's Law, innovation, and the growth of firms. *Am. Econ. Rev.* 52:1023-50

Marrett, C. B. 1971. On the specification of interorganizational dimensions. *Sociol Soc. Res.* 56:83-99

Mayer, K. B., Goldstein, S. 1961. *The First Two Years: Problems of Small Firm Growth and Survival.* Washington DC: GPO

Meyer, M. W. 1972. Size and the structure of organizations: a causal analysis. *Am. Sociol. Rev.* 37:434-41

Mindlin, S., Aldrich, H. E. 1975. Interorganizational dependence: a review of the concept and a reexamination of the findings of the Aston group. *Admin. Sci. Q.* 20:382-92

Mintzberg, H. 1973. *The Nature of Managerial Work,* New York: Harper & Row

Mohr, L. 1971. Organizational technology and organizational structure. *Admin. Sci. Q.* 16:444-59

Mueller, D. C. 1972. A life cycle theory of the firm. *J. Ind. Econ.* 20:199-219

Parsons, T. 1966. *Societies: Evolutionary and Comparative Perspectives.* Englewood Cliffs, NJ: Prentice-Hall

Pennings, J. 1973. Measures of organizational structure: a methodological note. *Am. J. Sociol.* 79:686-704

Pennings, J. M. 1975. The relevance of the structural-contingency model for organizational effectiveness. *Admin. Sci. Q.* 20:393-410

Penrose, E. T. 1952. Biological analogies in the theory of the firm. *Am. Econ. Rev. 42:804-19*

Perrow, C. 1970. *Organizational Analysis: A Sociological View.* Belmont, Calif: Wadsworth

Pfeffer, J. 1972a. Size and composition of corporate boards of directors. *Admin. Sci. Q.* 17:218-28

Pfeffer, J. 1972b. Merger as a response to organizational interdependence. *Admin. Sci. Q.* 17:382-94

Pfeffer, J. 1974. Administrative regulation and licensing: social problem or solution? *Soc. Probl.* 21:468-79

Pfeffer, J. 1976. Beyond management and the worker: the institutional function of management. *Acad. Manage. Rev.* 1:In press

Pfeffer, J., Leblebici, H. 1973a. The effect of competition on some dimensions of organizational structure. *Soc. Forces* 52:268-79

Pfeffer, J., Leblebici, H. 1973b. Executive recruitment and the development of interfirm organizations. *Admin. Sci. Q.* 18:445-61

Pfeffer, J., Nowak, P. 1976. Patterns of joint venture activity: implications for antitrust policy. *Antitrust Bull.* In press

Pfeffer, J., Salancik, G. R. 1974. Organizational decision making as a political process: the case of a university budget. *Admin. Sci. Q.* 19:135-51

Phillips, A. 1960. A theory of interfirm organization. *Q. J. Econ.* 74:602-13

Sahlins, M. D., Service, E. R. 1960 *Evolution and Culture.* Ann Arbor: Univ. Mich. Press

Scherer, F. M. 1970. *Industrial Market Structure and Economic Performance.* Chicago: Rand McNally

Schumpeter, J. A. 1934. *The Theory of Economic Development.* Cambridge: Harvard Univ. Press

Selznick, P. 1949. *TVA and the Grass Roots.* Berkeley: Univ. Calif. Press

Selznick, P. 1957. *Leadership in Administration.* Evanston, Ill: Row, Peterson

Selznick, P. 1960. *The Organizational Weapon.* Glencoe, Ill: Free Press

Starbuck, W. 1975. The organization and its environment. In *Handbook of Industrial and Organizational Psychology,* ed. M. Dunnette. Chicago: Rand McNally. In press

Staw, B. M., Szwajkowski, E. 1975. The scarcity-munificence component of organizational environments and the commission of illegal acts. *Admin. Sci. Q.* 20:345-54

Stigler, G. J. 1966. *The Theory of Price.* New York: Macmillan

Stinchcombe, A. L. 1965. Social structure and organizations. In *Handbook of Organizations,* ed. J. G. March, pp. 142-93. Chicago: Rand McNally

Thompson, J. D. 1967. *Organizations in Action.* New York: McGraw-Hill

Thornton, R., Nardi, P. M. 1975. The dynamics of role acquisition. *Am. J. Sociol.* 80:870-85

Wamsley, G., Zald, M. N. 1973. *The Political Economy of Public Organizations.* Lexington, Mass: Heath

Warren, R. 1967. The interorganizational field as a focus for investigation. *Admin. Sci. Q.* 12:396-419

Warren, R. Rose, S., Bergunder, A. 1974. *The Structure of Urban Reform.* Lexington, Mass: Heath

Weber, M. 1947. *The Theory of Social and Economic Organization.* Glencoe, Ill: Free Press

Weber, M. 1968. *Economy and Society.* New York: Bedminster

Weick, K. 1969. *The Social Psychology of Organizing.* Reading, Mass: Addison-Wesley

White, L. 1949. *The Science of Culture: A Study of Man and Civilization.* New York: Farrar

White, P. E. 1974. Resources as determinants of organizational behavior. *Admin. Sci. Q.* 19:366-79

Williamson, O. E. 1964. *The Economics of Discretionary Behavior: Managerial Objectives in a Theory of the Firm.* Englewood Cliffs, NJ: Prentice-Hall

Winter, S. 1971. Satisficing, selection, and the innovating remnant. *Q. J. Econ.* 85:237-61

Zachariah, M. 1971. The impact of Darwin's theory of evolution on theories of society. *Soc. Stud.* 62:69-76

Zald, M. N. 1970. Political economy: a framework for analysis. In *Power in Organizations,* ed. M. N. Zald, pp. 221-61. Nashville: Vanderbilt Univ. Press

Zald, M. N., Ash, R. 1966. Social movement organizations: growth, decay, and change. *Soc. Forces* 44:327-41

Zurcher, L. Curtis, R. 1973. A comparative analysis of propositions describing social movement organizations. *Sociol. Q.* 14:175-88

The Academic Library and Its Environment

Beverly P. Lynch

THE practical art of library organization and management is far ahead of its corresponding theory. The literature of librarianship reflects a preoccupation with the search for the one best way to organize the library, whereas practice encompasses a variety of organizational and managerial styles and configurations. Librarians know that an organizational structure suitable for a library of a liberal arts college in a rural setting probably is inappropriate for the library of a major urban college. They know that the management style and structure of the local college library differs from that of the local public library, although both libraries are in the same town. The thoughtful library manager recognizes individual differences in each library and structures his library accordingly.

Although many library schools, associations, and much library literature consider library problems by the type of library in which those problems occur, there has been no exploration of the differences arising from the environmental settings of libraries. It has been assumed that libraries are affected by their varying environments and that factors external to the library influence its internal operations. Although it has been recognized that external factors vary according to whether the library is a college, a public, or a school library, little is known about the impact of the environment upon the library.

Some of the classics in librarianship describe the library in its environmental context, but the more recent investigations of the library as an organization focus on intraorganizational phenomena.[1] Marchant studies the characteristics of the library's decision-making process and the impact of the process upon staff satisfaction.[2] Spence correlates measures of library size with various dimensions of library

---

Reprinted by permission of the American Library Association from *College and Research Libraries* 35(3): 126–32 (Mar. 1974).

structure.[3] Lynch measures the variability in the work of library departments before making predictions as to variations in the library's structure.[4] Each of these studies examines only internal characteristics of the library.

This preoccupation with internal factors has led to the relative neglect of interorganizational relationships within librarianship. Libraries "are embedded in an environment of other organizations as well as in a complex of norms, values, and collectivities of the society at large."[5] Librarians do recognize that the library is dependent to some degree upon its environment. Environmental factors within the university and the society at large have been identified as having an influence upon the library's structure.[6]

In the provocative article "The Changing Role of Directors of University Libraries," Arthur McAnally and Robert Downs describe characteristics of the university and society at large that affect the university library.[7] They suggest that the recent turnover in university library directors occured in response to the changing environment in which the university library is embedded: the library could not cope with the enormous expansion that took place within the university during the 1960s; the role of the library was reduced and its power diminished as the management patterns within the university changed; the expansion and fragmentation of knowledge influenced university curricula and design, and these patterns directly influenced the university library in terms of staffing patterns, responsibilities, decision making, and so forth.

The library can be viewed as an open system, affected by contingencies placed upon it by its environment. An open system is one in which some kind of exchange takes place between the system and its environment. The general perspective of the open system is that the organization obtains its resources and energy from its environment, transforms these resources into products, and exports the finished products or services back into the environment.[8] With the open system, the organization is capable of bringing in resources to modify its own internal workflows, structures, and procedures.

If the library is studied as a system interacting with its environment and bringing resources (human, financial, and material) into the library, the dynamic aspects of the library's internal organization, design, and structure can be better understood. Because the environment can influence internal workflows, structures, and procedures, a study of the library and its environment can help identify changing aspects of library organization and varying organizational patterns as well as lead to development of predictive models for library organization.

APPROACHES TO THE LIBRARY'S ENVIRONMENT

Several approaches can be used to examine the library's environment. The following four areas are covered in this study:

1. The nature of the environment itself.
2. The relationships among the libraries within a set of organizations.
3. The characteristics of the exchanges that take place among libraries.
4. The impact that the environment has upon the library's internal structures and operations.

THE NATURE OF THE ENVIRONMENT ITSELF

A consideration of the nature of the environment itself is a contextual approach that describes the organizational effects produced by larger social processes surrounding the organization. Although the Public Library Inquiry and the more recent study conducted by Allie Beth Martin explore certain societal-library relationships, and although several societal trends that affect the university library directly or indirectly have been identified, few library studies have explored the channels and types of influence exerted by the external environment upon interorganizational relations.[9]

There is no systematic, empirical evidence to confirm or deny the hypothesis that organizational change is increasingly externally induced.[10] Librarians generally assume that organizational change in the library is internally generated. It is frequently said that if the managerial style of the library director would change, or if the staff had broader participation in the decision making, the library's performance would change. Environmental factors leading to less participation in decision making have not been considered, nor have factors that could reduce the decision-making autonomy of the library itself been identified.

A second hypothesis derives from the contextual nature of the organizational environment: "the organization's ability to adapt is a function of its ability to learn and to perform according to changing environmental contingencies."[11] Most library literature calling for library application of computer technology or acquisition of current audiovisual materials supports the notion that the library must adapt or it will be replaced by different organizations.

It may be impossible to determine whether organizational change is internally or externally generated. An internal change may have external antecedents, and external events may have been initiated by internal sources. The point is that organizational change is influenced not only by internal factors. Librarians should be sensitive to these relationships.

RELATIONSHIPS AMONG ORGANIZATIONS WITHIN A SET OF ORGANIZATIONS

Another approach to the study of libraries and their environments is to examine the interactions of organizations within a network of organizations. This approach uses one organization as a referent and analyzes that organization's relationships with elements in its organizational set.[12]

There are several aspects of the organizational set that can be used in the analysis of the interactions.

1. Those organizations in the set upon which the focal organization depends can be identified and their interactions characterized. The environment of any organization consists of a set of input organizations and a set of output organizations. The input organizations are those upon which the organization depends for its resources. In the library environment, input organizations would include such organizations as publishers, whose materials are inputs into the library's resources; library schools, whose students are inputs into the library's staff; and state libraries, whose funds may partially support the library. The output organizations are those for whom the organization produces a product or service. Within the library's environment output organizations would include other libraries, industrial firms, and other organizations. (As this analysis is an organizational one, the individual client is excluded.)

2. The reliance on input from various organizational resources can be assessed. An organization may depend upon few or many input sources. Whether the concentration of library input resources is high or low probably affects the structure and functioning of the library. Use of a single jobber, hiring students from the same library school, receiving monies from the same library school, receiving monies from relatively few sources will have some impact upon the library.

3. Certain organizations within the same network are used by the focal organization for reference purposes. In addition to input and

output sets, the library environment also includes a set of comparative reference organizations. These organizations are used by the library as a standard of comparison in evaluating its own performance. A set of normative reference organizations is also included in the library environment in order to incorporate the values and goals of this set into the focal organization.

Comparative reference groups and normative reference groups of most academic libraries can be specifically identified. For example, the comparative reference group of the library of the University of Wisconsin probably contains the other Big Ten university libraries. Its normative reference group probably includes the Social Science Data and Program Library Service of the University of Wisconsin, which houses the collection of machine-readable data files in the social sciences, and the Bureau of Audio-Visual Instruction, which services all films used in the university.

4. A fourth dimension of the organization set is its size. Although the size of the organization set is to be distinguished from the size of the focal organization, it is likely that the two are correlated; the larger the library, the larger the set of organizations with which it interacts. Although the size of the library does influence many internal characteristics, little attention has been paid to the size of the organization set interacting with the library. It is likely that the library's internal structure and processes are significantly influenced by the number of organizations with which the library interacts.

An analysis of the organization sets for various types of libraries may provide new insights into understanding variations in internal structures and patterns of decision making. Such analyses could lead to new categories of library problems and to an identification of unrecognized organization sets. By comparing organization sets with the library as a focal point with organization sets of economic, political, educational, or other organizations, the structural arrangements for other types of organizations might be found inappropriate for academic libraries.

CHARACTERISTICS OF EXCHANGES AMONG ORGANIZATIONS

Organizational exchange is defined "as any voluntary activity between two organizations which has consequences, actual or antici- pated for the realization of the [organization's] respective goals or objectives."[13] Analysis of organizational exchange considers the content of the exchange itself and the organizational forces acting in the exchange. The analysis might examine the degree to which the exchange is formalized or given official sanction by the participating organization; the extent to which a coordinating mechanism has been established to operate the exchange; the degree of intensity or involvement demanded of the interacting organizations (the intensity can be measured by the size of the invested resources—staff activity, money, equipment, services—and by the frequency of interaction); and the extent of reciprocity, a critical dimension in the assessment of the relationships among autonomous organizations.

No doubt most librarians occasionally have asked a friend in another library to copy an article, answer a question, or help a patron. These activities can be described as informal exchanges between libraries. The librarian, as an agent of his library, in combination with others in his library doing the same thing, develops a system of informal exchange. This activity is quite different from a formal exchange arrangement sanctioned in the library to provide interlibrary loan, reference service, and other services. The new system of interlibrary loan in Wisconsin, WILS (Wisconsin Interlibrary Loan System), provides a coordinating mechanism different from the loan system previously operating in Wisconsin. Although there is no empirical evidence to describe the influence of the WILS system upon the individual libraries subscribing to it, many librarians working in those libraries are able to compare the two systems and identify differences in the characteristics of the exchange and in organizational patterns required to operate the exchange.

Organizations desiring to maintain autonomy might understandably show reluctance for exchanges where sacrifices exceed rewards. If library A enters into an exchange relationship with library B, A may assume that B will make demands on it. One of the norms of reciprocity implies that the exchange should be mutually beneficial and roughly equivalent.[14] The voluntary system of interlibrary loan, an example of a library exchange, was developed so that libraries would share resources in order to achieve the common goal of service to readers. If reciprocity is to occur, the needs of both participating libraries must be fulfilled by the exchange. In most cases of interlibrary loan, however, the loans are beneficial only to the receiving library; the general professional goal of service, which previously sustained the voluntary interlibrary loan system, now appears to be inadequate.

Two additional factors inhibit the sharing of library resources: money has not been widely used to facilitate the flow of resources, and each autonomous library is accountable to its own major source of legitimacy (which is usually also its source of direct financial support) and is evaluated in terms of specific kinds of services rendered to selected users. As more money is acquired for circulation and as library autonomy decreases, library cooperation may increase.

Analysis of exchange in terms of these organizational characteristics should lead to the development of models for library exchange, which could be used to identify constraints that may be imposed upon certain types of library exchange.

THE IMPACT OF THE ENVIRONMENT UPON INTRAORGANIZATIONAL PROPERTIES

The impact of the environment upon internal organizational design may provide the most immediate concern to librarians interested in the influence environmental factors might have upon library functions.

It has been suggested that complex, heterogeneous, and unstable environments impose more constraints and contingencies upon the organization and create greater decision-making uncertainty than environments that are simple, homogeneous, and stable.[15] In a study of industrial firms, those departments with more uncertain environments relied less on formal rules and procedures, had fewer reviews of job performance, and were generally less formal than those departments in organizations with more certain environments.[16] In a study of health and welfare agencies, those organizations that had more formal exchanges with other organizations reported more decentralized decision-making structures, were more innovative, and provided more formal mechanisms of communication.[17]

Not much is known about the impact of the environment upon the library's internal structure. When the influence of the environment is studied in a systematic manner, the many complexities of the library as an organization will be better understood.

ORGANIZATIONAL BOUNDARIES AND THE ROLE OF THE BOUNDARY SPANNER

The study of the library in its environmental context is not an easy task. Before any investigation is undertaken of library-environment relationships, the boundaries of the library must be identified. Organizational boundaries do vary. Whereas one library may include a catalog department, another may use cataloging data provided by an outside processing center. One library may operate its own bindery, most will not.

An organization tends to expand its boundaries in order to reduce or eliminate major constraints and contingencies imposed upon it. For example, the single, statewide library network strives to include all libraries within its boundaries. If the state's major university library were not included, the network would be unable to control the cooperation of that library. A constraint would be placed upon the voluntary network system because the university library could reduce or remove its participation at any time. Such a constraint is eliminated by including the university library formally within the boundaries of the network.

The open-system approach to organizational studies assumes that the elements composing the organization can be further distinguished as to those elements within the organization and those elements outside the organization. Such a separation, however, is sometimes difficult and problematic. Some elements are engaged in transactions between the organization and its environment and hence are in both systems. Within the academic library, for example, the faculty library committee may be inside or outside the boundaries of the library. The committee members form a part of another system, the faculty—a major component of the academic library's environment.

In the context of these two systems, library and faculty, the faculty library committee serves as an interacting link. An analysis of the interaction provided by the faculty library committee or other such "boundary-spanning" units can indicate the amount of information flowing across the library's boundaries. Furthermore, the amount of interaction taking place between the systems may have great impact upon the library and the rate of change occurring within it.[18]

The importance of organizational roles or job functions that span the boundaries of the library is relatively neglected by the subject literature. Boundary-spanning roles are defined "as those roles which link the focal organization with other organizations or social systems and are directly relevant for the goal attainment of the focal organization."[19] The qualification of goal attainment is crucial, for without it most people working in the library could be defined as boundary spanners. Because the library's boundary-spanning roles are limited to those between the library and the elements in its task environment, it becomes necessary to define the boundary itself before the boundary spanners are identified and characterized.[20]

SUMMARY

Librarians know that the organizational environment restricts what the library can do and influences individual characteristics of libraries. Little systematic investigation has been undertaken of library environments and the impact of those environments upon the individual library.

Four approaches to the study of library environments were outlined in this paper: identification of external environmental factors that may lead to some internal changes within the library; measurement of environmental impact upon internal structural arrangements in libraries; investigation of relationships that exist between the library and other organizations with which it must deal; and analysis of the characteristics of exchanges that occur between the library and other organizations. Organizational boundaries and the role of the "boundary spanner" are two other important areas of study.

Such investigations will broaden our understanding of constraints upon the library and will enable us to classify library environments and to develop analytical models that will provide the bases for assessing library/environmental relationships.

References

1. Carleton B. Joeckel, *The Government of the American Public Library* (Chicago: Univ. of Chicago Pr., 1937).
2. Maurice P. Marchant, "The Effects of the Decision Making Process and Related Organizational Factors on Alternative Measures of Performance in University Libraries" (unpublished Ph.D. dissertation, Univ. of Michigan, 1970).
3. Paul Herbert Spence, "A Comparative Study of University Library Organizational Structure" (unpublished Ph.D. dissertation, Univ. of Illinois, 1969).
4. Beverly P. Lynch, "Library Technology; a Comparison of the Work Functional Departments in Academic Libraries" (unpublished Ph.D. dissertation, Univ. of Wisconsin, Madison, 1972).
5. William M. Evan, "The Organization-Set: Toward a Theory of Inter-organizational Relations," in James D. Thompson, ed., *Approaches to Organizational Design* (Pittsburgh: Univ. of Pittsburgh Pr., 1966), p. 175–91.
6. Edward G. Holley, "Organization and Administration of Urban University Libraries," *CRL* 33:175–89 (May 1972).
7. Arthur M. McAnally and Robert B. Downs, "The Changing Role of Directors of University Libraries," *CRL* 34:103–25 (March 1973).

8. Daniel Katz and Robert L. Kahn, *The Social Psychology of Organizations* (New York: Wiley, 1966).
9. Robert D. Leigh, *The Public Library in the United States* (New York: Columbia Univ. Pr., 1950); Allie Beth Martin, ed., *A Strategy for Public Library Change* (Chicago: American Library Association, 1972).
10. Shirley Terreberry, "The Evolution of Organizational Environments," *Administrative Science Quarterly* 12:590–613 (March 1968).
11. Ibid.
12. Evan, "Organization-Set."
13. Sol Levine and Paul E. White, "Exchange as a Conceptual Framework for the Study of Interorganizational Relationships," *Administrative Science Quarterly* 5:583–601 (March 1961).
14. Anant R. Negandhi, ed., *Organization Theory in an Interorganizational Perspective* (Kent: Kent State University, Comparative Administration Research Institute of the Center for Business and Economic Research, 1971).
15. James D. Thompson, *Organization in Action* (New York: McGraw-Hill, 1967); Paul R. Lawrence and Jay W. Lorsch, *Organization and Environment* (Boston: Harvard University, 1967).
16. Lawrence and Lorsch, *Organization and Environment*.
17. Michael Aiken and Jerald Hage, "Organizational Interdependence and Inter-organizational Structure," *American Sociological Review* 33:912–30 (Dec. 1968).
18. Warren B. Brown, "Systems, Boundaries, and Information Flow," *Academy of Management Journal* 9:318–27 (Dec. 1966).
19. Michael Aiken and Jerald Hage, "Organizational Permeability, Boundary Spanners, and Organizational Structure," mimeographed (Madison: University of Wisconsin, Department of Sociology).
20. William R. Dill, "Environment as an Influence on Managerial Autonomy," *Administrative Science Quarterly* 2:409–43 (March 1958).

The Short and Glorious History of Organizational Theory

Charles Perrow

F ROM the beginning, the forces of light and the forces of darkness have polarized the field of organizational analysis, and the struggle has been protected and inconclusive. The forces of darkness have been represented by the mechanical school of organizational theory—those who treat the organization as a machine. This school characterizes organizations in terms of such things as:

- Centralized authority.
- Clear lines of authority.
- Specialization and expertise.
- Marked division of labor.
- Rules and regulations.
- Clear separation of staff and line.

The forces of light, which by midtwentieth century came to be characterized as the human relations school, emphasizes people rather than machines, accommodations rather than machine-like precision, and draws its inspiration from biological systems rather than engineering systems. It has emphasized such things as:

- Delegation of authority.
- Employee autonomy.
- Trust and openness.
- Concerns with the "whole person."
- Interpersonal dynamics.

Reprinted, by permission of the publisher, from ORGANIZATIONAL DYNAMICS, Summer 1973, © 1973 by AMACON, a division of American Management Association. All rights reserved.

THE RISE AND FALL OF SCIENTIFIC MANAGEMENT

The forces of darkness formulated their position first, starting in the early part of this century. They have been characterized as the scientific management or classical management school. This school started by parading simple-minded injunctions to plan ahead, keep records, write down policies, specialize, be decisive, and keep your span of control to about six people. These injunctions were needed as firms grew in size and complexity, since there were few models around beyond the railroads, the military, and the Catholic Church to guide organizations. And their injunctions worked. Executives began to delegate, reduce their span of control, keep records, and specialize. Planning ahead still difficult, it seems, and the modern equivalent is Management by Objectives.

But many things intruded to make these simple-minded injunctions less relevant:

1. Labor became a more critical factor in the firm. As the technology increased in sophistication it took longer to train people, and more varied and specialized skills were needed. Thus, labor turnover cost more and recruitment became more selective. As a consequence, labor's power increased. Unions and strikes appeared. Management adjusted by beginning to speak of a cooperative system of capital, management, and labor. The machine model began to lose its relevancy.

2. The increasing complexity of markets, variability of products, increasing number of branch plans, and changes in technology all required more adaptive organization. The scientific management school was ill-equipped to deal with rapid change. It had presumed that once the proper structure was achieved the firm could run forever without much tampering. By the late 1930s, people began writing about adaptation and change in industry from an organizational point of view and had to abandon some of the principles of scientific management.

3. Political, social, and culture changes meant new expectations regarding the proper way to treat people. The dark, satanic mills needed at the least a white-washing. Child labor and the brutality of supervision in many enterprises became no longer permissible. Even managers could not be expected to accept the authoritarian patterns of leadership that prevailed in the small firm run by the founding father.

4. As mergers and growth preceeded apace and the firm could no longer be viewed as the shadow of one man (the founding entre-

preneur), a search for methods of selecting good leadership became a preoccupation. A good, clear, mechanical structure would no longer suffice. Instead, firms had to search for the qualities of leadership that could fill the large footsteps of the entrepreneur. They tacitly had to admit that something other than either "sound principles" or "dynamic leadership" was needed. The search for leadership traits implied that leaders were made, not just born, that the matter was complex, and that several skills were involved.

ENTER HUMAN RELATIONS

From the beginning, individual voices were raised against the implications of the scientific management school. "Bureaucracy" had always been a dirty word, and the job design efforts of Frederick Taylor were even the subject of a congressional investigation. But no effective counterforce developed until 1938, when a business executive with academic talents named Chester Barnard proposed the first new theory of organizations: Organizations are cooperative systems, not the products of mechanical engineering. He stressed natural groups within the organization, upward communication, authority from below rather than from above and leaders who functioned as a cohesive force. With the spectre of labor unrest and the Great Depression upon him, Barnard's emphasis on the cooperative nature of organizations was well-timed. The year following the publication of his *Functions of the Executive* (1938) saw the publication of F. J. Roethelisberger and William Dickson's *Management and the Worker,* reporting on the first large-scale empirical investigation of productivity and social relations. The research, most of it conducted in the Hawthorne plant of the Western Electric Company during a period in which the workforce was reduced, highlighted the role of informal groups, work restriction norms, the value of decent, humane leadership, and the role of psychological manipulation of employees through the counseling system. World War II intervened, but after the war the human relations movement, building on the insights of Barnard and the Hawthorne studies, came into its own.

The first step was a search for the traits of good leadership. It went on furiously at university centers but at first failed to produce more than a list of Boy Scout maxims: A good leader was kind, courteous, loyal, courageous, etc. We suspected as much. However, the studies did turn up a distinction between "consideration," or employee-centered aspects of leadership, and job-centered, technical aspects labeled "initiating structure." Both were important, but the former received most of the attention and the latter went undeveloped. The former led directly to an examination of group processes, an investigation that has culminated in T-group programs and is moving forward still with encounter groups. Meanwhile, in England, the Tavistock Institute sensed the importance of the influence of the kind of task a group had to perform on the social relations within the group. The first important study, conducted among coal miners, showed that job simplification and specialization did not work under conditions of uncertainty and nonroutine tasks.

As this work flourished and spead, more adventurous theorists began to extend it beyond work groups to organizations as a whole. We now knew that there were a number of things that were bad for the morale and loyalty of groups—routine tasks, submission to authority, specialization of task, segregation of task sequence, ignorance of the goals of the firm, centralized decision making, and so on. If these were bad for groups, they were likely to be bad for groups of groups—i.e., for organizations. So people like Warren Bennis began talking about innovative, rapidly changing organizations that were made up of temporary groups, temporary authority systems, temporary leadership and role assignments, and democratic access to the goals of the firm. If rapidly changing technologies and unstable, turbulent environments were to characterize industry, then the structure of firms should be temporary and decentralized. The forces of light, of freedom, autonomy, change, humanity, creativity, and democracy were winning. Scientific management survived only in outdated textbooks. If the evangelizing of some of the human relations school theorists was excessive, and if Likert's System 4 or McGregor's Theory Y or Blake's 9 x 9 evaded us, at least there was a rationale for confusion, disorganization, scrambling, and stress: Systems should be temporary.

BUREAUCRACY'S COMEBACK

Meanwhile, in another part of the management forest, the mechanistic school was gathering its forces and preparing to outflank the forces of light. First came the numbers men—the linear programmers, the budget experts, and the financial analysts—with their PERT systems and cost-benefit analyses. From another world, unburdened by most of the scientific management ideology and untouched by the human relations school, they began to parcel things out and give some meaning to those truisms, "plan ahead," "keep records." Armed with emerging systems concepts, they carried the "mechanistic" analogy to its fullest—and it was very productive. Their work still goes on, largely untroubled by organizational theory; the theory, it seems clear, will have to adjust to them, rather than the other way around.

Then the works of Max Weber, first translated from the German in the 1940s—he wrote around 1910, incredibly—began to find their way into social science thought. At first, with his celebration of the efficiency of bureaucracy, he was received with only reluctant respect, and even with hostility. All writers were against bureaucracy. But it turned out, surprisingly, that managers were not. When asked, they acknowledged that they preferred clear lines of communication, clear specifications of authority and responsibility, and clear knowledge of whom they were responsible to. They were as wont to say "there ought to be a rule about this," as to say "there are too many rules around here," as wont to say "next week we've got to get organized," as to say "there is too much red tape." Gradually, studies began to show that bureaucratic organizations could change faster than nonbureaucratic ones, and that morale could be higher where there was clear evidence of bureaucracy.

What was this thing, then? Weber had showed us, for example, that bureaucracy was the most effective way of ridding organizations of favoritism, arbitrary authority, discrimination, payola and kickbacks, and yes, even incompetence. His model stressed expertise, and the favorite or the boss' nephew or the guy who burned up resources to make his performance look good was *not* the one with expertise. Rules could be changed; they could be dropped in exceptional circumstances; job security promoted more innovation. The sins of bureaucracy began to look like the sins of failing to follow its principles.

ENTER POWER, CONFLICT, AND DECISIONS

But another discipline began to intrude upon the confident work and increasingly elaborate models of the human relations theorists (largely social psychologists) and the uneasy toying with bureaucracy of the "structionalists" (largely sociologists). Both tended to study economic organizations. A few, like Philip Selznick, were noting conflict and differences in goals (perhaps because he was studying a public agency, the Tennessee Valley Authority) but most ignored conflict or treated it as a pathological manifestation of breakdowns in communication or the ego trips of unreconstructed managers.

But in the world of political parties, pressure groups, and legislative bodies, conflict was not only rampant, but to expected—it was even functional. This was the domain of the political scientists. They kept talking about power, making it a legitimate concern for analysis. There was an open acknowledgement of "manipulation." These were political scientists who were "behaviorally" inclined—studying and recording behavior rather than constitutions and formal systems of government—and they came to a much more complex view of organized activity. It spilled over into the area of economic organizations, with the help of some economists like R. A. Gordon and some sociologists who were studying conflicting goals of treatment and custody in prisons and mental hospitals.

The presence of legitimately conflicting goals and techniques of preserving and using power did not, of course, sit well with a cooperative systems view of organizations. But it also puzzled the bureaucratic school (and what was left of the old scientific management school), for the impressive Weberian principles were designed to settle questions of power through organizational design and to keep conflict out through reliance on rational-legal authority and systems of careers, expertise, and hierarchy. But power was being overtly contested and exercised in covert ways, and conflict was bursting out all over, and even being creative.

Gradually, in the second half of the 1950s and in the next decade, the political science view infiltrated both schools. Conflict could be healthy, even in a cooperative system, said the human relationists; it was the mode of resolution that counted, rather than prevention. Power became reconcepturalized as "influence," and the distribution was less important, said Arnold Tannenbaum, than the total amount. For the bureaucratic school—never a clearly defined group of people, and largely without any clear ideology—it was easier to just absorb the new data and theories as something else to be thrown into the pot. That is to say, they floundered, writing books that went from topic to topic, without a clear view of organizations, or better yet, producing "readers" and leaving students to sort it all out.

Buried in the political science viewpoint was a sleeper that only gradually began to undermine the dominant views. This was the idea, largely found in the work of Herbert Simon and James March, that because man was so limited—in intelligence, reasoning powers, information at his disposal, time available, and means of ordering his preferences clearly—he generally seized on the first acceptable alternative when deciding, rather than looking for the best; that he rarely changed things unless they really got bad, and even then he continued to try what had worked before; that he limited his search for solutions to well-worn paths and traditional sources of information and established ideas; that he was wont to remain preoccupied with routine, thus preventing innovation. They called these characteristics "cognitive limits on rationality" and spoke of "satisficing" rather than maximizing or optimizing. It is now called the "decision making" school, and is concerned with the basic question of how people make decisions.

This view had some rather unusual implications. It suggested that if managers were so limited, then they could be easily controlled. What was necessary was not to give direct orders (on the assumption that subordinates were idiots without expertise) or to leave them to their own devices (on the assumption that they were supermen who would somehow know what was best for the organization, how to coordinate with all the other supermen, how to anticipate market changes, etc.). It was necessary to control only the *premises* of their decisions. Left to themselves, with those premises set, they could be predicted to rely on precedent, keep things stable and smooth, and respond to signals that reinforce the behavior desired of them.

To control the premises of decision making, March and Simon outline a variety of devices, all of which are familiar to you, but some of which you may not have seen before in quite this light. For example, organizations develop vocabularies, and this means that certain kinds of information are highlighted, and others are screened out—just as Eskimos (and skiers) distinguish many varieties of snow, while Londoners see only one. This is a form of attention directing. Another is the reward system. Change the bonus for salesmen and you can shift them from volume selling to steady-account selling, or to selling quality products or new products. If you want to channel good people into a different function (because, for example, sales should no longer be the critical function as the market changes, but engineering aplications should), you may have to promote mediocre people in the unrewarded function in order to signal to the good people in the rewarded one that the game has changed. You cannot expect most people to make such decisions on their own because of the cognitive limits on their rationality, nor will you succeed by giving direct orders, because you yourself probably do not know whom to order where. You presume that once the signals are clear and the new sets of alternatives are manifest, they have enough ability to make the decision but you have had to change the premises for their decisions about their career lines.

It would take too long to go through the dozen or so devices, covering a range of decision areas (March and Simon are not that clear or systematic about them, themselves, so I have summarized them in my own book), but I think the message is clear.

It was becoming clear to the human relations school, and to the bureaucratic school. The human relationists had begun to speak of changing stimuli rather than changing personality. They had begun to see that the rewards that can change behavior can well be prestige, money, comfort, etc., rather than trust, openness, self-insight, and so on. The alternative to supportive relations need not be punishment, since behavior can best be changed by rewarding approved behavior rather than by punishing disapproved behavior. They were finding that although leadership may be centralized, it can function best through indirect and unobtrusive means such as changing the premises on which decisions are made, thus giving the impression that the subordinate is actually making a decision when he has only been switched to a different set of alternatives. The implications of this work were also beginning to filter into the human relations school through an emphasis on behavioral psychology (the modern version of the much maligned stimulus-response school) that was supplanting personality theory (Freudian in its roots, and drawing heavily, in the human relations school, on Maslow).

For the bureaucratic school, this new line of thought reduced the heavy weight placed upon the bony structure of bureaucracy by highlighting the muscle and flesh that make these bones move. A single chain of command, precise division of labor, and clear lines of communication are simply not enough in themselves. Control can be achieved by using alternative communication channels, depending on the situation; by increasing or decreasing the static or "noise" in the system; by creating organizational myths and organizational vocabularies that allow only selective bits of information to enter the system; and through monitoring performance through indirect means rather than direct surveillance. Weber was all right for a starter, but organizations had changed vastly, and the leaders needed many more means of control and more subtle means of manipulation than they did at the turn of the century.

THE TECHNOLOGICAL QUALIFICATION

By now the forces of darkness and forces of light had moved respectively from midnight and noon to about 4 A.M. and 8 A.M. But any convergence or resolution would have to be on yet new terms, for soon after the political science tradition had begun to infiltrate the established schools, another blow struck both of the major positions. Working quite independently of the Tavistock Group, with its emphasis on sociotechnical systems, and before the work of Burns and Stalker on mechanistic and organic firms, Joan Woodward was trying to see whether the classical scientific principles of organization made any sense in her survey of 100 firms in South Essex. She tripped and stumbled over a piece of gold in the process. She picked up the gold, labeled it "technology," and made sense out of her otherwise hopeless data. Job-shop firms, mass-production firms, and continuous-process firms all had quite different structures because the type of tasks, or the "technology," was different. Somewhat later, researchers in America were coming to very similar conclusions based on studies of hospitals, juvenile correctional institutions, and industrial firms. Bureaucracy appeared to be the best form of organization for routine operations; temporary work groups, decentralization, and emphasis on interpersonal processes appeared to work best for nonroutine operations. A raft of studies appeared and are still appearing, all trying to show how the nature of the task affects the structure of the organization.

This severely complicated things for the human relations school, since it suggested that openness and trust, while good things themselves, did not have much impact, or perhaps were not even possible in some kinds of work situations. The prescriptions that were being handed out would have to be drastically qualified. What might work for nonroutine, high-status, interesting, and challenging jobs performed by highly educated people might not be relevant or even beneficial for the vast majority of jobs and people.

It also forced the upholders of the revised bureaucratic theory to qualify their recommendations, since research and development units should obviously be run differently from mass-production units, and the difference between both of these and highly programmed and highly sophisticated continuous-process firms was obscure in terms of bureaucratic theory. But the bureaucratic school perhaps came out on top, because the forces of evil—authority, structure, division of labor, etc.—no longer looked evil, even if they were not applicable to a minority of industrial units.

The emphasis on technology raised other questions, however. A can company might be quite routine, and a plastics division nonroutine, but there were both routine and nonroutine units within each. How should they be integrated if the prescription were followed that, say, production should be bureaucratized and R&D not? James Thompson began spelling out different forms of interdependence among units in organizations, and Paul Lawrence and Jay Lorsch looked closely at the nature of integrating mechanisms. Lawrence and

Lorsch found that firms performed best when the differences between units were *maximized* (in contrast to both the human relations and the bureaucratic school), as long as the integrating mechanisms stood half-way between the two—being neither strongly bureaucratic nor nonroutine. They also noted that attempts at participative management in routine situations were counter-productive, that environments of some kinds of organizations were far from turbulent and customers did not want innovations and changes, that cost reduction, price, and efficiency were trivial considerations in some firms, and so on. The technological insight was demolishing our comfortable truths right and left. They were also being questioned from another quarter.

ENTER GOALS, ENVIRONMENTS, AND SYSTEMS

The final seam was being mined by the sociologists while all this went on. This was the concern with organizational goals and the environment. Borrowing from the political scientists to some extent, but pushing ahead on their own, this "institutional school" came to see that goals were not fixed; conflicting goals could be pursued simultaneously, if there were enough slack resources, or sequentially (growth for the next four years, then cost-cutting and profit-making for the next four); that goals were up for grabs in organizations, and units fought over them. Goals were, of course, not what they seemed to be, the important ones were quite unofficial; history played a big role; and assuming profit as the pre-eminent goal explained almost nothing about a firm's behavior.

They also did case studies that linked that organization to the web of influence of the environment; that showed how unique organizations were in many respects (so that, once again, there was no one best way to do things for all organizations); how organizations were embedded in their own history, making change difficult. Most striking of all, perhaps, the case studies revealed that the stated goals usually were not the real ones; the official leaders usually were not the powerful ones; claims of effectiveness and efficiency were deceptive or even untrue; the public interest was not being served; political influences were pervasive; favoritism, discrimination, and sheer corruption were commonplace. The accumulation of these studies presented quite a pill for either the forces of light or darkness to swallow, since it was hard to see how training sessions or interpersonal skills were relevant to these problems, and it was also clear that the vaunted efficiency of bureaucracy was hardly in evidence. What could they make of this wad of case studies?

We are still sorting it out. In one sense, the Weberian model is upheld because organizations are not, *by nature,* cooperative systems; top managers must exercise a great deal of effort to control them. But if organizations are tools in the hand of leaders, they may be very recalcitrant ones. Like the broom in the story of the sorcerer's apprentice, they occasionally get out of hand. If conflicting goals, bargaining, and unofficial leadership exist, where is the structure of Weberian bones and Simonian muscle? To what extent are organizations tools, and to what extent are they products of the varied interests and group strivings of their members? Does it vary by organization, in terms of some typological alchemy we have not discovered? We don't know. But at any rate, the bureaucratic model suffers again; it simply has not reckoned on the role of the environment. There are enormous sources of variations that the neat, though by now quite complex, neo-Weberian model could not account for.

The human relations model has also been badly shaken by the findings of the institutional school, for it was wont to assume that goals were given and unproblematical, and that anything that promoted harmony and efficiency for an organization also was good for society. Human relationists assumed that the problems created by organizations were largely limited to the psychological consequences of poor interpersonal relations within them, rather than their impact on the environment. Could the organization really promote the psychological health of its members when by necessity it had to define psychological health in terms of the goals of the organization itself? The neo-Weberian model at least called manipulation "manipulation" and was skeptical of claims about autonomy and self-realization.

But on one thing all the varied schools of organizational analysis now seemed to be agreed: organizations are systems—indeed, they are open systems. As the growth of the field has forced ever more variables into our consciousness, flat claims of predictive power are beginning to decrease and research has become bewilderingly complex. Even consulting groups need more than one or two tools in their kit-bag as the software multiplies.

The systems view is intuitively simple. Everything is related to everthing else, though in uneven degrees of tension and reciprocity. Every unit, organization, department, or work group takes in resources, transforms them, and sends them out, and thus interacts with the larger system. The psychological, sociological, and culture aspects of units interact. The systems view was explicit in the institutional work, since they tried to study whole organizations; it became explicit in the human relations school, because they were so concerned with the interactions of people. The political science and technology viewpoints also had to come to this realization, since they dealt with parts affecting each other (sales affecting production; technology affecting structure).

But as intuitively simple as it is, the systems view has been difficult to put into practical use. We still find ourselves ignoring the tenets of the open systems view, possibly because of the cognitive limits on our rationality. General systems theory itself has not lived up to its heady predictions; it remains rather nebulous. But at least there is a model for calling us to account and for stretching our minds, our research tools, and our troubled nostrums.

SOME CONCLUSIONS

Where does all this leave us? We might summarize the prescriptions and proscriptions for management very roughly as follows:

1. A great deal of the "variance" in a firm's behavior depends on the environment. We have become more realistic about the limited range of change that can be induced through internal efforts. The goals of organizations, including those of profit and efficiency, vary greatly among industries and vary systematically by industries. This suggests that the impact of better management by itself will be limited, since so much will depend on market forces, competition, legislation, nature of the work force, available technologies and innovations, and so on. Another source of variation is, obviously, the history of the firm and its industry and its traditions.

2. A fair amount of variation in both firms and industries is due to the type of work done in the organization—the technology. We are now fairly confident in recommending that if work is predictable and routine, the necessary arrangement for getting the work done can be highly structured, and one can use a good deal of bureaucratic theory in accomplishing this. If it is not predictable, if it is nonroutine and there is a good deal of uncertainty as to how to do a job, then one had better utilize the theories that emphasize autonomy, temporary groups, multiple lines of authority and communications, and so on. We also know that this distinction is important when organizing different parts of an organization.

We are also getting a grasp on the question of what is the most critical function in different types of organizations. For some organizations it is production; for others, marketing; for still others, development. Furthermore, firms go through phases whereby the initial development of a market or a product or manufacturing process or accounting scheme may require a non-bureaucratic structure, but once it comes on stream, the structure should change to reflect the changed character of the work.

3. In keeping with this, management should be advised that the attempt to produce change in an organization through managerial grids, sensitivity training, and even job enrichment and job enlargement is likely to be fairly ineffective for all but a few organizations. The critical reviews of research in all these fields show that there is no scientific evidence to support the claims of the proponents of these various methods; that research has told us a great deal about social psychology, but little about how to apply the highly complex findings to actual situations. The key word is *selectivity:* We have no broad-spectrum antibiotics for interpersonal relations. Of course, managers should be sensitive, decent, kind, courteous, and courageous, but we have known that for some time now, and beyond a minimal threshold level, the payoff is hard to measure. The various attempts to make work and interpersonal relations more humane and stimulating should be applauded, but we should not confuse this with solving problems of structure, or as the equivalent of decentralization or participatory democracy.

4. The burning cry in all organizations is for "good leadership," but we have learned that beyond a threshold level of adequacy it is extremely difficult to know what good leadership is. The hundreds of scientific studies of this phenomenon come to one general conclusion: Leadership is highly variable or "contingent" upon a large variety of important variables such as nature of task, size of the group, length of time the group has existed, type of personnel within the group and their relationships with each other, and amount of pressure the group is under. It does not seem likely that we'll be able to devise a way to select the best leader for a particular situation. Even if we could, that situation would probably change in a short time and thus would require a somewhat different type of leader.

Furthermore, we are beginning to realize that leadership involves more than smoothing the paths of human interaction. What has rarely been studied in this area is the wisdom or even the technical adequacy of a leader's decision. A leader does more than lead people; he also makes decisions about the allocation of resources, type of technology to be used, the nature of the market, and so on. This aspect of leadership remains very obscure, but it is obviously crucial.

5. If we cannot solve our problems through good human relations or through good leadership, what are we then left with? The literature suggests that changing the structures of organizations might be the most effective and certainly the quickest and cheapest method. However, we are now sophisticated enough to know that changing the formal structure by itself is not likely to produce the desired changes. In addition, one must be aware of a large range of subtle, unobtrusive, and even covert processes and change devices that exist. If inspection procedures are not working, we are now unlikely to rush in with sensitivity training, nor would we send down authoritative communications telling people to do a better job. We are more likely to find out where the authority really lies, whether the degree of specialization is adequate, what the rules and regulations are, and so on, but even this very likely will not be enough.

According to the neo-Weberian bureaucratic model, as it has been influenced by work on decision making and behavioral psychology, we should find out how to manipulate the reward structure, change the premises of the decision-makers through finer controls of the information received and the expectations generated, search for interdepartmental conflict that prevent better inspection procedures from being followed, and after manipulating these variables, sit back and wait for two or three months for them to take hold. This is complicated and hardly as dramatic as many of the solutions currently being peddled, but I think the weight of organizational theory is in its favor.

We have probably learned more, over several decade of research and theory, about the things that do *not* work (even though some of them obviously *should* have worked), than we have about things that do work. On balance, this is an important gain and should not discourage us. As you know, organizations are extremely complicated. To have as much knowledge as we do have in a fledgling discipline that has had to borrow from the diverse tools and concepts of psychology, sociology, economics, engineering, biology, history, and even anthropology is not really so bad.

Selected Bibliography

This paper is an adaptation of the discussion to be found in Charles Perrow, *Complex Organizations: A Critical Essay,* Scott, Foresman &

Co., Glenville, Illinois, 1972. All the points made in this paper are discussed thoroughly in that volume.

The best overview and discussion of classical management theory, and its changes over time is by Joseph Massie—"Management Theory" In the *Handbook of Organizations* edited by James March, Rand McNally & Co., Chicago, 1965, pp. 387-422.

The best discussion of the changing justifications for managerial rule and worker obedience as they are related to changes in technology, etc., can be found in Reinhard Bendix's *Work and Authority in Industry*, John Wiley & Sons, Inc., New York, 1956. See especially the chapter on the American experience.

Some of the leading lights of the classical view—F. W. Taylor, Col. Urwick, and Henry Fayol— are briefly discussed in *Writers on Organizations* by D. S. Pugh, D. J. Hickson and C. R. Hinings, Penguin, 1971. This brief, readable, and useful book also contains selections from many other schools that I discuss, including Weber, Woodward, Cyert and March, Simon, the Hawthorne Investigations, and the Human Relations Movement as represented by Argyris, Herzberg, Likert, McGregor, and Blake and Mouton.

As good a place as any to start examining the human relations tradition is Rensis Likert, *The Human Organization,* McGraw-Hill, New York, 1967. See also his *New Patterns of Management,* McGraw-Hill Book Company, New York, 1961.

The Buck Rogers school of organizational theory is best represented by Warren Bennis. See his *Changing Organizations,* McGraw-Hill Book Company, New York, 1966, and his book with Philip Slater, *The Temporary Society,* Harper & Row, Inc., New York, 1968. Much of this work is linked into more general studies, e.g., Alvin Toffler's very popular paperback *Future Shock,* Random House, 1970, and Bantam Paperbacks, or Zbigniew Brzezinsky's *Between Two Ages: America's Role in the Technitronic Era,* the Viking Press, New York, 1970. One of the first intimations of the new type of environment and firm and still perhaps the most perceptive is to be found in the volume by Tom Burns and G. Stalker, *The Management of Innovation,* Tavistock, London, 1961, where they distinguished between "organic" and "mechanistic" systems. The introduction, which is not very long, is an excellent and very tight summary of the book.

The political science tradition came in through three important works. First, Herbert Simon's *Administrative Behavior,* Macmillan Publishing Co., Inc., New York, 1948, followed by the second half of James March and Herbert Simon's *Organizations,* John Wiley & Sons, Inc., New York, 1958, then Richard M. Cyert and James

March's *A Behavioral Theory of the Firm,* Prentice-Hall, Inc., Englewood Cliffs, N.J., 1963. All three of these books are fairly rough going, though chapters 1, 2, 3, and 6 of the last volume are fairly short and accessible. A quite interesting book in this tradition, though somewhat heavygoing, is Michael Crozier's *The Bureaucratic Phenomenon,* University of Chicago, and Tavistock Publications, 1964. This is a striking description of power in organizations, though there is a somewhat dubious attempt to link organization processes in France to the cultural traits of the French people.

The book by Joan Woodward, *Industrial Organization: Theory and Practice,* Oxford University Press, London, 1965, is still very much worth reading. A fairly popular attempt to discuss the implications for this for management can be found in my own book, *Organizational Analysis: A Sociological View,* Tavistock, 1970, Chapters 2 and 3. The impact of technology on structure is still fairly controversial. A number of technical studies have found both support and nonsupport, largely because the concept is defined so differently, but there is general agreement that different structures and leadership techniques are needed for different situations. For studies that support and document this viewpoint see James Thompson, *Organizations in Action,* McGraw-Hill Book Company, New York, 1967, and Paul Lawrence and Jay Lorsch, *Organizations and Environment,* Harvard University Press, Cambridge, Mass., 1967.

The best single work on the relation between the organization and the environment and one of the most readable books in the field is Philip Selznick's short volume *Leadership in Administration,* Row, Peterson, Evanston, Illinois, 1957. But the large number of these studies are scattered about. I have summarized several in my *Complex Organizations: A Critical Essay.*

Lastly, the most elaborate and persuasive argument for a systems view of organizations is found in the first 100 pages of the book by Daniel Katz and Robert Kahn, *The Social Psychology of Organizations,* John Wiley and Co., 1966. It is not easy reading, however.

PART 2 THE MANAGEMENT PROCESS

The theory of complex organizations and the application of that theory to libraries was presented in Part 1. Part 2 considers the management of libraries and the manager's job.

Paul Howard's paper, "The Functions of Library Management," was published in 1940. It illustrates the thinking of American librarians on library management at that time. Howard, seeking to identify a theoretical framework for practicing library managers, applies the prevailing managerial thought of the time to library situations. Directing, ordering, supervising, organizing, controlling, evaluating, and representing are the processes of management in Howard's model. Howard elaborates on the importance of departmentalizing— how the library's work is divided, and of control—how the library's personnel are willing and able to carry out orders. His work adapts to libraries the thinking in other fields about the management of complex organizations. Many library managers applied his perspective to library operations. Library theorists did too. His view prevailed for two decades.

While most managers still would prefer the relative simplicity of Howard's model, Harold Koontz, in "The Management Theory Jungle Revisited," informs us that the theoretical perspectives are more complex than ever and points out the difficulties practicing managers have in making sense out of the various theories and empirical investigations based in the theory. Koontz identifies eleven major theoretical schools and characterizes the various approaches as a "jungle." He argues for a definition of management knowledge and for greater interaction between the practicing manager and the organizational theorist.

Andrew H. Van de Ven continues the theme of manager-theorist interaction. His review of the bestseller, *In Search of Excellence*, by Peters and Waterman, summarizes many of the contradictions which exist within organizations and the various paradoxes observable in organizations. Van de Ven urges the successful manager to help shape managerial theory. He applauds Peters and Waterman for generating ideas and providing a synthesis that may guide us to new theoretical perspectives.

The dynamics of change chronicled by Peters and Waterman are captured for academic libraries in the work of McAnally and Downs. Interviews with twenty-two university librarians provide the base for their paper on the turbulent world of university library management: "The Changing Role of Directors of University Libraries." McAnally and Downs asked why so much change was occurring at the top in major university libraries. Environmental issues including burgeoning enrollments, institutional leadership, explosion of knowledge, inflation, and a variety of internal factors are identified in relation to the crisis in library management. Many of the issues identified by the respondents in the McAnally and Downs paper suggest insights commented upon in the papers by Thomas J. Galvin and Richard De Gennaro and in the studies by Henry Mintzberg.

Galvin's article, "Beyond Survival . . . ," considers change in libraries. He offers the maxim, "Given a dynamic external environment, no institution can ever remain static. It is either improving or it is declining." Galvin emphasizes the ongoing effort required to manage a library successfully. He embraces the challenge of change and calls for new styles of leadership to guide and direct the inevitable change in library organization. In the article by John Gardner, "How to Prevent Organizational Dry Rot," organizational self-renewal is synonymous with organizational change. Gardner proposes nine rules the organization and its leadership should apply in order for the organization to flourish.

Mintzberg uses field investigations to support his view that managers do more than plan, organize, coordinate and control. His description of the manager's job in "The Manager's Job: Folklore and Fact," suggests that the manager has several important roles, that the manager's time is spent differently from what is popularly believed, and that managerial skills can be learned and practiced.

De Gennaro, while less optimistic that management can be taught, agrees with Mintzberg. He goes on to say that management is not yet a science, but it is an art. De Gennaro finds more credibility with library management as it is practiced than with management as it is theorized to be.

David Mechanic calls to our attention again the importance of the day-to-day activities in libraries and the power and influence held by the people who carry out these activities. The Mechanic paper anticipates the papers of Rosebeth Moss Kanter and Patricia Glass Schuman, also reproduced here. James March, in Part 1, and Mechanic approach the organization and its routine tasks from different perspectives. Each, however, emphasizes the importance of the regular, on-going, routine activity of the organization. Their insights are important ones for library managers to consider and reflect upon.

Two papers explore the role of women in the management of complex organizations and in libraries. Kanter, a sociologist, presents a thoughtful and systematic analysis of women in the organization. She suggests in "Women and the Structures of Organizations," that organizations have supported a masculine ethic with their continued emphasis on rationality and reason. Schuman, a librarian, extends many of Kanter's insights in her analysis of the role of women in libraries in her article, "Women, Power, and Libraries."

The final selection in this section is the classic by Robert L. Katz, "Skills of an Effective Administrator," in which he identifies the three basic skills every successful manager must have: technical, human, and conceptual.

The Functions of Library Management[1]

Paul Howard

T HE study of library management is based naturally upon the conception of the library as a form of cooperative enterprise. Cooperative enterprise may be defined as any activity in which individuals unite for the achievement of common objectives.

In every cooperative enterprise the activities of the individuals concerned are of two kinds—operational and managerial. Operational activities are those in which effort is exerted directly on the materials with which the enterprise is concerned, while managerial activities are those in which effort is exerted in facilitating the operational activities through the medium of personnel and through the environment in which the operational activities are manifested.

A common illustration of a very simple cooperative enterprise is that of two men moving an object. When they examine the object and the terrain over which they wish to move it and finally decide how they wish to go about moving the object, they are managing. If care is needed in placing the object in its destined position, one man may watch in order to tell the other just when the proper position is achieved. He is the manager. The actual exertion of force against the object is operational activity. All other activity mentioned is management. Both activities are essential to the conduct of the enterprise and each is found in every cooperative enterprise, whether it be moving objects or giving library service.

THE FUNCTIONS OF MANAGEMENT

The place of management in cooperative enterprise.—With the expansion of cooperative enterprise to include ever greater numbers of

Reprinted with permission from *The Library Quarterly*, V. 10 (July 1940), pp. 313–349. © 1940 by the University of Chicago.

people, wider territories, and more complex operations, it has become necessary to divide and subdivide operations until the units of any process are small enough to be within the range of one individual's powers. Such division has led to specialization on the part of individual workers and has, in turn, made possible further expansion of the enterprise. Indeed, it is impossible to tell whether the expansion of cooperative enterprise is responsible for specialization or whether specialization is responsible for the expansion. At any rate, they are mutually dependent.

Early in the division of duties those activities concerned with the management of the enterprise are usually separated from all others and become a distinct division of the work. This is true of any kind of enterprise that exists—commercial, governmental, or religious—and it is as true of libraries as of armies or factories or churches.

For the purpose of this study the term "management" will be used to denote activities which in library literature have often been called "administrative." The reason for adopting this term is because "administration" has been used loosely to include all types of activity, ranging from government of the library to typing letters or licking stamps. In a rather anomalous fashion administration is also considered by librarians to consist of those activities performed by employees situated in the hierarchy of positions somewhere between the board of trustees and the first assistants in departments. Such a misconception has hampered the growth of a theory of administration in library thinking. Library schools have not been blameless, for "management" has often been neglected in their courses. It has been hard to develop a definite idea of the functions of a catchall.

So, in order to forestall confusion resulting from the use of a term having so many varying meanings, "administration" will be abandoned in this study, and "management" will be considered to mean those activities which give direction to the group effort and which are intended to facilitate the union of the forces of cooperative enterprise. "Managers" will be considered to mean those persons who perform such operations, and the term will include all such persons from the trustees to the department heads or first assistants.

Historical development of the principles of management.—A history of the theory of management has not yet been written. In fact, the theory itself is only beginning to be enunciated, and, as in other new fields, thinking about a philosophy of management has not yet reached a definite stage. However, with the growth of communications and the industrial developments of the late nineteenth century, commercial enterprises began to expand to such a large scale that speculation on the principles of their management was inevitable. In the early 1880's, with the organization of the American Society of Mechanical Engineers, discussion of management was instituted,[2] and in 1886 Henry R. Towne presented a paper on "The engineer as economist,"[3] which argued that engineers must assume responsibility for the efficient operation of machines and thus for management.

The discussions of management which appeared in the American Society of Mechanical Engineers' *Transactions* were concerned largely with individual phenomena of management, but three problems were established: (1) wage incentives, (2) cost accounting, and (3) organization and system. The establishment of the magazine *System* was an outgrowth of the discussions of the last problem.[4]

However, it was not until the Eastern Rate Case Hearings in 1910-11 that it was discovered that management had developed "an integrated body of technique, a set of principles, and a philosophy."[5] The work of F. W. Taylor in the field of management became widely known as a result of these hearings, and for years the system which he advocated dominated thinking in the United States. The extent of this domination is indicated by Mr. Person's article, which mentions no evolution of the principles of management after Taylor. The principles enunciated by Taylor are:

1. Research is that which discovers and defines practicable objectives and formulates methods for their achievement
2. Standards are the enunciation of the results of research giving specifications for their application
3. Control through planning is the "organized predetermination and coordination of activities"
4. Cooperation is the final element in effective management and necessitates the precise execution of each element in the plan[6]

This synopsis ignores the idea of the functional manager which attracted so much attention to Taylor's work because this idea represented only a technique of management and contributed little to the concept of what management really is. Indeed, it can be maintained that the emphasis upon techniques, sponsored by many of Taylor's followers, hindered rather than aided the development of a philosophy of management.

During the same years that Taylor was developing his theories and techniques of scientific management Henri Fayol, working independently, was building up a theory of management which was in outline remarkably similar. The chief difference between Taylor's and Fayol's conception of management was that Taylor based management definitely upon the techniques of the industry involved, while Fayol maintained that successful management was less dependent upon the technical skill of the managers and more upon their skill in the functions of management.

Fayol defined administration as "to plan, organize, command, co-ordinate and control."[7] It should be stated that his "prevoyance"—which is here translated as "plan"—meant more than is usually meant by the word "plan" in that it included forecasting and preparing for the future.

Although Fayol was able to define administration and to state the elements contained in the concept, he did not go far beyond this. This does not mean that he was unaware of the methodology of admin-istration or the details, but he was still unable to classify the administrative activities accurately. This is implied in his statement accompanying the presentation of his fourteen principles of admin-istration:

> I shall leave the review of principles at this point, not because the list is exhausted—it has no precise limit—but because it seems to me particularly useful at the moment, to endow the theory of administration with about a dozen well-established principles.[8]

The fourteen principles enunciated by Fayol may be summarized under the following heads: (1) division of labor, (2) authority, (3) discipline, (4) unit of command, (5) unity of management, (6) subordination of individual interests to the common good, (7) remuneration, (8) centralization, (9) control, (10) order, (11) equity, (12) stability of staff, (13) initiative, and (14) *esprit de corps.*[9] In addition, Fayol listed sixteen administrative duties,[10] most of which can be compared with the fourteen principles, as was done by Urwick.

Taylor and Fayol may be considered as the founders of the theory of administration or management. Since their original presentation of the subject much has been written about it—many case studies and much repetitious material which has not advanced the theory a great way beyond the original concepts but which has served its purpose in disseminating the knowledge already developed.

The ideas of the leading authorities on the subject have been summarized by Lewis C. Sorrell, professor of transportation at the University of Chicago, who has tabulated the more important concepts of the nature of management and has attempted a reformu-lation of the concept of management through an analysis of its functions.[11] In this analysis he comes to a much neater and more definitive concept of management than have other writers. The seven functions of management which he presents are:

1. *Directing*—the thinking and deciding function, including planning, initiating, and devising
2. *Ordering*—formulating and issuing commands
3. *Supervising*—seeing whether orders are carried out, and seeing that orders are carried out
4. *Controlling*—producing in the workers the willingness and capacity to carry out the orders
5. *Organizing*—establishing definite relationships within an institution for the purpose of facilitating management and operation
6. *Evaluating*—determining the efficiency and effectiveness of the enterprise
7. *Representing*—personifying the enterprise to the owners and public

Sorrell's statement concerning the functions presented is as applicable to library management as to business management:

> The hypotheses suggested here is that the major functions (basic processes) of business management are roughly covered by the terms *directing, ordering, supervising, controlling, organizing, evaluating,* and *representing.* It is the task of the theory of business management to determine more precisely the *content* of each of these terms, the *methods and devices* employed in their performance, and the *relationship* which they sustain to each other in their functioning.

MANAGEMENT IN LIBRARY LITERATURE

In library literature surprisingly little can be found dealing with the nature and functions of library management, and that little is widely distributed throughout the entire period of time in which a theory of management has been developing.

In 1887 F. M. Crunden, librarian of the St. Louis Public Library, delivered an address before the American Library Association on "Business methods in library management." A short quotation demonstrates the state of advanced thinking at that time:

> The duties of a chief executive of a library differ in no essential from those of a manager of a stock company . . . . In both cases there is a board of directors to dictate the general policy, which the manager is to carry out. In both

cases the details are left to him; and, if he occupies a proper position in the esteem and confidence of the directors, they rely on him largely for suggestions as to measures for furthering the objects in view.

It seems hardly necessary to call attention to the librarian's function as purchasing agent.

The librarian, like the business superintendent, is expected to organize his subordinates so as to secure the most effective service at the least outlay for salaries.

In keeping his institution before the public, the librarian may profit by the methods of the business man.

Disaffection is contagious; a house divided against itself cannot stand; and a board of directors is not acting in accordance with approved business methods if it does not speedily secure harmony of action by removing the disturbing element.[12]

In these quotations we find four functions of management recognized in the following order: directing, organizing, representing, and controlling. Cruden's method of control is perhaps not in accord with the latest ideas on correct procedure, but it is especially interesting to note that he recognized control as a function of library management.

In 1894 Cruden again referred to the librarian as a manager and elaborated upon his function of representing the library to the people, "identifying himself with the library and standing for it before the public."[13]

It is to be regretted that with this early beginning a theory of library management was not more fully developed and that librarians should have become swamped in a consideration of techniques.

A later writer who conceived of management as something separate from library techniques was also librarian of the St. Louis Public Library—Arthur E. Bostwick, who has been active in the profession since 1895. Five essays published by Dr. Bostwick between the years 1902 and 1914[14] deal with purely administrative aspects of librarianship: "Lay control in libraries and elsewhere" (1903); " The whole duty of a library trustee: from a librarian's standpoint" (1906); "Conflicts of jurisdiction in library systems" (1914); "System in the library" (1909); and "Cost of administration" (1912). Other essays by Bostwick touch upon the theory of management but always in connection with techniques of operation.

Bostwick's theory of management, as gathered from these essays, may be stated as follows: The board of trustees *represents* to the public, *directs,* or as he put it, their function is "to consider what should be the results aimed at by the library, to formulate its conclusions, to communicate them to the librarian and then to hold him responsible for their attainment." It is implied in this statement that all other functions are exercised by the librarian, although Bostwick never published a classification of the duties of the librarian as an administrator.

That he recognized a separation of management from other operations is implied in an address delivered before the New Zealand Library Association in 1911.[15] In this address he discussed the development of the public library as an educational institution and the tendency of librarians to adopt the methods of business efficiency in the operation of the library, especially those methods advocated by F. W. Taylor. In the address there was no analysis of the functions of management, but there was a warning that American librarians were likely to carry these efficiency methods to such extreme lengths that they would fall into disreptute.

In the same year (1911) Willard Austen, assistant librarian of Cornell University, called attention to the possibility of applying the principles of adminstrative management to library problems.[16] It should be remembered that this was immediately after the famous Eastern Rate Case Hearings which brought the work of F. W. Taylor into great prominence.

Charles C. Williamson later called attention to the value of industrial methods in library work,[17] and in 1919 he stated that the principles of library management will represent a special application of psychology and sociology but that "no one has attempted yet to treat comprehensively the principles and philosophy of library service or library management."[18] This linking of a philosophy of library service with a philosophy of library management might lead to confusion, but it is an important basis for the approach to the study of library management.

Donald Coney in 1930 indicated that the solution of management problems in university libraries followed the principles of scientific management as in other fields.[19]

Despite this seeming recognition of the importance of the subject, P. C. Coetzee could state in 1935 that librarians have no clear idea of the functions and fundamentals of their profession, that they have made a fetish of technique to the exclusion of theorizing, and that training courses generally ignore the administrative aspects of library work.[20]

The most important recent work upon management in the library field is a collection of addresses delivered before the Library Institute at the University of Chicago in the summer of 1938.[21] This institute brought before a body of active librarians for perhaps the first time not only their own experts on management but leaders in management from other fields. Although most of the addresses dealt more with the practical than with the theoretical aspects of management, it is interesting to note that several did present ideas upon the nature of management. The Introduction to the volume indicated that management is beginning to receive from librarians some recognition as a distinct, integrated body of knowledge.[22] Among the addresses by librarians was one, delivered by Althea Warren, of the Los Angeles Public Library, in which the following functions of management were either stated or implied: organizing, directing, supervising, ordering, controlling, and representing.[23]

The development of the concept of management has been traced in the literature of business and in library literature. It has been discovered that, although students in the field of business have developed a much more extensive literature and have issued more definitive statements about the functions of management than have librarians, there are many points of agreement. With this fact in mind, it will be interesting to discuss the best of the statements concerning the nature of management in terms of library practice.

FUNCTIONS OF LIBRARY MANAGEMENT

If the basic activities of library managers can be determined, it will be but a step farther to detemine what factors exert a marked effect upon the exercise of these functions and from these data to infer something concerning the nature of management (as distinguished from operations) and thus to develop a theory and philosophy of library management.

The remainder of this study is devoted to an examination of a portion of library practice from this new viewpoint. It is intended to indicate some possibilities of this approach and to establish a hypothesis upon which further investigation may be based.

The seven functions of management—directing, ordering, supervising, controlling, organizing, evaluating, and representing—are broken down into their constituent parts and are discussed as essential portions of managerial activity in libraries.

DIRECTING

The first function of management to be considered is that of directing, which includes the establishment of objectives and the formulation of policies.

Establishment of objectives.—The objectives of a library are determined by the nature of its clientele, legal requirements, financial support, the presence of other social institutions, and by factors within the library itself. Any objectives established possess nature and scope. In other words, the management of the library decides what type of activities shall be conducted and how intensively and extensively these activities shall be carried on.

Nature of the objectives.—In the establishment of most libraries, as with other co-operative enterprises, it is doubtful whether much consideration is given to listing the things that the founders intend to accomplish. However, it may be taken for granted that in every case some definite result is expected. Whether this expected result is the elevation of the working man, a gain in prestige for the community, the establishment of a more universal culture, or any or all of innumerable benefits is not the immediate concern of this paper. The assumption upon which this argument is based is that libraries are established for some objective or set of objectives. These objectives may change as time passes, and their nature is a reflection of conditions within the community and within the library. The influences which affect the nature of a library's objectives may be summarized under the following headings:

1. Ideals and philosophy of the librarian
2. Nature of the library's clientele
3. Presence of other social institutions within the community
4. Governmental and legal conditions under which the library must operate
5. Financial support which the library can expect to receive
6. Organization of the library itself

An examination of these factors will show why there has been such a wide diversity in library service and in library standards.

A number of studies have been made concerning the nature of the library's clientele. Much of the work done at the Graduate Library School of the University of Chicago is concerned with this problem. In general, the method has been to classify readers into a number of categories based upon their occupations, their educations, and their stations in the economic strata. (Some attempt has been made to classify readers by maturity levels, but very little attention has been paid to ethnological factors in the characterization of readers.) The importance of these three ways of classifying readers—the library's clientele—should not be underestimated. Until some more accurate method is devised for determining the nature of its clientele, the library will have to depend upon such studies, or estimates, for its information about the people it is attempting to serve.

The ways in which governmental organization and legal considerations can affect the nature of objectives is demonstrated over and over in the history of American libraries and is admirably presented in Carleton B. Joeckel's *Government of the American public library.*[24] The nature of the library organization, the character of its officers, and the nature of its relation to other govermental bodies are usually defined by statute or charter, and though these factors have their greatest effect upon the scope of library service they also determine to a large extent the nature of the service which can be given.

Financial support which any co-operative enterprise receives is an effective determinant both of the scope of its activities and of their nature. It is easy to see that endowments for specific purposes do determine the nature of objectives. American history is filled with instances in which the power to control finances also became the power to control objectives. Awareness of this fact has been one of the most potent factors in the establishment of a fixed levy for library support. But, aside from this wilful though indirect control of the nature of library objectives through financial considerations, the amount of financial support and the financial ability of the community exert a marked influence upon the nature, as well as upon the extent, of library operations. Louis R. Wilson has shown that it is no accident that great library collections are concentrated in the prosperous regions of the United States.[25]

That the use of the public library is dependent upon a literate population is so evident that librarians no longer give this fact much consideration and thus do not always realize that historically and practically the library follows the school. The full effect of this one social institution upon the nature of library objectives has not been explored. However, the impracticability of establishing universal public library service before universal education is evident. It is likely that the spread of public education throughout the United States is one of the most potent factors in the spread of library service. Not only the fact of universal education but the nature of that education influences the nature of library objectives. It is interesting to speculate whether there is any relation between the establishment of vocational courses in public schools and the increase of nonfiction reading in libraries.

The presence and nature of other institutions as well as the school affect the nature of library objectives. Such institutions may be commercial, religious, or governmental in their nature, but each has its influence upon the things the library should be doing. Seaports have collections about navigation; libraries in industrial centers stress those branches of technology which are useful to their particular industries. The presence of a college in a small community inevitably affects the nature of the work the library is trying to do, and the intensity and nature of the religious life determine to a much greater extent than is often realized the type of library the community will have.

The four factors affecting the nature of library objectives—the library's clientele, the governmental and legal conditions, the financial support, the presence and nature of other institutions—all affect one another and to a large extent determine the conditions under which the fifth factor can operate. This factor, which is the organization of the library itself, grows more important as time passes and traditions within the organization become fixed.

Changes in organization and personnel often produce changes in objectives. The coming of a new librarian or the reorganization of the board of trustees sometimes produces profound changes in the type of things a library attempts to do. Of course, it is also true that changes in objectives necessitate changes in organization before the new objectives can be achieved. Too often this close relation between objectives and organization is not fully realized, and a library may pattern its organization upon that of another whose objectives are not at all comparable. Or, it is possible that after a change in library objectives the library may not be sufficiently reorganized to make achievement of the new objectives feasible.

This review of five factors which affect the nature of the library's objectives is intended merely as an outline and enters into details only enough to establish the possibility of further investigation either from the standpoint of an individual library or from the standpoint of the library movement as a whole.

In the same way a brief review of factors which affect the scope of library objectives indicates the things which the management must consider in any decision to limit or to expand the work which the library attempts.

Scope of the objectives.—The same factors which determine the nature of library objectives also play their part in determining the scope. There is such close relationship between these two qualities that it is often difficult to distinguish between them, and, moreover, such a distinction is often unimportant. For example, the Enoch Pratt Free Library, in common with other large public libraries, attempts to supply its clientele with authoritative books of popular nature on hygiene, physiology, nursing, and other medical subjects but does not attempt to build up a technical collection of medical works. Whether this limitation is of the nature or of the scope of its objectives is of less importance than the factors which have led to the decision to define the limits in this manner. If we grant that this decision is based upon the nature of its clientele, the state of its budget, the presence of other medical libraries in Baltimore, and the training of its staff in this field, then we must grant that if there is a realization of any considerable alteration in these conditions in the future, the present limitation should be reconsidered.

Notwithstanding the similarity of nature and scope, these two qualities of objectives may usually be distinguished. Nature may be compared to the constitution of a physical object, while scope may be compared to its dimensions and mass. Thus a library may decide to provide reference service in the field of history; but it may limit this to service within its main building or may decide to limit the scope of its history collection to general and basic works except in the history of its own community. Perhaps the most universal limitation in scope in library service is the limitation in hours of service. Twenty-four-hour library service is probably unheard of anywhere.

Consideration of these two examples indicates why there should be a distinction between the nature and the scope of library objectives although the same factors detemine each. It will be remembered that the six factors determining the nature of library objectives were listed in the approximate order of their importance as follows: (1) ideals and philosophy of the librarian; (2) nature of the clientele; (3) presence of other institutions; (4) government and legal conditions under which the library must operate; (5) financial support which the library can expect to receive; and (6) organization of the library itself. The importance of these factors in their effect upon the scope of library objectives requires that they be arranged in the following order: (1) financial support; (2) governmental and legal conditions; (3) ideals and philosophy of the librarian; (4) organization; (5) other institutions; and (6) nature of the clientele. This arrangement of factors is open to argument and will, of course, vary in individual cases.

The formulation of policies.—The second great division of the activities of directing is the formulation of policies. Policies are those broad rules for the conduct of an enterprise which are designed to aid in the achievement of its objectives. That the policies of a library should be based upon its objectives and should grow out of them may be accepted without question. The distinction between objectives and policies, on one hand, and between rules and policies, on the other hand, should be made clear. An example will serve to illustrate these distinctions. The familiar slogan "The best books for the greatest number at the least cost" is a statement of policy adopted by the American Library Association in furtherance of its objectives of universal library service. Anyone conversant with objectives of the association knows that this is merely a statement of policy rather than a definition of an objective. Individual libraries devise rules in accord with this policy. Rules fixing the length of the circulation period, the number of books issued to one individual, and establishing fines for violations of rules are based upon this or similar policies.

This introduction leads to the conclusion that the primary factors in the formulation of policies are the objectives that have been established. Other factors which affect the formulation of policies are those which also affect the establishment of objectives. The nature of the clientele, the legal basis of the organization, the amount of financial support, the presence of other institutions, and the organization of the library itself—all must be considered in determining how the library may best achieve its objectives.

Responsibility for directing.—The establishment of objectives and the formulation of policies in public libraries are usually centered in the board of trustees which, from a managerial standpoint, is comparable to the board of directors of a commercial firm. Most library writing on the subject states that the librarian is to carry out the policy of the board. However, in actual practice it is often the case that the librarian formulates the policies and presents them to the board for approval, and that the objectives and policies are in reality joint products of the board and the librarian. In the various divisions of the work the establishment of objectives and the formulation of policies are usually, in turn, the joint work of the librarian and the department head concerned.

In college and university libraries the function of directing is usually allocated in one of three ways: in a library committee of deans or of the faculty, in a library committee of trustees of the college (very rare), or in the chief administrative officer of the college. The exercise of this function is necessarily limited by the objectives and policies of the larger institution. Often the library committee serves in an advisory capacity only, and responsibility for the establishment of objectives and the formulation of policies belongs to the librarian alone.

ORDERING

The function of ordering has been defined as "formulating and issuing commands." It is through orders that policies established by the management are interpreted and applied to specific situations. Orders are of two kinds: general and specific, either of which may be temporary or permanent.

Factors in ordering.—The chief factors which affect the function of ordering are (1) the policies adopted; (2) the nature of the organization; and (3) the nature of the personnel.

Just as the formulation of policies is conditioned by the objectives of the library, so the function of ordering is conditioned by the policies thus formulated. It may be granted that policies are sometimes adopted which do not further progress toward established objectives, and that orders are sometimes given which run counter to library policies, but it will also be granted that this is bad practice.

Policies of the library have their greatest influence upon the content of the order, while the nature of the organization and the nature of the personnel have their greatest influence upon the formulation of the orders. It is evident that the management of two institutions which are attacking similar objectives in similar ways will issue orders dealing with practically the same type of things; but the ways in which the orders are issued will depend upon such things as the size of the organization, the territory covered, the means of communication available within the organization, the morale of the staff, the level of intelligence of the officials and subordinates, and the experience of the personnel.

General orders are issued to make the policies effective in situations which are likely to recur regularly and which affect the staff as a whole, while specific orders are called for under conditions such as: exceptional cases not covered by routine orders, emergencies, special adjustments between individuals or departments, and instructional situations in which a worker does not understand the exact nature of his duties. All orders, both general and specific, should have the following qualities: clearness, explicitness, confidence, courtesy, positiveness, and simplicity.[26]

Responsibility for ordering.—The idea of delegating authority is closely linked with the function of ordering in the minds of librarian writers. Librarians recognize that with the responsibility for any procedure there must be a corresponding degree of authority. Hence, the function of ordering is exercised almost entirely by the librarian and his subordinates. In practically every instance in which ordering is mentioned in library literature in connection with boards of trustees of public libraries the idea is stressed that the exercise of this function by such lay bodies is impractical and disturbing in its effects.

SUPERVISING

The loose use of terms in the literature of library management makes it difficult to determine the extent to which supervising is recognized as a function of management. For example, the statement is often found that one of the duties of the librarian is to direct the work of the assistants. It is likely that "direct" is used in such cases in much the same sense that "supervise" is used here—"seeing whether orders are carried out and seeing that orders are carried out." However, it is also possible that in these instances the word "direct" is used in the sense of establishing objectives and in supervising the way in which work is done.

In the definition of supervising used here, two phases of the task are indicated. The first phase, seeing whether orders are carried out, indicates a process of checking on the work of subordinates. One of the common devices for this checking is the report of progress by which the subordinate reports to his superior at intervals on the results of his efforts. The second phase, seeing that orders are carried out, is accomplished by several devices. Instructions may be issued as to how the work is to be done, and a deadline set for the completion of all or part of the task. Other devices, such as rewards and promotions for work accomplished, belong more properly with the function of controlling, which will be discussed later.

Factors affecting supervising.—Consideration of the factors which influence the activities labeled "supervising" indicates that there is a pattern which these functions of management follow. The chief factors which influence the function of ordering are the policies of the library, and in similar fashion the chief factors which influence the function of supervising are the orders which are to be followed. If the orders are specific and simple, the supervision is correspondingly direct and is limited to seeing that orders are obeyed. If orders are general and complicated, the supervision required is necessarily more detailed and more universally present.

The second factor which influences the function of supervising is the organization of the library. A highly centralized library system located in a single building may have a straight functional division of the library operations, and supervision of each function is established directly by the department head responsible for carrying out that function. However, as the system expands and branches are added, supervision becomes more complicated because functions become interlocked in the smaller units and because time and distance require the establishment of managers who are responsible for all library functions in each branch.

A third factor which influences supervising is the nature of the personnel. Intelligence, training, experience, and morale may all be considered as subdivisions of this factor. It is common experience that the lack of any one or all of these four qualities necessitates closer and more intensive supervision, and that as these qualities are established supervision may be relaxed.

Responsibility for supervising.—The responsibility for this activity of "seeing whether orders are carried out" extends throughout the managerial organization, although the degree of detail with which it is concerned varies with the rank of the person exercising the function. For example, a department head supervises the work of assistants more closely and with more concern for specific details than the assistant librarian or the librarian supervising the work of department heads, while trustees very rarely concern themselves with details at all.

It is important in the work of organizing the library that the management should indicate in what ways and by whom supervision will be carried out. The type of authority delegated to each manager and the nature of his supervisory relations to both subordinates and superiors should be stated in some detail.

CONTROLLING

Controlliing is probably one of the most universally recognized functions of library management. It is also one of the most elusive problems confronting the management because of the many intangible factors which become involved in its practice. Yet there are definite, concrete elements in control which may be listed under two heads: (1) the establishment of incentives, and (2) conditions of work. The incentives should include rewards for satisfactory services and penalties for unsatisfactory service, though most authorities[27] consider that rewards are more effective as incentives than are penalties. The factors in the conditions of work which affect controlling are basic rates of pay, hours, vacations, privileges, etc.

The change of method of control from that advocated by Crunden in 1887 is marked. Then control was simple and arbitrary, at least in theory. Today, however, with control being defined as "producing in the workers the willingness and capacity to carry out the orders," many devices are used to maintain control: salary schedules, annuities and pensions, efficiency or service ratings, staff meetings, leadership, and other devices of personnel management.[28]

Factors affecting control.—The exercise of the function of controlling is affected by several factors. As in all other phases of management, financial ability is an important consideration. It can be seen that the library with the greatest salary budget and with the greatest ability to give financial rewards for outstanding services will be able to produce for its organization the most able workers. The truth of this statement is becoming more and more evident with the spread of library service and the growth of competition between libraries. While the competition for workers was chiefly between the library profession and some other profession, certain intangible advantages of library work could offset financial disadvantage to some extent. But with a growth of competition between libraries themselves these intangible benefits are more or less equalized. Other ways in which financial ability affects controlling are through the provision of adequate staff, annuities and pensions, adequate equipment, and rewards in the form of vacations and leaves of absence.

The nature of the library organization and the nature of the personnel are other factors which affect the way in which controlling may be exercised. Large libraries may provide a greater number of grades in both salary schedules and schemes of service, and thus with a greater number of rewards to dispense many use them more frequently as a means of creating willingness and ability among the staff. On the other hand, the close associations established within a small staff in a small library make it possible for the management to be much more liberal in fitting the organization to individual variations. These individual variations and the nature of the personnel are important factors in determining the way in which the function of controlling is exercised. With the development of controlling from a process of eliminating those employees who do not conform to standards to a process of developing and stimulating the employees, personnel has become a factor of extreme importance in the exercise of this function.

The devices which are used in controlling are as varied and numerous as the situations which arise, but they may be classified in two main categories which conform to the two elements already mentioned: the establishments of incentives and conditions of work. Incentives are established in two ways: first by establishing rewards for satisfactory or outstanding services, and second by penalizing unsatisfactory services. Rewards may be any kind of satisfaction which the worker receives from accomplishment, while penalties may be any discomfort for disappointment which he receives. With these definitions in mind it is apparent that the activities which constitute the function of controlling are numerous and may lead to the establishment of intangible as well as tangible rewards. Thus the personal satisfaction which an employee receives from a well-executed performance may be a greater reward than his salary, and the rejection resulting from a failure may be a greater penalty than any material handicap. It is a task of library management to see that rewards become associated with the accomplishments which lead toward the achievement of library objectives, and that all penalties become associated with acts which defer the achievement of library objectives. It is also a task of library management to see that penalties become associated only with undesired acts and not with the management itself.

The conditions of work which a library may establish for its employees affect their ability and their desire to give adequate library service. Thus improper lighting and ventilation actually limit the physical efficiency of workers; inadequate equipment and poorly designed quarters hamper good work; and inadequate salaries and overwork destroy morale. The librarian who manages to correct such deficiencies does much to provide capable, enthusiastic, and loyal subordinates.

Responsibility for controlling.—The job of creating willingness and ability to perform the tasks of the library is spread throughout its management and to some extent is spread throughout the entire profession. The establishment of library schools is, in a sense, an effort by the profession and by society to perform a portion of this function through collective effort.

The delegation of the responsibility and authority for controlling extends from the trustees and librarian through the department heads, but it is likely that the librarian is the most important single factor in the performance of this function. His personality, fairness, judgment, and ability determine the effectiveness with which the function can be administered. An interesting device in controlling was established by Frederick W. Taylor's idea of functional foremen. An adaptation of this idea exists in the work of some children's and reference departments in which the heads of these departments control the work in these fields throughout the library system.

ORGANIZING

The organization of library work, together with the development of library techniques, has been one of the chief accomplishments of American librarianship. However, the problems of library organization have occupied the time and attention of librarians, sometimes almost to the exclusion of other functions of management.

Organizing is the process by which relationships within the library are established for the purpose of facilitating management and operation. Thus the function of organizing determines how the library's work will be divided, which persons shall be responsible for the various divisions, and the nature of the relations which shall exist between the various divisions and between the personnel of the divisions.

The two major phases of this activity of organizing are departmentation and personnel placement. There are also two subjects with which this activity deals—operations and management. Thus organizing may divide operations and place workers in each division, taking care to see that the relation between these divisions is clearly defined and thoroughly understood, and at the same time may divide management on a slightly different basis and select personnel for these divisions from an entirely different standpoint.

Factors affecting organizing.—The chief factors which influence the activities coming under the head of organizing are: (1) the library's objectives; (2) the nature of the community to be served; (3) the nature of the materials with which the library is concerned; (4) the type of staff; (5) the financial ability of the library; and (6) the physical plant.

Just as the nature of the objectives influences the way in which other managerial activities are exercised, so the nature of these objectives affects the type of organization which is set up to achieve them. An example of the difference in organization brought about by a change in objectives is shown by the establishment of browsing rooms in college libraries in recent years and by the establishment of readers' advisory services in public libraries. The things that a library is trying to do inevitably affect the stress that is placed upon its various departments and thus determine which departments shall be expanded, which shall be consolidated or eliminated, and what new departments shall be inaugurated.

The ways in which the nature of the community to be served influences the organizing activities of a library's management can be demonstrated by examining the organization of several types of libraries—such as a public library located in a large city, a county library, a state library commission, a college library, and a university library. We find that the decentralization of points of service in county and city libraries is probably a result of the wide areas of their communities; and yet state library commissions, with much larger areas to serve, usually are highly centralized and carry on their activities from the state captial. It is evident that other factors have prevented the library commissions from spreading their services in the way that city and county libraries do. In college and university libraries the parts of the organization having to do with business and maintenance may be omitted because the community which they serve—the college or the university—has provided these departments as part of the larger organization.

Other geographical factors also affect the work of organizing. Various factors in accessibility—such as the presence of rivers, lakes, railroads, parks, etc.—affect the placement of branches and the nature of the organization which serves these branches.

The type of materials which a library handles also affects the kind of organization which must be built up. The coming of film into the library picture has already influenced the organization of those libraries which are handling it, and it is likely that increased use of film by libraries will produce an even more profound effect upon the organization devoted to its exploitation. The same thing is true of devices for reproducing sound. The techniques of their handling and use present problems of organizing as well as problems of care.

The type of person available for employment, or the kind of staff which operates the library, has an enormous influence upon the way in which an organization can be established. In general, the more intelligent and experienced personnel requires less rigid demarcation in organizing. Often it becomes advisable to fit the organization to the personnel rather than the personnel to the organization. This is especially true in cases in which a ranking officer of the library is highly qualified in certain fields. A change of officials may mean a corresponding change in either the operational or managerial organization of the library. In the lower ranks of library service it is usually easier to shift staff members between departments in order to fit the personnel to the organization, but with the higher ranks the opposite may be true.

Since the financial ability of the library determines the size of the staff which can be employed and the extent to which library services can be expanded, it also determines to a great extent the type of organizing activity in which the library management may engage. Thus a library with a small income is forced to consolidate departments because of lack of staff and to relinquish services because of inability to finance them. Financial difficulties usually lead to centralization of operations and a change of organization to meet this concentration. Hence the impoverished library commissions are highly centralized, though they serve much greater areas than do county or city libraries.

The sixth major factor which influences the function of organizing is the nature of the library's physical plant. Although from an ideal standpoint it should be true that the type of organization developed determines the kind of plant in which the library should be housed, practically it is often the case that the organization must be fitted into an existing structure. Educational work with films is slighted because there is no projection booth in the library's auditorium, or the reference work cannot be organized on the subject-department basis because there are only two large reading-rooms. It is no accident that libraries did not organize for night service before the advent of electric lights. The history of library architecture is studded with examples of costly monuments which have hampered organizing efforts of their librarians and which have slowed the popularization of library service.

Organizing devices.—Two devices used in organizing libraries are departmentation and personnel placement.

"Departmentation" is a term borrowed from management in other fields, such as business management and governmental organization. It is used to designate the arrangement of an organization into units having a definite personnel and performing a definite portion of the work of the library. The results of this activity are apparent to any observer: each is usually designated by a name and thus becomes fixed upon the records of the institution; in addition, each unit has a definite task or set of tasks to perform, and thus instructions for performing the work of the enterprise are likely to be issued in the form of departmental memorandums or rules.

Departmentation is one of the managerial devices which is most susceptible of analysis. Departmentation is also one of the most effective devices of management. However, in a full-length study of the functions of management it should be recalled that departmentation is only one of the two devices by which the single function of organizing is given expression. Like other managerial devices, departmentation is not confined in its influence to one function. It provides a system of communication through which the managers can exercise all the functions of management,[29] and thus it becomes such a vital factor in management that it overshadows most of the true functions.

The second device by which the function of organizing is given expression is very closely related to departmentation. This device is personnel placement, which is the procedure by which the organizational units are manned. The effect of personnel upon departmentation is perhaps most easily illustrated by the way in which aptitudes and interests of high-ranking officials affect the grouping of departments under them. As departmentation is determined by variations in the nature of the work to be done, so personnel placement should be determined by variations in the qualifications of individuals as related to these variations in the nature of the work. Webster Robinson[30] discusses the various factors in personnel placement under such headings as "Physical variations," "Mental differences," "Education, training, and experience," "Job differences," and "Co-ordination of job requirements with personal qualifications." Personnel placement when co-ordinated with the function of controlling becomes a powerful aid and stimulus to effective library service.

Responsibility for organizing.—Although the responsibility for the use of these two devices of organizing rests primarily upon the librarian, it is often divided and portions of it are delegated to other library officials. Department heads are usually responsible for organizing intradepartmental activities. The problems of scheduling and personnel work are often delegated to an assistant librarian. The work of selecting employees and of training newly elected staff members is sometimes delegated to the assistant librarian and the head of a training class. Organizing is one of those functions of management which librarians usually feel should be delegated to the professional manager rather than left as the responsibility of the lay board.

EVALUATING

The sixth function of library management is evaluating, which has been defined as "determining the efficiency and effectiveness of the enterprise." Evaluating seeks to measure library accomplishments in comparison with library objectives and to determine to what degree these objectives are being achieved. In addition, evaluating seeks to determine the efficiency and effectiveness of specific items and procedures in the library's program. The exercise of this function permits an examination of each library procedure in relation to the way in which it performs the task for which it was designed, and so aids the library in following the course charted by its objectives and policies.

Evaluating is of two kinds: concrete and abstract. Concrete evaluation is concerned with those elements in library service which may be reduced to figures and measured statistically, while abstract evaluation is concerned with those intangible elements in library service which are not yet susceptible of measurement but whose existence can be perceived through observation and inference. The records of circulation, of registration, of library attendance, of book talks, of the number of questions answered, and of the size of the library's book collection furnish the raw material for concrete evaluation. The more difficult task of abstract evaluation must depend upon correlation of observed changes within the community with measured elements in library service and upon observations of the effects of library service upon individuals and groups. It is evident that as more and more of the elements of library work are subjected to concrete evaluation the task of abstract evaluation will become correspondingly easier.

Factors affecting evaluating.—The three chief factors which affect the exercise of this function of evaulating are: (1) the efficiency with which the function of organizing has been maintained; (2) the nature of the personnel; and (3) the financial ability of the library.

Perhaps the most influential of these factors is the efficiency with which the organizing has been done. This can facilitate evaluation, first, by providing means for the exercise of this function and, second, by establishing conditions throughout the library system which make comparisons possible both within the system and with other libraries.

The attitude of the personnel toward evaluation is a second important factor in facilitating this function. A staff which realizes the necessity of this activity and which is capable of recognizing pertinent data and recording it accurately can do much toward making a program of evaluating successful. Finally, the ability to interpret data is essential for success in such a program.

Evaluating is necessarily a costly activity, and a library which is hampered by lack of funds is often forced to eliminate all activities which are not obviously essential for immediate service to the public.

For this reason, inadequate financial support is usually fatal to any sustained program of evaluation. Many libraries are unable to determine their positions or to chart their courses effectively because they have not been able to afford the time or cost of the necessary records.

Devices used in evaluating.—The two most popular devices which librarians use in evaluating are surveying and reporting. The first is usually an activity conducted by an outside agency which employs a personnel not connected with the library surveyed. The persons conducting such surveys are usually qualified by training and experience to make a critical, impartial evaluation of the library and its service. The chief advantage of the survey is that its findings carry weight of authority and it can stress an abstract evaluation of library service with more success than can an evaluation by the library's own officers. The chief disadvantage of surveying as a device for evaluating is that there is no continuous process involved so that the examination must be made at a particular point in time and thus must necessarily be incomplete. However, surveying is probably the most effective method of evaluating yet evolved by librarians.

Reporting, the second device of evaluating, has been used more generally by librarians chiefly because it is a more continuous process and because its costs are hidden in the general operating expenses of the library, and it therefore seems to cost less than surveying. Potentially, reporting is more efficient for the following reasons: (1) reporting involves a continuous process and is more likely to show changes in library problems and service; (2) reporting becomes a part of the library routines and is more likely to be based upon typical library conditions; and (3) reporting is done by persons familiar with the library—persons who can evaluate details more nearly in their proper perspective than can experts less familiar with the library. However, it should be acknowledged that the intimate association of the library officials with the problems and operations of the library sometimes destroys their perspective and thus decreases the efficiency of reporting as a device of evaluating.

The use of these two devices is not necessarily confined to the annual reports of the librarian or to the occasional surveys of an entire library system by a group of outside experts. Reporting may be an evaluation by any library official upon any phase of library activity that is a regular part of his work. Thus daily circulation statistics, memorandums concerning activities or opportunities, and regular inventories are all a part of reporting. Surveying may be an evaluation by any library official when it is not a regular part of his work. Thus, the efforts of a newly elected staff member to learn the nature of a departmental collection, the assembly of data to aid in deciding upon the opening or closing of a branch, and the activities of a committee seeking to co-ordinate reference service may all be included as a part of surveying. Four distinct steps are involved in each of these devices (1) formulating the problem; (2) collecting and recording the data; (3) analyzing the data; and (4) interpreting the data.

Several instruments are available for use in connection with these devices of evaluating. One has long been familiar to librarians—the personnel report or efficiency record, which consists of a score sheet upon which are listed those qualities which the library management considers important in evaluating its employees. The library officials evaluate each of their subordinates in respect to the qualities listed and append to this concrete evaluation a set of remarks which attempt an abstract evaluation that the listing of qualities cannot reach.

A second instrument of evaluating which should prove invaluable as an aid to both surveying and reporting but which is almost entirely unknown to librarians is the standard of performance. It is the function of standards of performance to show the management how much and what quality of work each individual and each departmental unit should produce. These then form a basis for evaluating the worth of any procedure, unit, or individual in terms of a constant. The well-known standard of twenty thousand volumes circulated annually per librarian is an example of a common standard of performance. But establishment of standards should proceed cautiously until it is certain that they are just both to the institution and to the worker. Unjust standards—whether too high or too low— become serious disturbing factors in control. Industrial labor battles against the "stretch out" furnish ample evidence of this fact.

One means of determining standards of performance for library purposes may be roughly described as obtaining a consensus of opinion. This might be accomplished by forming a committee of the management and the employees to determine the results which might reasonably be expected of procedures, personnel, and departmental units. Each of these statements of expected results should show the quantity and quality of the work expected, and care should be taken to keep the standards within the range of ability of the average employee so that superior work might be recognized.

Factors which would affect the establishment of standards of performance are of three kinds. The first is the nature of the clientele, which might be described in terms of education, interests, and temperaments. The amount and type of education possessed by persons using the library will vary not only from branch to branch but among the departments of the main library and will inevitably affect the amount of work which can be done and the quality of the work required. Standards which do not reflect these varying conditions cannot be completely effective.

Interests of the clientele will also vary between the various branches and departments of a library. A branch in a residential district circulating popular literature almost exclusively will naturally be able to circulate more volumes per assistant than a branch in which reference work is heavy. It would be difficult for any person without experience in a particular branch to establish standards for that branch. These differences will affect not only the results of work by employees but also the results of procedures and the total work of the departmental unit. A more intangible factor which will affect the quantity and quality of the work is the temperament of the clientele. A downtown branch or department in which the clientele is hurried and perhaps more definite in its demands should be prepared to circulate books faster and to answer more reference questions than a branch in a residential district in which the patrons like to visit with one another and with the librarian. All these factors should be considered in the establishment of any standards of performance.

A second factor to be considered in the establishment of standards of performance is the nature of the equipment supplied for performance of the work. Three phases of this factor should be taken into consideration: first, labor-saving devices, which might include arrangement of buildings as well as automatic book-charging machines and other similar devices; second, the condition of the equipment and its effect upon the efficiency and effectiveness of the service; and third, the extent of standardization of equipment throughout the library system. The nature and condition of the book stock should also be considered.

A third factor in establishing standards of performance is the nature of the duties required. This factor may be subdivided into variety of duties, intensity, and objectives. It is easy to see that the librarian of a small branch who has to perform all library duties cannot be expected to give the same quality of service in special fields that the specialist at the main library can give. It is also easy to see that this branch librarian cannot be expected to meet the same standards of circulation as a circulation assistant at the main library or in a larger branch because of the number of other duties required. The intensity of the work also is a factor in the establishment of standards. The speed with which reference questions must be answered inevitably affects the quality of the answers, or the amount of work required to answer the questions inevitably affects the number of questions which might be answered. The objectives of the service will naturally vary from place to place within the system, and this variation will affect the quality and quantity of the results which might be expected. A unit whose chief objective is service to housewives will naturally have different standards from one whose chief objective is service to engineers.

Responsibility for evaluating.—In present library practice the function of evaluating is not highly developed and consequently there is no department dedicated to this activity. As a general rule, reporting is a duty of the librarian, who bases his evaluation upon reports submitted to him by department heads. Surveying, when it is an activity of an outside agency, is the responsibility of the trustees of the library, and the surveyors may be compared to accountants who make an audit of a business and report to the trustees and stockholders. When undertaken by the staff, surveying is usually delegated to a library officer or to a committee formed for this specific purpose.

REPRESENTING

The final class into which activities of library managers fall is that of representing. This function consists of those activities which form a liaison between the public and the library. The definition "personifying the enterprise to the owners and to the public" carries with it two ideas: the first gives a sense of a movement of communications outward from the library, while the second has the connotation of a movement of communications toward the library. The function of representing includes all those activities which present the library services and problems before the public or its representatives and all of those activities which provide for the presentation of public opinions and interests to the library organization.

Factors affecting representing.—In considering the elements which are likely to influence a program of representation, the two factors which first come to mind are (1) the avenues of communication available, and (2) the ability of the library's organization to utilize these avenues. In discussing the first factor, the term "avenues of communication" should be used in its broadest sense to include every agency through which ideas may be expressed—such as the press, the radio, and the library's own publications. Other mediums, including civic, social and religious organizations, service clubs, schools, and, in fact, every agency which tends to group people together, may be used as mediums of communication for presenting library services and library problems to the public. However, not all of these agencies are always available to the library. Practically every organization has its own problem of representing and thus creates a great deal of competition for library representation. Even the press and the radio must at times be closed to library affairs, and the objectives of some organizations require such vigorous campaigning that they cannot afford to allow any other use of their facilities. Such conditions vary from time to time and from place to place, and these variations affect the way in which the library may be presented to the public. In some cases certain avenues of communication may be preempted by other institutions, and the library may be obliged to develop new facilities or to campaign for a share of the existing medium. The growth of the Friends of the Library groups shows a recent development of new facilities for representing.

The second factor affecting representing—the library's ability to utilize these avenues of communication—is, in reality, a group of factors. One of these is the often-repeated factor—financial ability; another is the facility with which library officials or staff members can use the techniques and devices of representing; and a third is the capacity of the physical plant to facilitate representing. If a library's budget will allow the provision of a publicity agent, it is easy to see that its financial ability does aid in the exercise of the function of representing. On the other hand, financial inability to provide a publicity agent forces the shifting of this work into the hands of staff members who are often untrained and poorly fitted for such work. The ability to speak engagingly, to enlist sympathy and cooperation from others, to arrange interesting and striking exhibits, and to select those features of library service which appeal to public interest is an important asset in representation. In addition, an ability to perceive the problem and services of the library as a whole and in relation to the social structure of the community will affect any success in representing the library. In similar fashion, the library's physical plant is a factor in the way in which the function of representing can be carried on. The library cannot present its wares to the public as well from the suburbs as from the center of town. The possession of a printing press alters the problem of presenting library facts to the public, as does also the possession of an auditorium.

Devices of representing.—There are several devices of representing which libraries use. Reporting is a device of representing as well as of evaluating. Publicizing is perhaps the most-used device of representing. Personal appearances of staff members before groups and individuals for the purpose of extending library service to them or for presenting library needs or services may be termed a third device of representing. In addition to these three devices, means may be established for receiving representatives and delegations from other organizations in the community or for receiving individuals so that the library may be open to recommendations and to criticism.

Each of these devices may use several instruments as a means by which their objectives may be achieved. For example, instruments used in reporting are the annual report, minutes of a meeting, budget requests, and statistical reports to such bodies as the American Library Association. The library profession has developed additional instruments for reporting in its journals. The press, the radio, display windows, bibliographies, etc., are instruments of publicizing.

Responsibility for representing.—In a sense, the responsibility for representing is more widely diffused than for any other function. All employees of the library are representatives of the library in their contacts with the public. Members of the board of trustees are library representatives, and members of citizens' organizations also represent the library and present its case before the public. The librarian is especially the library's representative before official bodies and before the public. Publicity may be made the responsibility of a single library official or department, while responsibility for representing the library on special occasions may be delegated to any one of the library officials.

CONCLUSION

This survey of the seven functions of management as applied to library work is an effort to determine which activities of librarians are managerial in their nature and to indicate something of the relations that exist between such activities and library operations. It is not an attempt to define the principles of library management, nor is it an attempt to formulate rules for running a library. The analysis is not necessarily complete or final. Its chief value, in all probability, lies not in an accurate grouping of managerial activities in seven functions but in the fact that it proposes a reformulation of the concept of library management and an additional approach to librarianship.

It is the common experience of librarians as they ascend in the hierarchy of their profession that more and more of their time is drawn away from the procedures of library operation. A knowledge of the importance of managerial activities and of the relations existing between these activities and the success of library operations should go far toward compensating for the loss of those pleasant procedures which they must forego. In addition, a knowledge of the true function of library management should enable the library profession to select candidates for managerial positions much more accurately than is possible at the present time.

The classification of managerial activities into seven basic functions—directing, ordering, supervising, controlling, organizing, evaluating, and representing—is an attempt to think logically about the more neglected of the two fundamental divisions of library work.

The fact that managerial activity in libraries follows the pattern of managerial activity in all other cooperative enterprises makes the analysis easier and the findings relatively more important.

It should be possible to work from this, or a similar basis, toward the formulation of a comprehensive and definitive theory of library management.

References

1. Portion of Master's thesis, Graduate Library School, University of Chicago, 1939.
2. H. S. Person, "History and principles of management," in U.S. Department of Agriculture, Graduate School, *Administrative management* (Washington: U.S. Department of Agriculture, 1938), pp. 23–35.
3. American Society of Mechanical Engineers, *Transactions,* VII (1886), 428–32.
4. Person, *op. cit.,* p. 25.
5. *Ibid.,* p. 29.
6. *Ibid.,* p. 30.
7. L. Urwick, "The function of administration," in Luther Gulick and L. Urwick (eds.) *Papers on the science of administration* (New York: Institute of Public Administration, Columbia University, 1937), p. 119.
8. Henri Fayol, *Industrial and general administration* (Geneva: International Management Association, 1930), p. 32.
9. This summary taken from Urwick, *op. cit.,* p. 126.
10. *Op. cit.,* p. 42.
11. Professor Sorrell kindly consented to permit the author to quote from his unpublished class lecture on "The theory of business management."
12. Gertrude G. Drury, *The library and its organization* (New York: H. W. Wilson, 1924), pp. 83 and 84.
13. F. M. Crunden, "The librarian as administrator," *Library journal,* XIX (1894), 46.

14. *Library essays: papers related to the work of public libraries* (New York: H. W. Wilson, 1920).

15. "Two tendencies of American library work," *Library journal,* XXXVI (1911), 275-78.

16. "Efficiency in college and university library work," *Library journal,* XXXVI (1911), 566-69.

17. "Library service in a machine age," *Randolph Macon Woman's College bulletin,* V (1918-19), 21.

18. "Efficiency in library management," *Library journal,* XLIV (1919), 76.

19. "Scientific management and university libraries," in G. T. Schwenning (ed.), *Management problems* (Chapel Hill: University of North Carolina Press, 1930), pp. 168-98.

20. "Nuwe rigtings in die biblioteekwese," *South African libraries,* III (1935), 40-45.

21. C. B. Joeckel (ed.), *Current issues in library administration* (Chicago: University of Chicago Press, 1939).

22. *Ibid.,* p. vi.

23. "Administration of the public library of medium size," in *ibid.,* pp. 181-97.

24. Chicago University of Chicago Press, 1935.

25. *The geography of reading* (Chicago: University of Chicago Press, 1938).

26. An expansion of this analysis of ordering will be found in Ordway Tead, *The art of leadership* (New York: McGraw-Hill, 1935), pp. 152-62.

27. C. I. Barnard, *The functions of the executive* (Cambridge: Harvard University Press, 1938), pp. 139-60; and Webster Robinson, *Fundamentals of business organization* (New York: McGraw-Hill, 1925), pp. 74-75.

28. For a discussion of personnel work in libraries see John B. Kaiser, "Personnel: the key to administration," in C. B. Joeckel (ed.), *Current issues in library administration* (Chicago: University of Chicago Press, 1939), pp. 279-300; also Clara W. Herbert, *Personnel administration in public libraries* (Chicago: American Library Association, 1939).

29. See Barnard, *op. cit.,* pp. 106-13.

30. *Op. cit.,* pp. 76-106.

The Management Theory Jungle Revisited

Harold Koontz

N EARLY two decades ago, I became impressed by the confusion among intelligent managers arising from the wide differences in findings and opinions among academic experts writing and doing research in the field of management. The summary of these findings I identified as "the management theory jungle" [Koontz, 1961]. Originally written to clarify for myself why obviously intelligent academic colleagues were coming up with such widely diverse conclusions and advice concerning management, my summary was published and widely referred to under this title. What I found was that the thinking of these scholars fell into six schools or approaches in their analysis of management. In some cases, it appeared that, like the proverbial blind men from Hindustan, some specialists were describing management only through the perceptions of their specialties.

Judging by its reception over the years, the article and the concept of the "jungle" must have filled a need. In fact, so many inquiries have been made over the intervening years as to whether we still have a "management theory jungle" that I now believe the "jungle" should be revisited and reexamined. What I now find is that in place of the six specific schools identified in 1961, there are at least eleven approaches. Thus, the jungle appears to have become even more dense and impenetrable. But various developments are occurring that might in the future bring a coalescense of the various approaches and result in a more unified and useful theory of management.

Reprinted with permission from the *Academy of Management Review*, V. 5 (April 1980), pp. 175–187. © 1980 by the Academy of Management.

THE ORIGINAL MANAGEMENT
THEORY JUNGLE

What I found nearly two decades ago was that well-meaning researchers and writers, mostly from academic halls, were attempting to explain the nature and knowledge of managing from six different points of view then referred to as "schools." These were (1) the management process school, (2) the empirical or "case" approach, (3) the human behavior school, (4) the social system school, (5) the decision theory school, and (6) the mathematics school.

These varying schools, or approaches (as they are better called), led to a jungle of confusing thought, theory, and advice to practicing managers. The major sources of entanglement in the jungle were often due to varying meanings given common words like "organization," to differences in defining management as a body of knowledge, to widespread casting aside of the findings of early practicing managers as being "armchair" rather than what they were—the distilled experience and thought of perceptive men and women, to misunderstanding the nature and role of principles and theory, and to an inability or unwillingness of many "experts" to understand each other.

Although managing has been an important human task since the dawn of group effort, with few exceptions the serious attempt to develop a body of organized knowledge—science—underpinning practice has been a product of the present century. Moreover, until the past quarter century almost all of the meaningful writing was the product of alert and perceptive practitioners—for example, French industrialist Henry Fayol, General Motors executive James Mooney, Johns-Manville vice-president Alvin Brown, British chocolate executive Oliver Sheldon, New Jersey Bell Telephone president Chester Barnard, and British management consultant Lyndall Urwick.

But the early absence of the academics from the field of management has been more than atoned for by the deluge of writing on management from our colleges and universities in the past 25 years. For example, there are now more than 100 (I can find 97 in my own library) different textbooks purporting to tell the reader—student or manager—what management is all about. And in related fields like psychology, sociology, system sciences, and mathematical modelling, the number of textbooks that can be used to teach some aspect— usually narrow—of management is at least as large.

The jungle has perhaps been made more impenetrable by the

infiltration in our colleges and universities of many highly, but narrowly, trained instructors who are intelligent but know too little about the actual task of managing and the realities practicing managers face. In looking around the faculties of our business, management, and public administration schools, both undergraduate and graduate, practicing executives are impressed with the number of bright but inexperienced faculty members who are teaching management or some aspect of it. It seems to some like having professors in medical schools teaching surgery without ever having operated on a patient. As a result, many practicing managers are losing confidence in our colleges and universities and the kind of management taught.

It is certainly true that those who teach and write about basic operational management theory can use the findings and assistance of colleagues who are especially trained in psychology, sociology, mathematics, and operations research. But what dismays many is that some professors believe they are teaching management when they are only teaching these specialties.

What caused this? Basically two things. In the first place, the famous Ford Foundation (Gordon and Howell) and Carnegie Foundation (Pearson) reports in 1959 on our business school programs in American colleges and universities, authored and researched by scholars who were not trained in management, indicted the quality of business education in the United States and urged schools, including those that were already doing everything the researchers recommended, to adopt a broader and more social science approach to their curricula and faculty. As a result, many deans and other administrators went with great speed and vigor to recruit specialists in such fields as economics, mathematics, psychology, sociology, social psychology, and anthropology.

A second reason for the large number of faculty members trained in special fields, rather than in basic management theory and policy, is the fact that the rapid expansion of business and management schools occurred since 1960, during a period when there was an acute shortage of faculty candidates trained in management and with some mangerial experience. This shortage was consequently filled by an increasing number of PhDs in the specialized fields noted above.

THE CONTINUING JUNGLE

That the theory and science of management are far from being mature is apparent in the continuation of the management theory jungle. What has happened in the intervening years since 1961? The jungle still exists, and, in fact, there are nearly double the approaches to management that were identified nearly two decades ago. At the present time, a total of eleven approaches to the study of management science and theory may be identified. These are: (1) the empirical or case approach, (2) the interpersonal behavior approach, (3) the group behavior approach, (4) the cooperative social system approach, (5) the sociotechnical systems approach, (6) the decision theory approach, (7) the systems approach, (8) the mathematical or "management science" approach, (9) the contingency or situational approach, (10) the managerial roles approach, and (11) the operational theory approach.

Differences Between the Original and Present Jungle

What has caused this almost doubling of approaches to management theory and science? In the first place, one of the approaches found nearly two decades ago has been split into two. The original "human behavior school" has, in my judgment, divided itself into the interpersonal behavior approach (psychology) and the group behavior approach (sociology and cultural anthropology). The original social systems approach is essentially the same, but because its proponents seem to rest more heavily on the theories of Chester Barnard, it now seems more accurate to refer to it as the cooperative social systems approach.

Remaining essentially the same since my original article are (1) the empirical or case approach, (2) the decision theory approach, and (3) the mathematical or "management science" approach. Likewise, what was originally termed the "management process school" is now referred to more accurately as the operational theory approach.

New approaches that have become popular in the past two decades include the sociotechnical systems approach. This was first given birth by the research and writings of Eric Trist and his associates in the Tavistock Institute in 1951, but did not get many followers to form a clear-cut approach until the late 1960s. Also, even though the systems approach to any science or practice is not new (it was recognized in the original jungle as the "social systems" approach), its scholarly and widespread approach to management theory really occurred in the 1960s, particularly with the work of Johnson, Kast, and Rosenzweig (1963).

The managerial roles approach has gained its identification and adherents as the result of the research and writing of Henry Mintzberg

(1973, 1975), who prefers to call this approach the "work activity school."

The contingency or situational approach to management theory and science is really an outgrowth of early classical, or operational, theory. Believing that most theory before the 1970s too often advocated the "one best way," and often overlooking the fact that intelligent practicing managers have always tailored their practice to the actual situation, a fairly significant number of management scholars have begun building management theory and research around what should be done in various situations, or contingencies.

Many writers who have apparently not read the so-called classicists in management carefully have come up with the inaccurate shibboleth that classical writers were prescribing the "one best way." It is true that Gilbreth in his study of bricklaying was searching for the one best way, but that was bricklaying and not managing. Fayol recognized this clearly when he said "principles are flexible and capable of adaptation to every need; it is a matter of knowing how to make use of them, which is a difficult art requiring intelligence, experience, decision, and proportion" (1949, p. 19).

The Current Approaches to Management
Theory and Science

I hope the reader will realize that, in outlining the eleven approaches, I must necessarily be terse. Such conciseness may upset some adherents to the various approaches and some may even consider the treatment superficial, but space limitations make it necessary that most approaches be identified and commented on briefly.

The empirical or case approach. The members of this school study management by analyzing experience, usually through cases. It is based on the premise that students and practitioners will understand the field of management and somehow come to know how to manage effectively by studying managerial successes and failures in various individual cases.

However, unless a study of experience is aimed at determining *fundamentally* why something happened or did not happen, it is likely to be a questionable and even dangerous approach to understanding management, because what happened or did not happen in the past is not likely to help in solving problems in a most certainly different future. If distillation of experience takes place with a view to finding basic generalizations, this approach can be a useful one to develop or support some principles and theory of management.

The interpersonal behavior approach. This approach is apparently based on the thesis that managing involves getting things done through people, and that therefore the study of management should be centered on interpersonal relations. The writers and scholars in this school are heavily oriented to individual psychology and, indeed, most are trained as psychologists. Their focus is on the individual, and his or her motivations as a socio-psychological being. In this school are those who appear to emphasize human relations as an art that managers, even when foolishly trying to be amateur psychiatrists, can understand and practice. There are those who see the manager as a leader and may even equate managership and leadership—thus, in effect, treating all "led" activities as "managed." Others have concentrated on motivation or leadership and have case important light on these subjects, which has been useful to managers.

That the study of human interactions, whether in the context of managing or elsewhere, is useful and important cannot be denied. But it can hardly be said that the field of interpersonal behavior encompasses all there is to management. It is entirely possible for all the managers of a company to understand psychology and its nuances and yet not be effective in managing. One major division of a large American company put their managers from top to bottom through sensitivity training (called by its critics "psychological striptease") only to find that the managers had learned much about feelings but little about how to manage. Both research and practice are finding that we must go far beyond interpersonal relations to develop a useful science of management.

The group behavior approach. This approach is closely related to the interpersonal behavior approach and may be confused with it. But it is concerned primarily with behavior of people in groups rather than with interpersonal behavior. It thus tends to rely on sociology, anthropology, and social psychology rather than on individual psychology. Its emphasis is on group behavior patterns. This approach varies all the way from the study of small groups, with their cultural and behavioral patterns, to the behavioral characteristics of large groups. It is often called a study of "organization behavior" and the term "organization" may be taken to mean the system, or pattern, of any set of group relationships in a company, a government agency, a hospital, or any other kind of undertaking. Sometimes the term is used as Chester Barnard employed it, meaning "the cooperation of two or more persons," and "formal organization" as an organization with conscious, deliberate, joint purpose [1938, p. 65]. Chris Argyris has even used the term "organization" to include "*all* the behavior of *all* the participants" in a group undertaking [1957, p. 239].

It is not difficult to see that a practicing manager would not likely recognize that "operations" cover such a broad area of group behavior patterns. At the same time, many of the problems of managers do arise from group behavior patterns, attitudes, desires, and prejudices, some of which come from the groups within an enterprise, but many come from the cultural environment of people outside of a given company, department, or agency. What is perhaps most disturbing about this school of thought is the tendency of its members to draw an artificial and inaccurate line between "organization behavior" and "managing." Group behavior is an important aspect of managment. But it is not all there is to management.

The cooperative social system approach. A modification of the interpersonal and group behavior approaches has been the focus of some behavioral scientists on the study of human relationships as cooperative social systems. The idea of human relationships as social systems was early perceived by the Italian sociologist Vilfredo Pareto. His work apparently affected modern adherents to this school through his influence on Chester Barnard. In seeking to explain the work of executives, Barnard saw them operating in, and maintaining, cooperative social systems, which he referred to as "organizations" [1938, pp. 72-73]. He perceived social systems as the cooperative interaction of ideas, forces, desires, and thinking of two or more persons. An increasing number of writers have expanded this concept to apply to any system of cooperative and purposeful group inter-relationships or behavior and have given it the rather general title of "organization theory."

The cooperative social systems approach does have pertinence to the study and analysis of management. All managers do operate in a cooperative social system. But we do not find what is generally referred to as managers in *all* kinds of cooperative social systems. We would hardly think of a cooperative group of shoppers in a department store or an unorganized mob as being managed. Nor would we think of a family group gathering to celebrate a birthday as being managed. Therefore, we can conclude that this approach is broader than management while still overlooking many concepts, principles, and techniques that are important to managers.

The sociotechnical systems approach. One of the newer schools of management identifies itself as the sociotechnical systems approach. This development is generally credited to E. L. Trist and his associates at the Tavistock Institute of England. In studies made of production problems in long-wall coal mining, this group found that it was not enough merely to analyze social problems. Instead, in dealing with problems of mining productivity, they found that the technical system (machines and methods) had a strong influence on the social system. In other words, they discovered that personal attitudes and group behavior are strongly influenced by the technical system in which people work. It is therefore the position of this school of thought that social and technical systems must be considered together and that a major task of a manager is to make sure that these two systems are made harmonious.

Most of the work of this school has consequently concentrated on production, office operations, and other areas where the technical systems have a very close connection to people and their work. It therefore tends to be heavily oriented to industrial engineering. As an approach to management, this school has made some interesting contributions to managerial practice, even though it does not, as some of its proponents seem to believe, encompass all there is to management. Moreover, it is doubtful that any experienced manager would be surprised that the technology of the assembly line or the technology in railroad transportation or in oil companies affects individuals, groups, and their behavior patterns, the way operations are organized, and the techniques of managing required. Furthermore, as promising and helpful as this approach is in certain aspects of enterprise operations, it is safe to observe that there is much more to pertinent management knowledge than can be found in it.

The decision theory approach. This approach to management theory and science has apparently been based on the belief that, because it is a major task of managers to make decisions, we should concentrate on decision making. It is not surprising that there are many scholars and theorists who believe that because managing is characterized by decision making, the central focus of management theory should be decision making and that all of management thought can be built around it. This has a degree of reasonableness. However, it overlooks the fact that there is much more to managing than making decisions and that, for most managers, the actual making of a decision is a fairly easy thing—if goals are clear, if the environment in which the decision will operate can be fairly accurately anticipated, if adequate information is available, if the organization structure provides a clear understanding of responsibility for decisions, if competent people are available to make decisions, and if many of the other prerequisites of effective managing are present.

The systems approach. During recent years, many scholars and writers in management have emphasized the systems approach to the study and analysis of management thought. They feel that this is the most effective means by which such thought can be organized, presented, and understood.

A system is essentially a set or assemblage of things interconnected, or interdependent, so as to form a complex unity. These things may be physical, as with the parts of an automobile engine; or they may be biological, as with components of the human body; or they may be theoretical, as with a well-integrated assemblage of concepts, principles, theory, and techniques in an area such as managing. All systems, except perhaps the universe, interact with and are influenced by their environments, although we define boundaries for them so that we can see and analyze them both clearly.

The long use of systems theory and analyses in physical and biological sciences has given rise to a considerable body of systems knowledge. It comes as no surprise that systems theory has been found helpfully applicable to management theory and science. Some of us have long emphasized an arbitrary boundary of management knowledge—the theory underlying the managerial job in terms of what managers do. This boundary is set for the field of management theory and science in order to make the subject "manageable," but this does not imply a closed systems approach to the subject. On the contrary, there are always many interactions with the system environment. Thus, when managers plan, they have no choice but to take into account such external variables as markets, technology, social forces, laws, and regulations. When managers design an organizational structure to provide an environment for performance, they cannot help but be influenced by the behavior patterns people bring to their jobs from the environment that is external to an enterprise.

Systems also play an important part within the area of managing itself. There are planning systems, organizational systems, and control systems. And, within these, we can perceive many subsystems, such as systems of delegation, network planning, and budgeting.

Intelligent and experienced practicing managers and many management writers with practical experience, accustomed as they are to seeing their problems and operations as a network of interrelated elements with daily interaction between environments inside or outside their companies or other enterprises, are often surprised to find that many writers regard the systems approach as something new. To be sure, conscious study of, and emphasis on, systems have forced many managers and scholars to consider more perceptively the various interacting elements affecting management theory and practice. But it can hardly be regarded as a new approach to scientific thought.

The mathematical or "management science" approach. there are some theorists who see managing as primarily an exercise in mathematical processes, concepts, symbols, and models. Perhaps the most widely known of these are the operations researchers who have often given themselves the self-annointing title of "management scientists." The primary focus of this approach is the mathematical model, since, through this device, problems—whether managerial or other—can be expressed in basic relationships and, where a given goal is sought, the model can be expressed in terms which optimize that goal. Because so much of the mathematical approach is applied to problems of optimization, it could be argued that it has a strong relationship to decision theory. But, of course, mathematical modelling sometimes goes beyond decision problems.

To be sure, the journal *Management Science*, published by the Institute of Management Sciences, carries on its cover the statement that the Institute has as its purpose to "identify, extend, and unify scientific knowledge pertaining to management." But as judged by the articles published in this journal and the hundreds of papers presented by members of the Institute at its many meetings all over the world, the school seems to be almost completely preoccupied with mathematical models and elegance in simulating situations and in developing solutions to certain kinds of problems. Consequently, as many critics both inside and outside the ranks of the "management scientists" have observed, the narrow mathematical focus can hardly be called a complete approach to a true management science.

No one interested in any scientific field can overlook the great usefulness of mathematical models and analyses. But it is difficult to see mathematics as a school of chemistry, physics, or biology. Mathematics and mathematical models are, of course, tools of analysis, not a school of thought.

The contingency or situational approach. One of the approaches to management thought and practice that has tended to take management academicians by storm is the contingency approach to management. Essentially, this approach emphasizes the fact that what managers do in practice depends on a given set of circumstances—the situation. Contingency management is akin to situational management and the two terms are often used synonymously.

Some scholars distinguish between the two on the basis that, while situational management merely implies that what managers do depends on a given situation, contingency management implies an active interrelationship between the variables in a situation and the managerial solution devised. Thus, under a contingency approach, managers might look at an assembly-line situation and conclude that a highly structured organization pattern would best fit and interact with it.

According to some scholars, contingency theory takes into account not only given situations but also the influence of given solutions on behavior patterns of an enterprise. For example, an organization structured along the lines of operating functions (such as finance, engineering, production, and marketing) might be most suitable for a given situation, but managers in such a structure should take into account the behavioral patterns that often arise because of group loyalties to the function rather than to a company.

By its very nature, managerial practice requires that managers take into account the realities of a given situation when they apply theory or techniques. It has never been and never will be the task of science and theory to prescribe what should be done in a given situation. Science and theory in management have not and do not advocate the "best way" to do things in every situation, any more than the sciences of astrophysics or mechanics tell an engineer how to design a single best instrument for all kinds of applications. How theory and science are applied in practice naturally depends on the situation.

This is saying that there is science and there is art, that there is knowledge and there is practice. These are matters that any experienced manager has long known. One does not need much experience to understand that a corner grocery store could hardly be organized like General Motors, or that the technical realities of petroleum exploration, production, and refining make impracticable autonomously organized product divisions for gasoline, jet fuel, or lubricating oils.

The managerial roles approach. Perhaps the newest approach to management theory to catch the attention of academics and practitioners alike is the managerial roles approach, popularized by Henry Mintzberg (1973, 1975). Essentially this approach is to observe what managers actually do and from such observations come to conclusions as to what managerial activities (or roles) are. Although there have been researchers who have studied the actual work of managers, from chief executives to foremen, Mintzberg has given this approach sharp visibility.

By systematically studying the activities of five chief executives in a variety of organizations, Mintzberg came to the conclusion that executives do not act out the traditional classification of managerial functions—planning, organizing, coordinating, and controlling. Instead they do a variety of other activities.

From this research and the research of others who have studied what managers actually do, Mintzberg has come to the conclusion that managers act out a set of ten roles. These are:

A. Interpersonal Roles
   1. Figurehead (performing ceremonial and social duties as the organization's representative)
   2. Leader
   3. Liaison (particularly with outsiders)
B. Informational Roles
   1. Monitor (receiving information about the operation of an enterprise)
   2. Disseminator (passing information to subordinates)
   3. Spokesperson (transmitting information outside the organization)
C. Decision Roles
   1. Entrepreneur
   2. Disturbance handler
   3. Resource allocator
   4. Negotiator (dealing with various persons and groups of persons)

Mintzberg refers to the usual way of classifying managerial functions as "folklore." As we will see in the following discussion on the operational theory approach, operational theorists have used such managerial functions as planning, organizing, staffing, leading, and controlling. For example, what is resource allocation but planning? Likewise, the entrepreneurial role is certainly an element of the whole area of planning. And the interpersonal roles are mainly aspects of leading. In addition, the informational roles can be fitted into a number of the functional areas.

Nevertheless, looking at what managers actually do can have considerable value. In analyzing activities, an effective manager might wish to compare these to the basic functions of managers and use the latter as a kind of pilot's checklist to ascertain what actions are being overlooked. But the roles Mintzberg identifies appear to be inadequate. Where in them does one find such unquestionably important managerial activities as structuring organization, selecting and appraising managers, and determining major strategies? Omissions such as these can make one wonder whether the executives in his sample were effective managers. It certainly opens a serious question as to whether the managerial roles approach is an adequate one on which to base a practical theory of management.

The operational approach. The operational approach to management theory and science, a term borrowed from the work of P. W. Bridgman (1938, pp. 2-32), attempts to draw together the pertinent knowledge of management by relating it to the functions of managers. Like other operational sciences, it endeavors to put together for the field of management the concepts, principles, theory, and techniques that underpin the actual practice of managing.

The operational approach to management reognizes that there is a central core of knowledge about managing that exists only in management: such matters as line and staff, departmentation, the limitations of the span of management, managerial appraisal, and various managerial control techniques involve concepts and theory found only where managing is involved. But, in addition, this approach is eclectic in that it draws on pertinent knowledge derived from other fields. These include the clinical study of managerial activities, problems, and solutions; applications of systems theory; decision theory; motivation and leadership findings and theory; individual and group behavior theory; and the application of mathematical modeling and techniques. All these subjects are applicable to some extent to other fields of science, such as certain of the physical and geological sciences. But our interest in them must necessarily be limited to managerial aspects and applications.

The nature of the operational approach can perhaps best be appreciated by reference to Figure 1. As this diagram shows, the operational management school of thought includes a central core of science and theory unique to management plus knowledge eclectically drawn from various other schools and approaches. As the circle is intended to show, the operational approach is not interested in all the important knowledge in these various fields, but only that which is deemed to be most useful and relevant to managing.

The question of what managers do day by day and how they do it is secondary to what makes an acceptable and useful classification of knowledge. Organizing knowledge pertinent to managing is an indispensable first step in developing a useful theory and science of management. It makes possible the separation of science and techniques used in managing and those used in such nonmanagerial activities as marketing, accounting, manufacturing, and engineering.

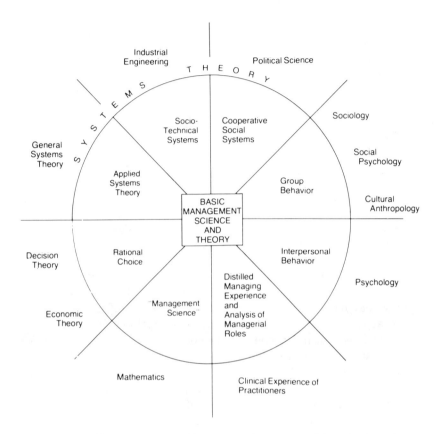

FIGURE 1   The Scope of Operational Science and Theory

It permits us to look at the basic aspects of management that have a high degree of universality among different enterprises and different cultures. By using the functions of managers as a first step, a logical and useful start can be made in setting up pigeonholes for classifying management knowledge.

The functions some theorists (including me) have found to be useful and meaningful as this first step in classifying knowledge are:

1. Planning: selecting objectives and means of accomplishing them.
2. Organizing: designing an intentional structure of roles for people to fill.

3. Staffing: selecting, appraising, and developing people to effectively fill organizational roles.
4. Leading: taking actions to motivate people and help them see that contributing to group objectives is in their own interests.
5. Controlling: measuring and correcting activities of people to ensure that plans are being accomplished.

As a second step in organizing management knowledge, some of us have found it useful to ask basic questions in each functional area, such as:

1. What is the nature and purpose of each functional area?
2. What structural elements exist in each functional area?
3. What processes, techniques, and approaches are there in each functional area and what are the advantages and disadvantages of each?
4. What obstructions exist in effectively accomplishing each function?
5. How can these obstructions be removed?

Those who, like me, subscribe to the operational approach do so with the hope of developing and identifying a field of science and theory that has useful application to the practice of managing, and one that is not so broad as to encompass everything that might have any relationships, no matter how remote, to the managerial job. We realize that any field as complex as managing can never be isolated from its physical, technological, biological, or cultural environment. We also realize, however, that some partitioning of knowledge is necessary and some boundaries to this knowledge must be set if meaningful progress in summarizing and classifying pertinent knowledge is ever to be made. Yet, as in the case of all systems analyses where system boundaries are set, it must be kept in mind that there is no such thing as a totally closed system and that many environmental variables will intrude on and influence any system proposed.

THE MANAGEMENT THEORY JUNGLE:
PROMISING TENDENCIES TOWARD
CONVERGENCE OF THEORIES

As can be seen from the brief discussions above of the schools and approaches to management theory and science, there is evidence that the management theory jungle continues to flourish and perhaps gets more dense, with nearly twice as many schools or approaches as were found nearly two decades ago. It is no wonder that a useful management theory and science has been so tardy in arriving. It is no wonder that we still do not have a clear notion of the scientific underpinnings of managing nor have we been able clearly to identify what we mean by competent managers.

The varying approaches, each with its own gurus, each with its own semantics, and each with a fierce pride to protect the concepts and techniques of the approach from attack or change, make the theory and science of management extremely difficult for the intelligent practitioner to understand and utilize. If the continuing jungle were only evidence of competing academic thought and research, it would not much matter. But when it retards the development of a useful theory and science and confuses practicing managers, the problem becomes serious. Effective managing at all levels and in all kinds of enterprises is too important to any society to allow it to fail through lack of available and understandable knowledge.

At the same time, there appears to be some reason to be optimistic, in that signs exist indicating tendencies for the various schools of thought to coalesce. Although the convergence is by no means yet complete, there is reason to hope that, as scholars and writers become more familiar with what managers do and the situations in which they act, more and more of these schools or approaches will adopt, and even expand, the basic thinking and concepts of the operational school of management.

While acknowledging that these are only indications and signs along the road to a more unified and practical operational theory of management, and that there is much more of this road to travel, let us briefly examine some of these tendencies toward convergence.

Greater Emphasis on Distillation of Basics
within the Empirical Approach

Within the many programs utilizing cases as a means of educating managers, there are indications that there now exists a much greater emphasis on distilling fundamentals than there was two decades ago. Likewise, in the field of business policy, by which terms most of these case approaches have tended to be known, there has been increased emphasis in teaching and research toward going beyond recounting what happened. One major result of all this has been a new emphasis on strategy and strategic planning. This has been nowhere more noteworthy than at the Harvard Business School, which is regarded as the cradle of the case approach. This has led many empiricists to come up with distilled knowledge that fits neatly into the operational theorist's classification of planning.

Recognizing that Systems Theory Is Not a Separate Approach

When systems theory was introduced into the management field some two decades ago, it was hailed by many as being a new way of analyzing and classifying management knowledge. But in recent years, as people have come to understand systems theory *and* the job of managing better, it has become increasingly clear that, in its essentials, there is little new about systems theory and that practicing managers as well as operational theorists had been using its basics (although not always the jargon) for a number of years. Nonetheless, as those in the field of operational management theory have more consciously and clearly employed the concepts and theory of systems, their attempts at developing a scientific field have been improved.

Recognizing that the Contingency Approach Is Not a New or Separate Approach

Although perceptive and intelligent managers and many management theorists have not been surprised by the realization, it is now clear that the contingency view is merely a way of distinguishing between science and art—knowledge and practice. As I pointed out earlier, these are two different things, albeit mutually complementary. Those writers and scholars who have emphasized contingency approaches have, to be sure, done the field of management theory and practice a great service by stressing that what the intelligent manager actually does depends on the realities of a situation. But this has long been true of the application of *any* science.

That contingency theory is really application in the light of a situation has been increasingly recognized, as is evidenced by a recent statement by one of its founders. Jay Lorsch recently admitted that the use of the term "contingency" was "misleading" [1977, pp. 2-14]. He appeared to recognize that an operational management theorist would necessarily become a situationalist when it came to applying management concepts, principles, and techniques.

Finding that Organization Theory Is Too Broad
an Approach

Largely because of the influence of Chester Barnard and his broad concept of "organization" as almost any kind of interpersonal relationships, it has become customary, particularly in some academic circles, to use the term "organization theory" to refer to almost any kind of interpersonal relationships. Many scholars attempted to make this field equal to management theory, but it is now fairly well agreed that managing is a narrower activity and that management theory pertains only to theory related to managing. Management theory is often thought of as being a subset of organization theory and it is now fairly well agreed that the general concept of organization theory is too broad.

This sign offers hope of clearing away some of the underbrush of the jungle.

The New Understanding of Motivation

The more recent research into motivation of people in organizational settings has tended to emphasize the importance of the organizational climate in curbing or arousing motives. The oversimplified explanations of motives by Maslow and Herzberg may identify human needs fairly well, but much more emphasis must be given to rewards and expectations of rewards. These, along with a climate that arouses and supports motivation, will depend to a very great extent on the nature of managing in an organization.

Litwin and Stringer [1968] found that the strength of such basic motives as needs for achievement, power, and affiliation, were definitely affected by the organizational climate. In a sample of 460 managers, they found a strong relationship between highly structured organizations and arousal of the need for power, and a negative relationship with the needs for achievement and affiliation. Likewise, in a climate with high responsibility and clear standards, they observed a strong positive relationship between this climate and achievement motivation, a moderate correlation to power motivation, and an unrelated to negatively related relationship with affiliation motivation.

The interaction between motivation and organizational climate not only underscores the systems aspects of motivation but also emphasizes how motivation depends on what managers do in setting and maintaining an environment for performance. These researches move the problem of motivation from a purely behavioral matter to one closely related to and dependent on what managers do. The theory of motivation, then, fits nicely into the operational approach to management theory and science.

The melding of motivation and leadership theory. Another interesting sign that we may be moving toward a unified operational theory of management is the way that research and analysis have tended to meld motivation and leadership theory. Especially in recent years, leadership research and theory have tended to emphasize the rather elementary propositions that the job of leaders is to know and appeal to things that motivate people and to recognize the simple truth that people tend to follow those in whom they see a means of satisfying their own desires. Thus, explanations of leadership have been increasingly related to motivation.

This melding of motivation and leadership theories has also emphasized the importance of organization climate and styles of leaders. Most recent studies and theories tend to underscore the importance of effective managing in making managers effective leaders. Implied by most recent research and theory is the clear message that effective leaders design a system that takes into account the expectancies of subordinates, the variability of motives between individuals and from time to time, situational factors, the need for clarity of role definition, interpersonal relations, and types of rewards.

As can be readily seen, knowledgeable and effective managers do these things when they design a climate for performance, when goals and means of achieving them are planned, when organizational roles are defined and well structured, when roles are intelligently staffed, and when control techniques and information are designed to make self-control possible. In other words, leadership theory and research are, like motivation, fitting into the scheme of operational management theory, rather than going off as a separate branch of theory.

The New Managerially Oriented "Organization
Development"

Both "organization development" and the field ordinarily referred to as "organization behavior" have grown out of the interpersonal and group behavior approaches to management. For a while, it seemed that these fields were far away and separate from operational management theory. Now many of these scientists are seeing that basic management theory and techniques, such as managing by objectives and clarifying organization structure, fit well into their programs of behavioral intervention.

A review of the latest organization behavior books indicates that some authors in this field are beginning to understand that behavioral elements in group operations must be more closely integrated with organization structure design, staffing, planning, and control. This is a promising sign. It is a recognition that analysis of individual and group behavior, at least in managed situations, easily and logically falls into place in the scheme of operational management theory.

The Impact of Technology: Researching an Old Problem

That technology has an important impact on organizational structure, behavior patterns, and other aspects of managing has been recognized by intelligent practitioners for many years. However, primarily among academic researchers, there has seemed to be in recent years a "discovery" that the impact of technology is important and real. To be sure, some of this research has been helpful to managers, especially that developed by the sociotechnical school of management. Also, while perceptive managers have known for many years that technology has important impacts, some of this research has tended to clarify and give special meaning to this impact.

The impact of technology is easily embraced by operational management theory and practice. And it should be. It is to be hoped that scholars and writers in the area of technological impacts will soon become familiar with operational management theory and incorporate their findings and ideas into that operational framework. At the very least, however, those who subscribe to the operational approach can incorporate the useful findings of those who emphasize the impact of technology.

Defections Among "Management Scientists"

It will be recalled that in the discussion of schools or approaches to management, one of them is identified as the mathematical or "management science" approach. The reader has also undoubtedly noted that "management science" was put in quotation marks; the reason for so doing is that this group does not really deal with a total science of management but rather largely with mathematical models, symbols, and elegance.

There are clear signs among the so-called management scientists that there are defectors who realize that their interests must go far beyond the use of mathematics, models, and the computer. These especially exist in the ranks of operations researchers in industry and government, where they are faced daily with practical management problems. A small but increasing number of academics are also coming to this realization. In fact, one of the leading and most respected academics, one widely regarded as a pioneer in operations research, C. West Churchman, has (in conversations with me) been highly critical of the excessive absorption with models and mathematics and, for this reason, has even resigned from the Operations Research Society.

There is no doubt that operations research and similar mathematical and modeling techniques fit nicely in the planning and controlling areas of operational management theory and science. Most operational management theorists recognize this. All that is really needed is for the trickle of "management science" defectors to become a torrent, moving their expertise and research more closely to a practical and useful management science.

Clarifying Semantics: Some Signs of Hope

One of the greatest obstacles to disentangling the jungle has long been, and still is, the problem of semantics. Those writing and lecturing on management and related fields have tended to use common terms in different ways. This is exemplified by the variety of meanings given to such terms as "organization," "line and staff," "authority," "responsibility," and "policies," to mention a few. Although this semantics swamp still exists and we are a long way from general acceptance of meanings of key terms and concepts, there are some signs of hope on the horizon.

It has become common for the leading management texts to include a glossary of key terms and concepts and an increasing number of them are beginning to show some commonality of meaning. Of interest also is the fact that the Fellows of the International Academy of Management, composed of some 180 management scholars and leaders from 32 countries of the world, have responded to the demands of its members and have undertaken to develop a glossary of management concepts and terms, to be published in a number of languages and given wide circulation among many countries.

Although it is too early to be sure, it does appear that we may be moving in the direction necessary for the development of a science—the acceptance of clear definitions for key terms and concepts.

THE NEED FOR MORE EFFORT IN DISENTANGLING THE JUNGLE

Despite some signs of hope, the fact is that the management theory jungle is still with us. Although some slight progress appears to be occurring, in the interest of a far better society through improved managerial practice it is to be hoped that some means can be found to accelerate this progress.

Perhaps the most effective way would be for leading managers to take a more active role in narrowing the widening gap that seems to exist between professional practice and our college and university business, management, and public administration schools. They could be far more vocal and helpful in making certain that our colleges and universities do more than they have been in developing and teaching a theory and science of management useful to practicing managers. This is not to advocate making these schools vocational schools, especially since basic operational management theory and research are among the most demanding areas of knowledge in our society. Moreover, these schools are *professional* schools and their task must be to serve the professions for which they exist.

Most of our professional schools have advisory councils or boards composed of influential and intelligent top managers and other leading citizens. Instead of these boards spending their time, as most do, in passively receiving reports from deans and faculty members of the "new" things being done, these boards should find out more of what is going on in managerially related teaching and research and insist that some of these be moved toward a more useful operational science of management.

References

Argyris, C. *Personality and organization.* New York: Harper & Brothers, 1957.

Barnard, C. I. *The functions of the executive.* Cambridge, Mass.: Harvard University Press, 1938.

Bridgman, P. W. *The logic of modern physics.* New York: Macmillan, 1938.

Fayol, H. *General and industrial management.* New York: Pitman, 1949.

Gordon, R. A.; & Howell, J. E. *Higher education for business.* New York: Columbia University Press, 1959.

Johnson, R. A.; Kast, F. E.; & Rosenzweig, J. E. *The theory and management of systems.* New York: McGraw-Hill, 1963.

Koontz, H. The management theory jungle. *Academy of Management Journal,* 1961, *4* (3), 174-188.

Litwin, G. H.; & Stringer, R. A., Jr. *Motivation and organization climate.* Boston: Harvard Graduate School of Business Administration, 1968.

Lorsch, J. W. Organization design: A situational perspective. *Organizational Dynamics,* 1977, *6* (2), 12-14.

Mintzberg, H. *The nature of managerial work.* New York: Harper & Row, 1973.

Mintzberg, H. The manager's job: Folklore and fact. *Harvard Business Review,* 1975, *53* (4), 49-61.

Pierson, F. C. *The education of American businessmen: A study of university-college programs in business adminstration.* New York: McGraw-Hill, 1959.

In Search of Excellence: A Review*

Andrew H. Van de Ven

S ELDOM does a management text achieve the public attention and media acclaim this book has. As of this writing, *In Search of Excellence* ranks second on the *New York Times* list of best-selling books and has been on the list for ten weeks. There is little need, therefore, to review the book in detail, since most *A S Q* readers have probably already read the book or reviews of it in *Time, Fortune,* and other popular magazines and newspapers. What is needed is an assessment of the contribution this book makes to administrative science.

Most likely, readers already know that the book is about 43 well-run American companies, as determined by a variety of criteria, including average return on equity and compound asset growth over a 20-year period. After extensive interviews and qualitative observations in these companies—such as 3M, IBM, Delta Airlines, Hewlett-Packard, and McDonald's—the authors distill their findings into eight prescriptive characteristics that make up the body of the book:

1. A bias for action—do it, try it, don't analyze the problem to death. "You more likely act yourself into feeling, than feel yourself into action" (p. 74).
2. Close to the customer. "If you can't understand the customers, you won't understand the business . . . .The answer on how much service is enough or what kind of quality is right lies in the marketplace" (p. 170).

---

*By Thomas J. Peters and Robert H. Waterman, Jr. New York: Harper & Row, 1982, 360 pp.

3. Autonomy and entrepreneurship. "Innovation success is a numbers game . . . . Make sure you generate a reasonable number of mistakes" (p. 208). The well-run companies foster innovation through "skunk works," a mythology and role models, suboptimal division, internal competition—the market is brought inside—and an intense communication system.
4. Productivity through people. The excellent companies treat their employees—not technology—as the root source of quality and productivity gains. "Respect for the individual is a central belief. The key to a people orientation is trust . . . [and] a great number of people programs" (p. 242).
5. Hands-on, value driven—MBWA (management by wandering around). "If asked to provide an all-purpose bit of advice, we might be tempted to reply, 'Figure out your value system. Decide what your company stands for . . . . Set and demand standards of excellence.' Anybody who accepts mediocrity—in school, in job, in life—is a guy who compromises. And when the leader compromises, the whole damn organization compromises" (pp. 280, 285).
6. Stick to the knitting. "Never acquire a business you don't know how to run . . . . The qualitative guiding value and the hands-on approach are at war with diversification. Diversification dilutes the guiding qualitative theme—in part because the acquired firm undoubtedly has different shared values, but also because themes such as quality tend to lose meaning when the organization strays far afield" (p. 293).
7. Simple form, lean staff. "Most acronyms stink. Not KISS: Keep It Simple, Stupid! One of the key attributes of the excellent companies is that they have realized the importance of keeping things simple despite overwhelming genuine pressures to complicate things" (p. 63).
8. Simultaneous loose-tight properties—both centralized and decentralized. "Autonomy is a product of discipline. The discipline (a few shared values) provides the framework. It gives people confidence (to experiment) stemming from stable expectations about what really counts. The 'rules' in the well-run companies have a positive cast. They deal with quality, service, innovation, and experimentation. They focus on expanding and building, the opposite of restraining. The value set is for all seasons" (p. 324).

In short,

The excellent companies were, above all, brilliant on the basics. Tools didn't substitute for thinking. Intellect didn't overpower wisdom. Analysis didn't impede action. Rather, these companies worked hard to keep things simple in a complex world. They persisted. They insisted on top quality. They fawned on their customers. They listened to their employees and treated them like adults. They allowed their innovative product and service "champions" long tethers. They allowed some chaos in return for quick action and regular experimentation. (p. 13)

The book is exceptionally well written and emotionally energizing—it's enough to send you forth whistling the IBM company song. The apparent redundancy throughout the book is inevitable, given the interrelatedness of the eight characteristics and the many different organizational settings to which they apply and which the authors flesh out with their rich vignettes, stories, and tales. The data presented to develop and support the eight characteristics would, by most scientific standards, not be admissible evidence of valid knowledge. But this is not a theory-testing effort; it is a rich display of idea generation and synthesis that may lead to the creation of a new theory.

So what ideas does this book contribute to advance administrative theory? Each reader is likely to have a different answer. For me, the central contribution of the book is a better appreciation of the paradoxes inherent in the nature of man and organization. Most administrative theories begin with or search for internal consistencies in the nature of man and organizations and relegate contradictions, as indicators of either poor theory or anomalies, to an area outside the bounds of the theory. Correspondingly, most administrative theories are static and are rightly criticized for their inability to explain the dynamics of change and development in organizational form and individual behavior. There is a growing realization that a dynamic theory that can explain both stability and change should begin with and directly address the tensions and conflicts inherent in human institutions. Peters and Waterman have begun in this way.

The eight characteristics of successful companies represent individual and organizational dilemmas in the management of attention. As the authors state, "The excellent companies have learned how to manage paradox" (p. 100). Peters and Waterman examine this paradox by first focusing on the contradictions that are built into human nature.

1. We like to think of ourselves as winners, but our talents are normally distributed. "We are not as good as we would like to believe, but rubbing our noses daily in that reality doesn't do us a bit of good" (p. 55).
2. While we have a very limited capacity to process information explicitly with our left brain, our unconscious mind (the right brain) is very powerful in being able to accumulate a vast storehouse of patterns.
3. While we are all creatures of our environment—very sensitive and responsive to external rewards and punishments—we are also strongly driven from within, self-motivated.
4. We desperately need meaning in our lives and will sacrifice a great deal to

institutions that will provide meaning for us. Yet we simultaneously need independence, to feel as though we are in charge of our destinies, and to have the ability to stick out.

5. For all the focus on self-interest rationality in management theory, organizational participants spend a majority of their working time doing things that are not in their self-interest.

But the paradoxes don't stop with the individual; they are pervasive throughout the well-run organizations. Reading between the lines in chapters 5 to 12, the reader finds the following organizational paradoxes:

1. Small is beautiful in order to get or stay big.
2. Flexible overall organization structures result in rigid subgroup structures. Organizations designed with impeccable micrologic often result in non-sense macro-logic.
3. To grow, organizations must often diversify, but to be successful, they must stick to their knitting, i.e., not diversify too much.
4. Organizations develop systems for strategic planning but, in the process, often lose strategic thinking. Long-range planning means emphasizing certain short-run activities.
5. The efficiency benefits provided by specialization; as well as centralized support services, are often destroyed by separating planners from doers and accountability from responsibility, respectively. In excellent companies, tidiness is sacrificed and redundancy is permitted to increase efficiency.
6. Attempts to structure innovative groups (e.g., skunk works) annihilates them. Since innovation is a numbers game, institutional leaders must manage a Darwinian evolutionary process in hopes that mutations emerge.
7. Organizations hire a heterogeneous work force, but want homogeneous values.
8. Organizations must develop tight values and beliefs in order to have loose structures and systems. The soft "touchy-feely" human component of the enterprise has become hard.

Current administrative theory does not explain or incorporate these contradictions and trade-offs inherent in organizational life. Is an internally consistent theory of these externally inconsistent dilemmas possible? I doubt if contingency theory is helpful here, since the paradoxes operate simultaneously and in joint situations. Yet, if Peters and Waterman are correct, successful practitioners have apparently developed such a theory—implicitly or explicitly—since the excellent companies have somehow learned to manage these paradoxes. The starting points in developing such a theory, the authors suggest, are to replace the rational actor with a complex social actor—a human being with inbuilt strengths, weaknesses, contradictions, and irrationalities—and to replace a steady-state view of social systems with a dynamic tension-strung view, in which groups of people interact with a fast-paced and ever-changing array of forces, both within and outside the organization. The theory would emphasize a return of the institutional school of Barnard, Selznick, Bennis, and Burns. It would center on transforming leadership, corporate culture, and organizational evolution. Transforming leadership goes beyond instrumental leadership by focusing on the ethics and value judgments that are implied when leaders and followers raise one another to higher levels of motivation and morality. Culture and shared values are important in unifying the social dimensions of any organization into an institutional character with a distinctive competence. A temporal evolutionary view is needed not only to keep an organization adaptive, but also to understand the processes in which individual and organizational dilemmas unfold and are addressed over time.

Peters and Waterman conclude that most current theory "is not loose enough to consider the relative lack of structure and the need for a wholly new management logic to ensure continuous adaptation in large enterprises" (p. 107). While the authors do not provide the alternative theory that they call for, they have provided a rich and valuable source of qualitative stories, vignettes, and paradoxes that administrative scientists need to begin to take into account. That alone makes this book a significant contribution to advancing administrative science.

The Changing Role of Directors of University Libraries

Arthur M. McAnally and Robert B. Downs

T RADITIONALLY the directorship of a major university library has been a lifetime post. Once a librarian achieved such a position of honor and leadership in the profession, he usually stayed until he reached retirement age. In the 1960s, however, an increasing number of incidents occurred which indicated that all was not well in the library directors' world, resulting in a vague feeling of uneasiness. Then in one year, 1971-72, the seriousness of the situation became dramatically evident: seven of the directors of the Big Ten university libraries (plus the University of Chicago) left their posts, only one a normal retirement for age. These are major universities on the national scene whose directorships had been stable in the past.

To discover how widespread this condition might be, an investigation has been undertaken among the seventy-eight largest university libraries—members of the Association of Research Libraries. Exactly one-half of the directors were found to have changed within the past three years, four of them twice. This is an extraordinarily high rate of change. If such a rate were to continue, the average span of service for directors would be five to six years. Next, to find out if the development was related to size of the library, those university libraries holding more than 2,000,000 volumes were compared with the twenty smallest libraries in the association. Size apparently has some bearing, but does not appear to be a major factor: while 60 percent of the larger libraries had changed directors, 45 percent of the smaller ones did, too. The authors are well aware that the directors of libraries

Reprinted by permission of the American Library Association from *College and Research Libraries* 34(2): 103–25 (Mar. 1973).

in many small universities—as well as those in intermediate and large institutions—are in severe difficulty or under intense pressure. Oddly, the chief librarians of colleges and junior colleges do not appear to be affected. The problem seems to be limited to university librarians only.

Several explanations of the phenomenon have been offered. Edward G. Holley observed the trend during visits to a number of urban university libraries in 1971: "At the end of the sixties it has not been uncommon for chief librarians, who by any objective standards served their institutions well, to retire early from their directorships, some with sorrow, some with relief, and a few with bitterness. Very few have retired with the glory and honor that used to accompany extraordinary accomplishments in building resources and expanding services."[1] Holley attributed the condition partly to changing attitudes of the library staffs. On the other hand, Raynard C. Swank questioned whether many directors really had retired in great favor in the past. He also suggested that the present high rate of change might be due partly to a large number of directors who were appointed some thirty years ago all nearing retirement age about the same time.[2] Others believe that the problem reflects a highly critical attitude towards the university library itself rather than just criticism of the directors. Still others conclude that an era is ending and old ways are having to give way to new: those who will not or cannot adapt are finished. The suggestion also was made that a few of the changes might be attributable to weaknesses among the directors. Though each of these explanations may have some validity, the full story is far more complicated.

Directors who have recently quit their jobs should be authoritative spokesmen on the subject. The authors corresponded or discussed the subject, therefore, with twenty-two directors or former directors whom they knew well personally.[3] Each was asked for his opinions about the causes of the extraordinary turnover in directorships and to suggest possible remedies. Every one replied, and many gave keen analyses of the causes as well as suggesting steps that should be taken.

BACKGROUND FACTORS

The numerous changes in directorships indicate that some fundamental dissatisfactions have arisen within university libraries or their environment in recent years. The underlying causes may be deep-seated and varied. Thus the director might be under fire, as he unquestionably is, because he is the most visible representative of an agency that is under attack, the university library itself. Therefore, recent trends in society and the university were examined, as well as movements in university administration, the world of scholarship and research, and the publishing and information world, as well as the university library itself.

Growth of enrollment. The extraordinary growth in enrollments in higher education during the decade of the sixties forced the university itself to make many changes to attempt to cope with the flood of students. Total enrollments grew from almost four million to approximately eight million. The number of graduate students tripled, from 314,000 to more than 900,000. The tremendous increase produced changes in the university far beyond merely making it larger. It became a far more complicated institution.[4]

University expansion began long before the sixties, of course. Probable effects upon the university library were noted in 1958 by Donald Coney, and the title of his article is prophetic: "Where Did You Go? To the Library. What Did You Get? Nothing."[5] Except for the creation of undergraduate libraries in some of the larger universities beginning at Harvard in 1948, few changes were made to cope with the rising flood. Most universities remained oriented basically to the single-copy research concept.

Changes in the presidency. Growth in size of the institution placed great pressure upon the president, and other factors added to his problems: rising expectations, growing militancy of students and faculty, disillusionment and a newly critical attitude towards higher education on the part of the general public that developed as a result of student activism, political pressure from hostile legislators or governors, growing powers exerted by state boards of control, and, to cap it all, financial support that began to decline or at least levelled out. Harried from all sides, forced to act often on bases of emergency or expediency, and with little time left for academic affairs, the position of the president has become almost untenable.

It is not surprising that the average tenure of university presidents in the United States is now a short five years. Chancellor Murphy of UCLA stated that the office of president or chancellor has become impossible, and suggested a maximum term of ten years. He observed that "The chief executive of an institution makes his greatest creative impacts in the first five to eight years. He may need a few more years to follow through in the implementation of these creative impacts. Beyond that, however, the housekeeping function inevitably becomes larger, and much of the vitality, drive, and creativity declines."[6]

President Lyman of Stanford noted that directors of libraries appeared to be in the same situation as presidents. Herman H. Fussler added that the tenure of all senior university administrators—not only presidents but also vice-presidents and deans—had declined considerably in recent years. He asked, why should librarians expect to be different?[7] Booz, Allen & Hamilton predicted that term appointments for presidents might become common, and that even peer election could come in the late seventies.[8]

Proliferation in university management. To cope with the greatly intensified pressures on the president, and in the belief that universities were undermanaged, nearly every university in the country has added substantially to its central management staff. The most striking increase has been in number of vice-presidents.

The proliferation of vice-presidents was noted and commented on by several directors: Lewis C. Branscomb, Thomas R. Buckman, Richard N. Logsdon, Robert Miller, and Edward B. Stanford. All observed that this movement has had the effect of interposing a layer of administrative officers between the chief librarian and the president. The director no longer has direct access to the president; thus the role of the library in the university and the power of the library to present its case has been reduced. Logsdon commented that unfortunately the presidents rarely have utilized existing administrators, such as directors of libraries, who have a broad overview of the university, to help with the growing burden of general administrative affairs.[9]

Changes in the world of learning and research. Several factors beyond the obvious one of expansion of existing graduate programs and establishment of new programs have affected the university and its library. A major instance is the continued fragmentation of traditional academic disciplines. New specializations continue to break off from older fields; each, of course, smaller than the original. One authority has referred to the trend as "the Balkanization" of learning.[10] Another movement of the sixties which is having a major impact on libraries is the emergence of interdisciplinary programs, including area studies. New social concerns and the demands for relevance also foster the growth of interdisciplinary institutes and other irregular patterns outside of established fields. Even engineering is moving towards a juncture with the sciences. To help cope with the flood of students, teaching methods have turned increasingly to larger classes, increased use of teaching assistants for regular classes, and, to a lesser degree, the newer media, such as closed-circuit TV.

These changes in the world of learning may presage a fundamental reorientation, according to Peter F. Drucker. "The emergence of knowledge as central to our society and the foundation of economy and social action drastically changes the position, the meaning, and the structure of knowledge . . . . Knowledge areas are in a state of flux. The existing faculties, departments, and disciplines will not be appropriate for long. Few are ancient to begin with, of course . . . . The most probable assumption is that every single one of the old demarcations, disciplines and faculties is going to become obsolete and a barrier to learning as well as to understanding. The fact that we are shifting rapidly from a Cartesian view of the universe, in which the accent has been on parts and elements, to a configuration view, with the emphasis on wholes and patterns, challenges every single dividing line between areas of study and knowledge."[11]

All the foregoing movements have implications for the libraries. As was remarked by Warren J. Haas, the rise of small new specializations tends to drive up the price of books and journals because the clienteles are small. Interdisciplinary studies tend to weaken the old system of departmental libraries. Spread-out departmental libraries do not serve the new needs well, and no university can afford to create the many new branch libraries presently being demanded. The multitudes of teaching assistants are not adept at utilizing the library in their teaching. Furthermore, the large numbers of students in single courses demand more copies of any title than the library is able to provide. Few libraries are equipped or staffed or budgeted to add the newer media to their services, and most are not oriented in that direction. The effects of all these patterns of scholarship upon library resources have been ably summarized by Douglas W. Bryant.[12]

The information explosion. The constantly accelerating production of knowledge has been so widely publicized that it hardly calls for comment. When the knowledge produced by the world up to 1900 is doubled by 1950, and doubles again by 1965, as has been estimated, the term "explosion" seems applicable. As early as 1945, Vannevar Bush wrote that "Professionally our methods of transmitting and reviewing the results of research are generations old and by now totally inadequate for their purpose . . . ."[13] No significant changes have occurred since Bush's statement. By 1970, a national Committee on Research in the Life Sciences concluded that "Investigators in the life sciences have not been able to cope with the waves of information since 15 years ago."[14] The rate of growth in science and technology seems fairly constant at 10 percent a year, which means a doubling every eight years.

University libraries quite obviously were going to be overwhelmed by this flood sooner or later; the velocity of change produces a faster expansion of knowledge than can be appraised, codified, or organized. Fremont Rider first called attention to the problem in 1944, pointing out that research libraries were doubling in size every sixteen years.[15] The annual studies at Purdue since 1965 indicate that the rates of growth discovered by Rider have continued unabated through 1971.[16]

So long as financial support of the university and its library grew steadily year after year, university libraries could hope at least to keep their heads above water. They clearly were in a very precarious position at best, however, and anyone could foresee that when hard times came, as they inevitably would, sooner or later, there would be serious difficulties. Those times have now arrived.

Hard times and inflation. The current financial problems of universities hardly need documentation. Earl F. Cheit in a study for the Carnegie commission on Higher Education and the Ford Foundation calls it "the new depression."[17] Budgets have actually been cut, or the rate of increase slowed drastically.

Planning and budgeting. A static budget when coupled with inflation spells real trouble for universities. All have begun to reassess goals and functions, and to try to improve their planning and budgeting processes. State boards of control appear strongly interested in program planning and budgeting systems, even though these devices have doubtful validity for colleges and universities. Clearly, long and short range planning and analytical budgeting are going to be a way of life in universities henceforth.

One of the budgets likely to be looked at hard with an eye to cutting is that of the university library, partly because it looms large. Certainly libraries can no longer count on steady increases in rate of publication. In addition, libraries are harder hit than most parts of the university, especially in regard to acquisitions, because the rate of inflation (or increases, if we accept the subject-fragmentation factor as one cause for increases in the price of materials) is higher than it is in other aspects of our economy. The declining status of the director of libraries in the administrative family also tends to reduce his effectiveness in presenting library needs.

Technology. Ever since Vannevar Bush proposed the Memex in 1945—the storage of all the information a research scholar needs in microform within the space of a desk, recallable at will—technology has been seen as a promising means of coping with the ever-growing flood of knowledge. Microtext has been adopted readily by university libraries, though it should be noted that government agencies do not allow the counting of materials in microtext in basic reports on resources. There have been many experiments with the computer, especially in computerized bibliography, the best examples being the National Library of Medicine's MEDLARS (now succeeded by MEDLINE), and *Chemical Abstracts.* Many experiments have been undertaken, numerous books have appeared on the subject, and the federal government has established a special agency on scientific information. One director declared in 1971 that "Computerization of information, long hoped by some to be the solution to library costs, is for that purpose substantially bankrupt."[18] This judgment may seem harsh, but it reflects general disappointment. Perhaps everyone, including librarians, had over-optimistic expectations. Time may change the situation, but it is now thirty-seven years since Vannevar Bush's proposal was first advanced.

Changing theories of management. Certain new theories of management emerged beginning in the early 1960s. Based on psychology and the study of human relations in an organization, the new ideas appeared first in business and industry and subsequently spread to governmental agencies. The new theories are characterized by the growing involvement of people in organizational decision-making, loosening of the traditional hierarchial structure, what might be called creative tensions, growing complexity, constant change, and open-endedness. Leadership is with a soft voice at a low key. Motivation and morale are stressed. Several excellent books on the new system have appeared.[19] One of the cycle theories, an aspect of the open-end concept, is that management is in constant change and that a successful organization evolves through five stages, the last of which is collaboration.[20]

The new theories seem especially suitable to an academic organization, because it is made up of intellectual and rational men, it is bureaucratic, and hardly compatible with the principles of hierarchy and obedience. One of the particular virtues of the new management plans for a university is that it tends to provide a defense in depth for the institution, when it comes under attack. It marshals all resources (administration, faculty, students, staff, and regents) against any onslaught. Predictions are that universities generally will adopt the new methods.[21] Ideas about participatory mangement in university administration are documented well by Henry L. Mason in a study promoted by AAUP.[22] Mason, in turn, reflects the ideas of Demerth, Millet, Carson, Kerr, and other authorities in academic management.

Unionization. Social conditions are changing, and therefore management needs to change. Factors promoting acceptance of the new theories of management include the growing educational level of workers, social disillusionment, activism including a demand for a share in the government of the enterprise, the need for more effective use of employee knowledge and spirit, the protection which they provide against outside attacks, and unionization. The unionization even of faculties, long regarded as unlikely, appears to be on the increase.[23] Participatory management may be an acceptable alternative. However, tight money and the over-supply of Ph.D.'s may speed the trend of college and university faculties to unionize "at a revolutionary pace."[24] Even the AAUP is moving away from its former cooperative attitude towards a position of being spokesman for the faculty as a defender of all faculty interests, including salaries, class size, and similar concerns. Unionization is one form of participation in management.

Increasing control by state boards. State boards of regents for higher education are becoming increasingly powerful and exerting more and more control over state-supported institutions. In part, this movement is a result of public disillusionment about higher education, especially universities where the student activist movement has been most evident, and partly it is a production of legislative wishes. Such boards, in some instances, are adding highly qualified specialists to their staff, developing long-term master-plans to which the universities must conform, and emphasizing the budgeting process. Many already budget by formulas, and nearly all are strongly interested in program planning and budgeting systems. In a number of states they are creating new community and junior colleges which are less subject to public disfavor, and also are politically popular. The junior institutions draw heavily on both state building and state operating funds for higher education. Typical of the movement towards stronger control is the recent reorganization of the State Board of Governors in 1971 by the North Carolina Legislature, giving the board complete authority to determine functions, educational activities, academic programs, and degrees. Previous assignments of functions or responsibilities to designated institutions were cancelled.[25] The state boards appear to be using for overall research and planning the National Center for Higher Education Management Systems (NCHEMS) of the Western Interstate Commission for Higher Education, at Boulder, Colorado. The center's studies and recommendations therefore are of basic importance.

University libraries are becoming more and more subject to the state boards, especially in the budgeting process and in their demands for more effective cooperation among all state academic libraries. The coming pattern of state budgetary controls for university libraries was predicted ten years ago. McAnally found in a survey in 1962 that a majority of state boards were not yet using formulas for university library budgets (even though some already had formulas for college libraries), because of the complexity of the problem, but that many were interested in the subject.[26] Now there is a definite trend towards formulas for budgeting for university libraries, and many state boards also are considering PPBS.[27] The Washington "Evergreen" formula, developed by business officers, in cooperation with the state's college and university libraries, is typical of the newer, complex formulas. It has certain disadvantages for university libraries.[28] McAnally and Ellsworth had referred to the dangers of equalitarianism in formula budgeting for university libraries. If graduate programs and quality are not given adequate weight, this could be an end result. It remains to be seen what the effect of PPBS will be on university libraries, if this budgeting system is adopted widely.

No national system for information. The last of the background problems for libraries is the failure to achieve an effective national system for the sharing of information. The present uncoordinated system was reasonably satisfactory around the turn of the century when advances in knowledge were slow and leisurely. The information explosion is now producing an enormous wealth of knowledge, published and distributed according to the techniques of 1900, which is beyond control and a source of frustration, dismay, and continual irritation to scholars. Steps such as interlibrary loan, cooperative acquisitions plans, union lists and catalogs, and the Center for Research Libraries have been useful, but too little and ineffective, and hardly acknowledged by the community of scholars. Control is not necessarily a library problem, though librarians seem to catch the brunt of the blame. Instead, many agencies ought to be helping solve the problem: the various professional associations in different subjects, publishers of books and journals, computer and information specialists, foundations, and last, but not least, the federal government. Information is a resource of national importance; certainly the center of an effective system will be enormous in size and complexity. The federal government has made some useful efforts toward the control of scientific information, but only in medicine has the work been supported adequately.

In any event, university libraries receive the principal blame for failure to solve the problem of access, with the result that the director of the library has lost stature and prestige within his institution.

Buckman believes that some substantial progress must be made towards the solution of major national problems, such as this one, before the director of libraries can hope to regain his proper status within the university.[29]

INTERNAL PROBLEMS

Many of the newer problems facing directors of university libraries have their origins in changing social conditions or within the institution as it attempts to adjust to these social trends. Some of his problems, however, have developed within the university library itself. Few of the internal problems are new; mainly, they are expansions of existing or latent difficulties.

Greatly Intensified Pressures

The most obvious change in the director's job is the extraordinary increase in the pressures exerted upon him. Many of the directors with whom the authors corresponded wrote quite feelingly upon this point. A few key phrases describe the situation succinctly. Herman Fussler observed that "the pressures on the library and director have changed by one or two orders of magnitude in the past twenty years . . . the librarian sits between the anvil of resources and the hammer of demands . . . . The strain is greater, just as it is for presidents of universities."

Louis Kaplan wrote, "Administration is never easy, and there were problems galore even when money was plentiful . . . . I had lived through the 'glory' years . . . ." Louis Branscomb noted that "It has become a matter of running faster on the treadmill every year in order to stay where you were the year before." One director said that at his first interview the new president informed him that he did not believe in buying books, and later elaborated this statement. Another reported that the president had refused to see him for ten years. David Otis Kelley suggested that the university should have "a younger man to sit on this hot seat." Edward B. Stanford referred to the "present climate of creeping discontent that pervades the faculty, students and staff on so many large campuses." Ralph Parker observed that "I have found the life of a Dean on this campus to be much cosier than the life of a librarian." And the title of a talk by Warren B. Kuhn describes the situation vividly: "in the Director's office, it's 'High Noon' every day!"

Writers on management agree that to a certain degree stress

stimulates executives to better performance. But they also agree that excessive stress is harmful. As the pressures on the director increase, he has a tendency to become more and more decisive in attempting to cope with the growing multitude of problems alone, until he ultimately offends too many people or else concludes that the rewards are no longer worth the cost.

Pressure sources. The growing pressures on the director are exerted by five different groups. They are, in probable order of magnitude, the president's office, the library staff, the faculty, students, and, in publicly supported universities, state boards of control. It may seem odd to list the library faculty as high as second, but in those cases in which the principal cause for the director quitting his position can be identified, the library staff ranks second.

Unquestionably, the president's office, including not only the president but also the academic vice-president and particularly the financial vice-president, bring the strongest pressures to bear on the director. In part, this is because the president is the most powerful man in the university, in part because he reflects institutional opinion. The president's office is a source of many of the director's frustrations. Numerous directors commented on this problem, and on the deterioration of these relationships. As already pointed out, the proliferation of top-level administrators has severed the director from direct contact with the president, interposed a layer of officers between the two, and reduced the ability of the library to present its case. Directors also have realized, as Thomas R. Buckman remarked, that they have no power base on which to operate, and others noted that the director could not even get to the point of a showdown, much less win one. All presidents are harried, some are inexperienced, and others may come from nonlibrary oriented fields such as the sciences.

One of the major frustrations of the director may be with the financial vice-president. Robert Vosper calls attention to a prediction by a social scientist as early as 1961, of coming conflicts between the library and budgetary authorities.[30] The rate of growth of libraries observed by Rider and others obviously had to end eventually. The director sees clearly the financial needs produced by the ever-growing flood of publications, increased enrollment, expanding graduate programs, rising expectations and demands, and inflation, but may not be able to convince the budget officer of the acuteness of library needs. Besides, the financial vice-president may have no new money, is reluctant to make cuts elsewhere for the library, which he may regard as a "bottomless pit," or may have less money than previously. Financial demands pressed hard are likely to see the director relieved of his post. A noteworthy example of this fact occurred in one of the great Ivy League schools—when the director wrote bluntly and bitterly about financial support, on the first page of his annual report (his only or last recourse?), he was immediately relieved and transferred to the School of Religion. The financial problems of the university library are not likely to decrease for the indefinite future.

Staff pressures. It may seem strange that the director should be under attack from his own staff, or fail to receive badly needed support in relations with the administration and faculty, but it is so in many cases. Robert Miller wrote: "In recent years there has been pressure exerted upon the library administrator by the library staff, the overt features including a strengthened organization, unionization, requests for participation in administrative decision-making, faculty status, etc. To me and to other benevolent and beloved administrators, this is an attack on the father image which I have long fancied. I know one man who felt this so keenly that he resigned."

Nowadays the library staff, both the academic or professional and the nonprofessional, are far better educated than in the past. Most librarians hold at least a master's degree, and many higher degrees. They also are more socially conscious, action-oriented, and impatient—in common with the rest of our society. They want and expect a share in policy decisions affecting themselves and the library.[31] The rise of library specialists in university libraries also is producing severe strains on the library's administrative structure, and represents a force for change in administrative practices, according to Eldred Smith.[32]

A particular problem that has not yet surfaced fully is that the director has two staffs, one academic or professional and one clerical or nonacademic. The latter is the larger of the two. Different administrative styles are needed for each. There is some danger that the two groups might end up in opposition to each other, especially if the nonacademic group unionizes and the academic group does not.

The old methods of organization may no longer be acceptable, but good alternatives are difficult to find. Booz, Allen & Hamilton identify the problem in their Columbia study.[33] In any event, new administrative styles are being called for, and those directors who will not or cannot adapt to the newer ways may be lost.

Faculty sources. The latent conflict of interests between librarians and the faculty were commented upon recently by Robert H. Blackburn and Richard H. Logsdon. Blackburn stated that librarians have the books, professors have the students.[34] Logsdon pointed out that the typical faculty member wants complete coverage in his

324 MANAGEMENT STRATEGIES FOR LIBRARIES

subject and centralized service; the professor sees the size of the
library budget and regards the library as an empire with all kinds of
staff help when the professor cannot even have a secretary. As one
director wrote, these and other frustrations lead to "a gradual building
up of small things into big, lose a friend here and there every year, and
there's bound to be a critic in almost every department."[35] A simple
but cynical explanation of the growing problem in faculty relations
may be financial—when there is not even money enough for any raises
for the faculty, faculty support for other university functions inevitably declines. The growing militancy in society generally also may be
a factor in bringing existing problems to the fore.

Student pressure. Students do not yet have the power in the
university for which they are agitating, but their power is growing.
They, too, are action oriented, and are demanding improvements in
library service. "Under pressure from students and faculty there has
been a forced change in academic library priorities," Robert A. Miller
finds. "Service is more important, or holds more immediacy than
collection building. More service is wanted and in more depth . . . reference to limitations of funds, space, personnel is not accepted as a
sound reply, but only as an alibi for non-performance."[36] When there is
no new money, improved service must come at the cost of collections.
A special problem is that most university libraries have over-
emphasized services to research, so that except in those institutions
where there is an undergraduate library, the collections tend to be
single-copy collections. Professors, when they select books, prefer to
cover as much of the new literature in their fields as possible, and are
reluctant to spend money on extra copies, even of important titles.
Approval plans also produce only single copies. To cap the problem,
changing emphases of human rights over property rights lead to
losses—not nearly as great as faculty and students think, but certainly
causing a very serious problem in public relations.

Declining Ability of Library to Meet Needs

Apparently the university library is becoming increasingly less able
to meet the legitimate needs of its university community. The causes
have already been outlined in background factors: the information
explosion, inflation, more students, and continued fragmentation of
the traditional disciplines, coupled with hard times. A recent study at
Harvard concluded that with 8,000,000 volumes the library was less
able to cope with the demands of scholars than it was when it had only
4,000,000 volumes. Ralph Ellsworth, in his 1971-72 annual report at

Colorado, came to the same conclusion. David Kaser states plaintively: "The lugubrious fact is that our ability to supply the books and journals needed by Cornell teaching and research programs is rapidly diminishing, and no one seems to know what to do about it. Computerization of information, cooperation, and microminiaturization have not provided solutions . . . .The somber conclusion fast being arrived at by the library staff is that the only solutions likely to be effective are (1) more money, or (2) a substantially reduced academic program for the library to serve, neither of which appears imminent. The library needs, and would welcome, advice in this matter."[37] Another director observed that "when the library is unable to perform at the level of satisfaction to the faculty, the head of the library is held personally responsible and it is assumed that he is incapable of being Director."

Lack of Goals and Planning

Like the university itself, the library has rarely done a good job of planning, either long-range or short-range. One director remarked: "Many university librarians have rigid, pre-conceived notions about the proper objectives of their libraries. The traditional library objectives summarized cynically in such phrases as 'more of the same' and 'bottomless pit' are probably unrealistic, and yet little is offered in their place."[38] Now that higher education and all its parts are under critical review, the lack of realistic, practicable, and accepted goals, and of long-range planning, is a major handicap. There are some noteworthy exceptions, such as UCLA, Columbia, and Illinois. Several writers have discussed this problem.[39]

Inability to Accommodate to Educational Changes Quickly

The university library, like the university itself, is a bureaucracy which is difficult to change, even though the need may be recognized by nearly everyone concerned. In addition, the university library may have large collections, sometimes built up over centuries, research collections which cannot be changed quickly; the library is housed in a great building or buildings which would cost millions to replace; and its staff of specialists has been developed over a period of years. The two groups most impatient for new philosophies and new types of services are the students and the president's office. Inability to make changes rapidly, even though he tried, cost at least one director his job.

Decline in Status of the Director

This subject has been dealt with previously, but is so important to the welfare of the library, as well as to the director personally, that it should be noted again in a consideration of internal problems. The director no longer is in the upper level of university management and cannot participate in institutional policy decisions, including planning and budgeting. Partly the decline is due to lack of basic support. The director seldom has an opportunity to defend the library, or if he does, no one wishes to listen to him. And on him now falls the chief burden of asking for institutional book funds as well as staff money. Many directors commented on this aspect and asserted that it made real achievements impossible and reduced the attractiveness of the position.

Declining Financial Support

When financial support for the universities slows down, stands still, or decreases, the library must suffer too. A static or declining budget causes especially acute problems in the library, because of the continuing proliferation of publications and increases in the prices of print well above the national average. A number of directors, in discussing this problem, referred to "housekeeping" or "caretaker-level" funding. Booz, Allen & Hamilton warns that the president is inclined to look at the library budget as a place to economize. There is widespread evidence that the percentage of the total educational and general budget allotted to the university library has declined in recent years, including some of our most distinguished universities. The national situation cannot be determined readily; however, *Statistics of Southern College and University Libraries,* which reports percentages spent on the library, reveals that decreases slightly outnumber increases over the past five years, but decreases outnumber increases two to one over a ten-year period.

Renewed Questioning of Centralization

Every director is probably aware of the declining efficiency of the general library and the old departmental library system in meeting new needs and rising expectations. Interdisciplinary studies and fragmenting disciplines are not served well by the system, and libraries have no funds to expand. Peter Drucker expects the entire university curriculum to be reorganized;[40] if so, this problem may well increase. Every director also is aware of the rise of many office collections, unoffical institute libraries funded from grants, and departmental reading rooms supplied personally by the faculty. All these developments indicate growing dissatisfaction with centralized controls. "Institutionalizing library resources inevitably denies individual faculty members the degree of control they would prefer . . . . Add to this the even stronger desire on the part of professional schools to be autonomous within the university and you have another set of frictions."[41]

No Effective Sharing of Resources,
Computerization, Microminiaturization

Failure to make substantial progress on these national problems is blamed on the library and its director, and some believe it an important factor in the decline of prestige of the director.

Old-Style Management

As noted above, the traditional hierarchical and authoritative style of management is increasingly unacceptable. As one director observed, it "no longer has any purchase in the market place." Many directors are unwilling or unable to adapt. In addition, the director's office now operates in a condition of constant change, intense pressures, and great complexity. These factors are of crucial importance to the director personally, demanding the highest administrative abilities as well as durability, flexibility, and determination.

SOLUTIONS AND CHANGES

It is far easier to identify the multitude of problems facing the university library and its director than it is to find solutions to these troubles. Nevertheless, there are answers to some problems and partial solutions to others. Perhaps the most important fact for the director to recognize is that old ways are being questioned and that changes are evolving; he should be receptive to continuing change, both for his library and for himself personally, and try to see that the best possible

choices are made among various alternatives. The university library
obviously will survive, for it is a fundamental part of the university,
but its nature will continue to be transformed. What happens to the
individual director may not be important, heartless though this may
seem. Either he adapts to new ways, or another person will be brought
in who has the qualities needed in the new era. But what happens to
the leadership of the library embodied in the position of director of
libraries is exceedingly important.

Solutions to National Problems

To restore the confidence of the university in the library and its
director, there has to be "general acceptance and implementation of
some significant national programs that really come to grips with
fundamental problems of providing information and knowledge for
people working in the universities . . . .They probably won't get it fully
until he and his colleagues attack the national problems in such a way
that the local university library becomes a manageable operation."[42]
   Unfortunately, the problems are so vast that there seems to be
little that the individual director can do. Instead, the solutions must
come at the national level. No *deus ex machina* is likely to appear any
time soon from the computer-information world, microminiaturization or other technologies; it is   therefore the responsibility of
librarians to develop answers, even though they may be only partial
and prove temporary. However, the librarian can make his views
known and speak out vigorously about the urgent need to national
agencies which are in a stronger position to attack the problems. These
include the Association of Research Libraries, agencies of the federal
government, and the American Library Association. Efforts of the Association of Research Libraries to promote a national acquisitions
program and to develop plans for more effective sharing of resources
for research are constructive, but the organization is dependent upon
the federal government and foundations for research funds, and is not
funded to operate any continuing program. Nonetheless, its leadership
is vitally important in the overall situation. Only the federal
government can provide the sizeable funds needed for a proper
national plan. There are four comprehensive federal agencies in the
field—the National Commission on Libraries, the Library of Congress,
the National Science Foundation, and the Department of Health,
Education, and Welfare—none of which is funded properly for the
task, nor has national responsibility for information been fully
accepted by the government. The American Library Association can

be helpful but has many diverse interests and at present has internal management problems.

Current developments of promise are the recently completed ARL interlibrary loan cost study, the same organization's current study of the feasibility of a computerized national referral center, and ongoing studies of national-regional periodicals resources centers or lending libraries by the National Commission on Libraries, ARL, and the Center for Research Libraries. Both the Association of Research Libraries and the Center for Research Libraries have broadened their membership considerably in recent years, thereby increasing their strength. ARL has adopted automatic membership criteria based on 50 percent of the ARL averages on certain factors. Some librarians see networks as an answer, but existing examples are uncoordinated and vary widely in scope and in value. It should be noted again that political pressures are strong for more and more effective cooperation, especially from state boards of higher education and from HEW.

Better Planning

Failure to plan for the future has been one of the major weaknesses of university libraries in general, a condition which many authorities agree must be corrected in the seventies. "Planning is the orderly means used by an organization to establish effective control over its own future ... to be effective any plan ... must be logical, comprehensive, flexible, action-oriented, and formal. Furthermore, it must extend into the future and involve human resources."[43] In an era of change in the university and of static financial support, the allocation of resources becomes especially important. The components of comprehensive library planning include (1) university requirements and expectations for library services; (2) the library's own objectives and plans in support of academic programs and general learning needs; and (3) library resources (financial, personnel, collections, facilities, and equipment) needed to implement agreed-upon plans. There are four ways to accommodate change. (1) Appoint a new chief librarian. (2) Call in an outside consultant. So far as the director is concerned, results are the same as (1) four times out of five, especially if the university calls for the consultant. (3) Establish a committee within the library organizational structure as a research and planning group.[44] (4) Appoint a staff officer in the director's office for planning and research, to do some of the work and to assist the staff committee. Kaser points out that in the university "academic decision making ... is not accomplished through the organizational tree that we have come to associate with large organizations. Such a structure does exist in universities, but it exists for nonacademic decisions; academic decisions . . . are rather initiated and made by faculty members as individuals and with practically no centralized control over them."[45] Implications for the library are obvious.

Improved Budgeting

During this period of hard times for the university, the university library must improve its budgeting and control practices greatly if it is to receive its fair share of limited resources. The old add-on type budget is gone, at least for a while and perhaps forever. Librarians need to prove their value to the classroom faculty as well as to the university administration—libraries are indispensable, but how indispensable? Libraries now have to demonstrate their importance to the educational program of the institution. There also must be more accountability—directors must provide better justifications for budget increases. Some steps that the director should take include adding a business-trained budget manager to the library staff for budget preparation; enlisting the support of instructional departments in preparing budgets; seeking faculty and administrative recognition of the fact that any new academic program requires money and that special financial aid should be given to the library for it; making productivity and cost benefit analyses regularly; participation in computerized networks and information-sharing systems; and having the director sit on the highest university policy board.[46] A discovery of considerable significance was made by Kenneth S. Allen, who found among thirteen sampled institutions that "the percentage of educational and general expense funds allocated to the library appears to be favorably influenced by having faculty status."[47] Further study is needed to see if this is true nationally.

State boards of higher education clearly are going to affect budgeting practices of state-supported university libraries, as previously observed, for their financial control is growing rapidly. The methods they adopt will govern library methods. Six types of budgets currently are in use: the traditional budget by objects of expenditure, program budget, performance budget, Planning, Programming and Budgetary Systems, formula budgeting, and combinations.[48]

New Organizational Patterns

If present trends in the academic programs of the university continue—breakoff of new subjects from old disciplines, growth of interdisciplinary studies and area studies, rise of programs oriented towards current social problems, more independent study programs, and more adult education work, or if indeed there will be entirely different curricula by 1980 as suggested by some—then the university library may have to make considerable change in its organizational structure to accommodate to university needs. Some modifications are needed already, for internal as well as external reasons; our present patterns are over seventy-five years old.

At present, no one knows with any certainty exactly what changes in organization may be needed. The most interesting suggestions to date, the Booz, Allen & Hamilton proposals (limited to staff and service only) for Columbia University libraries, appear unwieldy and cumbersome. The experiment should be watched with interest. The company reflects a business-industrial management firm's approach. In any event, the director needs to be aware that organizational changes may be needed, and to remain open-minded and flexible on the subject.

Services Vs. Collection-Building

The director must recognize that the emphasis in university libraries is shifting from collection-building to services, under growing pressures from students and faculty, and that the library must conform. Library staffs also seem to be becoming more service conscious and program oriented. When financial support is static, there is no place to obtain the money for improved services other than book and journal funds. Therefore, the percentage of the library budget allotted to acquisitions will decline, unfortunate as this is for the world of scholarship in general and the university in particular. In its most affluent days, no library was able to acquire more than a portion of the world's published output.

Every director has been made increasingly aware of the growing dissatisfactions with library service. Formerly faculty members and students were reluctant to voice criticism and make suggestions; nowadays, neither seems to hesitate to make attacks. Failing to receive satisfaction, they may go to the president or to the campus newspaper. Courteous hearings and boxes for complaints and suggestions are useful. Another evidence that every director must be aware of is the rapid growth in recent years of alternatives to standard library service-office collections, unofficial institute libraries, faculty-supplied departmental reading rooms, and the like. Dougherty suggests that a new attitude and new types of service may be needed for the latter group.[49]

Undergraduate libraries (or learning resources centers as some state boards prefer to call them) seem successful and desirable, and are popular with students. They are possible, however, only in large university libraries. They help improve service, but there seems to be little or no correlation between the presence of such a unit and the tenure of the director.

Collecting Policies

Several changes in collecting policies may be desirable. The first and most obvious change is that, with stable or declining funds, the library needs to be more selective in choosing from the world's output. Unless the library receives a book and journal budget that increases steadily at least 12 percent a year, the recent rate of inflation in the price of print, library intake will decline. There is a trend towards selection by library specialists. Blanket order and approval plans are becoming widespread. Both movements seem to be satisfactory and acceptable to the faculty. When book funds decline, many libraries tend to protect their periodical subscriptions first.

Institutional pride and rules of agencies for counting library statistics emphasize the codex book and the journal. Microprint is well used by libraries but is not acceptable for the basic count. Libraries need to widen their collecting net to include information in other forms, including the so-called newer media and information on computer tapes or discs. Douglas Bryant has pointed out the growing variety of forms that must be collected.[50]

Rare books. Some presidents, legislators, and state boards have long looked askance at the use of budgetary funds for the purchase of rare books *per se.* Now the attitude appears to be spreading to the faculty and to students. A little checking with faculty members in almost any department except history, English, and classics or other humanitites is likely to prove startling. Neither scientists nor social scientists are likely to appreciate the need. Perhaps the attitude is a product of severe financial problems, or McLuhanism, or strong emphasis on the current problems of our society. The director may be well advised to use only gift funds for such purposes, and to publicize this policy among the faculty. "Friends of the Library" organizations can be quite helpful in providing funds for "frosting on the cake."

More copies of important books or current titles in heavy demand ought to be purchased. Most university libraries, with the exception of those with undergraduate units, are basically single-copy libraries. The most severe criticism of every university library in the country probably is the inability of students or faculty to secure a copy of a high-demand title when needed. Changes in acquisitions policies clearly are required.

Institutionalization of Resources

Some loosening of centralized control over resources and services may be in order. This will seem downright heresy to some, and an encouragement of inefficiency and wastefulness by others. But the fact is that this is already occurring. Professional associations in medicine and law in concerted campaigns have gained a great deal of independence for their schools, including their libraries. Other professional associations are beginning to work on similar programs. The rise of many unofficial office collections, institute libraries, and departmental reading rooms has already been noted. The library itself cannot establish the needed new branches to serve interdisciplinary and similar new programs, due to the financial pinch. Actually, at least two great university libraries have always been federations of libraries—Harvard and Cornell. The financial and supportive aspects of allowing some degree of freedom were suggested by Donald Coney in the 1950s. When asked why he allowed so many independent branch libraries at Berkeley, he replied, "We get more money that way." Cooperation and a new kind of personalized service to meet new needs are suggested by Dougherty.[51] Holley suggests that coordinated decentralization as at Harvard should be looked at, as well as the view that after a certain size has been reached, some form of decentralization may be both necessary and desirable.[52]

Directors undoubtedly need all the help they can find nowadays, and by cooperation they can maintain some degree of coordination which might otherwise be lost. As the rate of acquisitions declines, libraries may have excess staff in their acquisitions and cataloging departments which could be utilized. Policies on these matters need to be reviewed, and either re-affirmed or modified.

Status of the Director

Most directors commented on the decline in status of the office of director, reflected in the interposition of layers of vice-presidents between the president and the director. Some decline in general approval of the library itself also seems to be evident. This is unfortunate for the director, but very serious indeed for the university library itself. The library's representative usually no longer participates in institutional policy decision making processes, and cannot present the library's case at the top level.

Buckman believes that the four requirements to restoring confidence and credibility in the director, and by implication the library, are: (1) some effective attack on major national problems; (2) establishing an effective working relationship with the administrative officers of the university; (3) providing a framework in which the director can operate effectively within the university's power structure and (4) setting reasonable and widely understood goals for the library.[53] Branscomb suggests that this may be a problem to be worked out individually on each campus, rather than by a considered attack from research libraries as a group.[54] Booz, Allen & Hamilton propose that the director be made a vice-president.[55] The vice-president needs to adopt a university-wide viewpoint when this is done. The idea is attractive, and has been implemented at Columbia, Texas, and Utah, the two latter perhaps for different reasons. An important factor, for directors considering such a move, may be that the office should be a vice-president for information services for the entire campus, assuming responsibilities for the newer media, even closed-circuit TV and certain aspects of computerized information services. Separate budgeting for the latter units seems fundamental.

The status of the director is sometimes a negotiable matter which should be dealt with as one of the conditions of appointment. The rank of dean may be negotiable; the status of vice-president possibly not. The welfare of the library itself as well as the opportunity for achievement by the director of course are involved.

Term Appointments

One of the solutions proposed by several directors is appointment for a fixed term, perhaps for ten years, perhaps for five years, with one renewal possible.[56] If Chancellor Murphy is correct, and if the post of director is comparable to that of a president, then his observation that an individual's major creative contributions are made within the first three to five years, with ten years the maximum time needed to complete programs, the idea should be considered carefully by the profession. Both the library and the individual are certain to suffer when the director remains in the position past his period of optimum contribution.

Several universities presently have term appointments for deans and other such administrators—with extensions possible—Cornell, Texas, and Illinois. The de facto tenure period for directors of ARL libraries over the past three years has averaged between five and six years. Vosper does note, however, that very short terms inhibit planning and focused concentration, such as the three year elective term in Japanese academic libraries.

If term appointments are adopted, some orderly plans or structure to facilitate wise change in administation must be formulated. So far there is none, though at West Virginia a president acquires retirement privileges after five years, and at Kentucky deans who return to teaching retain their salaries at the expense of the general admin-istration. A majority of directors who have quit their posts have gone into teaching, but there are limitations to this concept—many universities have no library school, and the ability of schools to absorb a succession of directors may be limited. Others have become curators of special collections, taken early retirement, or moved to another university. If peer appointment should come for presidents, as has been suggested, it might also apply to directors. In such circum-stances, moving to a lesser position in the library would become more practicable. In any event, the profession needs to give some thought to the problem of how to make such changes feasible rather than traumatic.

Increase the Percentage of
Nonprofessional Staff

Some twenty-five years ago university libraries in the United States generally had a 1:1 ratio between professional librarians and sup-porting staff. Then following a series of articles by Archie McNeal and others in the middle 1950s, pointing out that perhaps two-thirds of the work in an academic library could be done successfully and more economically by nonprofessional people, libraries generally moved to a staff composition of two nonprofessionals to one professional. With few exceptions, this distribution is common among university libraries today.

Among Canadian university libraries the ratios are different: from three-to-one up to five-to-one. The movement began in the catalog department at the University of British Columbia; when catalogers complained about the amount of routine and clerical work they were doing, the library increased the size of the supporting staff to what they deemed proper. Canadian university libraries have close working relations, and the movement spread rapidly. The new ratios are reported to be acceptable and satisfactory.

This subject requires further examination on the part of directors and their staffs. The education of the entire population has improved greatly in the last fifteen to twenty years, from which it follows that nonprofessional personnel ought to be able to carry more higher level duties. A careful survey of student opinion about the central library at the University of Oklahoma revealed that the four areas of greatest dissatisfaction fell within the province of the nonprofessional staff. Obviously the library needs more assistants.[57] Eldred Smith also had speculated that the university library may not need many more academic or professional staff, but better qualified and more specialized individuals.[58] Harold F. Wells suggests that the ratio of clerical to professional ought to be five-to-one; adding that all staff are better educated, one year is a short period of graduate education, the Army is very dependent on sergeants, and libraries ought to upgrade clericals and assign more duties to them.[59] A tentative inquiry about a research grant to establish the proper ratio was unsuccessful.

In relation to nonacademic staff members, there are three special problems for the director: they may fit a somewhat different administrative pattern, no one knows what are the proper relationships between the academic and the nonacademic staff, and clerical assistants appear to be more likely to join a union.[60] Booz, Allen & Hamilton proposals in the Columbia study attempt to come to grips with the problem, one of the first efforts to date. Other approaches need to be explored. In one major university library, the two groups have already come into conflict. The problems will grow in proportion to increases in size of the assistant group.

CHANGING PATTERNS OF MANAGEMENT

New management styles rapidly are replacing the old traditional techniques in the university library world. The trend has been observed and commented on by several librarians who have made surveys of university library management around the country during the last two years: Edward G. Holley, Maurice P. Marchant, Eldred Smith, and Jane G. Flener.[61] Involving increased staff participation in the management of the library to one degree or another, they are called participatory management, collegial management, or democratic administration. The theory and principles have been drawn from two different sources, business and industry, and academia itself. The new styles are being adopted rapidly because the arguments in their favor are persuasive. They draw in to the solution of problems a diverse group of good minds with varied viewpoints, thereby improving the quality as well as the effectiveness of decision making. They are the answer to growing staff pressures, particularly from the academic or professional staff, for participation in planning and policy decisions, as well as administrative affairs affecting themselves. They tend to improve the morale and dedication of the staff. They marshall the entire staff in defense of the library against attacks from outside, thus relieving and supporting the director, a defense in depth, as it were. The director has to surrender some of his old authority, and becomes more of a leader. His influence may not be diminished, but it must be exerted in different ways.

There are three principle styles, two based on business and industry, the other on university academic practices. The three might be called the business management plan, the unionization method, and collegial management or academic plan. A director may not be free to choose among them. If his university has not, and probably will not, grant academic status to librarians, such as the Ivy League universities, he must choose one of the first two. If the professional staff already has faculty status, then he would be wise to accept that style. A show of hands recently in the Association of Research Libraries indicated that three-fourths of the directors already had academic status or were interested in seeking it for their staffs. If a staff is unionized already, a new director has no choice. All of the new styles are so new, comparatively speaking, that there are still wide variations in practice in all three groups. Each may be successful. The director who enters upon any one of the paths grudgingly and because he is forced to, and drags his heels all the way, however, is likely to find himself in trouble after a short time.

Business management plan. Examples of libraries experimenting with the professional but not academic approach (i.e., their staffs do not have faculty status nor are they unionized) are Cornell, Columbia, UCLA, and recently Harvard. The method may give more options to the director, and allow him to make more decisions concerning the degree of staff participation. There are no firm outside models; therefore, the director and his staff have to make many basic and difficult decisions. A director who goes into this system determined to cede only what he has to treads a very difficult and possible dangerous path. There is likely to be a latent restlessness in the staff which will burst forth if there is even slight provocation. Given hard work, good judgment, and cooperation from both sides the method should be successful.

It is interesting to note that Booz, Allen & Hamilton Inc., in their original report of 1970 on *Problems in University Library Management,* make no mention of staff participation matters. Subsequent papers by Seashore and Bolton of the firm's staff, however, stressed the desirability of extensively involving the staff in management, and their recommendations in the Columbia study also emphasize this feature. A representative of the firm declined to commit himself about faculty status for librarians.

Unionization. Management by collective bargaining probably produces the most drastic changes in management of all the three methods. In some respects it is the newest and least-known of all. Chicago, California (Berkeley) to a certain extent, and the City University of New York are examples. A guide exists on the subject of unionization of library staff.[62] De Gennaro believes that unionism and participatory management are incompatible; which will emerge as the trend of the future is still uncertain.[63] One university library union, it should be noted, includes both professional and nonprofessional staff members.

Factors that might tend to lead to unionization are large size and unsatisfactory business management types of participative management. The larger the staff, the more difficult it is to develop participatory management plans that will effectively involve all of the staff. Academic, faculty, or collegial management seems less likely to lead to unionization of the professional staff, but if the classroom faculty is unionized, the library faculty undoubtedly will be included.

Academic management. The model for the third or academic style lies in the university itself—administration of a college. The director should be comparable to the dean of a college or perhaps a vice-president, and the professional staff to a college faculty. Like the first method, however, it has both advantages and disadvantages. First, despite many libraries working in this direction for a number of years—Illinois, Minnesota, Oklahoma, Ohio State, Oregon, Penn State, Miami, and Kentucky, for example—there are still about as many variations as there are in the first method. Excellent statements of principles under this system are those produced by Miami, Houston, Oregon, Minnesota, and Oklahoma. Numerous problems exist; the transition is neither simple nor easy. The director has less choice about the degree of participation in management which is to exist; he has more than many think, but the example of faculty-dean is close at hand, and there the respective roles are well-established and clear. To find out what the role of a director may be in such a plan, he has only to examine the role of the dean. A guide to the effects of academic status upon organization and management is that by

McAnally.[64] It should be noted that a dean of a nondepartmentalized college tends to have considerably more power and influence than a dean of a college with many departments. The role of a dean of libraries in a large university library which has to be subdivided into both academic and administrative departments is quite different. Middle management tends to be much stronger in this case. Both types of colleges flourish in American universities. Another disadvantage of the system is that numerous time-consuming committees are required. The excesses to which committee operation could be carried were illustrated at the Library of Congress by a pioneer in participative management, Luther Evans.[65] Committees of classroom faculty members produce certain problems and this is an area the director needs to watch.

The advantages of academic management or operation as a college are substantial. It provides recognition of the library as an academic unit. The methods of management fit the standard university pattern, hence are accepted readily by administration, classroom faculty, and the library staff. It draws in to planning, solution of problems, and management generally a wide variety of backgrounds and knowledge, so that decision-making tends to be better and the decisions accepted more readily. It promotes continuing education and professional growth, and increased professionalization. Morale is higher. One study indicates that it tends to improve financial support of the library.[66] Another indicates that the classroom faculty tends to be better satisfied with the library when the library operates as a faculty-academic unit.[67]

Productivity. Productivity under participatory management has been questioned by Lynch.[68] Her comments would seem to apply to business-style participatory management, academic management, and the unionization method alike. Marchant, however, points out that "While group decision-making alone appears to be neither adequate nor necessary to assure high productivity, it has been found to be generally characteristic of high-production organizations."[69] In a highly professionalized staff, his observation would seem particularly applicable. Any director who is convinced that the traditional hierarchical and authoritarian approach should be retained because it is best for the university would be well-advised to start looking for a new job, or a series of them, in view of current management trends.

Uncertain place of the supporting staff. Currently in university libraries in the United States, as previously observed, the supporting staff outnumbers the professional or academic staff two to one. The proportion is likely to rise during the next five years to the three to one up to five to one common in Canadian university libraries. The place of the nonprofessional staff in the management system, however, is still generally uncertain. Only in unionism is its role clear. Obviously, there must be solutions found for the proper involvement of the supporting staff in the government and management of the university library. Its members are better educated and better qualified than they were twenty years ago, and they will perform two-thirds to four-fifths of all work done in libraries. Various plans should be tried to find the best. Currently most nonacademic staff members operate under rules set by the university personnel office.

QUALITIES OF A MODEL DIRECTOR

The qualities required of a director of libraries are the same as they have always been. Certain aspects, however, receive more emphasis nowadays than they did in the past. First, the director must be more flexible and adaptable; the old certainties are being questioned or are gone, and the university library will continue to undergo changes. He must be willing to accept change as a way of life, and be open-minded about alternatives. Any man (or woman) unwilling to operate in such a milieu, or unable to accept uncertainty as a way of life should not undertake the management of a university library for the years immediately ahead. Second, he must possess a stable and equable temperament, and the ability to keep his emotional balance under the constant tensions that come at him from all directions. The tensions are unlikely to decrease. The apothegm of a former president seems appropriate: "If you can't stand the heat, stay out of the kitchen!" Third, he must have endurance. Luther Evans, who once described the qualities of a good library administrator, chose the term "endurance" instead of the term "vigor," which business and industry favored.[70] His choice seemed odd in the 1940s, but more apt now.

Finally, the director must be exceptionally persuasive. Ability to present library interests and needs effectively to the administration, classroom faculty, students, and state boards is essential. He must have facts derived from continuous planning and from continuing cost studies, including cost-benefit, but he also needs to have a personality that commands attention and respect. The new type of leadership within the library requires that he be a leader and not merely an authority. Sometimes it seems that a worker of miracles is wanted—a search committee for a new director of one of the major university libraries specified a mature and experienced man having at least ten

years of professional career yet to go who would be able to persuade the
university to increase financial support of the university library in an
era of declining institutional income!

References

1. Edward G. Holley, "Organization and Administration of Urban University Libraries," CRL 33:175–89 (May 1972).
2. Raynard C. Swank, Discussion with Arthur McAnally, Chicago, January 1972.
3. Lewis C. Branscomb, Thomas R. Buckman, Robert Carmack, Herman H. Fussler, John A. Heussman, Edward G. Holley, Robert K. Johnson, Louis Kaplan, David Otis Kelley, Roy L. Kidman, Warren B. Kuhn, Frank A. Lundy, John P. McDonald, Stanley McElderry, Robert A. Miller, Ralph H. Parker, Benjamin B. Richards, Eldred R. Smith, Edward B. Stanford, Lewis F. Steig, Raynard C. Swank, and Robert Vosper.
4. For a brief survey of some of these changes, not only in size but in other areas, and their probable effects on the university library, see President Richard Lyman (Stanford), "New Trends in Higher Education: The Impact on the University Library," Association of Research Libraries, *Minutes of the Twenty-Eighth meeting, May 14-15, 1971.* (Washington: A.R.L., 1971) p. 3–7. Also Booz, Allen & Hamilton Inc. "Trends in Higher Education and Their Implications for University Libraries and University Library Management," p. 11–20 of their *Problems in University Library Management* (Washington, D.C.: Association of Research Libraries, 1970).
5. Donald Coney, "Where Did You Go? To The Library, What Did You Get? Nothing," CRL 19:179-84 (May 1958).
6. Franklin D. Murphy, "Some Reflections on Structure," in John Coffrey, ed. *The Future Academic Community: Continuity and Change.* (Washington, D.C.: American Council on Education, 1969), p. 88–94.
7. Herman H. Fussler, Letter to Arthur McAnally, March 8, 1972, p. 2.
8. Earl C. Bolton, "Response of University Library Management to Changing Models of University Governance and Control," *CRL* 33:308 (July 1972).
9. Richard N. Logsdon, Letter to Arthur McAnally, August 10, 1972.
10. Jean Mayer, "The College and University: A Program for Academic Renewal," *Harvard Bulletin* (Nov. 16, 1970), p. 21–27.
11. Peter F. Drucker, *The Age of Discontinuity, Guidelines to Our Changing Society* (N.Y.: Harper & Row, 1969), P. 389–90.
12. Douglas W. Bryant, "Problem of Research Libraries: Development of Resources," *A.C.L.S. Newsletter* v. 22, no. 1 (Jan. 1971) p. 3–8.
13. Vannevar Bush, "As We May Think," *Atlantic Monthly* v. 176, no. 1 (July 1945), p. 101–08.
14. National Research Council. Committee on Research in the Life Sciences.

The Life Sciences: Recent Progress and Application to Human Affairs, the World of Biological Research, Requirements for the Future. (Washington: The National Academy of Sciences, 1970), p. 406.

15. Fremont Rider, *The Scholar and the Future of the Research Library, a Problem and Its Solution* (New York: Hadham Press, 1944).
16. O. C. Dunn, et al. *The Past and Likely Future of 58 Research Libraries, 1951-1980: A Statistical Study of Growth and Change* (Lafayette, Ind.: University Libraries and Audio-visual Center, 1965-).
17. Earl F. Cheit, *The New Depression in Higher Education, A Study of Financial Conditions at 41 Colleges and Universities; A General Report for the Carnegie Commission on Higher Education and the Ford Foundation* (New York: McGraw-Hill, 1971).
18. Cornell University Libraries. *Report of the Director of the University Libraries, 1970/71* (Ithaca, N.Y.: Cornell University Libraries, 1971), p. 7.
19. Representative leaders include Chris Argyris, *Understanding Organizational Behavior* (Homewood, Ill.: Dorsey Press, 1960) and his *Interpersonal Competence and Organizational Effectiveness* (Homewood, Ill.: Dorsey Press, 1962); Rensis Likert, *New Patterns of Management* (New York: McGraw-Hill, 1961); Peter F. Drucker, *The Effective Executive* (New York: Harper & Row, 1967); Robert A. Sutermeister, *People and Productivity;* 2d ed. (New York: McGraw-Hill, 1969); Alfred J. Marrow, et al., *Management by Participation; Creating a Climate for Personal and Organizational Development* (New York: Harper & Row, 1967); and Harlon Cleveland, *The Future Executive* (New York: Harper & Row, 1972). A good summary of the early movement is Timothy Hallimen, *New Directions in Organization Theory* (Santa Monica, Calif.: RAND Corp., Sept. 1968. p-3936).
20. Larry E. Greiner, "Evolution and Revolution as Organizations Grow," *Harvard Business Review* v. 50, no. 4 (July-Aug. 1972), p. 37–46.
21. See for example Earl C. Bolton, *Response of University Management,* p. 308.
22. Henry L. Mason, *College and University Government, A Handbook of Principle and Practice* (New Orleans: Tulane University, 1972).
23. See for example Myron Lieberman, "Professors, Unite!" *Harper's Magazine* v. 243, no. 1457 (Oct. 1971), p. 61–70; and Terence N. Tice, ed. *Faculty Power: Collective Bargaining on Campus* (Ann Arbor, Mich.: Institute of Continuing Legal Education, 1972).
24. "Unionization of Faculty Expected to Pick up Speed Because of Tight Money and Ph.D.s," *College Management* 6:38 (Sept. 1971).
25. "Analysis of an Act to Consolidate the Institutions of Higher Education in North Carolina, Session Laws of 1971, Proceedings, Chapter 1244, Ratified 30 October 1971."
26. Arthur M. McAnally, "Budgets by Formula," *Library Quarterly* 33:159-171 (April 1963).
27. Kenneth S. Allen, *Current and Emerging Budgeting Techniques in*

Academic Libraries, Including a Critique of the Model Budget Analysis Program of the State of Washington (Seattle: April, 1972).

28. Washington (State), Office of Interinstitutional Business Studies, *A Model Budget Analysis System for Program 05 Libraries* (Olympia, Wash.: 1970).

29. Thomas R. Buckman, Letter to Arthur McAnally, June 8, 1972, p. 2.

30. Second U.S.-Japan Conference of University Library Directors, Oct. 17-20, 1972. Robert Vosper, "The Role of the University Library Director: Principal Issues of the Seventies," p. 7. The social scientist is Richard L. Meier. See "Information Input Overload: Features of Growth in the Communications-Oriented Institutions" LIBRI 13:11, 1963.

31. See L. Carroll De Weese, "Status Concerns of Library Professionalism," *CRL* 33:31-38 (Jan. 1972). Also Edward G. Holley, "Organization and Management." Also Maurice P. Marchant, "Participative Management as Related to Personnel Development," *Library Trends* 20:48-59 (July 1971). Directors who have commented on this point, besides Robert Miller, included Edward B. Stanford, Lewis C. Branscomb, David Kaser, and Richard H. Logsdon.

32. Eldred R. Smith, *The Specialist in the Academic Research Library, a Report to the Council on Library Resources.* [Berkeley, Calif.] May 1971.

33. Booz, Allen & Hamilton Inc. *Organization and Staffing of the Libraries of Columbia University: A Summary of a Case Study.* (Washington, D.C.: Association of Research Libraries, 1972). (The full study will be published in two volumes.)

34. Robert T. Blackburn, "College Libraries: Paradoxical Failures; Some Reasons and a Possible Remedy," *CRL* 29:171-77 (May 1968).

35. Richard H. Logsdon, "Librarian and the Scholar: Eternal Enemies," *Library Journal* 95:2871-74 (Sept. 15, 1970).

36. Robert A. Miller, Letter to Arthur McAnally dated March 17, 1972. Also, see Hendrik Edelman, "Motherhood, the Growth of Library Collections, Freedom of Access and Other Issues," Cornell University Libraries *Bulletin,* no. 176 (April 1972), p. 5-6. See also Eldred R. Smith, "The Specialist in the Academic Research," p. 34.

37. Cornell University Libraries. *Annual Report of the Director, 1970/71* (Ithaca, N.Y.: The Libraries, 1971), p. 7.

38. Thomas R. Buckman, Letter to Arthur McAnally, dated June 8, 1972.

39. See Booz, Allen & Hamilton Inc. *Problems in University Library Management.* Also David Kaser, "Planning in University Libraries; Context and Processes," *Southeastern Librarian* 21:207-13 (Winter 1971). For a pioneering effort in long range planning, see Marion Milczewski, "Cloak and Dagger in University Library Administration," *CRL* 13:117-21 (April 1952).

40. Peter F. Drucker, *The Age of Discontinuity, Guidelines to Our Changing Society* (New York: Harper & Row, 1969).

41. Richard H. Logsdon, Letter to Arthur McAnally, August 8, 1972.

42. Thomas R. Buckman, Letter.
43. Earl C. Bolton, *Response of University Management,* p. 309. See also Booz, Allen & Hamilton Inc. *Problems in University Library Management,* p. 5-6 *et passim.*
44. Robert P. Haro, "Change in Academic Libraries," *CRL* 33:97-103 (March 1972).
45. David Kaser, "Planning in University Libraries," p. 288.
46. These and other excellent suggestions are made by Kenneth S. Allen, *Current and Emerging Budgeting,* p. 37-46. See also Booz, Allen & Hamilton Inc. *Problems in University Library Management.*
47. Kenneth S. Allen, *Current and Emerging Budgeting,* p. 40.
48. Ibid., p. 18.
49. Richard M. Dougherty, "The Unserved—Academic Library Style," *American Libraries* 2:1055-58 (Nov. 1971).
50. Douglas Bryant, "Problems of University Libraries: Development of Resources," *ACLS Newsletter,* v. 22, no. 1 (Jan. 1971), p. 3-8.
51. Richard M. Dougherty, "The Unserved."
52. Edward G. Holley, "Organization and Administration," p. 186-87.
53. Thomas R. Buckman, Letter.
54. Lewis C. Branscomb, Letter to Arthur McAnally, April 3, 1972.
55. Booz, Allen & Hamilton Inc. *Organization and Staffing of the Columbia University Library: A Summary of the Case Study.* Also their *Problems in University Library Management,* cited previously.
56. Herman H. Fussler and Robert Vosper, op. cit., Larry Powell made a similar observation to Vosper.
57. University of Oklahoma Library Ad Hoc Committee on Library Service. *Final Report of a User Survey of the Bizzell Memorial Library with Special Reference to Problems.* (Norman, Okla.: July 1972).
58. Eldred Smith, "Academic Status for College and University Librarians— Problems and Prospects," *CRL* 31:7-13 (Jan. 1970), p. 11.
59. Harold F. Wells, Telephone conversation with Arthur McAnally, July 8, 1972.
60. Edward G. Holley, "Organization and Administration," p. 182.
61. All have been cited already except Jane G. Flener: "Staff Participation in Management in Large University Libraries," *Indiana University Library News Letter,* v. 8, no. 1 (Oct. 1972) p. 1-3.
62. Melvin S. Goldstein, *Collective Bargaining in the Field of Librarianship* (Brooklyn, N.Y.: 1968).
63. Richard De Gennaro, "Participative Management or Unionization," *CRL* 33:173-74 (May 1972).
64. Arthur M. McAnally, "Status of the University Librarian in the Academic Community," in *Research Librarianship, Essays in Honor of Robert B. Downs,* ed. by Jerrold Orne (New York: Bowker, 1971), p. 19-50. Administrative operation is p. 31-46.
65. Luther H. Evans, "The Administration of a Federal Government

Agency," *L.C. Information Bulletin,* Sept. 20-26, 1949, Appendix, p. 1–9,
See also his annual reports of the period.
66. Kenneth S. Allen, *Current and Emerging Budgeting.* Thirteen institutions.
67. Maurice P. Marchant, *Participative Management,* p. 54. Also Lewis C.
Branscomb, letter to Arthur McAnally, April 3, 1972.
68. Beverly Lynch, "Participatory Management in Relation to Library
Productivity," *CRL* 33:382-90 (Sept. 1972).
69. Maurice P. Marchant, *Participative Management,* p. 48.
70. Luther H. Evans, "The Administration of a Federal."

Beyond Survival: Library Management for the Future

Thomas J. Galvin

THERE is a growing negativism among library administrators reflected in a persistent emphasis on "survival," on "survivalism"—both personal and institutional—often accompanied by an apparent desire to avoid and resist change at all costs—a kind of desperate determination to preserve the institutional status quo. This kind of determined effort to resist institutional change is one of the least constructive managerial responses. Every library director must understand and accept the fact that institutional change is both inevitable and desirable. The logic of this view is imbedded in a very simple formulation that I modestly refer to as Galvin's first law of institutional dynamics: Given a dynamic external environment, no institution can ever remain static. It is either improving or it is declining.

Library directors should be cautioned against the trap of attempting to deal with the present environment as though it were the environment of the past, or expending energy in the hopeless task of trying to alter the present to make it more closely resemble the past. In a document that I consider required reading for all academic library managers, a document prepared by the Carnegie Commission on Higher Education entitled *Priorities for Action,* the authors describe the pernicious symptomology of this highly destructive cast of managerial mind:

A traumatic loss of a sense of assured progress, of the inevitability of a better future, has occurred. Instead, there has developed more of a nostalgia for a Paradise Lost. The tone of so much academic thought now is more an attitude of how to hold on to as much of the past as possible—or even to

Reprinted from *Library Journal* (Sept. 15, 1976), pp. 1833–1836. Published by R.R. Bowker Co. (a Xerox company). Copyright © 1976 by Xerox Corporation.

retrieve lost aspects of it—rather than of how to confront the future directly; of how to avoid change, since most possible changes are thought to be unfavorable or even disastrous, rather than of how to plan and support constructive new developments. The prevalent attitude is more to look back with longing than to look ahead with hope—the situation may be bad but it cannot be improved: the Golden Age of the past is more attractive than any conceivable prospects for the future.

William Birenbaum, writing in the *Chronicle of Higher Education* about the fiscal plight of the City University of New York, is highly specific both in identifying the grave dangers inherent in this kind of administrative nostalgitis. He suggests ways in which managers can respond affirmatively to the question, "Is there institutional life after retrenchment?":

> To avoid death, one *must* imagine a future beyond retrenchment. Without either a history or a *vision of tomorrow,* everything collapses into the moment, the essence of which is to survive. Survival is guided by self interest, transitory and negotiable, like the stocks on yesterday's market. In this defeat, the University (substitute "library") is beginning to feel like a jungle in which little bands of cannibals are secretly sharpening their spears back in the departmental villages.

It is critical for the manager who seeks not merely to survive, but to flourish in difficult times, to recognize that the managerial environment is by its very nature a *dynamic* one. Much managerial energy continues to be expended in pursuit of the false and hopeless goal of achieving stasis. My teacher of library administration used to talk about the successful administrator as a person who had "administered himself out of a job." Either he was naïve in his understanding of the basic character of library administration, or, more likely, I was naïve in my understanding of what he was trying to convey. If so, this is a naïveté that is still rather widely shared. I am speaking of the incorrect perception of the managerial task as being one that comprises identifying a *finite* number of problems within an organization, and proceeding to deal definitely with each one in turn, until there are no more problems left to solve. This notion of the managerial role is based on the mistaken idea that some static state of perfection can be achieved within an organization—that the job of the library administrator is simply one of systematically setting things right and then just keeping them that way. This is a characteristic attitude that seems to be widely held by staff, and one of the major obstacles to mutual understanding and effective communication between staff and administrators.

MANAGEMENT IS PROBLEM SOLVING

The hard lesson—perhaps the most difficult one for most managers to learn and even more difficult to accept—is that the content of management *is* problem solving. If there were not always another problem waiting to replace the one that we've just dealt with, we'd be out of a job. As managers, it is essential that we and our staffs arrive at a clear understanding and acceptance of the fact that no matter how capable or industrious or dedicated we as administrators may become, we will never be able to set things wholly and permanently right, because every human organization will inevitably and continuously generate new problems. The very absence of new problems is often indicative of a corresponding absence of institutional progress. It is also often true that an inability to accept and live comfortably with this aspect of management is likely to engender highly counter-productive attitudes on the part of the manager, most notably a feeling that he or she is the object of persecution by both the staff and the clientele. That is trap that all administrators are inclined to fall into from time to time. Administrators must recognize that this attitude, if it is allowed to persist, is both dangerous and destructive to the administrator and to the organization.

DOCUMENTS ARE NOT SOLUTIONS

Another related notion that is both naïve and misleading is the view held by some managers that systems and documents, by themselves, possess problem-solving power. Their goal is to "perfect our documents and systems." My students in library management courses often express the view that policy statements are like preventive medicine—that either a given problem would never have arisen if an adequate policy statement had been in existence, or that such a statement would carry in it the resolution of any problem. In reality the scenario begins when somebody in authority recognizes that a problem exists within the library, and says, "Gee, we ought to have policy statement on that." With considerable effort, a document is drawn up setting forth a policy, a procedure, a methodology or a set of priorities which should govern future decisions.

The resulting document or system not only does not prevent the reoccurrence of the original problem or others like it, but often generates a whole new set of problems that either didn't exist before or that nobody identified as problems before.

This kind of experience may lead to a 180 degree reversal of attitude towards *any* systematic approach to larger policy questions, or even a cynical abandonment of any effort to provide a generalized policy-level context for approaching individual decisions. Thus, for example, Robert Townsend's characterization in *Up the Organization* of the process of developing written job descriptions:

> ... insane for jobs that pay $150 a week or more. At best, the job description freezes the job as the writer understood it at a particular instant in the past. At worst, they're prepared by personnel people who can't write and don't understand the jobs.

While the more experienced and/or more cynical among us may be tempted to nod in wry assent, most of us would recognize that the truth probably lies somewhere between the two extreme attitudes of naïve faith and cynicism. The important points are that no policy or procedure can ever be formulated for all time, and no policy statement, no matter how expertly prepared or written, ever in and of itself, solved a problem. The best materials selection policy never answered the question: "Shall we buy this book?" or "Will we need two prints of this film?" The best written, most comprehensive set of criteria for promotion and tenure never provided the answer to the question "Shall we recommend Ralph for tenure in recognition of his abilities, but in spite of his obvious limitations? Or, shall we get rid of him and replace him with somebody else who's more intelligent even if less pleasant? Or more pleasant, even if less intelligent? Or somebody who's more intelligent *and* more pleasant?"

The point is simply that documents and systems do not solve problems. People solve problems, and they can frequently do a better job of problem-solving with the aid of documents that have been thoughtfully prepared and policies that have been formulated and promulgated in a timely fashion.

PLANNING, ACCOUNTABILITY, FUNDING

Traditionally, planning was conceived of as something conducted wholly outside of the context of current operations, something oriented toward the long-term, and consisting of glowing predictions of a bibliographical millennium to come. The result was something like the effect of the old motion picture travelogues of the exotic south sea islands that used to fascinate me as a child, precisely because they had absolutely no direct relationship to either my present situation or to anything even remotely likely to happen to me in the foreseeable future.

Planning today has become an activity that is central to the ongoing program of the library. It occurs in a telescoped time frame, usually five years at maximum, rather than 10 or 20 years. It is as much, if not more concerned with how we are going to get there as it is with where exactly we are going as an institution, expressed in highly quantitative, very precise, extremely realistic terms. Finally, planning today is increasingly closely correlated with budget. Indeed, budget is a vehicle for the implementation of institutional plans and goals, rather than being, as in the past, simply a technique for obtaining and dispensing the largest possible piece of the institutional or governmental financial pie.

Traditionally, the effective library director has been thought to be one who brings to his board or his president or principal not merely problems, but problems accompanied by sound proposed solutions. This approach now is being extended to fiscal planning, so that the library director is increasingly expected not only to be concerned with disbursing funds, but also with generating income. This is, for the most part, an unfamiliar role for the library manager, as well as a difficult one. The library has not traditionally been an income-generating activity. It has no obvious paying clientele, nor any established capacity or means to generate significant revenues. A related problem for many libraries is the lack of any specific, identifiable constituency to act as concerned advocates for institutional needs and aspirations. I was visting recently on the campus of a large university where the library considers itself seriously underfinanced, and while its efforts to dramatize its fiscal plight have resulted in considerable sympathy from everybody on campus, no additional dollars have yet been forthcoming. The library director observed to me, somewhat ruefully, that the deans of the various schools in the university have the dominant voice in the distribution of institutional funds, and that, unfortunately, "the library is every dean's *second* priority."

THE BOTTOMLESS PIT

In this critical area of institutional and fiscal accountability we have not been, and generally are not now, in a particularly strong position to respond effectively. We have not always developed a sufficiently acute sense of collective urgency in taking an active role in assuring that the institutions for which we are responsible as managers will, indeed, survive. We have lacked adequate or effective means of identifying and describing the quality of our institutional product. It is service—by nature largely intangible and difficult to measure. Consequently, we are placed in a difficult posture with respect to accountability. We are neither able to plan on the basis of *how much might ultimately be enough,* nor have we been able to account in any very satisfactory way to fiscal authorities for precisely what we have accomplished with the resources that have already been made available to us. We have little more to offer than statistics of collection size and circulation, and we are discovering that these are data of dubious authenticity and even more dubious significance to funding authorities. The great danger, to borrow a phrase from Robert Munn, is that the library comes to resemble "a bottomless pit" in the eyes of those who make the ultimate funding decisions.

NEW MEASURES

We desperately need, as managers, to find alternative vehicles of institutional accountability. Adequate measures will probably place less emphasis on traditional quantitative indicators of library performance such as circulation and acquisitions data, and more emphasis on qualitative evidence of providing meaningful services to clients. In justifying our institutional existence we will need to become less materials oriented and more client oriented, to find ways to collect and quantify client attitudes towards the library and client estimates of its resources and services and to compare these data over time. Finally, and most central to effective planning, accountability, and budgeting, it will be essential that we devise and implement sound methods for establishing realistic, achievable, appropriate service goals and for reporting in a convincing and entirely candid manner the extent to which these goals have, or have not been realized.

Let me again quote the report of the Carnegie Commission on Higher Education in effectively highlighting the attitudinal barriers to urgently needed institutional change among administrators. The Commission speaks out against,

> ... the current survivalist mentality of higher education, particularly among administrators. The attitude is often one of maximum gain at no cost—the MAXIMIN PRINCIPLE; and since all institutional gains of importance have costs, the no-cost doctrine means no gains of importance. This is not only the result of the instinct of faculty members and administrators who feel themselves (often correctly) as being on the defensive, but also of the actions of many boards of trustees in selecting "consensual" administrators (concerned solely with mere consent) ... rather than builders .... The rational approach for a consensual administrator who wants to hold on to his job is to take no risks, to assume a posture of low visibility, to say nothing but to say it well, while still being "with it." The graceful protection of the status quo is the course of action for survival.

The acceptable alternative to the obsolete authoritarian style in management is not the form of consensual administration described by the Carnegie Commission, and regrettably widespread at present not only on college campuses, but in public school libraries as well. Management by mere consensus cannot be effective. The real alternative is to find and develop new styles of leadership—leadership that seeks consensus which is sound and responsive to present and future needs, but leadership that takes active responsibility for identifying appropriate directions for library development and for the vigorous, aggressive pursuit of clearly defined institutional and client interests. It is in the development of these new leadership styles and their mastery that the principle challenge as well as the chief opportunity for effective library management will be found.

The Manager's Job: Folklore and Fact

Henry Mintzberg

If you ask a manager what he does, he will most likely tell you that he plans, organizes, coordinates, and controls. Then watch what he does. Don't be surprised if you can't relate what you see to these four words.

When he is called and told that one of his factories has just burned down, and he advises the caller to see whether temporary arrangements can be made to supply customers through a foreign subsidiary, is he planning, organizing, coordinating, or controlling? How about when he presents a gold watch to a retiring employee? Or when he attends a conference to meet people in the trade? Or on returning from that conference, when he tells one of his employees about an interesting product idea he picked up there?

The fact is that these four words, which dominated management vocabulary since the French industrialist Henri Fayol first introduced them in 1916, tell us little about what managers actually do. At best, they indicate some vague objectives managers have when they work.

The field of management, so devoted to progress and change, has for more than half a century not seriously addressed *the* basic question: What do managers do? Without a proper answer, how can we teach management? How can we design planning or information systems for managers? How can we improve the practice of management at all?

Our ignorance of the nature of managerial work shows up in various ways in the modern organization—in the boast by the successful manager that he never spent a single day in a management training program; in the turnover of corporate planners who never quite understood what it was the manager wanted; in the computer consoles gathering dust in the back room because the managers never used the fancy on-line MIS some analyst thought they needed. Perhaps most important, our ignorance shows up in the inability of our large public organizations to come to grips with some of their most serious policy problems.

Somehow, in the rush to automate production, to use management science in the functional areas of marketing and finance, and to apply the skills of the behavioral scientist to the problem of worker motivation, the manager—that person in charge of the organization or one of its subunits—has been forgotten.

My intention in this article is simple: to break the reader away from Fayol's words and introduce him to a more supportable, and what I believe to be a more useful, description of managerial work. This description derives from my review and synthesis of the available research on how various managers have spent their time.

In some studies, managers were observed intensively ("shadowed" is the term some of them used); in a number of others, they kept detailed diaries of their activities; in a few studies, their records were analyzed. All kinds of managers were studied—foremen, factory supervisors, staff managers, field sales managers, hospital administrators, presidents of companies and nations, and even street gang leaders. These "managers" worked in the United States, Canada, Sweden, and Great Britain. In the ruled insert on page 115 is a brief review of the major studies that I found most useful in developing this description, including my own study of five American chief executive officers.

A synthesis of these findings paints an interesting picture, one as different from Fayol's classical view as a cubist abstract is from a Renaissance painting. In a sense, this picture will be obvious to anyone who has ever spent a day in a manager's office, either in front of the desk or behind it. Yet, at the same time, this picture may turn out to be revolutionary, in that it throws into doubt so much of the folklore that we have accepted about the manager's work.

I first discuss some of this folklore and contrast it with some of the discoveries of systematic research—the hard facts about how managers spend their time. Then I synthesize these research findings in a description of ten roles that seem to describe the essential content of all managers' jobs. In a concluding section, I discuss a number of implications of this synthesis for those trying to achieve more effective management, both in classrooms and in the business world.

SOME FOLKLORE AND FACTS ABOUT MANAGERIAL WORK

There are four myths about the manager's job that do not bear up under careful scrutiny of the facts.

1

Folklore: The manager is a reflective, systematic planner. The evidence on this issue is overwhelming, but not a shred of it supports this statement.

Fact: Study after study has shown that managers work at an unrelenting pace, that their activities are characterized by brevity, variety, and discontinuity, and that they are strongly oriented to action and dislike reflective activities. Consider this evidence:

Half the activities engaged in by the five chief executives of my study lasted less than nine minutes, and only 10 percent exceeded one hour.[1] A study of 56 U.S. foremen found that they averaged 583 activities per eight-hour shift, an average of 1 every 48 seconds.[2] The work pace for both chief executives and foremen was unrelenting. The chief executives met a steady stream of callers and mail from the moment they arrived in the morning until they left in the evening. Coffee breaks and lunches were inevitably work related, and ever-present subordinates seemed to usurp any free moment.

A diary study of 160 British middle and top managers found that they worked for a half hour or more without interruption only about once every two days.[3]

Of the verbal contacts of the chief executives in my study, 93 percent were arranged on an ad hoc basis. Only 1 percent of the executives' time was spent in open-ended observational tours. Only 1 out of 368 verbal contacts was unrelated to a specific issue and could be called general planning. Another researcher finds that "in *not one single case* did a manager report the obtaining of important external information from a general conversation or other undirected personal communication."[4]

No study has found important patterns in the way managers schedule their time. They seem to jump from issue to issue, continually responding to the needs of the moment.

Is this the planner that the classical view describes? Hardly. How, then, can we explain this behavior? The manager is simply responding to the pressures of his job. I found that my chief executives terminated many of their own activities, often leaving meetings before the end, and interrupted their desk work to call in subordinates. One president not only placed his desk so that he could look down a long hallway but also left his door open when he was alone—an invitation for subordinates to come in and interrupt him.

Clearly, these managers wanted to encourage the flow of current information. But more significantly, they seemed to be conditioned by their own work loads. They appreciated the opportunity cost of their own time, and they were continually aware of their ever-present obligations—mail to be answered, callers to attend to, and so on. It seems that no matter what he is doing, the manager is plagued by the possibilities of what he might do and what he must do.

When the manager must plan, he seems to do so implicitly in the context of daily actions, not in some abstract process reserved for two weeks in the organization's mountain retreat. The plans of the chief executives I studied seemed to exist only in their heads—as flexible, but often specific, intentions. The traditional literature notwithstanding, the job of managing does not breed reflective planners; the manager is a real-time responder to stimuli, an individual who is conditioned by his job to prefer live to delayed action.

2

Folklore: The effective manager has no regular duties to perform. Managers are constantly being told to spend more time planning and delegating, and less time seeing customers and engaging in negotiations. These are not, after all, the true tasks of the manager. To use the popular analogy, the good manager, like the good conductor, carefully orchestrates everything in advance, then sits back to enjoy the fruits of his labor, responding occasionally to an unforeseeable exception.

But here again the pleasant abstraction just does not seem to hold up. We had better take a closer look at those activities managers feel compelled to engage in before we arbitrarily define them away.

Fact: In addition to handling exceptions, managerial work involves performing a number of regular duties, including ritual and ceremony, negotiations, and processing of soft information that links the organization with its environment. Consider some evidence from the research studies:

A study of the work of the presidents of small companies found that they engaged in routine activities because their companies could not afford staff specialists and were so thin on operating personnel that a single absence often required the president to substitute.[5]

One study of field sales managers and another of chief executives suggest that it is a natural part of both jobs to see important customers, assuming the managers wish to keep those customers.[6]

Someone, only half in jest, once described the manager as that person who sees visitors so that everyone else can get his work done. In my study, I found that certain ceremonial duties—meeting visiting dignitaries, giving out gold watches, presiding at Christmas dinners—were an intrinsic part of the chief executive's job.

Studies of managers' information flow suggest that managers play a key role in securing "soft" external information (much of it available only to them because of their status) and in passing it along to their subordinates.

3

Folklore: The senior manager needs aggregated information, which a formal management information system best provides. Not too long ago, the words *total information system* were everywhere in the management literature. In keeping with the classical view of the manager as that individual perched on the apex of a regulated, hierarchical system, the literature's manager was to receive all his important information from a giant, comprehensive MIS.

But lately, as it has become increasingly evident that these giant MIS systems are not working—that managers are simply not using them—the enthusiasm has waned. A look at how managers actually process information makes the reason quite clear. Managers have five media at their command—documents, telephone calls, scheduled and unscheduled meetings, and observational tours.

Fact: Managers strongly favor the verbal media—namely, telephone calls and meetings. The evidence comes from every single study of managerial work. Consider the following:

In two British studies, managers spent an average of 66 percent and 80 percent of their time in verbal (oral) communication.[7] In my study of five American chief executives, the figure was 78 percent.

These five chief executives treated mail processing as a burden to be dispensed with. One came in Saturday morning to process 142 pieces of mail in just over three hours, to "get rid of all the stuff." This same manager looked at the first piece of "hard" mail he had received all week, a standard cost report, and put it aside with the comment, "I never look at this."

These same five chief executives responded immediately to 2 of the 40 routine reports they received during the five weeks of my study and to four items in the 104 periodicals. They skimmed most of these periodicals in seconds, almost ritualistically. In all, these chief executives of good-sized organizations initiated on their own—that is, not in response to something else—a grand total of 25 pieces of mail during the 25 days I observed them.

An analysis of the mail the executives received reveals an interesting picture—only 13 percent was of specific and immediate use. So now we have another piece in the puzzle: not much of the mail provides live, current information—the action of a competitor, the mood of a government legislator, or the rating of last night's television show. Yet this is the information that drove the managers, interrupting their meetings and rescheduling their workdays.

Consider another interesting finding. Managers seem to cherish "soft" information, especially gossip, hearsay, and speculation. Why? The reason is its timeliness; today's gossip may be tomorrow's fact. The manager who is not accessible for the telephone call informing him that his biggest customer was seen golfing with his main competitor may read about a dramatic drop in sales in the next quarterly report. But then it's too late.

To assess the value of historical, aggregated, "hard" MIS information, consider two of the manager's prime uses for his information—to identify problems and opportunities[8] and to build his own mental models of the things around him (e.g., how his organization's budget system works, how his customers buy his product, how changes in the economy affect his organization, and so on). Every bit of evidence suggests that the manager identifies decision situations and builds models not with the aggregated abstractions an MIS provides, but with specific tidbits of data.

Consider the words of Richard Neustadt, who studies the information-collecting habits of Presidents Roosevelt, Truman, and Eisenhower:

It is not information of a general sort that helps a President see personal stakes; not summaries, not surveys, not the *bland amalgams.* Rather ... it is the odds and ends of *tangible detail* that pieced together in his mind illuminate the underside of issues put before him. To help himself he must reach out as widely as he can for every scrap of fact, opinion, gossip, bearing on his interests and relationships as

President. He must become his own director of his own central intelligence.[9]

The manager's emphasis on the verbal media raises two important points:

First, verbal information is stored in the brains of people. Only when people write this information down can it be stored in the files of the organization—whether in metal cabinets or on magnetic tape—and managers apparently do not write down much of what they hear. Thus the strategic data bank of the organization is not in the memory of its computers but in the minds of its managers.

Second, the manager's extensive use of verbal media helps to explain why he is reluctant to delegate tasks. When we note that most of the manager's important information comes in verbal form and is stored in his head, we can well appreciate his reluctance. It is not as if he can hand a dossier over to someone; he must take the time to "dump memory"—to tell that someone all he knows about the subject. But this could take so long that the manager may find it easier to do the task himself. Thus the manager is damned by his own information systems to a "dilemma of delegation"—to do too much himself or to delegate to his subordinates with inadequate briefing.

4

Folklore: Management is, or at least is quickly becoming, a science and a profession. By almost any definitions of *science* and *profession,* this statement is false. Brief observation of any manager will quickly lay to rest the notion that managers practice a science. A science involves the enaction of systematic, analytically determined procedures or programs. If we do not even know what procedures managers use, how can we prescribe them by scientific analysis? And how can we call management a profession if we cannot specify what managers are to learn? For after all, a profession involves "knowledge of some department of learning or science" (*Random House Dictionary*).[10]

Fact: The managers' programs—to schedule time, process information, make decisions, and so on—remain locked deep inside their brains. Thus, to describe these programs, we rely on words like *judgment* and *intuition,* seldom stopping to realize that they are merely labels for our ignorance.

I was struck during my study by the fact that the executives I was observing—all very competent by any standard—are fundamentally

RESEARCH ON MANAGERIAL WORK

Considering its central importance to every aspect of management, there has been surprisingly little research on the manager's work, and virtually no systematic building of knowledge from one group of studies to another. In seeking to describe managerial work, I conducted my own research and also scanned the literature widely to integrate the findings of studies from many diverse sources with my own. These studies focused on two very different aspects of managerial work. Some were concerned with the characteristics of the work—how long managers work, where, at what pace and with what interruptions, with whom they work, and through what media they communicate. Other studies were more concerned with the essential content of the work—what activities the managers actually carry out, and why. Thus, after a meeting, one researcher might note that the manager spent 45 minutes with three government officials in their Washington office, while another might record that he presented his company's stand on some proposed legislation in order to change a regulation.

A few of the studies of managerial work are widely known, but most have remained buried as single journal articles or isolated books. Among the more important ones I cite (with full references in the footnotes) are the following:

Sune Carlson developed the diary method to study the work characteristics of nine Swedish managing directors. Each kept a detailed log of his activities. Carlson's results are reported in his book *Executive Behavior*. A number of British researchers, notably Rosemary Stewart, have subsequently used Carlson's method. In *Managers and Their Jobs*, she describes the study of 160 top and middle managers of British companies during four weeks, with particular attention to the differences in their work.

Leonard Sayles's book *Managerial Behavior* is another important re-

indistinguishable from their counterparts of a hundred years ago (or a thousand years ago, for that matter). The information they need differs, but they seek it in the same way—by word of mouth. Their decisions concern modern technology, but the procedures they use to make them are the same as the procedures of the nineteenth-century manager. Even the computer, so important for the specialized work of the organization, has apparently had no influence on the work procedures of general managers. In fact, the manager is in a kind of loop, with increasingly heavy work pressures but no aid forthcoming from management science.

Considering the facts about managerial work, we can see that the manager's job is enormously complicated and difficult. The manager ference. Using a method he refers to as "anthropological," Sayles studied the work content of middle- and lower-level managers in a large U.S. corporation. Sayles moved freely in the company, collecting whatever information struck him as important.

Perhaps the best-known source is *Presidental Power*, in which Richard Neustadt analyzes the power and managerial behavior of Presidents Roosevelt, Truman, and Eisenhower. Neustadt used secondary sources—documents and interviews with other parties—to generate his data.

Robert H. Guest, in *Personnel*, reports on a study of the foreman's working day. Fifty-six U.S. foremen were observed and each of their activities recorded during one eight-hour shift.

Richard C. Hodgson, Daniel J. Levinson, and Abraham Zaleznik studied a team of three top executives of a U.S. hospital. From that study they wrote *The Executive Role Constellation*. These researchers addressed in particular the way in which work and socioemotional roles were divided among the three managers.

William F. Whyte, from his study of a street gang during the Depression, wrote *Street Corner Society*. His findings about the gang's leadership, which George C. Holmans analyzed in *The Human Group*, suggest some interesting similarities of job content between street gang leaders and corporate managers.

My own study involved five American CEOs of middle-to large-sized organizations—a consulting firm, a technology company, a hospital, a consumer goods company, and a school system. Using a method called "structural observation," during one intensive week of observation for each executive I recorded various aspects of every piece of mail and every verbal contact. My method was designed to capture data on both work characteristics and job content. In all, I analyzed 890 pieces of incoming and outgoing mail and 368 verbal contacts.

---

is overburdened with obligations; yet he cannot easily delegate his tasks. As a result, he is driven to overwork and is forced to do many tasks superficially. Brevity, fragmentation, and verbal communication characterize his work. Yet these are the very characteristics of managerial work that have impeded scientific attempts to improve it. As a result, the management scientist has concentrated his efforts on the specialized functions of the organization, where he could more easily analyze the procedures and quantify the relevant information.[11]

But the pressures of the manager's job are becoming worse. Where before he needed only to respond to owners and directors, now he finds that subordinates with democratic norms continually reduce his freedom to issue unexplained orders, and a growing number of outside influences (consumer groups, government agencies, and so on) expect his attention. And the manager has had nowhere to turn for help. The first step in providing the manager with some help is to find out what his job really is.

BACK TO A BASIC DESCRIPTION OF MANAGERIAL WORK

Now let us try to put some of the pieces of this puzzle together. Earlier, I defined the manager as that person in charge of organization or one of its subunits. Besides chief executive officers, this definition would include vice presidents, bishops, foremen, hockey coaches, and prime ministers. Can all of these people have anything in common? Indeed they can. For an important starting point, all are vested with formal authority over an organizational unit. From formal authority comes status, which leads to various interpersonal relations, and from these comes access to information. Information, in turn, enables the manager to make decisions and strategies for his unit.

The manager's job can be described in terms of various "roles," or organized sets of behaviors identified with a position. My description, shown in *Exhibit I*, comprises ten roles. As we shall see, formal authority gives rise to the three interpersonal roles, which in turn give rise to the three informational roles; these two sets of roles enable the manager to play the four decisional roles.

Interpersonal roles

Three of the manager's roles arise directly from his formal authority and involve basic interpersonal relationships.

First is the *figurehead* role. By virtue of his position as head of an organizational unit, every manager must perform some duties of a ceremonial nature. The president greets the touring dignitaries, the foreman attends the wedding of a lathe operator, and the sales manager takes an important customer to lunch.

The chief executives of my study spent 12 percent of their contact time on ceremonial duties; 17 percent of their incoming mail dealt with acknowledgments and requests related to their status. For example, a letter to a company president requested free merchandise for a crippled schoolchild; diplomas were put on the desk of the school superintendent for his signature.

Duties that involve interpersonal roles may sometimes be routine, involving little serious communication and no important decision making. Nevertheless, they are important to the smooth functioning of an organization and cannot be ignored by the manager.

Because he is in charge of an organizational unit, the manager is responsible for the work of the people of that unit. His actions in this regard constitute the *leader* role. Some of these actions involve leadership directly—for example, in most organizations the manager is normally responsible for hiring and training his own staff.

In addition, there is the indirect exercise of the leader role. Every manager must motivate and encourage his employees, somehow reconciling their individual needs with the goals of the organization. In virtually every contact the manager has with his employees, subordinates seeking leadership clues probe his actions: "Does he approve?" "How would he like the report to turn out?" "Is he more interested in market share than high profits?"

The influence of the manager is most clearly seen in the leader role. Formal authority vests him with great potential power; leadership determines in large part how much of it he will realize.

EXHIBIT I The Manager's Roles

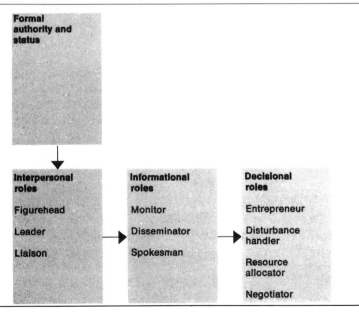

The literature of management has always recognized the leader role, particularly those aspects of it related to motivation. In comparison, until recently it has hardly mentioned the *liaison* role, in which the manager makes contacts outside his vertical chain of command. This is remarkable in light of the finding of virtually every study of managerial work that managers spend as much time with peers and other people outside their units as they do with their own subordinates—and, surprisingly, very little time with their own superiors.

In Rosemary Stewart's diary study, the 160 British middle and top managers spent 47 percent of their time with peers, 41 percent of their time with people outside their unit, and only 12 percent of their time with their superiors. For Robert H. Guest's study of U.S. foremen, the figures were 44 percent, 46 percent, and 10 percent. The chief executives of my study averaged 44 percent of their contact time with people outside their organizations, 48 percent with subordinates, and 7 percent with directors and trustees.

The contacts the five CEOs made were with an incredibly wide range of people: subordinates; clients, business associates, and suppliers; and peers—managers of similar organizations, government and trade organization officials, fellow directors on outside boards, and independents with no relevant organizational affiliations. The chief executives' time with and mail from these groups is shown in *Exhibit II*. Guest's study of foremen shows, likewise, that their contacts were numerous and wide ranging, seldom involving fewer than 25 individuals, and often more than 50.

As we shall see shortly, the manager cultivates such contacts largely to find information. In effect, the liaison role is devoted to building up the manager's own external information system—informal, private, verbal, but nevertheless, effective.

Informational roles

By virtue of his interpersonal contacts, both with his subordinates and with his network of contacts, the manager emerges as the nerve center of his organizational unit. He may not know everything, but he typically knows more than any member of his staff.

Studies have shown this relationship to hold for all managers, from street gang leaders to U.S. presidents. In *The Human Group*, George C. Homans explains how, because they were at the center of the information flow in their own gangs and were also in close touch with other gang leaders, street gang leaders were better informed than any

Exhibit II The Chief Executives' Contacts

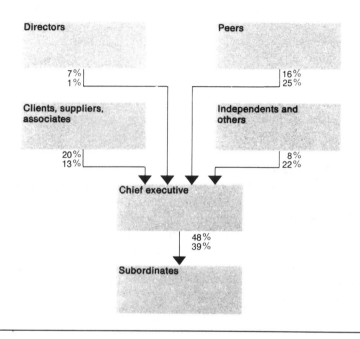

of their followers.[12] And Richard Neustadt describes the following account from his study of Franklin D. Roosevelt:

> The essence of Roosevelt's technique for information-gathering was competition. 'He would call you,' one of his aides once told me, 'and he'd ask you to get the story on some complicated business, and you'd come back after a couple of days of hard labor and present the juicy morsel you'd uncovered under a stone somewhere, and *then* you'd find out he knew all about it, along with something else you *didn't* know. Where he got this information from he wouldn't mention, usually, but after he had done this to you once or twice you got damn careful about *your* information.'[13]

We can see where Roosevelt "got this information" when we consider the relationship between the interpersonal and informational roles. As leader, the manager has formal and easy access to every member of his staff. Hence, as noted earlier, he tends to know more about his own unit than anyone else does. In addition, his liaison contacts expose the manager to external information to which his subordinates often lack access. Many of these contacts are with other managers of equal status, who are themselves nerve centers in their own organization. In this way, the manager develops a powerful data base of information.

The processing of information is a key part of the manager's job. In my study, the chief executives spent 40 percent of their contact time on activities devoted exclusively to the transmission of information; 70 percent of their incoming mail was purely informational (as opposed to requests for action). The manager does not leave meetings or hang up the telephone in order to get back to work. In large part, communication *is* his work. Three roles describe these informational aspects of managerial work.

As *monitor,* the manager perpetually scans his environment for information, interrogates his liaison contacts and his subordinates, and receives unsolicited information, much of it as a result of the network of personal contacts he has developed. Remember that a good part of the information the manager collects in his monitor role arrives in verbal form, often as gossip, hearsay, and speculation. By virtue of his contacts, the manager has a natural advantage in collecting this soft information for his organization.

He must share and distribute much of this information. Information he gleans from outside personal contacts may be needed within his organization. In his *disseminator* role, the manager passes some of his privileged information directly to his subordinates, who would otherwise have no access to it. When his subordinates lack easy contact with one another, the manager will sometimes pass information from one to another.

In his *spokesman* role, the manager sends some of his information to people outside his unit—a president makes a speech to lobby for an organization cause, or a foreman suggests a product modification to a supplier. In addition, as part of his role as spokesman, every manager must inform and satisfy the influential people who control his organizational unit. For the foreman, this may simply involve keeping the plant manager informed about the flow of work through the shop.

The president of a large corporation, however, may spend a great amount of his time dealing with a host of influences. Directors and shareholders must be advised about financial performance; consumer groups must be assured that the organization is fulfilling its social responsibilities; and government officials must be satisfied that the organization is abiding by the law.

Decisional roles

Information is not, of course, an end in itself; it is the basic input to decision making. One thing is clear in the study of managerial work: the manager plays the major role in his unit's decision-making system. As its formal authority, only he can commit the unit to important new courses of action; and as its nerve center, only he has full and current information to make the set decisions that determines the unit's strategy. Four roles describe the manager as decision-maker.

As *entrepreneur*, the manager seeks to improve his unit, to adapt it to changing conditions in the environment. In his monitor role, the president is constantly on the lookout for new ideas. When a good one appears, he initiates a development project that he may supervise himself or delegate to an employee (perhaps with the stipulation that he must approve the final proposal).

There are two interesting features about these development projects at the chief executive level.

First, these projects do not involve single decisions or even unified clusters of decisions. Rather, they emerge as a series of small decisions and actions sequenced over time. Apparently, the chief executive prolongs each project so that he can fit it bit by bit into his busy, disjointed schedule and so that he can gradually come to comprehend the issue, if it is a complex one.

Second, the chief executives I studied supervised as many as 50 of these projects at the same time. Some projects entailed new products or processes; others involved public relations campaigns, improvement of the cash position, reorganization of a weak department, resolution of a morale problem in a foreign division, integration of computer operations, various acquisitions at different stages of development, and so on.

The chief executive appears to maintain a kind of inventory of the development projects that he himself supervises—projects that are at various stages of development, some active and some in limbo. Like a juggler, he keeps a number of projects in the air; periodically, one comes down, is given a new burst of energy, and is sent back into orbit. At various intervals, he put new projects on-stream and discards old ones.

While the entrepreneur role describes the manager as the voluntary initiator of change, the *disturbance handler* role depicts the manager involuntarily responding to pressures. Here change is beyond the manager's control. He must act because the pressures of the situation are too severe to be ignored: strike looms, a major customer has gone bankrupt or a supplier reneges on his contract.

It has been fashionable, I noted earlier, to compare the manager to an orchestra conductor, just as Peter F. Drucker wrote in *The Practice of Management:*

> The manager has the task of creating a true whole that is larger than the sum of its parts, a productive entity that turns out more than the sum of the resources put into it. One analogy is the conductor of a symphony orchestra, through whose effort, vision and leadership individual instrumental parts that are so much noise by themselves become the living whole of music. But the conductor has the composer's score; he is only the interpreter. The manager is both composer and conductor.[14]

Now consider the words of Leonard R. Sayles, who has carried out systematic research on the manager's job:

> [The manager] is like a symphony orchestra conductor, endeavouring to maintain a melodious performance in which the contributions of the various instruments are coordinated and sequenced, patterned and paced, while the orchestra members are having various personal difficulties, stage hands are moving music stands, alternating excessive heat and cold are creating audience and instrument problems, and the sponsor of the concert is insisting on irrational changes in the program.[15]

In effect, every manager must spend a good part of his time responding to high-pressure disturbances. No organization can be so well run, so standardized, that it has considered every contingency in the uncertain environment in advance. Disturbances arise not only because poor managers ignore situations until they reach crisis proportions, but also because good managers cannot possibly anticipate all the consequences of the actions they take.

The third decisional role is that of *resource allocator.* To the manager falls the responsibility of deciding who will get what in his organizational unit. Perhaps the most important resource the manager allocates is his own time. Access to the manager constitutes exposure to the unit's nerve center and decision-maker. The manager is also charged with designing his unit's structure, that pattern of formal relationships that determines how work is to be divided and co-ordinated.

Also, in his role as resource allocator, the manager authorizes the important decisions of his unit before they are implemented. By retaining this power, the manager can ensure that decisions are interrelated; all must pass through a single brain. To fragment this power is to encourage discontinuous decision making and disjointed strategy.

There are a number of interesting features about the manager's authorizing others' decisions. First, despite the widespread use of capital budgeting procedures—a means of authorizing various capital expenditures at one time—executives in my study made a great many authorization decisions on an ad hoc basis. Apparently, many projects cannot wait or simply do not have the quantifiable costs and benefits that capital budgeting requires.

Second, I found that the chief executives faced incredibly complex choices. They had to consider the impact of each decision on other decisions and on the organization's strategy. They had to ensure that the decision would be acceptable to those who influence the organization, as well as ensure that resources would not be overextended. They had to understand the various costs and benefits as well as the feasibility of the proposal. They also had to consider questions of timing. All this was necessary for the simple approval of someone else's proposal. At the same time, however, delay could lose time, while quick approval could be ill considered and quick rejection might discourage the subordinate who had spent months developing a pet project.

One common solution to approving projects is to pick the man instead of the proposal. That is, the manager authorizes those projects presented to him by people whose judgment he trusts. But he cannot always use this simple dodge.

The final decisional role is that of *negotiator*. Studies of managerial work at all levels indicate that managers spend considerable time in negotiations: the president of the football team is called in to work out a contract with the holdout superstar; the corporation president leads his company's contingent to negotiate a new strike issue; the foreman argues a grievance problem to its conclusion with the shop steward. As Leonard Sayles puts it, negotiations are a "way of life" for the sophisticated manager.

These negotiations are duties of the manager's job; perhaps routine, they are not to be shirked. They are an integral part of his job, for only he has the authority to commit organizational resources in "real time," and only he has the nerve center information that important negotiations require.

The Integrated Job

It should be clear by now that the ten roles I have been describing are not easily separable. In the terminology of the psychologist, they

1. Where do I get my information, and how? Can I make greater use of my contacts to get information? Can other people do some of my scanning for me? In what areas is my knowledge weakest, and how can I get others to provide me with the information I need? Do I have powerful enough mental models of those things I must understand within the organization and in its environment?

2. What information do I disseminate in my organization? How important is it that my subordinates get my information? Do I keep too much information to myself because dissemination of it is time-consuming or inconvenient? How can I get more information to others so they can make better decisions?

3. Do I balance information collecting with action taking? Do I tend to act before information is in? Or do I wait so long for all the information that opportunities pass me by and I become a bottleneck in my organization?

4. What pace of change am I asking my organization to tolerate? Is this change balanced so that our operations are neither excessively static nor overly disrupted? Have we sufficiently analyzed the impact of this change on the future of our organization?

5. Am I sufficiently well informed to pass judgment on the proposals that my subordinates make? Is it possible to leave final authorization for more of the proposals with subordinates? Do we have problems of coordination because subordinates in fact now make too many of these decisions independently?

6. What is my vision of direction for this organization? Are these plans primarily in my own mind in loose form? Should I make them explicit in order to guide the decisions of others in the organization better? Or do I need flexibility to change them at will?

7. How do my subordinates react to my managerial style? Am I sufficiently sensitive to the powerful influence my actions have on them? Do I fully understand their reactions to my actions? Do I find an appropriate balance between encouragement and pressure? Do I stifle their initiative?

8. What kind of external relationships do I maintain, and how? Do I spend too much of my time maintaining these relationships? Are there certain types of people whom I should get to know better?

9. Is there any system to my time scheduling, or am I just reacting to the pressures of the moment? Do I find the appropriate mix of activities, or do I tend to concentrate on one particular function or one type of problem just because I find it interesting? Am I more efficient with particular kinds of work at special times of the day or week? Does my schedule reflect this? Can someone else (in addition to my secretary) take responsibility for much of my scheduling and do it more systematically?

10. Do I overwork? What effect does my work load have on my efficiency? Should I force myself to take breaks or to reduce the pace of my activity?

11. Am I too superficial in what I do? Can I really shift moods as quickly and frequently as my work patterns require? Should I attempt to decrease the amount of fragmentation and interruption in my work?

12. Do I orient myself too much toward current, tangible activities? Am I a slave to the action and excitement of my work, so that I am no longer able to concentrate on issues? Do key problems receive the attention they deserve? Should I spend more time reading and probing deeply into certain issues? Could I be more reflective? Should I be?

13. Do I use the different media appropriately? Do I know how to make the most of written communication? Do I rely excessively on face-to-face communication, thereby putting all but a few of my subordinates at an informational disadvantage? Do I schedule enough of my meetings on a regular basis? Do I spend enough time touring my organization to observe activity at first hand? Am I too detached from the heart of my organization's activities, seeing things only in an abstract way?

14. How do I blend my personal rights and duties? Do my obligations consume all my time? How can I free myself sufficiently from obligations to ensure that I am taking this organization where I want it to go? How can I turn my obligations to my advantage?

form a gestalt, an integrated whole. No role can be pulled out of the framework and the job be left intact. For example, a manager without liaison contacts lacks external information. As a result, he can neither disseminate the information his employees need nor make decisions that adequately reflect external conditions. (In fact, this is a problem for the new person in a managerial position, since he cannot make effective decisions until he has built up his network of contacts.)

Here lies a clue to the problems of team management.[16] Two or three people cannot share a single managerial position unless they can act as one entity. This means that they cannot divide up the ten roles unless they can very carefully reintegrate them. The real difficulty lies with the informational roles. Unless there can be full sharing of managerial information—and, as I pointed out earlier, it is primarily verbal—team management breaks down. A single managerial job cannot be arbitrarily split, for example, into internal and external roles, for information from both sources must be brought to bear on the same decisions.

To say that the ten roles form a gestalt is not to say that all managers give equal attention to each role. In fact, I found in my review of the various research studies that

. . . sales managers seem to spend relatively more of their time in the interpersonal roles, presumably a reflection of the extrovert nature of the marketing activity;

. . . production managers give relatively more attention to the decisional roles, presumably a reflection of their concern with efficient work flow;

. . . staff managers spend the most time in the informational roles, since they are experts who manage departments that advise other parts of the organization.

Nevertheless, in all cases the interpersonal, informational, and decisional roles remain inseparable.

TOWARD MORE
EFFECTIVE MANAGEMENT

What are the messages for management in this description? I believe, first and foremost, that this description of managerial work should prove more important to managers than any prescription they might derive from it. That is to say, *the manager's effectiveness is significantly influenced by his insight into his own work.* His performance depends on how well he understands and responds to the pressures and dilemmas of the job. Thus managers who can be introspective about their work are likely to be effective at their jobs. The ruled insert on pages 370–371 offers 14 groups of self-study questions for managers. Some may sound rhetorical; none is meant to be. Even though the questions cannot be answered simply, the manager should address them.

Let us take a look at three specific areas of concern. For the most part, the managerial logjams—the dilemma of delegation, the data base centralized in one brain, the problems of working with the management scientist—revolve around the verbal nature of the manager's information. There are great dangers in centralizing the organization's data bank in the minds of its managers. When they leave, they take their memory with them. And when subordinates are out of convenient verbal reach of the manager, they are at an informational disadvantage.

The manager is challenged to find systematic ways to share his privileged information. A regular debriefing session with key subordinates, a weekly memory dump on the dictating machine, the maintaining of a diary of important information for limited circulation, or other similar methods may ease the logjam of work considerably. Time spent disseminating this information will be more then regained when decisions must be made. Of course, some will raise the question of confidentiality. But managers would do well to weigh the risks of exposing privileged information against having subordinates who can make effective decisions.

If there is a single theme that runs through this article, it is that the pressures of his job drive the manager to be superficial in his actions—to overload himself with work, encourage interruption, respond quickly to every stimulus, seek the tangible and avoid the abstract, make decisions in small increments, and do everything abruptly.

Here again, the manager is challenged to deal consciously with the pressures of superficiality by giving serious attention to the issues that require it, by stepping back from his tangible bits of information in order to see a broad picture, and by making use of analytical inputs. Although effective managers have to be adept at responding quickly to numerous and varying problems, the danger in managerial work is that they will respond to every issue equally (and that means abruptly) and that they will never work the tangible bits and pieces of informational input into a comprehensive picture of their world.

As I noted earlier, the manager uses these bits of information to build models of his world. But the manager can also avail himself of the models of the specialists. Economists describe the functioning of markets, operations researchers simulate financial flow processes, and behavioral scientists explain the needs and goals of people. The best of these models can be searched out and learned.

In dealing with complex issues, the senior manager has much to gain from a close relationship with the management scientists of his own organization. They have something important that he lacks—time to probe complex issues. An effective working relationship hinges on the resolution of what a colleague and I have called "the planning dilemma."[17] Managers have the information and the authority; analysts have the time and the technology. A successful working relationship between the two will be effected when the manager learns to share his information and the analyst learns to adapt to the manager's needs. For the analyst, adaptation means worrying less about the elegance of the method and more about its speed and flexibility.

It seems to me that analysts can help the top manager especially to schedule his time, feed in analytical information, monitor projects under his supervision, develop models to aid in making choices, design contingency plans for disturbances that can be anticipated, and conduct "quick-and-dirty" analysis for those that cannot. But there can be no cooperation if the analysts are out of the mainstream of the manager's information flow.

The manager is challenged to gain control of his own time by turning obligations to his advantage and by turning those things he wishes to do into obligations. The chief executives of my study initiated only 32 percent of their own contacts (and another 5 percent by mutual agreement). And yet to a considerable extent they seemed to control their time. There were two key factors that enabled them to do so.

First, the manager has to spend so much time discharging obligations that if he were to view them as just that, he would leave no mark on his organization. The unsuccessful manager blames failure on the obligations; the effective manager turns his obligations to his own advantage. A speech is a chance to lobby for a cause; a meeting is a chance to reorganize a weak department; a visit to an important customer is a chance to extract trade information.

Second, the manager frees some of his time to do those things that he—perhaps no one else—thinks important by turning them into obligations. Free time is made, not found, in the manager's job; it is forced into the schedule. Hoping to leave some time open for contemplation or general planning is tantamount to hoping that the pressures of the job will go away. The manager who wants to innovate initiates a project and obligates others to report back to him: the manager who needs certain environmental information establishes channels that will automatically keep him informed; the manager who has to tour facilities commits himself publicly.

The Educator's Job

Finally, a word about the training of managers. Our management schools have done an admirable job of training the organization's specialists—management scientists, marketing researchers, accountants, and organizational development specialists. But for the most part they have not trained managers.[18]

Management schools will begin the serious training of managers when skill training takes a serious place next to cognitive learning. Cognitive learning is detached and informational, like reading a book or listening to a lecture. No doubt much important cognitive material must be assimilated by the manager-to-be. But cognitive learning no more makes a manager than it does a swimmer. The latter will drown the first time he jumps into the water if his coach never takes him out of the lecture hall, gets him wet, and gives him feedback on his performance.

In other words, we are taught a skill through practice plus feedback, whether in a real or a simulated situation. Our management schools need to identify the skills managers use, select students who show potential in these skills, put the students into situations where these skills can be practiced, and then give them systematic feedback on their performance.

My description of managerial work suggests a number of important managerial skills—developing peer relationships, carrying out negotiations, motivating subordinates, resolving conflicts, establishing information networks and subsequently disseminating information, making decisions in conditions of extreme ambiguity, and allocating resources. Above all, the manager needs to be introspective about his work so that he may continue to learn on the job.

Many of the manager's skills can, in fact, be practiced, using techniques that range from role playing to videotaping real meetings. And our management schools can enhance the entrepreneurial skills by designing programs that encourage sensible risk taking and innovation.

No job is more vital to our society than that of the manager. It is the manager who determines whether our social institutions serve us well or whether they squander our talents and resources. It is time to strip away the folklore about managerial work, and time to study it realistically so that we can begin the difficult task of making significant improvements in its performance.

References

1. All the data from my study can be found in Henry Mintzberg, *The Nature of Managerial Work* (New York: Harper & Row, 1973).
2. Robert H. Guest, "Of Time and the Foreman," *Personnel,* May 1956, p. 478.
3. Rosemary Stewart, *Managers and Their Jobs* (London: Macmillan, 1967); see also Sune Carlson, *Executive Behavior* (Stockholm: Strömbergs, 1951), the first of the diary studies.
4. Francis J. Aguilar, *Scanning the Business Environment* (New York: Macmillan, 1967), p. 102.
5. Unpublished study by Irving Choran, reported in Mintzberg, *The Nature of Managerial Work.*
6. Robert T. Davis, *Performance and Development of Field Sales Managers* (Boston: Division of Research, Harvard Business School, 1957); George H. Copeman, *The Role of the Managing Director* (London: Business Publications, 1963).
7. Stewart, *Managers and Their Jobs;* Tom Burns, "The Directions of Activity and Communication in a Departmental Executive Group," *Human Relations 7,* no. 1 (1954): 73.
8. H. Edward Wrapp, "Good Managers Don't Make Policy Decisions," HBR September-October 1967, p. 91; Wrapp refers to this as spotting opportunities and relationships in the stream of operating problems and decisions; in his article Wrapp raises a number of excellent points related to this analysis.
9. Richard E. Neustadt, *Presidential Power* (New York: John Wiley, 1960), pp. 153-154; italics added.
10. For a more thorough, though rather different, discussion of this issue, see Kenneth R. Andrews, "Toward Professionalism in Business Management," HBR March-April 1969, p. 49.
11. C. Jackson Grayson, Jr., in "Management Science and Business Practice," HBR July-August 1973, p. 41, explains in similar terms why, as chairman of the Price Commission, he did not use those very techniques that he himself promoted in his earlier career as a management scientist.
12. George C. Homans, *The Human Group* (New York: Harcourt, Brace & World, 1950), based on the study by William F. Whyte entitled *Street Corner Society,* rev. ed. (Chicago: University of Chicago Press, 1955).

13. Neustadt, *Presidential Power,* p. 157.
14. Peter F. Drucker, *The Practice of Management* (New York: Harper & Row, 1954), pp. 341-342.
15. Leonard R. Sayles, *Managerial Behavior* (New York: McGraw-Hill, 1964), p. 162.
16. See Richard C. Hodgson, Daniel J. Levinson, and Abraham Zaleznik, *The Executive Role Constellation* (Boston: Division of Research, Harvard Business School, 1965), for a discussion of the sharing of roles.
17. James S. Hekimian and Henry Mintzberg, "The Planning Dilemma," *The Management Review,* May 1968, p. 4.
18. See J. Sterling Livingston, "Myth of the Well-Educated Manager," HBR January-February 1971, p. 79.

Library Administration and New Management Systems

Richard De Gennaro

M ONSIEUR Jourdain, Molière's *Bourgeois Gentilhomme*, was surprised and pleased to learn that he had been speaking prose all his life without knowing it. I felt the same way when I finally learned that I had been a manager for 20 years without knowing it. Well, I always knew that I was a library *administrator*, but somehow I never thought of myself as a *manager* because that term connoted a kind of modern professionalism that the more familiar term *administrator*, lacked.

Ten years ago I attended the University of Maryland's excellent two-week development program for library administrators and was deeply impressed by the introductory courses and readings which covered the full range of subjects like McGregor's Theories X and Y, Management by Objectives (MBO), Program Budgeting (PPBS), Decision Theory, Cost-Benefit Analysis, Mathematical Modelling, Management Information Systems, etc. I came away thinking, somewhat naively, that business and other managers had mastered and were routinely using that arsenal of sophisticated management systems and techniques in their daily work, and that it was only library and perhaps academic administrators that were stuggling along with the traditional methods. It was clear that we librarians had a lot of catching-up to do.

It was with some hesitation that I accepted the directorship of a large library in 1970 because I believed that research libraries were becoming increasingly costly and complex organizations and that I lacked the formal management training and skills that the job required. Determined to remedy my lack of formal training, I enrolled in the Harvard Business School's Advanced Management Program, a

Reprinted from *Library Journal*, (Dec. 15, 1978), pp. 2477–2482. Published by R.R. Bowker Co. (a Xerox company). Copyright © 1978 by Xerox Corporation.

prestigious and expensive three-month program especially designed for high-level business, government, and military executives. I thought the "B-School" would work its magic and convert me from a self-taught library administrator into a certified modern manager, but I was disappointed.

Early in its history, the Harvard Business School developed the case method of instruction and it has used it almost exclusively in its teaching ever since. The case method can be very effective, but it was overused in the executive development program. In three months, we never read anything but cases, and since the cases were all efficiently reproduced and distributed in convenient packets, we never had the need or the occasion to use the rich resources of the Baker Library. In fact, we seldom had to read from a real book or journal. The classics of management science were rarely mentioned, and with the exception of a few sessions on decision theory and computer simulation, almost no mention was made of any of the new management systems that had been developed and were presumably being used routinely everywhere but in libraries. The Harvard program was useful, but it did not give me the management knowledge and skills that I needed and wanted: so I continued to read about management and to attend management institutes and workshops. (Among the best and most useful are the short programs offered by ARL's Office of Management Studies.) This reading and supplementary training helped me to develop and sharpen my management skills over the years. At the same time, I was gaining confidence and maturity and getting a lot of practical on-the-job experience.

I was also called upon to serve on a number of boards, commissions, and committees; this gave me the opportunity to work closely with and observe a peer group of top managers and executives, not only in libraries, but in universities, business firms, and government offices. I found that most of them, like me, had no special management training or education and were struggling, each in his or her own unscientific way, to do the management jobs to which they had been appointed. Some were more competent and effective than others, but previous formal management training seemed not to make any significant difference. Indeed, it was hard to tell who had training and who didn't. I noticed that there were few trained management experts in top level management positions. Instead, they were working as specialists in staff positions or as teachers, researchers, or consultants.

I could not see any real difference in what I was doing as a library director and what my peers in other fields were doing. After a while, I began to suspect that the reality of what we managers were experiencing in our day-to-day activities had more validity than the theoretical world of management that was being described in books and articles written by management professors and social scientists.

I was confirmed in that view when I read Henry Mintzberg's *The Nature of Managerial Work.*[1,2] Mintzberg, a McGill University management professor, had a much different view of management and the way managers worked than the conventional authors; that view checked with my own experience as a library administator. In order to find out and describe what managers actually did, he conducted a number of studies and also scanned the literature to integrate and synthesize the findings of other studies with his own.

HOW DO MANAGERS MANAGE?

The studies by Mintzberg and other researchers showed that from street gang leaders to the President of the United States, managers do not spend their time planning, organizing, coordinating, and controlling as the French industrialist, Henri Fayol said they did in 1916 and as most writers on management have continued to repeat ever since. They are not like the orchestra leader who directs the component parts of his organization with ease and precision. Instead, they spend their time reacting to crises, seizing special opportunities, attending meetings, negotiating, talking on the telephone, cultivating inter-personal and political relationships, gathering and disseminating information, and fulfilling a variety of ceremonial functions. Mintzberg says:

> I was struck during my study by the fact that the executives I was observing—all very competent by any standard—are fundamentally in-distinguishable from their counterparts of a hundred years ago (or a thousand years ago, for that matter). The information they needed differs, but they seek it in the same way—by word of mouth. Their decisions concern modern technology, but the procedures they use to make them are the same as the procedures of the 19th Century manager. Even the computer, so important for the specialized work of the organization, has apparently had no influence on the work procedures of general managers. In fact, the manager is in a kind of loop, with increasingly heavy work pressures but no aid forthcoming from management science.[3]

The Mintzberg view is by no means unique. There is a growing number of management scholars who are questioning the conventional view of management and what managers do. In a critical review of *On*

Management (Harper, 1976), a book of articles selected from 25 years of the *Harvard Business Review*, Albert Shapero, a management professor at the University of Texas, strikes a similar note:

> The term "management" conjures up images of control, rationality, systematics; but studies of what managers actually do depict behaviors and situations that are chaotic, unplanned, and charged with improvisation. The Managerial life at every level is reflexive—responding to calls, memos, personnel problems, fire drills, budget meetings, and personnel reviews. Occasionally, however, we find at managerial levels individuals who go 24 hours without being interrupted by meetings or phone calls. They are the long-range planners, the people in O.R., E.D.P., financial or market planning, or market research. Management is really for them. The bulk of the articles in *On Management* are concerned with ideas from the world of the staff functionary.[4]

ARE MANAGEMENT SYSTEMS REALLY USED?

What about the claims of widespread use of new scientific management systems and techniques? Is it really true that managers in business, government, and other institutions are using them extensively while we library administrators are lagging far behind?

Let's first look at what a few of the management experts say about the use of these systems in general, and then we will look at their use in libraries.

William R. Dill, dean of the Graduate School of Business Administration at New York University, makes this sober assessment:

> For all the progress we have made in developing good approaches to planning, forecasting, budgeting, and control, and for all the enthusiam we in schools of management have helped to build for these approaches, their use has been fitful and sporadic, even in the most analytically sophisticated and goal-oriented institutions. In corporations that are pointed out as models for what can be accomplished, the outputs of planning, budgeting, and modeling staffs are often quietly ignored by operating people when times are good; these outputs often seem irrelevant in times of sudden challenge or change. Analysis and planning are still far from foolproof ways to anticipate change and potential crises.[5]

Aaron Wildavsky, dean of the Graduate School of Public Policy at the University of California, Berkeley, has written a number of articles in which he argues convincingly, citing evidence and authorities, that the major modern information systems like PERT, MBO, PPBS, Social Indicators, and Zero Based Budgeting have not worked and cannot work. About PERT (Program Evaluation Review Technique), he says that "the few studies that exist suggest that outside of construction, where one activity tends to follow another, PERT is rarely successful."[6]

On MBO (Management by Objectives), he says: "The trouble with MBO is that the attempt to formalize procedures for choosing objectives without considering organizational dynamics leads to the opposite of what was intended—bad management, irrational choice, and ineffective decision-making."[7] "The main product of MBO, as experience in the United States federal government suggests, is, literally, a series of objectives. Aside from the unnecessary paper work, such exercises are self defeating because they become mechanisms for avoiding rather than making choices. Long lists of objectives are useless because rarely do resources remain beyond the first few."[8]

On PPBS, Wildavsky is equally harsh. He says that "Program budgeting does not work anywhere in the world it has been tried," and that "no one knows how to do program budgeting."[9] His assessments of Social Indicators and Zero Based Budgeting are in a similar vein.

These realistic assessments that we are getting from authorities like Mintzberg, Shapero, Dill, Wildavsky, and others should serve to remind us to maintain a healthy skepticism whenever we read about the effectiveness and widespread use of new management systems and techniques. We librarians should guard against the tendency we have to look for panaceas and to accept uncritically the claims and promises made on behalf of each new management theory or system that appears.

Consider the minimal impact on libraries as compared with the initial promise, for example, of PPBS, Operations Research, MBO, and even Participative Management.

To the best of my knowledge, PPBS has not been successfully implemented in a single library and I doubt that it ever will be.[10] Interest in it is rapidly waning.

The practical application of Operations Research in libraries has been extremely limited to date. One of the earliest and best known economic analyses of library decision making was done in the MIT Libraries in 1969. The report of that study came to this sobering conclusion: "Although helpful, an economic analysis of a university (or public) library is insufficient because libraries operate as political systems and thus improving libraries requires political analysis."[11] In an excellent article on library decision making, Jeffrey Raffel, an economist and co-author of the MIT study begins by saying that "in general, the more important the decision, the less beneficial a cost-benefit analysis is to library decision makers," and concludes by saying that "it is time that we all recognized the politics of libraries and acted accordingly."[12]

In a classic paper on Management by Objectives in academic libraries, James Michalko, after a thorough, critical review of the literature, recommends against the use of MBO in libraries on the grounds that it is a limited approach which is costly and difficult to implement and which yields uncertain results.[13]

Participative management is another "new" management technique that has been particularly oversold in the last decade. In fact, it is considered by many librarians to be the perfect management system. Good management has always included consultation and participation, it is just the name, the faddishness, and some of the formal structures that are new. When used properly and honestly, participative management is a useful process at all levels, and not just by top managers on major decisions as is sometimes assumed. It is essential that there be appropriate consultation and participation of interested and competent staff members on important decisions affecting them. But participative management will not bring the management millenium in libraries.

Participative management is not decision making by committee or by staff plebiscite. Good management requires that when all the facts have been gathered and analyzed and all the advice is in, the appropriate administrator has to make the decision and take responsibility for it. Knowing when and how to seek and take advantage of consultative advice and prior approval of decisions where appropriate is one of the most important managerial skills. Decisions should be made at the lowest competent level. The library's critical strategy decisions involve a world outside the library and must usually be made by the director and his chief associates. Staff committees can give good advice on such matters, but they simply do not have the information, the knowledge, or the perspective required to make those decisions—and they cannot take responsibility for the results.

One extreme form of participative management, the collegial or faculty system of governance, was developed for academic departments; it works badly there and worse or not at all in libraries. Where it appears to work, it is because those involved have tacitly made concessions to traditional hierarchical systems and the demands of the environment while preserving the collegial form. A library is not an academic department, it is a service organization and should be so administered. A librarian by any other name is still a librarian and it is time for mature acceptance of that fact.

Perhaps the reason that participative management has been embraced so enthusiastically and uncritically by librarians in recent years is not because of its management benefits, but because it appears to be the model that best justifies faculty status. It is assumed that because faculty members participate in a collegial academic decision-making process, that model is the appropriate one to use in libraries—if librarians are to achieve faculty status. Much of the library-based management literature since 1970 is self-serving and reflects a direct or indirect preoccupation with matters of staff status and benefits frequently hidden behind arguments for participative management. It is time that we recognize this natural bias and took steps to overcome it by giving more attention and weight to the more objective management literature from outside the library field.

Two recent articles on participative management in libraries, one by James Govan and the other by Dennis Dickenson, give encouraging evidence that the library profession is beginning to take a more realistic and balanced view of the advantages and limitations of participative management and collegial governance. Govan reminds us that:

> Librarians cannot afford to degrade services nor alienate their users in an effort, however enlightened or well-intentioned, to make their jobs more challenging and satisfying. Participation and consultation cost time and money and often, like faculty deliberations, produce rather conservative results. In this connection, it is useful to remember Maslow's belief that Theory Y is possible only in periods of affluence. It is also healthy to recall Drucker's statement that service institutions do not operate for the people who work in them.[4]

In his perceptive article, Dickenson tries to provide "an antidote for some of the more extreme and sometimes naive interpretations of participative management that appear from time to time in library literature."[15]

Peter Drucker summed up an important truth about management when he said in response to an interviewer's question about the efficacy of new management techniques: "The young people today expect to see business run by theory, knowledge, concepts, and planning. But then they find it is run like the rest of the world—by experience and expediency, by who you know, and by the hydrostatic pressure in your bladder."[16]

This is not just the way business in run, it is the way libraries are run as well. And it is the way they will continue to be run despite the current rhetoric about the managerial revolution that is being ushered in by the use of new quantitative and psychological management systems and theories.

Why? Because a library operates in a political environment and nearly all the really important decisions that are made at the highest levels have an overriding political component. They are rarely the product of cost-benefit analysis or Operations Research where the various factors are weighed and compared and the "best" or most cost-effective course is chosen. These management techniques can be useful sometimes to implement a program or a project in the most effective manner *after* the political decision to proceed has been made. They can also be useful in providing a rationale to support some essentially political decision that is being proposed or advocated, or to impress higher authorities or constituents with the competence of the managers and the rationality of their decision making process. Management systems, particularly PPBS, ZBB, and PERT are used in government and military bureacracies largely because they are mandated by law or regulation.

In the library world, as in education, business, and government, few major program decisions are made solely or even largely on the basis of careful studies of needs and costs. Consider, for example, decisions to build a new library building, to open a new departmental or branch library, to achieve excellence in some special subject discipline, or to embark on a major automation program. These program decisions are usually the result of an initiative or vision by an imaginative and powerful person, perhaps a library director, a dean, a president, a mayor, or other official. They are political, emotional, or even personal decisions—justified, rationalized, and perhaps implemented with the assistance of various kinds of analyses and studies, but seldom derived from them.

It is important that librarians understand how and why these really critical decisions are made so that they will not be disillusioned or discouraged when they discover that the "best," the most efficient, or the least expensive solution frequently loses out to the one that is the most politically expedient or attractive.

THE QUANTITATIVE APPROACH

I think it is important to make a distinction between the claims made on behalf of complex quantitative management systems such as Operations Research and Cost-Benefit Analysis, and the collection and analysis of quantitative data in libraries to assist in rational decision making. I am questioning the validity and usefulness of these complex systems, but I am not questioning the need for and use of quantitative studies for measuring and evaluating library services. Quite the contrary, we need to know more about libraries, their resources, and how they are actually used. We have relied historically upon input data, e.g., the number of books acquired, the number of serials subscribed to, the number of books circulated, the dollars spent, etc. The qualitative characteristics of these data are dubious; we desperately need reliable measures of library effectiveness.

Following the pioneering work by Fremont Rider[17] in 1940 on the growth of research libraries, there has been an increasing number of extremely valuable quantitative studies like those by Fussler,[18] Lancaster,[19] Buckland,[20] and other works of solid quality. The findings of such studies provide the theoretical foundations and practical knowledge that working library managers need to draw on to help them think clearly and creatively about library management and to make sound decisions based on valid data. This is especially true in this time of transition when the conventional wisdom of our profession will not suffice to see us through.

As one of the library managers for whose benefit and use such studies are presumably made, I thank the authors and urge them on to greater productivity and precision. I also urge them to try to keep their studies as simple as possible and to summarize their findings in readable English.

Unfortunately, a good deal of the quantitative research that is done in the library field is unintelligible, irrelevant, or too complicated and theoretical for any practical use in libraries. Much of it is written in the language of higher mathematics which is incomprehensible to most managers. This is particularly true of studies that are made by academics outside the library field such as statisticians, economists, psychologists, Operations Research people, etc. Their goal is not necessarily to do studies that are useful, but to demonstrate their mathematical prowess, to test theories and methodologies, to get published, and to award doctoral degrees to deserving graduate students. They select the library as their laboratory because it is convenient and because they think it is virgin territory ready for easy exploitation. They are more interested in the process than in the results.

The most useful library research is done by librarians or others with a serious long-term interest and involvement in libraries who work with librarians in a spirit of genuine collaboration. They are trying to make an impact. It is the difference between a class assignment and the real thing, between war games and war.

A notable exception to this criticism of academics is the landmark work by William J. Baumol and Matityahu Marcus, *Economics of Academic Libraries* (American Council on Education, Washington, D.C., 1973). These two economists went to unusual lengths to explain their statistical methods and to summarize their conclusions with refreshing brevity and clarity. As a consequence, their work is widely read and frequently cited.

Management scientists and other quantitatively oriented researchers frequently wonder why the results of quantitative research studies are not used more by practicing library managers in the decision making process.[21] One reason is that the mathematics and the methodologies required are far too complex and difficult for operating managers to learn and apply in their busy work environments. Few senior library administrators have the kind of staff support needed to successfully carry out complex analyses. Another and equally important reason is that the quantitative approach does not and cannot take into sufficient account the complex of political, organizational, and psychological factors that characterize the real work where people are more potent than numbers or logic.

The quality of many decisions could be significantly improved if we had more and better data, but many of the more important decisions have a relatively small quantitative component. As a library director, I seldom have a critical need for more quantitative data than are available from regularly kept statistics or by having someone make a special and usually simple survey and analysis of the problem. When the data are simply not available or too difficult to assemble, I can usually find a satisfactory way to manage without them. My real problem has nearly always been to correctly assess the political rather than the economic or quantitative factors. It is fairly easy to determine the most cost-effective course of action with or without detailed data. It is much harder to map out and implement a successful strategy for achieving it, to assess how the various persons and groups affected will perceive the manager's intentions, and how they will react to the decision. Someone said that quantification is not synonymous with management. Finding the best or most cost-effective course of action

388 MANAGEMENT STRATEGIES FOR LIBRARIES

is not the same as getting it accepted. Sometimes the quality of a decision is critical, other times, it is acceptance.

Effective decision making processes in large academic and public libraries involve complex sets of policies, procedures, and problems which require a variety of different kinds of information and approaches. Some decisions will be authoritarian, some will be collegial, some will be made by committees, and some will be made by combinations of the above. Library directors are not all-knowing, nor are the collective judgments of library faculties and committees infallible. Different situations call for different approaches. There are no simple formulas and no easy answers.

The new management systems that I have been discussing in this article divide into two general categories. There are *quantitative systems* such as Operations Research, PPBS, and ZBB, and *psychological* or *behavioral* systems such as Theory Y (and its variants) and MBO. In each system, there are a number of concepts, ideas, tools, and techniques that have validity and can be used to advantage by library managers, but as comprehensive systems they are all far too theoretical, complex, and simplistic to be applied successfully by ordinary managers in the day-to-day work environment. Few managers have the time or the specialized knowledge and skills required to make these systems work, and those that do are propably astute enough to manage as well or better without them.

In the hands of amateurs—and this is most of us—the quantitative systems frequently produce misleading and wrong solutions, while the psychological or behavioral systems can lead to the manipulation and misuse of people. The real danger with both kinds of management systems is that they offer mechanistic formulas for dealing with complex realities and keep us from thinking about and solving our management problems in practical, realistic, and common sense ways.

Despite the many claims to the contrary, management is not yet a science. It is still an art, but is very much an art that can and should be mastered and practiced by librarians.

References

1. Henry Mintzberg. *The Nature of Managerial Work,* Harper, 1973.
2. A very readable summary of Mintzberg's findings and views appeared in a much cited and reprinted article by him entitled "The Manager's Job: Folklore and Fact," *Harvard Business Review,* July-August 1975, p. 49-61.

3. Mintzberg, "The Manager's Job . . . " p. 54.
4. Albert Shapero, "What Management Says and What Managers Do," *Fortune,* May 1975, p. 275.
5. William R. Dill, "When Auld Acquaintance Be Forgot . . . From Cyert and March to Cyert vs. March," in: Richard M. Cyert, *The Management of Nonprofit Organizations,* Heath, 1975, p. 67.
6. Aaron Wildavsky, "Policy Analysis Is What Information Systems Are Not," Working Paper #53, July 1976, copy of a typescript of a paper delivered at the ASIS Conference, October 1976, p. 3.
7. Wildavsky, "Policy Analysis . . . " p. 5.
8. Wildavsky, "Policy Analysis . . . " p. 6.
9. Aaron Wildavsky, "Rescuing Policy Analysis from PPBS," *Public Administration Review,* March-April 1969, p. 193.
10. The reasons can be found in an authoritative study by Guy Joseph De Genaro, "A Planning-Programming-Budgeting System (PPBS) in Academic Libraries: Development of Objectives and Effectiveness Measures." Ph.D. dissertation, University of Florida, 1971.
11. Jeffrey A. Raffel, "From Economic to Political Analysis of Library Decision Making," *College & Research Libraries,* November 1974, p. 412.
12. Raffel, "From Economic to Political Analysis . . . ," p. 412, 421.
13. James Michalko, "Management by Objectives and the Academic Library: a Critical Overview," *Library Quarterly,* Vol. 45, No. 3, 1975, p. 235-52.
14. James F. Govan, "The Better Mousetrap: External Accountability and Staff Participation," *Library Trends,* Fall 1977, p. 264.
15. Dennis W. Dickenson, "Some Reflections on Participative Management in Libraries," *College & Research Libraries,* July 1978, p. 261.
16. Thomas J. Murray, "Peter Drucker Attacks: Our Top-heavy Corporations," *Dun's,* April 1974, p. 40.
17. Fremont Rider, *The Scholar and the Future of the Research Library,* Hadham Pr., 1944.
18. Herman H. Fussler & J. L. Simon, *Patterns in the Use of Books in Large Research Libraries,* Univ. of Chicago, Pr., 1969.
19. F. W. Lancaster, *The Measurement and Evaluation of Library Services,* Washington, D.C., Information Resources Press, 1977.
20. Michael K. Buckland, *Book Availability and the Library User,* Pergamon, 1975.
21. See for example: A. Graham McKenzie, "Whither Our Academic Libraries?" *Journal of Documentation, June 1976, p. 129.*

Sources of Power of Lower Participants in Complex Organizations

David Mechanic

T HIS paper explores various factors that account for the power of secretaries, hospital attendants, prison inmates, and other lower participants within organizations. Power is seen as resulting from access to and control over persons, information, and instrumentalities. Among the variables discussed affecting power are normative definitions, perception of legitimacy, exchange, and coalitions. Personal attributes related to power include commitment, effort, interest, willingness to use power, skills, and attractiveness. Finally, various attributes of social structure are discussed which also help to account for the power of lower participants: time spent in the organization, centrality of position, duality of power structures, and replaceability of persons.[1]

It is not unusual for lower participants[2] in complex organizations to assume and wield considerable power and influence not associated with their formally defined positions within these organizations. In sociological terms they have considerable personal power but no authority. Such personal power is often attained, for example, by executive secretaries and accountants in business firms, by attendants in mental hospitals, and even by inmates in prisons. The personal power achieved by these lower participants does not necessarily result from unique personal characteristics, although these may be relevant, but results rather from particular aspects of their location within their organizations.

Reprinted with permission from *Administrative Science Quarterly*, V. 7 (Dec. 1962) pp. 349–364.

INFORMAL VERSUS FORMAL POWER

Within organizations the distribution of authority (institutionalized power) is closely if not perfectly correlated with the prestige of positions. Those who have argued for the independence of these variables[3] have taken their examples from diverse organizations and do not deal with situations where power is clearly comparable.[4] Thus when Bierstedt argues that Einstein had prestige but no power, and the policeman power but no prestige, it is apparent that he is comparing categories that are not comparable. Generally persons occupying high-ranking positions within organizations have more authority than those holding low-ranking positions.

One might ask what characterizes high-ranking positions within organizations. What is most evident, perhaps, is that lower participants recognize the right of higher-ranking participants to exercise power, and yield without difficulty to demands they regard as legitimate. Moreover, persons in high-ranking positions tend to have considerable access and control over information and persons both within and outside the organization, and to instrumentalities or resources. Although higher supervisory personnel may be isolated from the task activities of lower participants, they maintain access to them through formally established intermediary positions and exercise control through intermediary participants. There appears, therefore, to be a clear correlation between the prestige of positions within organizations and the extent to which they offer access to information, persons, and instrumentalities.

Since formal organizations tend to structure lines of access and communication, access should be a clue to institutional prestige. Yet access depends on variables other than those controlled by the formal structure of an organization, and this often makes the informal power structure that develops within organizations somewhat incongruent with the formally intended plan. It is these variables that allow work groups to limit production through norms that contravene the goals of the larger organization, that allow hospital attendants to thwart changes in the structure of a hospital, and that allow prison inmates to exercise control over prison guards. Organizations, in a sense, are continuously at the mercy of their lower participants, and it is this fact that makes organizational power structure especially interesting to the sociologist and social psychologist.

Clarification of Definitions

The purpose of this paper is to present some hypotheses explaining why lower participants in organizations can often assume and wield considerable power which is not associated with their positions as formally defined within these organizations. For the purpose of this analysis the concepts "influence," "power," and "control" will be used synonymously. Moreover, we shall not be concerned with type of power, that is, whether the power is based on reward, punishment, identification, power to veto, or whatever.[5] Power will be defined as *any force that results in behavior that would not have occurred if the force had not been present.* We have defined power as a force rather than a relationship because it appears that much of what we mean by power is encompassed by the normative framework of an organization, and thus any analysis of power must take into consideration the power of norms as well as persons.

I shall also argue, following Thibaut and Kelley,[6] that power is closely related to dependence. To the extent that a person is dependent on another, he is potentially subject to the other person's power. Within organizations one makes others dependent upon him by controlling access to information, persons, and instrumentalities, which I shall define as follows:

a) *Information* includes knowledge of the organization, knowledge about persons, knowledge of the norms, procedures, techniques, and so forth.
b) *Persons* include anyone within the organization or any one outside the organization upon whom the organization is in some way dependent.
c) *Instrumentalities* include any aspect of the physical plant of the organization or its resources (equipment, machines, money, and so on).

Power is a function not only of the extent to which a person controls information, persons, and instrumentalities, but also of the importance of the various attributes he controls.[7]

Finally, following Dahl,[8] we shall agree that comparisons of power among persons should, as far as possible, utilize comparable units. Thus we shall strive for clarification by attempting to over-simplify organizational processes; the goal is to set up a number of hypothetical statements of the relationship between variables taken two at a time, "all other factors being assumed to remain constant."

A Classic Example

Like many other aspects of organizational theory, one can find a classic statement of our problem in Weber's discussion of the political bureaucracy. Weber indicated the extent to which bureaucrats may have considerable power over political incumbents, as a result, in part, of their permanence within the political bureaucracy, as contrasted to public officials, who are replaced rather frequently.[9] Weber noted how the low-ranking bureaucrat becomes familiar with the organization— its rules and operations, the work flow, and so on, which gives him considerable power over the new political incumbent, who might have higher rank but is not as familiar with the organization. While Weber does not directly state the point, his analysis suggests that bureaucratic permanence has some relationship to increased access to persons, information, and instrumentalities. To state the hypothesis suggested somewhat more formally:

H1 Other factors remaining constant, organizational power is related to access to persons, information, and instrumentalities.

H2 Other factors remaining constant, as a participant's length of time in an organization increases, he has increased access to persons, information, and instrumentalities.

While these hypotheses are obvious, they do suggest that a careful scrutiny of the organizational literature, especially that dealing with the power or counterpower of lower participants, might lead to further formalized statements, some considerably less obvious than the ones stated. This kind of hypothesis formation is treated later in the paper, but at this point I would like to place the discussion of power within theoretical context and discuss the relevance of role theory to the study of power processes.

IMPLICATIONS OF ROLE THEORY FOR THE STUDY OF POWER

There are many points of departure for the study of power processes within organizations. An investigator might view influence in terms of its sources and strategies; he might undertake a study of the flow of influence; he might concentrate on the structure of organizations, seeing to what extent regularities in behavior might be explained through the study of norms, roles, and traditions; and, finally, more psychologically oriented investigators might concentrate on the recipients of influence and the factors affecting susceptibility to influence attempts. Each of these points of departure leads to different theoretical emphases. For our purposes the most important emphasis is that presented by role theorists.

Role theorists approach the question of influence and power in terms of the behavioral regularities which result from established identities within specific social contexts like families, hospitals, and business firms. The underlying premise of most role theorists is that a large proportion of all behavior is brought about through socialization within specific organizations, and much behavior is routine and established through learning the traditional modes of adaptation in dealing with specific tasks. Thus the positions persons occupy in an organization account for much of their behavior. Norms and roles serve as mediating forces in influence processes.

While role theorists have argued much about vocabulary, the basic premises underlying their thought have been rather consistent. The argument is essentially that knowledge of one's identity or social position is a powerful index of the expectations such a person is likely to face in various social situations. Since behavior tends to be highly correlated with expectations, prediction of behavior is therefore possible. The approach of role theorists to the study of behavior within organizations is of particular merit in that it provides a consistent set of concepts which is useful analytically in describing recruitment, socialization, interaction, and personality, as well as the formal structure of organizations. Thus the concept of role is one of the few concepts clearly linking social structure, social process, and social character.

Many problems pertaining to a role theory have been raised. At times it is not clear whether role is regarded as a real entity, a theoretical construct, or both. Moreover, Gross has raised the issue of role consensus, that is, the extent to which the expectations impinging upon a position are held in common by persons occupying reciprocal positions to the one in question.[10] Merton has attempted to deal with inevitable inconsistencies in expectations of role occupants by introducing the concept of role-set which treats differences in expectations as resulting, in part, from the fact that any position is differently related to a number of reciprocal positions.[11] Furthermore, Goffman, has criticized role theory for its failure to deal adequately with commitment to roles[12]—a factor which Etzioni has found to be related intimately to the kind of power exercised in organizations.[13] Perhaps these various criticisms directed at role theory reflect its importance as well as its deficiencies, and despite the difficulties involved in role analysis, the concept of role may prove useful in various ways.

Role theory is useful in emphasizing the extent to which influence and power can be exercised without conflict. This occurs when power is integrated with a legitimate order, when sentiments are held in common, and when there are adequate mechanisms for introducing persons into the system and training them to recognize, accept, and value the legitimacy of control within the organization. By providing the conditions whereby participants within an organization may internalize the norms, these generalized rules, values, and sentiments serve as substitutes for interpersonal influence and make the workings of the organization more agreeable and pleasant for all.

It should be clear that lower participants will be more likely to circumvent higher authority, other factors remaining constant, when the mandates of those in power, if not the authority itself, are regarded as illegitimate. Thus as Etzioni points out, when lower participants become alienated from the organization, coercive power is likely to be required if its formal mandates are to be fulfilled.[14]

Moreover, all organizations must maintain control over lower participants. To the extent that lower participants fail to recognize the legitimacy of power, or believe that sanctions cannot or will not be exercised when violations occur, the organization loses to some extent, its ability to control their behavior. Moreover, in-so-far as higher participants can create the impression that they can or will exert sanctions above their actual willingness to use such sanctions, control over lower participants will increase. It is usually to the advantage of an organization to externalize and impersonalize controls, however, and if possible to develop positive sentiments toward its rules.

In other words, an effective organization can control its participants in such a way as to make it hardly perceivable that it exercises the control that it does. It seeks commitment from lower participants, and when commitment is obtained, surveillance can be relaxed. On the other hand, when the power of lower participants in organizations is considered, it often appears to be clearly divorced from the traditions, norms, and goals and sentiments of the organization as a whole. Lower participants do not usually achieve control by using the role structure of the organization, but rather by circumventing, sabotaging, and manipulating it.

SOURCES OF POWER OF LOWER PARTICIPANTS

The most effective way for lower participants to achieve power is to obtain, maintain, and control access to persons, information, and instrumentalities. To the extent that this can be accomplished, lower participants make higher-ranking participants dependent upon them.

Thus dependence together with the manipulation of the dependency relationship is the key to the power of lower participants.

A number of examples can be cited which illustrate the preceding point. Scheff, for example, reports on the failure of a state mental hospital to bring about intended reform because of the opposition of hospital attendants.[15] He noted that the power of hospital attendants was largely a result of the dependence of ward physicians on attendants. This dependence resulted from the physician's short tenure, his lack of interest in administration, and the large amount of administrative responsibility he had to assume. An implicit trading agreement developed between physicians and attendants, whereby attendants would take on some of the responsibilities and obligations of the ward physician in return for increased power in decision-making processes concerning patients. Failure of the ward physician to honor his part of the agreement resulted in information being withheld, disobedience, lack of cooperation, and unwillingness of the attendants to serve as a barrier between the physician and a ward full of patients demanding attention and recognition. When the attendant withheld cooperation, the physician had difficulty in making a graceful entrance and departure from the ward, in handling necessary paper work (officially his responsibility), and in obtaining information needed to deal adequately with daily treatment and behavior problems. When attendants opposed change, they could wield influence by refusing to assume responsibilities officially assigned to the physician.

Similarly, Sykes describes the dependence of prison guards on inmates and the power obtained by inmates over guards.[16] He suggests that although guards could report inmates for disobedience, frequent reports would give prison officials the impression that the guard was unable to command obedience. The guard, therefore, had some stake in ensuring the good behavior of prisoners without use of formal sanctions against them. The result was a trading agreement whereby the guard allowed violations of certain rules in return for cooperative behavior. A similar situation is found in respect to officers in the Armed Services or foremen in industry. To the extent that they require formal sanctions to bring about cooperation, they are usually perceived by their superiors as less valuable to the organization. For a good leader is expected to command obedience, at least, if not commitment.

FACTORS AFFECTING POWER

Expertise

Increasing specialization and organizational growth has made the expert or staff person important. The expert maintains power because high-ranking persons in the organization are dependent upon him for his special skills and access to certain kinds of information. One possible reason for lawyers obtaining many high governmental offices is that they are likely to have access to rather specialized but highly important means to organizational goals.[17]

We can state these ideas in hypotheses, as follows:

> H3 Other factors remaining constant, to the extent that a low-ranking participant has important expert knowledge not available to high-ranking participants, he is likely to have power over them.

Power stemming from expertise, however, is likely to be limited unless it is difficult to replace the expert. This leads to two further hypotheses:

> H4 Other factors remaining constant, a person difficult to replace will have greater power than a person easily replaceable.
> H5 Other factors remaining constant, experts will be more difficult to replace than nonexperts.

While persons having expertise are likely to be fairly high-ranking participants in an organization, the same hypotheses that explain the power of lower participants are relevant in explaining the comparative power positions of intermediate-and high-ranking persons.

The application of our hypotheses about expertise is clearly relevant if we look at certain organizational issues. For example, the merits of medical versus lay hospital administrators are often debated. It should be clear, however, that all other factors remaining unchanged, the medical administrator has clear advantage over the lay administrator. Where lay administrators receive preference, there is an implicit assumption that the lay person is better at administrative duties. This may be empirically valid but is not necessarily so. The special expert knowledge of the medical administrator stems from his ability legitimately to oppose a physician who contests an administrative decision on the basis of medical necessity. Usually hospitals are viewed primarily as universalistic in orientation both by the general public and most of their participants. Thus medical necessity usually takes precedence over management policies, a factor contributing to the poor financial position of most hospitals. The lay administrator is not in a position to contest such claims independently, since he usually lacks the basis for evaluation of the medical problems involved and also lacks official recognition of his competence to make such decisions. If the lay administrator is to evaluate these claims adequately on the basis of professional necessity, he must have a group of medical consultants or a committee of medical men to serve as a buffer between medical staff and the lay administration.

As a result of growing specialization, expertise is increasingly important in organizations. As the complexity of organizational tasks increases, and as organizations grow in size, there is a limit to responsibility that can be efficiently exercised by one person. Delegation of responsibility occurs, experts and specialists are brought in to provide information and research, and the higher participants become dependent upon them. Experts have tremendous potentialities for power by withholding information, providing incorrect information, and so on, and to the extent that experts are dissatisfied, the probability of organizational sabotage increases.

Effort and Interest

The extent to which lower participants may exercise power depends in part on their willingness to exert effort in areas where higher-ranking participants are often reluctant to participate. Effort exerted is directly related to the degree of interest one has in an area.

H6 Other factors remaining constant, there is a direct relationship between the amount of effort a person is willing to exert in an area and the power he can command.

For example, secretarial staffs in universities often have power to make decisions about the purchase and allocation of supplies, the allocation of their services, the scheduling of classes, and, at times, the disposition of student complaints. Such control may in some instances lead to sanctions against a professor by polite reluctance to furnish supplies, ignoring his preferences for the scheduling of classes, and giving others preference in the allocation of services. While the power to make such decisions may easily be removed from the jurisdiction of the lower participant, it can only be accomplished at a cost—the willingness to allocate time and effort to the decisions dealing with these matters. To the extent that responsibilities are delegated to lower participants, a certain degree of power is likely to accompany the responsibility. Also, should the lower participant see his perceived rights in jeopardy, he may sabotage the system in various ways.

Let us visualize a hypothetical situation where a department concludes that secretarial services are being allocated on a prejudicial basis as a result of complaints to the chairman of the department by several of the younger faculty. Let us also assume that, when the complaint is investigated, it is found to be substantially correct; that is, some of the younger faculty have difficulty obtaining secretarial services because of preferences among the secretarial staff. If in attempting to eliminate discretion by the secretarial staff, the chairman establishes a rule ordering the allocation of services on the basis of the order in which work appears, the rule can easily be made ineffective by complete conformity to it. Deadlines for papers, examinations, and the like will occur, and flexibility in the allocation of services is required if these deadlines are to be met. Thus the need for flexibility can be made to conflict with the rule by a staff usually not untalented in such operations.

When an organization gives discretion to lower participants, it is usually trading the power of discretion for needed flexibility. The cost of constant surveillance is too high, and the effort required too great; it is very often much easier for all concerned to allow the secretary discretion in return for cooperation and not too great an abuse of power.

H7 Other factors remaining constant, the less effort and interest higher-ranking participants are willing to devote to a task, the more likely are lower participants to obtain power relevant to this task.

Attractiveness

Another personal attribute associated with the power of low-ranking persons in an organization is attractiveness or what some call "personality." People who are viewed as attractive are more likely to obtain access to persons, and, once such access is gained, they may be more likely to succeed in promoting a cause. But once again dependence is the key to the power of attractiveness, for whether a person is dependent upon another for a service he provides, or for approval or affection, what is more relevant is the relational bond which is highly valued.

> H8 Other factors remaining constant, the more attractive a person, the more likely he is to obtain access to persons and control over these persons.

Location and Position

In any organization the person's location in physical space and position in social space are important factors influencing access to persons, information, and instrumentalities.[18] Propinquity affects the opportunities for interaction, as well as one's position within a communication network. Although these are somewhat separate factors, we shall refer to their combined effect as centrality[19] within the organization.

> H9 Other factors remaining constant, the more central a person is in an organization, the greater is his access to persons, information, and instrumentalities.

Some low participants may have great centrality within an organization. An executive's or university president's secretary not only has access, but often controls access in making appointments and scheduling events. Although she may have no great formal authority, she may have considerable power.

Coalitions

It should be clear that the variables we are considering are at different levels of analysis; some of them define attributes of persons, while others define attributes of communication and organization. Power processes within organizations are particularly interesting in that there are many channels of power and ways of achieving it.

In complex organizations different occupational groups attend to different functions, each group often maintaining its own power structure within the organization. Thus hospitals have administrators, medical personnel, nursing personnel, attendants, maintenance personnel, laboratory personnel, and so on. Universities, similarly, have teaching personnel, research personnel, administrative personnel, maintenance personnel, and so on. Each of these functional tasks within organizations often becomes the sphere of a particular group that controls activities relating to the task. While these tasks usually are coordinated at the highest levels of the organization, they often are not coordinated at intermediate and lower levels. It is not unusual, however, for coalitions to form among lower participants in these multiple structures. A secretary may know the man who manages the supply of stores, or the person assigning parking stickers. Such acquaintances may give her the ability to handle informally certain needs that would be more time-consuming and difficult to handle formally. Her ability to provide services informally makes higher-ranking participants in some degree dependent upon her, thereby giving her power, which increases her ability to bargain on issues important to her.

Rules

In organizations with complex power structures lower participants can use their knowledge of the norms of the organization to thwart attempted change. In discussing the various functions of bureaucratic rules, Gouldner maintains that such rules serve as excellent sub-stitutes for surveillance, since surveillance in addition to being expensive in time and effort arouses considerable hostility and antagonism.[20] Moreover, he argues, rules are a functional equivalent for direct, personally given orders, since they specify the obligations of workers to do things in specific ways. Standardized rules, in addition, allow simple screening of violations, facilitate remote control, and to some extent legitimize punishment when the rule is violated. The worker who violates a bureaucratic rule has little recourse to the excuse that he did not know what was expected, as he might claim for a direct order. Finally, Gouldner argues that rules are the "the 'chips' to which the company staked the supervisors and which they could use to play the game",[21] that is, rules established a punishment which could be withheld, and this facilitated the supervisors' bargaining power with lower participants.

While Gouldner emphasizes the functional characteristics of rules within an organization, it should be clear that full compliance to all the rules at all times will probably be dysfunctional for the organization. Complete and apathetic compliance may do everything but facilitate achievement of organizational goals. Lower participants who are familiar with an organization and its rules can often find rules to support their contention that they not do what they have been asked to do, and rules are also often a rationalization for inaction on their part. The following of rules becomes especially complex when associations and unions become involved, for there are then two sets of rules to which the participant can appeal.

What is suggested is that rules may be chips for everyone concerned in the game. Rules become the "chips" through which the bargaining process is maintained. Scheff, as noted earlier, observed that attendants in mental hospitals often took on responsibilities assigned legally to the ward physician, and when attendants refused to share these responsibilities the physician's position became extremely difficult.[22]

> The ward physician is legally responsible for the care and treatment of each ward patient. This responsibility requires attention to a host of details. Medicine, seclusion, sedation and transfer orders, for example, require the doctor's signature. Tranquilizers are particularly troublesome in this regard since they require frequent adjustment of dosage in order to get the desired effects. The physician's order is required to each change in dosage. With 150 patients under his care on tranquilizers, and several changes of dosages a week desirable, the physician could spend a major portion of his ward time in dealing with this single detail.
>
> Given the time-consuming formal chores of the physician and his many other duties, he usually worked out an arrangement with the ward personel, particularly the charge (supervisory attendant), to handle these duties. On several wards, the charge called specific problems to the doctor's attention, and the two of them, in effect, would have a consultation. The charge actually made most of the decisions concerning dosage change in the back wards. Since the doctor delegated portions of his formal responsibilities to the charge, he was dependent on her good will toward him. If she withheld her cooperation, the physician had absolutely no recourse but to do all the work himself.[23]

In a sense such delegation of responsibility involves a consideration of reward and cost, whereby the decision to be made involves a question of what is more valuable—to retain control over an area, or to delegate one's work to lower participants.

There are occasions, of course, when rules are regarded as illegitimate by lower participants, and they may disregard them. Gouldner observed that, in the mine, men felt they could resist authority in a situation involving danger to themselves.[24] They did not feel that they could legitimately be ordered to do anything that would endanger their lives. It is probably significant that in extremely dangerous situations organizations are more likely to rely on commitment to work than on authority. Even within nonvoluntary groups dangerous tasks are regarded usually as requiring task commitment, and it is likely that commitment is a much more powerful organizational force than coercive authority.

SUMMARY

The preceding remarks are general ones, and they are assumed to be in part true of all types of organizations. But power relationships in organization are likely to be molded by the type of organization being considered, the nature of organizational goals, the ideology of organizational decision making, the kind of commitment participants have to the organization, the formal structure of the organization, and so on. In short, we have attempted to discuss power processes within organizations in a manner somewhat divorced from other major organizational processes. We have emphasized variables affecting control of access to persons, information, and facilities within organizations. Normative definition, perception of legitimacy, exchange, and coalitions have all been viewed in relation to power processes. Moreover, we have dealt with some attributes of persons related to power: commitment, effort, interest, willingness to use power, skills, attractiveness, and so on. And we have discussed some other variables: time, centrality, complexity of power structure, and replaceability of persons. It appears that these variables help to account in part for power exercised by lower participants in organizations.

References

1. Paper presented at the Ford Foundation Seminar in the Social Science of Organizations, University of Pittsburgh, June 10–22, 1962.
2. The term "lower participants" comes from Amitai Etzioni, *A comparative analysis of complex organizations* (New York, 1961) and is used by him to designate persons in positions of lower rank: employees, rank-and-file, members, clients, customers, and inmates. We shall use the term in this paper in a relative sense denoting position vis-à-vis a higher-ranking participant.
3. Robert Biersted, An analysis of social power. *American Sociologist Review*, Vol. 15 (1950), pp. 730–38.
4. Robert A. Dahl. The concept of power. *Behavioral Science*, Vol.2 (1957), pp. 201–15.

5. One might observe, for example, that the power of lower participants is based primarily on the ability to "veto" or punish. For a discussion of bases of power, see John R. P. French, Jr., and Bertram Raven, The bases of social power, in D. Cartwright and A. Zander, eds., *Group dynamics* (Evanston, Ill.,1960), pp.607–23.

6. John Thibaut and Harold H. Kelley, *The Social Psychology of Groups* (New York, 1959). For a similar emphasis on dependence, see Richard M. Emerson, Power-Dependence Relationships, *American Sociological Review*, Vol. 27 (1962), pp. 31–41.

7. Although this paper will not attempt to explain how access may be measured, the author feels confident that the hypotheses concerned with access are clearly testable.

8. *Op. cit.*

9. Max Weber, The essentials of bureaucratic organization: An ideal-type construction, in Robert Merton *et al., Reader in bureaucracy* (Glencoe, Ill., 1952), pp. 18–27.

10. Neal Gross, Ward S. Mason, and Alexander W. McEachern. *Explorations in role analysis* (New York, 1958).

11. Robert Merton. The role-set: Problems in sociological theory, *British Journal of Sociology*, Vol. 8, 106–20.

12. Erving Goffman. *Encounters* (Indianapolis, Ind., 1961), pp. 85–152.

13. Etzoni, *op. cit.*

14. *Ibid.*

15. Thomas J. Scheff. Control over policy by attendants in a mental hospital. *Journal of Health and Human Behavior*, Vol. 2 (1961). pp. 93–105.

16. Gresham M. Sykes. The corruption of authority and rehabilitation, in A. Etzioni, ed., *Complex organizations* (New York, 1961). pp. 191–97.

17. As an example, it appears that 6 members of the cabinet, 30 important sub-cabinet officials, 63 senators, and 230 congressmen are lawyers (*New Yorker*, April 14, 1962, p. 62). Although one can site many reasons for lawyers holding political posts, an important one appears to be their legal expertise.

18. There is considerable data showing the powerful effect of propinquity on communication. For summary, see Thibaut and Kelley, *op. cit.*, pp. 39–42.

19. The concept of centrality is generally used in a more technical sense in the work of Bavelas, Shaw, Gilchrist, and others. For example, Bavelas defines the central region of a structure as the class of all cells with the smallest distance between one cell and any other cell in the structure, with distance measured in link units. Thus the most central position in a pattern is the position closest to all others. Cf. Harold Leavitt, Some effects of certain communication patterns on group performance, in E. Maccoby, T. N. Newcomb, and E. L. Hartley (eds.). *Readings in social psychology* (New York, 1958), p. 559.

20. Alvin W. Gouldner, *Patterns of industrial bureaucracy* (Glencoe, Ill., 1954).
21. *Ibid.,* p. 173.
22. Scheff, *op. cit.*
23. *Ibid.,* p. 97.
24. Gouldner, *op. cit.*

How to Prevent Organizational Dry Rot

John W. Gardner

Like people and plants, organizations have a life cycle. They have a green and supple youth, a time of flourishing strength, and a gnarled old age. We have all seen organizations that are still going through the diseases of childhood, and others so far gone in the rigidities of age that they ought to be pensioned off and sent to Florida to live out their days.

But organizations differ from people and plants in that their cycle isn't even approximately predictable. An organization may go from youth to old age in two or three decades, or it may last for centuries. More important, it may go through a period of stagnation and then revive. In short, decline is not inevitable. Organizations need not stagnate. They often do, to be sure, but that is because the arts of organization renewal are not yet widely understood. Organizations can renew themselves continuously. That fact has far-reaching implications for our future.

We know at least some of the rules for organizational renewal. And those rules are relevant for all kinds of organizations—U.S. Steel, Yale University, the U.S. Navy, a government agency, or your local bank.

The first rule is that the organization must have an effective program for the recruitment and development of talent. People are the ultimate source of renewal. The shortage of able, highly trained, highly motivated men will be a permanent feature of our kind of society; and every organization that wants its share of the short supply is going to have to get out and fight for it. The organization must have the kind of recruitment policy that will bring in a steady flow of able and highly motivated individuals. And it cannot afford to let those men go to seed, or get sidetracked or boxed in. There must be positive, constructive programs of career development. In this respect, local, state, and federal government agencies are particularly deficient, and have been so for many years. Their provisions for the recruitment and development of talent are seriously behind the times.

The second rule for the organization capable of continuous renewal is that it must be a hospitable environment for the individual. Organizations that have killed the spark of individuality in their members will have greatly diminished their capacity for change. Individuals who have been made to feel like cogs in the machine will behave like cogs in the machine. They will not produce ideas for change. On the contrary, they will resist such ideas when produced by others.

The third rule is that the organization must have built-in provisions for self-criticism. It must have an atmosphere in which uncomfortable questions can be asked. I would lay it down as a basic principle of human organization that the individuals who hold the reins of power in any enterprise cannot trust themselves to be adequately self-critical. For those in power the danger of self-deception is very great, the danger of failing to see the problems or refusing to see them is ever-present. And the only protection is to create an atmosphere in which anyone can speak up. The most enlightened top executives are well aware of this. Of course, I don't need to tell those readers who are below the loftiest level of management that even with enlightened executives a certain amount of prudence is useful. The Turks have a proverb that says, "The man who tells the truth should have one foot in the stirrup."

But it depends on the individual executive. Some welcome criticism, others don't. Louis Armstrong once said. "There are some people that if they don't know, you can't tell 'em."

The fourth requirement for the organization that seeks continuous renewal is fluidity of internal structure. Obviously, no complex modern organization can exist without the structural arrangements of divisions, branches, departments, and so forth. I'm not one of those who imagine that the modern world can get away from specialization. Specialization and division of labor are at the heart of modern organization. In this connection I always recall a Marx Brothers movie in which Groucho played a shyster lawyer. When a client commented on the dozens of flies buzzing around his broken-down office, Groucho said, "We have a working agreement with them. They don't practice law and we don't climb the walls."

But jurisdictional boundaries tend to get set in concrete. Pretty soon, no solution to a problem is seriously considered if there is any danger that it will threaten juridictional lines. But those lines aren't sacred. They were established in some past time to achieve certain objectives. Perhaps the objectives are still valid, perhaps not. *Most organizations have a structure that was designed to solve problems that no longer exist.*

The fifth rule is that the organization must have an adequate system of internal communication. If I may make a rather reckless generalization, I'd say that renewal is a little like creativity in this respect—that it depends on the existence of a large number of diverse elements in a situation that permits an infinite variety of combinations and recombinations. The enormous potentialities of the human brain are in part explainable in terms of such possibilities for combination and recombination. And such recombination is facilitated by easy communication, impeded by poor communication.

The sixth rule: The organization must have some means of combating the process by which men become prisoners of their procedures. The rule book grows fatter as the ideas grow fewer. Thus almost every well-established organization is a coral reef of procedures that were laid down to achieve some long-forgotten objective.

It is in our nature to develop an affection for customary ways of doing things. Some years ago a wholesale firm noted that some of its small shopkeeper customers were losing money because of antiquated merchandising methods. The firm decided that it would be good business to assit the shopkeepers in bringing their methods up-to-date, but soon discovered that many had no desire to modernize. They loved the old, money-losing ways.

Sometimes the organization procedures men devise to advance their purposes serve in the long run to block those purposes. This was apparent in an experience a friend of mine had in Germany in the last days of World War II. He was in Aachen, which had only recently been occupied by the American forces, when he received a message instructing him to proceed to London immediately. He went directly to U.S. Army headquarters, and showed the message to a sergeant in the Adjutant's office.

The sergeant said that the only plane for London within the next few days was leaving from the nearest airfield in thirty minutes. He added that the airfield was twenty-five minutes away.

It was discouraging news. My friend knew that he could not proceed to London without written orders, and that was a process that took from an hour to a couple of days in a well-established and smoothly functioning headquarters. The present headquarters had been opened the day before, and was in a totally unorganized state.

My friend explained his dilemma to the sergeant and handed over his papers. The sergeant scratched his head and left the room. Four minutes later he returned and said, "Here are your orders, sir."

My friend said he had never been in such an efficient headquarters. The sergeant looked at him with a twinkle in his eye and said, "Sir, it's just lucky for you we weren't organized!"

The seventh rule: The organization capable of continuous renewal will have found some means of combating the vested interests that grow up in every human institution. We commonly associate the term "vested interests" with people of wealth and power, but in an organization vested interests exist at every level. The lowest employees have their vested interests, every foreman has his, and every department head has his. Every change threatens someone's privileges, someone's authority, someone's status. What wise managers try to do, of course, is to sell the idea that in the long run everyone's overriding vested interest is in the continuing vitality of the organization itself. If that fails, everyone loses. But it's a hard message to get across.

Nowhere can the operation of vested interests be more clearly seen than in the functioning of university departments. There are exceptions, of course: some departments rise above their vested interests. But the average department holds like grim death to its piece of intellectual terrain. It teaches its neophytes a jealous devotion to the boundaries of the field. It assesses the significance of intellectual questions by the extent to which they can be answered without going outside the sacred territory. Such vested interests effectively block most efforts to reform undergraduate instruction.

The eighth rule is that the organization capable of continuous renewal is interested in what it is going to become and not what it has been. When I moved to New London, Connecticut, in 1938 I was astonished at the attitude of New Londoners toward their city's future. Having grown up in California, I was accustomed to cities and towns that looked ahead habitually (often with an almost absurd optimism). I was not prepared for a city that, so far as I could discover, had no view of its future, though it had a clear view of its past.

The need to look to the future is the reason so many corporations today have research and development programs. But an organization cannot guarantee its future by ritualistic spending on research. Its research-and-development program must be an outgrowth of a philosophy of innovation that guides the company in everything it does. The research program, which is a way of looking forward, cannot thrive if the rest of the organization has the habit of looking backward.

The ninth rule is obvious but difficult. An organization runs on motivation, on conviction, on morale. Men have to believe that it really makes a difference whether they do well or badly. They have to care. They have to believe that their efforts as individuals will mean something for the whole organization, and will be recognized by the whole organization.

Change is always risky, usually uncomfortable, often painful. It isn't accomplished by apathetic men and women. It requires high motivation to break through the rigidities of the aging organization.

So much for the rules.

One of the ominous facts about growth and decay is that the present success of an organization does not necessarily constitute grounds for optimism. In 1909 it would have been unwise to judge the future of the Central Leather Company by the fact that it ranked seventh in the nation in total assets. It would have been a disastrous long-term investment. A better bet would have been the relatively small Ford Motor Company which had been founded only six years earlier and was about to launch its Model T. As a company it wasn't huge or powerful, but to borrow a phrase from C. P. Snow, it had the future in its bones. (Not many of 1909's top twenty companies did— only four of them are in the top twenty today.)

Businessmen are fond of saying that, unlike other executives, they have a clear measure of present performance—the profit-and-loss statement. But the profits of today *may* be traceable to wise decisions made a good many years earlier. And current company officers may be making bad decisions that will spell disaster ten years from now.

I have collected many examples of organizations that experienced crises as a result of their failure to renew themselves. In the great majority, certainly nine out of ten, the trouble was not difficult to diagnose and there was ample warning of the coming catastrophe. In the case of a manufacturing concern that narrowly averted bankruptcy recently, the conditions that led to trouble were diagnosed by an outside consultant two years before the crisis came. In the case of another well-known organization, a published article outlined every essential difficulty that later led to disaster.

But if warning signals are plentiful, why doesn't the ailing organization take heed? The answer is clear: most ailing organizations have developed a functional blindness to their own defects. They are not suffering because they can't *solve* their problems but because they won't *see* their problems. They can look straight at their faults and rationalize them as virtues or necessities.

I was discussing these matters with a corporation president recently, and he said, "How do I know that *I* am not one of the blind ones? What do I do to find out? And if I am, what do I do about it?"

There are several ways to proceed. One way is to bring in an outside consultant who is not subject to the conditions that create functional blindness inside the organization.

A more direct approach, but one that is surrounded by subtle difficulties, is for the organization to encourage its internal critics. Every organization, no matter how far deteriorated, has a few stubbornly honest individuals who are not blinded by their own self-interest and have never quite accepted the rationalizations and self-deceptions shared by others in the organization. If they are encouraged to speak up they probably will. The head of a government agency said to me recently, "The shrewdest critics of this organization are right under this roof. But it would take a major change of atmosphere to get them to talk."

A somewhat more complicated solution is to bring new blood into at least a few of the key positions in the organization. If the top level of the organization is salted with vigorous individuals too new to be familiar with all the established ways of doing and thinking, they can be a source of fresh insights for the whole organization.

Still another means of getting fresh insights is rotation of personnel between parts of the organization. Not only is the individual broadened by the experience, but he brings a fresh point of view to his new post. After a few years of working together, men are likely to get so used to one another that the stimulus of intellectual conflict drops almost to zero. A fresh combination of individuals enlivens the atmosphere.

In the last analysis, however, everything depends on the wisdom of those who shape the organization's policy. Most policy makers today understand that they must sponsor creative research. But not many of them understand that the spirit of creativity and innovation so necessary in the research program is just as essential to the rest of the organization.

The future of this nation depends on its capacity for self-renewal. And that in turn depends on the vitality of the organizations and individuals that make it up. Americans have always been exceptionally gifted at organizational innovation. In fact, some observers say that this is the true American inventiveness. Thanks to that inventiveness we now stand on the threshold of new solutions to some of the problems that have destroyed the vitality of human institutions since the beginning of time. We have already made progress in discovering how we may keep our institutions vital and creative. We could do even better if we put our minds to it.

Women and the Structure of Organizations: Explorations in Theory and Behavior

Rosabeth Moss Kanter

T HIS is an "organizational" society. The lives of very few of us
are untouched by the growth and power of large, complex organizations in the twentieth century. The consequences of decisions made
in these organizations, particularly business enterprises, may affect
the availability of goods and services, the distribution of wealth and
privilege, and the opportunity for meaningful work. The distribution
of functions within organizations affects the quality of daily life for a
large proportion of working Americans: their opportunities for growth
and self-expression, for good or poor health, as well as their daily social
contacts. The distribution of power within organizations affects who
benefits, and to what degree, from the things organizations make
possible, and whose interests are served by the organization's decisions. Despite a prevalent image in social science of modern organizations as universalistic, sex-neutral tools, sex is a very important
determinant of who gets what in and out of organizations.

The ways in which women have been connected to organizations
and have operated within them, and whether these ways differ from
those of men, have been underinvestigated in social research. While
there is a relatively large and growing literature that documents the
degree to which women are socialized to perform different kinds of
activities from men (often activities with less power and monetary

I wish to thank the following people for their critical comments and support: Nancy
Chodorow, Susan Eckstein, Joan Huber, Barry Stein, Chris Argyris, Zick Rubin,
William Form, William Torbert, Caroline Butterfield, and Joanna Hiss.

reward), there has been less attention paid to the patterned relationships between women and men in organizations.

This paper is an attempt to define directions for an enlarged understanding of the sociology of organizations as it concerns women, and of the study of women as it contributes to a more comprehensive and accurate sociology of organizations. The focus throughout is solely on the United States and largely on the administrative levels of business organizations. In part, this was an attempt to place limits on an area with a vast amount of literature. But it is also because the administrative issues of business tended to provide the impetus for the early sociology of organizations. Business organizations, additionally, have great power in American society and, because they are successful, are assumed to be successfully managed, so that their organization and management has often served as a model for other systems. It is also in business organizations that women seem most conspicuously absent from positions of prestige and power.

MANAGEMENT: A MALE CATEGORY

Women generally do not hold positions of power and authority in organizations, especially in American industry. Those few women in management tend to be concentrated in lower-paying positions, in selected fields, in staff rather than line positions, and in less powerful, less prestigious organizations. In 1969 U.S. Census figures indicate that women constituted only 3.25 percent of the managers and administrators earning over $15,000 per year (before taxes), and 2.26 percent of those earning over $30,000 per year. Women themselves may make the choice not to compete for managerial positions. Educated women, for example, tend not to enter fields that are linked to, and are preparation for, management. A substantially higher proportion of female college graduates than male become "professional, technical, and kindred" workers rather than managers and administrators, for instance (77.4 percent as opposed to 58.9 percent—Bureau of the Census, 1973a). Women with doctorates generally do not take them in management-related fields, as figures on earned doctorates in the United States between 1960 and 1969 indicate.[1]

At least a portion of the evidence that women earn less than men can be accounted for by the fact that women hold jobs carrying less pay even in well-paid fields like management. Bureau of Labor Statistics figures indicate that in 1970 the median annual earnings of female managers and administrators (excluding farm administration) were around half of that for men, even in fields such as school administration and wholesale/retail trade, where female administrators are clustered. A recent national personnel survey of 163 U.S. companies discovered that the farther up the management ladder, even scarcer are the women. In over half of the companies, women held only 2 percent or less of the first-level supervisory jobs (including such positions as manager of secretaries); in *three quarters* of the companies, women held 2 percent or fewer of the middle-management jobs; and in *over three quarters* of the companies, they held *none* of the top-management jobs (*Personnel Policies Forum*, 1971).

The few management women are also clustered in particular kinds of organizations. The *Personnel Policies Forum* survey found that women were proportionately more represented in management in nonbusiness rather than in business organizations, and, within business, in nonmanufacturing rather than in manufacturing enterprises. A 1965 *Harvard Business Review* survey of 1,000 male and 900 female executives (the men were drawn from the *HBR* readership, but there were so few women among top executives that separate lists had to be used to locate them) found women disproportionately represented in the management of retail/wholesale trade (merchandising fields) and advertising, whereas men were disproportionately represented in the management of banking/investment/insurance companies (financial concerns) and industrial goods manufacturing (Bowman, Worthy, and Greyser, 1965). (Calculations based on 1969 U.S. Census figures confirm the clustering of women managers in retail trade and services, including stenographic services, and men in manufacturing.[2]) The *HBR* respondents, further, felt that opportunities for women in management lie only in: education, the arts, social services, retail trade, office management, personnel work, and nonmanagement positions. One third of the respondents felt, as of 1965, that there were *no* opportunities for women in the management of labor unions; construction, mining, and oil companies; industrial goods manufacturing; production; and top management in general (Bowman, Worthy, and Greyser, 1965). The *HBR* survey is also suggestive of the concentration of women in staff positions, where they tend not to have authority over subordinates, or in low-status areas. Women in the *HBR* study were heavily represented in marketing and office management (39 percent and 10 percent of the female respondents, respectively, as opposed to 16 percent and 3 percent of the males, respectively) and underrepresented in general management (10 percent of the women, compared with 40 percent of the men falling into this category). Similarly, the women were disproportionately found in small (and hence less powerful or statusful) organizations.

These data suggest that women are virtually absent from the management of large industrial enterprises and present to only a slightly greater degree in the management of retail or business-support service organizations. Even in areas in which the workers are likely to be female, their managers are likely to be male. The number of male and of female bank tellers in the United States in 1969 was nearly equal, for example (255,549 men and 220,255 women), but "bank officers and financial managers" were largely male (82.48 percent male and 17.52 percent female). Office workers are largely female, yet office *managers,* a relatively low-status management position, are still more likely to be male than female (59.64 percent male, 40.36 percent female) (calculations based on figures of Bureau of the Census, 1973a).

We need to know the barriers to women in organizational leadership and also what difference their presence makes: how culture and behavior are shaped by the sex distribution of managers. The behavior and experiences of the few women in management and leadership positions should be considered as a function of membership in male-dominated settings. (Some of the findings of the few studies done to date are reported later.) The politics and informal networks of management as influenced by its male membership should be further studied—e.g., the degree to which managerial as well as worker behavior and culture is shaped in part by the traditions, emotions, and sentiments of male groups.[3] How the culture and behavior of management is affected by (or reflected in) the sex ratio of managers is also important (e.g., how retail or service organizations differ from manufacturers), as well as the influence of the sex composition of management on its relations with other organizational strata.

OFFICE WORK: FEMALE FUNCTION

Women are to clerical labor as men are to management. According to Census Bureau data, there were over 10 million female "clerical and kindred workers" in the United States in 1969, 73.78 percent of the total employed workers in this category. Men in the clerical labor force tend to be concentrated in a few, physically oriented occupations where they far outnumber women (computer operators, messengers, mail carriers, shipping and receiving clerks, and stock clerks). The rest of the occupations, the core of office work, are heavily female. Women comprised 82.14 percent of the bookkeepers, 81.84 percent of the billing clerks, 68.96 percent of the payroll and timekeeping clerks, and 82.08 percent of the file clerks. In secretarial and related functions, men are as underrepresented as women are in management. Women comprised 93.46 percent of the stenographers in 1969, 94.18 percent of the typists, 94.65 percent of the receptionists, and 97.71 percent of the secretaries. In fact, these four positions account for nearly 40 percent of the 1969 female "clerical and kindred workers"; secretaries alone account for 25 percent of the 1969 female clerical labor force (calculations based on Bureau of the Census, 1973a). Labor Bureau statistics for 1970, calculated on a slightly different basis, show even fewer men in such positions: of the category "stenographers, typists, and secretaries," 98.6 percent are female and only 1.40 percent are male (Bureau of Labor Statistics, 1971). *Work in America* (1972), a task force report to HEW, has concluded that the job of secretary is symbolic of the status of female employment, both qualitatively and quantitatively. Office jobs for women have low status, little autonomy or opportunity for growth, and generally low pay.

Women did not always dominate the clerical labor force; office work in the nineteenth century was first a male job. The same turn-of-the-century period (1890-1910) that brought large organizations and the growth of the professional manager also witnessed the emergence of the modern office, with its invention of new roles for women. The three-person office of midnineteenth-century Dickens novels was socially reorganized into departments and functional areas headed by office managers, and this change—itself a product of bureaucraticization and machine technology—permitted the massive introduction of office machines. Though invented in the 1870s, the typewriter was not widely used until the twentieth century; but from 1900-20, office employment rose dramatically, and typing soon became women's work (Mills, 1951:192-93).

The rise in the employment of women in the office around the turn of the century was dramatic, and it corresponded to a large decrease in "household occupations" (servants, dressmakers and seamstresses outside of factories, and laundresses). In 1870 the "clerical group" (clerks, stenographers, typists, bookkeepers, cashiers, and accountants) accounted for less than 1 percent of the women employed outside of agriculture; by 1920 it accounted for over 25 percent of female nonagricultural employment (Hill, 1929:39). In 1880 the proportion of women in the clerical labor force as a whole was 4 percent; in 1890, 21 percent (Davies, 1974). By 1910, women were already 83.2 percent of the stenographers and typists; by 1920, they were 91.8 percent of the stenographers/typists and 48.8 percent of the bookkeepers, cashiers, and accountants (Hill, 1929:56-57). Between 1910 and 1920 the number of female clerks (excluding store clerks) quadrupled; female stenographers and typists more than doubled (Hill, 1929:33). Slightly more women were still employed in factory than in clerical jobs in 1920 (about 1.8 million and 1.5 million, respectively), but less than 1 percent of those in industry could be classified as managers, superintendents, or officials (calculations based on Hill, 1929: Table 115). The growth of modern administration brought women into domination in the office but absent in management. Whereas factory jobs were divided between men and women (though often sex-typed), clerical jobs rapidly became the work almost exclusively of women.

To what extent was the nature of office work and the structural position of office workers in organizations shaped by the "feminization" of the clerical labor force? Did the nature of this organizational status come to be defined in sex-role-appropriate terms,[4] and did the emergent relations between office work and the management for which it was done reinforce the female caste of the former and the masculine caste of the latter? Did the sexual stratification of these two organizational categories constitute a barrier to mobility between them? Sociologists have tended to neglect these questions. Studies of the history of the office, the social relations it entailed, and the structural relations between and within categories of clerical and managerial personnel have generally not been included in studies of modern organizations (Miller, 1950:303; Crozier, 1965:15). (The few pioneering studies include C. Wright Mills' *White Collar* [1951], Nancy Morse [1953] on job satisfaction of white-collar workers, and Michel Crozier [1965] on Parisian insurance office workers. Margery Davies' work in progress [1974] considers the social implications of the feminization of the clerical labor force.)[5]

The secretary may be a prototypical and pivotal role to examine; research should consider the place of this job in the clerical hierarchy, its relations to management, and whether its role demands bar women from moving into management positions. Even though private secretaries represent only a small proportion of the female clerical labor force, this position is sometimes the highest to which a woman office worker may aspire—the best-paid, most prestigious, and for secretaries of executives, one with "reflected power" derived from the status of the manager. It is also the job in which there are the most clearly defined male-female relations—the private secretary has been called an "office wife" (Mills, 1951).[6] My field work in a large New York-based corporation indicates that the traditional secretary-manager relationship has striking parallels to Weber's definition of "patrimonial rule" (Bendix, 1960:425), even though this relationship occurs within organizations that social scientists have assumed generally fit Weber's "bureaucratic" model. The relationship can be defined as "patrimonial" to the extent that managers make demands at their own discretion and arbitrarily recruit secretaries on the basis of appearance, personality, and other subjective factors rather than on skill, expect personal service, exact loyalty, and make secretaries part of their private retinue (e.g., expecting them to move when they move). Further, secretaries in many large organizations may derive their status from that of their boss, regardless of the work they do; a promotion for a secretary may mean moving on to a higher-status manager, whether or not her work changes or improves.[7] There may be no job descriptions, as there are for managerial positions, that help match the person's skills to the job or insure some uniformity of demands across jobs, so that there are often no safeguards to exploitation, no standards for promotion other than personal relationships, and no way of determining if a secretary can be moved to another job (all barriers to mobility out of the secretarial ranks for women).[8] The relation of the secretarial work force to management may be one of status in addition to function; e.g., secretaries may be chosen for the status they give their bosses in having educated, attractive secretaries, whether or not their skills are utilized, and acquisition of a secretary may be a status symbol in its own right in many organizations, signifying a manager's importance.[9]

Within the organizational structure secretarial positions are probably the most dramatic example of the much larger issue of the relationships between sex-typed roles. But the whole problem has, nevertheless, been largely neglected in organization research. Let us turn to a re-examination of historical models of organizations to see why.

EARLY MODELS OF ORGANIZATIONS: MANAGERIALISM AND A "MASCULINE ETHIC"

The period 1890-1910 brought what Daniel Bell (1957) has called "the breakup of family capitalism"—the beginnings of corporate mergers and finance capitalism (through bank intervention), which increasingly took (at least daily) control out of the hands of owners and put it in the domain of professional managers of large organizations. In 1941 James Burnham maintained that the character of twentieth-century economic organizational life was determined by this "managerial revolution" (Burnham, 1941). Whether or not capital owners actually did fade into the background, a point of some dispute (see Zeitlin, 1974), the rise of large organizations created a new and growing profession, with an internal decision-making monopoly and authority over those within the organization.

The advantages, authority, and control of the newly prominent managers required explanation and justification (Bendix, 1956). The new career managers lacked a class position buttressed by tradition that would provide grounds for legitimation, seeking it instead in the increasing professionalization of management, in the development of a "spirit of managerialism" that gave ideological coherence to the control of a relatively small and exclusive group of men over a large group of workers.[10] A social science both of management and of organizations grew with the growth of large organizations. This early organization theory aided legitimation of managerialism in several ways; first, by accepting, more or less uncritically, management's definition of itself, its tasks, and its importance; second, by providing both concepts (through research and writing) and an academic base (through schools of administration) that confirmed the power and per-quisites of managers as well as educating them to managerial theory.[11]

The class origins of early-to-midtwentieth-century top-business management—largely white, Protestant men from elite schools—and the connections of such a social base with managerial ideologies have been rather extensively documented (Burnham, 1941; Miller, 1950, 1952; Warner and Abegglen, 1955; Sutton et al., 1956). Given the virtually all-male occupancy of these positions, it is worth examining whether sexual status, in conjunction with class and ethnicity, was also reflected in managerial ideologies and models of organization, thus helping solidify the already apparent sex stratification of organizations.

A "masculine ethic" of rationality and reason can be identified in the early image of managers. This "masculine ethic" elevates the traits assumed to belong to men with educational advantages to necessities for effective organizations: a tough-minded approach to problems; analytic abilities to abstract and plan; a capacity to set aside personal, emotional considerations in the interests of task accomplishment; and a cognitive superiority in problem-solving and decision-making. These characteristics were assumed to belong to management in two early models of organizations. This view both supported managerial authority and served as intellectual blindfolds, limiting the utility of the models for social research.

RATIONAL MODELS

Social science first came to define modern organizations as rational instruments oriented to the attainment of specific goals, in which the unequal distribution of authority aided efficiency. (The classical "rational" models have already been criticized from a variety of perspectives, so that few social scientists today would actually agree to such limited definitions of organizations. See especially Argyris, 1957, 1972, 1973.)

During the same turn-of-the-century period that generated the growth of large organizations and professional management, Frederick I. Taylor introduced his theories of "scientific management" (the label was applied by Louis D. Brandeis in 1910) to American audiences, becoming a business consultant and prime creator of "classical" administrative theory. Taylor's premise was the application of the systematic analysis of science to management methods, emphasizing routines, order, logic, production planning, and cost analysis (Taylor, 1947; Tillett, Kempner, and Wills, 1970). His ideas influenced task specialization, time-and-motion studies, and assembly-line philosophies. Taylor's work also supported professional management at a time when unions were gaining in strength and employers were waging militant antiunion campaigns (Cochran, 1957). Taylor separated technical ability to perform a limited task from cognitive ability to abstract, plan, and logically understand the whole process; the latter was the special ability of management. Later Chester Barnard (1938) modified the idea of rationality; his conception of the rational organization was based on information and decisions rather than on routines and the orderly structuring of positions. He stressed communication (including informal channels) rather than hierarchy per se, but the need for a class of decisionmakers was clear. Goals were the special responsibility of the manager, whose functions included abstract generalizing and long-range planning. Authority was a necessary by-product of these decision-making functions (Tillett, Kempner, and Wills, 1970). (Herbert Simon has continued this tradition.)

Early organization theory thus developed rationality as the central ideal of formal organizations and hierarchy as the central structural principle. Organizations were considered tools for generating rational decisions and plans. Workers were motivated to participate on utilitarian grounds and could contribute specific skills, but the real effectiveness of the organization was seen to lie in the efforts of management to design the best way for individuals to fit together in an overall scheme. The rationality of the formal organization was thought to arise not so much from the nature of its participants as from the superiority of its plan, but the plan depended on rational decisionmakers. The design could minimize the nonrational, efficiency-undermining features of human beings to the extent that the participants consented to authority up the line. The very design of organizations thus was oriented toward, and assumed to be capable of, suppressing irrationality, personality, and emotionality, and people who had these unfortunate characteristics were devalued and kept from influencing the otherwise flawless machine. For Weber this gave bureaucratic organizations their advantage of efficiency over other types of corporate groups; bureaucracy was the truly "passionless" organization (Gerth and Mills, 1958:215-16).[12]

The development of the classical rational model limited research and theory in several directions. The model assumed that it was possible to design or engineer efficient structures, given specific, measurable goals. In emphasizing the goal-directed features of modern organizations, a consideration that in itself posed analytic difficulties,[13] it in turn focused attention on the visible, public-role players, the officials with the power to "speak for" and decide for the organization. The focus on goals in part legitimized managerial authority on other than political grounds, for managers were conceptualized as the keepers of the "goals," while workers were seen as free to act in terms of their own self-interest alone. An extension of the concern with goals and measures of output and efficiency was that the relative importance of sectors of an organization were seen in terms of their connection with the specific goals and/or production plans, and that segments of the system contributing in other ways—e.g., internal service or maintenance—were generally ignored in analysis. Given the concentration of women in such maintenance-support functions as office work, it was likely that the position of women and other such workers, the demands of their roles, their particular structural situation, and their contribution to the system would be under-examined, as indeed these issues have been in the organizational literature. Much research in the rational-model tradition emphasizes either structural design features or systems analyses of such issues as communication channels and horizontal and vertical linkages. Wider issues of organizational stratification, as opposed to narrower issues of the number and types of positions and their direct linkages, were generally not considered. Finally, the classical model also supported managerial authority and a masculine ethic of rationality. While organizations were being defined as sex-neutral machines, masculine principles were dominating their authority structures.

HUMAN-RELATIONS MODELS

The 1930s and 1940s gave rise to another model of organizations. A group of researchers working with Elton Mayo at Harvard Business School, beginning in the mid-1920s, discovered the importance for productivity of primary, informal relations among workers in the Hawthorne experiments (discussed later in this article; see also Roethlisberger and Dickson, 1939; Mayo, 1933).[14] This generated the concept of "informal organization" to include the emotional, non-rational, and sentimental aspects of human behavior in organizations, the ties and loyalties that affected workers. "Formal organization" came to refer to those features studied by the classical model, i.e., the organizational pattern designed by management: positions, functions, division of labor, relationships as defined by the organization chart, distribution of material rewards and privileges, and the official rules; "informal organization" to the social relations developed among workers beyond the formal ones given by the organization or to the actual behavior resulting from working relations rather than rote obedience to official rules (see Etzioni, 1964:40). The human-relations model assumed that people were motivated by social as well as economic rewards and that their behavior and attitudes were a function of group memberships. The model emphasized the roles of participation, communication patterns, and leadership style in effecting organizational outcomes.

While introducing social considerations and focusing on the human side of organizations, the human-relations analysts supported the concept of managerial authority and managerial rationality. In Mayo's view, workers were controlled by sentiment, emotion, and social instincts, and this phenomenon needed to be understood and taken into account in organizational functioning. Managers, on the other hand, were rational, logical, and able to control their emotions in the interests of organizational design (Mayo, 1933:122). Though the emphasis on informal, social factors could not be further from the factors considered important by scientific management, the view of the role of management in an organization was strikingly similar (Bendix, 1956:312). If the human-relations school's metaphor was the "family" rather than the "machine" of classical models, the organization was still thought to require a rational controller at its head. A consequence of this perspective, Reinhard Bendix has indicated, was a simplified version, which viewed the successful manager as the man who could control his emotions, whereas workers could not. Bendix quotes a 1947 management manual: "He [the leader] knows that the master of men has physical energies and skills and intellectual abilities, vision and integrity, and he knows that, above all, the leader must have emotional balance and control. The great leader is even-tempered when others rage, brave when others fear, calm when others are excited, self-controlled when others indulge" (Bendix, 1956:332). He found a strikingly similar description of the superiority of the manager lying in the manager's ability to control his emotions, in a 1931 volume. One does not have to look too far beyond such statements for the basis of the viewpoint of some managers in a 1965 survey that women were "temperamentally unfit" for management because they are too emotional (Bowman, Worthy, and Greyser, 1965).

Further, the literature on informal organization derived from the human-relations model, though introducing "non-rational" elements into organizational behavior, in practice turned out largely to *support* the rational bias of the formal system. Roethlisberger and Dickson as well as Warner and Low distinguished in their writing between the managerial elite's logic of efficiency and the workers' logic of sentiment. Informal organization was studied more often among workers or between workers and supervisor, leaving the impression that only workers have informal ties—managers do not (see Gouldner, 1959:407). There seems to be some support in the human-relations model, too, then, for managerial authority and the association of characteristics of the "masculine ethic" with management.

Research and theory based on the human-relations model proved limited in other ways. They tended to focus on informal work group relations in an abstract sense—independent of task, functional, or structural relationship to other organizational units, power and status outside of the group, or historical/cultural backdrop. Thus, many studies considered to be organizationally relevant were conducted in the laboratory in artificial situations rather than in the field. Findings about group cohesion, or leaders and subordinates, for example, were assumed to be generalizable over large numbers of kinds of groups, regardless of the complexities of the structural situations in which relationships in real organizations might be embedded.

Such, then, was the historical legacy of American organization theory. The early rational and human-relations models tended to support a managerial viewpoint that, in turn, can be seen to have latent functions as a "masculine ethic," congruent with the nearly exclusively male occupancy of the newly prominent careers in management and administration. The focus on managerial rationality could also justify the absence of women—the bearers of emotion—from power. At the same time, these leanings of traditional organization theory also had intellectual consequences, limiting its analytic perspective. Larger issues of organizational structure and stratification and their relation to social placement in the larger society, the differential distributions of men and women, and the consequences of these for organizational behavior—these questions were largely unnoticed. If the status quo of power in organizations and women's disadvantaged position was supported, it was as much because of intellectual blinders as because of deliberate intent. Theorists did not necessarily *want* to neglect women or keep them in their place, but the theorists tended not to see them because of the limits of the early models, and the theorists tended to assume that women were doing just what they ought to be doing: the office housework.

A STRUCTURALIST PERSPECTIVE
ON WOMEN AND ORGANIZATIONS

It is now time for use of a newer, more eclectic and integrated model, one that *can* examine structural issues in organizations and their consequences for behavior. This more recent model, which Amitai Etzioni has termed "structuralist" (1964:41) (though it also encompasses the work of Argyris, Katz and Kahn, neo-Marxists, and others), addresses itself to the weaknesses of the earlier theories and is capable of offering enlarged understanding of women's position and behavior in organizations. A structuralist perspective views the organization as a large, complex social unit in which many groups interact. These groups are defined both by their formal (task-related, functional) and informal connections and differentiations. The relative number and power of such organizational groupings, their tasks, and the ways in which they come into contact shape the nature of the organization. Groups may comprise different strata, like different social classes, with interests and values potentially in conflict, and integration between them limited by the potential for conflicts of interest. Those with power wield it in the interests of their own group as well as perhaps in the interests of the system as a whole (though in this model it is often difficult to define such collective interests). Self-interest, including material self-interest, is considered as potentially important as social needs, so that the formation of relationships should be seen in the more political sense of advantage to the person as well as in the human-relations sense of social satisfaction. Further, people are viewed as members of groups outside as well as inside of the organization, which both help to place them within the organization, give them status, define their involvement with it, and may or may not articulate with the organization's interests. Finally, the tasks of the organization and the tasks of those within it (the division of labor) are important because they define the number, interests, and relative arrangements of organizational classes as well as how informal relations may articulate with formal ones.

The "sex typing" of occupations and professions is relatively well known—the fact that many occupations are nearly exclusively filled by members of one sex and come to have a "gender," to be described in sex-role-appropriate terms. But to fully describe the position and behavior of women (and men) in organizations, we must understand not only their typical occupations (e.g., manager and secretary) but how these are *related* to one another and to the larger context of the organization as a social structure. Occupations carry with them membership in particular organizational classes. Each class may have its own internal hierarchy, political groupings and allegiances, interactional rules, ways of coming into contact with other classes, promotion rules, culture, and style, including demeanor and dress.[15] In many organizations, managers and clerical workers, for example, constitute two separate organizational classes, with separate hierarchies, rules, and reward structures, and practically no mobility between them. The managerial elite has the power and a group interest in retaining it. The position of clerical workers, on the other hand, is often anomalous: in contact with the organizational elite, dependent on, and in service to it, thus facilitating identification with it, but similar to other workers in subordination, lack of autonomy, and subjugation to routine (Crozier, 1965).

The economic concept of an "internal labor market" (Doeringer and Piore, 1971) is applicable here. When women enter an organization, they are placed not only in jobs but in an opportunity structure. Internal allocation of personnel is governed by hiring, promotion, and layoff rules within each structure, as well as by "suitability," as defined by the customs of each separate workplace. And ability in one workplace is not always transferable to others; what leads to success in one may even be dysfunctional for mobility into another. The rules of the internal labor market, Doeringer and Piore theorize, may vary from rigid and internally focused to highly responsive to external economic forces; rules also vary among organizational strata. They argue, for example, that there is a tendency for managerial markets, in contrast with other internal labor markets, to span more than one part of a company, to carry an implicit employment guarantee, and to reward ability rather than seniority (1971:3). But women participate in a different labor market than men, even within the same organization. Their "typical jobs" in the office carry with them not only sex-role demands but also placement in a class and hierarchy that itself limits mobility into positions of power.

The issue, thus, is not a mere division of labor between women and men but a difference of organizational class, at least on the administrative levels of modern organizations. Simplistically, women are part of a class rewarded for routine service, while men compose a class rewarded for decision-making rationality and visible leadership, and this potential membership affects even those found outside their own sexual class. This phenomenon constitutes the structural backdrop for an understanding of the organizational behavior of women and men.

Even though it is largely ignored in the organizational behavior literature, sex can be seen to be an important variable affecting the lives of groups, given the significant differences in the positions and power of women and men in society and in organizations. The sexual composition of a group appears to have impact on behavior around issues of power and leadership, aspirations, peer relations, and the relative involvement visibility or isolation/invisibility of members.

SEX AND ORGANIZATIONAL BEHAVIOR: FEMALE AND MALE SINGLE-SEXED GROUPS

Does a group of women behave differently from a group of men? The situations in which women and men find themselves are often so different that common-sense observation indicates a difference in both themes and process. Organizational research, on the other hand, has generally treated all groups of participants or workers alike, for the most part not distinguishing sex as a variable, and therefore implicitly assuming that gender does not make a difference in organizational behavior—reinforcing the mistaken idea that modern organizational life is universalistic and sex-neutral. Yet, even in the classic study that first discovered the importance of small, primary groups in worker behavior and opened the study of human relations in organizations, the sex of the groups studied varied and may have contributed to the different sets of specific findings. The experiments at the Hawthorne plant of Western Electric in the late 1920s and early 1930s developed the concept of informal organization by indicating how important a role the small group might play in worker productivity (cf. Roethlisberger and Dickson, 1939). These researchers have been examined and re-examined for all possible explanations of the findings, including, recently, operant conditioning (Parsons, 1974); sex composition is, to my knowledge, not mentioned among them. Three small groups were studied. In two sets of conditions, the Relay Assembly Test Room and the Mica Splitting Test Room, workers encouraged each other in raising productivity and believed that their efforts would be rewarded. In the third, the Bank Wiring Observation Room, workers developed an informal system that discouraged "rate busting" and kept productivity at an even keel, partly out of a mistrust in management— the belief that increased productivity would result in higher expectations, not higher rewards. There were differences among the three sets of conditions in size of group (fourteen in the third, vs. five or six in the first and second, depending on how the team is counted), nature of the task (a large number of units processed by individuals in the first two conditions, a small number of units in the third), experimental manipulations (like rest pauses), and "laboratory" vs. "natural" working conditions. But another striking difference is sex. The first two sets of groups, co-operative and trusting of management, were all female. The third, counterdependent, aggressively controlling, and suspicious, was all-male.

There is also evidence, if we reinterpret other studies not explicitly focused on sex, that women in female groups may be more oriented toward immediate relationships than men in male groups. Several studies of male professionals in organizations found a correlation between professionalism and a "cosmopolitan" rather than a local orientation. The exception was a study of nurses by Warren Bennis and colleagues. In this *female* group, the more professionally oriented nurses "did not differ from others in their loyalty to the hospital, and they were *more* apt than others, not less, to express loyalty to the local work group" (Blau and Scott, 1962:69). While Blau and Scott conclude that this is due to the limited visibility of the nurses' professional competence, other evidence indicates that this finding is consistent with a sex-linked interpretation. Constantini and Craik (1972) found, for example, that women politicians in California were oriented intraparty and locally rather than toward higher office, as men were.

Other evidence confirms that women in organizations, especially in the clerical class, limit their ambitions, prefer local and immediate relationships, and orient themselves to satisfying peer relationships. In a study of values of 120 occupational groups, secretaries, the only female group studied, were unique in placing their highest priorities on such values as security, love, happiness, and responsibility (Sikula, 1973). Female game-playing strategy in several laboratory studies was accommodative, including rather than excluding, and oriented toward others rather than toward winning, whereas the male strategy was exploitative and success-oriented (Vinacke, 1959; Uesugi and Vinacke, 1963). All-female group themes in a comparison of single-sex and mixed laboratory groups included affiliation, family, and conflicts about competition and leadership, self, and relationships, in contrast to the male themes: competition, aggression, violence, victimization, practical joking, questions of identity, and fear of self-disclosure (Aries, 1973). An earlier study compared all-male with all-female groups and found *no* significant differences in nine different conditions *except* persuasibility (higher in female groups) and level of aspiration (higher in male groups) (Cattell and Lawson, 1962).

In attitudinal studies distinguishing factors motivating increased performance as opposed to those merely preventing dissatisfaction ("hygiene" factors), attitudes toward interpersonal relations with peers constituted the only variable differentiating men and women.

(The women in two studies included those in both high-level and low-level jobs.) For woman, peer relationships were a motivational factor, whereas for men they were merely a hygiene factor (Davis, 1967:35-36). Structural factors can explain this. My field research in progress on a large New York-based corporation indicates that peer relations affect a woman's decision not to seek promotion into managerial ranks, where she will no longer be part of a group of women; for men, of of course, peer relations are a given throughout managerial ranks, and therefore, perhaps, more easily "taken for granted."

Other differences in male and female behavior in single-sex settings fail to be consistently demonstrated, as the Cattell and Lawson (1962) research, above, indicates. (See also Mann, 1959.) In studies of sex differences in the "risky shift," for example (the tendency for groups to make riskier decisions than individuals), there were *no* significant differences between male and female college students in initial conservatism or in the shift to risky decisions in the single-sex groups (Wallach, Kogan, and Bem, 1968). Organizational comparisons are rare, but Crozier's data on forty groups of French office workers revealed no difference in an atmosphere between male and female work groups; both kinds of groups showed the same wide range (1965:111).

Thus it is reasonable to hypothesize that groups of women differ from groups of men primarily in orientations toward interpersonal relationships and level of aspiration. One might interpret this as consistent with the training of women for family roles and thus label it a sex-linked attribute. But such orientations could also be seen as *realistic responses* to women's structural situation in organizations, of the kinds of opportunities and their limits, of the role demands in the organizational strata occupied by women, and of the dependence of women on relationships for mobility.

MIXED-SEX GROUPS

When men and women are together, in roughly equal numbers, as peers, tensions may emerge, and the behavior of each sex may be influenced. In Aries' laboratory study, people in two cross-sex groups were more tense, serious, self-conscious, and concerned with hetero-sexual attractiveness than those in the same-sex groups. Women generally spoke less than men (Aries, 1973). The sexual questions and "crosscultural" issues that can arise in mixed-sex groups are useful explanations for their tensions; William Foote Whyte has hypothe-sized, extrapolating from studies of the ethnic composition of groups, that "other things being equal, a one-sex work group is likely to be more cohesive" than a mixed-sex group (1961:511). Crozier's Parisian study found male-female conflicts when men and women worked in the same office (1965:110).

In addition to sexual and cultural issues, there are also status and power issues when men and women interact, a function of the structural positions and organizational class memberships of the sexes. Much social psychological research has indicated the importance of power and status in determining behavior in groups: e.g., those low in power tend to engage in more approval seeking, while those high in power engage in more influence attempts; those in low-status positions tend to communicate upward in a hierarchy, a form of "substitute locomotion" or "vicarious mobility." The differential behavior of the more and less powerful coincides with the observed group behavior of men and women. A field experiment tested more specifically the effects of high and low power on group relations, using thirty-two six-person groups at a one-day professional conference. Participants were labeled high-power or low-power on the basis of the prestige of their occupations, assumed to correlate with ability to influence. While the authors do not report the sex distribution of participants, it is likely from occupational sex-typing that men were found more often in the high-power category (psychiatrists, psychologists) and women in the low-power category (nurses, social workers, teachers). The researchers found that "highs" were liked more than "lows"; "highs" liked "lows" less than they liked other "highs"; "highs" talked more often than "lows"; "lows" communicated more frequently to "highs" than to other "lows"; and the amount of participation by "lows" was consistently overrated, as though people felt the "lows" talked too much (Hurwitz, Zander, and Hymovitch, 1968).

The interpretation is straightforward. In mixed groups of "peers," men and women may not, in fact, be equal, especially if their external statuses and organizational class memberships are discrepant. The resulting behavior, including frequency of participation, leadership, and conformity, may reflect status and power differences more than sex-linked personality traits.

THE EFFECTS OF SKEWED SEX RATIOS: THE LONE WOMAN IN THE MALE GROUP

The dynamic of interaction in settings with highly skewed sex ratios—numerical dominance by members of one sex and a "lone" or nearly alone member of the other sex—also deserves attention; in management and some professions, women are often one of very few women in a group of men. This makes "sex status" as important for interaction as occupational status (Epstein, 1970:1952).

Skewed sex ratios lend themselves, first, to cases of "mistaken identity"—to incorrect attributions. Lone women in male settings are sometimes initially misperceived as a result of their statistical rarity. The men with whom they come into contact may make a judgment about what a woman is doing in that particular situation, based on reasoning about the probabilities of various explanations, and may act toward her accordingly. This can be called "statistical discrimination" (Council of Economic Advisers, 1973:106), to distinguish it from prejudice; that is, an unusual woman may be treated as though she resembles women on the average. This may be the case every time someone assumes a female manager answering the telephone or sitting in an office is a secretary (cf. examples in Lynch, 1973; Epstein, 1970:191). Given the current occupational distribution, that person is likely to be correct a high proportion of the time. But the woman in question may still feel unfairly treated, as indeed she is, and there may be awkward exchanges while the woman's true identity is established.[16]

Attributions may also be made about the lone woman's expected informal role. These attributions put the woman in her place without challenging the male culture of the group. Field observations of lone women in male-dominated groups (including business meetings, academic conferences, sales training programs, and postprofessional training groups) have distinguished four kinds of roles attributed to lone women in male groups: "mother"; "sex object" or "seductress"; "pet" (group mascot); and "iron maiden" (militant and unapproachable) (Kanter, 1975). Such attributed roles affect both what the men in the group expect of the woman and how they interpret what she does. For her, the pressure is to confine her behavior to the limits of the role, whether or not it expresses her competence. Indeed, the roles provide a measure of security and uncertainty-reduction for some women, while others may devote time to struggling against the implications of the attributions. In either case, a woman's behavior in a situation like this is less likely to reflect her competencies, and it may take her longer to establish them, than at other times, when she is not a statistical rarity.

Several hypotheses are suggested. When a person is a statistical rarity, it may take her/him *more time* to untangle mistaken identities and establish a competence-based working relationship, particularly with members of the numerically dominant category. This may, in turn, generate a preference for minimizing change in work relations with peers, superiors/subordinates, or clients. As Epstein argues, "status discrepancies make continuous role definition necessary during interactions that should be routine" (1970:194). Margaret Cussler's sample of female executives in the 1950s suggests that this hypothesis may have some validity, for the women apparently changed work situations much less often than would be expected of male counterparts. Thus there may be a longer time-span for the establishment of competence-based relationships and a conservatism about changing relationships among "lone" women in male-dominated organizations.

Isolation and invisibility, self- as well as group-imposed, are often consequences of status as a lone woman in an otherwise all-male collectivity. In one study, six small training groups with only one woman each in a group of eight to twelve men were observed: three sensitivity training groups for business school students, and three work groups of psychiatric residents. In each case, the woman was eventually isolated, failed to become a leader or ally herself with the emergent leaders, and was defined by the researchers as a "casualty" of the groups. The researchers felt that the six groups' productivity tended to be low, in part because of the problematic interactions around the solo woman (Wolman and Frank, 1975). While the results of this study should not be taken as definitive,[17] they do suggest directions for further inquiry.

The female executives studied by Margaret Hennig (1970) support the isolation hypothesis. They reported that their most difficult relationships were with male peers when they (the women) were in the early to middle career. The women had little contact or relationship with the men, tried to be unobtrusive or invisible, and practiced strategies of conflict avoidance, as did lone professional women in Cynthia Epstein's research (1970:176). Epstein also suggests that team membership may be harder for the lone woman among male professional peers than for a man, pointing to institutionalized isolation (such as barriers to membership in male clubs or associations) as well as interactional isolation. As a consequence, she proposes that women have been less likely to be successful in fields that require participation on a team of peers as opposed to individual activity (1970:175).

Lone women may reinforce their own isolation by a series of accommodative strategies. The limiting of visibility ("taking a low profile") is one such accommodation to and reinforcement of isolation. Hennig's respondents reported early career strategies of trying to minimize their sexual attributes so as to blend unnoticeably into the predominant male culture:

> You dressed carefully and quietly to avoid attracting attention; you had to remember to swear once in a while, to know a few dirty jokes, and never to cry if you got attacked. You fended off all attempts of men to treat you like a woman: you opened doors before they could hold them, sat down before a chair could be held, and threw on a coat before it could be held for you [Hennig, 1970: vi–21].

In other reports, lone women managers have also participated in the limiting of the visibility of their competence by not taking credit for accomplishments or letting someone else take the credit (Lynch, 1973; Cussler, 1958). Some women, in interviews, even expressed pride that they could influence a group of men without the men recognizing the origin of the idea, or they rejoiced in the secret knowledge that they were responsible for their boss's success. (These reports match the Megaree finding reported below that high-dominance women may let a man assume official leadership while strongly influencing the decision.) Epstein (1970) points out that, in general, on elite levels women have less-visible jobs than men, promote themselves less often, feel the need to make fewer mistakes, and try to be unobtrusive.

With another context in mind, Seymour Sarason (1973) has argued that members of minority groups who have succeeded may try to limit the visibility of that success in fear of reprisals from the majority-dominant group, which might not be aware of the minority's success and might take action against it if known. He has reported a prevalent feeling among Jews that statistics about the high percentage of Jews in elite colleges such as Yale, for example, should not be broadcast. A concern like this, rather than a female sex-linked characteristic, could account for the woman manager's acceptance of the invisibility of her achievements. In the case of lone women, the pressure to adopt this stance must be even greater because of attributes like modesty assigned to the female stereotype.

This analysis suggests a re-examination of the "fear of success" in women hypothesis. Perhaps what has been called fear of success is really fear of visibility. In the original research by Matina Horner (1968) that identified this concept, women responded to a hypothetical situation in which a woman was at the top of her class in medical school—presumably a lone woman in a male peer group. Such a situation is the kind that creates pressure for a woman to make herself and her achievements invisible. When similar research was conducted using settings in which a woman is not a statistical rarity, "fear of success" imagery was greatly reduced (Tresemer, 1973).

WOMEN AND LEADERSHIP

If it's hard to demonstrate competence as a woman among men, it may be even harder to exercise leadership, given the current sex-stratification patterns in organizations. It is still an open question whether there are major sex differences in leadership *style* (Crozier, 1956: 126, finds none); but the structural and interactional context is certainly different for women. Taking directives from a woman has been anathema to most men and some women. In a 1965 *Harvard Business Review* survey of 1,000 male and 900 female executives, over two thirds of the men and nearly one fifth of the women reported that they themselves would not feel comfortable working for a woman. Very few of either sex (9 percent of the men and 15 percent of the women) felt that *men* feel comfortable working for a woman; and a proportion of the male respondents said that women did not belong in executive positions. A total of 51 percent of the men responded that women were "temperamentally unfit" for management, writing comments such as, "They scare male executives half to death . . . . As for an efficient woman manager, this is cultural blasphemy . . . " (Bowman, Worthy, and Greyser, 1965).

Male resentment of taking orders from a woman influenced the work flow and the interaction between waitresses and countermen in the restaurants studied by William Foote Whyte during World War II, a classic of organizational analysis. There were several devices in one restaurant by which countermen could avoid direct contact with waitresses (and hence direct orders) or could make their own decisions about the order in which to prepare food and drinks, thus taking initiative and forcing the waitresses to wait. Orders were written on slips and placed on a spindle, and a warming compartment imposed a high barrier between the waitresses and the countermen, thus eliminating face-to-face interaction. In a restaurant without these equalizing devices, satisfaction was low, and there was constant wrangling. Whyte's explanation is simple: People of higher status (men) like to do the directing for people of lower status (women) and resent reversals (1961: 128).

Even if women have formal authority, then, they may not necessarily be able to exercise it over reluctant subordinates. Margaret Cussler's (1958) study of female executives provides several examples of this. In one case a woman had formal leadership of a group of men, but the men did not accept this, reporting informally to her male superior. The subordinates further met together at lunch to share information, excluding her. More formal meetings then developed, "conceived of by the woman as meetings of her staff, by the men as a mutual protection society for the interchange of ideas" (1958:76–77).

At the same time, women tend to assume visible leadership reluctantly, in keeping with the invisibility of the lone woman mentioned earlier. A creative laboratory study discovered that for women the situational context rather than a dominant personality tended to predict a woman's exercise of visible leadership. Same-sex and cross-sex dyads were paired by scores on a "dominance" measure and given a task in which one member had to lead and one to follow. Assumption of leadership by high-dominance women paired with a low-dominance man was significantly lower than in any other pairing. The greatest assumption of leadership by high-dominance subjects occurred when a high-dominance man was paired with a low-dominance woman; the high- and low-dominance single-sex pairings showed about the same intermediate distribution of leadership. However, in the situation in which a high-dominance woman was paired with a low-dominance man, the *woman* made the final decision of who was to be the leader more often than in any other group, 91 percent of the time *appointing the man*. The study suggests that men are not necessarily more "dominant" in character than women, but women are more reluctant to assume leadership, particularly when the subordinate is male (Megaree, 1969). The leadership strategies chosen by successful women executives in Hennig's research (1970) tend to confirm this kind of laboratory finding. The women tended to minimize the authoritative exercise of power and maximize subordinate autonomy and learning through delegation.

But a leader's style may be ultimately less important for the impact on his or her subordinates than another resource unequally distributed between the sexes: power outside of the immediate work group. Early theory in organizational behavior assumed a direct relation between leader behavior and group satisfaction and morale. However, Donald Pelz discovered in the early 1950s that perceived external power was an intervening variable. He compared high- and low-morale work groups to test the hypothesis that the supervisor in high-morale groups would be better at communicating, more supportive, and more likely to recommend promotion. Yet, when he analyzed the data, the association seemed to be nonexistent or even reversed. In some cases supervisors who frequently recommended people for promotion and offered sincere praise for a job well done had *lower* morale scores. The differentiating variable was whether or not the leader had power outside and upward: influence on his or her own superiors and how decisions were made in the department. The combination of good human relations *and* power was associated with high morale. Human-relations skills and low power (a likely combination for women leaders) sometimes had negative consequences (Pelz, 1952).

The implications for female leadership in organizations are significant. A woman's generally more limited power (partly a function of her rarity and isolation in management), as well as her similarity to a subordinate clerical class rather than the elite, may interfere with her effective exercise of leadership *regardless* of her own style and competence. This hypothesis also helps explain the greater resistance to working for a woman. It also may account for the evidence of the importance of a male sponsor in the success of women executives (Cussler, 1958; Hennig, 1970). A high-status man bringing the woman up behind him may provide the visible sign that the woman does have influence upward. While sponsors serve multiple functions (e.g., coaching and socialization in the informal routines) and are found in the careers of men, the "reflected power" they provide may be even more pivotal for women.

CONCLUSION: WOMEN AND THE
INFRASTRUCTURE OF ORGANIZATIONS

Women's places in organizations have largely had limited visibility and low status; they have been part of the unexamined infrastructure. When men and women interact in organizations, they often do it across barriers like that of social class; women's mobility has largely been restricted to the infrastructure. In this the women within organizations have a kinship with the "women's auxiliary" outside of it—the network of wives of managers and leaders that perform unpaid tasks, play unofficial but normatively expected roles for the organization, and whose behavior can potentially affect relations in the official organization (Kanter, 1974). Just as managers have a group of women behind them in the office, they do at home, for male managers are largely married to women not employed in the paid labor force.[18]

I have suggested a few of the issues surrounding the sexual structure of organizations and groups that deserve further attention— from the problems of token women to the nature of internal labor markets for managers or secretaries. The sexual division of broad administrative classes was solidified very early in the history of large corporations. But the nature of organizational life for these broad groupings and other occupational subgroups, and how their opportunities and interactions vary in different kinds of organizations (e.g., those with fewer barriers to leadership for women), still require investigation. The ideological underpinnings of modern organizations, such as the connection between a "masculine ethic" and a "spirit of managerialism," need further examination. To understand the structural conditions for men and women in organizations and the organizational behavior of men and women is critical for both social inquiry and social change.

References

1. Data are from HEW, via a University of Minnesota publication, reprinted by the Women's Equity Action League, Washington, D.C., in 1974. M.D.s and other professional doctorates are not included. Women earned 11.63 percent of the total doctorates reported, but only 2.82 percent of the doctorates in business and commerce (a total of 86 women in 10 years), 5 percent of those in hospital administration (1 woman out of 20 doctorates), and none of those in trade or industrial training. Women earned 11.10 percent of all the social science doctorates but only 4.17 percent of those in industrial relations and 8.13 percent of those in public administration.

2. Of the managers and administrators earning over $15,000 per year, 26.1 percent of the women vs. 17.2 percent of the men are in retail trade, 25.8 percent of the women vs. 8.5 percent of the men are in "professional and related services," and 12.2 percent of the women vs. 26.7 percent of the men are in manufacturing. Women represent 9.3 percent of the total managers in services but only 1.52 percent of the total in manufacturing. Calculations from Census Bureau (1973b).

3. Several popularized accounts treat management as an expression of the instincts of male hunting bands and make management, indeed, seem charged with masculine culture and traditions. See Tiger (1969) and Jay (1967, 1971).

4. Margery Davies (1974) discovered that a 1916 *Ladies' Home Journal* article was already glorifying the feminine traits of stenographers: radiating sympathetic interest, agreeableness, courtesy. In 1900, however, the same magazine was urging women to stay out of offices.

5. See also recent journalistic accounts by Garson (1973) and Langer (1970); on secretaries see Benet (1973) and Halter *et al.* (1973).

6. A New York corporation informant, a former executive secretary promoted into management, told me that leaving her boss was like getting a divorce. For the first four months of her new job, she stopped in to see him every morning and hung her coat in her old office.

7. A manager of clerical employees told me that sometimes promotions mean that secretaries have *less* work to do and have trouble justifying their larger salaries to their peers. As with marriage, if a woman has the good fortune to be connected with a high-status male, she gets more money and does less work.

8. The large corporation in my research, beginning to design "upward mobility" programs for women, has discovered secretarial work to be arbitrary and particularistic. The change effort includes generating job descriptions and decoupling a secretary's status from her boss's so that she will no longer derive rank from him or necessarily move with him when he moves.

9. A chatty advice-to-managers book (Burger, 1964) devotes a chapter to "living with your secretary," with whom, the book declares, a man spends more of his waking hours than with his wife. She is a status symbol: "In many companies, a secretary outside your door is the most visible sign that you have become an executive; a secretary is automatically assigned to each executive, whether or not his work load requires one . . . . When you reach vice-presidential level, your secretary may have an office of her own, with her name on the door. At the top, the president may have two secretaries . . . . 'Miss Amy, please take a letter,' are words which have inwardly thrilled every young executive with a sense of his own importance . . . they symbolize power and status" (Burger, 1964: 219, 220).

10. Even today management has legitimacy issues. The tasks of management are largely intangible, and the results of managerial efforts depend largely on products of the work of other people. Technical expertise, according to analysts from Chester Barnard on, plays only a small role; indeed, many sociologists assume an organizational conflict between expertise and authority—i.e., between professionals and managers. The necessity (in economic and social terms) for large cadres of managers has yet to be demonstrated definitively (cf. the conflicting results of the several studies in Heydebrand, 1974). Barry Stein (1974) has marshaled evidence to indicate that the presumed efficiencies of scale in large organizations are often instead inefficiencies, and administrative costs are one important cause. A recent study of 167 large corporations over a 20-year period concludes that much of the variance in sales, earnings, and profit margins can be explained by factors other than the impact of management (Lieberson and O'Connor, 1972). To some extent, then, management may still have the tasks of justifying its necessity, importance, numbers, and privileges, though of course management in the 1970s is already very different in character from management of earlier years.

A provocative analogy could be made between management and fatherhood: necessary for conception but not visibly connected to or necessary for production thereafter. The uncertainty of management's actual connection to the results is like the uncertainty of paternity—the biological father can never be definitively identified. Yet in both cases control and the product's legitimacy are vested in the paternal figure. (I am indebted to Nancy Jay for the insight about fatherhood.)

11. The first school of business at an American university was the Wharton School, founded in 1884 at the University of Pennsylvania. Management as a separate field was not introduced until decades later, at the Harvard Business School. The connection between theory and practice is especially great in this field. Many social scientists consult to industry and teach at schools of administration. A great deal of the early research on organizations was done at the invitation of management. Both Frederick Taylor and Chester Barnard, influential early- and middle-organization theorists, had backgrounds in industry, Barnard as president of New Jersey Bell. In Reinhard Bendix's (1956) analysis of the development of American managerial ideology, social science was seen as playing a role in feeding concepts to management justifying authority and defining distance from workers. Alvin Gouldner goes even farther in connecting social science with legitimation of managerial authority (1959:414-15).

12. Weber's notion of the virtues of bureaucracy's exclusion of passion converges interestingly with Freud's argument that women—the bearers of passion and sexuality—must be excluded from the workaday world of men. Women, Freud wrote in *Civilization and Its Discontents* (1930), are driven by emotion and incapable of suppressing or sublimating their passions and sexual instincts as men could. Further, since the work of men in civilized societies removed them from their homes and families, women become hostile to the male world of organizations, constantly trying to lure men away from their higher, reasoned pursuits. Resisting female enticements, men carry on the burdens of government and rational thought; rationality is the male principle, in opposition to the female principle of emotionality. Men master their sexuality, in the Freudian view, while women cannot. It would be interesting to study the convergences of Weber and Freud, not only on male and female principles in organization life but also on the origin and nature of authority.

13. The literature abounds with examples of the difficulties one encounters in the concept of organizational goals. According to familiar analyses, goals may be: unclear, undefined, utopian, or nonoperational; precarious; changeable, in a process of goal succession or changing external conditions; ignored and/or deflected. There may be multiple goals, unstated goals, professed vs. operating goals, "task" vs. "maintenance" goals, and subgroup goals. There may be conflicts about which goals are thought appropriate by various segments of the organization, depending on their organizational position, internal or external constituency, and primary reference group. And there may be a wide gap between the stated goals of an organization and its functions for members or for society. See also Etzioni (1964).

14. Mary Parker Follett was among the influential figures in generating this more human approach to management and one of the only important female organization theorists. Her interest in management grew out of her experience with the administration of social-welfare organizations.

15. In a discussion of labor women, Patricia Cayo Sexton defines dress and hair style as well as personal appearance as a barrier to upward mobility,

since the styles of labor women are very different from those of more elite women (1974:392-93). Informants in a corporation told me that there was a "caste" barrier between secretaries and professional women visible in style differences: e.g., secretaries wore platform shoes while professional women wore pumps.

16. Sometimes the categorical attributions have extreme and negative implications: e.g., a female manager having a drink with her boss and assumed by a neighbor to be his mistress (Lynch, 1973:136). In another example, a woman executive was the only female present at an executive cocktail party at a New York hotel, when a drunk male guest entered, accosted her, and tried to tear her clothes off, assuming she was a call girl (Lynch, 1973:137).

17. Aside from *post hoc* reasoning, one of the researchers, a woman, was also a group leader in some of the groups and does not discuss the impact of her own presence as another woman in a *powerful* position.

18. A total of 93.19 percent of the male managers earning $15,000 or more in 1969 were married; 72.25 percent of their wives were not in the paid labor force (Bureau of Census, 1973b).

Bibliography

Argyris, Chris. 1957. *Personality and Organization.* New York: Harper & Brothers. 1972. *The Applicability of Organizational Sociology.* New York: Cambridge University Press. 1973. "Some Limits of Rational Man Organization Theory," *Public Administration Review* May-June: 253-67.

Barnard, Chester I. 1938. *The Functions of the Executive.* Cambridge, Mass.: Harvard University Press.

Bell, Daniel. 1956. "Work and Its Discontents: The Cult of Efficiency in America," *The End of Ideology,* rev. ed. New York: Collier Books, 1961, pp. 227-72. 1957. "The Breakup of Family Capitalism," *The End of Ideology,* rev. ed. New York: Collier Books, 1961.

Bendix, Reinhard. 1956. *Work and Authority in Industry: Ideologies of Management in the Course of Industrialization.* New York: Harper & Row. 1960. *Max Weber: An Intellectual Portrait.* Garden City, New York: Anchor Books, 1962.

Benet, Mary Kathleen. 1973. *The Secretarial Ghetto.* New York: McGraw-Hill.

Blau, Peter M., and Scott, W. Richard. 1962. *Formal Organizations.* San Francisco: Chandler.

Bowman, G. W.; Worthy, N. B.; and Greyser, S. A. 1965. "Are Women Executives People?," *Harvard Business Review* 43 July-August: 14-30.

Bureau of the Census, U.S. 1973a. *Occupational Characteristics.* Washington, D.C.: U.S. Government Printing Office. 1973b. *Occupations of Persons with Higher Earnings.*

Bureau of Labor Statistics, U.S. 1971. *Handbook of Labor Statistics.* Washington, D.C.: U.S. Department of Labor.

Burger, Chester. 1964. *Survival in the Executive Jungle.* New York: Macmillan.

Burnham, James. 1941. *The Managerial Revolution.* New York: John Day.

Cattell, Raymond B., and Lawson, Edwin D. 1962. "Sex Differences in Small Group Performance," *The Journal of Social Psychology* 58:141-45.

Cochran, Thomas C. 1957. *The American Business System: A Historical Perspective, 1900-1955.* Cambridge, Mass.: Harvard University Press.

Constantini, Edmond, and Craik, Kenneth H. 1972. "Women as Politicians: The Social Background, Personality, and Political Careers of Female Party Leaders," *Journal of Social Issues* 28:217-36.

Council of Economic Advisers. 1973. *Annual Report of the Council of Economic Advisers.* Washington, D.C.: U.S. Government Printing Office.

Crozier, Michel. 1965. *The World of the Office Worker,* trans. David Landau. Chicago: University of Chicago Press, 1971.

Cussler, Margaret. 1958. *The Woman Executive.* New York: Harcourt, Brace.

Davies, Margery. 1974. "Woman's Place Is at the Typewriter: The Feminization of the Clerical Labor Force." Waltham, Mass.: Brandeis University Department of Sociology.

Davis, Keith. 1967. *Human Relations at Work.* New York: McGraw-Hill.

Doeringer, Peter B., and Piore, Michael J. 1971. *Internal Labor Markets and Manpower Analysis.* Lexington, Mass.: D.C. Heath.

Epstein, Cynthia Fuchs. 1970. *Woman's Place: Options and Limits on Professional Careers.* Berkeley: University of California Press.

Etzioni, Amitai. 1964. *Modern Organizations.* Englewood Cliffs, N.J.: Prentice-Hall.

Freud, Sigmund. 1930. *Civilization and Its Discontents,* trans. James Strachey. New York: Norton, 1962.

Garson, Barbara. 1973. "Women's Work," *Working Papers for a New Society* 1 Fall: 5-14.

Gerth, Hans, and Mills, C. Wright (eds.). 1958. *From Max Weber: Essays in Sociology.* New York: Oxford University Press.

Gouldner, Alvin W. 1959. "Organizational Analysis," *Sociology Today: Problems and Prospects,* ed. R. K. Merton, L. Broom, and L. S. Cottrell, Jr. New York: Basic Books, pp. 440-28. Halter, Marilyn; Schneider, Eric. and Weiner, Lynn. 1973. "Report from the 'Enormous File': A Case Study of Office Work." Boston: Boston University Department of History.

Hennig, Margaret. 1970. "Career Development for Women Executives," unpublished doctoral dissertation. Cambridge, Mass.: Harvard University Graduate School of Business Administration.

Heydebrand, Wolf (ed.). 1974. *Comparative Organizations.* Englewood Cliffs, N.J.: Prentice-Hall.

Hill, Joseph A. 1929. *Women in Gainful Occupations, 1870-1920.* Census

Monographs IX. Washington, D.C.: U.S. Government Printing Office. New York: Johnson Reprint Corporation, 1972.

Horner, Matina. 1968. "Sex Differences in Achievement Motivation and Performance in Competitive and Non-Competitive Situations," unpublished doctoral dissertation. Ann Arbor, Mich.: University of Michigan.

Hurwitz, Jacob I.; Zander, Alvin F.; and Hymovich, Bernard. 1968. "Some Effects of Power on the Relations Among Group Members," *Group Dynamics* ed. D. Cartwright and A. Zander. New York: Harper & Row, pp. 291–97.

Jay, Anthony. 1967. *Management and Machiavelli: An Inquiry into the Politics of Corporate Life.* New York: Holt, Rinehart & Winston. 1971. *Corporation Man.* New York: Random House, Kanter, Rosabeth Moss. 1974. "The Auxiliary Organization." Waltham, Mass.: Brandeis University Department of Sociology. 1975. "Women in Organizations: Sex Roles, Group Dynamics, and Change Strategies," *Beyond Sex Roles,* ed. A. Sargent. St. Paul, Minn.: West Publishing.

Langer, Elinor. 1970. "Inside the New York Telephone Company," *Women at Work*, ed. W. L. O'Neill. Chicago: Quadrangle, 1972, pp. 305–60.

Lieberson, Stanley, and O'Connor, John F. 1972. "Leadership and Organizational Performance: A Study of Large Corporations," *American Sociological Review* 37 April: 117–30.

Lynch, Edith M. 1973. *The Executive Suite: Feminine Style:* New York: AMACOM.

Mann, R. D. 1959. "A Review of the Relationship between Personality and Performance in Small Groups," *Psychological Bulletin* 56:241–70.

Mayo, Elton. 1933. *The Human Problems of an Industrial Civilization.* New York: Macmillan.

Megaree, Edwin, I. 1969. "Influence of Sex Roles on the Manifestation of Leadership," *Journal of Applied Psychology* 53:377–82.

Miller, William. 1950. "The Recruitment of the American Business Elite," *Men in Business*, ed. W. Miller. Cambridge, Mass.: Harvard University Press. New York: Harper & Row, 1962. 1952. "The Business Elite in Business Bureaucracies: Careers of Top Executives in the Early Twentieth Century," *Men in Business,* ed. W. Miller. Cambridge, Mass.: Harvard University Press, pp. 286-305; New York: Harper & Row, 1962.

Mills, C. Wright. 1951. *White Collar: The American Middle Classes.* New York: Oxford University Press.

Morse, Nancy C. 1953. *Satisfaction in the White Collar Job.* Ann Arbor, Mich.: Survey Research Center, University of Michigan.

Parsons, H. M. 1974. "What Happened at Hawthorne?," *Science* 183 March: 922-32.

Pelz, Donald C. 1952. "Influence: A Key to Effective Leadership in the First-line Supervisor," *Personnel* 29:3-11. Report of a Special Task Force to the Secretary of Health, Education, and Welfare. 1972. *Work in America.* Cambridge, Mass.: MIT Press.

Roethlisberger, F. J., and Dickson, William J. 1939. *Management and the Worker.* Cambridge, Mass.: Harvard University Press.

Sarason, Seymour B. 1973. "Jewishness, Blackishness, and the Nature-Nurture Controversy," *American Psychologist* 28 November: 962-71.

Scott, W. Richard. 1964. "Theory of Organizations," *Handbook of Modern Sociology,* ed. R. E. L. Faris. Chicago: Rand McNally, pp. 485-529.

Sexton, Patricia Cayo. 1974. "Workers (Female) Arise!," *Dissent* Summer: 380-95.

Sikula, Andrew F. 1973. "The Uniqueness of Secretaries as Employees," *Journal of Business Education* 48 Fall: 203-5.

Stein, Barry A. 1974. *Size, Efficiency, and Community Enterprise.* Cambridge, Mass.: Center for Community Economic Development.

Sutton, Francis X.; Harris, Seymour E.; Kaysen, Carl; and Tobin, James. 1956. *The American Business Creed.* Cambridge, Mass.: Harvard University Press.

Taylor, Frederick W. 1947. *Scientific Management.* New York: Harper & Brothers.

Tiger, Lionel. 1969. *Men in Groups.* New York: Random House.

Tillett, Anthony; Kempner, Thomas; and Wills, Gordon (eds.). 1970. *Management Thinkers.* Baltimore, Md.: Penguin Books.

Tresemer, David. 1973. "Fear of Success: Popular but Unproven," *Psychology Today* 7 November.

Uesugi, Thomas K., and Vinacke, W. Edgar. 1963. "Strategy in a Feminine Game," *Sociometry* 26:35-88.

Vinacke, W. Edgar. 1959. "Sex Roles in a Three-person Game," *Sociometry* 22 December: 343-60.

Wallach, Michael A.; Kogan, Nathan; and Bem, Daryl J. 1968. "Group Influence on Individual Risk-taking," *Group Dynamics,* ed. D. Cartwright and A. Zander. New York: Harper & Row, pp. 430-43.

Warner, W. Lloyd, and Abegglen, James C. 1955. *Big Business Leaders in America.* New York: Harper & Brothers.

Winter, J. Alan. 1974. "Elective Affinities Between Religious Beliefs and Ideologies of Management in Two Eras," *American Journal of Sociology* 79 March: 1,134-50.

Wolman, Carol, and Frank, Harold. 1975. "The Solo Woman in a Professional Peer Group," *American Journal of Orthopsychiatry* 45: February.

Zeitlin, Maurice. 1974. "Corporate Ownership and Control: The Large Corporation and the Capitalist Class," *American Journal of Sociology* 79 March: 1,073-1,119.

Women, Power, and Libraries

Patricia Glass Schuman

PROFESSIONAL women hear a lot these days about the things mother never taught us. Still, there are things mother and father *did* teach us—and now we need to look at them as well. One significant lesson we learned was that it was not considered "proper" for women to discuss money, sex, or power. It really isn't "nice" to think about any of these things, or to admit that you want or have any of them.

"Power is America's last dirty word," says Rosabeth Kantor in her *Men and Women of the Corporation.* "People who have it deny it, people who want it do not want to appear to hunger for it; and people who engage in its machinations do so secretly." Power is a particularly distasteful word to most women. In an informal survey of my women friends, I asked what terms came to mind when they heard the word "power." The most common responses were: manipulation, control, dominance, ruthlessness, coercion, and anger.

THE DOUBLE BIND

"Power tends to corrupt. Absolute power corrupts absolutely." We usually drop the word "tends" from that famous statement and just say, "power corrupts." This view of power is certainly not confined to women. Men often find the raw concept of power somewhat repugnant. To women, however, the concept of power—of being powerful—is almost a societal taboo. Witness the clichés by which women's power has always been masked:

"The hand that rocks the cradle rules the world."

Reprinted from *Library Journal*, (Jan. 1984), pp. 42–47. Published by R.R. Bowker Co. (a Xerox company). Copyright © 1984 by Xerox Corporation.

"The iron hand in the velvet glove."
"The woman behind the throne."

These clichés may have been used historically to soften the news that women do have power, but they also imply a power of almost awesome proportions. This is the double bind—the myth of female weakness and female strength.

Images of the magical fertility goddess or the all-powerful mother abound in literature and history. Throughout history (and mythology) man has feared and worshipped her power. Joseph Campbell claims, in *The Mask of God,* that women's mythic power " . . . has been one of the chief concerns of the masculine part of the population . . . to break, control, and employ it for its own ends."

From the beginnings of time, women have been taught to submit, to give up their power. This in itself is an admission that women have power. In her *Man's World, Women's Place,* Elizabeth Janeway points out: "In mythic identification of power and weakness, women immolate themselves as a sign of strength. They are the givers. But how can one give if one does not possess riches and substances . . . Here is the paradox: women are weak because they can be strong only through giving. They are strong because they give what is needed, and this assures that their dominance will continue." Of course women's power has usually been private power, power within the family. The age-old power bargain states, in part, that "men rule the world, women rule the home."

During the past 20 years, women have made great strides—though not nearly great enough—in our struggle for equal rights and opportunity; in our fight to change the terms of the bargain. Yet we remain largely a powerless group—a majority not well organized, nor powerful enough to pass the Equal Rights Amendment.

THE CONDITIONED RESPONSE

Our lack of knowledge and understanding about power is largely a conditioned response. I am President of my own company. I'm told that I am the first woman to be nominated for treasurer of the American Library Association. *LJ*'s editors obviously thought enough of this article to publish it. Yet how do I want the reader to view me? Certainly not as "powerful." I want you to *like* me. To think I'm "good." Women are products of a compromised power group, taught to perceive ourselves as submissive, rather than as wielders of power and influence. Intellectually I know better, but emotionally . . .

I'm trying to get past my conditioning because I think it is essential that we understand power—understand what it is and where it comes from and how and when to use it.

THE WIDENING GAP

Why be concerned about women and power? Much of the library profession is female—part of the power structure. We're concerned, obviously, because the gains of the women's movement notwithstanding, women still have a long way to go. To put it in simple economic terms: in 1955, women earned 64.3 cents for every dollar men earned. In 1978, we earned 60 cents for every dollar. The earning gap is widening. Women have to work nine days to gross the same amount of money men do in five. Even those of us lucky enough to be "exceptions" are still grappling with the personal and emotional problems that come from trying to change very strong conditioning.

Women, as a group in our society, are still largely powerless. Women librarians are even more so. We may be members of a "women's profession," but the reality is that women hold only 15 percent of the directorships of libraries that belong to the Association of Research Libraries, 25 percent of top posts in library education, and only a third of the directorships in major public libraries. Even then, these positions are not in the largest and most prestigious institutions. Salary data also demonstrate that regardless of position or type of library, women continue to earn less than men. The gap widens at the highest levels.

Despite more than a decade of activism, there has been no clear improvement of the status of women in librarianship. The profession continues to evidence a clear pattern of dual career structures. Recent research and analysis by Kathleen Heim, Leigh Estabrook, and others suggests that salary discrimination exists, even when allowances are made for personal, career, and professional variations. There is segregation by type of library, with almost half of the men in the profession working in academic libraries. Women clearly dominate library services for schools and children. "Men hold major administrative positions in all types of libraries nearly three times as often as their proportion of the total work force would suggest, while women cluster in the lower levels of the organizational hierarchy," according to Heim.

Women librarians clearly lack economic power, but even more important, we lack structural power—the power to change and improve our institutions and our society.

POWER DEFINED

In order to achieve and use power, we must first define it. Max Weber's simple definition is a good starting point: "Power is the possibility of imposing one's will upon the behavior of other persons."

A person has power when she has the ability to mobilize resources (human and material), to apply negative or positive sanctions in order to get something done, to have her interest felt, to have effect on the decision-making process.

Power can be given, taken, assumed, inherited, vested, won, lost, used, abused, feared, and respected. Power comes with certain roles— mother, director, boss, expert.

Individuals and groups seek power to advance their own interests, to extend to others their personal and religious or social values. They use it to win support for their economic or social perception of the public good.

Power is neither moral nor immoral in itself, though it can be used for good or ill. As the late Saul Alinsky observed, "Power is an essential force always in operation either changing circumstances or opposing change—a gun may be used to take or save a life, to enforce slavery, or to achieve freedom. The morality of the use of power is not in the instrument but in the user."

HOW POWER WORKS

It is important to understand how power works, what differentiates those who exercise power from those who are subject to it, before dealing with the ethics of its use. Where does power come from, how does it grow, how is it transferred and used?

Sociologists, psychologists, management consultants, economists, and others have attempted to classify the types and sources of power. In a fascinating discussion in his recent book, *The Anatomy of Power*,

John Kenneth Galbraith defines three main types of power and where they come from:

Condign Power enforces submission through the threat of adverse unpleasant, or painful consequences—power by punishment.

Compensatory Power assures submission through affirmative rewards by giving something of value, like money.

Conditioned Power wins submission by changing belief, through persuasion, education, or social commitment to what seems "natural, and right." The submission reflects the so-called "preferred" course.

Individuals subject to power which uses punishments or rewards for enforcement are aware of their submission to it. However, conditioned power, relying upon belief, is subjective, neither those exercising it nor those subject to it are always aware that it is being exerted. We just *know* that "God is on our side." Advertising is a prevalent form of conditioned power, though not as reputable a form for teaching socially acceptable views as our educational system. "Power is served in many ways," says Galbraith. "No service is more useful than the cultivation of the belief that it *does not* exist."

Of course, all of these forms of power are interrelated. For example, although the reputation and use of condign power—punishment—has greatly declined in modern societies, its aura survives. For those who once possessed it as a "right," the image (conditioning) is still a factor in winning submission. "The husband, parent, teacher, and sheriff all have authority now in consequence of a past association with the right to inflict punishment."

One of Galbraith's major theses, of crucial importance to women, is that power in modern society is moving, through social and economic forces, from condign physical enforcement and compensatory monetary rewards to an ever-increasing reliance on the use of conditioned power, the power of belief. Of course those subject to this conditioned power are rarely aware of it. Submission to it usually reflects what we view as a "proper," "reputable," "acceptable," or "decent" behavior. We obey the law. We pay taxes. We accept the mores and taboos of society.

Another important point Galbraith makes is that: "something in the exercise of masculine authority must be attributed to the superior access of the male to condign power, to the greater physical strength of a husband and its use to enforce his will on a physically weaker and insufficiently acquiescent spouse. And no one can doubt the frequent efficiency of compensatory power, of reward in the form of clothing, jewelry, housing, entertainment. These have long and adequately demonstrated their utility in securing feminine compliance with masculine will."

Male power and female submission have relied much more completely, however, on the belief since ancient times that such submission is the natural order of things. "Men might love, honor, and cherish; it was for long accepted that women should love, honor, and *obey*." Granted, relief from the compensatory power wielded by men has been sought through the development of employment opportunities for women and by publicizing employment discrimination that keeps women in subordinate jobs. A major part of the effort has had to be "the challenge to belief—the belief that submission and subservience are normal, virtuous, and otherwise appropriate roles for women."

THE SOURCES OF POWER

Of course, all of these ways of enforcing power—reward, punishment, and conditioning—play various roles in the exercise of power. The question is, "What provides *access* to power, what *allows* its exercise?" Galbraith has three basic answers: personality, property, and organization. These are the ultimate sources of power. They almost always appear in some kind of combination and each relates to a type of power.

Galbraith contends that in modern society organizations (unions, governments, corporations, public agencies, special interest groups) are the key source of power, though certainly interrelated with other power sources. He quotes scholar, Charles Lindblom, to make his point: "Some people believe that wealth or property is the underlying source of power. But property is itself a form of authority created by government."

Galbraith uses the professional football team as a metaphor. The team, he says, uses all the sources and instruments of power and it is accepted that success depends on the effectiveness of their use. It uses the *personality* of the coaches and the more spectacular or effective players. It takes *property*, resources to support a major team. Most of all, the highly sophisticated *organization* of the teams and the game is essential.

The instruments of enforcement are the threat of condign rebuke from teammates, coach, and fans. The promise of compensatory power resides in the high salaries. Above all there is the highly developed training and conditioning required to win. "The team most strongly combining all of these elements of power will win; it will gain the submission of the opposing team. As in sport, so in life," says Galbraith. Men know this. How often do we hear women use the terms "end-run" or "teamwork" or say "There goes the ball-game"? That's not to say that we should.

POWER FOR WHAT?

The football team may be an analogy to the "norm" of how power is exercised. The dilemma for women is whether we want power in its usual form and for its usual ends. Power is neither moral nor immoral, it depends upon how it is used. To make a choice is to exercise power. If the choice is an effective one, it alters the status quo, it can change the distribution of power. There are no ethics inherent in power itself; there are only the ethics of the people who wield power. The key questions are: What do we want power for? How much do we have? How much do we want? How much risk are we willing to take? On what—or whose—terms?

THE ILLUSION OF POWER

Does power mean being the director of a library, more prestige, more money? Do we want to "buy in" on the societal terms men have set up and thus reap the rewards of power? Will we submit to "organizational goals," or will we enlarge and change them? If we want power, we must be aware of the danger of having the "illusions" and trappings of power, *without the impact*. To quote Galbraith once again, this time on modern corporations and public agencies like libraries:

> ... there is the illusion of individuals in these organizations that they have and are using power. As personality gives way to organization, there is inevitably a wider participation in the exercise of power. What once expressed the will of the boss is now the product of bureaucracy—of conference and committee and proposals passing up through the organizational hierarchy for modification, amendment, and ratification. In the older business enterprise, submission was to the owner; his word, as it was said, was law. In the modern large corporation, submission is to the bureaucratic processes in which many participate. The boss, as he may still be called, is the agent of those who instruct him; the power he is presumed

to exercise is at least partly the endowment of those who, sensitive to his vanity, attribute to him an authority that, were it real, would be disastrous. The modern corporate title expresses the reality: the chief executive officer—the CEO—is only the chief among those with executive authority. As with the modern corporation, so with the public agency. It, too, concentrates power and then distributes it among the individual participants.

The *illusion* of power is very seductive. I founded my company seven years ago, on a shoestring. We couldn't afford an office, so we worked out of my apartment. I had been a librarian and editor before that—all middle management positions. Suddenly I was a "president." Much to my amazement, as soon as I started calling myself "president," I began to be offered jobs as "president" of other publishing companies, positions no one would have *dreamed* of offering me three months earlier. I was the same person, with the same talents. Only the title had changed.

Illusions of power can also result from political and special issue organization. Just by forming an organization, making a speech, issuing statements, having meetings, we can create the illusion that we are exercising power, when in reality we are just spinning our wheels—marking time, feeling good, while others still hold the reins of power. We need to be able distinguish between this illusion and the practical effect—the results any such organization has.

ORGANIZING FOR POWER

Women also face danger in the power arena when we attempt to take and use power only as individuals—thinking that we are "different" than other women. We think we are somehow better, smarter, and more talented. We can stand alone. We don't *need* "organized" power. How many times have you heard other women disavow the "feminist" label? Letty Cottin Pogrebin, in a recent *New York Times* article, discussed several important and strong women who say they agree with feminist goals, but choose to disavow their feminism. She quotes Chris Craft, the TV commentator who sued the station that demoted her for being too old, unattractive, and not deferential to men: "I hate being categorized. Objectivity has always been my goal. If I said I'm a feminist, I'd never get another job as a reporter. I mean no slap against feminism, but this is my battle and mine alone."

Pogrebin suggests that women

resist being categorized because despite more than a decade of women's movement activism on everything from child care to homemaker's rights, the category "feminist" still conjures for many an image of a narrow, negative fringe group. I can vouch for the power of those preconceptions. I stand five feet, four inches tall. At virtually all my lecture appearances, believe it or not, someone says, "I thought you'd be bigger." Each of us who calls herself a feminist testifies that feminists come in all sizes, races, marital states, and sexual persuasions. Admission to our "category" is by commitment only.

Pogrebin compares Craft's desire for objectivity to Gloria Steinem's civil rights parody of the equal time rule: "O.K., we've heard from the black victims; now let's get the attack dog's side of the story." It's absurd to suggest that there are two sides to the denial of human rights to anyone. "Being a feminist—in favor of women's rights—should not stigmatize a woman; it should mark her as a person with rudimentary human concerns and female self-interest."

USING POWER

We run other risks, as well, in attempting to use power. One is exhibiting the classic behavior of the powerless—using whatever power we *do* gain in a oppressive way. In work situations, women are often said to hoard what little power they are given. Sometimes we think we need to do it all ourselves, to prove something. Often we don't delegate.

Rosabeth Kantor describes powerless people as those who supervise closely, focus on rules and procedures, are less willing to delegate, are territorial, attempt to hold on to the small "scraps of power" they may have. Contrast that with Carl Rogers' description of powerful people: "People who trust their own power do not need to have power over others. They are willing to foster and facilitate the latent strength in the other person. Constructive power can be released when people accept their own inner strength." Too often we see ourselves as the recipients of the benefits of power, rather than as a part of the power system. We see ourselves as the recipients of the benefits of networks, mentors, sponsors, and the like—rather than as those who pass on and share power.

POWER AND LIBRARIANSHIP

Women are members of a class that is perceived as powerless. As librarians, we are members of a profession that is perceived as powerless. The sociologists call librarianship a "semiprofession" because librarianship evidences three characteristics that are predominantly female: First, within the hierarchy of all occupations/professions, librarians are low in status, prestige, and income. Second, administrative positions are usually held by men. Third, men earn more than women when at equal levels of occupational and professional development.

We are, for the most part, an institution-based profession. Our goals and our services center around an institution over which we often have little control. Libraries are hierarchical institutions. Rarely do librarians have much to say in their workplace regarding hours, schedules, physical plant, or other conditions which affect the quality of their work.

We tend to do things *for* the people we serve. We rarely do things with them because we perceive ourselves as having little power to share.

REDEFINING POWER

The old cliché "information is power" has new meaning in a society that is rapidly changing from an industrial base to an information base. Over 50 percent of our Gross National Product is devoted to the production and distribution of information. Daniel Bell calls this a post-industrial society. Others say we're in the "age of information." If information is, or is rapidly becoming, one of the more effective tools with which to wield power, then the lack of it implies powerlessness. Librarianship is a profession ethically dedicated to the organization and dissemination of information—the dissemination, therefore, of knowledge and power. Our impact on existing and developing power structures could be massive. We can make a difference, changing who is information rich and who is information poor. In order to exploit this impact to its fullest, as women and as librarians, we must redefine power ourselves.

Forget Max Weber's definition of power as "imposing one's will on others." Let's redefine power as the ability to get cooperation. By that definition we have power when we can gain access to resources, information, and support and we mobilize these effectively to get things done. Rather than viewing power as something done *to us*, let's examine it as something we can *use*.

Remember there are no ethics of power. Power itself is neutral. Power can be used for either positive or negative ends. The use of power does not always have to result in a situation where "if I win, you lose." There is not just one "piece of the pie" to be shared among those of us who are the most dominant and aggressive—not unless we are willing to buy into a hierarchical system. It is a system within which much of the power is illusory—and we must not lose sight of this fact.

Unfortunately, as the members of a power-compromised group, women have few role models. Because of the position of women in society it is unlikely that any of us have escaped without some trauma to our self-perceptions. When we do have a chance to exercise power, we sometimes don't recognize it, we are sometimes frightened of it, and often we don't know how to use it. The problem is not ability, or opportunity, but an understanding and appreciation of the elements of power.

Despite the hierarchy and the ordained authority we may or may not have in our immediate workplace, there are many ways we can exercise power. The power we have is not ours through the authority of a title alone. We exercise power through friendships, personal traits, perceived expertise, confidence, status, seniority, and interpersonal skills. We have many more opportunities to exercise it than we realize. We are powerful not only when we control resources (money, personnel, equipment) and time (schedules, assignments). We are also powerful when we have access to people—supporters, backers, allies. We have power when we have control of, or access to, information. We have power when we understand how the system works and we have political access to it.

In order to gain and use power, women must join together, in an organized effort, for common goals. To operate only on "good will" and "principle" is not enough. What are these common goals? How can feminist power differ from the norm? Can we use power creatively, constructively, in life-enhancing ways? Will we use it to empower others?

POWER: CHANGING THE TERMS

How will we respond to the existing power establishment? Galbraith observes that the common response to an unwelcome exercise of power is to build a countering position of power. Usually we meet like with like, force with force, social conditioning with social conditioning. Yet consider the power—the impact—of those who have successfully refused to use power by traditional methods: Martin

Luther King's nonviolent resistance, Gandhi's use of Satyagraha. They changed the world by refusing to "buy in" on the usual terms. Realizing that there was no effective way to meet the power structure on its own terms, they changed the terms.

If we—as women and as librarians—accept the power bargain on the terms of the conventional wisdom of the hierarchy, we are subject to the dangers of what Warren Bennis terms "collective immorality." When moral, "good" people get together to make decisions for organizations, in order to preserve the values and goals of the institution, they often go against their individual ideals and principles. Loyalty is often held to be the highest good by an organization. Those who put the organization first in the narrowest sense, those people who unquestioningly follow the course perceived to be best for the organization, are often its most highly prized employees. Talent, ingenuity, innovation, intelligence, and creativity run a poor second in many organizational value systems.

That demand for loyalty, for adherence to the orthodoxy is perceived as the only way the organization can survive. Our first advice from the lawyer who drew up the papers to incorporate Neal-Schuman was: "Remember, your business is an entity unto itself. It's not an extension of you—it's something separate, something that has to be protected at all costs—even at the expense of the individuals involved." There are many valid reasons for protecting an organization, but unswerving and unquestioning loyalty is also the stuff from which both mediocrity and totalitarianism are made.

JOINING THE POWERLESS

Do we, as women, want to change our positions in libraries and in the world or do we want to change librarianship and the world? It has often been said that men are more effective when manipulating "things," but women are more effective when working with people. When we buy into the power structure of the hierarchy, with its punishments, rewards, and conditioning, we may think we have gained power, but in the end we are once again joining the ranks of the powerless. We may obtain personal gratification by "joining up" and offering unquestioning loyalty to the organization, but that route will leave us powerless to bring change or have real impact.

Merely replacing the male administrators with female administrators does not change the power structure. The key to truly feminist power lies in changing the terms of the existing power structure, not in becoming part of it. Women have discovered several effective routes to bring this change. We must build on them, even though they all involve challenges to the ways we traditionally value work and people, and to the ways in which people relate to each other. The new routes to using power to bring change begin with defining and confronting basic, yet neglected, issues of power and control.

SHARING POWER

To rescue our institutions, our libraries, from their debilitating foundations in traditional hierarchical authority, will first demand change within ourselves. We will not achieve true participatory power as long as we unquestioningly accept existing authority as legitimate. We will not be able to achieve the new forms of power as long as we remain content with the status quo, even when that status quo gives us a small share of the existing authority. This fundamental shift in the terms of power not only requires restructuring our workplaces, but also reeducating ourselves to a full awareness of the alternatives to the power assumptions that we now accept as reality—as the "way things are" and are supposed to be.

Networking is one fine example of a channel women are using to reach around existing power structures. Networks cut across institutional and hierarchical lines, offering open access to people, resources, and issues. There is no authority or leader at the top, as in conventional organizations. In a network, each individual is at the center. The routes to sharing power are direct; traditional boundaries disappear. Through networks we share power; we expand power. We empower both ourselves and others. We don't climb over others up some hierarchical pecking order.

Women have found the law to be another effective route to changing the terms of power. We didn't manage to pass the Equal Rights Amendment, but we have made progress in many areas of law. For example, there has been tremendous progress on the issue of comparable pay for comparable worth. Our progress toward acceptance of the concept that pay be equal not just for the same job, but for all jobs that call for comparable skills, effort, and responsibility has clearly changed the terms of power.

The current job market is rigged against women, who are concentrated in historically underpaid fields. These fields systematically pay less than male-dominated ones. The recent ruling in Tacoma,

Washington found "overt and institutionalized discrimination" in the state, thus reinforcing the doctrine of comparable worth that the Supreme Court acknowledged in 1981. The questions here go much deeper than the issue of whether or not librarians compare in worth to garbage collectors. Are librarians serving children or in schools worth as much as history bibliographers or online searchers?

A third route we have travelled since the beginning of the modern women's movement is consciousness raising. Frankly, I thought I was beyond all that, at least in terms of my professional life, until I started to examine my own reactions to power—how much I have, how much I use, and why and how I use it. I discovered how far I still have to go—not only to understand power, but even to feel comfortable using it. My discomfort with power is a clear result of my own conditioning, conditioning most women share.

Understanding power, feeling comfortable with it, and using it constructively is a building and learning process. Networking, consciousness raising, organized action, and pressure to change existing structures and laws are tested routes to power, valuable tools that we have at hand. We live in a world where the mind, through the pen, is literally more powerful than the sword. With it we can rewrite the terms of power—not only for women, but for all human beings.

Total power, omnipotence, is not available to any of us, nor would we want it. Our current impotence, our lack of power, is equally unacceptable. We can be, to coin a word, "partipotent." As women, we cannot accept the current terms of power which allow it to be concentrated in the hands of a few. Our task is to recast those terms and to share the power we gain. When we share power we empower others. When we share it, we bring power to all who are the victims of its traditional misuse.

Bibliography

Alinsky, Saul D. "Of Means and Ends," *Union Seminary Quarterly Review,* January 1967, p. 107-124.

Campbell, Joseph. *The Masks of God: Primitive Mythology.* Morrow, 1967.

Galbraith, John. *Anatomy of Power.* Houghton, 1983.

Heim, Kathleen. "The Demographic and Economic Status of Librarians in the 1970's, with Special Reference to Women," in *Advances in Librarianship, Vol. 12.* Academic Pr., 1982.

Heim, Kathleen, ed. *The Status of Women in Librarianship: Historical, Sociological, and Economic Issues.* Neal-Schuman, 1983.

Heim, Kathleen M. and Leigh S. Estabrook. *Career Profiles and Sex Discrimination in the Library Profession.* ALA, 1983.

Janeway, Elizabeth. *Man's World, Woman's Place: A Study in Social Mythology.* Morrow, 1967.

Kantor, Rosabeth Moss. "Power Failure in Management Circuits," *Harvard Business Review,* July-August 1979, p. 65-75.

Pogrebin, Letty Cottin. "Hers," *New York Times,* September 22, 1983, p. C2.

Rogers, Carl. *On Personal Power.* Delacorte, 1977.

Weber, Max. *Max Weber on Law and Economy in Society.* Harvard Univ. Pr., 1954.

Weibel, Kathleen and Kathleen M. Heim. *The Role of Women in Librarianship 1876-1976: The Entry, Advancement, and Struggle for Equalization in One Profession.* Oryx Pr. (A Neal-Schuman Professional Book), 1979.

Skills of an Effective Administrator

Robert L. Katz

ALTHOUGH the selection and training of good administrators is widely recognized as one of American industry's most pressing problems, there is surprisingly little agreement among executives or educators on what makes a good administrator. The executive development programs of some of the nation's leading corporations and colleges reflect a tremendous variation in objectives.

At the root of this difference is industry's search for the traits or attributes which will objectively identify the "ideal executive" who is equipped to cope effectively with any problem in any organization. As one observer of U.S. industry recently noted:

"The assumption that there is an executive type is widely accepted, either openly or implicitly. Yet any executive presumably knows that a company needs all kinds of managers for different levels of jobs. The qualities most needed by a shop superintendent are likely to be quite opposed to those needed by a coordinating vice president of manufacturing. The literature of executive development is loaded with efforts to define the qualities needed by executives, and by themselves these sound quite rational. Few, for instance, would dispute the fact that a top manager needs good judgment, the ability to make decisions, the ability to win respect of others, and all the other well-worn phrases any management man could mention. But one has only to look at the successful managers in any company to see how enormously their particular qualities vary from any ideal list of executive virtues."[1]

Author's note: This article is based on a study prepared under a grant from the Alfred P. Sloan Foundation.

Yet this quest for the executive stereotype has become so intense that many companies, in concentrating on certain specific traits or qualities, stand in danger of losing sight of their real concern: *what a man can accomplish.*

It is the purpose of this article to suggest what may be a more useful approach to the selection and development of administrators. This approach is based not on what good executives *are* (their innate traits and characteristics), but rather on what they *do* (the kinds of skills which they exhibit in carrying out their jobs effectively). As used here, a *skill* implies an ability which can be developed, not necessarily inborn, and which is manifested in performance, not merely in potential. So the principle criterion of skillfulness must be effective action under varying conditions.

This approach suggests that effective administration rests on *three basic developable skills* which obviate the need for identifying specific traits and which may provide a useful way of looking at and understanding the administrative process. This approach is the outgrowth of firsthand observation of executives at work coupled with study of current field research in administration.

In the sections which follow, an attempt will be made to define and demonstrate what these three skills are; to suggest that the relative importance of the three skills varies with the level of administrative responsibility; to present some of the implications of this variation for selection, training, and promotion of executives; and to propose ways of developing these skills.

THREE-SKILL APPROACH

It is assumed here that an administrator is one who (a) directs the activities of other persons and (b) undertakes the responsibility for achieving certain objectives through these efforts. Within this definition, successful administration appears to rest on three basic skills, which we will call *technical, human,* and *conceptual.* It would be unrealistic to assert that these skills are not interrelated, yet there may be real merit in examining each one separately, and in developing them independently.

Technical Skill

As used here, technical skill implies an understanding of, and proficiency in, a specific kind of activity, particularly one involving methods, processes, procedures, or techniques. It is relatively easy for us to visualize the technical skill of the surgeon, the musician, the accountant, or the engineer when each is performing his own special function. Technical skill involves specialized knowledge, analytical ability within that specialty, and facility in the use of the tools and techniques of the specific discipline.

Of the three skills decribed in this article, technical skill is perhaps the most familiar because it is the most concrete, and because, in our age of specialization, it is the skill required of the greatest number of people. Most of our vocational and on-the-job training programs are largely concerned with developing this specialized technical skill.

Human Skill

As used here, human skill is the executive's ability to work effectively as a group member and to build cooperative effort within the team he leads. As *technical* skill is primarily concerned with working with "things" (processes or physical objects), so *human* skill is primarily concerned with working with people. This skill is demonstrated in the way the individual perceives (and recognizes the perceptions of) his superiors, equals, and subordinates, and in the way he behaves subsequently.

The person with highly developed human skill is aware of his own attitudes, assumptions, and beliefs about other individuals and groups; he is able to see the usefulness and limitations of these feelings. By accepting the existence of viewpoints, perceptions, and beliefs which are different from his own, he is skilled in understanding what others really mean by their words and behavior. He is equally skillful in communicating to others, in their own contexts, what he means by *his* behavior.

Such a person works to create an atmosphere of approval and security in which subordinates feel free to express themselves without fear of censure or ridicule, by encouraging them to participate in the planning and carrying out of those things which directly affect them. He is sufficiently sensitive to the needs and motivations of others in his organization so that he can judge the possible reactions to, and outcomes of, various courses of action he may undertake. Having this sensitivity, he is able and willing to *act* in a way which takes these perceptions by others into account.

Real skill in working with others must become a natural, continuous activity, since it involves sensitivity not only at times of decision making but also in the day-by-day behavior of the individual. Human skill cannot be a "sometime thing." Techniques cannot be randomly applied, nor can personality traits be put on or removed like an overcoat. Because everything which an executive says and does (or leaves unsaid or undone) has an effect on his associates, his true self will, in time, show through. Thus, to be effective, this skill must be naturally developed and unconsciously, as well as consistently, demonstrated in the individual's every action. It must become an integral part of his whole being.

Because human skill is so vital a part of everything the administrator does, examples of inadequate human skill are easier to describe than are highly skillful performances. Perhaps consideration of an actual situation would serve to clarify what is involved:

When a new conveyor unit was installed in a shoe factory where workers had previously been free to determine their own work rate, the production manager asked the industrial engineer who had designed the conveyor to serve as foreman, even though a qualified foreman was available. The engineer, who reported directly to the production manager, objected, but under pressure he agreed to take the job "until a suitable foreman could be found," even though this was a job of lower status than his present one. Then this conversation took place:

Production Manager: "I've had a lot of experience with conveyors. I want you to keep this conveyor going at all times except for rest periods, and I want it going at top speed. Get these people thinking in terms of 2 pairs of shoes a minute, 70 dozen pairs a day, 350 dozen pairs a week. They are all experienced operators on their individual jobs, and it's just a matter of getting them to do their jobs in a little different way. I want you to make that base rate of 250 dozen pair a week work!" [Base rate was established at slightly under 75 percent of the maximum capacity. This base rate was 50 percent higher than under the old system.]

Engineer: "If I'm going to be foreman of the conveyor unit, I want to do things my way. I've worked on conveyors, and I don't agree with you on first getting people used to a conveyor going at top speed. These people have never seen a conveyor. You'll scare them. I'd like to run the conveyor at one-third speed for a couple of weeks and then gradually increase the speed.

"I think we should discuss setting the base rate [production quota before incentive bonus] on a daily basis instead of a weekly basis. [Workers had previously been paid on a daily straight piecework basis.]

"I'd also suggest setting a daily base rate at 45 or even 40 dozen pair. You have to set a base rate low enough for them to make. Once they know they can make the base rate, they will go after the bonus."

Production Manager: "You do it your way on the speed; but remember it's the results that count. On the base rate, I'm not discussing it with you; I'm telling you to make the 250 dozen pair a week work. I don't want a daily base rate."[2]

Here is a situation in which the production manager was so preoccupied with getting the physical output that he did not pay attention to the people through whom that output had to be achieved. Notice, first, that he made the engineer who designed the unit serve as foreman, apparently hoping to force the engineer to justify his design by producing the maximum output. However, the production manager was oblivious to (a) the way the engineer perceived this appointment, as a demotion, and (b) the need for the engineer to be able to control the variables if he was to be held responsible for maximum output. Instead the production manager imposed a production standard and refused to make any changes in the work situation.

Moreover, although this was a radically new situation for the operators, the production manager expected them to produce immediately at well above their previous output—even though the operators had an unfamiliar production system to cope with, the operators had never worked together as a team before, the operators and their new foreman had never worked together before, and the foreman was not in agreement with the production goals or standards. By ignoring all these human factors, the production manager not only placed the engineer in an extremely difficult operating situation but also, by refusing to allow the engineer to "run his own show," discouraged the very assumption of responsibility he had hoped for in making the appointment.

Under these circumstances, it is easy to understand how the relationship between these two men rapidly deteriorated, and how production, after two months' operation, was at only 125 dozen pairs per week (just 75 percent of what the output had been under the old system).

Conceptual Skill

As used here, conceptual skill involves the ability to see the enterprise as a whole; it includes recognizing how the various functions of the organization depend on one another, and how changes in any one part affect all the others; and it extends to visualizing the relationship of the individual business to the industry, the community, and the political, social, and economic forces of the nation as a whole. Recognizing these relationships and perceiving the significant elements in any situation, the administrator should then be able to act in a way which advances the over-all welfare of the total organization.

Hence, the success of any decision depends on the conceptual skill of the people who make the decision and those who put it into action. When, for example, an important change in marketing policy is made, it is critical that the effects on production, control, finance, research, and the people involved be considered. And it remains critical right down to the last executive who must implement the new policy. If each executive recognizes the over-all relationships and significance of the change, he is almost certain to be more effective in administering it. Consequently the chances for succeeding are greatly increased.

Not only does the effective coordination of the various parts of the business depend on the conceptual skill of the administrators involved, but so also does the whole future direction and tone of the organization. The attitudes of a top executive color the whole character of the organization's response and determine the "corporate personality" which distinguishes one company's ways of doing business from another's. These attitudes are a reflection of the administrator's conceptual skill (referred to by some as his "creative ability"—the way he perceives and responds to the direction in which the business should grow, company objectives and policies, and stockholders' and employees' interests.

Conceptual skill, as defined above, is what Chester I. Barnard, former president of the New Jersey Bell Telephone Company, is implying when he says: " . . . the essential aspect of the [executive] process is the sensing of the organization as a whole and of the total situation relevant to it."[3] Examples of inadequate conceptual skill are all around us. Here is one instance:

In a large manufacturing company which had a long tradition of job-shop type operations, primary responsibility for production control had been left to the foremen and other lower-level supervisors. "Village" type operations with small working groups and informal organizations were the rule. A heavy influx of orders following World War II tripled the normal production requirements and severely taxed the whole manufacturing organization. At this point, a new production manager was brought in from outside the company, and he established a wide range of controls and formalized the entire operating structure.

As long as the boom demand lasted, the employees made every effort to conform with the new procedures and environment. But when demand subsided to prewar levels, serious labor relations problems developed, friction was high among department heads, and the company found itself saddled with a heavy indirect labor cost. Management sought to reinstate its old procedures; it fired the production manager and attempted to give greater authority to the foremen once again. However, during the four years of formalized control, the foremen had grown away from their old practices, many had left the company, and adequate replacements had not been developed. Without strong foreman leadership, the traditional job-shop operations proved costly and inefficient.

In this instance, when the new production controls and formalized organizations were introduced, management did not foresee the consequences of this action in the event of a future contraction of business. Later, when conditions changed and it was necessary to pare down operations, management was again unable to recognize the implications of its action and reverted to the old procedures, which, under the circumstances, were no longer appropriate. This compounded *conceptual* inadequacy left the company at a serious competitive disadvantage.

Because a company's over-all success is dependent on its executives' conceptual skill in establishing and carrying out policy decisions, this skill is the unifying, coordinating ingredient of the administrative process, and of undeniable over-all importance.

RELATIVE IMPORTANCE

We may notice that, in a very real sense, conceptual skill embodies consideration of both the technical and human aspects of the organization. Yet the concept of *skill*, as an ability to translate knowledge into action, should enable one to distinguish between the three skills of performing the technical activities (technical skill), understanding and motivating individuals and groups (human skill), and coordinating and integrating all the activities and interests of the organization toward a common objective (conceptual skill).

This separation of effective administration into three basic skills is useful primarily for purposes of analysis. In practice, these skills are so closely interrelated that it is difficult to determine where one ends and another begins. However, just because the skills are interrelated does not imply that we cannot get some value from looking at them separately, or by varying their emphasis. In playing golf the action of the hands, wrists, hips, shoulders, arms, and head are all interrelated; yet in improving one's swing it is often valuable to work on one of these elements separately. Also, under different playing conditions the relative importance of these elements varies. Similarly, although all three are of importance at every level of administration, the technical, human, and conceptual skills of the administrator vary in relative importance at different levels of responsibility.

At Lower Levels

Technical skill is responsible for many of the great advances of modern industry. It is indispensable to efficient operation. Yet it has greatest importance at the lower levels of administration. As the administrator moves further and further from the actual physical operation, this need for technical skill becomes less important, provided he has skilled subordinates and can help them solve their own problems. At the top, technical skill may be almost nonexistent, and the executive may still be able to perform effectively if his human and conceptual skills are highly developed. For example:

In one large capital-goods producing company, the controller was called on to replace the manufacturing vice president, who had been stricken suddenly with a severe illness. The controller had no previous production experience, but he had been with the company for more than 20 years and knew many of the key production personnel intimately. By setting up an advisory staff, and by delegating an unusual amount of authority to his department heads, he was able to devote himself to coordination of the various functions. By so doing, he produced a highly efficient team. The results were lower costs, greater productivity, and higher morale than the production division had ever before experienced. Management had gambled that this man's ability to work with people was more important than his lack of a technical production background, and the gamble paid off.

Other examples are evident all around us. We are all familiar with those "professional managers" who are becoming the prototypes of our modern executive world. These men shift with great ease, and with no apparent loss in effectiveness, from one industry to another. Their human and conceptual skills seem to make up for their unfamiliarity with the new job's technical aspects.

At Every Level

Human skill, the ability to work with others, is essential to effective administration at every level. One recent research study has shown that human skill is of paramount importance at the foreman level, pointing out that the chief function of the foreman as an administrator is to attain collaboration of people in the work group.[4] Another study reinforces this finding and extends it to the middle-management group, adding that the administrator should be primarily concerned with facilitating communication in the organization.[5] And still another study, concerned primarily with top management, underscores the need for self-awareness and sensitivity to human relationships by executives at that level.[6] These findings would tend to indicate that human skill is of great importance at every level, but notice the difference in emphasis.

Human skill seems to be most important at lower levels, where the number of direct contacts between administrators and subordinates is greatest. As we go higher and higher in the administrative echelons, the number and frequency of these personal contacts decrease, and the need for human skill becomes proportionately, although probably not absolutely, less. At the same time, conceptual skill becomes increasingly more important with the need for policy decisions and broad-scale action. The human skill of dealing with individuals then becomes subordinate to the conceptual skill of integrating group interests and activities into a whole.

In fact, a recent research study by Professor Chris Argyris of Yale University has given us the example of an extremely effective plant manager who, although possessing little human skill as defined here, was nonetheless very successful:

This manager, the head of a largely autonomous division, made his supervisors, through the effects of his strong personality and the "pressure" he applied, highly dependent on him for most of their "rewards, penalties, authority, perpetuation, communication, and identification."

As a result, the supervisors spent much of their time competing with one another for the manager's favor. They told him only the things they thought he wanted to hear, and spent much time trying to find out his desires. They depended on him to set their objectives and to show them how to reach them. Because the manager was inconsistent and unpredictable in his behavior, the supervisors were insecure and continually engaged in interdepartmental squabbles which they tried to keep hidden from the manager.

Clearly, human skill as defined here was lacking. Yet, by the evaluation of his superiors and by his results in increasing efficiency and raising profits and morale, this manager was exceedingly effective. Professor Argyris suggests that employees in modern industrial organizations tend to have a "built-in" sense of dependence on superiors which capable and alert men can turn to advantage.[7]

In the context of the three-skill approach, it seems that this manager was able to capitalize on this dependence because he recognized the interrelationships of all the activities under his control, identified himself with the organization, and sublimated the individual interests of his subordinates to *his* (the organization's) interest, set his goals realistically, and showed his subordinates how to reach these goals. This would seem to be an excellent example of a situation in which strong conceptual skill more than compensated for a lack of human skill.

At the Top Level

Conceptual skill, as indicated in the preceding sections, becomes increasingly critical in more responsible executive positions where its effects are maximized and most easily observed. In fact, recent research findings lead to the conclusion that at the top level of administration this conceptual skill becomes the most important ability of all. As Herman W. Steinkraus, president of Bridgeport Brass Company, said:

> One of the most important lessons which I learned on this job (the presidency) is the importance of coordinating the various departments into an effective team, and, secondly, to recognize the shifting emphasis from time to time of the relative importance of various departments to the business.[8]

It would appear, then, that at lower levels of administrative responsibility, the principal need is for technical and human skills. At higher levels, technical skill becomes relatively less important while the need for conceptual skill increases rapidly. At the top level of an organization, conceptual skill becomes the most important skill of all for successful administration. A chief executive may lack technical or human skills and still be effective if he has subordinates who have strong abilities in these directions. But if his conceptual skill is weak, the success of the whole organization may be jeopardized.

IMPLICATIONS FOR ACTION

This three-skill approach implies that significant benefits may result from redefining the objectives of executive development programs, from reconsidering the placement of executives in organizations, and from revising procedures for testing and selecting prospective executives.

Executive Development

Many executive development programs may be failing to achieve satisfactory results because of their inability to foster the growth of these administrative skills. Programs which concentrate on the mere imparting of information or the cultivation of a specific trait would seem to be largely unproductive in enhancing the administrative skills of candidates.

A strictly informative program was described to me recently by an officer and director of a large corporation who had been responsible for the executive-development activities of his company, as follows:

"What we try to do is to get our promising young men together with some of our senior executives in regular meetings each month. Then we give the young fellows a chance to ask questions to let them find out about the company's history and how and why we've done things in the past."

It was not surprising that neither the senior executives nor the young men felt this program was improving their administrative abilities.

The futility of pursuing specific traits becomes apparent when we consider the responses of an administrator in a number of different situations. In coping with these varied conditions, he may appear to demonstrate one trait in one instance—e.g., dominance when dealing with subordinates—and the directly opposite trait under another set of circumstances—e.g., submissiveness when dealing with superiors. Yet in each instance he may be acting appropriately to achieve the best results. Which, then, can we identify as a desirable characteristic? Here is a further example of this dilemma:

A Pacific Coast sales manager had a reputation for decisiveness and positive action. Yet when he was required to name an assistant to understudy his job from among several well-qualified subordinates, he deliberately avoided making a decision. His associates were quick to observe what appeared to be obvious indecisiveness.

But after several months had passed, it became clear that the sales manager had very unobtrusively been giving the various salesmen opportunities to demonstrate their attitudes and feelings. As a result, he was able to identify strong sentiments for one man whose subsequent promotion was enthusiastically accepted by the entire group.

In this instance, the sales manager's skillful performance was improperly interpreted as "indecisiveness." Their concern with irrelevant traits led his associates to overlook the adequacy of his performance. Would it not have been more appropriate to conclude that his human skill in working with others enabled him to adapt effectively to the requirements of a new situation?

Cases such as these would indicate that it is more useful to judge an administrator on the results of his performance than on his apparent traits. Skills are easier to identify than are traits and are less likely to be misinterpreted. Furthermore, skills offer a more directly applicable frame of reference for executive development, since any improvement in an administrator's skills must necessarily result in more effective performance.

Still another danger in many existing executive development programs lies in the unqualified enthusiasm with which some companies and colleges have embraced courses in "human relations." There would seem to be two inherent pitfalls here: (1) Human relations courses might only be imparting information or specific techniques, rather than developing the individual's human skill. (2) Even if individual development does take place, some companies, by placing all of their emphasis on human skill, may be completely overlooking the training requirements for top positions. They may run the risk of producing men with highly developed human skill who lack the conceptual ability to be effective top-level administrators.

It would appear important, then, that the training of a candidate for an administrative position be directed at the development of those skills which are most needed at the level of responsibility for which he is being considered.

Executive Placement

This three-skill concept suggests immediate possibilities for the creating of management teams of individuals with complementary skills. For example, one medium-size midwestern distributing organization has as president a man of unusual conceptual ability but extremely limited human skill. However, he has two vice presidents with exceptional human skill. These three men make up an executive committee which has been outstandingly successful, the skills of each member making up for deficiencies of the others. Perhaps the plan of two-man complementary conference leadership proposed by Robert F. Bales, in which the one leader maintains "task leadership" while the other provides "social leadership," might also be an example in point.[9]

Executive Selection

In trying to predetermine a prospective candidate's abilities on a job, much use is being made these days of various kinds of testing devices. Executives are being tested for everything from "decisiveness" to "conformity." These tests, as a recent article in *Fortune* points out, have achieved some highly questionable results when applied to performance on the job.[10] Would it not be much more productive to be concerned with skills of doing rather than with a number of traits which do not guarantee performance?

This three-skill approach makes trait testing unnecessary and substitutes for it procedures which examine a man's ability to cope with the actual problems and situations he will find on his job. These procedures, which indicate what a man can *do* in specific situations, are the same for selection and for measuring development. They will be described in the section on developing executive skills which follows.

This approach suggests that executives should *not* be chosen on the basis of their apparent possession of a number of behavior characteristics or traits, but on the basis of their possession of the requisite skills for the specific level of responsibility involved.

DEVELOPING THE SKILLS

For years many people have contended that leadership ability is inherent in certain chosen individuals. We talk of "born leaders,"

"born executives," "born salesmen." It is undoubtedly true that
certain people, naturally or innately, possess greater aptitude or
ability in certain skills. But research in psychology and physiology
would also indicate, first, that those having strong aptitudes and
abilities can improve their skill through practice and training, and,
secondly, that even those lacking the natural ability can improve their
performance and over-all effectiveness.

The *skill* conception of administration suggests that we may hope
to improve our administrative effectiveness and to develop better
administrators for the future. This skill conception implies *learning
by doing*. Different people learn in different ways, but skills are
developed through practice and through relating learning to one's own
personal experience and background. If well done, training in these
basic administrative skills should develop executive abilities more
surely and more rapidly than through unorganized experience. What,
then, are some of the ways in which this training can be conducted?

Technical Skill

Development of technical skill has received great attention for
many years by industry and educational institutions alike, and much
progress has been made. Sound grounding in the principles, structures, and processes of the individual specialty, coupled with actual
practice and experience during which the individual is watched and
helped by a superior, appear to be most effective. In view of the vast
amount of work which has been done in training people in the
technical skills, it would seem unnecessary in this article to suggest

Human Skill

Human skill, however, has been much less understood, and only
recently has systematic progress been made in developing it. Many
different approaches to the development of human skill are being
pursued by various universities and professional men today. These are
rooted in such disciplines as psychology, sociology, and anthropology.

Some of these approaches find their application in "applied
psychology," "human engineering," and a host of other manifestations requiring technical specialists to help the businessman with
his human problems. As a practical matter, however, the executive

must develop his own human skill, rather than lean on the advice of others. To be effective, he must develop his own personal point of view toward human activity, so that he will (a) recognize the feelings and sentiments which he brings to a situation; (b) have an attitude about his own experiences which will enable him to re-evaluate and learn from them; (c) develop ability in understanding what others by their actions and words (explicit or implicit) are trying to communicate to him; and (d) develop ability in successfully communicating his ideas and attitudes to others.[11]

This human skill can be developed by some individuals without formalized training. Others can be individually aided by their immediate superiors as an integral part of the "coaching" process to be described later. This aid depends for effectiveness, obviously, on the extent to which the superior possesses the human skill.

For larger groups, the use of case problems coupled with impromptu role playing can be very effective. This training can be established on a formal or informal basis, but it requires a skilled instructor and organized sequence of activities.[12] It affords as good an approximation to reality as can be provided on a continuing classroom basis and offers an opportunity for critical reflection not often found in actual practice. An important part of the procedure is the self-examination of the trainee's own concepts and values, which may enable him to develop more useful attitudes about himself and about others. With the change in attitude, hopefully, there may also come some active skill in dealing with human problems.

Human skill has also been tested in the classroom, within reasonable limits, by a series of analyses of detailed accounts of actual situations involving administrative action, together with a number of role-playing opportunities in which the individual is required to carry out the details of the action he has proposed. In this way an individual's understanding of the total situation and his own personal ability to something about it can be evaluated.

On the job, there should be frequent opportunities for a superior to observe an individual's ability to work effectively with others. These may appear to be highly subjective evaluations and to depend for validity on the human skill of the rater. But does not every promotion, in the last analysis, depend on someone's subjective judgment? And should this subjectivity be berated, or should we make a greater effort to develop people within our organizations with the human skill to make such judgments effectively?

Conceptual Skill

Conceptual skill, like human skill, has not been very widely understood. A number of methods have been tried to aid in developing this ability, with varying success. Some of the best results have always been achieved through the "coaching" of subordinates by superiors.[13] This is no new idea. It implies that one of the key responsibilities of the executive is to help his subordinates to develop their administrative potentials. One way a superior can help "coach" his subordinate is by assigning a particular responsibility, and then responding with searching questions or opinions, rather than giving answers, whenever the subordinate seeks help. When Benjamin F. Fairless, now chairman of the board of the United States Steel Corporation, was president of the corporation, he described his coaching activities:

> When one of my vice presidents or the head of one of our operating companies comes to me for instructions, I generally counter by asking him questions. First thing I know, he has told me how to solve the problem himself.

Obviously, this is an ideal and wholly natural procedure for administrative training, and applies to the development of technical and human skill, as well as to that of conceptual skill. However, its success must necessarily rest on the abilities and willingness of the superior to help the subordinate.

Another excellent way to develop conceptual skill is through trading jobs, that is, by moving promising young men through different functions of the business but at the same level of responsibility. This gives the man the chance literally to "be in the other fellow's shoes."

Other possibilities include: special assignments, particularly the kind which involve inter-departmental problems; and management boards, such as the McCormick Multiple Management plan, in which junior executives serve as advisers to top management on policy matters.

For larger groups, the kind of case-problems course described above, only using cases involving broad management policy and interdepartmental coordination, may be useful. Courses of this kind, often called "General Management" or "Business Policy," are becoming increasingly prevalent.

In the classroom, conceptual skill has also been evaluated with reasonable effectiveness by presenting a series of detailed descriptions of specific complex situations. In these the individual being tested is asked to set forth a course of action which responds to the underlying forces operating in each situation and which considers the implications of this action on the various functions and parts of the organization and its total environment.

On the job, the alert supervisor should find frequent opportunities to observe the extent to which the individual is able to relate himself and his job to the other functions and operations of the company.

Like human skill, conceptual skill, too, must become a natural part of the executive's makeup. Different methods may be indicated for developing different people, by virtue of their backgrounds, attitudes, and experience. But in every case that method should be chosen which will enable the executive to develop his own personal skill in visualizing the enterprise as a whole and in coordinating and integrating its various parts.

CONCLUSION

The purpose of this article has been to show that effective administration depends on three basic personal skills, which have been called *technical, human,* and *conceptual.* The administrator needs: (a) sufficient technical skill to accomplish the mechanics of the particular job for which he is responsible; (b) sufficient human skill in working with others to be an effective group member and to be able to build cooperative effort within the team he leads; (c) sufficient conceptual skill to recognize the interrelationships of the various factors involved in his situation, which will lead him to take that action which is likely to achieve the maximum good for the total organization.

The relative importance of these three skills seems to vary with the level of administrative responsibility. At lower levels, the major need is for technical and human skills. At higher levels, the administrator's effectiveness depends largely on human and conceptual skills. At the top, conceptual skill becomes the most important of all for successful administration.

This three-skill approach emphasizes that good administrators are not necessarily born; they may be developed. It transcends the need to identify specific traits in an effort to provide a more useful way of looking at the administrative process. By helping to identify the skills most needed at various levels of responsibility, it may prove useful in the selection, training, and promotion of executives.

RETROSPECTIVE COMMENTARY

When this article was first published nearly 20 years ago, there was a great deal of interest in trying to identify a set of ideal personality traits that would readily distinguish potential executive talent. The search for these traits was vigorously pursued in the hope that the selection and training of managers could be conducted with greater reliability.

This article was an attempt to focus attention on demonstrable skills of performance rather than on innate personality characteristics. And, while describing the three kinds of administrative skill (technical, human, and conceptual), it also attempted to highlight the importance of conceptual skill as a uniquely valuable managerial capability, long before the concept of corporate strategy was well defined or popularly understood.

It still appears useful to think of managerial ability in terms of these three basic, observable skills. It also still appears that the relative importance of these skills varies with the administrative level of the manager in the organization. However, my experience over the past 20 years, in working with senior executives in a wide variety of industries, suggests that several specific points require either sharp modification or substantial further refinement.

Human Skill

I now believe that this kind of skill could be usefully subdivided into (a) leadership ability within the manager's own unit and (b) skill in intergroup relationships. In my experience, outstanding capability in one of these roles is frequently accompanied by mediocre performance in the other.

Often, the most internally efficient department managers are those who have committed themselves fully to the unique values and criteria of their specialized functions, without acknowledging that other departments' differing values have any validity at all. For example, a production manager may be most efficient if he puts all his emphasis on obtaining a high degree of reliability in his production schedule. He would then resist any external pressures that place a higher priority on criteria other than delivering the required output on time. Or a sales manager may be most efficient if he puts all his emphasis on maintaining positive relationships with customers. He would then resist all pressures that would emphasize other values, such as ease of production or selling the highest gross margin items. In each case, the manager will probably receive strong support from his subordinates, who share the same values. But he will encounter severe antagonism from other departments with conflicting values.

To the extent that two departments' values conflict with each other, skillful intergroup relationships require some equivocation. But compromise is often perceived by departmental subordinates as a "sellout." Thus the manager is obliged to choose between gaining full support from subordinates or enjoying full collaboration with peers and/or superiors. Having both is rarely possible. Consequently, I would revise my original evaluation of human skill to say now that internal *intragroup* skills are essential in lower and middle management roles and that *intergroup* skills become increasingly important in successively higher levels of management.

Conceptual Skill

In retrospect, I now see that what I called conceptual skill depends entirely on a specific way of thinking about an enterprise. This "general management point of view," as it has come to be known, involves always thinking in terms of the following: relative emphases and priorities among conflicting objectives and criteria; relative tendencies and probabilities (rather than certainties); rough correlations and patterns among elements (rather than clear-cut cause-and-effect relationships).

I am now far less sanguine about the degree to which this way of thinking can be developed on the job. Unless a person has learned to think this way early in life, it is unrealistic to expect a major change on reaching executive status. Job rotation, special interdepartmental assignments, and working with case problems certainly provide opportunities for a person to enhance previously developed conceptual abilities. But I question how easily this way of thinking can be inculcated after a person passes adolescence. In this sense, then, conceptual skill should perhaps be viewed as an *innate* ability.

Technical Skill

In the original article, I suggested that specific technical skills are unimportant at top management levels. I cited as evidence the many professional managers who move easily from one industry to another without apparent loss of effectiveness.

I now believe this mobility is possible only in very large companies, where the chief executive has extensive staff assistance and highly competent, experienced technical operators throughout the organization. An old, established, large company has great operational momentum that enables the new chief executive to concentrate on strategic issues.

In smaller companies, where technical expertise is not as pervasive and seasoned staff assistance is not as available, I believe the chief executive has a much greater need for personal experience in the industry. He not only needs to know the right questions to ask his subordinates; he also needs enough industry background to know how to evaluate the answers.

Role of the Chief Executive

In the original article, I took too simplistic and naïve a view of the chief executive's role. My extensive work with company presidents and my own personal experience as a chief executive have given me much more respect for the difficulties and complexities of that role. I now know that every important executive action must strike a balance among so many conflicting values, objectives, and criteria that it will *always* be suboptimal from any single viewpoint. *Every* decision or choice affecting the whole enterprise has negative consequences for some of the parts.

The chief executive must try to perceive the conflicts and trace accurately their likely impact throughout the organization. Reluctantly, but wittingly, he may have to sacrifice the interests of a single unit or part for the good of the whole. He needs to be willing to accept solutions that are adequate and feasible in the total situation rather than what, from a single point of view, may be elegant or optimum.

Not only must the chief executive be an efficient operator, but he must also be an effective strategist. It is his responsibility to provide the framework and direction for overall company operations. He must continually specify where the company will place its emphasis in terms of products, services, and customers. He must define performance criteria and determine what special competences the company will emphasize. He also needs to set priorities and time-tables. He must establish the standards and controls necessary to monitor progress and to place limits on individual actions. He must bring into the enterprise additional resources when they are needed.

Moreover, he must change his management style and strike different balances among his personal skills as conditions change or as his organization grows in size and complexity. The *remedial* role (saving the organization when it is in great difficulty) calls for drastic human action and emphasizes conceptual and technical skills. The *maintaining* role (sustaining the organization in its present posture) emphasizes human skills and requires only modest technical or strategic changes. But the *innovative* role (developing and expanding the organization) demands high competence in both conceptual and intergroup skills, with the technical contribution provided primarily by subordinates.

In my view, it is impossible for anyone to perform well in these continually changing roles without help. Yet because effective management of the total enterprise involves constant suboptimizing, it is impossible for the chief executive to get unanimous or continuous support from his subordinates. If he is overly friendly or supportive, he may compromise his effectiveness or his objectivity. Yet somewhere in the organization, he needs to have a well informed, objective, understanding, and supportive sounding board with whom he can freely discuss his doubts, fears, and aspirations. Sometimes this function can be supplied by an outside director, the outside corporate counsel, or the company auditor. But such a confidant requires just as high a degree of conceptual and human skills as the chief executive himself; and to be truly helpful, he must know all about the company's operations, key personnel, and industry. This role has been largely overlooked in discussions of organizational requirements, but in my view, its proper fulfillment is essential to the success of the chief executive and the enterprise.

Conclusion

I now realize more fully that managers at all levels require some competence in each of the three skills. Even managers at the lowest levels must continually use all of them. Dealing with the external demands on a manager's unit requires conceptual skill; the limited physical and financial resources available to him tax his technical skill; and the capabilities and demands of the persons with whom he deals make it essential that he possess human skill. A clear idea of these skills and of ways to measure a manager's competence in each category still appears to me to be a most effective tool for top management, not only in understanding executive behavior, but also in the selection, training, and promotion of managers at all levels.

References

1. Perrin Stryker, "The Growing Pains of Executive Development." *Advanced Management*, August 1954, p. 15.
2. From a mimeographed case in the files of the Harvard Business School; copyrighted by the President and Fellows of Harvard College.
3. *Functions of the Executive* (Cambridge, Harvard University Press, 1948), p. 235.
4. A. Zaleznik, *Foreman Training in a Growing Enterprise* (Boston, Division of Research, Harvard Business School, 1951).
5. Harriet O. Ronken and Paul R. Lawrence, *Administering Changes* (Boston, Division of Research, Harvard Business School, 1952).
6. Edmund P. Learned, David H. Ulrich, and Donald R. Booz, *Executive Action* (Boston, Division of Research, Harvard Business School, 1950).
7. *Executive Leadership* (New York, Harper & Brothers, 1953); see also "Leadership Pattern in the Plant," HBR January-February 1954, p. 63.
8. "What Should a President Do?" *Dun's Review*, August 1951, p. 21
9. "In Conference," HBR March-April 1954, p. 44.
10. William H. Whyte, Jr., "The Fallacies of 'Personality' Testing," *Fortune*, September 1954, p. 117.
11. For a further discussion of this point, see F. J. Roethlisberger, "Training Supervisors in Human Relations," HBR September 1951, p. 47.
12. See, for example, A. Winn, "Training in Administration and Human Relations," *Personnel*, September 1953, p. 139; see also, Kenneth R. Andrews, "Executive Training by the Case Method," HBR September 1951, p. 58.
13. For a more complete development of the concept of "coaching," see Myles L. Mace, *The Growth and Development of Executives* (Boston, Division of Research, Harvard Business School, 1950).
14. "What Should a President Do?" *Dun's Review*, July 1951, p. 14.

PART 3 THE WORK OF MANAGEMENT

Every library manager expects to plan, to make decisions affecting the library and its staff, and to worry about the design of jobs, the nature of the work, and the satisfaction of the people who do the library's work. Part 3 considers these aspects of the management process.

The papers presented here offer theoretical perspectives and empirical investigations on the design of libraries in terms of organizational structure and in terms of the work done in libraries. In 1973, Herbert Simon in his article, "Applying Information Technology to Organizational Design," observed that organizational structure would change as the technologies developed relating to information processing systems. The papers by Charles Martell and Mercedes Utawale, Thomas W. Shaughnessy, and Klaus Musmann offer testimony to that change. Although the papers were not written primarily to describe the change in libraries, and in library jobs brought about the introduction of new technologies, the descriptions emerge.

Within organizations, decision making is an organizational choice made among various alternatives. Four papers on decision making were selected to describe the complexity of the process and to call attention to several models of decision making. The emphasis in each of these selections is on decision making done by the library as organization rather than on decision making done by the library manager as individual. The rational model, the most common model, forms the basis of Simon's paper and Victor H. Vroom's. Simon suggests that the structure of the organization may look quite different if the organization is structured according to decision making and information-processing systems instead of collections of people. In Simon's view, the rapid development of the technology of information processing makes possible more rational decisions. The new technology also will change the internal structure of organizations.

Vroom, like Simon, assumes that within the organization there is agreement on objectives and that a set of common values exists. He also assumes that decision makers seek an effective decision which is dependent upon the quality or rationality of the decision and the acceptance of the decision by subordinates. Acceptance of the decision leads Vroom to a consideration of process and style of the leader as decision maker. The rational model assumes that the organization has agreed upon goals and a set of common values so the decisions on recommended courses of action will be the result of reasoned problem solving. The rational model of decision making has its base in the belief that the choice among the alternatives will enhance the agreed upon goals and will support the commonly held values. In the rational model the choice is deliberate and the implementation clear.

In his article, "From Economic To Political Analysis of Library Decision Making," Jeffrey A. Raffel brings the economic model and the political model to the understanding of decision making in libraries. In the context of the political model, decisions are made through conflict resolution. This model assumes that there is no single agreed upon goal in the organization. Instead, multiple values and objectives exist so that the decision, when made, will tend to favor one group over another. The choice among various alternatives generally is not linked to any agreed upon overall objectives. Negotiation, the formation of coalitions, and the notion of the "survival of the fittest" all play a part in this model. Reasoned problem solving does not occur in the political model.

Joseph McDonald's paper synthesizes for libraries some of the other theories on decision making. He links decision making to the need for information and offers a description of the various kinds of information required.

As was mentioned in Part 1, Charles Perrow has asserted that various attempts to change an organization through job design are likely to be ineffective. Others still are not sure; five papers in this section consider job design, job enrichment, and job enlargement.

The pioneering work of Frederick Herzberg and his colleagues began as efforts to motivate workers and to increase worker satisfaction on the job. Herzberg's theoretical work on motivation has its base in many studies on motivation conducted by Herzberg and his colleagues. While this work has been criticized for flaws in its methodology and its insignificant results, Herzberg's recommendations on job enrichment and job design has been adopted widely.

J. Richard Hackman et al, describe the theory of job enrichment and present a strategy for job redesign. The strategy is based on a set of diagnostic tools used to collect data about jobs and the people who do them and has been tested in a number of organizations. The jobs tested basically were clerical and routine in nature.

Martell and Untawale adopt the Hackman et al, strategy. In "Work Enrichment for Academic Libraries," they describe an actual library study in which jobs, mainly clerical and repetitive in nature, changed through the use of a strategy similar to that of Hackman's. The departmental structure in the library changed too. That change supports Simon's predictions as to the impact of information processing on organizational structure.

Shaughnessy, like Martell and Untawale, corroborates Simon's insights on the influence of technology and automation on organizational design. Shaughnessy also speculates on the effect of technology on the design of library jobs. Musmann's paper, "Socio-technical Theory and Job Design in Libraries," ranges widely. He comments on Herzberg's influence and offers some consideration of the impact of technology and automation on the design of library departmental structures and the design of library jobs.

The last two papers in this section deal with the complex issues of motivation and job satisfaction. Herzberg's work is carefully described in George D'Elia's paper. D'Elia's study is on the job satisfaction of a group of beginning librarians without considering the library settings in which they work. The study I conducted with JoAnn Verdin investigated job satisfaction among employees in particular library settings. The essential difference between these two studies on job satisfaction in libraries is that D'Elia studies professional librarians outside the context of their work environment; Lynch and Verdin study *all* full-time employees, librarians and others, in the context of the work environment and in the specific setting of the library department.

Applying Information Technology To Organization Design

Herbert A. Simon

IN the past, organization theory has been mainly concerned with what might be called "organization for production"—that is, with systems that use the services of substantial numbers of employees to generate, more or less continuously, some kind of output or "product."[1] The normative theory of organization, aimed at enhancing organizational efficiency and effectiveness, traditionally paid special attention to two problems: how to divide up the work for its efficient performance and in such a way as to keep the needs for coordination of the parts within manageable bounds; and how to construct and maintain mechanisms for coordinating the several organizational parts—especially authority mechanisms.

Research on "human relations" in organizations, beginning on a substantial scale in the 1930s, turned attention in organizational design to the linkage betwen the individual as organization member and the pattern of organizational activity. The principal normative concern here was to create organizational environments in which employees would be motivated to join the organization, to remain in it, and to contribute vigorously and effectively to its goals. As a result of theory and empirical research in human relations, the factory and office came to be viewed as relatively impoverished human environments—starving both the human mind and the human emotions. Proposals were advanced for the redesign of organizations in ways that would make work intellectually more stimulating (or less boring), and give the worker a greater feeling of participation in the decisions governing his activity. "Job enrichment" and "democratic management" are labels commonly applied to these emphases in organizational design.[2]

The human relations movement did not limit itself to redesigning organizations to achieve the traditional goals of organizational effectiveness and efficiency. It also raised fundamental value questions of whether organizations *should* be designed in these terms; or whether, on the other hand, there should be a deliberate sacrifice of effectiveness and efficiency in order to make work itself a rewarding and enjoyable part of human life. This value issue is sometimes obscured in the literature when the assumption is made, implicitly or explicitly, that "the happy employee is the productive employee." That assumption tends to prevail through the early writings on human relations; but has been frequently questioned or attacked in recent years by the social critics of the New Left.

I do not intend to enter into that controversy here. I raise the issue because I think the debate has been carried out on premises that are less and less valid in today's organizations, and will be still less valid in the organizations of the future. The attack on work in organizations as dehumanizing generally takes as its model of the organization a system engaged in mass repetitive processing of materials or symbols— the assembly line or a room full of clerks or draftsmen. Chaplin's movie, "Modern Times," exaggerates only slightly the portrait of the factory given in the human relations literature.

But with the introduction of highly automated machinery, and particularly with the introduction of mechanized information processing equipment, the assembly line becomes a rather rare form of organization of production, as does the repetitive unautomated clerical process. The human operative or clerk is less often a cog in the ongoing production process, or even the first-level controller of that process. He is more and more an observer, moderator, maintenance man, and repairman for a nearly autonomous process that can carry on for significant intervals of time without direct human intervention.

The question of whether "the happy employee is the productive employee" still needs asking under these new conditions of employment. But it is not obvious that the question will have the same answer it had in the past. The problems of cognitive impoverishment and alienation may be replaced by quite new problems—or may disappear altogether. My own assessment—based on direct observation and the studies of others of highly automated work situations— is that the new environment will be, for most workers, a more pleasant and humane environment than the old. We will need a great deal more experience with this new environment, however, to provide solid evidential foundations for that optimism.

But I am getting a bit ahead of my story, for I have not yet said why I think organizations are changing in the directions I have mentioned.

THE POST-INDUSTRIAL SOCIETY

Peter Drucker has used the phrase "post-industrial society" to describe the emerging world in which manufacturing production, and the activities associated with it, plays a much less central role than it did in the world of the past century. Organizations in the post-industrial society provide services, many of them intangible, more than they manufacture things. Already, a large part of the economic activity of our society consist in providing services for education, health, and leisure-time activities.

Providing services tends to pose different organizational problems from producing tangible goods. It is usually more difficult to define appropriate output measures for service organizations than for organizations that produce tangible commodities. Whatever problems are present in measuring the quality of goods are magnified greatly in measuring the quality of services. The point can be illustrated by comparing two versions of the same economic activity, first viewed as goods-producing activity, then as a service-producing activity: that is, producing *houses* and *housing* respectively.

A house is a tangible commodity that can be manufactured and distributed through the usual market mechanisms; housing is a bundle of services provided by a dwelling in the context of a neighborhood, with schools, streets, shopping facilities, and a pattern of social interaction among the inhabitants. However complex it may be to define the qualities of a house, narrowly conceived as a structure, it is far more complex to define the qualities of housing, in the sense of a situation that creates and supports a pattern of social activity.

Related to the tendency of organizations in our society to broaden the definition of their goals from the production of tangible commodities to the production of bundles of services that may or may not be associated with tangible commodities, is a tendency to broaden their concern for the externalities associated with their activities. Externalities are simply those consequences of action that are not charged, through the existing market mechanisms, to the actors. The classical example is the factory smoke whose social costs have not generally been paid by the consumers of the factory's product.

It may be that organizations producing services usually have more and larger externalities associated with their activities than organizations producing goods; it may be that we are simply becoming more sensitive in our society to the indirect consequences of organizational activity directed toward specialized goals; it may be that, with the growth of population and technology, the actual interdependencies of organizations, and hence the externalities they cause, are becoming more extensive and significant. Whatever the reasons—and all three of those mentioned probably contribute to the trend—organizational decision making in the organizations of the post-industrial world shows every sign of becoming a great deal more complex than the decision making of the past. As a consequence of this fact, the decision-making process, rather than the processes contributing immediately and directly to the production of the organization's final output, will bulk larger and larger as *the* central activity in which the organization is engaged.

In the post-industrial society, the central problem is not how to organize to produce efficiently (although this will always remain an important consideration), but how to organize to make decisions— that is, to process information. Until recent years, decision making was exclusively a human activity; it involved processes going on inside the human head and symbolic communication among humans. In our present world, decision making is shared between the human and mechanized components of man-machine systems, the machines being those devices we call computers. The division of labor between the human and computer components in these systems has changed steadily over the past 20 years, and we can expect it to continue to change as the sophistication of computer technology—and particularly computer programming or "software" technology—grows.

The anatomy of an organization viewed as a decision-making and information-processing system may look very different from the anatomy of the same organization viewed as a collection of people. The latter viewpoint, which is the traditional one, focuses attention on the groupings of human beings—that is, the departmentalization. The former viewpoint, on the other hand, focuses on the decision-making process itself—that is, upon the flows and transformations of symbols. If we carve an organization, conceptually, into subsystems on the basis of the principal components into which the decision-making process divides, we may, and probably will, arrive at a very different dissection than if we carve it into its departmental and subdepartmental components. Moreover, the greater the interdependencies among the departmental components, the greater will be the difference in these two ways of conceptualizing the organization.

Both of these viewpoints are useful and even essential in arriving at sound designs for organizations. In this analysis, I shall emphasize the less conventional point of view and shall discuss the decision-making process disembodied, so to speak, from the flesh-and-blood (or glass and metal, as the case may be) decision makers who actually carry out this process. Instead of watching a man or computer as information reaches him and he processes it and transmits new information in his turn, we will watch information as it flows from one man or computer to another and is transformed in the course of flow. This approach, if it has no other advantages (though I believe it does), will give us a fresh look at the design of organizations.

TWO REQUIREMENTS OF ORGANIZATIONAL DESIGN

The division of labor is quite as important in organizing decision making as in organizing production, but what is being divided is different in the two cases. From the information processing point of view, division of labor means factoring the total system of decisions that need to be made into relatively independent subsystems, each one of which can be designed with only minimal concern for its interactions with the others. The division is necessary because the processors that are available to organizations, whether humans or computers, are very limited in their processing capacity in comparison with the magnitude of the decision problems that organizations face. The number of alternatives that can be considered; the intricacy of the chains of consequences that can be traced—all of these are severely restricted by the limited capacities of the available processors.

Any division of labor among decisional subsystems creates externalities, which arise out of the interdependencies among the subsystems that are ignored. What is wanted is a factorization that minimizes these externalities and consequently permits a maximum degree of decentralization of final decision to the subsystems, and a maximum use of relatively simple and cheap coordinating devices like the market mechanism to relate each of the decisional subsystems with the others.

Not only must the size of decision problems handled by organizations be reduced to manageable proportions by factorization, but the number of decisions to be processed must be limited by applying good principles of attention management. Attention management for an organization means exactly what it means for an individual human being: processing capacity must be allocated to specific decision tasks, and if the total capacity is not adequate to the totality of tasks, then priorities must be set so that the most important or critical tasks are attended to.

The information-processing systems of our contemporary world swim in an exceedingly rich soup of information, of symbols. In a world of this kind, the scarce resource is not information; it is processing capacity to attend to information. Attention is the chief bottleneck in organizational activity, and the bottleneck becomes narrower and narrower as we move to the tops of organizations, where parallel processing capacity becomes less easy to provide without damaging the coordinating function that is a prime responsibility of these levels.

The richness of the informational environment and the scarcity of attention have many consequences for organizational design, some of which will be developed presently. At this point, only a couple of further comments need to be made. First, the difficulty of coping with the information-rich environment is compounded by the fact that most information relevant to top-level and long-run organizational decisions typically originates outside the organization, and hence in forms and quantities that are beyond its control. This means that the organization must have an "interface" for ingesting such information selectively, and for translating it into formats that are compatible with its internal information flows and systems.

Second, if attention is the scarce resource, then it becomes particularly important to distinguish between problems for decision that come with deadlines attached (real-time decision), and problems that have relatively flexible deadlines. Rather different system designs are called for to handle these different kinds of decisions.

In summary, the inherent capacity limits of information-processing systems impose two requirements on organizational design: that the totality of decision problems be factored in such a way as to minimize the interdependence of the components; and that the entire system be so structured as to conserve the scarce resource, attention. The organizational design must provide for interfaces to handle information that originates outside the organization, and special provision must be made for decisions that have particular time limits associated with them.

Applying these basic design requirements makes it easy to see the fallacy in some recent, and more or less abortive, approaches to the improvement of information systems: municipal data banks, and management information systems. There was great enthusiasm, only a couple of years ago, for developing comprehensive data banks for metropolitan areas—these data banks to incorporate in a single system all of the myriad pieces of information about land and its uses, and about people and their activities that are generated by the operations of urban government. As the result of several attempts to construct such systems, the enthusiasm has been much moderated, and several incipient undertakings of this kind have been abandoned. There were several reasons for the disenchantment that followed the initial attempts at constructing such systems. First, the data processing and data storage tasks proved much larger and more complex than had been imagined. Perhaps more crucial, it became less and less clear just how the data were to enter into the the decision-making process, or indeed to just what decisions they were relevant.

The lesson is clear. There is no magic in "comprehensiveness." It may be sufficient motive to climb a mountain "because it is there," but the mere existence of a mass of data is not a sufficient reason for collecting it into a single, comprehensive information system. Indeed, the problem is quite the opposite: of finding way of factoring decision problems in order to relate the several components to their respective relevant data sources. Analysis of the decision-making system and its data requirements must come first; only then can a reasonable approach be made to defining the data systems that will support the decision-making process.

The history of management information systems has been nearly the same as the history of municipal data banks. In the enthusiasm to make use of the enormous power of computers, there was a tendency, in designing such systems, to take the existing source records as starting point and to try to give top management access to all this information. The question was not asked, or not asked with sufficient seriousness, whether top management either wanted or needed such information, nor whether the information that top management needed and should want could in fact be derived from these particular source records. The systems were not designed to conserve the critical scarce resource—the attention of managers—and they tended to ignore the fact that the information most important to top managers comes mainly from external sources and not from the internal records that were immediately accessible for mechanized processing.

Thus many of the efforts to design information systems for municipalities and corporations fell into the fallacy of thinking that "more information is better." They took over, implicitly, the assumptions of a past society where information rather than attention was the scarce resource.

CHARACTERISTICS OF THE TECHNOLOGY

Good design requires bringing the desired ends into effective relation with the available means. To design effective decision making organizations, we must understand the structure of the decisions to be made; and we must understand the decision-making tools at our disposal, both human and mechanical—men and computers.

The Human Components

In our fascination with the new capabilities that computers offer us, we must be careful not to forget that our human decision makers have some pretty remarkable qualities too. Each human decision maker is provided with a sizeable memory that is stocked cumulatively over a long period of years with various kinds of relevant and irrelevant information and skills. Each is able to communicate in natural language with his fellows, either in direct face-to-face settings or by remote devices like the telephone.

Suppose, for example, that we were interested in designing an organization that would lead us to the most expert source of information in the United States about any particular question that happened to arise. Now this expert information is stored both in human heads and in books. Moreover, the information in books is also indexed in human heads, so that usually the most expeditious way to find the right book is to ask a human who is an expert on the subject the book deals with. Not only are books indexed in human heads, but people are also. Taking these resources into account, the most powerful information processing system for carrying out this search task is the aggregate of memory that is distributed among 200 million human heads, together with the telephone system that links these distributed memories. On receipt of the inquiry, I pick up the phone and call the person, among my acquaintances, whose field of expertness is as close as possible (it need not be very close at all). I ask him, not for the answer to the question, but for the name of the person in his circle of acquaintance who is closest to being an expert on the topic. I repeat the process until I have the information I want. It will be a rare instance when more than three or four calls are required.

Suppose that the question is whether whales have spleens. (I can't imagine why we want to know, but this example is as good as any other.) I call a biologist, who refers me to an ichthyologist, who refers me to a specialist on whales, who either knows the answer or can refer me to the book where I will find it.

I don't mean to propose that we junk all of our other information systems and place sole reliance on the telephone and the vast distributed memory with which it connects us. I am even a little reluctant to mention this particular technique publicly, because if it attains general popularity, we will all be busy answering the phone, and the trick will be spoiled for those of us who use it extensively. It does provide, however, a useful illustration of how we must think about information-processing systems—including human systems— their components and interconnections, if we are to design them well. We must learn to characterize them in terms of the sizes of their memories, the ways in which those memories are indexed, their processing rates, and the rapidity with which they can respond. The human components of information systems are just as describable as the machine components, and since World War II we have learned a great deal, through psychological research, about the parameters of the human system.

Our new and growing understanding of information processing enables us to look at familiar processing systems—man and telephone—in new ways. It also introduces us to new kinds of systems, which we put under the general label of "computers," that have capabilities of the most varied kinds.

The Computer as Memory

The computer is, first of all, a memory. I have already expressed my qualms about confusing the design of an information-*collecting* system with the design of an information-*processing* system. The fault, of course, is not in collecting information (although that may be costly in itself); it is in demanding the scarce attention of decision makers to the information that has been collected. Memories, as components of information-processing systems, need to be viewed as stores of *potential* information, which, if indexed effectively, can become available at a reasonable cost whenever it is needed as input to a decision-making process.

Consider a man who has collected a library of 30,000 books. Even if he reads one book a day—a pretty good clip—it will take him 100 years to read through all the shelves. We may even consider it a bit ostentatious of him to have collected more books than he can possibly read—as though he were trying to impress us with his learning.

However, we must not be too hasty in judging him. If his library is properly indexed, then our collector has potential access to *any* of the information in the 30,000 volumes. He is quite justified in collecting more volumes than he can read if he cannot predict in advance what particular information he will need in the future.

The computer memories that are employed today are not, in general, large compared with the paper-and-ink memories we call libraries. They are, in general, better indexed for rapid retrieval of information, and one of the important directions of technological progress since the computer has appeared on the scene has been our understanding of the indexing and information retrieval processes, and in our ability to carry these out mechanically.

The Computer as Processor

In addition to being a memory, the computer is also a processor that possesses quite general capabilities for handling symbols of all kinds, numerical and non-numerical. This is the computer's most novel feature. Nonhuman memories have been familiar to man since the invention of writing. Nonhuman symbol manipulation is something quite new, and even after 20 years, we are just beginning to glimpse its potential.[3]

Up to the present time, perhaps the most important use of the computer in decision making (though not the use that accounts for the bulk of computer time that is consumed by organizations) is to model complex situations, and to infer the consequences of alternative decisions. Some of this modelling makes use of mathematical techniques, like linear programming, that permit the calculation of optimal courses of action, hence serve as direct decision-making tools. In other forms of modelling, the computer serves as a simulator, calculating out the alternative histories of a system that would follow on different decision strategies.

The term "management information system" has generally been construed narrowly, and has been applied to large information storage and retrieval systems, like those mentioned earlier, in which the computer does only very simple processing of the information. The term would be better applied to the optimizing and simulation models that are increasingly used to illuminate various areas of management decision—models that are usually referred to as "operations research" and "strategic planning." Such models, however they are labelled, probably give us a better preview of the future uses of computers in organizational decision systems than do the explicitly named management information systems.

Let me cite one example of an area of application for a strategic planning model. In the next decades, our society faces some important and difficult policy decisions with respect to the production and use of energy. In the past, the national energy problem was perceived mostly as a resource problem, and it was left in considerable part to private management through market mechanisms. Today, we see that the use of energy has important indirect consequences for the environment, and we see also that the adequacy of fuel resources for producing energy will depend on such broader trends as the rates of development of industrializing countries and the decisions we made with respect to R & D into energy technology.

The number of important variables involved in the energy picture is so large, and the interconnections among variables so intricate, that common sense and everyday reasoning no longer provide adequate guides to energy policies—if, indeed, they ever did. Nor is there a simple organizational solution of a traditional kind: establishing a federal agency with comprehensive jurisdiction over energy problems, or, alternatively, tinkering with the market mechanism. Agency reorganization is no solution for at least two reasons. First, energy problems cannot be separated neatly from other problems. What would be the relation of a comprehensive jurisdiction over environmental problems? The fragmentation of responsibility for energy policy in the federal government today is a consequence of the intertwining of those problems with others. Second, even if there were such an agency, it too would need a systematic framework within which to take up its decision problems. Tinkering with market mechanisms raises the same difficulty—without a decision framework, we do not know how to tinker.

Hence, the most important organizational requirement for handling energy policy in an intelligent way is the creation of one or more models—either of an optimizing or simulation type—to provide coherence to the decision-making process. No doubt, it is of some importance to locate the responsibility for developing and exploiting such models in appropriate places in the governmental and industrial structure. But the mere existence of the models, wherever located, cannot but have a major impact on energy policy decisions. Surprisingly, for first comprehensive models of the energy system are just now under construction, although the need for them has been fairly obvious for some years. The tardiness of response to the need is evidence both of the novelty of the modelling technology and the novelty of looking at organization as a collection of decision systems rather than a collection of agencies and departments.[4]

Computer Access to External Information

A third point must be made about the characteristics of the computer as a component of the organization's information processing system. I have mentioned as one limitation of the management information systems of recent years their great reliance on information that is generated internally, within the organization itself—for example, production and accounting information. A major reason for the emphasis on internal information is that, since the organization controls the production of this information, it is not hard to produce it in machine-readable form. Then no costly step is involved in getting it inside the computer.

If we examine the kinds of external information that executives use, we find that a large proportion of it is simply natural language text—the pages of newspapers, trade magazines, technical journals, and so on. Natural language text can, of course, be stored in computer memory after it is translated into some machine-readable form—punched cards, magnetic tape, or the like. Once stored in memory, computer programs can be written to index it automatically and to retrieve information from it in response to inquiries of a variety of kinds.

The only barrier, therefore, to making available to the mechanized components of organizational information systems the same kind of external information that executives now rely upon is the cost of putting the information into machine-readable form. Technologically, the obstacle is not insuperable; it is possible to produce devices that will translate printed text into magnetic tape. The costs of doing this, however, are rather high, and the prospects do not appear bright for reducing them rapidly.

This particular Gordian knot should be cut, not united. Substantially every word that is now printed in a newspaper, journal, or book passes at some time during its prior history through a machine—typewritter or telesetting machine—that could produce a machine-readable version of the text at the same time that it produces the man-readable version, and at an insignificant incremental cost. Hence, we may look forward to a time in the near future when the written word will be almost universally available in both machine-readable and man-readable editions. Once the switchover begins, so that there is a market for the machine-readable versions, we can expect the conversion process to go very rapidly. It is a little like the telephone—the more people who have them, the more worthwhile to get one.

This development will open up a whole new range of application of computers to organization information systems. It will enable computers to serve as initial filters for most of the information that enters the organization from outside, and will thereby help reduce the attentional demands on executives.

Matching Techniques to Requirements

These comments will serve to indicate what is involved in fitting together the requirements of organization information systems with the characteristics of the information technology that is now available or emerging. The key to the successful design of information systems lies in matching the technology to the limits of the attentional resources. From this general principle, we can derive several rules of thumb to guide us when we are considering adding a component to an existing information-processing system.

In general, an additional component (man or machine) for an information-processing system will improve the system's performance only if:

1. Its output is small in comparison with its input, so that it conserves attention instead of making additional demands on attention;
2. It incorporates effective indexes of both passive and active kinds (active indexes are processes that automatically select and filter information for subsequent transmission);
3. It incorporates analytic and synthetic models that are capable not merely of storing and retrieving information, but of solving problems, evaluating solutions, and making decisions.

These heuristics are applicable to all components of information systems, not just to computers. It is a useful exercise, for example, to look at television in their light, as a component of a political information system. Television can be used to deliver lectures or to exhibit concrete scenes and events. As a source of lectures, its relatively undifferentiated mass audience is a severe handicap—for almost any individual member of the audience, we could devise a lecture that would be more appropriate than the one actually screened. In communicating information through pictures it has the further disadvantages of its inability to abstract, to generalize, or to sample properly from complex populations of events. It possesses no analytic capabilities other than those provided by the commentator.

To point to these severe deficiencies of television as a source of politically relevant information is not to deny its effects on the political system. The most obvious of these effects is its power to focus the attention of an entire society for a period of time on a particular set of events—whether these be trips to the moon, riots, or summit conferences. In general, television *informs* very little about such events, but it may succeed in evoking strong emotions simultaneously from millions of viewers, and consequently in rearranging the public agenda.

POLITICS AS INFORMATION PROCESSING

This last example, as well as the earlier example of energy policy, are illustrative of a broader point: that our political institutions are organizations, and that what we have said about the design of information-processing systems for organizations applies fully to the design of the decision-making components of the political system. Nowhere is the problem of attention management and the conservation of attention of greater importance than in the political process.

The themes of alienation of the electorate, and the need to "return government to the people," which have been prominent in recent public discussion of our institutions are, of course, not new to the American political scene. Cynicism about the political process is deeply ingrained in the American culture. For the most part, proposals for political reform have focused on strengthening controls over the professional full-time participants in the system, elected or appointed (e.g., recall elections, presidential primary), or on creating new channels of direct popular participation in decision making (e.g., the initiative and referendum, official provision for citizen participation in program administration).

As high technology has come to play a larger role in our society, and in the provision of governmental services in particular, the growing difficulties of assuring that participation will be informed participation have not gone unnoticed. Informed participation in decision is a problem not only for the part-time contributors to the system—the voters—but for elected representatives and high-level administrators as well. It is at the core of the familiar organizational problem of the relation of experts to laymen.

An Example of Poorly Informed Participation

The phosphate detergent fiasco is only the most recent of innumerable instances of the difficulties of settling technical issues with wide public involvement. A problem existed: excessive algal bloom in lakes. It was known that this condition only incurred in waters having a high level of organic nutrients; phosphate, in particular, was highly suspect as culprit. (Clear scientific evidence on the precise mechanisms of eutrophication, and the precise conditions under which it will or won't occur is nearly non-existent.) A substantial fraction of the phosphate in water is contributed by household detergents. There exist non-phosphate or low-phosphate detergents. Therefore—but the "therefore," however obvious it may seem, left unanswered most of the critical questions: Would removal of phosphate from household detergents do any good if other phosphate sources remained? Was phosphate, in fact, the principal culprit? What are the alternative methods, other than changing detergents, for eliminating phosphate from lakes? What are the properties of the alternative detergents, and what consequences would their use have? What would be the relative costs of various courses of action?

As our previous analysis should lead us to predict, the mass media had a large impact in focusing public attention on the eutrophication problem, and in creating insistent demands for forceful action. There is no difficulty in picturing on television a dead fish or (at least on color television) an algae-green lake. What the mass media could not do was to remove the scientific unknowns from the problem, or provide a systems analysis of alternatives. As a result of the pressure for action, the federal government came close to banning phosphate from detergents, but unfortunately had not done so by the time some of the difficulties and dangers of the alternatives had become known.

My intent here is not to suggest what the solution of the problem should have been, but to use these events to point to the weaknesses of our current decision-making processes in political matters where complex technical issues are involved. Most of the current proposals to remedy these weaknesses are of a traditional kind: create new organizations to provide the technical expertise that is now lacking. The two most prominent proposals are the creation or strengthening of organizations that would represent the consumer and the creation of organizations for technology assessment, these latter to be responsible to the legislative body.

So far as these proposals go, they seem to me sound, but I would warn that we should not expect too much from them. In particular, in talking about "consumer organizations," we must remember that that is precisely what a government is created to be, and thus new organizations of this kind are no more exempt from the iron law of bureaucracy than are existing institutions (as experience with trade unions, political parties, and the American Medical Association should have taught us).

The Contribution of Systems Analysis

If magic is to be performed, it will not come through the mere creation of new organizations. The problem is not primarily one of control but of information—not one of enforcing virtue but of discovering the path of virtue. We do not need new organizations so much as we need new decision processes. To illustrate my meaning, let me cite some happier examples than the phosphate debate of recent public discussion.

The struggles over the anti-ballistic missile and the supersonic transport are, to my mind, examples of what we may hope for in the way of informed discussion of highly technical and complex issues. This does not mean that the correct decisions were necessarily reached. I have no more infallible means for deciding that than did the disputants at the time of the debate. Honest and reasonable men could and did take either side of either question. But what distinguished these particular debates was that both sides were armed with sophisticated analyses based on man-years of careful study supported by quantitative models. For this reason, it was possible for the layman, with a reasonable expenditure of time, to understand where the differences lay—which disagreements about assumptions were responsible for the divergent conclusions reached. Moreover, for each of the decisions there was not a single analysis but several, prepared by protagonists that had different sets of interests and different viewpoints.

Thus, the ABM and SST decision processes were informed by analyses that met three essential criteria: comprehensiveness, technical sophistication, and pluralism. Satisfaction of these criteria does not guarantee that correct decisions are reached—in a world of uncertainty and conflict of interest, that guarantee can seldom be provided. It does tend to assure that the decisions reached are such as reasonable men of good will could arrive at. And it is the guarantee of due process, not the guarantee of infallibility, that democratic institutions require.

In making this plea for more and better systems analyses, and more and better institutional arrangements for carrying them out, I should not want to be thought to be urging centralization of any and all decisions. An equally important direction for improvement of decision processes is to instill new vigor into market mechanisms as an essential component of a decentralized society. Our growing awareness of the externalities, particularly environmental costs, that the price system has ignored in the past has caused something of a crisis of confidence in market mechanisms as social regulators and decision makers. Where externalities are present, there is an alternative, however, to centralization: incorporating the externalities in the pricing process. A tax on oxides of sulphur emitted into the atmosphere is an example of such a measure. To attack such a proposal as "a license to pollute" is to substitute sloganizing for problem solving. We need not only to solve the problems we perceive, but, in solving them, to minimize the drain on our scarce resources. Using the price system as motivator, where it is applicable, is one of the most powerful means available to us for enlisting a multitude of energies and minds into the search for least-cost solutions to our problems.

CONCLUSION

The major problems of governmental (and corporate and educational) organization today are not problems of departmentalization and coordination of operating units. Instead, they are problems of organizing information storage and information processing—not problems of the division of labor, but problems of the factorization of decision making. These organizational problems are best attacked, at least to a first approximation, by examining the information system in abstraction from agency and department structure.

With the rapid development of information-processing technology, the corporate and public decision-making processes are becoming immensely more sophisticated and rational than they were in past eras. If we require any proof for this, we need only compare the ABM debate (regardless of whether we like its outcome) with any debate on the Acropolis reported by Thucydides—or, for that matter, with any debate in the U.S. Congress in the first half of this century.

With the development of information-processing technology, we have a growing capacity to consider interactions and tradeoffs among alternatives and consequences; to cumulate our understanding of fragments of the whole problem by embedding these fragments in comprehensive models.

Barbara Ward and others have pointed out to us that the largest crises in our world today are crises of aspirations. The population problem is as old as Man. What is new about it today is that we are resolved not to accept a gloomy outcome, but to deal with it. For centuries, Man's actions have been creating all kinds of unintended and unexpected consequences. He could live in good conscience with his actions to the extent that he was unaware of these consequences. Today, we can trace minute and indirect effects of our behavior: the relation of smoking to cancer, the relation of the brittleness of eagles' eggs to the presence of DDT in the environment. With this new ability to trace effects, we feel responsible for them in a way we previously did not. The intellectual awakening is also a moral awakening.

The new problems created (or made visible) by our new scientific knowledge are symptoms of progress, not omens of doom. They demonstrate that Mankind now possess the analytic tools that are basic to understanding his problems—basic to understanding the human condition.

Of course, to understand problems is not necessarily to solve them. But it *is* the essential first step. The new information technology that we are creating enables us to take that step.

Some Further Reading

The premises about the nature of organizations upon which this essay rests are developed and documented in *Administrative Behavior* (Macmillan, 1947, 1957) and in the two final chapters of March and Simon, *Organizations* (Wiley, 1958). Fuller discussions of the potentialities of computers and systems design tools in organizations will be found in the last half of *The Shape of Automation* (Harper & Row, 1965) and in chapter 3 of *The Sciences of the Artificial* (M.I.T. Press, 1969).

I have proposed a taxonomy of species of information in my essay "Research for Choice," in W. R. Ewald, Jr. (ed.), *Environment and Policy: The Next Fifty Years* (Indiana University Press, 1968, pp. 360-380), and have drawn out the implications of attention scarcity for technology assessment in "Designing Organizations for an Information-Rich World," published in Martin Greenberger (ed.), *Computers, Communications, and the Public Interest* (Johns Hopkins Press, 1971, pp. 37-52).

References

1. It takes a bit of stretching to include military organizations in this category of "production organizations," and regulatory bodies do not really fit at all. However, most of the literature, empirical and theoretical, of organization theory in recent years has focused on industrial organizations and governmental agencies that provide public services, both of which categories do fit. I shall make no attempt here to discuss regulatory agencies. Military organizations, however, have a much larger component of information processing in their total pattern of activity than do, say, typical manfacturing organizations. Hence it is probably no accident that the concern with organizing for effective information processing first made its appearance on a large scale in military organizations, and that they have been and still are the initial testing grounds for most modern information processing technology.

2. The names of Lewin, Roethlisberger, Likert, MacGregor, and Argyris will identify the general range of approaches and emphases within the human relations movement. Many other names could, of course, be added to the list, which is only illustrative.

3. One evidence of the degree of novelty of the computer's capabilities is the resistance it evokes from those who refuse to see in it anything more than an enlarged desk calculator. Not since the Darwinian controversy of the past century have we seen such a passionate defense of the uniqueness of man against claims of kinship by systems that don't belong to his species.

4. We have now had a generation's experience with decision models for economic policy. The construction and testing of such models in the United States has been carried out in considerable part by nongovernmental agencies—the Cowles Foundation for Research in Economics, and The Brookings Institution, for example. Since the day when President Nixon declared himself to be a Keynesian, their impact on government decisions could no longer be in doubt, although the impact certainly preceded that declaration by a decade or more. The econometric models have generally used classical analytic mathematical techniques, but the computer has been essential to carrying out the calculations. A somewhat different example is provided by several linear programming models that have been constructed, mainly under university auspices, to guide water policy decisions. In both of these cases we see decision-making systems being designed in relative independence from reorganizations of a traditional kind. It is interesting to speculate whether all of the agency-shuffling reorganizations of federal agencies since 1937 have had as great an effect on public policy as these new decision-making systems.

Decision Making and the Leadership Process

Victor H. Vroom

T HIS article deals with the intersection of two areas of scientific inquiry and with the results of an extensive program of research to explore that intersection. The first area is the process of decision making. Recent developments in the theory of decision making suggest the usefulness of focussing on the processes by which decisions are made by individuals, groups and organizations.[1] Instead of treating the social system as a "black box," research underscores the necessity of identifying the processes which intervene between problem and solution—those which ultimately control the decisions that are made.

The second area of inquiry is the study of leadership. From its early beginnings in the search for universal leadership traits and from more recent efforts to uncover patterns of leader behavior which are consistently related to group effectiveness has come widespread support for situational or contingency conceptions of the leadership process. Such questions as, "Who would be the best leader?" or "How should a leader behave so as to stimulate the greatest productivity?" cannot be answered without a detailed knowledge of the situation.[2]

To put these two developments together, one can conceive of the leader's role, at least in part, as controlling the processes by which

The research on which this paper is based was sponsored by the Organizational Effectiveness Research Programs, Psychological Sciences Division Office of Naval Research. (Control No. NOO14-67-A0097-0027, Control Authority Identification No. NR-177-935.)

Reprinted with permission from *Journal of Contemporary Business* (Volume 3, no. 4), 1974, pp. 47–64.

decisions are made in that part of the organization for which he or she is responsible. The processes vary in a number of respects, but the one of most immediate interest and relevance to the study of leadership is the extent to which the leader encourages the participation of his or her subordinates in the decision-making process.

To illustrate this connection between leadership and decision making, assume that you are a manager who has five subordinates reporting to you.

Each subordinate has a clearly defined and distinct set of responsibilities. When one of them resigns to take a position with another organization due to a recent cost-cutting program which makes it impossible to hire new employees, you cannot replace this subordinate with someone else. Now it will be necessary to find some way to reallocate the departing subordinate's responsibilities among the remaining four in order to maintain the present workload and effectiveness of the unit.

The situation represents many circumstances faced by persons in leadership positions. There is some need for action—a problem exists and a solution, or decision, must be found. You, as leader, have some area of freedom or discretion (there are a number of possible ways in which the work can be reallocated), but there are also some constraints on your actions. For example, you cannot solve the problem by hiring someone from outside the organization. Furthermore, the solution is going to have effects on people other than yourself; your subordinates must carry out whatever decision is reached.

In this situation, one can envision a number of possible decision-making processes that could be employed. You could make the decision by yourself and announce it to your subordinates; you could obtain additional information from your subordinates and then make the decision; you could consult your subordinates, individually or collectively, before making the decision; or you could convene them as a group, share the problem and attempt to reach an agreement on the solution. These alternatives vary in terms of not cognitive but social processes—specifically, the amount and type of opportunity afforded subordinates to participate in the decision.

Two theoretically distinct sets of questions can be asked concerning the leader's choice of a decision process. One contains the normative questions about which process *should* be used to make the decision. The other set consists of descriptive questions concerning which decision-making process actually *would* be used. This article describes the results of a research program aimed at answering these sets of questions.

TOWARD A NORMATIVE MODEL

What would be a rational way of deciding on the form and amount of participation in decision-making to be used in different situations?

One can agree with the basic tenet of contingency theories that "leadership must depend upon the situation" but despair over the vacuous nature of this statement when faced with the task of specifying the kinds of situations which call for different approaches.

Clearly, one wants to select a decision process in a given situation that has the greatest likelihood of resulting in effective decisions, but the concept of effectiveness is far too general to be of much use for analytical purposes. There are at least three classes of outcomes that bear on the ultimate effectiveness of decisions:

- The quality or rationality of the decision.
- The acceptance or commitment on the part of subordinates to execute the decision effectively.
- The amount of time required to make the decision.

Research dealing with the effects of the degree of subordinate participation in decision making on each of these outcomes concluded:

> The results suggest that allocating problem-solving and decision-making tasks to entire groups requires a greater investment of manhours but produces higher acceptance of decisions and a higher probability that the decision will be executed efficiently. Differences between these two methods in quality of decisions and in elapsed time are inconclusive and probably highly variable .... It would be naive to think that group decision-making is always more "effective" than autocratic decision-making, or vice versa; the relative effectiveness of these two extreme methods depends both on the weights attached to quality, acceptance and time variables and on differences in amounts of these outcomes resulting from these methods, neither of which is invariant from one situation to another. The critics and proponents of participative management would do well to direct their efforts toward identifying the properties of situations in

which different decision-making approaches are effective rather than wholesale condemnation or deification of one approach.[3]

Vroom and Yetton described a taxonomy of decision processes that is used throughout this article. The taxonomy is shown in Table 1. Each process is represented by a symbol, e.g., AI, CI, GII; the first letter signifies the basic properties of the process (A stands for autocratic, C for consultative and G for group) and the Roman numerals constitute variants on that process. Thus, AI represents the first variant on an autocratic process and AII represents the second variant, etc.

The next step is to identify, in a manner consistent with available research evidence, properties of the situation that can be used in a model. In the model to be described, the situational attributes are characteristics of the problem to be solved or decision to be made

TABLE 1 Types of Management Decision Styles

AI	You solve the problem or make the decision yourself, using information available to you at that time.
AII	You obtain the necessary information from your subordinate(s), then decide on the solution to the problem yourself. You may or may not tell your subordinates what the problem is in getting the information from them. The role played by your subordinates in making the decision is clearly one of providing the necessary information to you, rather than generating or evaluating alternative solutions.
CI	You share the problem with relevant subordinates individually, getting their ideas and suggestions without bringing them together as a group. Then *you* make the decision that may or may not reflect your subordinates' influence.
CII	You share the problem with your subordinates as a group, collectively obtaining their ideas and suggestions. Then *you* make the decision that may or may not reflect your subordinates' influence.
GII*	You share a problem with your subordinates as a group. Together you generate and evaluate alternatives and attempt to reach agreement (consensus) on a solution. Your role is much like that of chairman. You do not try to influence the group to adopt "your" solution and you are willing to accept and implement any solution that has the support of the entire group.

*(GI is omitted because it applies only to more comprehensive models outside the scope of this article.)

rather than more general properties of the role of the leader. Table 2 shows the problem attributes in the present form of the model. For each attribute a question is provided that can be used by leaders in diagnosing problems. The terms used in Table 2 and the empirical basis for their inclusion in the model are described more completely in a more recent book by Vroom and Yetton.[4]

It has been found that trained managers can diagnose a particular problem quickly and quite reliably by answering this set of seven relevant questions. But how can such responses generate a prediction

TABLE 2 Problem Attributes Used in the Model

Problem Attributes	Diagnostic Questions
A. The importance of the quality of the decision.	Is there a quality requirement such that one solution is likely to be more rational than another?
B. The extent to which the leader possesses sufficient information/expertise to make a high-quality decision by himself or herself.	Do I have sufficient information to make a high-quality decision?
C. The extent to which the problem is structured.	Is the problem structured?
D. The extent to which acceptance or commitment on the part of subordinates is critical to the effective implementation of the decision.	Is acceptance of the decision by subordinates critical to effective implementation?
E. The prior probability that the leader's autocratic decision will receive acceptance by subordinates.	If I were to make the decision by myself, is it reasonably certain that it would be accepted by my subordinates?
F. The extent to which subordinates are motivated to attain the organizational goals as represented in the objectives explicit in the statement of the problem.	Do subordinates share the organizational goals to be obtained in solving the problem?
G. The extent to which subordinates are likely to be in conflict over preferred solutions.	Is conflict among subordinates likely in preferred solutions?

FIGURE 1 Decision Process Flow Chart

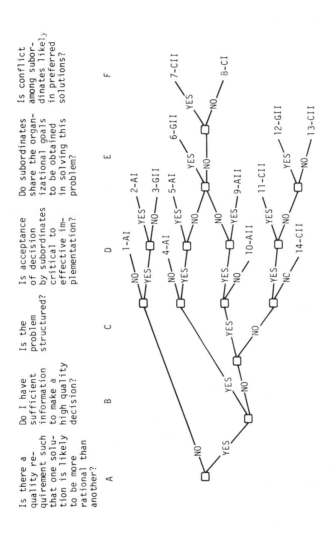

Is there a quality requirement such that one solution is likely to be more rational than another?

Do I have sufficient information to make a high quality decision?

Is the problem structured?

Is acceptance of decision by subordinates critical to effective implementation?

Do subordinates share the organizational goals to be obtained in solving this problem?

Is conflict among subordinates likely in preferred solutions?

A   B   C   D   E   F

concerning the most effective decision process to be employed by the leader? What kind of normative model of leadership style can be constructed using this set of problem attributes?

Figure 1 shows one such model expressed in the form of a decision tree, the seventh version of such a model that we have developed over the last 3 years. The problem attributes, expressed in question form, are arranged along the top of the figure. To use the model for a particular decision-making situation, one starts at the left-hand side and works toward the right asking oneself the question immediately above any box encountered. When a terminal node is reached, a number will be found designating the problem type and one of the decision-making processes appearing in Table 1.

AI is prescribed for four problem types (1, 2, 4, and 5); AII is prescribed for two problem types (9 and 10); CI is prescribed for only one problem type (8); CII is prescribed for four problem types (7, 11, 13, and 14); and GII is prescribed for three problem types (3, 6 and 12). The relative frequency with which each of the five decision processes would be prescribed for any manager would, of course, depend on the distribution of problem types encountered in his decision-making.

Rationale Underlying the Model

The decision processes specified for each problem type are not arbitrary. The model's behavior is governed by a set of principles intended to be consistent with evidence concerning the consequences of participation in decision-making on organizational effectiveness.

Two mechanisms underlie the behavior of the model. The first is a set of seven rules that protect the quality and acceptance of the decision by eliminating alternatives that risk one or the other of these decision outcomes. The second mechanism is a principle for choosing among alternatives in the feasible set where more than one exists.

The rules are examined first because they do much of the work of the model. As previously indicated, they intend to protect both the quality and acceptance of the decision.

Rules Protecting Decision Quality. In the form of the model shown, three rules protect decision quality.

- *The Information Rule.* If the quality of the decision is important and if the leader does not possess enough information or expertise to solve the problem by himself or herself, AI is eliminated from the feasible set. (Its use risks a low-quality decision.)
- *The Goal-Congruence Rule.* If the quality of the decision is important and

if the subordinates do not share the organizational goals to be obtained in solving the problem, GII is eliminated from the feasible set. (Alternatives that eliminate the leader's final control over the decision reached may jeopardize the quality of the decision.)

- *The Unstructured-Problem Rule.* In decisions in which the quality of the decision is important, if the leader lacks the necessary information or expertise to solve the problem alone, and if the problem is unstructured, i.e., he or she does not know exactly what information is needed and where it is located, the method used must provide not only for collection of information but also for collection in an efficient and effective manner. Methods that involve interaction among all subordinates with full knowledge of the problem are likely to be both more efficient and to generate a high-quality solution. Under these conditions, AI, AII and CI are eliminated from the feasible set. (AI does not allow the leader to collect the necessary information, and AII and CI represent more cumbersome, less effective and less efficient means of bringing the necessary information to bear on the solution of the problem than methods that permit persons with the necessary information to interact.)

Rules Protecting Acceptance. In addition to the decision quality rules, there are four rules to protect acceptance.

- *The Acceptance Rule.* If the acceptance of the decision by subordinates is critical to effective implementation, and if it is not certain that an autocratic decision made by the leader would receive that acceptance, AI and AII are eliminated from the feasible set. (Neither provides an opportunity for subordinates to participate in the decision and both risk the necessary acceptance.)
- *The Conflict Rule.* If the acceptance of the decision is critical; if an autocratic decision is not certain to be accepted; and if subordinates are likely to be in conflict or disagreement over the appropriate solution, AI, AII and CI are eliminated from the feasible set. (The method used in solving the problem should enable those disagreeing to resolve their differences with full knowledge of the problem. Accordingly, under these conditions, AI, AII and CI, which involve no interaction or only "one-on-one" relationships and, therefore, provide no opportunity for those in conflict to resolve their differences, are eliminated from the feasible set. Their use runs the risk of leaving some subordinates with less than the necessary commitment to the final decision.)
- *The Fairness Rule.* If the quality of decision is unimportant and if acceptance is critical and not certain to result from an autocratic decision, AI, AII, CI and CII are eliminated from the feasible set. (The method used should maximize the probability of acceptance as this is the only relevant consideration in determining the effectiveness of the decision. Under these circumstances, AI, AII, CI and CII, which create less acceptance or

commitment than GII, are eliminated from the feasible set. To use them is to run the risk of getting less than the needed acceptance of the decision.)

- *The Acceptance Priority Rule.* If acceptance is critical and is not assured by an autocratic decision, and if subordinates can be trusted, AI, AII, CI and CII are eliminated from the feasible set. (Methods that provide greater partnership in the decision-making process can provide greater acceptance without risking decision quality. Use of any method other than GII results in an unnecessary risk that the decision will not be fully accepted or receive the necessary commitment on the part of subordinates.)

After these seven rules have been applied to a given problem, a feasible set of decision processes is generated (see Table 3). Clearly, there are some problems types for which only one method remains in the feasible set and others for which five methods remain feasible.

Choosing Among Alternatives. When more than one method remains in the feasible set, there are a number of ways to choose among them. In Figure 1, the mechanism underlying choices utilizes the number of manhours used in solving the problem. Given a set of methods with equal likelihood of meeting both quality and acceptance requirements for the decision, it chooses that method that requires the least investment in manhours. On the basis of the empirical evidence summarized earlier, this is the method furthest to the left within the feasible set. For example, because AI, AII, CI, CII and GII are all feasible as in Problem Types 1 and 2, AI would be the method chosen.

The model just described seeks to protect the quality of the decision and to expend the least number of manhours in the process. Because it focuses on conditions surrounding making and implementing a particular decision rather than on any long-term considerations, it can be termed a short-term model.

However, it seems likely that leadership methods that may be optimal for short-term results may be different from those that would be optimal over a longer period of time. The manager who uses more participative methods could, in time, develop his or her subordinates, increasing not only the knowledge and talent that they could bring to bear on decisions but also their identification with the organization goals. A promising approach to development of a long-term model is one that places less weight on manhours as the basis for choice of method within the feasible set. Given a long-term orientation, one would be interested in the possibility of a tradeoff between manhours in problem solving and team development, both of which increase with participation. Viewed in these terms, the time-minimizing model places maximum relative weight on manhours and no weight on development, hence, it chooses the style furthest to the left within the feasible set. If these assumptions are correct, a model that places less weight on manhours and more weight on development would choose a style further to the right within the feasible set.

The model just described is the latest of a set of such models which have been devised over the last few years. Undoubtedly, it is not perfect and will be amended or altered as additional research evidence becomes available.

It should be noted that the domain of decisions to which this model has been addressed are what Maier, Solem and Maier refer to as "group problems," i.e., decisions which affect all or a major subset of the subordinates reporting to the leader.[5] However, a substantial number of problems confronting the leader may affect only one of his (her) subordinates. These "individual problems" fall outside the domain of the model described here, but a similar model has been developed to deal with them. This model utilizes additional decision processes, including delegation of the decision to the affected subordinate.[6] Substantial similarity between the problem attributes used for group and individual problems has made it possible to present the models in a single decision tree.

TABLE 3 Problem Types and the Feasible Set of Decision Processes

Problem Type	Acceptable Methods
1	AI, AII, CI, CII, GII
2	AI, AII, CI, CII, GII
3	GII
4	AI, AII, CI, CII, GII*
5	AI, AII, CI, CII, GII*
6	GII
7	CII
8	CI, CII
9	AII, CI, CII, GII*
10	AII, CI, CII, GII*
11	CII, GII*
12	GII
13	CII
14	CII, GII*

*Within the feasible set only when the answer to question F is Yes.

TOWARD A DESCRIPTIVE MODEL

In addition to the work dealing with the development of normative or prescriptive models, research also has been involved with descriptive questions involving how leaders do, in fact, behave when confronted with problems to solve or decisions to make. What considerations affect the decision processes they employ? What factors both within their personal makeup and in the situations they face cause leaders to retain or share their decision-making power with their subordinates? In what respects is their behavior similar to or different from the normative model?

Two different research methods have been used in an attempt to answer such questions. The first investigation utilized a method that can be referred to as "recalled problems." Over 500 managers from 11 different countries representing a variety of firms were asked to provide a written description of a problem that they had recently had to solve. The problems varied in length from one paragraph to several pages and covered virtually every facet of managerial decision making. For each case, the manager was asked to indicate which of the decision processes shown in Table 1 was used to solve the problem. Finally, each manager was asked to answer the questions shown in Table 2 corresponding to the problem attributes used in the normative model.

These data made it possible to determine the frequency with which the managers' decision process was similar to that of the normative model. It also illustrated the factors in their description of the situation which were associated with the use of each decision process. This investigation provided interesting results but, more important, it provided the basis for a second more powerful method for investigating the same questions. This second method, "standardized problems," used the actual cases written by the managers in the construction of a standardized set of cases, each of which depicts a manager faced with a problem to solve or decision to make. In each case, a leader is asked to assume the role of the manager faced with the situation described and to indicate which decision process he or she would use if faced with that situation.

Several such sets of cases have been developed. In early research, each set consisted of 30 cases corresponding to the definition of group problems. Recently a set of 48 cases, one-half group problems and one-half individual problems, has been used for research purposes.[7]

Composition of each set of standardized cases was in accordance with multifactorial experimental design. The seven problem attributes used in the normative model varied in each case and variation in each attribute was independent of other attributes, allowing assessment of the effects of each problem attribute on the decision processes used by a given manager.

The cases spanned a wide range of managerial problems, including production scheduling, quality control, portfolio management, personnel allocation and R & D project selection. To date, several thousand managers in the United States and abroad have been studied using this approach.

It is not possible to summarize everything learned in the course of this research within the limits of this article, but, some of the highlights are presented. Since the results obtained from the two research methods—recalled and standardized problems—are consistent, the major results can be presented independent of the method used.

Major Results

Perhaps the most striking finding is the weakening of the widespread view that participativeness is a general trait that individual managers exhibit in different amounts. To be sure, there were differences *among* managers in their general tendencies to utilize participative methods as opposed to autocratic ones. On the standardized problems, these differences accounted for about 10 percent of the total variance in the decision processes. Furthermore, managers who tended to use more participative methods such as CII and GII, with group problems also tended to use more participative methods, like delegation, for dealing with individual problems.

However, these differences in behavior among managers were small in comparison with differences *within* managers. On the standardized problems, no manager indicated that he or she would use the same decision process on all problems or decisions, and most managers use all methods, in some circumstances.

Some of this variance in behavior within managers can be attributed to widely shared tendencies to respond to some situations by sharing power and to other situations by retaining it. It makes more sense to talk about participative and autocratic situations than to talk about participative and autocratic managers. In fact, on the standardized group problems, the variance in behavior across problems or cases is about three times as large as the variance across managers and, on standardized individual problems, situational variance exceeds variance among people by a factor of five.

What are the characteristics of an autocratic as opposed to participative situation? This answer constitutes a partial descriptive model of this aspect of the decision-making process and has been the goal of much of the research conducted. From observations of behavior on both recalled and standardized problems, it is clear that the decision-making process employed by a typical manager is influenced by a large number of factors, many of which also show up in the normative model. Following are several conclusions substantiated by the results on both recalled and standardized problems: Managers use decision processes providing less opportunity for participation (1) when they possess all the necessary information, (2) when the problem they face is well-structured rather than unstructured, (3) when their subordinates' acceptance of the decision is not critical for the effective implementation of the decision or when the prior probability of acceptance of an autocratic decision is high, and (4) when the personal goals of their subordinates are *not* congruent with the goals of the organization as manifested in the problem.

These findings concern relatively common or widely shared ways of dealing with organizational problems. Other results suggest that managers have different ways of "tailoring" their decision process to the situation. Theoretically, these can be thought of as differences among managers in decision rules about when to encourage participation. Statistically, they are represented as interactions between situational variables and personal characteristics.

For example, consider two managers who have identical distributions of the use of the five decision processes shown in Table 1 on a set of 30 cases. In a sense, they are equally participative (or autocratic); however, the situations in which they permit or encourage participation in decision making on the part of their subordinates may be very different. One may restrict the participation of subordinates to decisions without a quality requirement, whereas, the other may restrict their participation to problems with a quality requirement. The former would be more inclined to use participative decision processes (like GII) on decisions such as what color the walls should be painted or when the company picnic should be held. The latter would be more likely to encourage participation in making decisions that have a clear and demonstrable impact on the organization's success in achieving its external goals.

Use of the standardized problem set permits the assessment of such differences in decision rules that govern choices among decision-making processes. Because the cases are selected in accordance with an experimental design, they can indicate differences in the behavior of managers attributable not only to the existence of a quality requirement in the problem but also to the existence of acceptance requirements, conflict, information requirements, etc.

Behavior of the Model vs. Manager Behavior

The research using recalled and standardized problems has also permitted examination of similarities and differences between the behavior of the normative model and the behavior of a typical manager. This analysis reveals, at the very least, what behavior changes can be expected if managers began using the normative model as the basis for choosing their decision-making processes.

A typical manager says he or she would (or did) use the same decision process as that in Figure 1 in about 40 percent of group problems. In two-thirds of the situations, his or her behavior is consistent with the feasible set of methods proposed in the model. However, in the remaining one-third of the situations, the behavior violates at least one of the seven rules underlying the model. Results show significantly higher agreement with the normative model for individual problems than for group problems.

The four rules designed to protect the acceptance or commitment of the decision have substantially higher probabilities of being violated than the three rules designed to protect the quality or rationality of the decision. One of the acceptance rules, the Fairness Rule (Rule 6), is violated almost 75 percent of the time that it could have been violated. On the other hand, one of the quality rules, the Information Rule (Rule 1), is violated in only about 3 percent of occasions in which it is applicable. If we assume for the moment that these two sets of rules have equal validity, the findings strongly suggest that the decisions made by typical managers are more likely to prove ineffective due to deficiencies of acceptance by subordinates than due to deficiencies in decision quality.

Another striking difference between the behavior of the model and the typical manager is that model behavior shows far greater variance with the situation. If a typical manager voluntarily used the model as the basis for choosing his or her methods of making decisions, this manager would become both more autocratic and more paticipative. He or she would employ autocratic methods more frequently in situations in which subordinates were unaffected by the decision. Also, this manager would use participative methods more frequently when his or her subordinates' cooperation and support were critical and/or their information and expertise were required.

It should be noted that the typical manager to whom we refer is merely a statistical average of the several thousand who have been studied over the last 3 or 4 years; thus, there is great deal of variation around that average. As evidenced by their behavior on standardized problems, some managers already behave in a manner that is highly consistent with the model, while others' behavior is clearly at variance with it.

IMPLICATIONS FOR LEADERSHIP TRAINING

The research program just summarized was conducted in order to shed new light on the causes and consequences of decision-making processes used by leaders in formal organizations. The course of the research shows that the data collection procedures, with appropriate additions and modifications, might also serve a useful function in leadership development. From this realization evolved an important by-product of the research activities—a new approach to leadership training based on the concepts in the normative model and the empirical methods of the descriptive research.

A detailed description of this training program and of initial attempts to evaluate its effectiveness is based on the premise that one critical skill required of all leaders is the ability to adapt their behavior to the demands of the situation and that a component of this skill involves selecting the appropriate decision-making process for each problem or decision he or she confronts. The purpose of the program is *not* to "train" managers to use the model in their everyday decision-making activities. Instead, the model serves as a device for encouraging managers to examine their leadership styles and for coming to a conscious realization of their own, often implicit, choices among decision processes, including their similarity and dissimilarity with the model. By helping managers to become aware of their present behavior and of alternatives to it, the training provides a basis for rethinking one's leadership style to be more consistent with goals and objectives. Succinctly, the training is intended to transform habits into choices rather than to program a leader with a particular method of making choices.

A fundamental part of the program in its present form is the use of a set of standardized cases previously described in connection with the descriptive phase of the research. Each participant specifies the decision process to be employed if he or she were the leader described in the case. Responses to the entire set of cases (usually 30 or 48) are processed by the computer which generates a highly detailed analysis of the leadership style. The responses for all participants in a single course typically are processed simultaneously, permitting the calculation of differences between the person and others in the same program.

In its present form, a single computer printout for a person consists of three 15″ × 11″ pages, each filled with graphs and tables highlighting different features of behavior. Understanding the results requires a detailed knowledge of the concepts underlying the model, something already developed in one of the previous phases of the training program. The printout is accompanied by a manual that aids in explaining the results and provides suggested steps to be followed in extracting full meaning from the printout.

Following are a few of the questions that the printout answers:

- How autocratic or participative am I in my dealings with subordinates in comparison with other participants in the program?
- What decision processes do I use more or less frequently than the average?
- How close does my behavior come to that of the model? How frequently does my behavior agree with the feasible set? What evidence is there that my leadership style reflects the pressure of time as opposed to a concern with the development of my subordinates? How do I compare in these respects with other participants in the class?
- What rules do I violate most frequently and least frequently? On what cases did I violate these rules? Does my leadership style reflect more concern with getting decisions that are high in quality or with getting decisions that are accepted?

When a typical manager receives the printout, he or she immediately tries to understand what this means about himself or herself. After most of the major results are understood, this manager goes back to the set of cases to reread those in which he or she has violated rules. Typically, managers show an interest in discussing and comparing their results with others in the program, so groups of four to six persons gather to do this—a process which has been included as part of the program.

It should be emphasized that this method of providing feedback on leadership style is just one part of the total training experience which encompasses more than 30 hours over 3 successive days. To date, no long-term evaluations of its effectiveness have been undertaken but initial results appear quite promising.

SUMMARY

This article provides a brief overview of some of the principal results of a research program aimed at increasing understanding of certain facets of the leadership process, most notably the role of the leader in the decision-making process. Two goals guide the inquiry; the first is normative and concerns the role that leaders should play in the process of making decisions. The second goal is descriptive and involves the role that leaders do play in the decision-making process. The normative model presented is one form of contingency model, stressing that leaders should adapt their role in the decision-making process to the demands of the situation. Further, results show that leaders do attempt to adapt their behavior to the situation, although in ways that are not perfectly consistent with the normative model. Finally, an approach to leadership training is described which utilizes the concepts of the normative model and some empirical research methods in an attempt to develop more effective leadership in organizations.

References

1. J. G. March and H. A. Simon, *Organizations* (New York: Wiley, 1958); R. M. Cyert and J. G. March, *A Behavior Theory of the Firm* (Englewood Cliffs, N.J.: Prentice-Hall, 1963); A. Newell and H. A. Simon, *Human Problem Solving* (Englewood Cliffs, N.J.: Prentice-Hall, 1972).
2. F. E. Fiedler, *A Theory of Leadership Effectiveness* (New York: McGraw-Hill, 1967); V. H. Vroom, "Leadership," *Handbook of Industrial and Organizational Psychology*, M. Dunnette, ed. (Chicago: Rand McNally, 1976).
3. V. H. Vroom, "Industrial Social Psychology," in G. Lindzey and E. Aronson, eds., *Handbook of Social Psychology,* Vol. 5 (Reading, Mass.: Addison-Wesley, 1970), pp. 239-240.
4. V. H. Vroom and P. W. Yetton, *Leadership and Decision-Making* (Pittsburgh: University of Pittsburgh Press, 1973).
5. N. R. F. Maier, A. R. Solem and A. A. Maier, *Supervisory and Executive Development: A Manual for Role Playing* (New York: Wiley, 1957).
6. V. H. Vroom and A. G. Jago, "Decision-Making As a Social Process: Normative and Descriptive Models of Leader Behavior," *Decision Sciences,* Vol. 5 (1974), pp. 743-769.
7. *Ibid.*

From Economic to Political Analysis of Library Decision Making*

Jeffrey A. Raffel

In 1969 the M.I.T. Press published a new volume, *Systematic Analysis of University Libraries: An Application of Cost-Benefit Analysis to the M.I.T. Libraries,* which might have signaled the entrance of economic analysis into the area of library decision making. As co-author of the book, I anxiously awaited the reviews I hoped would follow.[1] To date all reviews missed what I regard as the major point of the book: *Although helpful, an economic analysis of a university (or public) library is insufficient because libraries operate as political systems and thus improving libraries requires political analysis.*

The purpose of this paper is not only to argue that political analysis of university and public libraries should be undertaken in conjunction with economic analyses but also to apply a specific theoretical framework and concept to university and public libraries. The improvement of libraries requires an expansion of analysis beyond technical discussions of procedural changes and per item costs to the broader utilization of social science theory and research.

In the past two decades both economists and political scientists

*My frequent co-author, Robert Shishko, has tried to impart the essence of cost-benefit analyses to his audience by telling them about an economist who, when asked if he liked sex, replied immediately, "What are the alternatives?" I thank Bob Shishko for helping me to learn enough about economic analysis to criticize it, and I thank David Schulz and Daniel Rich for their insightful comments on earlier drafts of this paper.

Reprinted by permission of the American Library Association from *College and Research Libraries* 35(6): 412–23 (Nov. 1974).

have expanded their field of inquiry. Economists have become crucial figures in the analysis of governmental policy, especially in the measurement and analysis of governmental effectiveness through the methodology of cost-benefit analysis.[2] Political scientists have at the same time shifted their focus toward nongovernmental institutions, with some analyzing what were once thought to be nonpolitical governmental institutions (e.g., schools) and others, nongovernments (e.g., private governments). As Mancur Olson has recently observed, the social science disciplines differ by their approaches and theoretical frameworks rather than by their subject matter.[3] Thus libraries, be they primarily publicly or privately operated, are fair game for the frameworks of political scientists and economists.

Each discipline includes an array of theoretical frameworks. The overall approach of systems analysis stands out within each discipline as a fruitful way to improve libraries, specifically cost-benefit analysis in economics and Estonian systems analysis in political science.

ECONOMIC ANALYSIS

Brief Description

"Basically, economic analysis is the study of choice: the allocation of scarce resources among alternative uses, and the distribution of outputs among alternative uses—that is, the classic questions of what and how much to produce, and who gets what products."[4] Cost-benefit analysis is a subfield of economic analysis: a specific application of economic analysis to nonmarket activity. We have defined cost-benefit analysis as the analytical examiniation of the costs and benefits of alternatives designed to meet specified objectives under various contingencies or states of the world.[5] Some differentiate cost-*benefit* analysis from cost-*effectiveness* analysis; the former referring to long-range financial effects (e.g, increased dollar income) and the latter to short-ranged measured output in nonfinancial terms (e.g., number of books circulated).[6] Although systems analysis has been used to refer to cost-benefit analyses, because its use is much more widespread, having application in areas from computer technology to political analysis, we define systems analysis as the study of systems of complexes or organized and interrelated parts, in terms of inputs, outputs, and internal functioning.[7]

Our definition of cost-benefit analysis has already included most of the elements of the basic analytical framework: costs, benefits, alternatives, and contingencies. What then is cost-benefit analysis? It is a way of looking at the world. Usually one starts from a set of objectives that a decision maker has in mind. The analyst finds measures of the extent to which the objectives may be met. For example, if an objective of a library were to provide reading material to library users, then one measure of meeting this objective would be annual book circulation. One then examines the alternatives for fulfilling each objective.

By constructing models (e.g., formulas, computer simulations), the analyst relates each alternative to its corresponding costs and benefits (i.e., the degree to which objectives are met). The model is used across several contingencies or states of the world. Given the costs and benefits associated with each alternative in each contingency, a criterion or measure of preferredness (e.g., maximizing profits) is selected and the "best" alternative is chosen.

Figure 1 illustrates the cost-benefit procedure. Note that the method is actually circular—objectives are revised in light of feasibility and costs, new alternatives are created, models are refined, and the decision process is continuously in motion.

FIGURE 1 The Basic Cost-Benefit Framework

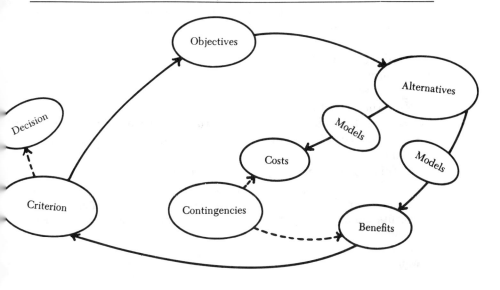

Brief Critique

The elements of the cost-benefit analysis model serve as the basis for a brief critique of the method. Attempts to define library objectives can lead to clarifications of purpose, yet they often result in futile searches for well-hidden goals obscuring the true clients of the library.[8] While efforts to generate alternatives to perform library services more efficiently and effectively are made, the question of the practicality and feasibility of radically different ideas weights the ultimate analysis against innovative options. Relating costs to alternatives becomes the key task, and numbers generated through cost modeling become the foci of economy drives. Benefit modeling, however, is weakest when the alternatives are most innovative, e.g., public library programs based on distributing paperback books for disadvantaged patrons, university libraries handing out free copies of required articles to students.[9] Because the contingencies studied most are those thought to affect costs, not benefits, inflation of prices is emphasized over inflation of goals in serving users.

Each of these difficulties is related to the political context in which the economic study is conceived, implemented, and received. The basic political problem with economic analysis transcends operational and day-to-day difficulties and political intrigue. The basic political problem centers on political conflict inherent in all our institutions, including libraries. It is this conflict that is inappropriately dealt with or ignored in economic analysis.

The Political Problem with Economic Analysis: An Example

Near the end of the data collection stage, the economic systems analysis of the Massachusetts Institute of Technology (M.I.T.) libraries yielded a list of twenty library alternatives with associated costs and benefits.[10]

At this stage in the analysis several points were evident:

1. Several alternatives were not worth considering. Alternatives offering fewer benefits at a higher cost than comparable alternatives were discarded. For example, storing books off campus rather than on campus saved no money and resulted in losses of benefits to library users.
2. Many conclusions with major policy implications were already warranted. For example, inexpensive storage appeared to offer little financial savings at a fairly high cost in benefits to a majority of the M.I.T. community.

3. Although alternatives could be described in terms of costs and benefits with respect to the two major library objectives, more information was required to select and recommend a subset of alternatives. For example, should the cost of reproducing copies of library materials be reduced or should many course-required articles be distributed free of charge? Should either be done with or without a decentralization of library space?[11]

It is at this point that cost-benefit analysis (and economic analysis) comes to a grinding halt. Cost-benefit analysis assumes that the objectives, even if unclear at the beginning of the analysis, can be specified at some point to the satisfaction of the decision maker. Cost-benefit analysts recognize that multiple objectives may exist and suggest that the tradeoffs, the extent to which meeting one objective leads to a failure to meet other objectives, be specified and clearly displayed. But did our analysis indicate objectives that could be agreed upon?

We decided to present the data on alternatives derived from our analysis to the individual members of the university community, thus to allow each to act as if he or she were the ultimate decision maker.[12] Because it would have been too costly to reach all members of the community, we drew a random sample of undergraduate students, graduate students, and faculty and research staff and presented them with twenty alternative changes, with a brief description of costs and relevant benefit considerations, for the M.I.T. libraries. Respondents were given budgets of $0, $100,000, and $200,000 to spend for changes in the libraries.

The analysis of the survey clearly indicates that different sub-groups of the M.I.T. community either had different objectives in mind or viewed different means as being best for meeting common objectives:

> The general conclusion is that the three major campus groups differ in the systems they would like the library to adopt. Undergraduates seek to expand and centralize the reserve collection by cutting research services. Graduate students add lower Xerox prices and increased access to this list of desired systems and would prefer to cut seating rather than cataloging. The faculty are the most willing to alter book storage and cataloging and relatively less desirous of a centralized reserve system . . . .
>
> The less a respondent reported using the libraries the more likely he was to select saving money on book storage and seating and to spend it on lower Xerox rates, departmental libraries, and an all-Xerox reserve system. Low users thus tend to be outside-use oriented. The high users prefer expanding seating, acquisitions, reference, and access to other collections. The high

users thus are research oriented. We have concluded that the library has traditionally served one clientele, the research oriented. There now appears to be, however, a second clientele, who spend few hours in the library and seek not the space but the materials in its collection. We believe, with as yet no proof, that many of those oriented to outside use prefer to work outside the library but are forced, primarily by the reserve system, to work in the library. We hypothesize that these users (and many other potential users) could be served by a library emphasizing distribution as well as in-house facilities and services.[13]

The M.I.T. analysis indicates that the alternatives faced by the M.I.T. library and university administrators involved major choices among various subgroups on campus. Furthermore, the analysis strongly suggests that decisions now favor faculty far more than students.

The political problem with economic analysis is that there is no economic way to resolve differences among alternatives meeting different objectives held by different subgroups; where political conflict exists a political solution must be found.[14] This is not news to most economists. What library decision makers require is help in resolving these political conflicts. Presumably political analysis can help.

POLITICAL ANALYSIS

Political scientists would not agree on the nature of analysis necessary to deal with such political conflict. Some would argue that an analysis should begin with a positivist or descriptive analysis of libraries with a focus on who decides and by what process. Others would argue that an explicitly normative or value based analysis, with a major focus on issues of equity and responsiveness, is required. Because neither of these approaches has been applied to libraries, a first step falling between the normative and positive poles of political systems analysis has been chosen here. Below, David Easton's descriptive framework is used to raise the normative questions which library decision makers should be addressing.[15]

Easton defines politics as the authoritative allocation of values for a society. In the past, many governmental institutions, perhaps education is the best example, have been viewed as being outside of the realm of politics. In 1969, in an introduction to a reader on the politics of education, the editor stated that "The idea that politics and *public education* are intimately related was practically unthinkable as recently as a decade ago . . . . At the very least, any governmental process involving authoritative decisions on matters of public relevance is of a political nature."[16] Thus an entire literature dealing with the politics of education has developed.[17] Certainly it would not be inappropriate to raise issues concerning the politics of public libraries and libraries at public universities.

Studying the politics of university libraries derives from another expansion of political analysis to the area of private government.[18] Public governments have been defined as "those general as well as special-purpose associations and agencies either to which all inhabitants of a given locality are subject or of which all citizens are members"; and *private governments* are "those limited-purpose associations or organizations, usually voluntary in membership, which exist both alongside and subordinate to public governments."[19] Examples of private governments are corporations, trade unions, professional associations, and universities. Indeed, the public versus private distinction has become increasingly blurred, especially as applied to universities, within the past decade.[20] The basic questions one asks about private governments are political: Are (and can) private governments (be) democratic?[21] Related questions include: Who gets what, when, and how?[22]

Although many alternative models of the political process exist, I believe that Easton's framework provides a useful analytical scheme for beginning a political analysis of libraries.[23]

Easton's Framework for Political Analysis

Easton's model (see Figure 2) is simple in its conception but complex in its full description. Dye describes the theoretical framework succinctly:

> One way to conceive of public policy is to think of it as a response of a political system to forces brought to bear upon it from the environment. Forces generated in the environment which affect the political system are viewed as inputs. The environment is any condition or circumstance defined as external to the boundaries of the political system. The political system is that group of interrelated structures and processes which functions authoritatively to allocate values for a society. Outputs of the political system are authoritative value allocations of the system, and these allocations constitute public policy.
>
> Systems theory portrays public policy as an output of the political system. The concept of "system" implies an indentifiable set of institutions

and activities in society that function to transform demands into authoritative decisions requiring the support of society. The concept of "systems" also implies that elements of the system are interrelated, that the system can respond to forces in its environment, and that it will do so in order to preserve itself. Inputs are received into the political system in the form of both demands and support. Demands occur when individuals or groups, in response to real or perceived environmental conditions, act to affect public policy. Support is rendered when individuals or groups accept the outcome of elections, obey the laws, pay their taxes, and generally conform to policy decisions. Any system absorbs a variety of demands, some of which conflict with each other. In order to transform these demands into outputs (public policies), it must arrange settlements and enforce these settlements upon the parties concerned. It is recognized that outputs (public policies) may have a modifying effect on the environment and the demands arising from it, and may also have an effect upon the character of the political system. The system preserves itself by: (1) producing reasonably satisfying outputs, (2) relying upon deeply rooted attachments to the system itself, and (3) using, or threatening to use force.[24]

POLITICAL ANALYSIS AND UNIVERSITY LIBRARIES

System Boundaries and Legitimacy

The first question that arises is whether we can determine the boundaries of a political system. Throughout the M.I.T. library study

FIGURE 2 The Systems Model

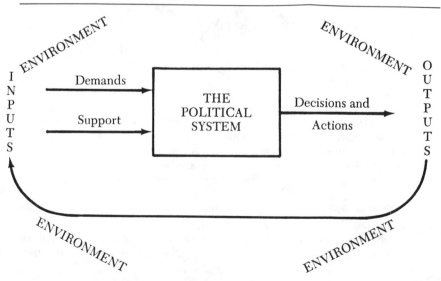

we felt too constrained by the definition of the system we were studying, "the M.I.T. libraries." The use and evaluation of a university library are not independent of the book stores within (and without) the university. To declare one a legitimate item for analysis and the other as outside of the area of analysis may be to miss the dynamics of the situation. It was surprising to discover that a high-level, library acquisitions department staff member had not only made no effort to buy books from the Harvard Coop but also had never even been to this store, one of the world's largest bookstores. We were surprised to receive veiled threats by a department chairman after we had measured his departmental library's floor-space without his permission. The quality of departmental libraries must surely determine the nature and degree of use of the main libraries. What units should be included in the library decision maker's domain?

Output and Benefits

Unlike Easton, it seems that the most fruitful political analysis must begin with the output stage of the political process. The analysis of output, done within the cost-benefit framework of the M.I.T. study, provides some significant information and raises some important questions.

The best tool available for analyzing policy was (and often is) the library budget. But budgets are usually input based (e.g., cost of books purchased, cost of personnel salaries) rather than output or policy derived (e.g., cost of providing student services for coursework). Perhaps even more interesting, the M.I.T. library budget, divided into parts among discipline-related libraries, was considered confidential. To paraphase one library administrator, "If the social scientists knew what we were spending on the physical science library, they'd start asking for more funds."

A program budget analysis of the M.I.T. library seems to show quite clearly who benefits from the current decision-making system. Only 23 percent of the total budget is used for providing required reading and facilities for studying, i.e., less than a quarter of the budget is devoted to nonresearch, course-related student services. Of course, this overstates the antistudent bias, for undergraduate and particularly graduate students devote much effort to research both inside and outside of courses.

As noted in the discussion of the cost-benefit analysis of the M.I.T. libraries, the survey analysis challenges the myth of a unitary community.[25] In fact it suggests that the allocation of benefits, if not costs, is weighted in favor of faculty and staff. Why should this be so?

Demand and Democratic Process

The concept of demand is a crucial one in Easton's framework. An analysis of demands made upon library administrators at M.I.T. would probably indicate that a small number of senior faculty are the primary demanders. The library advisory committee contained no students; the administrators themselves spoke almost entirely of faculty complaints.[26] What channels, both formal and informal, are required for those affected by decisions concerning libraries to be adequately heard?

The concept of demand is a crucial one in Easton's framework. An analysis of demands made upon library administrators at M.I.T. would probably indicate that a small number of senior faculty are the Easton concentrates on the reasons for the weeding of demands and the attrition of preferences in the input stage of the political process. We should ask, as does Easton, what institutions exist to filter and channel demands to library decision makers? How successful are different kinds of people within the university community in making their demands heard? To what extend should access be equalized?

The mobilization of bias should also be considered crucial by library analysts. Several political scientists have criticized their discipline for the substantive conclusion that American institutions are open and responsive to minority groups.[27] They argue that this optimistic substantive conclusion derives in part from a methodological problem, analyzing only decisions made by public bodies. Bachrack and Baratz ask, "Can the researcher overlook the chance that some person or association could limit decision-making to relatively noncontroversial matters, by influencing community values and political procedures and rituals?"[28] By limiting political analysis to overt decisions, the role that elites play in mobilizing bias, i.e., in defining the nature and states of the political game, is overlooked.

The mobilization of bias plays a critical role in library policy. One of our early suggestions at M.I.T. was that the price of reproducing pages of library materials within M.I.T.'s libraries should be reduced. Although the price was later decreased, the action was based upon an agreement that decreasing the price would ultimately increase revenue (i.e., elastic demand) and the system would remain self-supporting. *But why should the dissemination of information by copying be self-supporting, and who is disadvantaged by this decision rule?* Whereas many faculty have research grants, departmental resources, and relatively high incomes, students are at a relative disadvantage in the marketplace. Libraries do not break even on providing books. Should they break even on copying materials for dissemination?

One economist has made an argument that could have been based on the mobilization of bias concept:

> Or why do not librarians diminish their stock of hard-cover books and acquire in their stead substantial inventories of paperbacks which they would then give away free? We are inclined to reply, "Why, that would be crazy: our budget would soon be exhausted." And yet that is exactly what librarians are doing now except instead of giving books away free they are giving staff services away free.[29]

Keller calls for implicit (or explicit) pricing of library services.[30]

Easton's framework, indeed all political frameworks, should include a basic economic concept of exit. Hirschman argues that one mechanism of voicing disapproval within the political as well as economic sector is exit, e.g., leaving the organization or not consuming the product.[31] To what extent do potential library users seek other sources of information because of library ineffectiveness? To what extent do some groups lack an effective means of influencing library decision makers by their inability to exit?

The larger question that each of these points concerning demand raises is the appropriateness of democratic norms for library decision making. Should libraries be run more democratically than they now are?

Decision Making and Selecting Decision Makers

The analysis of decisions and decision makers is a crucial aspect of Easton's framework. The analysis of library decision making must reach beyond the traditional organizational bounds of the exercise of rationality. Lakoff has expressed the criticisms of traditional organizational analysis as follows:

> The study of organizational decision-making studiously avoids asking the kind of questions that would render the study of decision-making genuinely political. It does not ask what constituencies are involved, or how the legislative is related to the executive, or how the authority of the decision-maker is made accountable to those he represents. It does not ask whether

the system is constitutional or just, legitimate or illegitimate. Instead the study of decision-making in organizations is confined to the question of whether and to what extent the functions of management are exercised rationally. The stress, in other words, is clearly on administration rather than government, on the integrative function of social organization, on improving the efficiency of the decision-maker. There is practically no attention paid to the question of whether people who are members of the organization or who are served by it have or ought to have control over it, whether they have any right (a term which would probably be considered altogether unscientific by students of organization) to be consulted in the decision-making process or indeed to decide what form the process will take.[32]

In this conventional sense, the study of organizations, despite its focus on decision-making, has been quite apolitical.

Dye's identification of barriers limiting rational decision making, in many ways analogous to criticisms of the use of cost-benefit analysis in libraries, might serve as a starting point for an analysis of library decision making. they are restated below as hypotheses.

1. There are no community values which are usually agreed upon, but only the values of specific groups and individuals, many of which are conflicting.
2. The many conflicting values cannot be compared or weighted: for example, it is impossible to compare or weight the value of individual dignity against the loss of rare books.
3. The environment of library policy makers, particularly the power and influence system, renders it impossible for them to see or accurately weight many community values, particularly those values which have no active or powerful proponents.
4. Library policy makers are not motivated to make decisions on the basis of community goals, but instead try to maximize their own rewards—power, status, money, etc.
5. Library policy makers are not motivated to maximize net goal achievement, but merely to satisfy demands for progress; they do not search until they find "the one best way" but halt their search when they find an alternative which "will work."
6. Large investments in existing programs and policies (e.g., cataloging systems, library buildings, and other "sunk costs") prevent policy makers from reconsidering alternatives foreclosed by previous decisions.
7. There are innumerable barriers to collecting all of the information required to know all possible policy alternatives and the consequences of each alternative, including the cost of information gathering, the availability of the information, and the time involved in its collection.

8. Neither the predictive capacities of the social and behavioral sciences nor the predictive capacities of the physical and biological sciences are sufficiently advanced to enable policy makers to understand the full range of consequences of each library policy alternative.
9. Library policy makers, even with the most advanced computerized analytical techniques, do not have sufficient intelligence to calcute accurately cost-benefit ratios when a large number of diverse political, social, economic, and cultural values are at stake.
10. Library policy makers have personal needs, inhibitions, and inadequacies which prevent them from performing in a highly rational manner.
11. Uncertainty about the consequences of various policy alternatives compels policy makers to stick as closely as possible to previous policies to reduce the likelihood of disturbing, unanticipated consequences.
12. The segmentalized nature of policy making in large library bureaucracies makes it difficult to coordinate decision making so that the input of all of the various specialists is brought to bear at the point of decision.[33]

Testing these hypotheses requires an analysis of the values and personal goals of library decision makers, the power of competing interests in universities, the incentive structures surrounding library administrators, and the nature of information available to decision makers. Significant normative questions follow. Should library decision makers be more representative of those who use the libraries? Should the incentive structure for advancement in library administration be altered to better reflect user and potential user demand?

LESSONS FOR LIBRARIANS

Unfortunately, whereas economists can advocate that library decision makers try to maximize benefits at a given budget level, political scientists can offer no clear-cut decision rule as an alternative. This paper ends with questions that library decision makers should ask, but no simple answers of what actions to take if answers are found can be offered at this point.[34] Future research is needed, although this obviously will not solve all the political problems of librarians.

Following the more complete Easton model, library decision makers should ask themselves:

1. What is the relevant library system? Have I excluded a key component that determines user behavior but has traditionally fallen outside my purview? Can I coordinate decisions between my area and the additional area?

2. What are the *environmental* constraints that appear to limit my discretion? Can they be altered?

3. What groups (and individuals) make *demands*? Are they representative of the potential users of the library? What preferences do not become demands? Are new or revised mechanisms needed to encourage more demands?

4. What is the general climate of opinion with respect to the library, e.g., *support* for library? Has the climate provided me with so much latitude that demands remain unmet? What assumptions (of users or administrators) limit the consideration of alternative policies? Who benefits from these assumptions? Who does not benefit? Can the assumptions be changed?

5. *Who plays a role in decisions* about library allocations? To what extent are users or potential users involved? To what extent are those affected by decisions helping to make them?

6. Who *benefits* from (and pays for) the library? Does the budget show this? What services serve what groups? How well are they served?

7. What *feedback* is available to the decision maker to evaluate current allocations? What mechanisms for feedback exist? Are they successful in bringing evaluations of users to decision makers? Do nonusers have access and do they use feedback systems?

In brief, political systems analysis is analogous to economic systems analysis: it is a way of thinking.

Woodrow Wilson, asked whether he had much difficulty in accustoming himself to practical politics, stated that after his experience in university politics at Princeton everything else seemed simple. It is time that we all recognized the politics of libraries and acted accordingly.

References

1. Jeffrey A. Raffel and Robert Shishko, *Systematic Analysis of University Libraries: An Application of Cost-Benefit Analysis to the M.I.T. Libraries* (Cambridge, Mass.: M.I.T. Press, 1969). Our M.I.T. editor said goodbye to us with the comment, "I hope you get some reviews." When we replied, "You mean some *good* reviews," she responded, "No, just some reviews."

2. General references in the area of cost-benefit analysis include Charles I. Hitch and Roland N. McKean, *The Economics of Defense in the Nuclear Age* (Cambridge, Mass.: Harvard Univ. Pr., 1960); and David Novick, ed., *Program Budgeting: Program Analysis and the Federal Budget* (Cambridge, Mass.: Harvard Univ. Pr., 1965). References on the "economics of information" can be found in Harold Anker Olsen, *The*

Economics of Information: Bibliography and Commentary on the Literature (Washington, D.C.: ERIC Clearinghouse on Library and Information Sciences, 1971). (ED 044 545).

3. Mancur Olson, "Economics, Sociology, and the Best of All Possible Worlds," *The Public Interest,* no. 12 (Summer 1968), p.96-118.

4. Olsen, *Economics of Information,* p.1.

5. Jeffrey A. Raffel and Robert Shishko, "Cost-Benefit Analysis for Library Administrators," paper presented to Massachusetts Chapter of the Special Libraries Association on March 11, 1969, in Boston, Massachusetts.

6. Melvin R. Levin and Alan Shank refer to cost-benefit analysis "as a measurement technique in which the total costs of a given project or program are compared with the probable total benefit . . . .The result is a numerical ratio . . . ." Cost-effectiveness is viewed as a variation of cost-benefit analysis where the output is expressed in "raw form without conversion to dollars." See Levin and Shank, eds., *Educational Investment in an Urban Society: Costs, Benefits, and Public Policy* (New York: Teachers College Press, 1970), p.1-2.

   Using this distinction, I refer primarily to cost-effectiveness analysis in its application to libraries and cost-benefit analysis as the general approach.

7. Raffel and Shishko, "Cost-Benefit Analysis," p.2.

8. Late in the M.I.T. analysis it became evident that an advertising objective of the library was also significant; that is, librarians wanted to encourage those in the university community to increase their use of the library. Thus attempts were made to entice book use by lavishly furnishing lounges in the libraries. This goal was rarely acknowledged.

9. In the M.I.T. study we tried to resolve this problem by asking potential users to judge benefits themselves.

10. Raffel and Shishko, *Systematic Analysis of University Libraries,* p.50-55.

11. Ibid., p.46-67.

12. Terry N. Clark, in an unpublished paper titled "Please Cut the Budget Pie" (research paper #37 of the Comparative Study of Community Decision-Making, Summer [1972], develops a further rationale and somewhat different methodology to measure citizen preferences for various public policies.

13. Raffel and Shishko, *Systematic Analysis of University Libraries,* p.65.

14. There is a literature in economics (welfare economics and public choice economics) on this subject. The proposed solutions include: (1) maximizing total utility across individuals—but this requires the interpersonal comparison of utility and the measure of utility, both problematic procedures; (2) transforming costs and benefits into dollars and maximizing the net figure—but the full transformation is usually impossible and questions like those raised in the first method still arise;

and (3) only taking those actions that make no one worse off and at least one person better off—but this case arises infrequently in the era of declining or steady budgets.

I am indebted to the critiques of cost-benefit analysis by Aaron Wildavsky. See his "The Political Economy of Efficiency: Cost-Benefit Analysis Systems Analysis and Program Budgeting," *Public Administration Review* 26:292-310 (Dec. 1966); and "Rescuing Policy Analysis from PPBS," in *Public Administration Review: PPBS Reexamined* 29:189-202 (March/April 1969).

15. David Easton, *A Systems Analysis of Political Life* (New York: Wiley, 1965).
16. Alan Rosenthal, ed., *Governing Education: A Reader on Politics, Power, and Public School Policy (Garden City, N.Y.: Anchor Books, 1969), p.viii-ix.*
17. See Frederick Wirt and Michael Kirst, *The Political Web of American Schools* (Boston: Little, 1972), for one volume applying Easton's framework to the politics of education.
18. See Sanford A. Lakoff and Daniel Rich, eds., *Private Government: Introductory Readings* (Glenview, Ill.: Scott, Foresman, 1973), for an excellent discussion of the rationale for studying the politics of private government and case studies, including the politics of university governance.
19. Ibid., p.3.
20. See Sanford Lakoff, "Private Government in the Managed Society," in Lakoff and Rich, eds., *Private Government,* p.218-42.
21. Lakoff and Rich. *Private Government,* preface.
22. Harold Lasswell, *Politics: Who Gets What, When, and How* (Glencoe, Ill.: Free Press, 1958).
23. Thomas Dye recently described several models used in analyzing public policy: (a) elite-mass model, (b) group model, (c) incremental model, (d) institutional model, (e) systems model, and (f) rational model. See Thomas R. Dye, *Understanding Public Policy* (Englewood Cliffs, N.J.: Prentice-Hall, 1972).
24. Dye, *Understanding Public Policy,* p.18-19. Dye's conceptualization is based upon David Easton, "An Approach to the Analysis of Political Systems," *World Politics* 9:383-400 (1957); and Easton, *A Framework for Political Analysis* (Englewood Cliffs, N.J.: Prentice-Hall, 1965).
25. In the preference survey at the $0 budget level, although differences were small, faculty were somewhat more satisfied as measured by the percentage desiring changes from current allocations.
26. The reader should note that this paper is not an indictment of M.I.T. in particular, although there is evidence that the libraries are governed in the same way as are other elements of the university (e.g., health services, graduate school).
27. These arguments relate to a larger battle among elitists, pluralists, neoelitists, and so on. See Dye, *Understanding Public Policy.*

28. Peter Bachrach and Morton S. Baratz, *Power and Poverty: Theory and Practice* (New York: Oxford Univ. Pr., 1970), p.9.
29. John E. Keller, "Program Budgeting and Cost Benefit Analysis in Libraries," *College & Research Libraries* 30:160 (March 1969).
30. It should be noted that many university libraries charge fees for use, for reproduction and for organizational users. My own opinion is that fees for the former are far too high and the latter far too low. In any event, both require further political analysis.
31. Albert Hirschman, *Exit, Voice, and Loyalty* (Cambridge, Mass.: Harvard Univ. Pr., 1970).
32. Lakoff, "Private Government in the Managed Society," p.229.
33. Dye, *Understanding Public Policy.*
34. Note that analogous questions arise about public libraries. Political scientist Edward Banfield is one of a few people to raise explicit political questions about public libraries. Banfield begins his discussion of urban libraries with the question of their purpose. "It [the urban library] is trying to do some things that it probably cannot do, and it is doing others that it should not do."

    In Easton's terms the question expands: (a) What is the relevant *system?* Educational institutions? Information institutions? (b) What are the *outputs* of the library? What groups does it serve? How well does it serve them? (c) Why does the library try to serve these groups? What *demands* does it try to meet? What preferences never become demands? What tasks might it accomplish that are not now viewed as appropriate?

    Banfield argues that libraries should serve "serious," not "light," readers; the latter group could be served by rental and paperback libraries. But most serious readers can pay for the services they receive. Should the general public then pay for a subgroup to receive the services?

    Perhaps what Banfield is trying to communicate is that although the *cost* of library services may serve as the focal point for library decision making and public concern (e.g., closing and reduction in services of public libraries), the basic problem of public libraries is not an economic problem. Rather, we have not examined library priorities and reallocated library resources to meet changing political circumstances. Only a political analysis will indicate why this is so and what changes should be made.

    See Edward C. Banfield, "Some Alternatives for the Public Library," in Ralph W. Conant, ed., *The Public Library and the City* (Cambridge, Mass.: M.I.T. Press, 1965), p.102-13.

Aspects of Managing Information and Making Decisions

Joseph McDonald

INTRODUCTION

There are many different ways to examine the presence and operation of "information" in an organization. But invariably information and decision making are conjoined, for obvious reasons. If decisions do not need to be made, there is no reason to have information. Conversely, information that is not used (or intended to be used) to make decisions is like science which is not communicated: pointless. Therefore this paper uses Yovits's definition of information: "Data of value in decision making;"[1] and we will examine four aspects of the information/decision making interaction: *context, theory, organization and presentation, and uses.*

The design of an organization can help or impede the flow of information. Furthermore, because of "task uncertainty" organizations must process information in order to accomplish work. We will examine Jay Galbraith's Information Processing Model of organization design and posit it as the context for our further inquiry into information and decision making.

Decision making and its close ally, problem solving, have attracted the attention of a variety of psycho-sociological researchers as well as mathematicians. We intend to limit our concern to administrative decision making and to look to some of the classic discussions of it: March and Simon, Etzioni, and Lindblom. Along with this we will also discuss briefly the latest theoretical work being done on information and decision making, specifically, M. C. Yovit's studies in information flow analysis.

In our third step from the abstract to the concrete we will examine what is typically considered to be "information" in, particularly, industrial and business organizations; management information systems (MIS); and the emerging, and relatively crude, decision support systems (DSS). It would seem that Yovits's work will advance our understanding of DSS even if the advance is (to use a hard science analogy) like the advance from phlogiston in our understanding of combustion.

Finally, we will attend to the very concrete world of the uses of information and examine it as power and control. Throughout, a major focus of the paper will be on the costs of information.

It is important for the reader to understand that this paper is not an exhaustive one. Its purpose is to move along the "cutting edge," to suggest areas for further investigation. Accordingly, at the end, we present some hypotheses which lend themselves to development and testing in an area of information science where variables can be easily identified but are difficult to quantify and test.

CONTEXT

At the risk of oversimplification, there appear to be two basic types of decision making in any organization. There is the relatively routine decision making with structured inputs. This is largely the domain of the functional specialist at many levels and appears to be the area where operations research as an aid to decision making has had the greatest impact. The other type of decision is that made under ambiguity and in the midst of complexity. Sometimes called strategic decision making, it is open-ended and dynamic. Bayesian analysis, linear programming, queuing theory, and investment analysis are of relatively little help in strategic decision making.

It is important then to have in mind the kind of decision called for when considering the processing of information for making that decision.

Jay Galbraith had developed a model for organization design called the Information Processing Model and which is most fully elaborated in his book, *Organization Design.*[2] The model is particularly helpful in setting the organizational context for our inquiry because it emphasizes the reality of information flows within organizations and incorporates both routine and strategic decision making.

According to Galbraith, the organization design problem is one of achieving coherence among strategy, organizing mode, and integration of individuals. Beginning with the task—which is, after all, the fundamental raison d'etre of the organization—he lets it vary to see how organizing modes can be adjusted to achieve coherence, and makes two propositions:

1. The greater the task uncertainty, the greater the amount of information that must be processed among decision makers during task execution in order to achieve a given level of performance.
2. Uncertainty is the difference between the amount of information required to perform the task and the amount of information already possessed by the organization.

The amount of information required to perform a task is suggested by:

• The diversity of goals and the amount of internal diversity (division of labor)
• Level of goal performance required to remain productive in the organization's chosen domain

Unfortunately, "at the moment the information-processing load of a task and the information processing capacity of an organization cannot be measured accurately . . . . This is due partially to the difficulty of goal performance . . . . However, organizations can detect changes in variables affecting information . . . . Thus, when the task changes, the organization must change."[3] And, of course, we can determine empirically the change in quantity and quality of information required when the task changes.

As an organization moves from less task uncertainty to greater task uncertainty it coordinates its activities in ways which enable it to increase the amount of information which can be processed. As the organization's size increases and as the need for more information-processing capacity increases, organizations appear to rely on the following key coordinating mechanisms: hierarchy of authority; rules and procedures; planning and goal setting; and narrowing span of control.

These four coordinating mechanisms can be used, exclusively, up to a certain point when, because of the number of exceptions and the increasing task uncertainty, organizations must either reduce the need for information processing or increase their capacity to process information. Whatever is done has costs for an organization, and these must be carefully considered.

Reducing the need for information is accomplished by:

• Environmental management. An organization can attempt to reduce uncertainty about critical events. Examples of this are increased efficiency in order to guarantee access to scarce resources; cartels, and so forth. Alternatively an organization can modify its domain and its relationships with elements in its domain. (It is interesting to observe libraries moving in this direction as uncertainty increases.)

- Creation of slack resources. This requires a reduction in the level of performance which leads to a reduction in the number of exceptions that occur and has the effect of reducing task uncertainty.
- Creation of self-contained tasks. This can be accomplished by:

  1. Reducing the amount of output diversity faced by a single collection of resources. A university may create several completely self-contained libraries to serve different cohorts on the campus population (or different campuses). In practice, many individual libraries are organized this way with severe departmentalization, for example, of technical services and public service tasks. When a reference librarian files in the card catalog, not only is the filing probably less accurate but information to determine priorities (service or filing) must be processed. It is probably much better to risk some unproductive time "on the desk," than to accept mediocre service and poor filing.
  2. Reducing the division of labor. Less specialization means each individual must do more things. But that reduces the amount of information which must be processed between specialists while increasing information to be processed by an individual.

Increasing the capacity to process information is accomplished by:

- Investment in vertical information systems. Information is collected at the points of origination and directed to appropriate places in the hierarchy.
- Creation of lateral relations. "Lateral relations permit the moving of decisions to lower levels of the organization and yet guarantee that all information is included in the process."[4] However, this strategy requires greater amounts of managerial time spent in group meetings and the overhead expense of liaison and integrating roles.

Galbraith hypothesizes these five strategies as an exhaustive set of alternatives. "The organization must adopt at least one of the five strategies when faced with greater uncertainty. If it does not consciously choose one of the five, then slack, reduced performance standards will happen automatically. The task information requirements and the capacity of the organization to process information are always matched."[5]

THEORY

At the risk, again, of oversimplification, administrative decision making (sometimes called policy making) can be seen under two heads: the "classic" rational-comprehensive approach and the limited, incremental approach. A "third" approach, or "mixed-scanning," proposed by Amitai Etzioni, is more or less a synthesis of the first two.

James G. March and Herbert A. Simon state, "Most human decision making, whether individual or organizational, is concerned with the discovery and selection of satisfactory alternatives; only in exceptional cases is it concerned with the discovery and selection of optimal alternatives. To optimize requires processes several orders of magnitude more complex than those required to "satisfice." An example is the difference between searching a haystack to find the sharpest needle in it and searching the haystack to find a needle sharp enough to sew with."[6]

The "satisficing" approach to decision making is a step forward from the rationality of the "economic man" or the rational man of modern statistical decision theory. But it deals with the organizational decisions primarily in terms of the cognitive processes of decision makers and does not examine the interaction between the decision maker and the environment.

The major alternative to the rational or comprehensive approach is "incrementalism." Charles E. Lindblom, in "The Science of 'Muddling Through'"[7] argues that policy making is not a comprehensive process but is made on the basis of marginal or incremental differences in its value consequences.

His comparison of the two methods is worth reproducing:

Rational-Comprehensive (Root)	Successive Limited Comparisons (Branch)
1a. Clarification of values or objectives distinct from and usually prerequisite to empirical analysis alternative policies.	1b. Selection of value goals and empirical analysis of the needed action are not distinct from one another but are closely intertwined.
2a. Policy-formulation is therefore approached through means-end analysis: First the ends are isolated, then the means to achieve them are sought.	2b. Since means and ends are not distinct, means-end analysis is often inappropriate or limited.

Rational-Comprehensive (Root)	Successive Limited Comparisons (Branch)
3a. The test of a "good" policy is that it can be shown to be the most appropriate means to desired ends.	3b. The test of a "good" policy is typically that various analysts find themselves directly agreeing on a policy (without their agreeing that it is the most appropriate means to an agreed objective).

4a. Analysis is comprehensive; every important relevant factor is taken into account.	4b. Analysis is drastically limited:
	  i) Important possible outcomes are neglected.
	  ii) Important alternative potential policies are neglected
	  iii) Important affected values are neglected.

5a. Theory is often heavily relied upon.	5b. A succession of comparisons greatly reduces or eliminates reliance on theory.[8]

Etzioni attempts to combine the comprehensive and incremental approaches in what he terms a "mixed-scanning" approach.[9] While incremental decision making is the usual approach, he argues that it is frequently necessary to take a global view of things. The problem with mixed scanning is that it is frequently difficult to combine the short-range planning which leads to incremental decision making and the long-term comprehensive planning involved in global decision making.

But what is the role of information in decision making? Do we know how decision makers use information? M. C. Yovits, C. R. Foulk, and L. L. Rose describe research which has been underway at Ohio State University to develop a fundamental and general theory of information flow and analysis. Using the earlier quoted definition of information, "data of value in decision making," they have developed a model of a Generalized Information System (GIS). This model has been used to simulate the use of information by an Ohio farmer and has also been used with a mathematically abstracted decision situation. The basic theoretical and conceptual development and the simulation examples and results are reported in the *Journal of the American Society for Information Science.*[10]

The GIS model is based on three hypotheses:

1. Information is data of value in decision making.
2. Information gives rise to observable effects through the decision-making process.
3. Information feedback exists so that the (decision maker) will adjust his assessment of the decision situation for later similar decisions.[11]

The GIS considers primarily the average "rational" man who attempts to meet two objectives when faced with a decision. He wants to choose the "best" course of action (COA) and by choosing a course of action he tries to learn all that he can about "the total current decision situation."

A decision maker, according to Yovits, "will learn about the particular decision situation and environment as follows:" 1) He predicts likely outcomes for various COA on the basis of all information available to him at the time. He will, in fact, relate the current situation to other past decisions he has made. 2) He chooses a COA according to some criteria. 3) He compares the actual resulting observables against his predicted observables by means of feedback. 4) He updates his total model of the situation as a result of this process (learning). 5) When the opportunity arises, he returns to step (1) and makes subsequent similar decisions, reiterating the procedure.[12]

The uncertainties surrounding a decision can be classed:

- State-of-nature, encompassing "the uncontrollable external conditions that will determine the various outcomes."
- Executional, which appears in two ways:
  1. The decision maker must identify the courses of action available to him.
  2. He "must determine likely outcome for each course of action under consideration."
- Goals, which relates outcomes to goal achievement.

Furthermore, each uncertainty has both "structural" and "relational" contexts. "The (decision maker) has structural uncertainty about the number of relevant states of nature, the number of viable alternatives, and the number of outcomes that can occur as a result of executing the alternatives."

"Once the structure is identified . . . he must then resolve relational uncertainties. What is the probability a given state of nature prevails? What is the probability that a given (course of action) will result in a specific outcome? What is the probable value of each outcome relative to a goal attainment?"[13]

The theory (and model) then goes on to define a number of factors at issue in decision making, including such concepts as quantity of information, as well as a number of states and relationships.

Finally, states Yovits, "It is our ultimate goal to apply this theory to real and useful situations and to describe and measure the significance and value of information in these situations. We hope to apply this to information systems development, database management systems, information retrieval, and to decision systems in general."[14]

ORGANIZATION AND PRESENTATION

It is useful at this juncture to take some bearings. "Information" and "decision-making" mean different things to different investigators (and ordinary professionals). In this paper we are trying to "unbundle" a variety of meanings and then link specific understandings of "information" with specific understandings of "decision making."

Our working definition of information (because it links to decision making) is, "data of value in decision making." The obvious assumption is that decision making requires certain data. What kinds of data, how much data, when should the data be acquired, when and how are the data used, are questions that are only now beginning to be answered—and that quite tentatively. But some work is being done. For example, Yovits and others have trenchant observations to make which tend to cut short untested conventional wisdom on these questions. We will examine a set of these observations below.

"Decision making" we define as converting information into action. The two definitions together come close to being a tautology, but a circular definition is avoided by envisioning this *schema*:

Information (i.e., data) → Decision Making → Action

"Classic" theory on decision making has decision makers gathering a lot of information and making the best rational decision—or gathering a lot of information and making a "satisficing" decision—or gathering enough information to advance matters a little bit at a time—or gathering a lot of information on some things, a little on others and combining levels of information, as appropriate, to make a decision which deals with both fundamental matters and less weighty concerns at the same time.

However, decision making in organizations operates on two levels, or, perhaps more accurately, on a continuum with administrative, "managerial" policy making at one end and routine, perhaps repetitive decision making at the other. The design or structure of organizations is determined by the need of organizations to process information (to make decisions) in quantities determined by the uncertainty of a given organization's task(s). And uncertainty is defined as the relative difference in the amount of information required and the amount possessed by the organization.

From all of the foregoing, it is not difficult to hypothesize that information is crucial to an organization's well-being. Assuming such to be the case, it would seem appropriate to assure the manager—the decision maker at one end of the continuum responsible for the organization's well-being—a large, full flow of information, letting him choose what he needs to make decisions. Russell Ackoff strongly suggests that is not the thing to do.[15]

Ackoff identifies "five common and erroneous assumptions underlying the design of most management information systems (MIS)." These are:

1. Give them more. Managers suffer more from an overabundance of irrelevant information than from a lack of relevant information.
2. The manager needs the information that he wants. "One cannot specify what information is required for decision-making until an explanatory model of the decision process and the system involved has been constructed and tested." This is usually not done and since the manager, accordingly, does not know what he needs to know, wants "everything"—to be "safe."
3. Give the manager the information he needs and decision making will improve. "It is necessary to determine how well managers can use needed information." If the decision process is complex and managers cannot use information well, decision rules and performance feedback (perhaps à la Yovits) are needed to improve decision making, not more information.
4. More communication means better performance. MIS can provide many segments of an organization with current information on what other segments are doing and how well. Seldom does better interdepartmental communication of this kind mean better coordination and improved organizational performance.
5. A manager does not have to understand how an information system works, only how to use it. "No MIS should ever be installed unless the managers

for whom it is intended are trained to evaluate and hence control it rather than be controlled by it."

With these caveats in mind we can briefly explore MIS and the currently faddish evolution from MIS, Decision Support Systems (DSS).

One way of looking at DSS is to see it as a third generation attempt to apply systems thinking and computer technology to the manager's domain. The first generation could be called "Electronic Data Processing." Then came MIS and now, DSS. What is the difference?

EDP/MIS	DSS
Passive Use	Active use
Clerical activities	Line, staff and management activities
Oriented toward mechanical fficiency	Oriented toward overall effectiveness
Focus on the past	Focus on the present and future
Emphasis on consistency	Emphasis on flexibility and ad hoc utilization[16]

MIS provides routine data as the result of the automation of certain functions within an organization. DSS attempts to interact with the decision maker, to allow him to introduce variables which the system can then manipulate. DSSs probably begin their lives as pieces of an MIS. Put another way, a DSS is a sophisticated MIS.

There appear to be seven distinct types of DSS:

1. "File drawer" systems allow immediate access to data items.
2. Data analysis systems allow the manipulation of data by means of operators tailored to the task and setting or operators of a general nature.
3. Analysis information systems provide access to a series of databases and small models.
4. Accounting models calculate the consequences of planned actions on the basis of accounting definitions.
5. Representational models estimate the consequences of actions on the basis of models that are partially nondefinitional.
6. Optimization models provide guidelines for action by generating the optimal solution consistent with a series of constraints.

7. Suggestion models perform mechanical work leading to a specific suggested decision for a fairly structured task.[17]

MIS and DSS, when designed and use properly, can provide the manager with a great deal of information (or access to information) for decision making that would otherwise be unobtainable, practically speaking. But the nagging questions still remain: is all that information needed? Does it really lead to better decisions, especially strategic decisions? Part of the answer appears to be that DSS can be a useful and convenient tool for operating middle managers. For policy making, MIS and DSS appear considerably less useful.

SOME QUESTIONS FOR THE FUTURE

It is fair to say we have a very incomplete understanding of how organizations generate information internally, how information gets into organizations for outside, what the differences between these two types of information are, and how information is used and disseminated within organizations.[18]

Furthermore there are large questions about how managers use information to make, especially, strategic decisions. Mintzberg analyzes it this way in a discussion of skills in decision making under ambiguity:

> Management students should learn how to build informal information networks, find sources of information and extract what they need, validate information, assimilate it and build effective mental models. Furthermore, they should learn how to disseminate information, express their ideas effectively, and speak formally as representatives of organizations.[19]

We need much knowledge on what it is managers are really deciding when they make decisions. A decision to alter the design of an organization may, fundamentally, be a decision to increase power and control. Accordingly, the information going into that decision is, in reality, probably structured and used differently than if it were to be used to improve the competitive position of the organization. Yet it may be precisely the same set of "facts and figures."

Although we have not stressed it here, routine decision making (and its supporting information) is taken for granted in most organizations, and very little is known about the continuum between strategic and routine decision making. Does a succession of routine decision making "force" the strategic decision? Does the strategic decision "force" a long series of routine decisions? Mintzberg states:

> Most characteristic of top manager decision making is the unstructured situation. The manager must first decide when a decision must be made; he must then diagnose the situation and plan an approach to it; he must search for solutions and evaluate their consequences; finally, he must select an alternative. This, of course, is only the tip of the iceberg, for as we have seen, a 'decision' is in fact a series of nested smaller decisions one at a time; he juggles a host of them, dealing with each intermittently, all the while attempting to develop some integration among them . . . . It is not the decision making under certainty, risk, or even uncertainty of the textbook that the manager faces, but decision making under ambiguity. Very little information is given to the manager faced with a strategic issue, and almost none of that is structured.[20]

Have managers not been doing this? Have they learned how to do it "on the job"? Or, do managers actually require relatively very little information to make sound decisions, as opposed, say, to an accountant who requires complete and full information to make routine financial decisions? Leon D. Harmon's computer experiments at the Bell Telephone Labs were designed to determine the least amount of visual information a picture can contain and still be recognizable. Relatively little information was required. Could the brain's associative powers do the same for management (strategic) information and decision making? The suspicion is that organizational uses of information for management decision making are unlike the uses of information in scientific and technical matters. Routine decision making may be—perhaps should be—"scientific." But beyond that we know virtually nothing.

In conclusion, one could ask, what does all of this have to do with the information professional? The answer is itself a matter for further exploration. Information handlers have typically concerned themselves with acquiring, processing, and disseminating preorganized data. This is not useless but it is limiting. Should the information professional lay stake to the entire information domain? Is it finally appropriate and necessary to combine the skills of the information scientist, the computer scientists, and the librarian into an information resources manager? Or would that concentrate too much power in the hands of a few? Is "information" still too large and diverse, too uncontrollable a phenomenon to comprehend in one discipline and set of skills? Is an essentially fragmented approach to organizational information still desirable? Or necessary? Or beneficial?

References

1. M. C. Yovits et al., "Information Flow and Analysis," *Journal of the American Society for Information Science* 32 (May 1981): 187.
2. Jay Galbraith, *Organization Design* (Reading, MA: Addison-Wesley, 1977).
3. Galbraith, pp. 38-99.
4. Galbraith, p. 55.
5. Ibid.
6. James G. March and Herbert A. Simon, *Organizations* (New York: John Wiley and Sons, 1958), p. 141.
7. Charles E. Lindblom, "The Science of Muddling Through," *Public Administration Review* 19 (June 1959): 79-88.
8. Ibid., p. 81.
9. Amitai Etzioni, "Mixed-Scanning: A 'Third' Approach to Decision-Making," *Public Administration Review* 27 (December 1967), pp. 385-92.
10. Yovits, pp. 187-210.
11. Ibid., p. 188.
12. Ibid., p. 189.
13. Ibid.
14. Ibid., p. 200.
15. Russell L. Ackoff, "Management Misinformation Systems," in *Key Papers in the Design and Evaluation of Information Systems*, ed. Donald King (White Plains: Knowledge Industry Publication, 1978), pp. 335-44.
16. Steven Alter, *Decision Support Systems: Current Practice and Continuing Challenges.* (Reading, MA: Addison-Wesley, 1980).
17. Ibid., p. 74.
18. Lyman W. Porter and Karlene H. Roberts, "Communication in Organizations," in *Handbook of Industrial and Organizational Psychology* ed. Marvin D. Dunnette (Chicago: Rand McNally, 1976), p. 1562-63.
19. Henry Mintzberg, *The Nature of Managerial Work* (Englewood Cliffs: Prentice-Hall, 1980), p. 190.
20. Ibid., p. 191.

A New Strategy for Job Enrichment

J. Richard Hackman, Greg Oldham, Robert Janson, and Kenneth Purdy

Practitioners of job enrichment have been living through a time of excitement, even euphoria. Their craft has moved from the psychology and management journals to the front page and the Sunday supplement. Job enrichment, which began with the pioneering work of Herzberg and his associates, originally was intended as a means to increase the motivation and satisfaction of people at work—and to improve productivity in the bargain.[1-5] Now it is being acclaimed in the popular press as a cure for problems ranging from inflation to drug abuse.

Much current writing about job enrichment is enthusiastic, sometimes even messianic, about what it can accomplish. But the hard questions of exactly what should be done to improve jobs, and how, tend to be glossed over. Lately, because the harder questions have not been dealt with adequately, critical winds have begun to blow. Job enrichment has been described as yet another "management fad," as "nothing new," even as a fraud. And reports of job-enrichment failures are beginning to appear in management and psychology journals.

This article attempts to redress the excesses that have characterized some of the recent writings about job enrichment. As the technique increases in popularity as a management tool, top managers inevitably will find themselves making decisions about its use. The intent of this paper is to help both managers and behavioral scientists become better able to make those decisions on solid basis of fact and data.

Succinctly stated, we present here a new strategy for going about the redesign of work. The strategy is based on three years of collaborative work and cross-fertilization among the authors—two of whom are academic researchers and two of whom are active practitioners in job enrichment. Our approach is new, but it has been tested in many organizations. It draws on the contributions of both management practice and psychological theory, but it is firmly in the middle ground between them. It builds on and complements previous work by Herzberg and others, but provides for the first time a set of tools for *diagnosing* existing jobs—and a map for translating the diagnostic results into specific action steps for change.

What we have, then, is the following:

1. A theory that specifies when people will get personally "turned on" to their work. The theory shows what kinds of jobs are most likely to generate excitement and commitment about work, and what kinds of employees it works best for.
2. A set of action steps for job enrichment based on the theory, which prescribe in concrete terms what to do to make jobs more motivating for the people who do them.
3. Evidence that the theory holds water and that it can be used to bring about measurable—and sometimes dramatic—improvements in employee work behavior, in job satisfaction, and in the financial performance of the organizational unit involved.

THE THEORY BEHIND THE STRATEGY

What makes people get turned on to their work? For workers who are really prospering in their jobs, work is likely to be a lot like play. Consider, for example, a golfer at a driving range, practicing to get rid of a hook. His activity is *meaningful* to him: he has chosen to do it because he gets a "kick" from testing his skills by playing the game. He knows that he alone is *responsible* for what happens when he hits the ball. And he has *knowledge of the results* within a few seconds.

Behavioral scientists have found that the three "psychological states" experienced by the golfer in the above example also are critical in determining a person's motivation and satisfaction on the job.

Experienced meaningfulness: The individual must perceive his work as worthwhile or important by some system of values he accepts.

Experienced responsibility: He must believe that he personally is accountable for the outcomes of his efforts.

Knowledge of results: He must be able to determine, on some fairly regular basis, whether or not the outcomes of his work are satisfactory.

When these three conditions are present, a person tends to feel very good about himself when he performs well. And those good feelings will prompt him to try to continue to do well—so he can continue to earn the positive feelings in the future. That is what is meant by "internal motivation"—being turned on to one's work because of the positive internal feelings that are generated by doing well, rather than being dependent on external factors (such as incentive pay or compliments from the boss) for the motivation to work effectively.

What if one of the three psychological states is missing? Motivation drops markedly. Suppose, for example, that our golfer has settled in at the driving range to practice for a couple of hours. Suddenly a fog drift in over the range. He can no longer see if the ball starts to tail off to the left a hundred yards out. The satisfaction he got from hitting straight down the middle—and the motivation to try to correct something whenever he didn't—are both gone. If the fog stays, it's likely that he soon will be packing up his clubs.

The relationship between the three psychological states and on-the-job outcomes is illustrated in Figure 1. When all three are high, then internal work motivation, job satisfaction, and work quality are high, and absenteeism and turnover are low.

FIGURE 1 Relationships Among Core Job Dimensions, Critical Psychological States, and On-the-Job Outcomes

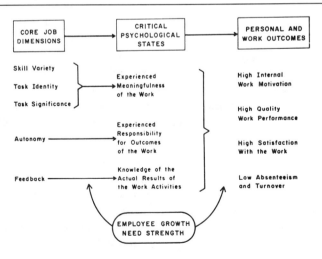

What job characteristics make it happen? Recent research has identified five "core" characteristics of jobs that elicit the psychological states described above.[6-8] these five core job dimensions provide the key to objectively measuring jobs and to changing them so that they have high potential for motivating people who do them.

• Toward meaningful work. Three of the five core dimensions contribute to a job's meaningfulness for the worker:

1. Skill Variety—the degree to which a job requires the worker to perform activities that challenge his skills and abilities. When even a single skill is involved, there is at least a seed of potential meaningfulness. When several are involved, the job has the potential of appealing to more of the whole person, and also of avoiding the monotony of performing the same task repeatedly, no matter how much skill it may require.
2. Task Identity—the degree to which the job requires completion of a "whole" and identifiable piece of work—doing a job from beginning to end with a visible outcome. For example, it is clearly more meaningful to an employee to build complete toasters than to attach electrical cord after electrical cord, especially if he never sees a completed toaster. (Note that the whole job, in this example, probably would involve greater skill variety as well as task identity.)
3. Task Significance—the degree to which the job has a substantial and perceivable impact on the lives of other people, whether in the immediate organization or the world at large. The worker who tightens nuts on aircraft brake assemblies is more likely to perceive his work as significant than the worker who fills small boxes with paper clips—even though the skill levels involved may be comparable.

Each of these three job dimensions represents an important route to experienced meaningfulness. If the job is high in all three, the worker is quite likely to experience his job as very meaningful. It is not necessary, however, for a job to be very high in all three dimensions. If the job is low in any one of them, there will be a drop in overall experienced meaningfulness. But even when two dimensions are low the worker may find the job meaningful if the third is high enough.

• Toward personal responsibility. A fourth core dimension leads a worker to experience increased responsibility in his job. This is *autonomy*, the degree to which the job gives the worker freedom, independence, and discretion in scheduling work and determining how he will carry it out. People in highly autonomous jobs know that they are personally responsible for success and failures. To the extent that their autonomy is high, then, how the work goes will be felt to depend more on the individual's own efforts and initiative rather than on detailed instructions from the boss or from a manual of job procedures.

• Toward knowledge of results. The fifth and last core dimension is *feedback*. This is the degree to which a worker, in carrying out the work activities required by the job, gets information about the effectiveness of his efforts. Feedback is most powerful when it comes directly from the work itself—for example, when a worker has the responsibility for gauging and otherwise checking a component he has just finished, and learns in the process that he has lowered his reject rate by meeting specifications more consistently.

• The overall "motivating potential" of a job. Figure 1 shows how the five core dimensions combine to affect the psychological states that are critical in determining whether or not an employee will be internally motivated to work effectively. Indeed, when using an instrument to be described later, it is possible to compute a "motivating potential score" (MPS) for any job. The MPS provides a single summary index of the degree to which the objective characteristics of the job will prompt high internal work motivation. Following the theory outlined above, a job high in motivating potential must be high in at least one (and hopefully more) of the three dimensions that lead to experienced meaningfulness and high in both autonomy and feedbacks as well. The MPS provides a quantitative index of the degree to which this is in fact the case (see Appendix for detailed formula). As will be seen later, the MPS can be very useful in diagnosing jobs and in assessing the effectiveness of job-enrichment activities.

Does the theory work for everybody? Unfortunately not. Not everyone is able to become internally motivated in his work, even when the motivating potential of a job is very high indeed.

Research has shown that the *psychological needs* of people are very important in determining who can (and who cannot) become internally motivated at work. Some people have strong needs for personal accomplishment, for learning and developing themselves beyond where they are now, for being stimulated and challenged, and so on. These people are high in "growth-need strength."

Figure 2 shows diagrammatically the proposition that individual growth needs have the power to moderate the relationship between the characteristics of jobs and work outcomes. Many workers with high growth needs will turn on eagerly when they have jobs that are high in the core dimensions. Workers whose growth needs are not so strong

FIGURE 2 The Moderating Effect of Employee Growth-Need Strength

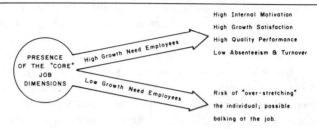

may respond less eagerly—or, at first, even balk at being "pushed" or "stretched" too far.

Psychologists who emphasize human potential argue that everyone has within him at least a spark of the need to grow and develop personally. Steadily accumulating evidence shows, however, that unless that spark is pretty strong, chances are it will get snuffed out by one's experiences in typical organizations. So, a person who has worked for twenty years in stultifying jobs may find it difficult or impossible to become internally motivated overnight when given the opportunity.

We should be cautious, however, about creating rigid categories of people based on their measured growth-need strength at any particular time. It is true that we can predict from these measures who is likely to become internally motivated on a job and who will be less willing or able to do so. But what we do not know yet is whether or not the growth-need "spark" can be rekindled for those individuals who have had their growth needs dampened by years of growth-depressing experience in their organizations.

Since it is often the organization that is responsible for currently low levels of growth desires, we believe that the organization also should provide the individual with the chance to reverse that trend whenever possible, even if that means putting a person in a job where he may be "stretched" more than he wants to be. He can always move back later to the old job—and in the meantime the embers of his growth needs just might burst back into flame, to his surprise and pleasure, and for the good of the organization.

FROM THEORY TO PRACTICE:
A TECHNOLOGY FOR JOB ENRICHMENT

When job enrichment fails, it often fails because of inadequate *diagnosis* of the target job and employees' reactions to it. Often, for example, job enrichment is assumed by management to be a solution to "people problems" on the job and is implemented even though there has been no diagnostic activity to indicate that the root of the problem is in fact how the work is designed. At other times, some diagnosis is made—but it provides no concrete guidance about what specific aspects of the job require change. In either case, the success of job enrichment may wind up depending more on the quality of the intuition of the change agent—or his luck—than on a solid base of data about the people and the work.

In the paragraphs to follow, we outline a new technology for use in job enrichment which explicitly addresses the diagnostic as well as the action components of the change process. The technology has two parts: (1) a set of diagnostic tools that are useful in evaluating jobs and people's reactions to them prior to change—and in pinpointing exactly what aspects of specific jobs are most critical to a successful change attempt; and (2) a set of "implementing concepts" that provide concrete guidance for action steps in job enrichment. The implementing concepts are tied directly to the diagnostic tools; the output of the diagnostic activity specifies which action steps are likely to have the most impact in a particular situation.

The diagnostic tools. Central to the diagnostic procedure we propose is a package of instruments to be used by employees, supervisors, and outside observers in assessing the target job and employees' reactions to it.[9] These instruments gauge the following:

1. The objective characteristics of the jobs themselves, including both an overall indication of the "motivating potential" of the job as it exists (that is, the MPS score) and the score of the job on each of the five core dimensions described previously. Because knowing the strengths and weaknesses of the job is critical to any work-redesign effort, assessments of the job are made by supervisors and outside observers as well as the employees themselves—and the final assessment of a job uses data from all three sources.

2. The current levels of motivation, satisfaction, and work performance of employees on the job. In addition to satisfaction with the work itself, measures are taken of how people feel about other aspects of the work setting, such as pay, supervision, and relationships with co-workers.

3. The level of growth-need strength of the employees. As indicated earlier, employees who have strong growth needs are more likely to be more responsive to job enrichment than employees with weak growth needs. Therefore, it is important to know at the outset just what kinds of satisfactions the people who do the job are (and are not) motivated to obtain from their work. This will make it possible to identify which persons

are best to start changes with, and which may need help in adapting to the newly enriched job.

What, then, might be the actual steps one would take in carrying out a job diagnosis using these tools? Although the approach to any particular diagnosis depends upon the specifics of the particular work situation involved, the sequence of questions listed below is fairly typical.

Step 1. Are motivation and satisfaction central to the problem? Sometimes organizations undertake job enrichment to improve the work motivation and satisfaction of employees when in fact the real problem with work performance lies elsewhere—for example, in a poorly designed production system, in an error-prone computer, and so on. The first step is to examine the scores of employees on the motivation and satisfaction portions of the diagnostic instrument. (The questionnaire taken by employees is called the Job Diagnostic Survey and will be referred to hereafter as the JDS.) If motivation and satisfaction are problematic, the change agent would continue to Step 2; if not, he would look to other aspects of the work situation to identify the real problem.

Step 2. Is the job low in motivating potential? To answer this question, one would examine the motivating potential score of the target job and compare it to the MPS's of other jobs to determine whether or not *the job itself* is a probable cause of the motivational problems documented in Step 1. If the job turns out to be low on the MPS, one would continue to Step 3; if it scores high, attention should be given to other possible reasons for the motivational difficulties (such as the pay system, the nature of supervision, and so on).

Step 3. What specific aspects of the job are causing the difficulty? This step involves examining the job on each of the five core dimensions to pinpoint the specific strengths and weaknesses of the job as it is currently structured. It is useful at this stage to construct a "profile" of the target job, to make visually apparent where improvements need to be made. An illustrative profile for two jobs (one "good" job and one job needing improvement) is shown in Figure 3.

Job A is an engineering maintenance job and is high on all of the core dimensions; the MPS of this job is a very high 260. (MPS scores can range from 10 to about 350; an "average" score would be about 125.) Job enrichment would not be recommended for this job; if employees working on the job were unproductive and unhappy, the reasons are likely to have little to do with the nature or design of the work itself.

FIGURE 3 The JDS Diagnostic Profile for a "Good" and a "Bad" Job

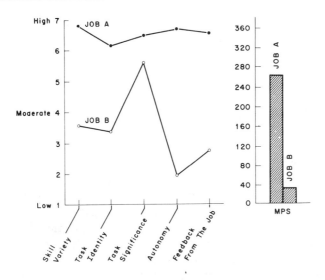

Job B, on the other hand, has many problems. This job involves the routine and repetitive processing of checks in the "back room" of a bank. The MPS is 30, which is quite low—and indeed, would be even lower if it were not for the moderately high task significance of the job. (Task significance is moderately high because the people are handling large amounts of other people's money, and therefore the quality of their efforts potentially has important consequences for their unseen clients.) The job provides the individuals with very little direct feedback about how effectively they are doing it; the employees have little autonomy in how they go about doing the job; and the job is moderately low in both skill variety and task identity.

For Job B, then, there is plenty of room for improvement—and many avenues to examine in planning job changes. For still other jobs, the avenues for change often turn out to be considerably more specific: for example, feedback and autonomy may be reasonably high, but one or more of the core dimensions that contribute to the experienced meaningfulness of the job (skill variety, task identity, and task significance) may be low. In such a case, attention would turn to ways to increase the standing of the job on these latter three dimensions.

Step 4. How "ready" are the employees for change? Once it has been documented that there is need for improvement in the job—and the particularly troublesome aspects of the job have been identified—

then it is time to begin to think about the specific action steps which will be taken to enrich the job. An important factor in such planning is the level of growth needs of the employees, since employees high on growth needs usually respond more readily to job enrichment than do employees with little need for growth. The JDS provides a direct measure of the growth-need strength of the employees. This measure can be very helpful in planning how to introduce the changes to the people (for instance, cautiously versus dramatically), and in deciding who should be among the first group of employees to have their jobs changed.

In actual use of the diagnostic package, additional information is generated which supplements and expands the basic diagnostic questions outlined above. The point of the above discussion is merely to indicate the kinds of questions which we believe to be most important in diagnosing a job prior to changing it. We now turn to how the diagnostic conclusions are translated into specific job changes.

The implementing concepts. Five "implementing concepts" for job enrichment are identified and discussed below.[10] Each one is a specific action step aimed at improving both the quality of the working experience for the individual and his work productivity. They are: (1) forming natural work units; (2) combining tasks; (3) establishing client relationships; (4) vertical loading; (5) opening feedback channels.

The links between the implementing concepts and the core dimensions are shown in Figure 4—which illustrates our theory of job

FIGURE 4 The Full Model: How Use of the Implementing Concepts Can Lead to Positive Outcomes

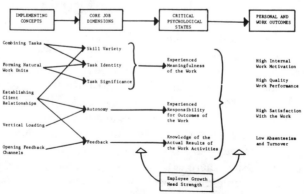

enrichment, ranging from the concrete action steps through the core dimensions and the psychological states to the actual personal and work outcomes.

After completing the diagnosis of a job, a change agent would know which of the core dimensions were most in need of remedial attention. He could then turn to Figure 4 and select those implementing concepts that specifically deal with the most troublesome parts of the existing job. How this would take place in practice will be seen below.

• Forming natural work units. The notion of distributing work in some logical way may seem to be an obvious part of the design of any job. In many cases, however, the logic is one imposed by just about any consideration except job-holder satisfaction and motivation. Such considerations include technological dictates, level of worker training or experience, "efficiency" as defined by industrial engineering, and current workload. In many cases the cluster of tasks a worker faces during a typical day or week is natural to anyone *but* the worker.

For example, suppose that a typing pool (consisting of one supervisor and ten typists) handles all work for one division of a company. Jobs are delivered in rough draft or dictated form to the supervisor, who distributes them as evenly as possible among the typists. In such circumstances the individual letters, reports, and other tasks performed by a given typist in one day or week are randomly assigned. There is no basis for identifying with the work or the person or department for whom it is performed, or for placing any personal value upon it.

The principle underlying natural units of work, by contrast, is "ownership"—a worker's sense of continuing responsibility for an identifiable body of work. Two steps are involved in creating natural work units. The first is to identify the basic work items. In the typing pool, for example, the items might be "pages to be typed." The second step is to group the items in natural categories. For example, each typist might be assigned continuing responsibility for all jobs requested by one or several specific departments. The assignments should be made, of course, in such a way that workloads are about equal in the long run. (For example, one typist might end up with all the work from one busy department, while another handles jobs from several smaller units.)

At this point we can begin to see specifically how the job-design principles relate to the core dimensions (cf. Figure 4). The ownership fostered by natural units by work can make the difference between a feeling that work is meaningful and rewarding and the feeling that it is irrelevant and boring. As the diagram shows, natural units of work are directly related to two of the core dimensions: task identity and task significance.

A typist whose work is assigned naturally rather than randomly—say, by departments—has a much greater chance of performing a whole job to completion. Instead of typing one section of a large report, the individual is likely to type the whole thing, with knowledge of exactly what the product of the work is (task identity). Furthermore, over time the typist will develop a growing sense of how the work affects co-workers in the department serviced (task significance).

  • Combining tasks. The very existence of a pool made up entirely of persons whose sole function is typing reflects a fractionalization of jobs that has been a basic precept of "scientific management." Most obvious in assembly-line work, fractionalization has been applied to nonmanufacturing jobs as well. It is typically justified by efficiency, which is usually defined in terms of either low costs or some time-and-motion type of criteria.

It is hard to find fault with measuring efficiency ultimately in terms of cost-effectiveness. In doing so, however, a manager should be sure to consider *all* the costs involved. It is possible, for example, for highly fractionalized jobs to meet all the time-and-motion criteria of efficiency, but if the resulting job is so unrewarding that performing it day after day leads to high turnover, absenteeism, drugs and alcohol, and strikes, them productivity is really lower (and costs higher) than data on efficiency might indicate.

The principle of combining tasks, then, suggests that whenever possible existing and fractionalized tasks should be put together to form new and larger modules of work. At the Medfield, Massachusetts plant of Corning Glass Works the assembly of a laboratory hot plate has been redesigned along the lines suggested here. Each hot plate now is assembled from start to finish by one operator, instead of going through several separate operations that are performed by different people.

Some tasks, if combined into a meaningfully large module of work, would be more than an individual could do by himself. In such cases, it is often useful to consider assigning the new, larger task to a small *team* of workers—who are given great autonomy for its completion. At the Racine, Wisconsin plant of Emerson Electric, the assembly process for trash disposal appliances was restructured this way. Instead of a sequence of moving the appliance from station to station, the assembly now is done from start to finish by one team. Such teams include both men and women to permit switching off the heavier and more delicate aspects of the work. The team responsible is identified on the appliance. In case of customer complaints, the team often drafts the reply.

As a job-design principle, task combination, like natural units of work, expands the task identity of the job. For example, the hot-plate assembler can see and identify with a finished product ready for shipment, rather than a nearly invisible junction of solder. Moreover, the more tasks that are combined into a single worker's job, the greater the variety of skills he must call on in performing the job. So task combination also leads directly to greater skill variety—the third core dimension that contributes to the overall experienced meaningfulness of the work.

• Establishing client relationships. One consequence of fractionalization is that the typical worker has little or no contact with (or even awareness of) the ultimate user of his product or service. By encouraging and enabling employees to establish direct relationships with the clients of their work, improvements often can be realized simultaneously on three of the core dimensions. Feedback increases, because of additional opportunities for the individual to receive praise or criticism of his work outputs directly. Skill variety often increases, because of the necessity to develop and exercise one's interpersonal skills in maintaining the client relationship. And autonomy can increase because the individual often is given personal responsibility for deciding how to manage his relationships with the clients of his work.

Creating client relationships is a three-step process. First, the client must be identified. Second, the most direct contact possible between the worker and the client must be established. Third, criteria must be set up by which the client can judge the quality of the product or service he receives. And whenever possible, the client should have means of relaying his judgments directly back to the worker.

The contact between worker and client should be as great as possible and as frequent as necessary. Face-to-face contact is highly desirable, at least occasionally. Where that is impossible or impractical, telephone and mail can suffice. In any case, it is important that the performance criteria by which the worker will be rated by the client must be mutually understood and agreed upon.

• Vertical loading. Typically the split between the "doing" of a job and the "planning" and "controlling" of the work has evolved along with horizontal fractionalization. Its rationale, once again, has been "efficiency through specialization." And once again, the excess of specialization that has emerged has resulted in unexpected but significant costs in motivation, morale, and work quality. In vertical loading, the intent is to partially close the gap between the doing and the controlling parts of the job—and thereby reap some important motivational advantages.

Of all the job-design principles, vertical loading may be the single most crucial one. In some cases, where it has been impossible to implement any other changes, vertical loading alone has had significant motivational effects.

When a job is vertically loaded, responsibilities and controls that formerly were reserved for high levels of management are added to the job. There are many ways to accomplish this:

- Return to the job holder greater discretion in setting schedules, deciding on work methods, checking on quality, and advising or helping to train less experienced workers.
- Grant additional authority. The objective should be to advance workers from a position of no authority or highly restricted authority to positions of reviewed, and eventually, near-total authority for his own work.
- Time management. The job holder should have the greatest possible freedom to decide when to start and stop work, when to break, and how to assign priorities.
- Troubleshooting and crisis decisions. Workers should be encouraged to seek problem solutions on their own, rather than calling immediately for the supervisor.
- Financial controls. Some degree of knowledge and control over budgets and other financial aspects of a job can often be highly motivating. However, access to this information frequently tends to be restricted. Workers can benefit from knowing something about the costs of their jobs, the potential effect upon profit, and various financial and budgetary alternatives.

When a job is vertically loaded it will inevitably increase in *autonomy*. And as shown in Figure 4, this increase in objective personal control over the work will also lead to an increased feeling of personal responsibility for work, and ultimately to higher internal work motivation.

- Opening feedback channels. In virtually all jobs there are ways to open channels of feedback to individuals or teams to help them learn whether their performance is improving, deteriorating, or remaining at a constant level. While there are numerous channels through which information about performance can be provided, it generally is better for a worker to learn about his performance *directly as he does his job*—rather than from management on an occasional basis.

Job-provided feedback usually is more immediate and private than supervisor-supplied feedback, and it increases the worker's feelings of personal control over his work in the bargain. Moreover, it avoids many of the potentially disruptive interpersonal problems that can develop when the only way a worker has to find out how he is doing is through direct messages or subtle cues from the boss.

Exactly what should be done to open channels for job-provided feedback will vary from job to job and organization to organization. Yet in many cases the changes involve simply removing existing blocks that isolate the worker from naturally occurring data about performance—rather than generating entirely new feedback mechanisms. For example:

- Establishing direct client relationships often removes blocks between the worker and natural external sources of data about his work.
- Quality-control efforts in many organizations often eliminate a natural source of feedback. The quality check on a product or service is done by persons other than those responsible for the work. Feedback to the workers—if there is any—is belated and diluted. It often fosters a tendency to think of quality as "someone else's concern." By placing quality control close to the worker (perhaps even in his own hands), the quantity and quality of data about performance available to him can dramatically increase.
- Tradition and established procedure in many organizations dictate that records about performance be kept by a supervisor and transmitted up (not down) in the organizational hierarchy. Sometimes supervisors even check the work and correct any errors themselves. The worker who made the error never knows it occured—and is denied the very information that could enhance both his internal work motivation and the technical adequacy of his performance. In many cases it is possible to provide standard summaries of performance records directly to the worker (as well as to his superior), thereby giving him personally and regularly the data he needs to improve his performance.
- Computers and other automated operations sometimes can be used to provide the individual with data now blocked from him. Many clerical operations, for example, are now performed on computer consoles. These consoles often can be programmed to provide the clerk with immediate feedback in the form of a CRT display or a printout indicating that an error has been made. Some systems even have been programmed to provide the

operator with a positive feedback message when a period of error-free performance has been sustained.

Many organizations simply have not recognized the importance of feedback as a motivator. Data on quality and other aspects of performance are viewed as being of interest only to management. Worse still, the *standards* for acceptable performance often are kept from workers as well. As a result, workers who would be interested in following the daily or weekly ups and downs of their performance, and in trying accordingly to improve, are deprived of the very guidelines they need to do so. They are like the golfer we mentioned earlier, whose efforts to correct his hook are stopped dead by fog over the driving range.

THE STRATEGY IN ACTION: HOW WELL DOES IT WORK?

So far we have examined a basic theory of how people get turned on to their work; a set of core dimensions of jobs that create the conditions for such internal work motivation to develop on the job; and a set of five implementing concepts that are the action steps recommended to boost a job on the core dimensions and thereby increase employee motivation, satisfaction, and productivity.

The remaining question is straightforward and important: *Does it work?* In reality, that question is twofold. First, does the theory itself hold water, or are we barking up the wrong conceptual tree? And second, does the change strategy really lead to measurable differences when it is applied in an actual organizational setting?

This section summarizes the findings we have generated to date on these questions.

Is the job-enrichment theory correct? In general, the answer seems to be yes. The JDS instrument has been taken by more than 1,000 employees working on about 100 diverse jobs in more than a dozen organizations over the last two years. These data have been analyzed to test the basic motivational theory—and especially the impact of the core job dimensions on worker motivation, satisfaction, and behavior on the job. An illustrative overview of some of the findings is given below.[10]

1. People who work on jobs high on the core dimensions are more motivated and satisfied than are people who work on jobs that score low on the

dimensions. Employees with jobs high on the core dimensions (MPS scores greater than 240) were compared to those who held unmotivating jobs (MPS scores less than 40). As shown in Figure 5, employees with high MPS jobs were higher on (a) the three psychological states, (b) internal work motivation, (c) general satisfaction, and (d) "growth" satisfaction.

FIGURE 5 Employee Reactions to Jobs High and Low in Motivating Potential for Two Banks and a Steel Firm

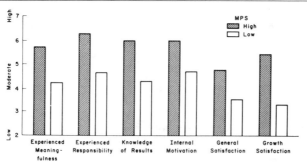

2. Figure 6 shows that the same is true for measures of actual behavior at work—absenteeism and performance effectiveness—although less strongly so for the performance measure.

FIGURE 6 Absenteeism and Job Performance for Employees with Jobs High and Low in Motivating Potential

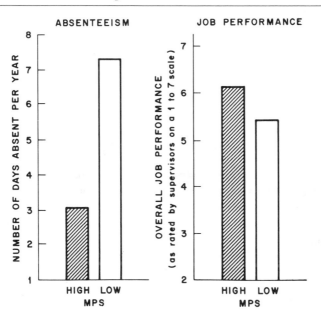

3. Responses to jobs high in motivating potential are more positive for people who have strong growth needs than for people with weak needs for growth. In Figure 7 the linear relationship between the motivating potential of a job and employees' level of internal work motivation is shown, separately for people with high versus low growth needs as measured by the JDS. While both groups of employees show increases in internal motivation as MPS increases, the *rate* of increase is significantly greater for the group of employees who have strong needs for growth.

FIGURE 7 Relationship Between the Motivating Potential of a Job and the Internal Work Motivation of Employees (Shown separately for employees with strong versus weak growth-need strength.)

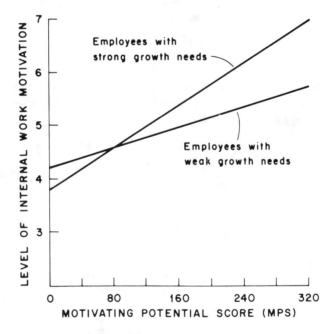

How does the change strategy work in practice? The results summarized above suggest that both the theory and the diagnostic instrument work when used with real people in real organizations. In this section, we summarize a job-enrichment project conducted at The Travelers Insurance Companies, which illustrates how the change procedures themselves work in practice.

The Travelers project was designed with two purposes in mind.

One was to achieve improvements in morale, productivity, and other indicators of employee well-being. The other was to test the general effectiveness of the strategy for job enrichment we have summarized in this article.

The work group chosen was a keypunching operation. The group's function was to transfer information from printed or written documents onto punched cards for computer input. The work group consisted of ninety-eight keypunch operators and verifiers (both in the same job classification), plus seven assignment clerks. All reported to a supervisor who, in turn, reported to the assistant manager and manager of the data-input division.

The size of individual punching orders varied considerably, from a few cards to as many as 2,500. Some work came to the work group with a specified delivery date, while other orders were to be given routine service on a predetermined schedule.

Assignment clerks received the jobs from the user departments. After reviewing the work for obvious errors, omissions, and legibility problems, the assignment clerk parceled out the work in batches expected to take about one hour. If the clerk found the work not suitable for punching it went to the supervisor, who either returned the work to the user department or cleared up problems by phone. When work went to operators for punching, it was with the instruction, "Punch only what you see. Don't correct errors, no matter how obvious they look."

Because of the high cost of computer time, keypunched work was 100 percent verified—a task that consumed nearly as many man-hours as the punching itself. Then the cards went to the supervisor, who screened the jobs for due dates before sending them to the computer. Errors detected in verification were assigned to various operators at random to be corrected.

The computer output from the cards was sent to the originating department, accompanied by a printout of errors. Eventually the printout went back to the supervisor for final correction.

A great many phenomena indicated that the problems being experienced in the work group might be the result of poor motivation. As the only person performing supervisory functions of any kind, the supervisor spent most of his time responding to crisis situations, which recurred continually. He also had to deal almost daily with employees' salary grievances or other complaints. Employees frequently showed apathy or outright hostility toward their jobs.

Rates of work output, by accepted work-measurement standards, were inadequate. Error rates were high. Due dates and schedules frequently were missed. Absenteeism was higher than average, especially before and after weekends and holidays.

The single, rather unusual exception was turnover. It was lower than the companywide average for similar jobs. The company has attributed this fact to a poor job market in the base period just before the project began, and to an older, relatively more settled work force—made up, incidentally, entirely of women.

The diagnosis. Using some of the tools and techniques we have outlined, a consulting team from the Management Services Department and from Roy W. Walters & Associates concluded that the keypunch-operator's job exhibited the following serious weaknesses in terms of the core dimensions.

- Skill variety: there was none. Only a single skill was involved—the ability to punch adequately the data on the batch of documents.
- Task identity: virtually nonexistent. Batches were assembled to provide an even workload, but not whole identifiable jobs.
- Task significance: not apparent. The keypunching operation was a necessary step in providing service to the company's customers. The individual operator was isolated by an assignment clerk and a supervisor from any knowledge of what the operation meant to the using department, let alone its meaning to the ultimate customer.
- Autonomy: none. The operators had no freedom to arrange their daily tasks to meet schedules, to resolve problems with the using department, or even to correct, in punching, information that was obviously wrong.
- Feedback: none. Once a batch was out of the operator's hands, she had no assured chance of seeing evidence of its quality or inadequacy.

Design of the experimental trial. Since the diagnosis indicated that the motivating potential of the job was extremely low, it was decided to attempt to improve the motivation and productivity of the work group through job enrichment. Moreover, it was possible to design an experimental test of the effects of the changes to be introduced: the results of changes made in the target work group were to be compared with trends in a control work group of similar size and demographic make-up. Since the control group was located more than a mile away, there appeared to be little risk of communication between members of the two groups.

A base period was defined before the start of the experimental trial period, and appropriate data were gathered on the productivity, absenteeism, and work attitudes of members of both groups. Data also were available on turnover; but since turnover was already below average in the target group, prospective changes in this measure were deemed insignificant.

An educational session was conducted with supervisors, at which they were given the theory and implementing concepts and actually helped to design the job changes themselves. Out of this session came an active plan consisting of about twenty-five change items that would significantly affect the design of the target jobs.

The implementing concepts and the changes. Because the job as it existed was rather uniformly low on the core job dimensions, all five of the implementing concepts were used in enriching it.

- Natural units of work. The random batch assignment of work was replaced by assigning to each operator continuing responsibility for certain accounts—either particular departments or particular recurring jobs. Any work for those accounts now always goes to the same operator.
- Task combination. Some planning and controlling functions were combined with the central task of keypunching. In this case, however, these additions can be more suitably discussed under the remaining three implementing concepts.
- Client relationships. Each operator was given several channels of direct contact with clients. The operators, not their assignment clerks, now inspect their documents for correctness and legibility. When problems arise, the operator, not the supervisor, takes them up with the client.
- Feedback. In addition to feedback from client contact, the operators were provided with a number of additional sources of data about their performance. The computer department now returns incorrect cards to the operators who punched them, and operators correct their own errors. Each operator also keeps her own file of copies of her errors. These can be reviewed to determine trends in error frequency and types of errors. Each operator receives weekly a computer printout of her errors and productivity, which is sent to her directly, rather than given to her by the supervisor.
- Vertical loading. Besides consulting directly with clients about work questions, operators now have the authority to correct obvious coding errors on their own. Operators may set their own schedules and plan their daily work, as long as they meet schedules. Some competent operators have been given the option of not verifying their work and making their own program changes.

Results of the trial. The results were dramatic. The number of operators declined from ninety-eight to sixty. This occured partly through attrition and partly through transfer to other departments. Some of the operators were promoted to higher-paying jobs in departments whose cards they had been handling—something that had never occurred before. Some details of the results are given below.

- Quantity of work. The control group, with no job changes made, showed an increase in productivity of 8.1 percent during the trial period. The experimental group showed an increase of 39.6 percent.
- Error rates. To assess work quality, error rates were recorded for about forty operators in the experimental group. All were experienced, and all had been in their jobs before the job-enrichment program began. For two months before the study, these operators had a collective error rate of 1.53 percent. For two months toward the end of the study, the collective error rate was 0.99 percent. By the end of the study the number of operators with poor performance had dropped from 11.1 percent to 5.5 percent.
- Absenteeism. The experimental group registered a 24.1 percent decline in absences. The control group, by contrast, showed a 29 percent *increase*.
- Attitudes toward the job. An attitude survey given at the start of the project showed that the two groups scored about average, and nearly identically, in nine different areas of work satisfaction. At the end of the project the survey was repeated. The control group showed an insignificant 0.5 percent improvement, while the experimental group's overall satisfaction score rose 16.5 percent.
- Selective elimination of controls. Demonstrated improvements in operator proficiency permitted them to work with fewer controls. Travelers estimates that the reduction of controls had the same effect as adding seven operators—a saving even beyond the effects of improved productivity and lowered absenteeism.
- Role of the supervisor. One of the most significant findings in the Travelers experiment was the effect of the changes on the supervisor's job, and thus on the rest of the organization. The operators took on many responsibilities that had been reserved at least to the unit leaders and sometimes to the supervisor. The unit leaders, in turn, assumed some of the day-to-day supervisory functions that had plagued the supervisor. Instead of spending his days supervising the behavior of subordinates and dealing with crises, he was able to devote time to developing feedback systems, setting up work modules and spearheading the enrichment effort—in other works, managing. It should be noted, however, that helping supervisors change their own work activities when their subordinates' jobs have been enriched is itself a challenging task. And if appropriate attention and help are not given to supervisors in such cases, they rapidly can become disaffected—and a job-enrichment "backlash" can result.[11]

Summary. By applying work-measurement standards to the changes wrought by job enrichment—attitude and quality, absenteeism, and selective administration of controls—Travelers was able to estimate the total dollar impact of the project. Actual savings in salaries and machine rental charges during the first year totaled $64,305. Potential savings by further application of the changes were put at $91,937 annually. Thus, by almost any measure used—from the work attitudes of individual employees to dollar savings for the company as a whole—The Travelers test of the job-enrichment strategy proved a success.

CONCLUSIONS

In this article we have presented a new strategy for the redesign of work in general and for job enrichment in particular. The approach has four main characteristics:

1. It is gounded in a basic psychological theory of what motivates people in their work.
2. It emphasizes that planning for job changes should be done on the basis of *data* about the jobs and the people who do them—and a set of diagnostic instruments is provided to collect such data.
3. It provides a set of specific implementing concepts to guide actual job changes, as well as a set of theory-based rules for selecting *which* action steps are likely to be most beneficial in a given situation.
4. The strategy is buttressed by a set of findings showing that the theory holds water, that the diagnostic procedures are practical and informative, and that the implementing concepts can lead to changes that are beneficial both to organizations and to the people who work in them.

We believe that job enrichment is moving beyond the stage where it can be considered "yet another management fad." Instead, it represents a potentially powerful strategy for change that can help organizations achieve their goals for higher quality work—and at the same time further the equally legitimate needs of contemporary employees for a more meaningful work experience. Yet there are pressing questions about job enrichment and its use that remain to be answered.

Prominent among these is the question of employee participation in planning and implementing work redesign. The diagnostic tools and implementing concepts we have presented are neither designed nor intended for use only by management. Rather, our belief is that the effectiveness of job enrichment is likely to be enhanced when the tasks of diagnosing and changing jobs are undertaken *collaboratively* by management and by the employees whose work will be affected.

Moreover, the effects of work redesign on the broader organization remain generally uncharted. Evidence now is accumulating that when jobs are changed, turbulence can appear in the surrounding organization—for example, in supervisory-subordinate relationships, in pay and benefit plans, and so on. Such turbulence can be viewed by management either as a problem with job enrichment, or as an opportunity for further and broader organizational development teams of managers and employees. To the degree that management takes the latter view, we believe, the oft-espoused goal of achieving basic organizational change through the redesign of work may come increasingly within reach.

The diagnostic tools and implementing concepts we have presented are useful in deciding on and designing basic changes in the jobs themselves. They do not address the broader issues of who plans the changes, how they are carried out, and how they are followed up. The way these broader questions are dealt with, we believe, may determine whether job enrichment will grow up—or whether it will die an early and unfortunate death, like so many other fledgling behavioral-science approaches to organizational change.

Appendix:

For the algebraically inclined, the Motivating Potential Score is computed as follows

$$MPS = \left[\frac{\text{Skill Variety} + \text{Task Identity} + \text{Task Significance}}{3} \right] \times \text{Autonomy} \quad \times \text{Feedback}$$

It should be noted that in some cases the MPS score can be *too* high for positive job satisfaction and effective performance—in effect overstimulating the person who holds the job. This paper focuses on jobs which are toward the low end of the scale—and which potentially can be improved through job enrichment.

Acknowledgments: The authors acknowledge with great appreciation the editorial assistance of John Hickey in the preparation of this paper, and the help of Kenneth Brousseau, Daniel Feldman, and Linda Frank in collecting the data that are summarized here. The research activities reported were supported in part by the Organizational Effectiveness Research Program of the Office of Naval Research, and the Manpower Administration of the U.S. Department of Labor, both through contracts to Yale University.

References

1. F. Herzberg, B. Mausner and B. Snyderman, *The Motivation to Work* (New York: John Wiley & Sons, 1959).
2. F. Herzberg, *Work and the Nature of Man* (Cleveland: World, 1966).
3. F. Herzberg, "One More Time: How Do You Motivate Employees?" *Harvard Business Review* (1968), pp. 53-62.
4. W. J. Paul, Jr.; K. B. Robertson and F. Herzberg, "Job Enrichment Pays Off," *Harvard Business Review* (1969), pp. 61-78.
5. R. N. Ford, *Motivation Through the Work Itself* New York: American Management Association, 1969).
6. A. N. Turner and P. R. Lawrence, *Industrial Jobs and the Worker* (Cambridge, Mass.: Harvard Graduate School of Business Administration, 1965).
7. J. R. Hackman and E. E. Lawler, "Employee Reactions to Job Characteristics," *Journal of Applied Psychology Monograph* (1971), pp. 259-286.
8. J. R. Hackman and G. R. Oldham, *Motivation Through the Design of Work: Test of a Theory,* Technical Report No. 6, Department of Administrative Sciences, Yale University, 1974.
9. J. R. Hackman and G. R. Oldham, "Development of the Job Diagnostic Survey," *Journal of Applied Psychology* (1975), pp. 159-170.
10. R. W. Walters and Associates, *Job Enrichment for Results* (Cambridge, Mass.: Addison-Wesley, 1975).
11. E. E. Lawler III; J. R. Hackman, and S. Kaufman, "Effects of Job Redesign: A Field Experiment," *Journal of Applied Social Psychology* (1973), pp. 49-62.

Work Enrichment for Academic Libraries

Charles Martell and Mercedes Untawale

AMERICAN workers at all levels are expressing more job dissatisfaction than at any point in the last 28 years. Middle managers are more unhappy and feel less secure than ever before.[1] Librarians talk about burnout and staff exhibit higher levels of stress and anxiety. Meanwhile, computerized systems continue to alter work relationships. They change the way in which we look at our work, at ourselves, and at one another.

Librarians talk of boredom. Work doesn't have the same meaning for some that it did at first. They lack challenge. They lack a sense of commitment. Change has frequently brought new tasks but not new roles. Some library staff feel that the quality of their work life is unsatisfactory. Furthermore, despite forms of participation, they are not usually involved in the big decisions (e.g., the decision to introduce a computer system into the workplace, or how jobs will be changed).

What can be done about the feelings of dissatisfaction, anxiety, and lack of commitment? How can the process by which far-reaching technologies are introduced into the workplace be humanized? New techniques and skills can be adopted. What may be required, however, is the redesign of jobs and the redesign of libraries as organizations.[2] This may lead to a shift in the locus of power and influence in libraries to include more basic decision-making authority and responsibility by staff members at lower levels in the library.

QUALITY OF WORK LIFE

Warren J. Haas suggests that "this is a time for imagination, innovation, and experiment—not for stereotyped response to over-

Reprinted with permission from *The Journal of Academic Librarianship*, vol. 8 (1983), pp. 339–343. © 1983 by Mountainside Publishing, Inc.

simplified problems."[3] The quality of work life (QWL) movement can make valuable contributions in this area. QWL can be defined as "the degree to which members of a work organization are able to satisfy important personal needs through their experiences in the organization."[4] This includes:

- Participation in decision making
- Freedom and independence
- Challenge
- Use of a variety of valued skills and abilities
- Expression of creativity
- Opportunity for learning

The focus on individual needs contrasts sharply with traditional personnel systems that center on the productive capacity of the employee. Proponents of QWL are able to demonstrate that work can be redesigned to meet the psychological needs of the employee (e.g., feelings of self-esteem, competency, and self-actualization), while simultaneously encouraging improvement in productivity norms.

In subsequent issues of the *Journal of Academic Librarianship*, a series of themes related to QWL will be explored: job redesign, the impact of technology on the workplace, productivity, burnout, organization design, and motivation. Case studies will be presented for some themes.

Job enrichment, a popular form of job redesign, is described in this issue. The case study prepared by Mercedes Untawale discusses how the introduction of automated systems necessitated changes in workflow and work assignments. Although Untawale was entirely unaware of job enrichment and QWL principles, her job change strategy offers interesting parallels to them. Her actions led to the redesign of jobs, and resulted in a significant increase in both the speed with which books flowed through the Processing Division and, quite inadvertently, the QWL of the staff. It is likely that other library managers are also struggling and solving job change problems with techniques similar to those espoused by QWL advocates. One purpose of this series of articles is to highlight these contributions.

Job Enlargement

Among the earliest techniques to target the psychological needs of the employee was job enlargement. *Enlargement occurs when the variety of tasks contained within a job is increased.* The technique was originally promoted because it seemed to address needs that were unmet by other pre-and post-World War II job design programs. Higher levels of job satisfaction and a reduction in absenteeism were recorded. However, these benefits were short-lived. Analysis later revealed that job enlargement does not benefit three critical psychological states: (1) experienced meaningfulness of the work; (2) experienced responsibility for outcomes of the work; and (3) knowledge of the actual results of the work activities. To overcome these shortcomings, four job attributes that were purposefully excluded from most nonsupervisory jobs in the past must be reconsidered. They are: autonomy, control, decision making, and feedback.[5] Developed during the 1960s, the technique of job enrichment owes much of its success to the deliberate manner in which the four attributes are built into the basic design package.

Job Enrichment

Job enrichment is the process by which a person gains greater control over those factors that directly affect his or her job. It stresses the humanizing and self-fulfilling potential of an expanded organizational role. Included are *scheduling* (when you do what during the day), *decision making* (meaningful involvement in the decisions that affect your tasks, your job, and your role within the library), *meaning* (who does your work help and how important does it seem to you), and *feedback* (the information that you receive on how your efforts contribute to the goals of your unit, the library, and most importantly, users).

The decision to begin a job enrichment program should only be made after analysis has revealed the true nature of the problem. Some factors may be entirely unrelated to how the work is designed: pay and other reward structures; faulty computer systems; types of supervision; and inadequate design features in the production system are but a few. In "A New Strategy for Job Enrichment," Hackman et al. present a set of diagnostic tools to be used and a set of implementing concepts. Hackman recommends that the following questions be answered:

1. Are motivation and satisfaction central to the employee's problem?
2. Is the job low in motivating potential?
3. What specific aspects of the job are causing the difficulty?
4. How ready is the employee for change?[6]

The Job Diagnostic Survey (JDS) can be used to examine the need for a job enrichment program and to indicate the specific factors to be changed. The JDS can also provide clues to staff growth-need strengths (e.g., need for challenge and personal accomplishment). Staff with high growth needs tend to show greater responsiveness to job enrichment than staff with low growth needs.

The case study that accompanies this article demonstrates how changes were introduced in the design of jobs for a materials processing unit that resulted in an enriched level of work. Although an ad hoc, relatively unplanned strategy developed, the results are not unlike formal enrichment strategies typical of other industrial and service sectors.

HOW TO DEVELOP ENRICHED WORK

Changes in the design of jobs in the Processing Division were necessitated by the introduction of two automated systems: (1) the in-house acquisition system, and (2) the RLIN system. The design changes were not planned in advance. This is typical. Fortunately, the alterations enriched the quality of work life in the Processing Division. The effort was successful because of unusually astute and imaginative supervision and an equally supportive, well-trained staff. Change is not always so beneficial. Frequently there is little understanding or sensitivity exhibited where the concerns of staff intersect with the perceived need for computer-driven technical innovation. A technology is introduced and the staff are expected to comply with the technical imperatives demanded of the new system.

How can library supervisors and staff develop enriched work? First, supervisors can assess the QWL in their units. Since supervisors have a basic responsibility to ensure that the work of their units is accomplished successfully, improvements in the design of work must take place within this broad constraint. Observation and discussion with staff can serve to uncover tasks and jobs that are weak in this area. Second, through study and analysis, the supervisor can learn about and consider the use of a repertoire of job redesign techniques. Third, in conjunction with staff, supervisors can develop and implement plans for enriching selected activities. Supervisors may need the support of the library administration when the job redesign skills available in the library are not sufficient to solve identified problems. Even the identification of problems can be difficult. The hiring of a consultant might be necessary.

Specific steps

Library staff can take these steps. First, think about your job based on the topics discussed in this article. Read materials from the list of selected resources found at the end of the article. What QWL features does your job have? What features does it lack? Think about the individual tasks that you perform. List everything that comes to mind (e.g., too challenging or not challenging enough, too much responsibility or not enough responsibility). For each item on your list, estimate whether or not it can be reasonably changed. If it can be changed, try to determine how this might be accomplished. If it cannot be changed, state why. Discuss these items with your supervisor. The relationship between supervisor and staff should be one of mutual support, trust, openness, and respect. If these characteristics do not exist, the potential for effective change toward job enrichment is seriously handicapped. In these instances, the first requirement may be general improvement in the organizational climate.

CONCLUSIONS

"Redesigning a job often appears seductively simple. In practice, it is a rather challenging enterprise. It requires a good deal more energy than most other organizational development activities."[7] Experts with many years experience frequently encounter almost insurmountable difficulties. Large corporations have the resources to employ, or hire as consultants, experts who can plan and direct job redesign programs. Academic libraries have no such luxury. Improvements that we make are likely to occur because of a unique blend of circumstances: a high level of administrative support; a core of middle managers who want to use work enrichment techniques; staff who can identify problems that can be solved within reasonable organizational constraints; and staff who want to initiate and assist in the planning and implementing of a job redesign program.

Most attempts to enrich work involve an entire unit and not just a single employee. An individual can choose to volunteer for job rotation or take on additional responsibilities. More extensive changes may require cooperation, expertise, and commitment that involve others in the unit, the department, or even the library as a whole. Obviously, this is far more complicated. With the background provided here, with information gleaned from other material on the subject, and with individual analysis of the work environment, perhaps some areas can be identified for improvement in a specific library. Planning and implementing specific programs will challenge the best in every librarian.

References

1. "A continuing study of 250,000 workers by Opinion Research Corp., Princeton, N.J., shows only 57% of middle managers view their companies favorably, down from 73% three to five years ago." "Labor Letter," *Wall Street Journal,* October 26, 1982, p. 1.
2. Charles Martell, *The Client-Centered Academic Library: An Organizational Model,* (Westport, CT, Greenwood, 1983).
3. Warren J. Haas, "The Impact of Institutional Change on Research Libraries in the United States," in *Issues in Library Administration,* eds. Warren M. Tsuneishi, Thomas R. Buckman and Yukihisa Suzuki (New York: Columbia University Press, 1974), p. 11.
4. J. Lloyd Suttle, "Improving Life at Work—Problems & Prospects," in *Improving Life at Work: Behavioral Science Approaches to Organizational Change,* eds. J. Richard Hackman and J. Lloyd Suttle (Santa Monica, CA: Goodyear Publishing, 1977), p. 4.
5. J. Richard Hackman and Edward E. Lawler III, "Employee Reactions to Job Characteristics," *Journal of Applied Psychology Monograph 55,* no. 3 (June 1971): 284.
6. J. Richard Hackman, et al., "A New Strategy for Job Enrichment," *California Management Review* 17 (Summer 1975): 61-62.
7. J. Richard Hackman, "Work Design," in *Improving Life at Work: Behavioral Science Approaches to Organizational Change,* eds. J. Richard Hackman and J. Lloyd Suttle (Santa Monica, CA: Goodyear Publishing, 1977): 150.

List of Selected Resources

Alber, A. and Blumberg, M. "Team vs. Individual Approaches to Job Enrichment Programs," *Personnel* 58:1 (January-February 1981): 63-75.

Bohlander, George W. "Implementing Quality-of-Work Programs: Recognizing the Barriers," *MSU Business Topics* (Spring 1979): 33-40

Cummings, Thomas G. and Srivastva, Suresh. *Management of Work: A Sociotechnical Systems Approach.* Kent, Ohio: Kent State University Press, 1977.

Davis, Louis E. and Taylor, James C., eds. *Design of Jobs.* Middlesex, England: Penguin Books, 1972.

Davis, Louis E. and Cherns, Albert B., eds. *The Quality of Working Life.* New York: Free Press, 1975. 2 v.

Glaser, Edward M. *Productivity Gains Through Workplace Improvements:* New York: Harcourt Brace Jovanovich, 1976.

Hackman, J. Richard and Suttle, J. Lloyd, eds. *Improving Life at Work: Behavioral Science Approaches to Organizational Change.* Santa Monica, CA: Goodyear, 1977.

Hackman, J. Richard. "The Design of Work in the 1980s," *Organizational Dynamics* (Summer 1978): 317.

Lawler, Edward III et al., eds. *Organizational Assessment: Perspectives on the Measurement of Organizational Behavior and the Quality of Working Life.* New York: Wiley, 1980.

Martell, Charles. "Improving the Effectiveness of Libraries Through Improvements in the Quality of Working Life," *College & Research Libraries* 42 (September 1981): 435-46.

Rosow, Jerome M. "Quality of Work Life Issues for the 1980s," *Training and Development Journal* 35, (March 1981):33-52. Reprinted from *Work in America: The Decade Ahead* (New York: Van Nostrand Reinhold, 1979).

Walton, Richard. "Work Innovations in the United States," *Harvard Business Review* (July-August 1979): 88-98.

Warr, Peter, ed. *Personal Goals and Work Design.* London: Wiley, 1975.

Work in America. Cambridge, Mass.: MIT Press, 1973. Report of a Special Task Force to the Secretary of Health, Education and Welfare.

A CASE STUDY: UNIVERSITY OF CALIFORNIA, BERKELEY.

Prior to the introduction of automation the Processing Division received and processed material purchased through the Acquisition Department. This entailed matching material with a manual order record, marking items with appropriate ownership and location stamps, routing material, approving invoices for payment, and dealing with vendor correspondence. In 1975-76 the Division had 6.5 full-time staff and two 15-hour-per-week student positions. The Division handled 41,434 items during the fiscal year.

During this period, the goals were to: improve work procedures; upgrade positions; improve individual work assignments; provide staff with a comprehensive profile of the workflow in technical service units; promote a greater understanding of public service needs; and improve communication between the Division and other library units. Some of these goals were achieved through job rotation and increased training opportunities. Staff toured branch libraries and technical service units (e.g., Serials Payment Division). They were encouraged to participate in library committee work and to attend workshops.

Efforts were made to improve work assignments by making each staff member responsible for handling all correspondence, reports, and invoices for a selected group of vendors. Staff were urged to communicate directly with both main and branch library selectors on problems related to order records and to the receipt of material. These actions led to an increased understanding of the purpose, functions, and workflow of monographic processing. However, positions were still at the Library Assistant I and II ranks without much hope for advancement to the III and IV ranks. (See Figure 1 for organization chart of Processing Division.)

In preparation for automation, various studies and workflow analyses were conducted by the Systems Office, and a special study team was assigned to make recommendations for improvements in the cataloging and processing operations. These activities culminated in the issuance of a directive, *Technical Service Goals, Problems, Objectives, Prospects 1977/78,* by the Associate University Librarian for Technical Services. This directive had important implications for the Processing Division:

FIGURE 1 Processing Division—Organization Chart

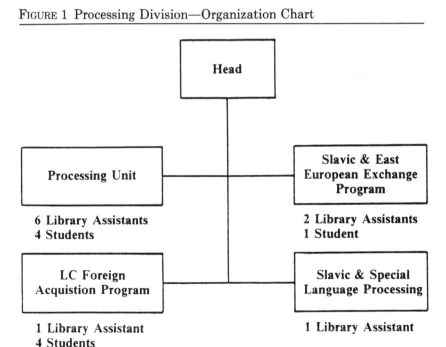

Head

Processing Unit

6 Library Assistants
4 Students

Slavic & East European Exchange Program

2 Library Assistants
1 Student

LC Foreign Acquistion Program

1 Library Assistant
4 Students

Slavic & Special Language Processing

1 Library Assistant

1. Transferring most tasks performed by the Preliminary Cataloging Division, Catalog Department, to the Processing Division.
2. Merging the processing functions of the Gift and Exchange Division with the Processing Division.
3. Processing completely (e.g., copy cataloging) some categories of material at the point of receipt in the library.

Use of the Research Libraries Information Network (RLIN) online cataloging system to search for cataloging copy at the point of receipt was the first step toward automated processing. An RLIN terminal was installed in March 1977, and staff received training to search and select cataloging copy for use by the Catalog Department. The Division also became responsible for the sorting and distribution of material returned from binding, a function previously performed by the Preliminary Cataloging Division—a division subsequently phased out.

Initial training efforts were partially successful. Formerly, the staff were responsible only for verifying that the correct item had been received. Now they were also expected to recognize various material types and to initiate the appropriate cataloging treatment. The absence of guidelines for book distribution and the lack of clear instructions on the cataloging copy needed by the Catalog Department created additional confusion. The Catalog Department itself was trying to adjust to the enormous changes generated by the adoption of the RLIN system. Requirements were constantly changing as modifications were made. Once the need for regular consultation between the Catalog Department and the Processing Division was recognized, the author was invited to work with Catalog Department planning groups to develop procedures for streamlining the growing number of interdependent functions. Support from the head of the Catalog Department was a critical factor in solving mutual problems and developing an attitude of cooperation between the two units.

Initially, staff were wary of the "machine." Soon they found the new technology exciting. After learning to use the computer terminals, staff began to enjoy the new system. Their ability to process material more effectively led to a greater sense of achievement. In a few months they would begin to work with a second automated system—the library acquisition in-process automated control system. In February 1977, the first order records were keyed into the Catalog Supplement—now called Catalog 2: Books. The Catalog Supplement contained on-order, in-process, temporarily cataloged and fully cataloged material. This system grew very rapidly and somewhat haphazardly.

Until the new system was fully operational, the staff maintained the manual system as a backup.

Procedures for processing material through the in-house and RLIN systems were worked out after the fact and too often on an ad hoc basis. Since these procedures were in a state of constant change it was difficult to keep the staff well informed and well trained. A sketchy manual was produced, and as "fine tuning" of the system progressed, a more detailed manual was developed. Training was to become a major factor in the successful operation of the automated systems. Meanwhile, backlogs started to accumulate. Because of these backlogs and the pressure on the staff, the discontinuance of the manual system was suggested and supported.

Automation changed the workflow of monographic material and introduced many new functions. The whole concept of the Processing Division as a check-in unit was altered. The processing staff made more and more decisions that affected the entire routing and handling of books up to the point of cataloging. Processing became responsible for much of the correcting and updating of existing records, the keying of bibliographical records for material that had no existing record in the Catalog Supplement, the searching for cataloging copy, and the handling of the traditional functions of invoice approval, claiming, and vendor correspondence.

As job complexity increased it was possible to justify the reclassification of several positions. With the increased responsibility staff experienced greater job satisfaction as they realized that their efforts resulted in a record of receipt, the creation and upgrading of bibliographic records that assisted public access to library materials, and the generation of cataloging copy that helped to speed material to library users. However, to minimize eye strain and fatigue, a policy was established to limit terminal keying time to two one-hour sessions per day for each staff member. This limitation complicated scheduling. To alleviate this problem, staff were made responsible for scheduling their own work, and were encouraged to learn all functions performed in the Division. They were also given responsibility for the supervision and training of new staff, the handling of special categories of materials such as art exhibition catalogs, and searching for in-process materials needed by library users.

Once it became apparent how efficient the routines were in improving throughput time, other types of monographic material handled or received by other units began to be routed through Processing. This included material received as gifts and exchanges, monographic standing orders through the Serials Department, depository material from the Documents Department and Library of Congress Foreign Acquisition Program materials. The routing of all monographic material through the same pipeline promoted standardization of records and the most effective routing of material. This resulted in a tremendous increase in workload. The number of items handled by Processing increased from 41,434 in 1975/76 to 81,677 in 1978/79. The library administration was very supportive and increased staffing from time to time.

In March 1980, the processing unit began to perform online cataloging for selected categories of material. Again, the staff were required to learn new routines. They approached this new assignment with great enthusiasm. By now, the staff had developed the feeling that there was nothing that they could not accomplish. One concern was that by performing so many different functions the quality of work might suffer. Just the opposite proved true. Although involved in almost all receiving and cataloging functions, the staff made fewer errors and experienced increased job satisfaction.

The Processing Division has evolved from a receiving unit into a major bibliographic unit that combines the receipt functions with precataloging and other cataloging functions. Earlier, bits and pieces of these functions were scattered and there was unnecessary duplication in the handling of material. Functions traditionally performed only by the Catalog Department or the Acquisition Department have become intermixed, and departmental lines have become less clearly defined. The staff has increased to 10.5 full-time equivalents plus 135 student assistant hours per week. A total of 112,089 items were

FIGURE 2 Average Number of Items Processed Per Employee

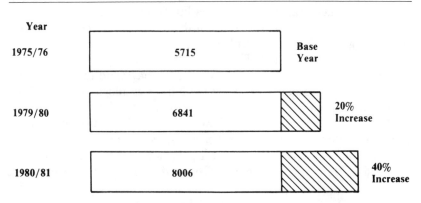

Year		
1975/76	5715	Base Year
1979/80	6841	20% Increase
1980/81	8006	40% Increase

handled in 1980/81. This represents a 171 percent increase over 1975/76 against a 90 percent increase in staff size (see Figure 2). Most items were processed within two weeks of receipt. Rush material was usually processed in two days. No backlogs have developed in recent years.

Currently, the library is exploring the possibility of cataloging more material at the point of receipt, of developing more areas of special responsibility, and of training branch library staff to key records directly into the data base to avoid unnecessary routing of material. Also, job rotation opportunities may be developed within the Division for staff in other technical service departments performing related processing functions.

Technology and Job Design in Libraries: A Sociotechnical Systems Approach

Thomas W. Shaughnessy

THIS paper attempts to relate recent organizational theories and changes in library technology to the practice and quality of library work. Library organizations are considered in this paper as open, sociotechnical systems—that is, they are systems embedded in an environment that is influenced by a culture and its values and practices. Further, in any purposive organization in which people work, the desired output of the organization is achieved through the joint operation of a social system and a technical system.[1] The sociotechnical approach to organizational behavior encompasses three aspects: an organization's environments, its social system, and its technical system.

The term *sociotechnical system* appears to have been coined in 1951 by Eric Trist, who was then associated with the Tavistock Institute of Human Relations, together with K. W. Bamforth. Their study of the effects of mechanization in the British coal-mining industry led them to develop the concept of a working group as neither a technical system (as posed by Babbage and Taylor) nor a purely social system (as propounded by the Human Relations school) but as an interdependent sociotechnical system.[2] According to Emery and Trist, social relationships are not determined by technology nor is the manner in which a job is performed determined by the social or psychological characteristics of the workers. The social and technical requirements and operations are *mutually* interactive.[3]

Reprinted with permission from *The Journal of Academic Librarianship*, vol. 3 (1977), pp. 269–272. © 1977 by Mountainside Publishing, Inc.

Although most of the research on sociotechnical systems has focused on industrial organizations and blue-collar workers, this approach also seems applicable to service institutions.[4] In fact, this approach is particularly effective when applied to the design of jobs and work roles that are both more satisfying to their occupants and more effective in meeting organizational requirements.[5]

ORGANIZATIONAL ENVIRONMENTS

The influence of the environment has been discussed by a number of writers.[6] Emery and Trist have hypothesized that there are four "ideal types" of environments which comprise the causal texture of an organization. One of these types is the "turbulent field," which seems to describe the environment surrounding most organizations. In a turbulent field, the accelerating rate and complexity of change exceed the component systems' capacities for prediction and control of the consequences of their actions.[7]

Organizations exist in multiple environments, and each environment takes part in modifying the internal structure of organizations within it. Terreberry states that there are conditions that occur externally to an organization over which it has little or no control.[8] The organization must either adapt to, buffer, or level its environmental turbulence. The author notes that the capacity of any system for adapting is inversely related to its dependence upon instinct, habit, or tradition. Organizational change is, for the most part, externally induced, and organizational survival is a function of the "ability to learn and to perform according to changing contingencies in the environment.[9]

The organization differentiates its internal structure so that each unit or department within the organization can better cope with that part of the external environment relevant to it.[10] One might hypothesize that libraries as complex organizations have differentiated (or departmentalized) to respond more effectively to parts of their external environment: user needs, supplier requirements, and the objectives of their parent organizations.

TECHNOLOGY

The methods an organization utilizes to transform input (people, information, materials) into output constitute the organization's technology. The significant role that technology plays in organizations has been addressed by a number of social scientists. Hage and Aiken have stated that technology is likely to determine whether an organization's structure is formalized or nonformalized and whether it has a diverse or relatively simple division of labor; further, both the technology of an organization and its social structure influence the nature of its goals.[11] Woodward, in her study of approximately 100 manufacturing firms in Great Britain, found that organization and management practices varied depending on the type of technology employed.[12] Many of Woodward's findings were later corroborated by Zwerman's study of 55 firms situated in the United States.[13] Harvey, in a study of the structural characteristics of some 43 organizations, found that where there is a diffuse, highly changing technology, management tends to become more organic (and less mechanistic) in both structure and style.[14] Two other researchers, Burns and Stalker, arrived at a similar conclusion: A mechanistic system of management might be more appropriate for a stable technology, but an organic system is more effective in a rapidly changing technology.[15]

Technology, as used in this context, is defined very broadly as the combination of skills, equipment, facilities, tools, and relevant specialized knowledge needed to bring about transformations in materials, information, and people. It also includes the body of ideas that expresses the goals of work, its importance, rationale, and underlying theory.[16] Perrow defines technology as the action performed on an object in order to change it with or without the use of tools or mechanical devices.[17]

In addition to these definitions, several models of technology have been set forth in the literature. Hickson and others analyze an organization's technology in terms of three dimensions: materials (inputs), operations (transformation processes), and knowledge (the competence and skill needed to convert input into output).[18] Thompson's approach goes beyond the industrial organization to include human service agencies and institutions.[19] Mediating technology, he suggests, involves the joining or linking of clients, customers, and others who are or wish to be interdependent.

Few attemps, unfortunately, have been made to evaluate the impact of library technology on organizational behavior and work systems, although a number have skirted the issue, including the Booth-Ricking report,[20] the Booz, Allen and Hamilton study,[21] the *Jobs in Instructional Media* report,[22] and a few doctoral dissertations. Although the first three studies place considerable emphasis on task analysis, they tend to ignore the importance of technology, which frequently determines the nature of the tasks to be performed. Vorwerk's study approaches library organization from a contingency theory perspective and includes several environmental factors, one of which is technology, whose impact, however, is not explored in detail.[23]

Two studies that do address the role of technology are both dissertations, one by Lynch[24] and the other by Sloan.[25] The Lynch study attempted to identify the respective technologies employed in 15 departments in three academic libraries in relation to four dimensions which form technological boundaries: materials, operations, production, and knowledge.[26] Although her data gathering instruments were able to discriminate among the departments with respect to the technology utilized, the differences were small. Further, the slight variations that were discovered may have been due to the fact that Lynch combined professional and nonprofessional employees in the departments. Her findings that library work in these departments is predictable (regular search strategies) and routine (relatively low-knowledge requirements) are extremely interesting but tentative, pending replication and refinement of the study.[27]

The Sloan study, based on data gathered at 11 research libraries in the Northeast, approached collection development as a discrete, definable sociotechnical subsystem operating within the large academic research library. Utilizing four organizational variables (organizational environment, formal organizational structure, task structure, and technology), the study sought to explore the organization of collection development activities and its relationship to its environment.[28] The technologies required for collection development include the use of blanket order and approval plans, subject specialists, policy statements, and participation in resource-sharing networks.[29] Admitting the exploratory purpose of the study, the author tentatively concludes that organizational structure is related to the nature of the environment and type of technology.However, of the four components of technology described above, only the use of subject specialists was examined in detail.[30]

Once again, the research seems to raise more questions than it answers. Perhaps the significance of this study and Lynch's is that both make a sustained attempt to rationalize organizational behavior while underscoring the importance of technology as a determinant of organizational structure and job design.

Based on this brief and far from comprehensive review of the literature, it appears that a research gap continues to exist concerning the effects of technology on library work systems and organizational design. Further, research findings are far more conclusive in non-library areas. Given the pragmatic orientation of the library field and its lack of a strong tradition of research, its slowness in capitalizing upon relevant research findings in other disciplines is not suprising.

Nevertheless, speculations can be made on the role technology has played in setting the pattern of library organization. For example, was the division of the library into technical, public, and administrative service functions a response to clientele needs, or was it due to a "technological imperative"? Is division by format (serials, documents, monographs, maps, and nonprint media) based on user requirements or on evolving library technology? And might not the tripartite reorganization plan for Columbia University libraries[31] be more reflective of technological and other internal considerations than it is of user needs?

SOCIAL REQUIREMENTS AND JOB DESIGN

As has already been indicated, a number of writers have studied technology as a determinant of certain gross features of organizational structure. Others, such as Lawrence, go so far as to suggest that technology also influences the behavior of organizational members, and that it is an immediate determinant of individual and group work systems, and indirectly a determinant of social structure and norms.[32] In addition, a growing body of data indicates that technology is a major factor in the quality of the working life of employees in an organization.[33]

In library organizations, specifically in the technical services area, the advent (or disappearance) of the library jobber has significantly affected the work of the acquisitions librarian. Similarly, the ready availability of catalog copy (through OCLC or some other source) for a larger and larger percentage of titles must be having an impact on the work and job satisfaction of the cataloger.[34] Indeed, one can hardly imagine what the closing of card catalogs, as has been discussed in a recent report, will require in terms of the redesign of existing positions and work systems.[35]

In the public services area, technology is having similar repercussions. How has the availability of on-line bibliographic data searching affected the work of information specialists? A recent report published by the System Development Corporation states that of 801 literature searchers surveyed, almost half indicated that on-line searching increased their workloads; of 472 managers queried, 76 percent reported that on-line searching increased staff productivity.[36] To what extent have new reference tools, such as citation indexes and pathfinders, modified the work of the reference librarian? How has the new information and referral technology affected staff work in libraries?

Not unexpectedly, administrative and organizational change may be called for if libraries wish fully to capitalize on electronic technology. Atkinson has suggested that, because electronics are distance independent, the concept of the central library is going out of style.[37] Thus, the decentralization of service functions and the centralization of administrative responsibilities by means of electronic protocols should accelerate. Such technologically induced change will affect virtually every aspect of librarianship.

Perhaps in many libraries these questions are premature, if not irrelevant. But in an ever-increasing number of libraries of all types these questions hold significance not only for organizational effectiveness but also for the job potential of employees.

The manner in which individual workers will respond to new technology or changes in existing technology will depend in large part on the policies and means used to incorporate them into the organization. If the new technology is simply superimposed, staff will inevitably become anxious, alienated, and perhaps incompetent. "Organizations have to be redesigned both in structure and function to use any new technology humanely and well . . . ."[38]

Davis and Taylor have observed that one of the most salient characteristics of the new technology is that it absorbs routine activities and changes the social structure of the organization. It frequently suggests new roles for employees, requiring diagnostic competencies and skills related to regulation, monitoring, and adjustment processes.[39] Under these conditions, an employee's *role* may possibly be enlarged as his *job* diminishes—that is, worker roles may become more complex and demanding as jobs become simpler.[40]

As technological change is introduced into a growing number of libraries and as worker expectations become tangibly greater, two managerial strategies seem to be particularly appropriate. One is to develop a sociotechnical systems approach to the analysis of organizational behavior. The second is to research the impact of technology on work systems and to establish a basis for the enrichment and redesign of jobs. The sociotechnical systems design differs from other approaches because it simultaneously attends to the technical and production requirements of the work and to the psychosocial requirements of individual employees and working groups.[41]

Although a considerable amount of study has been devoted to the design of job methods, comparatively little has been done in the area of job content. Yet several research studies suggest that job content can inspire motivation and result in decreased absenteeism and turnover, increased production, and job satisfaction.[42] The earlier, vertical approach to job content was merely incremental—do more of what you are already doing—whereas the present, horizontal approach attempts to give the individual worker a feeling of increased responsibility for the job as a whole, as well as some measure of autonomy. The enrichment of previously fragmented, routine jobs fosters task identity and at the same time gives employees an opportunity to use more fully their skills and abilities and to be challenged by their work.[43]

It is not just new technology alone that calls for job design, which is defined as "the specification of the contents, methods and relationships of jobs in order to satisfy technological and organizational requirements, as well as the social and personal requirements of the job-holder."[44] The remaining two elements in the sociotechnical model are equally important: environmental demands and psychosocial values. The latter values have been eloquently described by Terkel[45] and Dickson[46] among others, and environmental factors have been investigated by a score of writers and researchers, many of whom have already been cited.

In view of the technological changes and environmental turbulence affecting libraries, and the psychosocial response of librarians to their work, immediate steps toward job design seem necessary. In fact, the results of several surveys concerning the job satisfaction of librarians support this position. Presthus reported in 1970 that two thirds of the librarians responding to a survey would not choose librarianship as a career, if given another chance, due to their marginal job satisfaction.[47] Kortendick and Stone reported in 1971 that a number of librarians whom they studied were discouraged by the large amount of clerical and subprofessional work they were performing.[48] And in 1974, Plate and Stone reported that of 237 librarians surveyed, only 27 reported that they held particularly good feeling about their jobs.[49]

These findings, as well as increasing worker expectations, suggest that more attention needs to be given to the possible benefits—organizational as well as personal—deriving from job design, and to the quality of working life in libraries. The sociotechnical systems approach, by integrating all these aspects of work, can provide an appropriate theoretical framwork within which these issues might be addressed.

References

1. Louis E. Davis, "The Coming Crisis for Production Management: Technology and Organization," in *Design of Jobs*, Louis E. Davis and J.C. Taylor (Eds.) (London: Penguin, 1972), p. 423.
2. E.L. Trist and K.W. Bamforth, "Some Social and Psychological Consequences of the Longwall Method of Coal Getting," *Human Relations*, 4 (February, 1951): 3-38.
3. F.E. Emery and E.L. Trist, "Socio-technical Systems," in *Management Sciences: Models and Techniques*, C.W. Churchman and M. Verhulst (Eds.) (New York: Pergamon, 1960), pp. 83-97.
4. Robert T. Keller, "A Look at the Sociotechnical System," *California Management Review*, 15 (Fall, 1972): 91.
5. James C. Taylor, "The Human Side of Work: The Socio-Technical Approach to Work System Design," (Los Angeles: UCLA Graduate School of Management, 1975): 4-5 (mimeo).
6. Shirley Terreberry, "The Evolution of Organizational Environments," *Administrative Science Quarterly*, 12 (March, 1968): 590-613.
7. F. Emery and E. Trist, "The Causal Texture of Organizational Environments," *Human Relations*, 18 (February, 1965): 21-31.
8. Terreberry, *op. cit.* p. 610-11.
9. Ibid., p. 600.
10. J.W. Lorsch and P.R. Lawrence, *Organization and Environment: Managing Differentiation and Integration*, (Homewood, Ill.: Richard D. Irwin, 1969), pp. 24-30.
11. J. Hage and M. Aiken, "Routine Technology, Social Structure, and Organization Goals," *Administrative Science Quarterly*, 14 (September, 1969): 367.
12. Joan Woodward, *Industrial Organization: Behavior and Control* (London: Oxford University Press, 1965).
13. W.L. Zwerman, *New Perspectives on Organization Theory* (Westport, Conn.: Greenwood, 1970).
14. E. Harvey, "Technology and the Structure of Organization," *American Sociological Review*, 33 (April, 1968): 247-59.
15. T. Burns and G.M. Stalker, *The Management of Innovation* (London: Tavistock, 1961), pp. 4-8.
16. L.E. Davis, "Job Satisfaction Research: The Post-Industrial View," in *Design of Jobs*, L.E. Davis and J.C. Taylor (Eds.) (London: Penguin, 1972), pp. 158-59.
17. C. Perrow, "A Framework for the Comparative Analysis of Organizations," *American Sociological Review*, 32 (April, 1967): 194–208.

18. D.J. Hickson, D.S. Pugh, and D.C. Pheysey, "Operations Technology and Organization Structure: An Empirical Reappraisal," *Administrative Science Quarterly*, 14 (September, 1969): 380.
19. J.D. Thompson, *Organizations in Action* (New York: McGraw-Hill, 1967), pp. 15-18.
20. M. Ricking and R. Booth, *Personnel Utilization in Libraries: A Systems Approach* (Chicago: American Library Association, 1974).
21. Booz, Allen, and Hamilton Inc., *Organization and Staffing of the Libraries of Columbia University* (Washington, D.C.: Association of Research Libraries, 1972).
22. C.J. Wallington, *Jobs in Instructional Media* (Bethesda, Md.: ERIC Document Reproduction Service, ED 037088, 1970).
23. R.J. Vorwerk, "The Environmental Demands and Organizational States of Two Academic Libraries" (Ph.D. dissertation, Indiana University, 1970).
24. B. Lynch, "Library Technology: A Comparison of the Work of Functional Departments in Academic Libraries" (Ph.D. dissertation, University of Wisconsin, 1972).
25. E. Sloan, "The Organization of Collection Development in Large University Research Libraries," (Ph.D. dissertation, University of Maryland, 1973).
26. Lynch, "Library Technology," pp. 19-20.
27. Lynch based her analysis on a model developed by Charles Perrow. See "A Framework for the Comparative Analysis of Organizations," *American Sociological Review*, 32 (April 1967): 194-208.
28. Sloan, "Organization of Collection Development," p. 1.
29. Ibid., pp. 71-72.
30. Ibid., p. 124.
31. Booz, Allen and Hamilton, *op. cit.*
32. Paul R. Lawrence, "Technical Inputs," in *Systems Analysis in Organizational Behavior,* John A. Seiler (Ed.) (Homewood, Ill.: Irwin-Dorsey, 1967), p. 133.
33. L.E. Davis and J.C. Taylor, "Technology Effects on Job, Work, and Organizational Structure: A Contingency View," in *The Quality of Working Life,* Vol. 1, L.E. Davis and A.B. Cherns (Eds.) (New York: The Free Press, 1975), pp. 220-41. See also L.E. Bjork, "An Experiment in Work Satisfaction," *Scientific American,* 232 (March, 1975): 17-23.
34. John Goodell, "A Case Study of Catalogers in Three University Libraries Using Work Sampling" (Ph.D. dissertation, Florida State University, 1971), pp. 115-116.
35. *The Future of Card Catalogs* (Washington, D.C.: Association of Research Libraries, 1975).
36. J. Wanger, M. Fishburn, and C. Cuadra, *On Line Impact Study (A Brief Summary Report)* (Santa Monica, Calif.: System Development Corporation, 1975), pp. 17-18.

37. *The Future of Card Catalogs*, pp. 36-37.
38. *Information Technology: Some Critical Implications for Decision Makers* (New York: Conference Board, 1972), p. 55.
39. L.E. Davis and J.C. Taylor, "Technology, Organization, and Job Structure," (University of California, Los Angeles, Graduate School of Management, 1975), p. 8 (mimeo).
40. L.E. Davis, "Introduction," in *Design of Jobs*, L.E. Davis and J.C. Taylor (Eds.) (London: Penguin, 1972), pp. 11-13.
41. Taylor, "The Human Side of Work," p. 2.
42. See L.E. Davis and J.C. Taylor (Eds.), *Design of Jobs*, and R.N. Ford, *Motivation Through the Work Itself* (New York: American Management Association, 1969).
43. J.R. Hackman and E.E. Lawler, "Conditions Under Which Jobs Will Facilitate Internal Motivation: A Conceptual Framework," in *Design of Jobs*, p. 150.
44. L.E. Davis, "The Design of Jobs," *Industrial Relations*, 6 (October, 1966), p. 21.
45. Studs Terkel, *Working* (New York: Pantheon, 1974).
46. Paul Dickson, *The Future of the Workplace* (London: Weybright and Tally, 1975).
47. R. Presthus, *Technological Change and Occupational Response: A Study of Librarians* (Final Report). (Washington, D.C.: U.S. Office of Education, 1970), pp. 69, 108.
48. J. Kortendick and E. Stone, *Job Dimensions and Educational Needs in Librarianship* (Chicago: American Library Association, 1971), pp. 80, 280.
49. K.H. Plate and E. Stone, "Factors Affecting Librarians' Job Satisfaction: A Report of Two Studies," *Library Quarterly*, 44 (April, 1974): 102-04.

Socio-Technical Theory and Job Design in Libraries

Klaus Musmann

Socio-technical theory has been called an ecological focus that provides meaningful insight into the structure of organizations and job content. Socio-technical theory considers organizations to be purposive and postulates that organizations interact with their surrounding social and technological environment across permeable boundaries. Technology is considered a significant variable that interacts jointly with social and personal variables to form the system that carries out the purposes of an organization. It considers the individuals within the organization to be purposive, whole human beings who reflect and shape the values of society in interaction with technology as they seek to satisfy their own as well as the organization's needs. Applications of socio-technical concepts appear to develop satisfying, yet economically efficient jobs.[1]

Past studies of job satisfaction have been and are still being carried out mostly by psychologists or sociologists. According to Davis, most of these studies are tainted by major flaws. Job satisfaction is treated as an end in itself and reveals little about cause-and-effect relationships.[2] Psychologists have not examined variables that are influenced by technology and have ignored the interaction between social and technical systems. Furthermore, most such studies have failed to examine the job itself. Psychological studies, which have recommended job enlargement as a means to increase job satisfaction, have examined the relationship between repetitive work and monotony and between task length and satisfaction, but they have never examined the relevant technology largely responsible for many of the dehumanizing tasks found in industrial work situations.

More recent job satisfaction research, under the influence of socio-

Reprinted by permission of the American Library Association from *College and Research Libraries* 39(1): 20–28 (Jan. 1978); Copyright © 1978 by the American Library Association.

technical theory, has focused upon three distinct areas of research, namely (1) on the work itself, (2) on the individual versus the organization, and (3) on job design.

This paper will focus upon these three areas and will attempt to explore some of the problem areas of job design for library employees. Hertzberg, Paul, Likert, and Lawler have written extensively on the relationship of motivation and satisfaction to the intrinsic, substantive contents of jobs.[3] In the area of the individual versus the organization, attention has been focused upon the interaction between technology and social organization in shaping the roles of individuals. Models of jobs and organizations have been designed that are motivating and satisfying to individuals and groups and suitable to an organization and its technology.

Here the researchers have been concerned about the impact of the changing technology and the social environment and personal values in conflict with organizational concepts that are outmoded for our time. Writings on job design have focused upon responsible, autonomous job behavior as the key to a successful interrelationship among individuals, organizations, and technology.

Autonomous behavior is defined as self-regulation of work content and structure within the job, self-evaluation of performance, and participation in the setting of job goals and objectives. Responsible job behavior includes acceptance by the individual or group for the cycle of activities to complete the services and accountability for the quantity and quality of the output. It also includes recognition of the interdependence of an individual on others for completion of the cycle of activities.[4]

Successful job design seems to depend upon finding satisfactory solutions to bridge the needs of the organization and its technology and the desires and demands of the employed individuals. At the same time, the organization must make sure that the objectives of its subunits are relevant to an organization's overall goal objectives and that the organization remains adaptive to its environment.[5]

LIBRARY TECHNOLOGY AND THE ENVIRONMENT

Few, if any, of these concepts have found their way into the field of library literature, although the evolution of socio-technical systems theory has been taking place over the past fifteen years.

One of the few writers in our field has been Beverly P. Lynch, who recently published two articles in *College & Research Libraries.*[6] In her first article she attempted to delineate the environment of the academic library, and in the second one she employed Perrow's model of organizational technology to compare the work of fifteen different departments in three academic libraries. Her articles did not focus directly upon job design and satisfaction in libraries, but she did touch upon important aspects that are ultimately related to successful job design. Lynch adapted Perrow's model of technology to the environment of the library in the following manner.[7]

1. Materials technology, i.e., the nature of the raw material entering a department. The essential characteristic was the perception of the material's predictability or unpredictability.
2. Operations technology, i.e., the techniques employed to change the raw material into a finished product. The essential characteristic was whether a department's operation was routine or nonroutine.
3. Knowledge technology, i.e., the knowledge required by the library's staff to convert the raw materials into the finished product. The essential characteristic was whether a particular department's knowledge was sufficient to complete the tasks.

Lynch found that the nature of the work performed in the various departments (reference, catalog, serials, acquisitions, circulation, and searching) was very similar regardless of a department's functions. In terms of predictability of the material, the routineness of operations, and the knowledge necessary to perform the required tasks, relatively minor differences emerged between departments. The final conclusions of her study were that the technologies of all departments consisted of predictable events, routine operations, and relatively low knowledge requirements.[8]

But a word of caution is in order here. Lynch's model of library technology was a measurement of attitudes about work rather than an evaluation of the work itself. Furthermore, her questionnaires were distributed to all full-time employees, including both professional and clerical staff members. This factor alone would certainly introduce a high degree of bias toward routine operations and low knowledge requirements because of the large number of clerical employees engaged in such operations.

In her article on the environment of the academic library, Beverly Lynch states that librarians generally think of organizational change in the library as being internally generated. She writes that "it is frequently said that if the managerial style of the library director would change or if the staff had broader participation in the decision making, the library's performance would change."[9] Of course, environmental factors, i.e., external events, could greatly influence the decision-making power within the library and may well reduce the decision-making autonomy of the library itself. Lynch goes on to say that it may be difficult to determine whether organizational change is initiated by internal or external antecedents, but the main point is that librarians must be aware of external as well as internal events that are shaping the library's organizational structure.[10]

It is important to note that complex, heterogeneous, and unstable environments impose greater constraints and contingencies upon an institution than environments that are simple, homogeneous, and stable.[11] Departments with uncertain environments rely less on formal rules and procedures, have fewer job performance reviews, and are less formal overall than departments with stable environments. Such findings are, of course, essential for any serious study of job satisfaction.

The stability of our environment has to be determined before we can begin to design jobs in library organizations that are satisfactory not only to the individuals employed in libraries but also to the aims of the library itself. Unfortunately, little is known about the impact of the environment upon the library's internal structure. However, Beverly Lynch has at least made a start in analyzing some of the underlying factors essential to applying the principles of socio-technical theories to libraries.

THE STIGMATIZATION OF THE NONPROFESSIONAL

Lynch found that the technology of the library consists of predictable events and of routine operations and that it requires relatively low knowledge to perform the required tasks in most departments of an academic library. If we accept her findings as accurate, we have an immediate area of potential for job dissatisfaction due to the nature of the work itself.

Unfortunately, Lynch did not make a distinction between the work performed by professional and clerical employees since she was primarily interested in the technology of departments and their alleged differences. But the area of professional versus clerical work contains another potential for job dissatisfaction for both clerical and professional library employees in addition to the problem area of the work itself. Most theories regarding work motivation have held that nonprofessionals are not concerned with self-actualization but are merely interested in extrinsic factors, i.e., pay, so that they may be able to purchase satisfaction away from their jobs. It has been assumed that "lower-order needs are barely met (i.e., pay) and that therfore higher-order, intrinsic factors (i.e., self-actualization) cannot be met."[12]

Self-actualization is said to be important because it is supposed to improve the efficiency and effectiveness of employees in organizations by meeting their personal needs. However, a substantial body of literature exists that refutes such claims. Jerome Seliger quotes the work of David Sirota, who tested such claims and found no correlation between ego fulfillment and personal or organizational effectiveness.[13] But self-actualization exists as a normative and popular value in the society at large and must therefore be treated in an organization as if it were a real need.

Self-actualization, freedom, independence, and specialized knowledge are associated with professional standing in our society. Our society appears to value professionalism to a very high degree, and most people want to be called professionals. In a society that values professionalism, individuals who occupy nonprofessional positions are stigmatized.[14] Although nonprofessionals could enter a work situation imbued with values similar to those held by professionals, the nonprofessionals' work experience will soon teach them that their "careers" are not as important as those of the professionals in the same work situation, and attitudes toward their work may be affected adversely.[15] If nonprofessionals enter the organization in expectation of job satisfaction and status and find low status and boring, routine work instead, then it seems reasonable to expect that they will become alienated either psychologically or behaviorally in regard to the organization's objectives.[16]

We know that librarians have a high status than the clerical support staff and that the latter find themselves stigmatized by the low status of their occupation. In fact, individuals in high-status occupations have a vested interest in encouraging stigmatization because of their own insecurity regarding their occupational status. It is possible that librarians encourage such stigmatization because of the fear that their own status might be threatened by the low status clerical employees as "peers" in the hierarchy of the organization. It has been stated that such low status transference "seems to be a very general anxiety, felt most strongly perhaps by just those groups which have most recently achieved some degree of status."[17]

PROFESSIONALISM AND
ORGANIZATIONS

Professionalism is seen by some students of organizations as the successor to bureaucracy. A professional's loyalties are to the profession and go beyond the confines of an organization's rules and regulations. The professional has the personal freedom to be independent of the organization. Ronald Corwin, in a study of conflict in nursing roles, has stated that a professional is concerned with an expanding body of knowledge that may change the accepted practice in an organization. In contrast, a bureaucrat is concerned with preserving the routine elements inherent in an institution. Corwin found that those individuals who were considered professional had more role conflict in regard to their status within the organization than those who did not have a professional degree.[18]

Another study found that a basic conflict exists between the salaried professionals and the bureaucracies that employ them. Peter Blau and Richard Scott, in their book *Formal Organizations*, viewed the professional's expertise and the bureaucrat's discipline as alternative methods of coping with uncertainty. The professional's loyalty to the profession is a dilemma that "affects wider and wider circles as the number of people subject to these conflicting control mechanisms grows."[19] More and more professionals work in bureaucratic organizations, and the operations of bureaucracies are becoming increasingly professionalized.

Seliger speaks of a built-in conflict between the values and obligations associated with professionalism and organization structure and cites as evidence the organization of professional social workers in task groupings that "are more consistent with orientation toward the organization."[20] They are compelled to meet more of the organization's goals than the goals of their profession. He states that, as a general principle, specialist groupings are associated with professional orientation while task groupings are not. These findings appear to have a direct bearing on the organizational structure of libraries. Certainly, the recent reorganization of Columbia University is a step toward a specialist grouping and away from the traditional organization of large academic libraries.

REWARDS AND MOTIVATION

If we now turn away from the area of the individual versus the organization and toward job design, we will have to examine Maslow's hierarchy of needs. His theory has been widely accepted in the area of job motivation together with Herzberg's motivation-hygiene theory. Maslow categorized various human needs into five basic groups, which he labled as follows:

1. The need for self-actualization
2. The need for self- and group-esteem
3. The needs for love and belongingness
4. The need for safety
5. The physiological needs[21]

In this paper we are primarily concerned with the need for self-actualization and the needs for self- and group-esteem. According to Maslow, these are the higher-order needs that can be perceived only after partial fulfillment of the lower-order needs. Self-actualization is thought of as being a realization of every person's full potential. This state is thought of as making life more meaningful and assumes that the self-actualized person continually seeks such a psychological state. No empirical support for such a theory exists.[22] But it appears that Maslow's hierarchy has found nearly universal acceptance.

Herzberg's theory, too, has found wide acceptance. It states that motivation is dependent upon two different components: hygiene factors and motivation factors. Job dissatisfaction ensues, according to Herzberg, when hygiene factors deteriorate to a level below which the employee considers acceptable. Hygiene factors do not motivate the employee, but they do eliminate job dissatisfaction. Motivation factors are those factors that satisfy and motivate the individual, but they have little or no effect on job dissatisfaction itself. Herzberg has been criticized extensively for the many methodological errors in his study, and his hypothesis has made poor showings in retesting situations.[23]

Herzberg argues that job factors that define the job context are of little importance to the employee. Ullrich, on the other hand, argues convincingly that Herzberg is wrong in his findings. As in the case with salaries, there is usually no direct relationship between the efforts individuals invest in their jobs and the quality of the working conditions they receive in return. No matter how hard individuals work, their working conditions will remain virtually unchanged, as will their job security and their status within the organization.

Even if improvements in these conditions were aspired to by an individual, the lack of environmental potential would render motivation under such conditions unrealistic. Where promotional opportunities offer the potential for improved working conditions and status, the increase in need satisfaction may be so small that they are deemed without practical value. In Ullrich's words:

> the reader is undoubtedly familiar with cases in which improvements in working conditions earned by a promotion consists of having a coat tree, a larger desk, or some other trivial addition brought to the individual's place of work. How much harder is one going to work to earn a coat tree?[24]

Financial incentives provided by most employers fall into a similar category. The salaries paid by most employers serve more to encourage employees to establish and to maintain employment rather than encourage greater motivation on the part of the employees. Most employers establish salary schedules that limit the salary to each given type of job. Usually salaries conform to those of other employers in similar locations. Usually employers pay neither more nor less than their competitors.[25]

It is clear that under such a system salaries will not be an incentive to individual productivity. Regardless of whether an individual works harder than anyone else, the salary of this employee will remain the same. Even pay raises are considered by Ullrich to be of marginal importance in motivating employees since most pay raises are not substantial enough to have any real impact on an individual's salary. Furthermore, pay raises are granted, not because of individual effort, but are given equally to everyone as a cost-of-living increment or as an automatic step increase for seniority. Goal-seeking behavior, i.e., motivation, is uncalled for under such conditions. If money is to be used for employee motivation financial rewards must be substantial. Where individuals aspire toward greater incomes, money can be used to bring about goal-seeking behavior.[26]

In summary, then, we can state that where rewards are provided by the formal work environment, which are perceived by employees as being average or better, satiation may occur. Ullrich states, and here he is in partial agreement with Maslow, that "needs can be fulfilled in the short run to levels at which further goal-seeking behavior ceases because aspirations cease to rise."[27] He feels that certain forms of technology, work methods, etc., limit an employee's ability to seek fulfillment for higher-order needs and thereby discourage goal-seeking behavior. Under such conditions, individuals will favor behavior that supports the status quo, and the organization itself will move toward homeostasis and will become resistant to change.[28]

The continued existence of good working conditions does not depend upon the daily activities of an employee to attain the objectives of the organization. The rewards of good working conditions are automatically granted as long as the employee agrees to maintain the status quo. The formation of motivation requires the formation of an action goal. The recognition or creation of an unfulfilled employee aspiration is the beginning of initiating employee motivation.

Achievement, recognition, responsibility, and the work itself can be thought of as providing fulfillment of Maslow's higher-order needs for an individual. These need fulfillments can be obtained in proportion to the employee's activity level. Achievement is a transitory experience, and individuals must maintain a high degree of performance to continually increase their feelings of achievement. But if employees are to achieve fulfillment of their higher-order needs in the work environment, they will have to be given substantial control over their own tasks. The individual employee would gain authority and would experience at the same time an increased commitment to the organization's objectives.[29]

SPONTANEITY AND WORK

Our conception of work has undergone dramatic changes over the past thirty years. Work may still be a burdensome imposition while leisure is a world of freedom and spontaneity. Apparently, people aspire to enjoy their work as they do their leisure. It has been frequently noted that pleasurable experiences possess a degree of spontaneity that is lacking in most work situations. Similarly, pleasurable experiences lose some of their value when their spontaneity is lost. Someone's hobby may well lose its enjoyment when it becomes a full-time job. This implies that the work of an individual may contain the potential for need fulfillment, but work may "impose temporal limitations on activities which cause these activities to be undertaken past the point at which aspired levels of fulfillment have been obtained."[30]

The spontaneity of pleasurable activities is determined by two unique characteristics. Such activities are structured in a way that allows the individual to move toward or away from the activity and pleasurable activities that appear to exist as alternatives to one another. Having satisfied one desire, one may undertake a second activity at one's own choice. These prerequisites to spontaneity are lacking in most work environments. Usually, one has neither the option to cease working nor the opportunity to find alternative work activities. Most of our work in libraries tends to be structured in a way that does not permit spontaneity.

The successful pursuit of need fulfillment depends on individuals' ability to pursue their needs as they experience them, but also on the availability of aspired need fulfillment. Timing is one of the most important and frequently overlooked factors in the design of jobs. This is precisely the reason why academic work is so attractive because of the freedom given to the individual in designing both job content and temporal arrangements for task completion. Such decision making should be left to individual employees. It would increase the enjoyment of their work. It should be stressed that employees enjoy their labor because it provides aspired increments in their rate of need fulfillment. This is not the same as saying that individuals work because they enjoy their work. It merely means that high morale may follow successful, goal-seeking behavior.[31]

INNOVATIVE LIBRARY
REORGANIZATION

Recently, two studies were published that seem to forebode well for the future of job design in librarianship. One is the Booz, Allen & Hamilton study of Columbia University's libraries,[32] and the other one is Ricking and Booth's *Personnel Utilization in Libraries*.[33] Both sides, although prepared for quite different purposes, illustrate innovative concepts in library management.

As mentioned earlier, Columbia University's reorganization is a step forward toward professionalization of librarianship, at least at the senior level. This library was reorganized into a resources group, a services group, and a support group. The resources group comprises primarily senior professionals who are responsible for planning and carrying out collection development and preservation, in-depth reference and research assistance, classroom instruction, and original cataloging.

All of the foregoing services are thoroughly professional in nature and would certainly score quite differently on Beverly Lynch's technology scale. But most important of all, at least as far as job satisfaction for professional librarians is concerned, they would free the professional from the stultifying routine of functional, assembly-line type of production work and would fully utilize the professional's talents that are underutilized in the more traditional types of organizations in research libraries.

The library is also committed to an individualized career development program for the staff. According to the proposal, "highly individualized" programs would be prepared for each staff member by top management with the active participation of all librarians.[34] The study also includes staff development plans for specialists and for the clerical staff. The plan specifies help and encouragement to develop individual career interests and to fulfill individual career goals. Expanded levels of professional capabilities are thought of as benefiting the library by building a more dynamic staff.

Professional competency, in addition to administrative responsibility, as demonstrated through individual initiative, was singled out as "the central criterion for a successful career."[35] Professional staff evaluation would be based upon employees' performances of current responsibilities as well as on their progress toward long-term professional growth and development. Evaluation of supervisors' capacities to motivate the staff toward the organization's objectives and their own professional motivation and attitudes are also proposed by this study.

Again, all of these proposals center upon the development of the staff and the professionalization of librarianship. Unfortunately, the study is silent on the actual design of satisfying jobs for either professional or clerical employees. Position classifications and general job descriptions are given, although the actual tasks that are to be performed by each employee are omitted.

The Booz study did not consider the variable of technology and the impact it has on the social system of the library, nor did it spell out the amount of control individuals would have over the content of their own jobs. Of course, job design and employee motivation were not of central importance to the Booz study. But it is surprising that the authors failed to approach the library as a socio-technical system, especially in view of the sweeping changes they proposed for the organizational structure of the library. We know that technical changes have a direct bearing not only on the tasks that are to be performed and on the work-role relationship but that they also affect the absolute and relative rewards as well as the status of different groups within an organization. The authors' extensive bibliography did not reveal a single reference to socio-technical research findings, although they did consider Columbia University's libraries as a system and were concerned about the library's responsiveness to its environment.

TASK ANALYSIS

The objectives of Ricking and Booth, on the other hand, were to get away from position classification and to reveal the nature of the work itself in order to determine in an objective way a basis for job design through task analysis. In contrast to most other studies on library job descriptions, which are usually descriptions of general and rather vague duties, their task analysis is specific and spells out in detail the exact functions and duties of librarians, technicians, and clerical workers for various library subsystems.

They have taken a systems approach and considered the entire spectrum of the library's goals and objectives, its programs, and the tasks needed to accomplish its purpose. It is beyond the scope of this paper to consider the many additional aspects of their approach.

In their opinion, task analysis and job design cannot be approached unless one considers the organizational goals and objectives as well as the motivation of the employees who perform the actual work. In a quote from Chris Argyris' *Personality and Organization*, they point out that

> Theoretically, this means that healthy adults will tend to obtain optimum personality expression while at work if they are provided with jobs which permit them to be more active than passive; more independent than dependent; to have longer rather than shorter time perspectives; to occupy higher positions than their peers; to have control over their world; and to express many of their deeper, more important abilities.[36]

Furthermore, they agree that traditional organization theory is incongruent to the development of healthy human beings and that rigidly traditional work environments lead to "psychological failure," particulary as one goes down the line of command and "jobs become more and more mechanized."[37]

In contrast with the traditional process-centered approach, they state that the worker-centered approach is more suitable to today's society inasmuch as it emphasizes the participation of the employee in decision making and gives meaning to the work situation. Job enlargement and job rotation are additional approaches to relieve the monotony of routine jobs. A number of libraries have assigned professional staff to subject areas where they have complete control from acquisition through cataloging and reference service within a given subject area. They conclude their survey with Davis' job-centered approach, which states that no job can be adequately designed without considering the variables of the processes, the worker, and the organization as well as the variables arising from their interaction.[38]

Ricking and Booth recommend some form of participatory management for all functions they describe in their model. Closer harmony between the employees and the organization will be the result of such participation. In addition, they express the hope that an employee's competency and personal job satisfaction will continue to grow over the years. To encourage such a development, they suggest that libraries adopt the following recommendations:

> (1) Creative job design, based on the goals of the individual as well as those of the organization; (2) involvement of the individual in determining the organization's purpose, goals, objectives, and programs; and (3) a flexible career movement within the agency as programs change and individuals develop.[39]

CONCLUSIONS

The Ricking and Booth study is an excellent and innovative approach to personnel utilization in libraries. But as was the case with the earlier discussed studies, the problem of creative job design and employee motivation on all levels is never fully explored. But their task listing provides us with a solid and detailed description of the actual library tasks. With this information at our disposal we should be able to design jobs that meet the requirements of socio-technical theory. Of course, a listing of tasks is not enough.

We will have to plan for the compatibility between the values of our culture and the value of our libraries, the autonomy of the individual and the control imposed by our institutions, the demands of the work system itself and the responses employees are equipped to give. We will have to plan for a minimum of rigidity in the application of technology upon job content and structure. Modern organizational planning should develop minimal critical tasks necessary to achieve the goals of our organizations instead of imposing detailed specifications and restrictions on jobs.

Libraries are in an excellent position to offer potential for self-actualization and fulfillment of employees' needs at both the professional and the support level because library work is socially significant and can easily be restructured to achieve individual and organizational compatibility.[40]

References

1. Louis E. Davis, *Job Satisfaction Research: The Post-Industrial View* (Los Angeles: University of California, Institute of Industrial Relations, 1971), p. 185-86.
2. Ibid., p. 181.
3. See the detailed bibliographical survey in Davis, *Job Satisfaction*, p. 188.
4. Ibid., p. 190.
5. Ibid., p. 191.
6. Beverly P. Lynch, "The Academic Library and Its Environment," *College & Research Libraries* 35, 126-32 (March 1974), and "A Framework for a Comparative Analysis of Library Work," *College & Research Libraries* 35:432-43 (Nov. 1974).
7. Lynch, "Framework," p. 440.
8. Lynch, "Framework," p. 441.
9. Lynch, "Academic Library," p. 128.
10. Lynch,. "Academic Library," p. 128.
11. Lynch, "Academic Library," p. 130.
12. Jerome S. Seliger, *The Effects of Position Classification on Need Satisfaction and Work Attitudes* (Dissertation, Univ. of Southern California, 1974).
13. Ibid., p. 5.
14. Ibid., p. 13.
15. Ibid., p. 17-18.
16. Ibid., p. 37.
17. Ibid., p. 24-25.
18. Ibid., p. 10.
19. Ibid., p. 42.
20. Ibid., p. 240.
21. Robert A. Ullrich, *A Theoretical Model of Human Behavior in Organizations* (Morristown, N.J.: General Learning Press, 1972). p. 7.
22. Ibid., p. 9.
23. Ibid., p. 18.
24. Ibid., p. 189.
25. Ibid., p. 186.
26. Ibid., p. 188.
27. Ibid., p. 190.
28. Ibid., p. 191.
29. Ibid., p. 199.

30. Ibid., p. 196.
31. Ibid., p. 196.
32. Booz, Allen & Hamilton Inc., *Organization and Staffing of the Libraries of Columbia University* (Westport, Conn.: Redgrave, 1973).
33. Myrl Ricking and Robert E. Booth, *Personnel Utilization in Libraries* (Chicago: American Library Assn., 1974).
34. Booz, *Organization and Staffing*, p. 154-55.
35. Ibid., p. 156.
36. Ricking, *Personnel Utilization*, p. 26.
37. Ibid., p. 27.
38. Ibid., p. 29.
39. Ibid., p. 31.
40. Kenneth H. Plate and Elizabeth W. Stone, "Factors Affecting Librarian's Job Satisfaction: A Report of Two Studies," *Library Quarterly* 49:99 (April 1974).

One More Time: How Do You Motivate Employees?

Frederick Herzberg

How many articles, books, speeches, and workshops have pleaded plaintively, "How do I get an employee to do what I want him to do?"

The psychology of motivation is tremendously complex, and what has been unraveled with any degree of assurance is small indeed. But the dismal ratio of knowledge to speculation has not dampened the enthusiasm for new forms of snake oil that are constantly coming on the market, many of them with academic testimonials. Doubtless this article will have no depressing impact on the market for snake oil, but since the ideas expressed in it have been tested in many corporations and other organizations, it will help—I hope—to redress the imbalance in the aforementioned ratio.

'MOTIVATING' WITH KITA

In lectures to industry on the problem, I have found that the audiences are anxious for quick and practical answers, so I will begin with a straightforward, practical formula for moving people.

What is the simplest, surest, and most direct way of getting someone to do something? Ask him? But if he responds that he does not want to do it, then that calls for a psychological consultation to determine the reason for his obstinacy. Tell him? His response shows

---

Author's note: I should like to acknowledge the contributions that Robert Ford of the American Telephone and Telegraph Company has made to the ideas expressed in this paper, and in particular to the successful application of these ideas in improving work performance and the job satisfaction of employees.

that he does not understand you, and now an expert in communication methods has to be brought in to show you how to get through to him. Give him a monetary incentive? I do not need to remind the reader of the complexity and difficulty involved in setting up and administering an incentive system. Show him? This means a costly training program. We need a simple way.

Every audience contains the "direct action" manager who shouts, "Kick him!" And this type of manager is right. The surest and least circumlocuted way of getting someone to do something is to kick him in the pants—give him what might be called the KITA.

There are various forms of KITA, and here are some of them:

Negative physical KITA. This is a literal application of the term and was frequently used in the past. It has, however, three major drawbacks: (1) it is inelegant; (2) it contradicts the precious image of benevolence that most organizations cherish; and (3) since it is a physical attack, it directly stimulates the autonomic nervous system, and this often results in negative feedback—the employee may just kick you in return. These factors give rise to certain taboos against negative physical KITA.

The psychologist has come to the rescue of those who are no longer permitted to use negative physical KITA. He has uncovered infinite sources of psychological vulnerabilities and the appropriate methods to play tunes on them. "He took my rug away"; "I wonder what he meant by that"; "The boss is always going around me"—these symptomatic expressions of ego sores that have been rubbed raw are the result of application of:

Negative Psychological KITA. This has several advantages over negative physical KITA. First, the cruelty is not visible; the bleeding is internal and comes much later. Second, since it affects the higher cortical centers of the brain with its inhibitory powers, it reduces the posibility of physical backlash. Third, since the psychological pains that a person can feel is almost infinite, the direction and site possibilities of the KITA are increased many times. Fourth, the person administering the kick can manage to be above it all and let the system accomplish the dirty work. Fifth, those who practice it receive some ego satisfaction (oneupmanship), whereas they would find drawing blood abhorrent. Finally, if the employee does complain, he can always be accused of being paranoid, since there is no tangible evidence of an actual attack.

Now, what does negative KITA accomplish? If I kick you in the rear (physically or psychologically), who is motivated? *I* am motivated, *you* move! Negative KITA does not lead to motivation, but to movement. So:

Positive KITA. Let us consider motivation. If I say to you, "Do this for me or the company, and in return I will give you a reward, an incentive, more status, a promotion, all the quid pro quos that exist in the industrial organization," am I motivating you? The overwhelming opinion I receive from management people is, "Yes, this is motivation."

I have a year-old Schnauzer. When it was a small puppy and I wanted it to move, I kicked it in the rear and it moved. Now that I have finished its obedience training, I hold up a dog biscuit when I want the Schnauzer to move. In this instance, who is motivated—I or the dog? The dog wants the biscuit, but it is I who want it to move. Again, I am the one who is motivated, and the dog is the one who moves. In this instance all I did was apply KITA frontally; I exerted a pull instead of a push. When industry wishes to use such positive KITAs, it has available an incredible number and variety of dog biscuits (jelly beans for humans) to wave in front of the employee to get him to jump.

Why is it that managerial audiences are quick to see that negative KITA is *not* motivation, while they are almost unanimous in their judgement that positive KITA *is* motivation? It is because negative KITA is rape, and positive KITA is seduction. But it is infinitely worse to be seduced than to be raped; the latter is an unfortunate occurrence, while the former signifies that you were a party to your own downfall. This is why positive KITA is so popular: it is a tradition; it is in the American way. The organization does not have to kick you; you kick yourself.

Myths about Motivation

Why is KITA not motivation? If I kick my dog (from the front or the back), he will move. And when I want him to move again, what must I do? I must kick him again. Similarly, I can charge a man's battery, and then recharge it and recharge it again. But it is only when he has his own generator that we can talk about motivation. He then needs no outside stimulation. He *wants* to do it.

With this in mind, we can review some positive KITA personnel practices that were developed as attempts to instill "motivation":

1. *Reducing time spent at work*—This represents a marvelous way of motivating people to work—getting them off the job! We have

reduced (formally and informally) the time spent on the job over the last 50 or 60 years until we are finally on the way to the "6½-day weekend." An interesting variant of this approach is the development of off-hour recreation programs. The philosophy here seems to be that those who play together, work together. The fact is that motivated people seek more hours of work, not fewer.

2. *Spiraling wages*—Have these motivated people? Yes, to seek the next wage increase. Some medievalists still can be heard to say that a good depression will get employees moving. They feel that if rising wages don't or won't do the job, perhaps reducing them will.

3. *Fringe benefits*—Industry has outdone the most welfare-minded of welfare states in dispensing cradle-to-the-grave succor. One company I know of had an informal "fringe benefit of the month club" going for a while. The cost of fringe benefits in this country has reached approximately 25% of the wage dollar, and we still cry for motivation.

People spend less time working for more money and more security than ever before, and the trend cannot be reversed. These benefits are no longer rewards; they are rights. A 6-day week is inhuman, a 10-hour day is exploitation, extended medical coverage is a basic decency, and stock options are the salvation of American initiative. Unless the ante is continuously raised, the psychological reaction of employees is that the company is turning back the clock.

4. *Human relations training*—Over 30 years of teaching and, in many instances, of practicing psychological approaches to handling people have resulted in costly human relations programs and, in the end, the same question: How do you motivate workers? Here, too, escalations have taken place. Thirty years ago it was necessary to request, "Please don't spit on the floor." Today the same admonition requires three "please"s before the employee feels that his superior has demonstrated the psychologically proper attitudes toward him.

The failure of human relations training to produce motivation led to the conclusion that the supervisor or manager himself was not psychologically true to himself in his practice of interpersonal decency. So an advanced form of human relations KITA, sensitivity training, was unfolded.

5. *Sensitivity training*—Do you really, really understand yourself? Do you really, really, really trust the other man? Do you really, really,

really, really cooperate. The failure of sensitivity training is now being explained, by those who have become opportunistic exploiters of the technique, as a failure to really (five times) conduct proper sensitivity training courses.

With the realization that there are only temporary gains from comfort and economic and interpersonal KITA, personnel managers concluded that the fault lay not in what they were doing, but in the employee's failure to appreciate what they were doing. This opened up the field of communications, a whole new area of "scientifically" sanctioned KITA.

6. *Communications*—The professor of communications was invited to join the faculty of management training programs and help in making employees understand what management was doing for them. House organs, briefing sessions, supervisory instruction on the importance of communication, and all sorts of propaganda have proliferated until today there is even an International Council of Industrial Editors. But no motivation resulted, and the obvious thought occurred that perhaps management was not hearing what the employees were saying. That led to the next KITA.

7. *Two-way communication*—Management ordered morale surveys, suggestion plans, and group participation programs. Then both employees and management were communicating and listening to each other more than ever, but without much improvement in motivation.

The behavioral scientists began to take another look at their conceptions and their data, and they took human relations one step further. A glimmer of truth was beginning to show through in the writings of the so-called higher-order-need psychologists. People, so they said, want to actualize themselves. Unfortunately, the "actualizing" psychologists got mixed up with the human psychologists, and a new KITA emerged.

8. *Job participation*—Though it may not have been the theoretical intention, job participation often became a "give them the big picture" approach. For example, if a man is tightening 10,000 nuts a day on an assembly line with a torque wrench, tell him he is building a Chevrolet. Another approach had the goal of giving the employee a *feeling* that he is determining, in some measure, what he does on his job. The goal was to provide a *sense* of achievement rather than a

substantive achievement in his task. Real achievement, of course, requires a task that makes it possible.

But still there was no motivation. This led to the inevitable conclusion that the employees must be sick, and therefore to the next KITA.

9. *Employee counseling*—The initial use of this form of KITA in a systematic fashion can be credited to the Hawthorne experiment of the Western Electric Company during the early 1930's. At that time, it was found that the employees harbored irrational feelings that were interfering with the rational operation of the factory. Counseling in this instance was a means of letting the employees unburden themselves by talking to someone about their problems. Although the counseling techniques were primitive, the program was large indeed.

The counseling approach suffered as a result of experiences during World War II, when the programs themselves were found to be interfering with the operation of the organizations, the counselors had forgotten their role of benevolent listeners and were attempting to do something about the problems that they heard about. Psychological counseling, however, has managed to survive the negative impact of World War II experiences and today is beginning to flourish with renewed sophistication. But, alas, many of these programs, like all the others, do not seem to have lessened the pressure of demands to find out how to motivate workers.

Since KITA results only in short-term movement, it is safe to predict that the cost of these programs will increase steadily and new varieties will be developed as old positive KITAs reach their satiation points.

HYGIENE VS. MOTIVATORS

Let me rephrase the perennial question this way: How do you install a generator in an employee? A brief review of my motivation-hygiene theory of job attitudes is required before theoretical and practical suggestions can be offered. The theory was first drawn from an examination of events in the lives of engineers and accountants. At least 16 other investigations, using a wide variety of populations (including some in the Communist countries), have since been completed, making the original research one of the most replicated studies in the field of job attitudes.

The findings of these studies, along with corroboration from many other investigations using different procedures, suggest that the factors involved in producing job satisfaction (and motivation) are separate and distinct from the factors that lead to job dissatisfaction. Since separate factors need to be considered, depending on whether job satisfaction or job dissatisfaction is being examined, it follows that these two feelings are not opposites of each other. The opposite of job satisfaction is not job dissatisfaction but, rather, *no* job satisfaction; and, similarly, the opposite of job dissatisfaction is not job satisfaction, but *no* job dissatisfaction.

Stating the concept presents a problem in semantics, for we normally think of satisfaction and dissatisfaction as opposites—i.e., what is not satisfying must be dissatisfying, and vice versa. But when it comes to understanding the behavior of people in their jobs, more than a play on words is involved.

Two different needs of man are involved here. One set of needs can be thought of as stemming from his animal nature—the built-in drive to avoid pain from the environment, plus all the learned drives which become conditioned to the basic biological needs. For example, hunger, a basic biological drive, makes it necessary to earn money, and then money becomes a specific drive. The other set of needs relates to that unique human characteristic, the ability to achieve and, through achievement, to experience psychological growth. The stimuli for the growth needs are tasks that induce growth; in the industrial setting, they are the *job content*. Contrariwise, the stimuli inducing pain-avoidance behavior are found in the *job environment*.

The growth or *motivator* factors that are intrinsic to the job are: achievement, recognition for achievement, the work itself, responsibility, and growth or advancement. The dissatisfaction-avoidance or *hygiene* (KITA) factors that are extrinsic to the job include: company policy and administration, supervision, interpersonal relationships, working conditions, salary, status, and security.

A composite of the factors that are involved in causing job satisfaction and job dissatisfaction, drawn from samples of 1,685 employees, is shown in *Exhibit I*. The results indicate that motivators were the primary cause of satisfaction, and hygiene factors the primary cause of unhappiness on the job. The employees, studied in 12 different investigations, included lower-level supervisors, professional women, agricultural administrators, men about to retire from management positions, hospital maintenance personnel, manufacturing supervisors, nurses, food handlers, military officers, engineers, scientists, housekeepers, teachers, technicians, female assemblers, accountants, Finnish foremen, and Hungarian engineers.

They were asked what job events had occurred in their work that

EXHIBIT I Factors Affecting Job Attitudes, as Reported in 12 Investigations

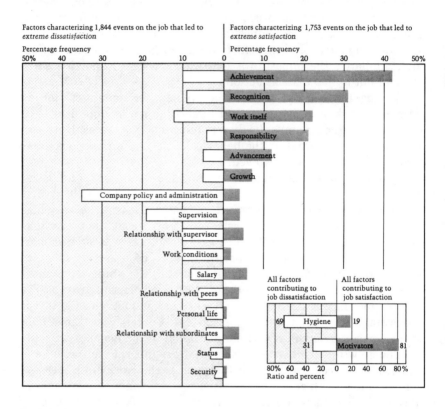

had led to extreme satisfaction or extreme dissatisfaction on their part. Their responses are broken down in the exhibit into percentages of total "positive" job events and of total "negative" job events. (The figures total more than 100 percent on both the "hygiene" and "motivators" sides because often at least two factors can be attributed to a single event; advancement, for instance, often accompanies assumption of responsibility.)

To illustrate, a typical response involving achievement that had a negative effect for the employee was, "I was unhappy because I didn't do the job successfully." A typical response in the small number of positive job events in the Company Policy and Administration grouping was, "I was happy because the company reorganized the section so that I didn't report any longer to the guy I didn't get along with."

As the lower right-hand part of the exhibit shows, of all the factors contributing to job satisfaction, 81 percent were motivators. And of all the factors contributing to the employees' dissatisfaction over their work, 69 percent involved hygiene elements.

Eternal Triangle

There are three general philosophies of personnel management. The first is based on organizational theory, the second on industrial engineering, and the third on behavioral science.

The organizational theorist believes that human needs are either so irrational or so varied and adjustable to specific situations that the major function of personnel management is to be as pragmatic as the occasion demands. If jobs are organized in a proper manner, he reasons, the result will be the most efficient job structure, and the most favorable job attitudes will follow as a matter of course.

The industrial engineer holds that man is mechanistically oriented and economically motivated and his needs are best met by attuning the individual to the most efficient work process. The goal of personnel management therefore should be to concoct the most appropriate incentive system and to design the specific working conditions in a way that facilitates the most efficient use of the human machine. By structuring jobs in a manner that leads to the most efficient operation, the engineer believes that he can obtain the optimal organization of work and the proper work attitudes.

The behavioral scientist focuses on group sentiments, attitudes of individual employees, and the organization's social and psychological climate. According to his persuasion, he emphasizes one or more of the various hygiene and motivator needs. His approach to personnel management generally emphasizes some form of human relations education, in the hope of instilling healthy employee attitudes and an organizational climate which he considers to be felicitous to human values. He believes that proper attitudes will lead to efficient job and organizational structure.

There is always a lively debate as to the overall effectiveness of the approaches of the organizational theorists and the industrial engineer. Manifestly they have achieved much. But the nagging question for the behavioral scientist has been: What is the cost in human problems that eventually cause more expense to the organization—for instance, turnover, absenteeism, errors, violation of safety rules, strikes, restriction of output, higher wages, and greater fringe benefits? On the other hand, the behavioral scientist is hard put to document much

EXHIBIT II   'Triangle' of Philosophies of Personnel Management

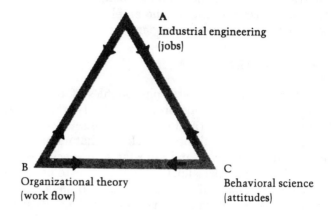

A
Industrial engineering
(jobs)

B
Organizational theory
(work flow)

C
Behavioral science
(attitudes)

manifest improvement in personnel management, using his approach.

The three philosophies can be depicted as a triangle, as is done in *Exhibit II*, with each persuasion claiming the apex angle. The motivation-hygiene theory claims the same angle as industrial engineering, but for opposite goals. Rather than rationalizing the work to increase efficiency, the theory suggests that work be *enriched* to bring about effective utilization of personnel. Such a systematic attempt to motivate employees by manipulating the motivator factors is just beginning.

The term *job enrichment* describes this embryonic movement. An older term, job enlargement, should be avoided because it is associated with past failures stemming from a misunderstanding of the problem. Job enrichment provides the opportunity for the employee's psychological growth, while job enlargement merely makes a job structurally bigger. Since scientific job enrichment is very new, this article only suggests the principles and practical steps that have recently emerged from several successful experiments in industry.

Job Loading

In attempting to enrich an employee's job, management often succeeds in reducing the man's personal contribution, rather than giving him an opportunity for growth in his accustomed job. Such an endeavor, which I shall call horizontal job loading (as opposed to vertical loading, or providing motivator factors), has been the problem of earlier job enlargement programs. This activity merely enlarges the meaninglessness of the job. Some examples of this approach, and their effect, are:

Challenging the employee by increasing the amount of production expected of him. If he tightens 10,000 bolts a day, see if he can tighten 20,000 bolts a day. The arithmetic involved shows that multiplying zero by zero still equals zero.

Adding another meaningless task to the existing one, usually some routine clerical activity. The arithmetic here is adding zero to zero.

Rotating the assignments of a number of jobs that need to be enriched. This means washing dishes for a while, then washing silverware. The arithmetic is substituting one zero for another zero.

Removing the most difficult parts of the assignment in order to free the worker to accomplish more of the less challenging assignments. This traditional industrial engineering approach amounts to subtraction in the hope of accomplishing addition.

These are common forms of horizontal loading that frequently come up in preliminary brainstorming sessions on job enrichment. The principles of vertical loading have not all been worked out as yet, and they remain rather general, but I have furnished seven useful starting points for consideration in *Exhibit III*.

A Successful Application

An example from a highly successful job enrichment experiment can illustrate the distinction between horizontal and vertical loading of a job. The subjects of this study were the stockholder correspondents employed by a very large corporation. Seemingly, the task required of these carefully selected and highly trained correspondents was quite complex and challenging. But almost all indexes of performance and job attitudes were low, and exit interviewing confirmed that the challenge of the job existed merely as words.

A job enrichment project was initiated in the form of an experiment with one group, designated as an achieving unit, having its job enriched by the principles described in *Exhibit III*. A control group continued to do its job in the traditional way. (There were also two "uncommitted" groups of correspondents formed to measure the so-called Hawthorne Effect—that is, to gauge whether productivity and attitudes toward the job changed artificially merely because employees sensed that the company was paying more attention to them

EXHIBIT III Principles of Vertical Job Loading

Principle	Motivators involved
A. Removing some controls while retaining accountability	Responsibility and personal achievement
B. Increasing the accountability of individuals for own work	Responsibility and recognition
C. Giving a person a complete natural unit of work (module, division, area, and so on)	Responsibility, achievement, and recognition
D. Granting additional authority to an employee in his activity; job freedom	Responsibility, achievement, and recognition
E. Making periodic reports directly available to the worker himself rather than to the supervisor	Internal recognition
F. Introducing new and more difficult tasks not previously handled	Growth and learning
G. Assigning individuals specific or specialized tasks, enabling them to become experts	Responsibility, growth, and advancement

in doing something different or novel. The results for these groups were substantially the same as for the control group, and for the sake of simplicity I do not deal with them in this summary.) No changes in hygiene were introduced for either group other than those that would have been made anyway, such as normal pay increases.

The changes for the achieving unit were introduced in the first two months, averaging one per week of the seven motivators listed in *Exhibit III*. At the end of six months the members of the achieving unit were found to be outperforming their counterparts in the control group, and in addition indicated a marked increase in their liking for their jobs. Other results showed that the achieving group had lower absenteeism and, subsequently, a much higher rate of promotion.

Exhibit IV illustrates the changes in performance, measured in February and March, before the study period began, and at the end of each month of the study period. The shareholder service index represents quality of letters, including accuracy of information, and speed of response to stockholders' letters of inquiry. The index of a

EXHIBIT IV   Shareholder Service Index in Company Experiment [Three-month cumulative average]

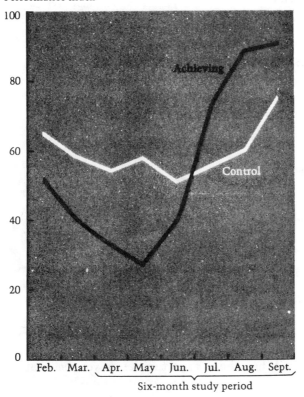

[Three-month cumulative average]

Performance index

current month was averaged into the average of the two prior months, which means that improvement was harder to obtain if the indexes of the previous months were low. The "achievers" were performing less well before the six-month period started, and their performance service index continued to decline after the introduction of the motivators, evidently because of uncertainty over their newly granted responsibilities. In the third month, however, performance improved, and soon the members of this group had reached a high level of accomplishment.

Exhibit V shows the two groups' attitudes toward their job, measured at the end of March, just before the first motivator was

EXHIBIT V   Changes in Attitudes Toward Tasks in Company
Experiment [Changes in mean scores over six-month period]

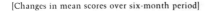

[Changes in mean scores over six-month period]

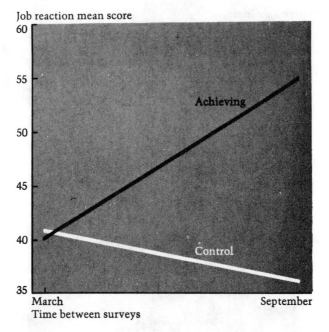

introduced, and again at the end of September. The correspondents
were asked 16 questions, all involving motivation. A typical one was,
"As you see it, how many opportunities do you feel that you have in
your job for making worthwhile contributions?" The answers were
scaled from 1 to 5, with 80 as the maximum possible score. The
achievers became much more positive about their job, while the
attitude of the control unit remained about the same (the drop is not
statistically significant).

How was the job of these correspondents restructured? *Exhibit VI*
lists the suggestions made that were deemed to be horizontal loading,
and the actual vertical loading changes that were incorporated in the
job of the achieving unit. The capital letters under "Principle" after
"Vertical loading" refer to the corresponding letters in *Exhibit III*. The
reader will note that the rejected forms of horizontal loading correspond
closely to the list of common manifestations of the phenomenon.

EXHIBIT VI   Enlargement vs. Enrichment of Correspondents' Tasks in Company Experiment

Horizontal loading suggestions (rejected)	Vertical loading suggestions (adopted)	Principle
Firm quotas could be set for letters to be answered each day, using a rate which would be hard to reach.	Subject matter experts were appointed within each unit for other members of the unit to consult with before seeking supervisory help. (The supervisor had been answering all specialized and difficult questions.)	G
The women could type the letters themselves, as well as compose them, or take on any other clerical functions.	Correspondents signed their own names on letters. (The supervisor had been signing all letters.)	B
All difficult or complex inquiries could be channeled to a few women so that the remainder could achieve high rates of output. These jobs could be exchanged from time to time.	The work of the more experienced correspondents was proofread less frequently by supervisors and was done at the correspondents' desks, dropping verification from 100% to 10%. (Previously, all correspondents' letters had been checked by the supervisor.)	A
The women could be rotated through units handling different customers, and then sent back to their own units.	Production was discussed, but only in terms such as "a full day's work is expected." As time went on, this was no longer mentioned. (Before, the group had been constantly reminded of the number of letters that needed to be answered.)	D
	Outgoing mail went directly to the mailroom without going over supervisors' desks. (The letters had always been routed through the supervisors.)	A
	Correspondents were encouraged to answer letters in a more personalized way. (Reliance on the form-letter approach had been standard practice.)	C
	Each correspondent was held personally responsible for the quality and accuracy of letters. (This responsibility had been the province of the supervisor and the verifier.)	B, E

STEPS TO JOB ENRICHMENT

Now that the motivator idea has been described in practice, here are the steps that managers should take in instituting the principle with their employees:

1. Select those jobs in which (a) the investment in industrial engineering does not make changes too costly, (b) attitudes are poor, (c) hygiene is becoming very costly, and (d) motivation will make a difference in performance.

2. Approach these jobs with the conviction that they can be changed. Years of tradition have led managers to believe that the content of the jobs is sacrosanct and the only scope of action that they have is in ways of stimulating people.

3. Brainstorm a list of changes that may enrich the jobs, without concern for their practicality.

4. Screen the list to eliminate suggestions that involve hygiene, rather than actual motivation.

5. Screen the list for generalities, such as "give them more responsibility," that are rarely followed in practice. This might seem obvious, but the motivator words have never left industry; the substance has just been rationalized and organized out. Words like "responsibility," "growth," "achievement," and "challenge," for example, have been elevated to the lyrics of the patriotic anthem for all organizations. It is the old problem typified by the pledge of allegiance to the flag being more important than contributions to the country—of following the form, rather than the substance.

6. Screen the list to eliminate any *horizontal* loading suggestions.

7. Avoid direct participation by the employees whose jobs are to be enriched. Ideas they have expressed previously certainly constitute a valuable source for recommended changes, but their direct involvement contaminates the process with human relations *hygiene* and, more specifically, gives them only a *sense* of making a contribution. The job is to be changed, and it is the content that will produce the motivation, not attitudes about being involved or the challenge inherent in setting up a job. That process will be over shortly, and it is what the employees will be doing from then on that will determine their motivation. A sense of participation will result only in short-term movement.

8. In the initial attempts at job enrichment, set up a controlled experiment. At least two equivalent groups should be chosen, one an experimental unit in which the motivators are systematically in-

troduced over a period of time, and the other one a control group in which no changes are made. For both groups, hygiene should be allowed to follow its natural course for the duration of the experiment. Pre- and post-installation tests of performance and job attitudes are necessary to evaluate the effectiveness of the job enrichment program. The attitude test must be limited to motivator items in order to divorce the employee's view of the job he is given from all the surrounding hygiene feelings that he might have.

9. Be prepared for a drop in performance in the experimental group the first few weeks. The changeover to a new job may lead to a temporary reduction in efficiency.

10. Expect your first-line supervisors to experience some anxiety and hostility over the changes you are making. The anxiety comes from their fear that the changes will result in poorer performance for their unit. Hostility will arise when the employees start assuming what the supervisors regard as their own responsibility for performance. The supervisor without checking duties to perform may then be left with little to do.

After a successful experiment, however, the supervisor usually discovers the supervisory and managerial functions he has neglected, or which were never his because all his time was given over to checking the work of his subordinates. For example, in the R&D division of one large chemical company I know of, the supervisors of the laboratory assistants were theoretically responsible for their training and evaluation. These functions, however, had come to be performed in a routine, unsubstantial fashion. After the job enrichment program, during which the supervisors were not merely passive observers of the assistants' performance, the supervisors actually were devoting their time to reviewing performance and administering thorough training.

What has been called an employee-centered style of supervision will come about not through education of supervisors, but by changing the jobs that they do.

CONCLUDING NOTE

Job enrichment will not be a one-time proposition, but a continuous management function. The initial changes, however, should last for a very long period of time. There are a number of reasons for this:

The changes should bring the job up to the level of challenge commensurate with the skill that was hired.

Those who have still more ability eventually will be able to demonstrate it better and win promotion to higher-level jobs.

The very nature of motivators, as opposed to hygiene factors, is that they have a much longer-term effect on employees' attitudes. Perhaps the job will have to be enriched again, but this will not occur as frequently as the need for hygiene.

Not all jobs can be enriched, nor do all jobs need to be enriched. If only a small percentage of the time and money that is now devoted to hygiene, however, were given to job enrichment efforts, the return in human satisfaction and economic gain would be one of the largest dividends that industry and society have ever reaped through their efforts at better personnel management.

The argument for job enrichment can be summed up quite simply: If you have someone on a job, use him. If you can't use him on the job, get rid of him, either via automation or by selecting someone with lesser ability. If you can't use him and you can't get rid of him, you will have a motivation problem.

Reprints of this article are available at $1.00 each (minimum order $5.00) from Harvard Business Review, Soldiers Field, Boston, Mass. 02163, telephone (617) 495-6192.

The Determinants of Job Satisfaction Among Beginning Librarians

George P. D'Elia

J OB satisfaction is defined as an employee's affective response to his job environment. It is a state of mind inferred from an employee's response to the question, "How satisfied are you with your job?" Whether this state of mind affects the employee's performance is still open to question, but the traditional notions that a happy worker is a productive worker or that a productive worker is a happy worker have an appealing face validity. At the very least, an analysis of job satisfaction within an organization provides an important diagnostic assessment of the health of that organization. Employee reactions to organizational structure, job classifications, personnel policies, professional milieu, social environment, working conditions, and other organizational characteristics are one form of feedback to the administration pertaining to its performance. The usefulness of such feedback appears to be self-evident, and recent papers by Plate and Stone (1), Vaughn and Dunn (2), and Wahba (3) have focused the profession's attention upon job satisfaction in librarianship. The purpose of this paper is to present a methodology for continuing the study of job satisfaction in librarianship and to explore the determinants of job satisfaction among librarians.

METHODOLOGICAL CONSIDERATIONS

Before reviewing the relevant literature of job satisfaction in librarianship it would be worthwhile to discuss briefly two important

Reprinted with permission from *The Library Quarterly*, V. 49 (July 1979), pp. 283–302. © 1979 by The University of Chicago.

methodological considerations: a conceptual model of job satisfaction and its operationalization through instrumentation.

Job satisfaction is considered to be a function of the interaction of the employee with his job environment. The employee experiences the various characteristics operating within his job environment and reacts to those characteristics on the basis of his own personal requirements. These personal requirements have been described variously in terms of the employee's motivations, expectations, or self-concept. Among these, the motivation model appears to be pre-eminent both in terms of the volume and richness of the research which it has generated and in terms of its simplicity and utility. A motivation model of job satisfaction posits that an employee works in order to gratify his physical, social, and psychological needs. To the degree that these needs are gratified, the employee is satisfied. Thus, a motivation model identifies three sets of variables: the needs of the employee, the characteristics of the job environment as perceived by the employee, and the degree of satisfaction experienced by the employee.

It is important to note that these three sets of variables are conceptually different and therefore should be independently measured. Available instrumentation should be evaluated on the basis of the clarity and precision with which these constructs have been operationalized as evidenced by its reported statistical reliability and validity. Among the numerous instruments available for use in job-satisfaction research there are, unfortunately, many which confuse these variables and thus yield ambiguous and useless data.

Research into Job Satisfaction in Librarianship

Three papers have been identified which have reported research into job satisfaction in librarianship.[1] All three papers employed a descriptive analysis of the data. Plate and Stone and Vaughn and Dunn simply enumerated the data and reported percentages, while Wahba used t-tests to describe differences between male and female librarians.

A primary goal of applied research is to draw inferences from data and then to use these inferences as guides for action. To the extent that a descriptive analysis of data does not attempt to control for concomitant variation among the independent variables and does not test for a relationship between the dependent variable and the array of independent variables, it does not permit the drawing of inferences and hence is limited in its usefulness as a mode of research. A descriptive analysis of data for a particular case study does yield useful information, providing that these data can be compared to standardized norms and providing that an established set of relationships exists such that the comparisons are amenable to meaningful interpretation. Unfortunately, the state of the art in research on job satisfaction in librarianship is such that neither norms nor relationships have been established. These three studies are, therefore, limited in their usefulness. In addition, each has a methodological flaw which further compromises its results.

The Plate and Stone study.—Plate and Stone employed Herzberg's (7) two-factor theory of job satisfaction as the conceptual basis for their study. Generally, motivation theories of job satisfaction, with the exception of Herzberg's, posit that any characteristic of the job environment is potentially related to the degree of job satisfaction experienced by an employee. In effect, any job characteristics can be an inducement to satisfaction or dissatisfaction depending upon the need requirements of the employee. Herzberg disagrees, however, and proposes that there are two different types of job characteristics: motivator factors and hygiene factors. The motivator factors, which are characteristic of the employee's involvement with the content of the job itself, can by their presence induce job satisfaction but cannot by their absence induce job dissatisfaction. The hygiene factors, which are characteristic of the context or the environment in which the job is performed, can by their absence induce job dissatisfaction but cannot by their presence induce job satisfaction. This two-factor theory was first proposed in 1959 and it has generated a considerable amount of research. The results of this research are controversial, but there is sufficient documentation to indicate that the two-factor theory is instrument bound, that is, Herzberg's results can be replicated only by using his methodology.[2]

Herzberg employs a critical incident technique in which an employee is asked to describe situations in which he experienced job satisfaction and then to describe situations in which he experienced job dissatisfaction. These incidents are then interpreted and coded by the researcher. This method, by its very form, forces the employee to describe satisfying factors and dissatisfying factors separately, it permits the employee to accept responsibility for his good feelings and to ascribe to others the responsibility for his bad feelings, it is open to subjectivity on the part of the researcher who interprets and codes the employee's responses, and it yields data that are analyzed in a superficial manner (simple enumeration of satisfying and dissatisfying factors and their frequency of occurance expressed in percentages.)

Numerous attempts at replicating Herzberg's results using more sophisticated statistical methodologies have either failed or proven inconclusive. Thus a number of organizational behaviorists have concluded that the two-factor theory is a consequence of its simplistic methodology and have suggested that the two-factor theory be laid to rest so as not "to allow the direction of motivational research or actual administrative decisions to be dictated by the seductive simplicity of the two-factor theory" (10, p. 173). Plate and Stone's paper should be read with this caveat in mind.

The Vaughn and Dunn study.—Vaughn and Dunn's study of job satisfaction in six university libraries employed an instrument with questionable face validity. The Job Description Index (JDI)[3] specifically asks the employee to describe the characteristics of his job environment, not to reveal his feelings about the job. Thus the JDI does not measure an employee's job satisfaction, but rather measures an employee's perception of the presence or absence of certain characteristics in the job environment. These characteristics are the work itself, the supervisory climate, the interpersonal climate, the pay conditions, and promotion opportunities. While these characteristics are related to job satisfaction they do not measure job satisfaction. Thus the data collected and presented by Vaughn and Dunn are really a descriptive analysis of the characteristics of the job environments in six university libraries. Since the relationship between these five job characteristics and the job satisfaction of the librarians working in these libraries has not been established, the data have no clear interpretation.

The Wahba study.—Wahba's study of job satisfaction of librarians was based upon a need-gratification model and employed the Need Satisfaction Questionnaire (NSQ)[4] to collect the data. The NSQ addresses itself to five needs: security, social, esteem, autonomy, and self-actualization. For each of these needs the NSQ, as amended by Wahba, asks the employee to respond to the following questions: (1) How much of the characteristic is there now (in the job environment)? (2) How much of the characteristic do you think there should be? (3) How important is characteristic to you? The response to question 1 is called the need-fulfillment score, and it is considered to be a measure of job satisfaction—"the higher the value of the need fulfillment score, the higher the perceived satisfaction . . ." (3, p. 47). Question 1, however, does not ask about job satisfaction. It specifically asks the employee to estimate the degree to which he perceives a specific job characteristic to be present in his job environment. Thus question 1 does not measure job satisfaction nor, for that matter, does it measure need fulfillment. Question 3 yields a need-importance score, but it is not considered to be important in the analysis of the data. A third score, the need-deficiency score, is computed as the difference between the employee's responses to questions 1 and 2. It is interpreted as another measure of satisfaction—"the higher the need deficiency score, the higher . . . the dissatisfaction of the need . . . "(3, p. 47).

This type of scale, a difference score, suffers from two serious limitations. The validity of the scale is suspect since it incorporates the error of measurement of question 1 and the error of measurement of question 2. It is possible that any given need-deficiency score is nothing more than measurement error. Cronbach and Furby (21) demonstrate that all such difference scores are systematically related to random error of measurement and advise that such scores should not be used. Even if this error-of-measurement problem could be surmounted, the need-deficiency score is not independent of either question 1 or question 2. Thus, when Wahba reports four significantly different need-deficiency scores between male and female librarians, neither she nor the reader is able to determine whether these differences are attributable to error, to differences between the responses of males and females to question 1, to differences between the responses of males and females to question 2, or to a combination of all of the above. Under these circumstances, Wahba's conclusion that female librarians are treated differently than their male counterparts and consequently experience less job satisfaction is without foundation.

In view of the previously discussed conceptual model of job satisfaction, it is apparent that these three studies of job satisfaction in librarianship are limited in their usefulness because of weaknesses in conceptualization, instrumentation, and analysis.

OBJECTIVES

Using a motivation model of job satisfaction, this study seeks to identify those factors related to the job satisfaction of a sample of librarians. These factors include the vocational needs of the librarians and the characteristics of the job environments in which the librarians work. In addition, two demographic variables are also tested—the sex of the librarian and the type of library in which the librarian works.

INSTRUMENTATION

The Minnesota Importance Questionnaire (MIQ) (22) was used to measure the vocational needs of the librarians in the sample, the Minnesota Job Description Questionnaire (MJDQ) (23) was used to measure a librarian's perceptions of the characteristics of his job environment, and the Minnesota Satisfaction Questionnaire (MSQ) (24) was used to measure a librarian's satisfaction with each of these job characteristics. All three instruments measure the same job-related dimensions. They are as follows: ability utilization (AU), achievement (Ach), activity (Act), advancement (Adv), authority (Au), company policies and practices (CPP), compensation (Com), co-workers (Cow), creativity (Cre), independence (Ind), moral values (MV), recognition (Rec), responsibility (Res), security (Sec), social service (SSe), social status (SSt), supervision-human relations (SHR), supervision-technical competence (ST), variety (Var), and working conditions (WC). Thus, the MIQ measures the importance of each dimension to an employee, the MJDQ measures the degree to which an employee perceives that dimension to be present in his job environment, and the MSQ measures the degree of satisfaction experienced by the employee with each of the dimensions. In addition, the MJDQ and the MSQ measure the dimension of autonomy on the job (Aut), and the MSQ also yields a general satisfaction scale score, which is a measure of an employee's overall satisfaction with his job. All three instruments have demonstrated reliability and validity, and all three instruments have been used extensively in vocational research.

DATA COLLECTION

A group of 314 prospective graduates was identified at six library schools. Each of these students was contacted personally by the researcher or by cooperating members of the faculties at the library schools. The students were advised of the nature of the study, their cooperation was solicited, and some preliminary data were collected. Subsequently, a packet of materials containing the MIQ, the MJDQ, and the MSQ was mailed directly to each student, now a librarian, with return postage to the researcher. At the time of these follow-up mailings the librarians had been in their respective job environments for periods ranging from six to eighteen months. A total of 228 completed MJDQs and MSQs were returned for a response rate of .73, and 193 MIQs were returned for a response rate of .61. The MIQ is considerably longer than either the MJDQ or the MSQ, which probably accounted for the lower response rate.

The sample was selected for the following reasons: (1) to limit the study to nonsupervisory librarians; (2) to satisfy the author's interest in the adjustment of new librarians to the job environments of librarianship; and, more importantly, (3) to minimize the possible effect of withdrawal from the profession by new librarians which at one time was reported by Drennan and Darling (25) to be very high for both sexes. The incidence of quitting a job is a classic correlate of job dissatisfaction. While studying the job satisfaction of a sample of recently graduated librarians runs the risk of not allowing for professional growth and development, studying a sample of more vocationally mature librarians runs the risk of not taking into account those librarians who may have quit out of dissatisfaction. While each of these alternatives suffers from a serious limitation, the difficulty of contacting former librarians is greater than the problem of trying to generalize from a sample of recently graduated librarians to a sample of more vocationally mature librarians. To the extent that vocational muturity is a function of the age and work experience of the employee, it is possible to test for the influence of these variables upon the members of the sample. These tests are reported in the data analysis, and they demonstrate that the sample has generalizability.

DATA ANALYSIS

When testing a single hypothesis, a researcher ordinarily accepts a probability of .05 of rejecting a true null hypothesis (type 1 error). This probability of a type 1 error increases, however, as the number of tests increases. For example, if a test were conducted on each of the twenty scales of the MIQ with α = .05, then the simultaneous error rate (the probability of making at least one type 1 error) would be equal to .64 if the tests were independent of each other[5] and 1.0 if the tests were not independent of each other.[6] In order, therefore, to minimize the simultaneous error rate in the analysis of the data, all tests were conducted at α = .01.

The Vocational Maturity of the Sample

Assuming that the need profile of a vocationally mature librarian would have been affected by his age and work experience, the

TABLE 1   One-Way Analysis of Variance of the MIQ Scale Scores* by Previous Work Experience

	TOTAL (N = 182)		GROUP 2 (N = 43)		GROUP 3 (N = 37)		GROUP 4 (N = 102)		
	$\bar{X}$	SD	$\bar{X}$	SD	$\bar{X}$	SD	$\bar{X}$	SD	F†
AU	1.59	.55	1.42	.60	1.57	.52	1.67	.53	3.236
Ach	1.60	.62	1.54	.58	1.63	.61	1.61	.64	.263
Act	−.06	.82	−.05	.81	−.05	.71	−.06	.87	.005
Adv	.83	.67	.92	.51	.76	.81	.81	.68	.606
Au	−.37	.72	−.49	.70	−.26	.68	−.36	.74	1.052
CPP	1.11	.61	1.23	.63	1.12	.62	1.06	.59	1.211
Com	.64	.84	.73	1.04	.60	.69	.60	.80	.393
Cow	.63	.67	.54	.62	.62	.69	.66	.69	.498
Cre	1.27	.65	1.13	.57	1.18	.48	1.35	.73	1.893
Ind	−.09	.81	−.17	.74	−.15	.76	−.03	.85	.646
MV	1.58	1.26	1.69	1.25	1.70	1.31	1.49	1.26	.582
Rec	.81	.65	.80	.58	.64	.68	.88	.66	1.899
Res	1.18	.67	1.09	.51	1.15	.70	1.23	.72	.666
Sec	.57	.82	.60	.84	.56	.81	.57	.83	.037
SSe	1.34	.99	1.27	.95	1.73	.61	1.22	1.09	3.916
SSt	−.56	.80	−.77	.67	−.64	.82	−.45	.83	2.689
SHR	.88	.65	.89	.56	.86	.60	.88	.70	.027
ST	.56	.69	.53	.60	.54	.66	.59	.74	.129
Var	.25	.73	.20	.65	.27	.70	.26	.77	.138
WC	.75	.69	.66	.81	.81	.53	.77	.69	.531

NOTE.—Group 1 = no previous work experience, excluded because N = 11; group 2 = previous nonprofessional work experience in a library; group 3 = previous nonlibrary work experience; group 4 = previous work experience both in and out of libraries.

*MIQ scale scores generally range from −2.00 to +2.00. The Work Adjustment Project suggests the following key for interpretation: Above 1.5 = high-level need; 1.0–1.5 = moderate-level need; .0–.3 = low-level need; less than .0 = very low-level need.

†$F_{.99}$ (2,179) ≈ 4.73.

vocational needs of the members of the sample were tested for any significant relationships with age and previous work experience. The members of the sample were divided into four groups: those with no previous work experience, those with previous nonprofessional work experience in a library, those with previous nonlibrary work experience, and those with previous work experience both in and out of libraries. Those members of the sample with no previous work experience were excluded from the analysis because of an insufficient number of cases (N = 11). The MIQ scale scores of the remaining three groups were submitted to a one-way analysis of variance. The results of this analysis, reported in Table 1, indicated no significant differences among the group means. Correlation analyses between the

TABLE 2   Pearson Correlation Coefficients Between the MIQ Scale Scores and the Age of the Librarians ($3N = 193$)

Ability utilization (AU)	.09
Achievement (Ach)	.05
Activity (Act)	.08
Advancement (Adv)	$-.02$
Authority (Au)	.17
Company policies and practices (CPP)	$-.11$
Compensation (Com)	$-.03$
Co-workers (Cow)	.00
Creativity (Cre)	.19*
Independence (Ind)	$-.01$
Moral values (MV)	$-.11$
Recognition (Rec)	.04
Responsibility (Res)	.14
Security (Sec)	.09
Social service (SSe)	.14
Social status (SSt)	.11
Supervision–human relations (SHR)	$-.13$
Supervision–technical competence (ST)	$-.09$
Variety (Var)	$-.02$
Working conditions (WC)	$-.03$

*$r_{.99}$ (192) $\approx$ .185.

MIQ scale scores and the ages of the members of the sample, reported in Table 2, resulted in only one weak significant relationship. Thus it appears that the results of this study can be generalized to a population of experienced librarians. It should be noted, however, that these results do not preclude the possibility that the vocational needs of librarians could change with experience over time.

Factors Related to Job Satisfaction

Sex and type of librarian.—The twenty-two scale scores of the MSQ were tested for significant differences between male and female librarians using t-tests. This analysis, reported in Table 3, resulted in no significant t-ratios, indicating that there was no difference in the degree of job satisfaction reported by male and female librarians in the sample. The sample was also divided into groups of librarians representative of the type of library in which the librarians worked. These groups were public services librarians in academic libraries, technical services librarians in academic libraries, public services librarians in public libraries, school librarians, and special librarians. Technical services librarians in public libraries were excluded from the analysis because of an insufficient number of cases ($N = 4$). The twenty-two scale scores of the MSQ were tested for significant differences among these five groups of librarians using a one-way analysis of variance. This analysis, reported in Table 4, resulted in significant F-ratios for the creativity, independence, social service, and social status scales, thus indicating that significant differences do exist among the five groups for each of these four scales.

In order to determine which groups differ from which other groups, the data for these four scales were submitted to the Scheffé procedure[7] for multiple comparisons among group means. The results of this analysis indicated that the mean creativity scale score of the school

TABLE 3 t-Tests for the MSQ Scale Scores* for Male and Female Librarians

	MALES (N = 43)		FEMALES (N = 185)		
	$\bar{X}$	SD	$\bar{X}$	SD	t†
AU	3.14	1.17	3.18	1.38	− .17
Ach	3.23	1.02	3.38	1.19	− .74
Act	3.33	1.19	3.46	1.11	− .70
Adv	2.79	1.19	2.56	1.17	1.18
Au	2.95	.72	3.26	.75	−2.43
CPP	2.61	1.09	2.48	1.08	.70
Com	2.84	1.19	2.92	1.17	− .44
Cow	3.79	.97	3.51	1.07	1.59
Cre	2.79	1.28	3.30	1.30	−2.34
Ind	3.21	.86	3.45	.94	−1.56
MV	3.58	.96	3.96	.97	−2.30
Rec	3.14	.94	2.94	1.04	1.18
Res	2.95	1.36	3.30	1.23	−1.65
Sec	3.77	1.02	3.65	1.11	.61
SSe	3.61	1.03	3.83	1.04	−1.27
SSt	2.81	1.01	2.86	.95	− .28
SHR	2.47	1.10	2.57	1.38	− .41
ST	2.81	1.14	3.02	1.36	− .90
Var	3.49	1.10	3.48	1.09	.04
WC	3.44	.67	3.32	1.20	.65
Aut	3.26	1.20	3.56	1.06	−1.67
General satisfaction scale score	65.90	12.28	67.94	13.53	− .90

*The MSQ employs a five-point scale where 1 = not satisfied with the aspect of his job, 2 = only slightly satisfied, 3 = satisfied, 4 = very satisfied, and 5 = extremely satisfied.
†$t_{.99}(\infty) = 2.58$.

TABLE 4 One-Way Analysis of Variance of the MSQ Scale Scores by Type of Library Job Environment

	Total (N = 224)		Group 1 (N = 36)		Group 2 (N = 34)		Group 3 (N = 63)		Group 5 (N = 54)		Group 6 (N = 37)		F*
	$\bar{X}$	SD	$\bar{X}$	SD	$\bar{X}$	SD	$\bar{X}$	SD	$\bar{X}$	SD	$\bar{X}$	SD	
AU	3.16	1.34	3.25	1.36	3.00	1.52	3.19	1.29	3.29	1.35	2.95	1.25	.54
Ach	3.35	1.15	3.69	1.09	3.24	1.13	3.35	1.15	3.30	1.13	3.19	1.27	1.10
Act	3.44	1.13	3.22	1.31	3.59	1.40	3.41	.98	3.61	.88	3.32	1.25	.89
Adv	2.58	1.16	2.67	1.43	2.71	1.29	2.40	.99	2.52	.98	2.76	1.23	.79
Au	3.21	.76	3.39	.69	3.23	.89	3.08	.68	3.20	.83	3.22	.71	.97
CPP	2.53	1.08	2.42	1.05	2.47	1.11	2.37	1.02	2.70	1.14	2.70	1.05	1.09
Com	2.88	1.16	2.75	1.23	2.76	1.18	2.70	1.01	3.11	1.08	3.08	1.38	1.41
Cow	3.56	1.06	3.72	.97	3.47	1.31	3.73	.81	3.28	1.20	3.62	1.01	1.68
Cre	3.19	1.31	3.47	1.28	2.65	1.55	2.86	1.29	3.72	1.09	3.22	1.08	5.57*
Ind	3.40	.92	3.53	.88	4.00	.98	3.17	.75	3.17	.97	3.43	.87	6.10*
MV	3.90	.97	4.00	.95	4.12	.91	3.71	1.05	3.80	1.00	4.08	.83	1.58
Rec	2.97	1.02	3.08	1.18	3.06	1.23	3.00	.93	2.80	.92	3.00	.97	.58
Res	3.25	1.26	3.44	1.27	3.06	1.54	3.02	1.29	3.50	1.04	3.27	1.19	1.49
Sec	3.71	1.07	3.67	1.15	4.00	1.21	3.56	.96	3.69	1.01	3.76	1.14	.99
SSe	3.79	1.03	4.19	.86	2.88	.91	4.00	.89	4.04	.85	3.51	1.19	12.18*
SSt	2.85	.97	2.86	.96	3.24	1.13	2.97	.80	2.72	.90	2.46	1.04	3.47*
SHR	2.57	1.33	2.83	1.58	2.59	1.35	2.65	1.22	2.37	1.28	2.43	1.30	.82
ST	3.00	1.32	3.28	1.50	2.88	1.39	3.22	1.28	2.59	1.17	3.03	1.26	2.24
Var	3.47	1.09	3.50	1.25	3.00	1.21	3.67	.98	3.63	.98	3.32	1.03	2.64
WC	3.34	1.11	3.61	.93	3.29	1.19	3.38	1.07	3.04	1.30	3.49	.87	1.77
Aut	3.52	1.09	3.72	1.23	3.35	1.10	3.30	1.06	3.70	.96	3.59	1.12	1.59
General satisfaction scale score	67.61	13.33	70.31	14.57	66.47	14.89	66.73	11.63	67.78	11.85	67.27	15.53	.50

NOTE.—Group 1 = public services librarians in academic libraries; group 2 = technical services librarians in academic libraries; group 3 = public services librarians in public libraries; group 4 = technical services librarians in public libraries, excluded because $N = 4$; group 5 = school librarians; group 6 = special librarians.

*$F_{.99}(4, \infty) = 3.32$.

librarians was significantly higher than the mean creativity scale scores of the technical services librarians in academic libraries and public services librarians in public libraries; that the mean independence scale score of the technical services librarians in academic librarians; and that the mean social service scale score of the technical scores of the public services librarians in public libraries and school librarians; and that the mean social service score of the technical services librarians in academic libraries was significantly lower than the mean social service scale scores of public services librarians in both academic and public libraries and school librarians.

The Scheffé procedure did not reveal any significant differences among group means for the social status scale, despite the significant F-ratio related to this scale.

These results suggest that school librarians tend to derive greater satisfaction from the creative aspects of their job than do other librarians, and that technical services librarians in academic libraries tend to derive greater satisfaction from the independent nature of their job (that is, the chance to work alone) and lesser satisfaction from the service aspects of their jobs than do other librarians. While these differences are intriguing, the reader should not overlook the considerable evidence of lack of differentiation in the degree of job satisfaction reported by the five groups of librarians. In my opinion, these analyses indicate that the degree of job satisfaction reported by the librarians in the sample was not a function of the sex of the librarians or the type of library in which the librarians worked.

Job environment.—The twenty scale scores of the MIQ measuring the vocational needs of the librarians and the twenty-one scale scores of the MJDQ measuring the librarians' perceptions of the characteristics of their job environments were entered into simple correlation analyses with the general satisfaction scale scores of the MSQ, which measures the librarians' overall satisfaction with their jobs. The results of these analyses, reported in Table 5, indicate only two relatively weak significant relationships between the MIQ scale scores and the general satisfaction scale score, and eighteen weak to strong significant relationships between the MJDQ scale scores and the general satisfaction scale score. These results indicate that the need profiles of satisfied and dissatisfied librarians were quite similar, while the job environments in which satisfied and dissatisfied librarians worked were perceived to be quite dissimilar. It appears, therefore, that the principle factors related to the job satisfaction experienced by the librarians in the sample were the characteristics of the library job environments in which they worked. Because of the concomitant variation among the MJDQ scale scores, however, this analysis does

TABLE 5   Pearson Correlation Coefficients between the MIQ and MJDQ Scale Scores and the General Satisfaction Scale Scores

	MIQ (N = 193)	MJDQ (N = 228)
Ability utilization (AU)	.17	.51*
Achievement (Ach)	.03	.46*
Activity (Act)	.26†	.20*
Advancement (Adv)	−.04	.35*
Authority (Au)	.03	.21*
Company policies and practices (CPP)	−.05	.38*
Compensation (Com)	−.22†	.30*
Co-workers (Cow)	.06	.15
Creativity (Cre)	.17	.48*
Independence (Ind)	.04	.16
Moral values (MV)	.03	.00
Recognition (Rec)	.04	.43*
Responsibility (Res)	.12	.49*
Security (Sec)	−.08	−.03
Social service (SSe)	.12	.28*
Social status (SSt)	−.01	.33*
Supervision–human relations (SHR)	−.05	.51*
Supervision–technical competence (ST)	−.02	.42*
Variety (Var)	.17	.31*
Working conditions (WC)	−.13	.32*
Autonomy (Aut)	. . .	.36*

*$r_{.99}(227) = .172$.
†$r_{.99}(192) = .185$.

not indicate which of these job characteristics are the prinicpal determinants or predictors of job satisfaction. In order to answer this question, the twenty-one scale scores of the MJDQ were entered into a stepwise multiple regression analysis with the general satisfaction scale scores.

Supervision–human relations and ability utilization.—The results of this analysis, reported in Table 6, indicate that the twenty-one scales of the MJDQ account for approximately .48 of the variance of the general satisfaction scale scores, and that, of these twenty-one scales of the MJDQ, the supervision–human relations scale and the ability-utilization scale clearly are the most highly correlated with the general satisfaction scale score (r = .51 for each) and together account for the greatest degree of variation in that score (R^2 = .38). It would be inappropriate, however, to conclude from this analysis that supervision–human relations is the most important characteristic in the job environment related to job satisfaction. It should be noted that the

TABLE 6   Multiple Regression Analysis* of the General Satisfaction Scale Scores with the Scale Scores of the MJDQ

	R	R^2	R^2 Change
SHR	.51	.26	.26
AU	.62	.38	.12
SSt	.63	.40	.02
ST	.65	.42	.02

NOTE.—The remaining 17 variables only accounted for an additional .06 of the variance of the general satisfaction scale scores.

*Variables were entered into the regression equation one at a time in a stepwise fashion. R is the coefficient of multiple correlation, and it is an index of the correlation of the regression equation with the dependent variable. R^2 is the coefficient of multiple determination, and it measures the proportionate reduction of total variation in the dependent variable associated with the use of the set of independent variables entered in the regression equation.

supervision–human relations scale was entered into the regression analysis before the ability-utilization scale simply because its r of .513 exceeded the r of the ability-utilization scale (.509) by .004. This margin of difference is clearly within the realm of chance, and thus the ability-utilization scale could just as easily have been entered first.

What is important is that together, regardless of which scale is entered first, the supervision–human relations scale (which measures the respondent's assessment of the human relations skills of his immediate supervisor) and the ability-utilization scale (which measures the respondent's assessment of the degree to which his job allows him to make full use of his abilities) account for .38 of the variance of the general satisfaction scale scores.

As has been previously noted, the scale scores of the MJDQ tend to be correlated among themselves. Thus it is interesting to observe in the correlation matrix in Table 7 that the ability-utilization scale is correlated with the achievement scale (.67), the creativity scale (.80), the recognition scale (.54), and the responsibility scale (.70), while the supervision–human relations scale is correlated with the company policies and practices scale (.67) and the supervision–technical scale (.54). It is apparent, therefore, that the ability-utilization scale is related to a cluster of job characteristics, measured by the achievement, creativity, recognition, and responsibility scales, which appears to be associated with mastery of the job content, and that the supervision–human relations scale is related to a cluster of job characteristics, measured by the company policies and practices, and supervision–technical scales, which appears to be associated with the supervisory climate of the job environment.

TABLE 7 Correlation Matrix of the MJDQ Scale Scores

	AU	Ach	Act	Adv	Au	CPP	Com	Cow	Cre	Ind	MV	Rec	Res	Sec	SSe	SSt	SHR	ST	Var	WC	Aut
AU																					
Ach	.67																				
Act	.22	.27																			
Adv	.42	.43	.01																		
Au	.20	.13	.22	.11																	
CPP	.34	.33	.05	.42	.12																
Com	.21	.15	-.04	.36	.17	.21															
Cow	.08	.08	.15	.12	.13	.23	.26														
Cre	.78	.61	.21	.41	.29	.34	.12	.01													
Ind	.11	.09	.42	.21	.08	.06	.00	.12	.13												
MV	.00	.05	-.03	.01	.09	.21	.06	.07	-.04	-.07											
Rec	.54	.66	.09	.52	.18	.38	.29	.08	.55	.13	-.04										
Res	.70	.59	.22	.46	.26	.32	.14	-.05	.79	.23	-.03	.55									
Sec	-.12	-.13	.14	-.09	.15	.07	.03	.26	-.13	.29	.23	.00	-.11								
SSe	.39	.41	.22	.15	.22	.09	.18	.15	.39	.06	.03	.24	.29	.02							
SSt	.26	.39	.23	.24	.18	.13	.26	.16	.25	.11	.01	.38	.24	.09	.33						
SHR	.38	.33	.10	.37	.33	.67	.26	.26	.42	.09	.10	.45	.44	.10	.22	.23					
ST	.25	.37	.02	.42	.17	.47	.19	.15	.23	.13	.18	.42	.31	.05	.05	.20	.54				
Var	.36	.37	.55	.13	.32	.09	.04	.23	.49	.27	-.04	.27	.38	.09	.36	.28	.24	.07			
WC	.26	.32	-.03	.21	.06	.43	.32	.35	.13	-.09	.22	.28	.07	.18	.18	.24	.35	.24	.05		
Aut	.39	.30	.25	.27	.23	.20	.01	.04	.56	.33	-.08	.40	.70	.03	.17	.23	.29	.19	.43	-.04	

In order to determine whether these two clusters of scales are indeed indicative of underlying dimensions in the data, the correlation matrix of the MJDQ scale scores was submitted to a factor analysis. The results of this analysis, reported in Table 8, indicate that these two dimensions, as well as three others apparently not related to job satisfaction, do indeed underlie the data. The first factor extracted, with principle loadings by the ability-utilization, achievement, creativity, responsibility, and autonomy scales, appears to be measuring those job characteristics associated with mastery of the job. The second factor extracted, with principal loadings by the company policies and practices, supervision–human relations, and working-conditions scales, appears to be measuring those job characteristics associated with the supervisory climate of the job environment. Thus

TABLE 8   Factor Matrix* of MJDQ Scale Scores

| | \multicolumn{5}{c}{Factors} | | | |
	1	2	3	4	5
AU	.67	.05	.37	.30	−.06
Ach	.51	.03	.50	.40	−.03
Act	.27	−.02	.25	−.13	.56
Adv	.25	.10	.13	.67	.03
Au	.30	.24	.13	−.04	.20
CPP	.28	.61	−.03	.40	−.03
Com	−.03	.24	.31	.32	−.02
Cow	−.09	.41	.28	.05	.25
Cre	.86	.02	.23	.21	−.01
Ind	.10	−.09	−.07	.23	.71
MV	−.06	.34	.02	−.01	−.02
Rec	.42	.09	.30	.58	.03
Res	.83	−.04	.05	.37	.09
Sec	−.17	.32	.03	−.06	.42
SSe	.31	.07	.50	−.02	.08
SSt	.15	.09	.45	.23	.18
SHR	.42	.64	.01	.32	.06
ST	.20	.39	−.02	.49	.04
Var	.50	.05	.36	−.15	.46
WC	−.04	.52	.39	.23	−.10
Aut	.62	−.05	−.05	.19	.33
Total variance (.51)	.28	.09	.07	.04	.03
Common variance	.55	.17	.13	.08	.06

Note.—The factor loadings can be interpreted as the correlation coefficient between each scale and the underlying factors in the data.

*Principal axes technique, varimax rotation.

it does appear that the supervision–human relations and ability-utilization scales are representative of clusters of job characteristics identified as the supervisory climate of the job environment and as the mastery of the job content.

SUMMARY AND DISCUSSION

The principal objective of this study was to identify those factors which are most highly related to job satisfaction among librarians. To this end, data were collected from a sample of librarians as to their sex, the type of library in which they worked, the degree to which they felt certain vocational needs to be important to them, the degree to which they perceived certain characteristics to be operating in their job environments, and the degree of job satisfaction which they reported experiencing from their work.

The analyses of these data revealed no differences in the degree of job satisfaction experienced by male and female librarians. These results contradict Wahba's conclusion that female librarians are more dissatisfied than male librarians. My contention is that the discrepancy between the results of this study and the results of the Wahba study are due to the psychometrically faulty instrumentation used by Wahba. It is possible, however, that differences in the career ladders of male and female librarians could eventually lead to differences in the degree of job satisfaction experienced by male and female librarians. Since the respondents in this study were beginning librarians, this possibility remains to be tested.

The analyses of the data revealed no meaningful pattern of differences in the degree of job satisfaction experienced by public or technical services librarians in academic libraries, public services librarians in public libraries, school librarians, or special librarians. The data analyses also revealed no systematic relationship between the vocational needs of the librarians and their degree of job satisfaction, but did reveal a strong systematic relationship between the job satisfaction of the librarians and the characteristics of the job environments in which they worked.

It was found that the two job characteristics most highly related to job satisfaction tended to be the supervision–human relations and ability-utilization scales. It was also found that these two scales were representative of two underlying dimensions within the data. These dimensions were identified as the supervisory climate of the job environment and the intrinsic factors related to mastery of the job itself, such as ability utilization, achievement, creativity, responsibility, autonomy, and recognition.

At first reading these results may appear comparable to those of Plate and Stone. There is however, a very important difference between these sets of conclusions. Plate and Stone, using Herzberg's two-factor theory of job satisfaction, concluded that the presence of motivator factors such as a sense of achievement and recognition were related to job satisfaction, but that the absence of these factors from the job environment would not produce job dissatisfaction, and that a poor supervisory climate in the job environment would produce job dissatisfaction but that a good supervisory climate would not, in and of itself, produce job satisfaction. The results of this study contradict the conclusions of Plate and Stone and indicate very clearly that there is a positive relationship between job satisfaction and a job environment which is characterized by both a good supervisory climate and the presence of factors related to mastery of the job itself.

Indeed, the data indicate that not only is a good supervisory climate satisfying in itself, but that it appears to be a necessary precondition for librarians to experience satisfaction with the characteristics related to mastery of the job itself. An examination of the relevant MJDQ scale items will highlight this connection. Three items attempt to measure specific characteristics of the supervisory climate: (ST) the technical competence of the supervisor, (SHR) the interpersonal skills of the supervisor, and (CPP) the manner in which administrative policies are executed. Two items attempt to measure an employee's mastery of the job content: (AU) use of individual abilities and (Ach) feeling of accomplishment with the job. The remaining four items of interest appear to measure characteristics related to the mastery of a job and to a supervisory climate which permits the exercise of professional judgment: (Aut) planning work with little supervision, (Res) the freedom to use personal judgment, (Cre) the chance to try new methods of performing the job, and (Rec) receiving recognition for a job well done. These items are indicative of job characteristics associated with personal initiative, individual responsibility, and the exercise of professional judgment in the performance of the job.

It appears, therefore, that there is an integral relationship between a supervisory climate which is conducive to the exercise of individual initiative and professional judgment and the librarian's experience of mastering a job. These two dimensions are, in turn, most strongly related to the degree of job satisfaction reportedly experienced by the librarians in the study. These results tend to indicate that a participatory administrative style, or perhaps even a laissez-faire style, is conducive to job satisfaction among librarians. They also suggest that an assessment of job satisfaction among the personnel of a libray would be a useful diagnostic tool for evaluating the performance of library administrators. In order to facilitate this diagnostic review, it would be advisable to develop standardized instruments for measuring job satisfaction among librarians and for measuring the characteristics operating in the job environments of librarianship. Such standardized instrumentation would lend itself to the development of normative data against which the data generated by local librarians could be compared for diagnostic purposes.

References

1. There is another study which, while not specifically addressed to job satisfaction, does deal with the subject of staff satisfaction in libraries. Marchant (4) has published a book, based upon his doctoral dissertation, in which he develops and tests a model which proposes that participative management leads to staff satisfaction, which in turn positively affects library performance. In my opinion, however, the Marchant study does not demonstrate a command of the complex theoretical issues involved in the investigation of job satisfaction, employee performance, or organizational effectiveness which mitigate against the simplistic set of relationships proposed by Marchant. While Marchant claims that his data support his conclusions, the numerous methodological weaknesses of the study counsel against such assertions. The reader is referred to Lynch (5) for a detailed analysis and evaluation of the study and to Marchant (6) for a rebuttal.
2. This body of literature is quite large. In my opinion, the most salient studies are the following: Ewen (8); Burke (9); Dunnette, Campbell, and Hakel (10); House and Wigdor (11); Lindsay, Marks, and Gorlow (12); Behling, Labovitz, and Kosmo (13); Hinton (14); Hulin and Waters (15); Waters and Waters (16); Wall (17); Gorden, Pryor, and Harris (18); and Ondrach (19).
3. For a review of the Job Description Index, see Robinson, Athanasiou, and Head (20, pp. 105-7).
4. For a review of the Need Satisfaction Questionnaire, see Robinson et al. (20 pp. 148-51).
5. $\alpha_c = 1 - (1 - \alpha)^m = 1 - (1 - .05)^{20} = .64$.
6. $\alpha_c = \alpha m = .05(20) = 1.0$. For a detailed discussion of simultaneous error rate, see Harris (26), Kirk (27), and Winer (28).
7. The Scheffé procedure for multiple comparisons is preferable in this case to the Tukey Honestly Significant Difference (HSD) for pairwise comparisons because the Scheffé procedure is not sensitive to unequal cell sizes, while the Tukey HSD is.

Bibliography

1. Plate, Kenneth H., and Stone, Elizabeth W. "Factors Affecting Librarians' Job Satisfaction: A Report of Two Studies." *Library Quarterly* 44 (April 1974): 97-110.
2. Vaughn, William J., and Dunn, J. D. "A Study of Job Satisfaction in Six University Libraries," *College and Research Libraries* 35 (May 1974): 163-77.
3. Wahba, Susanne P. "Job Satisfaction of Librarians: A Comparison between Men and Women." *College and Research Libraries* 36 (January 1975): 45-51.
4. Marchant, Maurice P. *Participative Management in Academic Libraries.* Westport, Conn.: Greenwood Press, 1976.
5. Lynch, Beverly. "Participative Management in Relationship to Library Effectiveness." *College and Research Libraries* 33 (September 1972): 382-90.
6. Marchant, Maurice P. "And a Response." *College and Research Libraries* 33 (September 1972): 391-97.
7. Herzberg, Frederick; Mausner, Bernard; and Snyderman, Barbara. *The Motivation to Work.* New York: John Wiley & Sons, 1959.
8. Ewen, Robert B. "Some Determinants of Job Satisfaction: A Study of the Generality of Herzberg's Theory." *Journal of Applied Psychology* 48 (June 1964): 161-63.
9. Burke, Ronald J. "Are Herzberg's Motivators and Hygienes Unidimensional?" *Journal of Applied Psychology* 50 (August 1966): 317-21.
10. Dunnette, Marvin D.; Campbell, John P.; and Hakel, Milton D. "Factors Contributing to Job Satisfaction and Job Dissatisfaction in Six Occupational Groups." *Organizational Behavior and Human Performance* 2 (May 1967): 143-74.
11. House, Robert J., and Wigdor, Lawrence A. "Herzberg's Dual Factor Theory of Job Satisfaction and Motivation: A Review of Evidence and a Criticism." *Personnel Psychology* 20 (Winter 1967): 369-89.
12. Lindsay, Carl A.; Marks, Edmond; and Gorlow, Leon. "The Herzberg Theory: A Critique and Reformulation." *Journal of Applied Psychology* 51 (August 1967): 330-39.
13. Behling, Orlando; Labovitz, George; and Kosno, Richard. "The Herzberg Controversy: A Critical Appraisal." *Academy of Management Journal* 11 (March 1968): 99-108.
14. Hinton, Bernard L. "An Empirical Investigation of Herzberg's Methodology and Two-Factor Theory." *Organizational Behavior and Human Performance* 3 (August 1968): 286-309.
15. Hulin, Charles L., and Waters, L. K. "Regression Analysis of Three Varations of the Two-Factor Theory of Job Satisfaction." *Journal of Applied Psychology* 55 (June 1971): 211-17.
16. Waters, L. K., and Waters, Carrie W. "An Empirical Test of Five

Versions of the Two-Factor Theory of Job Satisfaction." *Organizational Behavior and Human Performance* 7 (February 1972): 18-24.

17. Wall, Toby. "Ego-Defensiveness as a Determinant of Reported Differences in Sources of Job Satisfaction and Job Dissatisfaction." *Journal of Applied Psychology* 58 (August 1973): 125-28.

18. Gorden, Michael E.; Pryor, Norman M.; and Harris, Bob. "An Examination of Scaling Bias in Herzberg's Theory of Job Satisfaction." *Organizational Behavior and Human Performance* 11 (February 1974): 106-21.

19. Ondrach, D. A. "Defense Mechanisms and the Herzberg Theory: An Alternate Test." *Academy of Management Journal* 17 (March 1974): 79-89.

20. Robinson, John P.; Athanasiou, Robert; and Head, Kendra B. *Measures of Occupational Attitudes and Occupational Characteristics.* Ann Arbor: Institute for Social Research, University of Michigan, 1976.

21. Cronbach, Lee J., and Furby, Lita. "How We Should Measure Change— or Should We?" *Psychological Bulletin* 74 (August 1970): 68-80.

22. *Manual for the Minnesota Importance Questionnaire.* Minnesota Studies in Vocational Rehabilitation, no. 28. Minneapolis: Work Adjustment Project, Industrial Relations Center, University of Minnesota, 1971.

23. *The Measurement of Occupational Reinforcer Patterns.* Minnesota Studies in Vocational Rehabilitation, no. 25. Minneapolis: Work Adjustment Project, Industrial Relations Center, University of Minnesota, 1968.

24. *Manual for the Minnesota Satisfaction Questionnaire.* Minnesota Studies in Vocational Rehabilitation, no. 22. Minneapolis: Work Adjustment Project, Industrial Relations Center, University of Minnesota, 1967.

25. Drennan, Henry T., and Darling, Richard L. *Library Manpower, Occupational Characteristics of Public and School Librarians.* Washington, D.C.: Bureau of Adult and Vocational Education, U.S. Office of Education, 1966.

26. Harris, Richard J. *A Primer of Multivariate Statistics.* New York: Academic Press, 1975.

27. Kirk, Roger E. *Experimental Design: Procedures for the Behavioral Sciences.* Belmont, Calif.: Brooks/Cole Publishing Co., 1968.

28. Winer, B. J. *Statistical Principles in Experimental Design.* New York: McGraw-Hill Book Co., 1971.

Job Satisfaction in Libraries: Relationships of the Work Itself, Age, Sex, Occupational Group, Tenure, Supervisory Level, Career Commitment, and Library Department

Beverly P. Lynch and Jo Ann Verdin

THREE schools of thought describe the more than 3,000 theoretical studies and empirical investigations of the many factors relating to job satisfaction (1). One school, the physical-economic school, has its base in the works of Taylor and others working in the 1920s who considered the influence of the physical arrangement of work, fatigue, and pay on job satisfaction. Another, the human-relations school, shaped by the Hawthorne studies and the later work at the universities of Michigan and Ohio State, emphasizes the relationships of good supervision, informal work groups, and friendly employer-employee relationships on satisfaction. The third, the work-itself school, investigates the effects of challenging work on the attainment of job satisfaction. Much of the interest in job satisfaction stems from the assumption that a high level of satisfaction will lead to a high level of job performance, although some evidence suggests that a high level of job performance in itself can lead to good job satisfaction (2).

Reprinted with permission from *The Library Quarterly*, V. 53 (Oct. 1983), pp. 434–447.
© 1983 by The University of Chicago. All rights reserved.

Prompted by the presumed relationships of job satisfaction to job performance and stimulated by the general acceptance of the human-relations theory, a number of studies have appeared recently on the job satisfaction of librarians. The close connection perceived as existing between job satisfaction and the quality of library service leads librarians to want to determine what factors may be related to the satisfaction of staff members.

The library studies on various aspects of job satisfaction have sought to identify those factors most highly related to job satisfaction. Only two of the ten studies reviewed below have investigated satisfaction in the context of specific libraries. Only one of these compares libraries or library units on levels of job satisfaction. Only one investigates the satisfaction of all occupational groups within libraries.

Plate and Stone (3) analyzed data from 162 American and 75 Canadian librarians in terms of Herzberg's motivation and hygienic theory (4). Their findings corresponded to those of Herzberg. The chief satisfying factors were achievement and recognition. The chief dissatisfying factors were institutional policy and administration, supervision, and interpersonal relationships.

Wahba (5) compared the job satisfaction of 202 male and female librarians working in twenty-three academic libraries. She concluded that women are more dissatisfied than men in the needs categories of security, esteem, autonomy, and self-actualization, with the exception of social needs, which were similar for both men and women.

D'Elia (6) measured the attitudes of 314 librarians who had graduated from six library schools and, at the time of study, had been working in their jobs for periods of six to eighteen months. He, in contrast to Wahba, found no significant differences between male and female librarians on job satisfaction. Previous work experiences was not related to job satisfaction, nor was the type of library or type of service in which the librarians were working. D'Elia concluded from his data that the nature of the supervisory climate is important to job satisfaction, as are factors which lead to the mastery of the job itself. He suggested that a participatory management style is conducive to job satisfaction among librarians.

Vaughn and Dunn (7) measured differences in levels of satisfaction among librarians in six university libraries, and, in one of these libraries, among the various departments. They audited the attitudes of library employees about pay, work, promotional opportunities, co-workers, and supervisors. The results enabled comparisons among the libraries and the departments, although no library department or library scored very differently from the others on these various dimensions. Vaugh and Dunn observed that "age seems to have a predictable influence upon job satisfaction. Generally, the young are more dissatisfied than the old" (7, p.166). They did not test this observation.

Prybil (8) examined the relationship between job satisfaction and occupational groups in a single university library. All full-time library staff members were placed into three groups, those librarians with a masters degree from accredited library school, the clerical personnel and others without a graduate library degree, and the maintenance and custodial staff assigned to the library. No significant relationships emerged between satisfaction and occupational group. The clerical workers as a group seemed most satisfied with their jobs, but the results suggest that the satisfaction of library personnel is not related directly to the three occupational groups chosen for the study.

Chwe (9) sought evidence to support the hypothesis that reference librarians working in academic libraries were more satisfied than catalog librarians. His hypothesis grew out of other studies which indicate that "less esteem and less preference are associated with cataloging than with reference service among library professionals" (9, p. 139). He found no difference in the overall job satisfaction between the 183 reference librarians and 170 catalog librarians who participated in the study.

Roberts (10) conducted a study of job satisfaction among the graduates of the Post-Graduate School of Librarianship and Information Studies, Sheffield University. His data suggest that overall job satisfaction increases as librarians settle into their work, make adjustments to the job, and gain in experience and confidence. According to the Roberts study, the length of time the person has worked in a particular library may influence the level of job satisfaction he or she reports.

Jones (11, pp. 133–51), as part of a larger study, asked 146 librarians in the Library Association's professional register during the year 1966, who were still employed in libraries and still on the register in 1976, how satisfied they were with their careers so far in terms of professional development and how they rated their present positions in terms of job satisfaction. The respondents reported high degrees of satisfaction. The study indicated that satisfaction tended to increase with experience, mobility, with seniority of the post, and with managerial level.

Scamell and Stead (12) analyzed the relationships between age, tenure, and job satisfaction for sixty-four librarians participating in management development program for members of the Special Library Association. Thus, they studied the relationships of the variables for a particular occupational group rather than for people working within a particular organization. No significant differences were found between age and job satisfaction or between tenure and job satisfaction in this Scamell and Stead study. They continued to explore job satisfaction for librarians, extending their investigations to the relationships of role conflict and role clarity with job satisfaction (13).

The present study continues to explore the relationship of sex, occupational group, age, and length of service on the job with satisfaction of librarians and other working in libraries. In addition, it explores the relationship of supervisory level, career orientation, and departmental affliation. The general hypothesis guiding the investigation was that differences in job satisfaction will be found among library units and among occupational groups within library units. Our concern was not to apply comprehensive measures of job satisfaction to librarians. It was to suggest that library studies on job satisfaction would be more useful to the profession if placed within the context of the work environments in which librarians find themselves. Most library studies on satisfaction have been of the occupational group outside of the work setting. This study is placed in the context of university libraries. Its theoretical base, in the general context of the work-itself school, determined the nature of the satisfaction measure.

DATA AND METHOD

The investigation reported here was part of a larger study conducted in 1971–72 in three university libraries in the United States. An effort was made to match the libraries according to size of budget, size of staff, and number of doctoral programs maintained by the universities in which the libraries are located. As the libraries were guaranteed anonymity, their exact size, location, and historical development cannot be disclosed. All full-time employees in the departments assigned the functions of book selection, acquisitions, cataloging, circulation, and reference were asked to respond to a questionnaire on various aspects of their work. Although the five operational functions were studied in all three libraries, the organizational patterns so varied that six departments were studied in one library, five in the second, and four in the third. A total of 521 questionnaires were distributed; 384 were returned, for a response rate of 73 percent.

The index to job satisfaction was based upon a satisfaction scale developed by Jerald Hage and Michael Aiken (14). Four questions form the scale: (1) How satisfied are you with your present job when you compare it with similar positions in other departments or other libraries? (2) How satisfied are you with the progress you are making toward the goals that you have set for yourself in your present position? (3) How satisfied are you with your present job when you consider the expectations you had when you took the job? (4) How satisfied are you with your present job in light of your career expectations?

The index measures satisfaction in the context of the work itself. The questions forming the index address the respondent's attitudes toward his or her present job, perceived progress toward work-related goals, as well as the comparison of the current job and the expectations about the job and about the career.

Responses to each of the four questions were summed to derive the satisfaction score. Each question was weighted equally. The reliability of the satisfaction scale, measured by Cronback's α, is .8. A low score indicates high satisfaction; a high score indicates low satisfaction. The possible scores on satisfaction range from 4 (high satisfaction) to 28 (low satisfaction).

The employee characteristics measured were age, sex, occupational level described as professional or nonprofessional, and whether the respondent is a supervisor. Tenure, that is, years worked in the particular library, total years of library experience, and length of time in the present job also were measured.

Four categories describe supervisory level: no supervisory responsibility, direct the work of others, head of a unit or section, and department head. Career orientation was measured by means of the question, "What do you think you will be doing five years from now?" The fourteen possible responses were collapsed into five categories: plan to leave the labor force or work in a library part-time, go into another type of work, return to the university for more education, work in the same library, and work in a different library.

LIMITATIONS

The limitations of this study and of all studies of library satisfaction should be taken into account when reviewing the findings and the conclusions based upon the findings. One cannot generalize about all libraries or library staff members from this investigation. The data are derived from questionnaires sent in 1971–72 to all full-time staff members in the functional departments of the main library of three large research libraries. No investigation was made at that time of the environmental conditions of each library or of each department. The assumption was that the three libraries were similar in terms of the nature of their collections, clientele, staff, and institutional mission.

Studies of organizational phenomena are difficult and expensive to carry out. Scientific method requires large, carefully drawn samples in order to generalize about particular populations, yet only a few investigations of organizations are able to meet this requirement. In order to aid in understanding organizational phenomena, we must do the best we can within the resources available. The important work of Hage and Aiken (14), for example, is based upon the study of sixteen social welfare and health organizations in one large midwestern city. Hage and Aiken's reports of their investigations of these organizations have furthered the understanding of the behavior of all kinds of organizations.

Plate and Stone (3), Wahba (5), and D'Elia (6) studied the job satisfaction of professional librarians without placing their investigations within the context of the libraries in which their respondents worked. D'Elia concludes his paper: "(These results) suggest that an assessment of job satisfaction among the personnel of a library would be a useful diagnostic tool for evaluating the performance of library administrators. In order to facilitate this diagnostic review, it would be advisable to develop standarized instruments for measuring job satisfaction among librarians and for measuring the characteristics operating the job environments of librarianship. Such standardized instrumentation would lend itself to the development of normative data against which the data generated by local librarians could be compared for diagnostic purposes" (6, p. 301). D'Elia's recommendation, while appealing in its simplicity, is based upon assumptions relating to the similarity of libraries as organizations, upon normative data that do not change over time, upon the ability of the profession to develop and collect such data, and upon the primacy of the satisfaction of the professional librarian. The practitioner may find D'Elia's suggestion dangerous, for it suggests that career decisions be guided by the application D'Elia proposes.

Vaughn and Dunn (7) and Prybil (8) place their investigations within the context of the work environment. Their efforts to discover and to understand the variations in job satisfaction within the library work setting are useful when compared with the results reported in this paper.

The data analyzed here were collected in the early 1970s, but, ten years later, they offer a solid base for comparative purposes, even if they do not represent the present situation in the three libraries studied.

HYPOTHESES AND FINDINGS

Seven hypotheses guided the investigation: (1) there is no significant difference between men and women library employees on satisfaction; (2) there is no significant difference between the age of the library employee and job satisfaction; (3) there is no significant difference between the tenure of the employee and job satisfaction; (4) there is no significant difference between the career commitment of library employees and job satisfaction; (5) there is no significant difference between supervisory level and job satisfaction; (6) there is no significant difference among the functional departments on job satisfaction; and (7) there is no significant difference between occupational group and job satisfaction.

The hypotheses were tested individually using the entire sample. One-way analysis of variance was used. The results are presented in Table 1.

The F test, calculated using one-way analysis of variance, is applied under the assumption of homogeneity of variance. Further, the F distribution is "robust with respect to violation of the assumption of homogeneity of population-error variances provided that the number of observations in the sample is equal. For samples of unequal size however, violations of the homogeneity assumption can have a marked effect on the test significance" (15, p. 61). Because the sample sizes were unequal in this study, a test of homogeneity of variance (Bartlett–Box F) was made. No significant differences were found, thus indicating that the F test of significance is appropriate for this analysis.

The F test is an overall test, indicating that there is a significant difference between at least two of the groups. In order to examine the situation further, Duncan's new multiple-range test is applied. This pairwise comparison of the means indicates which of the groups are significantly different (15, pp. 93–94; 16, pp. 67–72). The Duncan procedure was used when more than two groups were compared.

TABLE 1   One-Way Analysis of Variance Satisfaction of Employees (Total Sample)

Hypothesis	$\bar{X}$	SD	F
Sex of library employee:			
Female ($N = 320$)	14.84	6.09	.29
Male ($N = 64$)	14.39	5.88	. . .
Age of library employee (years):			
< 25 ($N = 119$)	17.16	6.00	5.33***
25–29 ($N = 75$)	14.89	5.83	. . .
30–34 ($N = 35$)	13.17	5.65	. . .
35–39 ($N = 24$)	14.12	5.09	. . .
40–44 ($N = 34$)	11.55	5.07	. . .
45–49 ($N = 28$)	14.82	5.20	. . .
50–54 ($N = 26$)	12.61	7.11	. . .
55–59 ($N = 17$)	15.00	7.21	. . .
> 60 ($N = 23$)	12.00	4.11	. . .
Years worked at library:			
< 1 ($N = 67$)	14.04	4.76	2.21*
1–2 ($N = 105$)	15.94	6.63	. . .
3–4 ($N = 75$)	15.92	6.25	. . .
5–6 ($N = 45$)	13.95	5.52	. . .
7–8 ($N = 20$)	14.50	6.28	. . .
9–10 ($N = 18$)	14.55	5.57	. . .
11–14 ($N = 19$)	11.47	5.77	. . .
15–24 ($N = 22$)	12.45	4.75	. . .
> 25 ($N = 12$)	14.83	8.07	. . .
Total years experience:			
< 1 ($N = 42$)	14.64	4.53	2.20*
1–2 ($N = 75$)	15.45	6.85	. . .
3–4 ($N = 83$)	16.57	6.05	. . .
5–6 ($N = 40$)	13.90	4.73	. . .
7–8 ($N = 27$)	15.00	7.21	. . .
9–10 ($N = 31$)	13.06	5.96	. . .
11–14 ($N = 31$)	12.96	5.39	. . .
15–24 ($N = 33$)	13.09	5.70	. . .
> 25 ($N = 17$)	13.94	6.96	. . .
Time in current job:			
< 3 months ($N = 29$)	13.86	4.16	.98
3–6 months ($N = 20$)	15.45	6.40	. . .
6–12 months ($N = 59$)	14.15	6.11	. . .
1–2 years ($N = 117$)	15.62	6.29	. . .
3–5 years ($N = 100$)	14.72	6.00	. . .
> 6 years ($N = 56$)	13.92	6.37	. . .
Career orientation:			
Out of full-time work force ($N = 77$)	14.18	6.15	12.25***
Other type of work ($N = 74$)	18.25	5.49	. . .
More library education ($N = 22$)	15.72	6.15	. . .
Work at same library ($N = 121$)	12.43	5.72	. . .
Work at different library ($N = 58$)	15.39	5.47	. . .

TABLE 1 *(continued)*

Hypothesis	$\bar{X}$	SD	F
Supervisory level:			
No supervisory responsibility (N = 245)	15.64	6.03	6.24***
First-level supervisor (N = 70)	14.10	6.30	...
Unit manager (N = 52)	12.73	5.42	...
Department head (N = 17)	11.11	3.96	...
Department affiliation:			
Reference (N = 41)	12.21	5.36	3.46**
Acquisitions (N = 62)	14.03	5.48	...
Cataloging (N = 143)	14.45	5.76	...
Serials (N = 55)	15.89	6.53	...
Circulation (N = 70)	16.25	6.54	...
Search (N = 11)	17.45	6.53	...
Occupational group:			
Nonprofessional (N = 244)	15.47	6.03	10.56***
Professional (N = 137)	13.40	5.91	...

NOTE.—Totals may not reach 384 due to missing data. Figures shown in parentheses are frequencies.
***$P < .001$.
**$P < .01$.
*$P < .05$.

The analysis of variance conducted on all respondents indicated that the only hypothesis accepted was number one, there is no significant difference between men and women library employees. D'Elia also reported that the satisfaction of library employees is unrelated to sex. The present study finds the job satisfaction reported by people working in the three libraries in this study was not a function of sex.

The present investigation supports the findings of other studies that job satisfaction is a function of the age of the employee. The least satisfied group of employees was the group under twenty-five years of age. This group differed significantly from all other groups, except those twenty-five to twenty-nine and fifty-five to fifty-nine years old.

The relationship of the tenure of employees and job satisfaction has been investigated in the studies of librarians by Roberts, who found that the length of time a person has worked in a particular library may influence the level of job satisfaction reported, and Scammel and Stead, who found no significant difference between tenure and satisfaction. Significant differences emerge in the present study. People with more years of experience report higher job satisfaction than other groups, and people who had worked in the particular library a relatively shorter period of time reported lower satisfaction than employees who have worked longer in the library.

In terms of total years of experience working in libraries, the 3–4 year group displayed the lowest job satisfaction and differed significantly from those working in the field for 5–6, 9–10, 11–14, and 15–24 years. Among those working in the same library, persons with 1–2 or 3–4 years of experience in that library were significantly less satisfied than those who had worked 11–14 or 15–24 years in that library.

The career commitment of the individuals participating in this study is influenced by job satisfaction. Those who plan to be working in the same library five years hence are significantly more satisfied than persons with other plans. Those who intend to go into a different type of work altogether are significantly less satisfied than those who plan to change libraries, drop out of the full-time work force, or who plan to stay in the library.

Whether the respondent was a supervisor influenced the levels of job satisfaction reported in this study. Department heads report the highest levels of job satisfaction. The differences were significant among the respondents with no supervisory responsibility when compared with unit and department heads. Persons with no supervisory responsibility report the lowest satisfaction.

Significant differences also emerged according to the departmental affiliations of respondents. When aggregating responses from all employees, the employees in reference departments reported significantly higher levels of job satisfaction than the employees of any other department except acquisitions.

Significant differences also emerged between the occupational groups. Professional librarians differed from nonprofessional employees on job satisfaction, the professional librarians reporting higher satisfaction than the other members of the staff. The results of the one-way analysis of variance reported in Table 1 suggest that, within the library context, the satisfaction of the professional employees may vary significantly from that of the nonprofessional employees. Other studies of job satisfaction in libraries for the most part investigate only the job satisfaction of the professional librarian. Only Prybil investigated the differences among occupational groups. In contrast to the present study, Prybil found no significant differences among the three groups: librarians, clerical staff, and maintenance and custodial staff.

Differences between the occupational groups is an important finding, not only for the researcher, but for the library manager who is making personnel policy. In order to examine more closely the

TABLE 2   Results of One-Way Analysis of Variance Satisfaction by Work Groups (P)

HYPOTHESIS	WORK GROUP		
	Nonprofessional	Professional	Combined Group
Sex	—	—	—
Age	***	—	***
Years worked at library	—	—	*
Total years experience	—	—	*
Time in current job	*	—	—
Career orientation	***	*	***
Supervisory level	—	*	***
Department affiliation	**	—	***

***$P < .001$.
**$P < .01$.
*$P < .05$.
—$P > .05$.

differences in the occupational groups, separate analyses were made of the professional and nonprofessional groups. A summary of the results is presented in Table 2.

For nonprofessional employees, age, time in current job, career orientation, and departmental affiliation were related to satisfaction.

Among professional employees, satisfaction was related to career orientation and supervisory level. Those with greater supervisory responsibility reported greater satisfaction. Reference librarians reported higher levels of satisfaction than librarians in other units, but, like Chwe's results, not at levels of significant difference.

Of the 137 professional respondents, twenty-four, or 17 percent, indicated their intent to leave the full-time work force or go into another type of work. Of these twenty-four, twelve were over the age of fifty-five, suggesting that retirement was a primary reason for their decision. Fifty-four, or 40 percent of the professionals, and sixty-seven, 27 percent of the nonprofessionals, expected to be working in the same library.

SUMMARY AND DISCUSSION

This study of job satisfaction in three academic libraries investigates the job satisfaction of all full-time employees, professional and nonprofessional, working in the functional departments of acquisitions, cataloging, circulation, and reference. The investigation differs from most other studies on satisfaction reported in the library literature. These studies, for the most part, have their base in the human-relations school. They investigate the attitudes of professional librarians as a class, selected either from a group of recent graduates or attendees at various seminars and conferences.

The present study, conducted in the context of the work situation, uses as a measure of satisfaction a four-item questionnaire that addresses the respondent's attitudes toward his or her present job and progress toward work-related goals, together with a comparison of the current job and the respondent's expectations about his or her job and career. Not all employees seek challenging work or value it. The theoretical question, "Do employees who do *not* value or seek mentally challenging work get the same satisfaction from their work as those who seek such work?" has not been addressed in this study. The assumption underlying the study and the measures of satisfaction used in it is that work means the same thing to all library employees, and that the satisfaction or lack of it, placed in the context of the work itself, also has the same meaning.

Relatively high levels of satisfaction were reported across the library units. Fifty-four (40 percent) of the professional respondents and sixty-seven (27 percent) of the nonprofessional respondents expect to be working in the same library five years hence. More of the satisfied people are going to stay in the same place.

Among the librarians, those working in reference departments reported the highest levels of satisfaction, followed closely by the librarians working in circulation departments. Among the nonprofessional employees, those working in reference departments reported the highest levels of satisfaction. Reference service is considered by some to have more esteem than other aspect of library work (9, p. 139). The response of the professional and nonprofessional employees in the reference departments may be reflecting that esteem, or it may be that reference work is more varied and nonroutine than that of other departments, or the response may be reflecting reasons not pursued in this study. Further investigations on satisfaction and the nature of the work could be illuminating.

In contrast to the professional librarians in circulation who reported relatively high levels of satisfaction, nonprofessional employees in circulation departments reported very low levels of satisfaction. In the case of the professional in the circulation departments, the work, being predominantly supervision, may be a major factor. Since this investigation was conducted, two of the libraries have automated fully their circulation departments. Assuming that the nature of the work of the nonprofessional employee has changed substantially since the automated systems were introduced, a subsequent study could offer insights as to employee satisfaction in relation to the nature of the work itself.

Overall, the professional group differs significantly from the nonprofessional group on job satisfaction. This is an important finding. Some library managers intuitively recognize the differences among the occupational groups and will work within a framework of differing reward structures and different approaches to employee selection, training, and systems of performance appraisal. Other managers do not recognize such differences, tending to view all of the unit's employees in the same way. That different occupational groups within the same functional unit may have differing degrees of satisfaction toward their work has been underestimated by some library managers theorists writing about library organization.

The total sample in this study is heavily female (82 percent). Of the professional respondents, ninety-seven, or 71 percent, are female. No difference emerged among the male or the female respondents on satisfaction.

The study reports significant differences among supervisory levels on job satisfaction. Within the job satisfaction literature there is almost a universal finding of a positive relationship between job level and job satisfaction. The present study is no exception. No nonprofessionals are department heads, for academic libraries generally require library education and training for jobs at the level of department head. On-the-job training alone does not lead to entry into this level.

The new entrants into the library or into the profession report some of the lowest levels of satisfaction. As the length of time in the profession increases, the reported levels of satisfaction also rise. The latter finding is not surprising. It would be expected that the longer an employee is on the job the more he or she would accommodate to the work situation, or, if dissatisfaction continued, the employee would leave. The low levels of job satisfaction reported by those at the beginning of their careers is more troublesome, suggesting that a new professional, just starting to work in a library, may find it difficult to accommodate to working within an organizational context or within a framework of group expectations, work-flow demands, or individual library standards. It also suggests that the nature of the entry-level work for professionals in large research libraries may be more routine and "nonprofessional" than librarians expect. Further investigation of the job satisfaction of entry-level librarians within the context of the work itself could be of assistance in understanding the various reasons for the low levels of satisfaction reported.

This study was guided by an interest in job satisfaction within the work setting. Its intent was to investigate, within large research libraries, some of the correlates of job satisfaction found in other library studies on job satisfaction. It has demonstrated that job satisfaction can vary from one library unit to another and from one occupational group to another within the same library. It has raised questions about why satisfaction varies from unit to unit and, within the same unit, from one occupational group to another.

Studies on job satisfaction in libraries will be fruitful if conducted within the framework of the work itself, seeking correlates relating to the work, the nature of the job, and the characteristics of the work unit. Further study of career commitment also may offer insights to the profession, as well as to managers of large research libraries. Organizational issues, issues of job design, and the varying nature of library work will provide more understanding as to why some library workers in specific departments are happier with their work than are others.

References

1. Locke, Edwin A. "The Nature and Causes of Job Satisfaction." In *Handbook of Industrial and Organizational Psychology,* edited by Marvin D. Dunnette. Chicago: Rand McNally College Publishing Company, 1976.
2. Schwab, Donald P., and Cummings, Larry L. "Theories of Performance and Satisfaction: A Review," *Industrial Relations* 9 (October 1970): 408-30.
3. Plate, Kenneth H., and Stone, Elizabeth W. "Factors Affecting Librarians' Job Satisfaction: A Report of Two Studies." *Library Quarterly* 44 (April 1974): 97-110.
4. Herzberg, Frederick; Mausner, Bernard; and Snyderman, Barbara. *The Motivation to Work.* 2d ed. New York: John Wiley & Sons, 1959.
5. Wahba, Susanne P. "Job Satisfaction of Librarians: A Comparison between Men and Women." *College & Research Libraries* 36 (January 1975): 45-51.
6. D'Elia, George P. "The Determinants of Job Satisfaction among Beginning Librarians." *Library Quarterly* 49 (July 1979): 283-302.
7. Vaughn, William J., and Dunn, J. D. "A Study of Job Satisfaction in Six University Libraries." *College & Research Libraries* 35 (May 1974): 163-77.
8. Prybil, Lawrence D. "Job Satisfaction in Relation to Job Performance and Occupational Level." *Personnel Journal* 52 (February 1973): 94-100.
9. Chwe, Steven Seokho. "A Comparative Study of Job Satisfaction:

Catalogers and Reference Librarians in University Libraries." *Journal of Academic Librarianship* 4 (July 1978): 139-43.

10. Roberts, Norman. "Graduates in Academic Libraries: A Survey of Past Students of the Post-Graduate School of Librarianship and Information Studies, Sheffield University, 1964/65-1970/71." *Journal of Librarianship* 5 (April 1973): 97-115.

11. Jones, Noragh. *Continuing Education for Librarians.* Leeds: Leeds Polytechnic School of Librarianship, 1977.

12. Scamell, Richard W., and Stead, Bette Ann. "A Study of Age and Tenure as It Pertains to Job Satisfaction." *Journal of Library Admimistration* 1 (Spring 1980): 3-18.

13. Scamell, Richard W., and Stead, Bette Ann. "A Study of the Relationship of Role Conflict, the Need for Role Clarity, and Job Satisfaction for Professional Librarians." *Library Quarterly* 50 (July 1980): 310-23.

14. Hage, Jerald, and Aiken, Michael. "Program Change and Organizational Properties: A Comparative Analysis." *American Journal of Sociology* 72 (March 1967): 503-19.

15. Kirk, Roger E. *Experimental Design: Procedures for the Behavioral Sciences.* Belmont, Calif.: Brooks/Cole Publishing Company, 1968.

16. Huck, Schuyler W.; Cormier, William H.; and Bounds, William G., Jr. *Reading Statistics and Research.* New York: Harper & Row Publishers, 1974.

List of Contributors

Howard E. Aldrich is Professor, Department of Sociology, University of North Carolina, Chapel Hill.

Peter M. Blau is Quetelet Professor, Department of Sociology, Columbia University, and Distinguished Professor, Department of Sociology, State University of New York at Albany.

Donald Coney (1901-1973) was University Librarian and Professor of Librarianship, the University of California, Berkeley.

Richard M. Cyert is President of Carnegie-Mellon University.

Richard De Gennaro is Director of Libraries, University of Pennsylvania.

George P. D'Elia is Director of the Library School, University of Minnesota.

William J. Dickson and Fritz J. Roethlisberg conducted the famous studies at the Western Electric Hawthorn Plant that revealed the importance of social interaction and psychological factors in relation to worker productivity.

Richard M. Dougherty is Director of the Library and Professor of Library Science, University of Michigan.

Robert B. Downs is Dean of Library Administration Emeritus, University of Illinois at Urbana-Champaign.

Thomas J. Galvin is Dean, Graduate School of Library and Information Science, University of Pittsburgh.

John W. Gardner's work has demonstrated his concern about the domination of technology and bureaucracy over the individual and the direction of American society.

J. Richard Hackman is Professor, School of Organization and Management and Department of Psychology, Yale University.

Fred J. Heinritz is Professor, School of Library Science, Southern Connecticut State College.

Frederick Herzberg is Distinguished Professor of Management, University of Utah.

Paul Howard, the first head of the American Library Association's Washington Office, retired in 1970 as Executive Secretary of the Federal Library Committee.

Rosabeth Moss Kanter is Professor of Sociology, Yale University.

Fremont E. Kast is Professor, Department of Management and Organization, University of Washington.

Robert L. Katz has taught in the graduate schools of business at Dartmouth, Harvard, and Stanford universities

Howard Koontz is Professor, Graduate School of Management, UCLA.

Beverly P. Lynch is the University Librarian, University of Illinois at Chicago.

Arthur M. McAnally (1911-1972) was Director of Libraries at the University of Oklahoma.

Joseph McDonald is Director, Brooklyn Center Library, Long Island University.

James G. March is Professor of Management, Political Science, and Sociology at Stanford University.

Maurice P. Marchant is Professor, Library School, Brigham Young University.

Charles Martell is Associate Director of Libraries, California State University, Sacramento.

David Mechanic is Professor of Sociology, University of Wisconsin, Madison.

Henry Mintzberg is Professor, Faculty of Management, McGill University.

Klaus Musmann is Head Acquisitions Librarian, Los Angeles County Law Library.

Charles Perrow is Professor of Sociology, Yale University.

Jeffrey Pfeffer is Professor of Organizational Behavior, Graduate School of Business and Department of Sociology, Stanford University.

Rose B. Phelps (1893-1974) was Professor of Library Science, University of Illinois.

Jeffrey A. Raffel is with the Division of Urban Affairs, University of Delaware.

Fritz J. Roethlisberger and William J. Dickson conducted the famous studies at the Western Electric Hawthorn Plant that revealed the importance of social interaction and psychological factors in relation to worker productivity.

James E. Rosenzweig is Professor, Department of Management and Organization, University of Washington.

Patricia Glass Schuman is President, Neal-Schuman Publishers, Inc.

Thomas W. Shaughnessy is Director of the Library, University of Missouri.

Herbert A. Simon is Richard King Mellon University Professor of Computer Sciences and Psychology, Carnegie-Mellon University.

Frederick W. Taylor (1856-1915) is considered the father of scientific management.

Mercedes Untawale is Assistant Head, Bibliographic Services, Catalog Department, University of California, Berkeley.

Andrew H. Van de Ven is 3M Professor of Human Systems Management and Director of the Strategic Management Research Center, University of Minnesota.

Jo Ann Verdin is Assistant Professor, College of Business Administration, University of Illinois at Chicago.

Victor H. Vroom is Professor of Psychology and Administrative Sciences, Yale University.

Max Weber (1864-1920) a German sociologist, was highly influential in the fields of organization theory, political and economic development, and the comparative study of societies and religion, industrial society, and social stratification.

Index